Financial Decisions for Retirement

Huebner School Series   *H. King McGlaughon, Jr., Editor*

Individual Medical Expense Insurance
Thomas P. O'Hare

Meeting the Financial Need of Long-Term Care
Burton T. Beam, Jr., and Thomas P. O'Hare

Financial Planning: Process and Environment
Don A. Taylor and C. Bruce Worsham (eds.)

Fundamentals of Insurance Planning
Burton T. Beam, Jr., Eric A. Wiening, and David L. Bickelhaupt

Fundamentals of Financial Planning
David M. Cordell (ed.)

Fundamentals of Income Taxation
James F. Ivers III (ed.)

McGill's Life Insurance
Edward E. Graves (ed.)

McGill's Legal Aspects of Life Insurance
Edward E. Graves and Burke A. Christensen (eds.)

Group Benefits: Basic Concepts and Alternatives
Burton T. Beam, Jr.

Planning for Retirement Needs
David A. Littell and Kenn Beam Tacchino

Fundamentals of Investments for Financial Planning
Walt J. Woerheide and David M. Cordell

Fundamentals of Estate Planning
Constance J. Fontaine

Estate Planning Applications
Ted Kurlowicz

Planning for Business Owners and Professionals
Ted Kurlowicz, James F. Ivers III, and John J. McFadden

Financial Planning Applications
Thomas P. Langdon and William J. Ruckstuhl

Advanced Topics in Group Benefits
Burton T. Beam, Jr., and Thomas P. O'Hare (eds.)

Executive Compensation
John J. McFadden (ed.)

Health and Long-Term Care Financing for Seniors
Burton T. Beam, Jr., and Thomas P. O'Hare

Financial Decisions for Retirement
David A. Littell and Kenn Beam Tacchino

Huebner School Series

Financial Decisions for Retirement

David A. Littell
Kenn Beam Tacchino
Richard A. Dulisse
Constance J. Fontaine
Edward E. Graves
Walt J. Woerheide

The American College Press/*Bryn Mawr, Pennsylvania*

This publication is designed to provide accurate and authoritative information about the subject covered. While every precaution has been taken in the preparation of this material, the authors and The American College® assume no liability for damages resulting from the use of the information contained in this publication. The American College is not engaged in rendering legal, accounting, or other professional advice. If legal or other expert advice is required, the services of an appropriate professional should be sought.

Library of Congress Control Number 2004118161
ISBN 1932819177

Printed in the United States of America

About the Authors

David A. Littell, JD, is Joseph E. Boettner Chair in Financial Gerontology and professor of taxation at The American College. He holds a BA in Psychology from Northwestern University and a JD from the Boston University School of Law. He was previously an attorney with Saul, Ewing, Remick & Saul, and Paul Tanker & Associates, both Philadelphia-based firms.

Kenn Beam Tacchino, JD, LLM, is a consultant to The American College and a professor of taxation and financial planning at Widener University. He received his BA from Muhlenberg College, his law degree (JD) from Western New England Law School, and his LLM from Widener University School of Law. Kenn is a member of the American Bar Association and the National Council on Aging. He previously worked for Massachusetts Mutual Life Insurance Company and Prentice-Hall.

Richard A. Dulisse, MSFS, MSM, CLU, ChFC, CFP, is assistant pro–fessor of financial planning at The American College. He is a member of the Society of Financial Service Professionals and the National Association of Insurance and Financial Advisors (NAIFA).

Constance J. Fontaine, JD, LLM, CLU, ChFC, is Larry R. Pike Chair in Insurance and Investments and associate professor of taxation at The American College. She received her BA from Beaver College, her JD from Widener University School of Law, and her LLM from Villanova University School of Law. She is a member of the Pennsylvania Bar Association, the honor society of Phi Kappa Phi, and the International Legal Fraternity of Phi Delta Phi.

Edward E. Graves, MA, CLU, ChFC, is Charles J. Zimmerman Chair in Life Insurance Education and associate professor of insurance at The American College. A graduate of California State University at Los Angeles, he earned his MA from the Wharton School of the University of Pennsylvania. He is a member of the Society of Financial Service Professionals and the International Association of Financial Planning.

Walt J. Woerheide, PhD, is professor of investments at The American College. His bachelor's degree is from Brown University, and his MBA and PhD are from Washington University in St. Louis. He is a past president of both the Academy of Financial Services and the Midwest Finance Association

Contents

7 Retirement Investment Strategies: The Distribution Period 7.1
Walt J. Woerheide

8 Annuities—Part I 8.1
Richard A. Dulisse

9 Annuities—Part II 9.1
Richard A. Dulisse

Acknowledgments

The authors are grateful to many individuals for their valuable contributions to this book. We would like to express our special appreciation to American College faculty members Richard A. Dulisse, Constance J. Fontaine, Edward E. Graves, and Walt J. Woerheide for writing chapters for this text.

We also thank Susan Doherty and Patricia C. Berenson, production assistants, and Charlene McNulty, production group leader, for their excellent skills and patience in deciphering, typing, and formatting this document; Wendy de Pinho, manuscript editor, for the outstanding job she did editing this textbook; Keith de Pinho, senior editor, and Robert Murphy, manuscript editor, for additional editing and proofreading; Lynn Hayes, editorial director, for meticulous final layout and pagination; Patricia Cheers, permissions editor, for expediting reprints; Ryan M. Emery, senior instructional designer/multimedia developer, for creating and updating graphics; and Virginia E. Webb, librarian, and Mary Anne Adler, library assistant, for help with research and references.

Financial Decisions for Retirement

1

The Nature and Scope of Retirement Planning

Kenn Beam Tacchino

Chapter Outline

Although the discipline of retirement planning is relatively new, it is rapidly evolving into one of the most important elements of comprehensive financial planning. Consider this: In 1930 only one in 10 workers was covered by a pension program and Social Security did not exist in the United States. Today, survey after survey indicates that retirement planning is a top consumer priority. For planners wishing to become first-rate advisors to their senior clients, the study of retirement planning is arguably the key component to establishing their credibility. This is not to say that retirement planning is exclusively about older clients. On the contrary, retirement planning spans the client's life cycle and is all too often misunderstood by clients as a financial planning process restricted to later life.

This chapter will set the stage for your study of retirement planning by identifying the key components of the retirement planning process. It will then explore the greatest threats to retirement security facing clients. The chapter will then turn its attention to the resources available to helping clients achieve financial security in retirement. Finally, the discipline of financial gerontology will be studied with the hope of showing financial planners that there is more to the world of retirement than can be defined by the dollar.

KEY COMPONENTS OF THE RETIREMENT PLANNING PROCESS

In order to understand the discipline of retirement planning, financial services professionals must better understand:

- retirement alternatives
- planning for retirement
- the retirement planning environment
- the steps in the retirement planning process
- the five phases of retirement planning
- the key questions that define the retirement planning discipline

Defining Retirement Alternatives

Retirement defies a singular definition because there are too many variables, lifestyle choices, and contingencies that make it unique for each client. For example, some clients may view retirement as a long-deserved rest, filled with travel and a carefree, low responsibility existence (can anyone say Hakuna Matata?). Others may be retiring from a paying job to take on the demanding role of caregiver for a loved one. Still others may be thinking of retirement as a second, albeit more laid-back, career. For many, it may be a combination of all three.

For some, retirement starts with the last day they *have to* work, for others it starts with the last day they *want to* work, and for others it starts with the last day they *can* work. Retirement goals and expectations vary by individuals—even husbands and wives may have conflicting goals! Health and frailty exposures during retirement vary by individual as well. Some clients will enjoy the blessings of good health and will be able to continue their active lifestyles well into retirement. Other clients will need to alter everything to accommodate health concerns. Another variable that confounds retirement is financial status. Some clients will spend their lives living hand to mouth, while others will have significant discretionary income. What's more, even if clients have a precise picture of what retirement should look like, their expectations and obligations may change over time—both before and after retirement begins. It is within this chaotic environment that financial service professionals must help their clients plan for the moving target of retirement.

Defining Planning—Retirement Style

Whether retirement is a reaction to an unexpected situation or has been carefully thought out starting at the outset of a client's career, one axiom holds true: "It is never too early or too late to plan for retirement." At any stage of the client's life cycle, retirement planning is about recognizing the threats to security later in life and taking actions to mitigate the negative consequences that might ensue. Retirement planning is about helping clients to achieve financial independence and understand the physical health and emotional demands of later life. It is about making dreams come true and planning to avoid nightmares.

It is important to point out that there is no brush which paints all individuals. Some are destined for a secure retirement and the planner's role is to help enhance their security. Others are destined for rough financial times and the planner's role is to help the client achieve the best level of security possible.

The Retirement Planning Environment

To better serve clients in the retirement planning process, planners should be aware of the following factors which help to define the retirement planning environment as we know it today

The Graying of America

The graying of America is a colloquial phrase which describes the gerontological concept of population aging. Population aging occurs when the proportion of older people relative to younger generations increases. There are approximately 35 million people in the United States aged 65 or older. This currently accounts for about 13 percent of the total population. This older population will double to 70 million by 2030 as the baby boomers start to join this cohort. In effect, it is possible to envision a country of Floridas as time goes on because over one in five Americans will be over age 60 by 2040.

The Increase in Longevity

baby boomers

It is predicted that one in nine *baby boomers* (people born between 1946 and 1964) will live to be at least age 90. In addition, the number of those 85 years old and older will quadruple by 2050.

- The number of centenarians worldwide is projected to increase sixteen-fold by 2050 and to reach 1.1 million persons. (The U.S. Census Bureau currently estimates that nearly 66,000 Americans are over the age of 100, compared with about 3,500 in 1990.) In addition, life at age 100 is surprisingly healthy.

life span

- Scientists are debating about what is the maximum potential *life span* (the life span is the maximum potential age of human beings). Most believe it is 120 years (some argue more!).

Long life is more prevalent in women. Women account for 58 percent of those over age 65 and 70 percent of those 85 or older. In addition, the older population will become more ethnically and racially diverse as time goes by. Of those aged 65 or older now, about 84 percent are non-Hispanic whites. By 2050, that number will be 64 percent. One final important fact—the longer a client lives, the better the chances for a client to see a very advanced age (see figure 1-1).

The Changing Nature of Retirement Living

In the middle of the 20th century, renowned American illustrator Norman Rockwell may have pictured retirement and senior citizenship as an older lady in a rocking chair covered by a shawl with a cat cuddled up at her side. If Rockwell were alive today, the picture would be much different! Seniors are better educated, are taking better care of themselves, and are living longer and healthier lives than previous generations. Tennis anyone?

active life expectancy

Active life expectancy (the measure of the number of years a person can expect to live without a disability) is increasing as well as life expectancy (more than 8 out of 10 Americans over the age of 65 are now able to take care of themselves in the routine activities of daily living, an 8.9 percent increase since 1982).

Planners must keep in mind that the insurgence of over 77 million baby boomers into the retirement landscape promises to change the very face of retirement. Totally new patterns of product and service consumption, wealth transfer, travel and leisure, and health management will emerge. Consider, historically, how boomers changed the face of education, housing, and the financial markets at different stages of their life cycle. Why should retirement be any different?

FIGURE 1-1
The Longer You Live. . .The Longer You Live

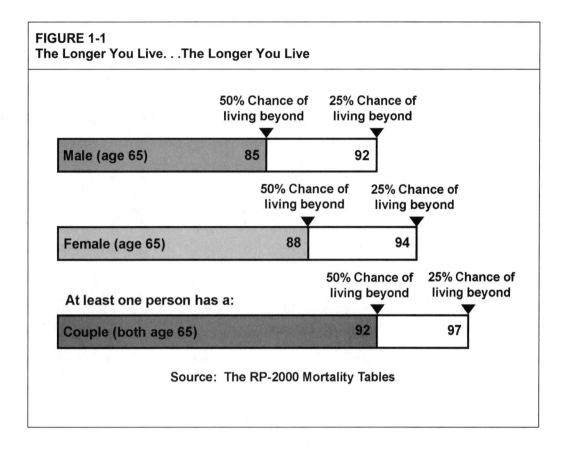

Source: The RP-2000 Mortality Tables

The Need for Caregiving

Another responsibility changing the nature of retirement is caregiving. The retirees of today and tomorrow are increasingly responsible for caring for parents, children, and grandchildren.

John Adams once said there are two types of people in the world, those who are committed to an ideal, and those who require the commitment of others. Throughout our careers, we are committed to accomplishing our ideals. In retirement, we are typically committed to the needs of our loved ones or require the commitment of our loved ones for our needs. Women account for approximately 72 percent of caregivers in the United States. Collectively, family caregivers spend $2 billion of their assets each month to assist relatives. And nearly 90 percent of baby boomers say taking care of their parents is among their top three life priorities. In addition, we often think of caregivers as young and healthy. This is not always the case; for example, a 70-year-old daughter with health issues of her own may be taking care of a 92-year-old mother. Finally, apparently a parent's job never ends! According to the U.S. Census Bureau, about 5.5 million children (or 7.7 percent of all children in the

United States) were living in homes with a grandparent. Three-quarters of the time the grandparent maintains the home. Remember that Norman Rockwell retirement picture? Now picture a grandmother playing catch with her granddaughter as the mother gets into the car to go to work.

Steps in the Retirement Planning Process: Planner Perspective

The process for retirement planning is similar to the process for financial planning, and includes the following steps:

- Establishing client/planner relationships
- Determining goals and expectations and gathering client data
- Analyzing and evaluating the client's financial status
- Developing and presenting the retirement plan
- Implementing the retirement plan
- Monitoring the retirement plan

Financial services professionals intending to offer retirement planning services must also be ready to motivate the client concerning the need to save and plan for the future. Finally, they must be able to educate clients about the realistic possibility that they have to achieve their goals and to suggest alternative strategies when applicable.

Step 1: Establish Client/Planner Relationships

It is essential to establish a working relationship with the client. This involves the identification and explanation of issues, concepts, and products related to the retirement process. The planner should describe the services he or she provides, the steps involved in the process, and the documentation required from the client (such as summary plan descriptions, tax forms, investment summaries, and other information). To better enable effective relationships, planners are expected to understand the aging process and the myriad of financial and non-financial issues involved with senior living.

Step 2: Determine Goals and Expectations and Gather Client Data

This step begins by listening to clients' goals and hopes for retirement. Listening skills are important because it is easy for planners to impose their concept of retirement on clients or to assume what they believe to be important is also important to clients. Clients have a variety of objectives that range from never having to work again to working full time during retirement. Clearly, planners have their work cut out for them as they deal with a plethora of expectations and, in some cases, help frame the expectations of their clients through the education process.

> ## YOUR FINANCIAL SERVICES PRACTICE:
> ## IMPORTANT FACT-FINDING TOOLS
>
> In addition to the typical information concerning assets and liabilities, securities holdings, and annual income, retirement planners need to look at the following:
>
> - wills and trusts
> - long-term care policies
> - Social Security statements
> - employer health benefit policies
> - employer summary plan descriptions
> - employer benefit statements

This is especially true when the clients' expressed goals are vague or imprecise. For example, a goal of retiring in comfort does not provide enough information to direct the remainder of the planning process.

In addition to sorting through the various lifestyle options for retirement, planners must also focus at this stage on conducting a financial inventory of retirement assets and an assessment of the strategies clients have available to them. For example, a planner must account for all resources allocated to retirement and all opportunities a client has, such as the ability to contribute to a Roth IRA or the availability of a 401(k) plan at his or her place of work.

Step 3: Analyze and Evaluate the Client's Financial Status

In this step, the planner looks at the client's current situation as well as his or her future goals in order to evaluate the appropriate strategies for that particular client. This includes the performance of a retirement needs analysis as well as the analysis of the client's risk tolerance, risk management strategies, and risk exposures. For example, does the client have adequate disability insurance and long-term care insurance? Do his or her current investment allocations adequately achieve his or her financial goals? Is the client currently saving enough for retirement? What tax planning and distribution strategies are available, and do they make sense for the client's situation? Planners need to evaluate and analyze current retirement plan exposures (for example, premature distribution tax), current retirement plans, Social Security benefits, and current retirement strategies.

Step 4: Develop and Present the Retirement Plan

The planner should develop and prepare a client-specific retirement plan tailored to meet the client's goals and objectives and commensurate with the client's values, objectives, temperament, and risk tolerance. In addition to the client's current financial position, the plan should include the client's projected retirement status under the status quo as well as projected statements if the planner's recommendations are followed. The planner should also provide a current asset allocation statement along with strategy recommendations and a statement that assumes that recommendations will be followed. Investments should be summarized, and the planner should propose an investment policy statement and additional policy recommendations. The plan should also include an assessment of distribution options and tax strategies for retirement. Finally, the plan should list prioritized action items and address issues such as housing and health care.

After developing and preparing the plan, the planner should present the plan to the client and review it with him or her. The planner should collaborate with the client to ensure that the plan meets the client's goals and objectives, and the planner should revise it as appropriate.

Step 5: Implement the Retirement Plan

geriatric care manager

The planner should assist the client in implementing the recommendations. Typically this requires coordinating with other professionals, such as social workers, *geriatric care managers* (social service professionals with expertise in devising, monitoring, and coordinating care plans for older people), human resource professionals, accountants, attorneys, real estate agents, investment advisers, stock brokers, and insurance agents.

Step 6: Monitor the Retirement Plan

After the plan is implemented, the planner should periodically monitor and evaluate the soundness of recommendations and review the progress of the plan with the client. The planner should discuss and evaluate changes in the client's personal circumstances, such as family births or deaths, illness, divorce, or change in job status. Any relevant changes in tax laws, benefit and pension options, and the economic environment should be reviewed and evaluated before the planner makes recommendations to accommodate new or changing circumstances.

The Five Phases of Retirement Planning: Client Perspective

Despite the fact that retirement is a moving target that defies a singular definition because it will be different for different people, retirement planning occurs throughout the client's life cycle and is typically evidenced by the following phases:

- saving
- increased preparation and visualization
- decision making
- transitioning to retirement and settling into the retirement lifestyle
- coping with frailty

YOUR FINANCIAL SERVICES PRACTICE: INTERNET HELP FOR PLANNERS AND THEIR CLIENTS

Planners and practitioners alike will find the following Web sites useful:

1. *www.ssa.gov*—This site allows individuals to project the benefits they will receive from Social Security; it also provides a great deal of information regarding Social Security.
2. *www.EBRI.org*—The home page of the Employee Benefit Research Institute presents updates, databases, and surveys that have been recently issued.
3. *www.ASEC.org*—The American Savings Education Council provides the ballpark estimate calculator that enables people to calculate their savings need for retirement. It also contains links to different financial calculators.
4. *www.irs.gov*—The IRS Web site provides useful publications on all sorts of retirement issues.
5. *www.benefitscheckup.org*—A new service that allows seniors, their families, and caregivers to quickly and easily identify what programs and services they may qualify for and how to access them.

Note that the phases tend to be a continuum of experiences that may or may not be demarcated by a singular event.

The *savings phase* starts as soon as possible after the client's career begins. During the time, clients will be preoccupied with other competing savings objectives, such as buying a home and family-building expenses. The planner's role in the savings phase is to motivate the client to save for retirement and to educate the client about the importance of starting early. Establishing good retirement savings habits despite the lure of more short-term goals is essential to retirement security because of the miracle of compound interest. Think of clients buying retirement on the installment plan; the sooner they pay, the less it costs. Also, during this period clients often change jobs and the planner's role is to make sure that retirement

rollover

savings are not cannibalized for other uses. *Rollovers,* tax-free transfers from one tax-qualified vehicle (for example, an employer plan) to another (for example, an IRA) can be a key service the planner provides for his client at this stage.

The *increased preparation and visualization phase* cannot be identified with any particular age. In fact, the earlier it starts, the better for retirement security purposes. In this phase, the client kicks retirement planning into high gear. Often the focus on retirement goals is spurred by parents retiring. At this time, children begin to see the parents' plight and realize they want to emulate the positive and not repeat the negative. In the savings phase, the motivation to plan and save came from the planner. In the increased preparation phase, it is the client who sees the need to increase 401(k) contributions or make paying off the house before retirement a priority. To initiate the increased preparation phase, planners should use a retirement calculator to identify the amount needed to be saved for retirement (and at the same time wake up clients concerning their future).

The second part of the phase sees the clients becoming even more focused. The concept of what retirement should be begins to crystallize in their minds. Now the need to meet with a planner becomes more important and possibly more productive. In some cases, they begin to understand that limiting expenses can be just as important a goal as increasing savings. One strategy often suggested by planners during the visualization phase is to save all raises that are earned in the 5 or 6 years prior to retirement. By putting their salary increase into a 401(k), Roth, or conventional IRA, the clients will not only save more for retirement, but will also lock in spending habits and learn not to grow their lifestyle and budget—an important lesson for retirement.

The *decision phase* is often characterized by the imminent event of retirement. The year before, year of, and year after retirement bring with them myriad planning choices and challenges. Clients in the decision phase have often grown tired of their current career. They need to be prepared for a non-working environment or a phased retirement. They often look to restructure asset allocation (often unnecessary because certain retirement assets will not be used for 20 or more years in the future). Sometimes they think of moving into retirement because their children have completed college, they are empty nesting, or they received an inheritance. Other times, age drives the decision of when to retire. However, planners should educate clients that health and money are more accurate drivers of the retirement decision. During the decision phase, planners need to advise clients on a variety of issues, such as pension distributions, when to start Social Security, and how to convert assets into retirement income.

The *retirement transition and lifestyle phase* follows immediately after retirement. It is often accompanied by a surge of increased spending on travel and other recreational pursuits and a focus on adapting to a changed environment. Travel, golf, gardening, and volunteer work often occupy the client's calendar. Communications with former coworkers take on a different character. Grandparenting joys may become part of the lifestyle. Planners must be ready to help with the psychological and emotional needs that accompany these changes. The client-planner relationship goes beyond financial solutions at this time. Once clients have settled into retirement, planners must help them to adjust their spending plans accordingly. Often caregiving responsibilities will become the clients' "new career." As time passes, the nature of the clients environment also changes. Friends and family may die or move away. Relationships with former coworkers grow remote. Events with other seniors take on more importance. By this time, planners need to help clients decide to move near family or to a continuing care retirement community. From a financial situation, clients become more asset rich and income poor.

The *frailty phase* of retirement planning is not dependent on any specific age, but is evidenced by dealing with health issues, caregiving for a spouse, and the loss of mobility. Clients in this phase tend to become more lonely and dependent on others. Proximity to medical services and community services becomes more important. Issues such as forfeiting a driver's license and coping with loss dominate clients' lifestyles. At this stage, the planner can be of service by directing clients to social services. It is also heartening to planners to see that they have helped to council clients to have sufficient resources. The loss of physical independence can be softened by financial independence.

Questions that Define the Retirement Planning Discipline

The essence of retirement planning is to answer clients' questions concerning a variety of issues. For example, with regard to Social Security, clients will be concerned with the inner workings of the system. They will ask what type of benefits it provides and when they should start taking those benefits. They also will want to know what lies ahead for the future of the Social Security system. Answers to these questions about Social Security can be found in chapter 2.

With regard to employer pensions, clients will be concerned with maximizing the tax efficiencies inherent in employer plans. Clients want to understand what benefits the employer plans provide. They also will want to know how nonqualified plans and IRAs can be used to enhance retirement security. Chapters 3 and 4 discusses these issues.

Clients also want planners to answer the questions of whether they can afford to retire. Chapter 5 explains how clients can accumulate sufficient wealth to sustain their preretirement lifestyle without outliving their income.

Clients are also concerned with investment strategies they can use during the accumulation period and the liquidation period. Chapters 6 and 7 discuss investment strategies and asset allocation decisions.

Clients are also curious about how annuities fit into their retirement plan. Chapters 8 and 9 examine various types of annuities and explain how to use annuities to transfer the risk of investing and living too long.

A major concern for clients entering the retirement period is how to properly plan for distributions from qualified plans. They need to be made aware of the available distribution options and they need guidance in order to navigate the maze of choices. Distribution issues are covered in chapters 10 and 11.

downsize

Other questions arise regarding housing. Where should clients live? Should they *downsize*—that is, sell their home to free up assets for retirement use while they move to more senior-friendly housing? These issues and more will be discussed in chapter 12.

The insurance products available for retirement are also of great importance. Clients wonder if and how much long term care insurance they will need: They also need to understand Medicare. They ask which Medigap works best. These issues are answered in chapter 13.

Finally, clients want to know about the intersection of retirement planning and estate planning. In many ways, retirement planning and estate planning have contradictory goals. For example, retirement planners may advise their clients to use a life annuity to protect against living too long. An estate planner, on the other hand, may advise against the use of a life annuity to provide for heirs. Estate planning issues will be discussed in chapter 14.

Throughout your study of retirement planning, keep in mind that planning is more art than science. Be flexible, and encourage your clients to do the same. Together the client and planner can create a bright future and a successful financial solution.

THREATS TO RETIREMENT SECURITY

We stated earlier in this chapter that a key component of retirement planning is recognizing the threats to retirement security and taking actions to mitigate their consequences. A variety of threats and the strategies for overcoming them will be discussed throughout this text. At this point, however, it may be appropriate to identify in one place the major macro concerns that threaten retirement security in the United States. These include:

- *The knowledge gap*—Because of the difficulty in understanding portfolio design and financial planning for retirement, many consumers make serious mistakes. Professional advice is needed, but in many cases people go without it.
- *The biology of aging*—Distressing as it may sound, biologists tell us that as a biological organism we are here to reproduce and nature doesn't have much need for us after that. Planners must be able to provide advice about the myriad issues concerning the aging process through retirement and during the frailty period.
- *Shortcomings of the current system*—Our pension and Social Security system works well in many instances. However, there are many security issues still remaining. These include the transition from coverage under defined-benefit plans to coverage under defined-contribution plans, overuse of employer stock, cutbacks in retiree medical coverage, potential liabilities for the Pension Benefit Guarantee Corporation, and a shortfall in funding for the Social Security system.
- *Unique risks facing women*—Retirement planning is sometimes thought of as a women's issue because of the unique threats to the financial security of older women.

The Knowledge Gap

Despite recent governmental and private-sector policy initiatives to foster financial literacy, a significant financial crisis awaits those who lack the investment sophistication to manage their retirement funds and the financial planning awareness to correctly asses the myriad and complex decisions they will soon encounter. For example, it is not unusual to find a plan participant with significant money in his or her 401(k) account who does not know the difference between a money market fund and a mutual fund. When you ask the participant, he or she will tell you that the money is invested in a 401(k) plan, but will not know the particular investment vehicle. According to a Transamerica Retirement Services survey, 71 percent of workers either strongly agree or agree somewhat that they do not know as much about investing as they should. Further evidence of the investment gap comes from a 2002 study by the National Center for Policy Analysis, which found that many participants barely keep up with inflation because they invest too conservatively. Finally, according to the Investment Company Institute, three out of five plan participants have not reallocated their contributions or plan assets since joining the plan. A case can be made that this inactivity stems from the participant's discomfort with the plan's investment choices rather than from a thoroughly researched buy-and-hold strategy.

The investment knowledge gap is closely paralleled by the financial planning gap. Statistics indicate that too many workers do not know (even remotely) how much savings they will need to provide adequate retirement income. Even when retirement income needs have been calculated, preparation to accumulate the necessary funds is often inadequate. According to a Transamerica Center for Retirement Studies Small Business Retirement Survey, 55 percent of workers either strongly agree or somewhat agree with the statement that they could work until age 65 and still not save enough to meet their retirement needs.

Workers are also uninformed about other planning issues. Many do not own or understand long-term care insurance. Many fail to grasp the concept of annuitization, and others are unfamiliar with the retirement tax rules. One author succinctly says it all:

> Evidence indicates that at every step a significant faction of participants make serious mistakes. A quarter of those eligible to participate in a plan choose not to. Fewer that 10 percent of those who participate contribute the maximum. Over half fail to diversify their investments, many over-invest in company stock, and almost none rebalance their portfolios in response to age or market returns. Most important, many cash out when they change jobs. And very few buy an annuity at retirement.[1]

Not shockingly, the Employee Benefits Research Institute (EBRI) has concluded that the bottom line does not look promising for workers planning to retire. According to the EBRI, "The total annual national retirement income shortfall will grow to as much as $57 billion by 2030, an increase of approximately $25 billion from its projected level in 2005. During the decade ending in 2030, aggregate retiree income shortfall could exceed $500 billion." Much more could be said about the knowledge gap and the lack of financial fundamentals that are prevalent. Worse, however, is that even when greater degrees of sophistication exist, the ability of the participant is often no match for the complex decisions that are necessary for a financially successful retirement. Many can drive a car; some can change their oil; few, however, can rebuild an engine. Professional service will be required for successful results, and far too many individuals are not getting professional counseling.[2]

The Biology of Aging

The title of Art Linkletter's best-selling book says it all: *Old Age is Not for Sissies.* It goes without saying that aging is often characterized by an increased likelihood of disease and dependence and that the physical limitations that define the aging process threaten retirement security. What's more, frailty is an equal threat to retirement security. An individual client's propensity to face frailty or dementia issues depends on a myriad of factors including genetics, behavioral factors, and social factors. It is important to note that people differ not only in how they age, but also in the way they react to the changes taking place in their bodies.

lentigo

The litany of biological changes in the aging process includes mundane changes such as gray hair and *lentigo* (discoloration or spotting that occurs on the face, backs of the hands, and forearms of people over 50) to serious changes such as dementia, heart disease, osteoporosis, and loss of muscle mass (which may contribute to crippling falls). Even chronic problems like arthritis, hearing impairment, and vision issues threaten to restructure living patterns.

activities of daily living (ADLs)

The most common result of negative consequences stemming from the biology of aging is the need for long-term care. According to LIMRA, over 4.5 million people over age 65 have difficulty carrying out *activities of daily living (ADLs)*. Although definitions differ, ADLs include mobility restrictions (for example, transferring from bed to a chair), dressing, bathing, self feeding, and toileting. Other people have dementia. Still others need help with *instrumental activities of daily living (IDALs)*. IDALs include an ability to do light housework, prepare meals, grocery shop, use the telephone, use transportation, keep track of money or bills, and manage medicines.

instrumental activities of daily living (IDALs)

The economic effect of these issues pales in comparison to the human effect. However, the economic implications are a real threat to retirement security. Planners who have become trusted advisors must be ready to adjust budgets and otherwise adapt the financial picture. In addition, they must

---

YOUR FINANCIAL SERVICES PRACTICE: THE BIOLOGY OF AGING—SOME GOOD NEWS

Although aging issues have serious economic implications and threaten to restructure living patterns in many instances, planners and clients should take heart in the following:

- According to a Baltimore longitudinal study on aging, only 10 percent of people over 65 ever develop dementia.
- There is no single pattern for aging. It varies widely from person to person.
- Many losses of function once thought to be age-related can be stopped or slowed.
- Lifestyle changes can fend off or slow age-related diseases such as arthritis, diabetes, heart disease, and stroke. In addition, weight training is proving remarkably useful in ameliorating age-related loss in strength, even in women in their 90s.
- More seniors engage in regular physical exercise than young adults.

---

educate clients about powers of attorney, living wills, and other financial services. Finally, they may need to help clients and their families make decisions regarding when to give up a driver's license, when to move to assisted living, and other related issues.

Shortcomings of the Current System

Our current pension and Social Security system has many shortcomings which threaten retirement security. For example, a subtle yet important threat to retirement security both in the United States and worldwide concerns the type of plan coverage that employees receive. There has been a slow and steady erosion of coverage under defined-benefit systems. According to the EBRI, the percentage of families with defined-benefit coverage has decreased from over 60 percent in 1992 to fewer than 45 percent today. EBRI research shows that in 1975, there were approximately 175,000 defined-benefit plans; by 2001, there were just 36,000 defined-benefit plans left. The rise of the defined-contribution model (for example, 401(k) plans) and the fall of the defined-benefit model have signaled a shift in risk from the employer (who is better able to handle risk) to the employee. In any defined-contribution system, the risk of investment performance falls on the employee. In a defined-benefit plan, the employer must weather turbulent market cycles. In addition, defined-benefit plans have the advantage of being based on a client's final average salary, which typically accounts for pre-retirement inflation. The now predominant defined-contribution system provides benefits based on career average salaries and does not fully account for inflation prior to retirement. In many instances, this will lead to a decline in the wealth needed for retirement. Finally, defined-benefit plans often provide a significant replacement ratio (percentage of final salary) for a long-term employee in the form of an annuity (with the annuity's potential for mortality gain). With a defined-contribution plan, lump-sum distributions are more common and in some cases they will not be used wisely.

In essence, the planner must help clients overcome this changing paradigm by enabling clients to better handle risk and by educating them concerning the sophisticated financial decisions that formerly were left to the employer.

Another gap in the current system centers on the preponderance of money invested in employer stock. For example, before its collapse, Enron employees had over 55 percent of their 401(k) money in employer stock. According to Hewitt Associates, 23 percent of 401(k) plans offer a match in company stock and 85 percent of 401(k) plans have restrictions on the sale of company stock. This factor plus the use of employee stock ownership plans and stock bonus plans, not to mention the use of stock incentives in the non-qualified plan arena, make it so that there is overexposure in company stock by a significant group in almost all age cohorts. The cornerstone principal of diversification is being ignored by too many for too long. Even worse is that an employee's risk is doubled because investment risk and job security are centered on one company.

Other issues of concern with the current system include:

- *Cutbacks in employer-sponsored medical coverage for retirees*—In 1998, two-thirds of large employers offered retiree health benefits; in 2004, only one-third did. In addition, in 2004 79 percent of employers increased retiree premiums.

- *Potential liabilities for the Pension Benefit Guaranty Corporation (PBGC)*—The PBGC protects nearly 44 million workers in more than 32,000 private defined-benefit plans. In a recent year, it paid benefits of $2.5 billion to nearly 1 million people. The guaranteed benefit is around $4,000 per month. According to the PBGC, if its financial condition continues to worsen, years down the road there could be a choice between cuts in benefits, increases in premiums, a congressional bailout, or all of the above. High-profile cases such as US Air, United, TWA, Polaroid, Singer, LTV Steel, Bethlehem Steel, Grand Union, Caldor, and Bradlees have helped to push the PBGC from a $9.7 billion surplus to an $11.2 billion deficit in a short time span. Further erosion of the stock market will threaten this vital cog in retirement security unless Congress takes action to protect it.

- *Changes to Social Security*—When it first started, Social Security had an acceptable ratio of workers to retirees to make the system work. As time goes by, however, the ratio will diminish and those working will not be able to pay for the benefits of those who are retired. Because of this, changes must be made to the system to sustain its future viability. In all likelihood, part of those changes will be benefit cuts which will erode income for retirees.

- *Private pension availability*—Clients who work for medium- and large-sized employers typically have an advantage over their counterparts in small firms. One fact of life in retirement planning is that as the size of the organization increases, the chance of having a pension program increases. For example:
  - Eighty-five percent of workers at employers with 100 or more employees have an employment-based plan available to them
  - Fifty percent of workers at employers with 25–99 employees have an employment-based plan available to them.
  - Twenty percent of workers at employers with less than 25 employees have an employment-based plan available to them.
  - The Employee Benefits Research Institute (EBRI) says over 25 million employees working for small businesses are not covered by company pension plans.

Unique Problems for Women

Women have unique problems that make it difficult to achieve a financially successful retirement. For one thing, women are less likely to have a pension at work than men because they historically work in industries that ignore pensions. Second, they have lower earnings, which obviously make it harder to save for retirement. Third, they experience higher turnover than men, so they are more adversely affected by plan vesting schedules. Fourth, they outlive men, so all else being equal; will need to save more than men. Fifth, they are more likely to be caregivers than men and thus often forgo income to care for a loved one. Sixth, they are more likely to be single or widowed and the burden of retirement in these instances is not shared. And finally, according to studies, they invest pension assets too conservatively and thus self-inflict an additional savings burden. Table 1-1 gives some indication of just how much women feel they are lagging behind their male counterparts in being prepared financially for retirement.

THE RETIREMENT LADDER

Traditional thinking indicates that financial needs during retirement are met from three primary sources—often referred to as the legs of the three-legged stool. The sources include Social Security benefits, employer-sponsored pension plan benefits, and personal savings. In recent years, however, the traditional view of the three-legged stool has often been criticized as being inadequate. For this reason, let us now think of the stool being replaced by a retirement ladder (figure 1-2). The ladder acknowledges that retirement security is dependent upon many additional factors. Let's take a closer look.

TABLE 1-1
Gender Comparisons among Workers

Retirement Confidence

Overall confidence in having enough money to live comfortably throughout retirement:

Males:	29 percent very confident 47 percent somewhat confident 24 percent not confident	Females:	17 percent very confident 48 percent somewhat confident 35 percent not confident

Confidence in doing a good job of preparing financially for retirement:

Males:	28 percent very confident 49 percent somewhat confident 23 percent not confident	Females:	18 percent very confident 49 percent somewhat confident 32 percent not confident

Confidence levels about having enough money to take care of long-term care expenses in retirement:

Males:	16 percent very confident 39 percent somewhat confident 44 percent not confident	Females:	10 percent very confident 33 percent somewhat confident 56 percent not confident

Retirement Preparations

Have saved for retirement:

Males:	69 percent in 2002 68 percent in 2001 79 percent in 2000 71 percent in 1999 69 percent in 1998 70 percent in 1997	Females:	64 percent in 2002 62 percent in 2001 72 percent in 2000 70 percent in 1999 57 percent in 1998 68 percent in 1997

Have done a retirement savings needs calculation:

Males:	37 percent in 2002 44 percent in 2001 58 percent in 2000 54 percent in 1999 49 percent in 1998 39 percent in 1997	Females:	27 percent in 2002 35 percent in 2001 49 percent in 2000 44 percent in 1999 40 percent in 1998 32 percent in 1997

Retirement planning and saving status:

Males:	6 percent ahead of schedule 39 percent on track 26 percent a little behind 　　schedule 28 percent a lot behind schedule	Females:	4 percent ahead of schedule 30 percent on track 25 percent a little behind 　　schedule 37 percent a lot behind schedule

Source: 2002 Retirement Confidence Survey, Employee Benefit Research Institute, American Savings Education Council, Mathew Greenwald & Assts. Reprinted by permission.

FIGURE 1-2
The Ladder of Retirement Security

Social Security

The federal Social Security system provides retirement benefits (as well as disability benefits, survivor's benefits, and Medicare benefits) to a large portion of the workers and their dependents in the United States. Almost all employees living in the United States are covered by the program. Two statistics clearly demonstrate the importance of Social Security benefits: (1) around 90 percent of all individuals aged 65 and older report Social Security benefits as a source of income, and (2) Social Security represents more than 40 percent of total income for this group (see figure 1-3). For most Americans, Social Security benefits alone will not provide adequate retirement income, especially for higher-income employees, whose percentage of salary replaced by Social Security benefits is smaller (around 20 percent of income for those in the highest quintile).

Whether the current system remains the same or is reduced because of funding problems, Social Security should not be overly relied upon. The retirement planner must understand that Social Security is an important stream of income but, especially for the more highly compensated worker, it will not provide anywhere near the preretirement income replacement ratio needed for a secure retirement. For lower-income individuals, Social Security becomes a much more central source of retirement income. However, even for a single individual retiring with an annual income of $24,000, Social Security provides a replacement ratio of only 43.2 percent—nowhere near the amount necessary for a secure retirement. Factoring in the additional possibility of future reductions in Social Security, everyone planning for retirement should be aware that other sources of retirement income are necessary for a secure retirement.

Company-Sponsored Retirement Plans

Nearly 95 million Americans are covered by a company-sponsored retirement plan. As we already mentioned, one form of plan is a defined-benefit plan. Defined-benefit plans provide a specified benefit, usually in the form of a life annuity beginning at a specified normal retirement age.

The major strengths of the defined-benefit plan include the following: First and foremost is that for the long-term employee, the defined-benefit plan often provides a substantial benefit for the entire life of both the retiree and his or her spouse. Another important feature of the defined-benefit plan is that benefits can be based upon the employee's service prior to the establishment of the plan. This is significant when a company that has not had a plan now wants to provide for the retirement income of current long-term employees.

Another form of coverage comes from defined-contribution plans. In every defined-contribution plan, as money is contributed to the plan, it is allocated to

FIGURE 1-3
Income Sources as a Percent of Personal Income by Personal Income Quintile for Persons Age 65 and Older in 2002

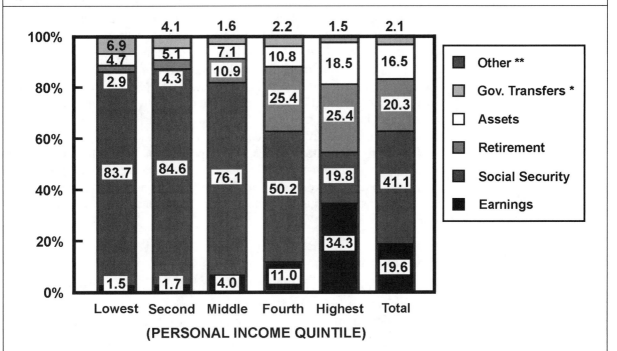

* Government cash transfers include unemployment compensation, workers'
  compensation, veterans benefits, SSI, public assistance, and education assistance.
** Other income includes child support, alimony payments, and family financial assistance.
Note: Because the smallest value of one category "Others" cannot be shown and labeled,
  numbers do not sum to 100 percent.
Source: March 2003 current Population Survey.

individual accounts for each worker. In some plans, the employer contributes a fixed payment to each worker's account each year. In other plans, the employer can contribute a discretionary amount each year. Benefits are based on the size of the account—which equals contributions plus any gains or losses, income, expenses, and (in some cases) forfeitures allocated to the account. To participants, the defined-contribution plan looks simple—like a bank account—and they see their accounts increase with contributions and investment earnings. Finally, many types of defined-contribution plans allow individual participants to select investment alternatives.

The role of the private pension and the expertise of the financial service professional cannot be overstated. Planners must properly evaluate the client's plan. Planners also must understand the difference between the defined-benefit approach and the defined-contribution approach, the impact of retiring at various ages, the effect of changing jobs, and so on. Also, as defined-contribution plans become more prominent, retirement planners have some new accountabilities: counseling clients about appropriate investment choices under the plan and helping clients determine how much to contribute to employee pretax savings plans, such as 401(k) plans. One topic that was not discussed here but is another important role for retirement planners is counseling clients on the taxation of pension distributions. This important area is covered in depth in later chapters.

Income from private pensions is an important source of retirement income. However, only slightly more than 30 percent of the population aged 65 and older have pension income and, to the surprise of many, pension income for current retirees represents only about 20 percent of total retirement income (see table 1-2).

Personal Savings

Just from watching the news, most of us are aware of the low savings rate for Americans today. In the 1960s, the average savings rate was almost 7.4 percent, but in the most recent 10-year period, the average rate was below 5 percent.

TABLE 1-2
Sources of Income for Persons 65 and Older

Source	Approximate Percentage of 65 + Cohort Who Have It	Approximate Mean Amount from Source	Approximate Median Amount from Source
Social Security	89	$10,000	$ 9,900
Interest income	53	3,400	600
Pension income	31	13,000	8,400
Dividend income	23	3,600	800
Earnings income	16	28,000	15,000
Rents, royalties, estates or trusts	8	8,000	3,000
Survivor benefits	5	9,000	5,500
SSI	4	4,200	3,400

Source: March 2003 Current Population Survey and AARP Public Policy Institute

Something also looks wrong when comparing the savings rate in the United States with that of other parts of the world. Households in Europe and Japan have boosted savings dramatically in recent years. In the same time span, the U.S. savings rate stayed below 5 percent. In all, it is hard to imagine that individuals are generally saving enough to be ready for retirement.

The goal of any successful retirement savings program is to accumulate enough assets to reach some targeted amount. How this amount is calculated is quite complex, and is the subject of chapter 5. Once the accumulation goal is chosen, the saver needs a strategy of how to reach it. In plotting a strategy, the individual must understand that three components affect the outcome. They include the length of the accumulation period (accumulation of capital is affected profoundly by the length of the accumulation period; the longer an amount is invested and allowed to accumulate, the greater the effect of compounding), the rate of return (clients should be counseled to invest for the long haul), and the amount invested (the rate of return on an investment of $0 is zero percent).

Over 50 percent of people aged 65 and older have interest income and approximately 25 percent have dividend income. For many, personal savings will also be found in extra savings put into IRAs and 401(k) plans. Government statistics (see figure 1-3 and table 1-2), however, put the money coming from these sources in the pension category.

Informed Planning

One of the key rungs on the ladder of retirement success is proper planning. In a recent study, more than 90 percent of human resource and financial managers believed that employees are ill prepared to make their own retirement decisions (see the previously discussed "Knowledge Gap"). In the same study, 86 percent of human resource and financial managers felt that their employees needed financial advice regarding retirement assets above and beyond the current educational information they were receiving. Because fiduciary liability concerns often make the plan sponsor hesitant to provide advice, third-party advice becomes increasingly important.

This represents a huge opportunity and challenge for financial services professionals. Professionals who can meet this need can provide a necessary service to business clients and also increase their individual client base. Consider this:

- According to one study, investment education has replaced health care as the top concern for employee benefit professionals and employers.
- Seminar presentations are an invaluable service that financial services professionals can provide; 401(k) participation jumps 17 percent when seminars are offered. Contribution rates are also up.
- According to one research study, the most important priority for plan sponsors over the next 5 to 10 years is employee education.

- Sixty-two percent of employers offer retirement education.
- Only one of every two plan sponsors feels they have sufficient time and resources to fulfill their fiduciary responsibility to provide adequate information to educate plan participants.

One final point: One of the great myths of our time is that the Internet will replace retirement planners. A recent survey of affluent clients revealed that although high-income clients use the Internet for supplemental retirement planning advice and information, they still prefer working directly with their financial advisor.

The retirement planner, *working in conjunction with the Internet* and perhaps a better-informed consumer, is still an integral part of the process. The trusted advisor will no sooner be replaced by Internet information than movie theaters were replaced by videos. According to Relia Star Financial Group, 65-year-olds without a written financial plan are twice as likely to find retirement a time of financial worry as their counterparts who have a plan.

Insurance Solutions

A key resource for retirement security is sufficient insurance protection in all forms of insurance. In all phases of life, an insurance checkup is needed to ensure financial security. From renter's insurance to long-term care, seniors often find themselves lacking the protection they need. Insurance solutions will be discussed in detail in a later chapter. However, at this point it is worth noting that clients who have Medigap coverage, long-term care insurance, and other protections will *be* more financially secure and will *feel* more secure than clients who do not have these protections. One fact that may help to illustrate this concerns a recent Fidelity Investments estimate. According to the estimate, the average 65-year old couple retiring today will need $190,000 to cover medical tests over the next 15 to 20 years. The estimate includes expenses with Medicare premiums, Medicare cost-sharing provisions, and prescription drug costs. As if the $190,000 figure were not disturbing enough, the Fidelity estimate does not account for other health expenses such as over-the-counter medications, dental service, and long-term care.

Fiscal Welfare/Social Assistance

fiscal welfare

social assistance

For clients of limited means, one of the keys to financial security in retirement concerns fiscal welfare and social assistance. *Fiscal welfare* is an indirect payment made to individuals through the tax system. An example is the retirement savings contribution credit (discussed later). *Social assistance* is a type of social benefit which contains eligibility criteria designed in part to encourage the able-bodied poor to work by providing minimal benefits.

An example of social assistance would be supplemental security income (discussed later). Planners need to assist clients in understanding these important social programs. For this reason, a closer study of these programs is in order.

The retirement savings contributions credit is a tax credit of up to $1,000 ($2,000 if married filing jointly) which is given as an incentive for lower-income clients to save for their future. It is available to your client if they make an "eligible contribution" which includes a contribution to a traditional or Roth IRA; a 401(k), 403(b), or 457 plan; a SIMPLE, or a salary reduction SEP (SARSEP).

The credit applies to individuals with incomes up to $25,000 ($37,500 for a head of household) and married couples, filling jointly, with incomes up to $50,000. The client must also be at least age 18, not a full-time student, and not claimed as a dependent on another person's return.

The credit is a percentage of the qualifying contribution amount, with the highest rate for taxpayers with the least income, as shown in table 1-3.

TABLE 1-3
Retirement Savings Contribution Credit

Credit Rate	Income for Married, Joint	Income for Head of Household	Income for Others
50%	up to $30,000	up to $22,500	up to $15,000
20%	$30,001–$32,500	$22,501–$24,375	$15,001–$16,250
10%	$32,501–$50,000	$24,376–$37,500	$16,251–$25,000

When figuring this credit, your clients must subtract the amount of distributions they have received from their retirement plans from the contributions they have made. This rule applies for distributions starting 2 years before the year the credit is claimed and ending with the filing deadline for that tax return. Form 8880, "Credit for Qualified Retirement Savings Contribution," is used to figure the amount of credit, which is then reported on Form 1040 or Form 1040A.

Supplemental Security Income (SSI)

Supplemental Security Income (SSI) is a benefit program administered by the Social Security Administration that pays monthly income to clients who are 65 or older, blind, or disabled. An individual client who qualifies for the full benefit can receive close to $600 per month and a couple can receive close to $900 per month. In addition, state supplements may increase these amounts, depending on your client's state of residence.

In a recent year, almost 4 percent of the population 65 and older received an average of $4,200 in SSI. Since the benefits are need based, the key question planners must answer is whether their clients are eligible. Because of the complexities involved (including the rules for living with another person and citizenship), it is necessary to work with the Social Security Administration to determine eligibility after you have helped the client conduct a financial inventory. As a general rule, to qualify a client must have limited resources and income (as well as meet other criteria). Assets will be limited to $2,000 ($3,000 per couple), but they do not include the home, car, household goods, and other items. The amount of income a client can have each month and still get SSI depends partly on where the client lives. The federal payment is based on countable income. Examples used in Social Security publications show clients getting reduced benefits even when their earned or unearned income (including Social Security) exceeded $500 per month.[3]

Older Americans Act (OAA)

A third and related topic under this section concerns the *Older Americans Act (OAA)*. This law assists senior Americans in living independently and has generated several topics of importance for lower-income clients and others. Services include the National Older Americans Volunteer Program, nutrition programs for seniors, and the nursing home ombudsman program (in which nursing home residents are provided an advocate for resolution of concerns about quality of services and conditions of nursing facilities). The OAA is administered on the national level through the Administration on Aging (AOA). On a state level, administration occurs at the State Unit on Aging (SUA). More importantly, all states have set up Area Agencies on Aging (AAA). The AAA can be an invaluable resource for your clients.

Topics covered by the AAA include:

- finding OAA-funded transportation services (trips to doctors and shopping)
- contracting with the service providers for delivery of services (meals, legal services)
- assessments for Medicaid qualification
- in-home supportive services
- helping children resolve a variety of issues when parents live far away and need care

Perhaps most importantly, AAA can put older persons in touch with OAA services that have an impact on finances (for example, Medigap counseling) and therefore make for a great networking opportunity.

eldercare locator

One of the provisions of the OAA is the eldercare locator. The *eldercare locator* allows clients, their caregivers, and their planners to call a toll-free number (1-800-677-1116 or www.eldercare.gov) and talk to someone who can facilitate help. The specialist who answers the call will want to know the county, city, or zip code of the elder person who needs assistance and a brief description of the problem. He or she will then access general agency information, hotlines, and special services offered in the area and a list of information and referral assistance providers that are available. For example,

---

> ### YOUR FINANCIAL SERVICES PRACTICE:
> ### BENEFITS CHECK-UP
>
> This free National Council on Aging-sponsored Web site (www.ncoa.org) is a direct-access consumer Web site that informs clients and their planners about benefits that may be available. Over 1,100 federal, state, and local benefit programs are maintained in the system. Compare this with the government's version, www.govbenefits.gov, which references only 50 federal programs. Clients are asked to take 10–15 minutes to complete confidential questionnaires (no names, addresses, or Social Security numbers are required). Benefits Check-Up then applies the information in the questionnaire to its database and searches for programs for people age 55 and older that may pay for some of their costs of prescription drugs, health care, utilities, and other essential items and services. Benefits Check-Up gives the client a personalized report that lists programs he or she may qualify for, telephone numbers, and directions on how to sign up for these programs. For more information, visit www.benefitscheckup.org, or the National Council on Aging Web site (www.ncoa.org) for a direct link.

they may provide information on local home and community-based care services, such as meal delivery, transportation assistance, and chore service. They can also provide information on housing options, community senior centers, adult day care, respite care options, and specialized services for seniors with Alzheimer's, cancer, or heart disease.

A recent offshoot of the renewal of the OAA (2000), the Family Caregiver Support Group helps people who are providing primary care for spouses, parents, older relatives, and friends. The program calls for all states to have five basic services for family caregivers: information to caregivers about available services, assistance to caregivers in gaining access to services, individual counseling, support groups and caregiver training, and *respite care* (to enable caregivers to be temporarily relieved from their caregiving responsibilities).

respite care

For the caregiver, personal respite varies as much as the individual and could mean, for example, attending a doctor's appointment or going shopping; taking the opportunity to nap, bathe, or otherwise rejuvenate himself or herself; attending a church service or seeing a movie; taking a much-needed vacation; pampering oneself with a hair appointment or manicure; scheduling elective surgery; or simply visiting friends or relatives. (For more information on caregiver support, see the Administration on Aging Web site, www.aoa.gov.)

Part-Time Wages

Over 2 million people or 23 percent of the 65–69 cohort remain in the labor force. In addition, according to a recent AARP survey, 66 percent of older workers plan to work well into their retirement years. For all people aged 65 and older, 16.3 percent have earned income and the median income is $15,000. Seniors continue to work for a variety of reasons, including these:

- They enjoy work.
- They wish to keep health insurance or other benefits.
- They see work as a source of status.
- They find recreational pursuits unsatisfactory.
- They need to spend physical and mental energy in a meaningful way.
- They need to avoid social isolation.
- They feel successful at work.
- They want money to buy extras or make ends meet.

No matter what the reason, people receive significant income from full-time and part-time wages in retirement. Planners find it difficult to account for this income in the early stages of the planning process because they feel that despite clients' intentions to work, health concerns may impede their goal. On the other hand, planners faced with clients who started planning too

phased retirement

late in life for retirement can consider a *phased retirement* (a reduction in hours and commitments rather then a complete removal from the workforce) or a second career of part-time work as a viable planning strategy.

Inheritances

For some clients, inheritances will add to their financial security in retirement. According to AARP, only 15 percent of baby boomers expect to receive any future inheritances. The median value of inheritances already received by baby boomers was $47,900, and less than 2 percent received over $100,000. It is important to know that the bulk of wealth is concentrated in the hands of the wealthiest 10 percent. It's also important to know that parents are living longer and spending down accumulated assets or have annuitized their wealth so that second generation inheritances are unlikely. This does not mean that clients will not get an inheritance from their parents. It does mean, however, they should not count on inheritances as a financial planning tool.

Other Forms of Support

There are a variety of other sources of retirement income, including:

- *home equity*—for many, this represents the largest asset they will have in the later retirement years. Strategies such as downsizing to free up cash or using a reverse mortgage may be considered.
- *life insurance*—receiving life insurance from a deceased spouse or cashing out a whole life policy may provide retirement protection for

some. In addition, under the so-called pension-maximization technique, life insurance may be used as a substitute for a joint and survivor annuity.

- *family business assets*—if a client owned his or her own business, he or she may be able to capitalize on the business by selling it at retirement.
- *rental property*—some clients may receive rental income from property they own.

FINANCIAL GERONTOLOGY

In order to better serve clients and to prosper in the senior market, financial service professionals need to better understand the emerging discipline of financial gerontology. Financial gerontology is a field of study concerned with the dynamics of financial security, well-being, and the quality of life within and across generations. Students of financial gerontology explore the relationships of economic forces to gerontological trends and emphasize the theories and data of gerontology as part of holistic financial services.

Planners who have an understanding of financial gerontology are less likely to miscalculate solutions for senior clients and are more likely to convince a senior client and his or her family to take the proper course of action.

The demographics of the marketplace are an interesting place to start our brief overview of financial gerontology. Most planners are aware of the baby boom generation and its 77 million participants. However, few are aware that the children of these boomers—the so-called *echo boomers* (people born between 1977 and 1994) are 72 million strong. Of key concern to the gerontologist and to the financial service professional is the elderly dependency ratio. The *elderly dependency ratio* is the number of persons 65 or older per 100 persons of working age (18–64). It will increase from 20 per 100 in 1990 to 30 per 100 in 2030. The increase in this ratio is causing concerns for government systems like Social Security, Medicare, and Medicaid. In addition, the very nature of senior living will be affected by the increase in the dependency ratio, which coincides with the aging to the baby boomer generation.

The biology of aging was mentioned earlier as one of the threats to retirement security. The biology of aging, health, and wellness are also important topics in financial gerontology. Planners should be aware that heart disease and cancer are responsible for two-thirds of all deaths among people age 65 to 84. Planners should also understand that socioeconomic factors positively affect health for a variety of reasons, including increased likelihood of having health insurance, access to good health care, and access to preventative care, such as mammograms. For planning purposes, active life expectancy (the measure of the number of years a person can expect to live without a disability) is a key factor.

echo boomers

elderly dependency ratio

Financial gerontology is also concerned with the economic status of the aged. Fortunately, there is good news in this area because the economic status for older Americans has improved over recent decades. As late as 1966, nearly one out of three Americans age 65 or older lived in poverty. Today it is below 11 percent. Despite impressive gains in income and wealth, it is important to recognize that the gains have been unevenly distributed. The death of a spouse or a decline in health often triggers a financial crisis for seniors (especially for racial and ethnic minorities). What's more, women of all ages are more likely to be poor then men. Finally, the young-old have a significant income advantage over the old-old.

Deciding when to retire is another issue of concern in the field of financial gerontology. Professionals who receive intrinsic rewards from work often delay retirement, whereas people who work at routine and unchallenging jobs all their lives are eager to retire. Some people who are not financially ready will time their own retirement on the basis of their desire to trade work for leisure. Factors that influence retirement include

- The rules of the job
- The meaning of work
- Health
- Income
- Family responsibilities

Some will seek joint retirement, in which dual worker couples retire at the same time. Others will seek sequential retirement—either the husband or wife retires first while the other continues to work. Often availability and affordability of health insurance drives the decision for sequential retirement.

The transition from work to retirement is another major issue in financial gerontology. So-called crisp retirement, which is an abrupt departure from a lifetime career, is how it will work for some who plan and for those who find themselves unexpectedly forced out of work. However, gerontologists point out that it is difficult to define retirement as leaving one's main work when most people do not have lifetime employment with a single firm. In addition, many Americans do not leave the labor force completely when they leave their full-time jobs. In one study, 25 percent went to part-time work on the same job and 25 percent switched to different jobs. For these blurred retirements, there is still a gradual transition with the work and retirement roles overlapping. For others, *bridge jobs* span the period between full-time employment in a career and permanent retirement. Clients who find themselves permanently retired may experience retirement as a busy time. Clients have to adjust to a new social identity, but most healthy retirees sustain busy and active lives.

Satisfaction with retirement is another major topic of financial gerontology. There are two theories used to explain how well people adjust

crisis theory

continuity theory

The Age Discrimination and Employment Act (ADEA)

to retirement. The *crisis theory* views the occupational role as the major source of personal validation. The loss of work is a wrenching experience that deprives clients of status and a meaningful role in society. The *continuity theory* stresses the persistence of personal identity through the expansion of other roles. Retirees who fall into this more prevalent category are more likely to experience retirement in a positive way.

In many instances, studies have shown that happiness in retirement is associated with good health, adequate income, and access to a social support system. People who are married have more positive attitudes in retirement, higher satisfaction with retirement, and better adaptation to retirement than those who are not married.

Employment prospects for older workers are yet another concern for financial gerontologists. *The Age Discrimination and Employment Act* (ADEA) has made it illegal to discriminate against workers over 40 since 1967. Technically under the law, older workers can't be fired, demoted, or receive reduced salaries without good cause. However, the ADEA has not eliminated discrimination in hiring and firing, nor has it effectively combated bias against older workers. What's worse, older workers who lose their jobs take longer then other workers to find a new job and are more likely to take a pay cut when they do.

Financial gerontologists recognize that the living arrangements of senior clients are critically important to their quality of life. The issue of whether to remain in their own home or move (and if so, when) is a major choice faced by retirees. For those who choose to age in place, an accommodation must be made between the aging individual and his or her retirement home. For example, many older people could benefit from modifications to their homes that could promote self-care and safe independent living. These include grab bars and handrails in the shower area, stair lifts, push bars on doors because knobs may be hard to turn, accessible kitchens, and lighting improvements. A different set of strategies is necessary for those who choose to move near family or to an assisted living or continuing care retirement community. (More on this in a later chapter.)

Other areas of study in financial gerontology include:

- family relationships and social support networks (women are typically better off than men in these areas) and family caregiving
- marriage and widowhood (widowed men are seven times more likely to remarry then widowed women)
- migration of retirees to Sun Belt states such as Florida and Arizona in the search for warm climates and reasonably priced retirement housing
- grandparents raising grandchildren
- changes in the population pyramid (the population pyramid reflects the distribution of a population by age and gender)

- the squaring of the mortality curve (delaying illness and morbidity as long as possible)
- the types of government programs and social services available to aging Americans
- understanding the differences between male and female clients (for example, women are more likely then men to acknowledge their need for assistance and to seek help from others, and women are more likely then men to receive social support and to have an adequate social network)

Although there is more to gerontology and financial gerontology then the brief overview we just studied, a more detailed discussion is beyond the scope of this chapter.

CONCLUSION

It may be useful to conclude our overview of the nature and scope of retirement with a review of governmental support for the issue.

One encouraging fact about retirement is that it is currently receiving widespread governmental and consumer support. Tax preferences for employer pension plans are the single largest tax expenditure, exceeding subsidies for home mortgages and health benefits. The general accounting office estimates that preferences exceed $76 billion. In addition, expenditures for Keogh plans were $5 billion and expenditures for IRAs were $12.2 billion.

Looking at it another way, Roth IRAs, a fairly new governmental policy, have become a popular way to save for retirement. Ownership of Roth IRAs has increased dramatically. Roth IRAs are being opened by younger clients and also by people who didn't have traditional IRAs. Additionally, the percentage of American households having some type of IRA has grown to 41 percent because of the popularity of the Roth IRA.

Roth IRAs, SIMPLE pensions (discussed in a later chapter), and age weighted or cross-tested profit-sharing plans (also discussed in a later chapter) are just a few of the newer options in the retirement planning arsenal.

Finally, the government left no doubt that its policies were retirement friendly when it enacted major tax legislation in the spring of 2001. The Economic Growth and Tax Relief Reconciliation Act of 2001 (EGTRRA) adopted many of the provisions that had been proposed in a retirement security summit several years earlier. They included:

- increases in the defined-contribution limit
- increases in the annual limit on compensation
- increases in the defined-benefit limit

- faster vesting schedules for employer matching contributions
- catch-up provisions that allow extra retirement savings for those who are 50 and older

In total, these and other changes (discussed further in chapter 3) make it easier and more effective for clients to save for retirement. More importantly, the government has weighed in strongly in favor of a policy that will promote retirement savings and retirement security.

NOTES

1. Mannell and Surdon, "Avoiding Mistakes in Your 401(k) Plan," *The Boston Globe,* February 4, 2004.
2. The preceding section was reprinted with permission from the following: Kenn Beam Tacchino, "Beyond Retirement Seminars: A Suggested Model for Closing the Knowledge Gap," *Journal of Financial Service Professionals*, March 2005, 43–54.
3. The preceding section is reprinted with permission from the following: Kenn Beam Tacchino, "Retirement Planning—The Rest of the Story," *Journal of Financial Service Professionsals*, May 2003, 10–12.

2

Social Security

Kenn Beam Tacchino

Chapter Outline

BACKGROUND/HISTORY

Social Security

Social Security is arguably the most important retirement plan in the United States. Social Security is much more than retirement, however. Technically, *Social Security* is the old-age, survivors, disability, and health insurance (OASDHI) program of the federal government. In addition to retirement benefits, the Social Security system also provides benefits to disabled workers and to families of workers who have died, retired, or become disabled. Currently, approximately 52 million Americans—one out of every six—receive retirement, survivors, and disability benefits from Social Security. In addition, the hospital insurance (HI) program provides health care coverage through Medicare to retirees, the disabled, and their families.

Historically, Social Security has been a work in progress. The system has been changed a number of times to meet the ever-changing needs of the people it serves. Currently further changes are being debated in Washington. When these changes are sorted out they will represent another chapter in a long and storied history for the Social Security system. For an overview of the history of Social Security, see the timeline in table 2-1.

For retirement planning purposes, planners need to be familiar with the entire Social Security system. This chapter focuses on OASDI benefits, which include old-age retirement benefits, disability benefits, and survivor benefits. Medicare, along with other retiree health care issues, will be discussed in a later chapter. Finally, this chapter will review who is covered under the OASDI program, who pays for it, and what benefits are provided. In addition, tax issues are discussed.

EXTENT OF COVERAGE

Close to 90 percent of the workers in the United States are in covered employment under the Social Security program. This means that these workers have wages (if they are employees) or self-employment income (if they are self-employed) on which Social Security taxes must be paid. For this reason, it is important for the retirement planner to understand potential clients who are not covered under the Social Security program. The following are the major categories of workers who may not receive benefits under the program:

TABLE 2-1
History of Social Security

1935	FDR signs the Social Security Act providing for old-age insurance
1939	Survivors benefits are added
1940	First benefits are paid out
1950	Truman extends coverage to many farm and domestic workers, state and municipal employees, and some professionals
1956	Disability coverage added by Eisenhower; women become eligible for some benefits at 62 rather than 65
1965	Johnson adds Medicare
1972	Benefit increases pegged to the cost of living
1983	Social Security Reform Act

- people with less than 40 quarters of coverage (discussed later)
- civilian employees of the federal government who were employed by the government prior to 1984 and who are covered primarily under the Civil Service Retirement System. Coverage for new civilian federal employees under the entire program was one of the most significant changes resulting from the 1983 amendments to the Social Security Act. It should be noted, however, that all federal employees have been covered under Social Security for purposes of Medicare since 1983.
- railroad workers. Under the Railroad Retirement Act (RRA), employees of railroads have their own benefit system that is similar to OASDI. However, they are covered under Social Security for purposes of Medicare. In addition, there are certain circumstances under which railroad workers receive benefits from the Social Security program even though their contributions were paid to the railroad program.
- employees of state and local governments unless the state has entered into a voluntary agreement with the Social Security Administration. However, this exemption applies only to those employees who are covered under their employer's retirement plan. Under an agreement with the Social Security Administration, the state may either require that employees of local governments also be covered or allow local governments to decide whether to include their employees. In addition, the state may elect to include all or only certain groups of its employees. Prior to 1984, states and local government units were allowed to withdraw their employees from Social Security coverage. However, this withdrawal privilege is no longer available.
- American citizens working abroad for foreign affiliates of U.S. employers, unless the employer owns at least a 10 percent interest in the foreign affiliate and has made arrangements with the Secretary of the

Treasury for the payment of Social Security taxes. However, Americans working abroad are covered under Social Security if they are working directly for U.S. employers rather than for their foreign subsidiaries.

- ministers who elect out of coverage because of conscience or religious principles
- workers in certain jobs, such as student nurses, newspaper carriers under age 18, and students working for the school at which they are regularly enrolled or doing domestic work for a local college club, fraternity, or sorority
- certain family employment. This includes the employment of a child under age 18 by a parent. This exclusion, however, does not apply if the employment is for a corporation owned by a family member.
- certain workers who must satisfy special earnings requirements. For example, self-employed persons are not covered unless they have net annual earnings of $400 or more.

One last point concerning the extent of coverage—many of the groups not covered (for example, federal workers in the civil service retirement system and railroad workers covered by the RRA) have significant pensions that account for the lack of Social Security coverage. In addition, nonworking spouses (those with less than 40 quarters of coverage) may be entitled to a spousal benefit under the system. In other words, many of those excluded from coverage are "taken care of" in other ways.

BREADTH OF COVERAGE

According to the Social Security Administration, Social Security replaces about 40 percent of the average worker's preretirement earnings. For more affluent clients, this percentage will be lower, however, because of the way benefits are structured to favor lower-paid workers over higher-paid workers (see figure 2-1). America's reliance on Social Security, particularly for middle- and lower-income Americans, is staggering. Consider this:

- Only about 10 percent of American senior citizens live in poverty; without Social Security it would be nearly 50 percent.
- For nearly two-thirds of seniors (65 percent), Social Security is their major source of income. In other words, it is more than one-half of what they have to live on in retirement.
- Social Security is the only source of income for nearly one-third of seniors.

One can conclude from these statistics that the breadth and importance of the Social Security system is divided along (for lack of a better term) "class"

FIGURE 2-1
Social Security Replacement Ratios for Retiree and Family

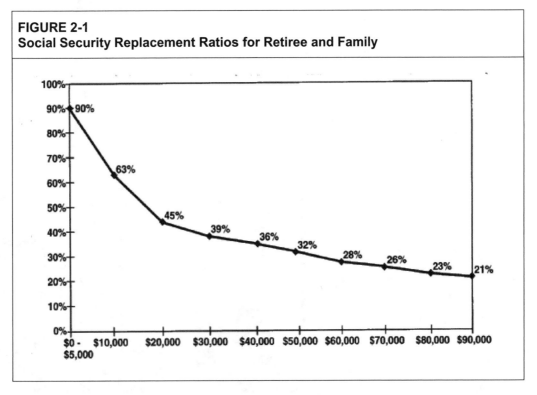

lines. For people in the upper-middle- and upper-income groups, Social Security, while important, is not vital. For people below those levels, however, Social Security is crucial to financial well being. (See figure 2-2.)

FUNDING

All benefits of the OASDI program are financed through a system of payroll and self-employment taxes paid by all persons covered under the program. Employers of covered persons are also taxed.

taxable wage base

FICA tax

Currently, an employee and his or her employer pay a tax of 7.65 percent each on the first $90,000 of the employee's wages. This is called the *taxable wage base*. Of this tax rate, 6.2 percent is for OASDI and 1.45 percent is for Medicare. (This is also called the *FICA tax*—Federal Insurance Contributions Act.) The 1.45 percent Medicare tax rate is also levied on all wages in excess of $90,000. The tax rates are currently scheduled to remain the same after 2005. However, the wage bases are adjusted annually for changes in the national level of wages. The tax rate for the self-employed is 15.3 percent on the first $90,000 of self-employment income and 2.9 percent on the balance of any self-employment income. (This is also known as the *SECA tax*—Self-Employment Contributions Act.) The SECA tax is equal to the combined

SECA tax

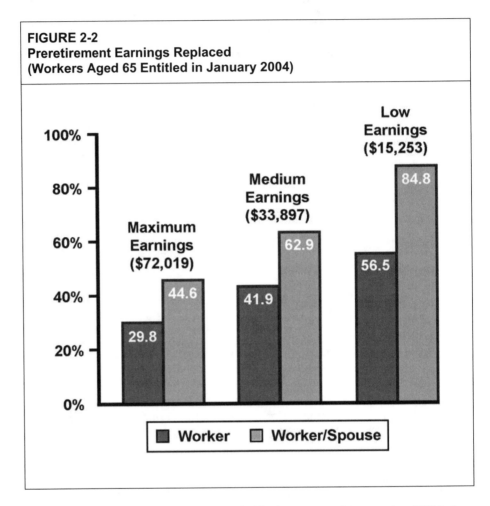

FIGURE 2-2
Preretirement Earnings Replaced
(Workers Aged 65 Entitled in January 2004)

employee and employer rates. An individual must continue paying FICA (or SECA) taxes as long as he or she continues employment, even if Social Security benefits have already begun.

Over the years, both the tax rate and the wage base have been dramatically increased to finance increased benefit levels under Social Security as well as new benefits that have been added to the program. Table 2-2 shows the magnitude of these increases for selected years.

The Social Security program is essentially based on a system of pay-as-you-go financing with limited trust funds. This means that current payroll taxes and other contributions the program receives are used to pay the current benefits of persons who are no longer paying Social Security taxes because of death, old age, or disability. This is in direct contrast to private insurance or retirement plans, which are based on advance funding, whereby assets are accumulated from current contributions to pay the future benefits of those making the contributions.

TABLE 2-2
Changes in Tax Rate and Wage Base under Social Security

Year	Wage Base	Tax Rate	Maximum Employee Tax
1950	$ 3,000	1.50%	$ 45.00
1955	4,200	2.00	84.00
1960	4,800	3.00	144.00
1965	4,800	3.65	174.00
1970	7,800	4.80	374.40
1975	14,100	5.85	824.85
1980	25,900	6.13	1,587.67
1985	39,600	7.05	2,791.80
1986	42,000	7.15	3,003.00
1987	43,800	7.15	3,131.70
1988	45,000	7.51	3,379.50
1989	48,000	7.51	3,604.80
1990	51,300	7.65	3,924.45
1991	first 53,400	7.65	
	next 71,600	1.45	5,123.30
1992	first 55,500	7.65	
	next 74,700	1.45	5,328.90
1993	first 57,600	7.65	
	next 77,400	1.45	5,528.70
1994	first 60,600	7.65	
	additional wages	1.45	*
1995	first 61,200	7.65	
	additional wages	1.45	*
1996	first $62,700	7.65	
	additional wages	1.45	*
1997	first $65,400	7.65	
	additional wages	1.45	*
1998	first $68,400	7.65	
	additional wages	1.45	*
1999	first $72,600	7.65	
	additional wages	1.45	*
2000	first $76,200	7.65	
	additional wages	1.45	*
2001	first 80,400	7.65	
	additional wages	1.45	*
2002	first $84,900	7.65	
	additional wages	1.45	*
2003	first $87,000	7.65	
	additional wages	1.45	*
2004	first $87,900	7.65	
	additional wages	1.45	*
2005	first $90,000	7.65	
	additional wages	1.45	*

* No determinable maximum because of unlimited wage base for Medicare tax

Social Security Trust Funds[*]

- Disability
- Old-age and survivors
- Medicare Part A
- Medicare Part B

[*] Out of every dollar paid in Social Security taxes, 69 cents goes to the old-age and survivors trust fund, 19 cents goes to the Medicare trust fund, and 12 cents goes to the disability trust fund.

All payroll taxes and other sources of funds for Social Security (such as income tax on Social Security benefits and interest earned by the current surplus) are deposited into four trust funds: an old-age and survivors fund, a disability fund, and two Medicare funds. Benefits and administrative expenses are paid out of the appropriate trust fund from contributions to that fund and any interest earnings on excess contributions. The Social Security program does have limited reserves to serve as emergency funds in periods when benefits exceed contributions, such as in times of high unemployment. However, these reserves are currently relatively small and could pay benefits for only a limited time if contributions to a fund ceased.

In the early 1980s, considerable concern arose over the potential inability of payroll taxes to pay promised benefits in the future. Through a series of changes, the most significant being the 1983 amendments to the Social Security Act, these problems were addressed for the OASDI portion of the program—at least in the short run. The changes approached the problem from two directions. On the one hand, payroll tax rates were increased; on the other hand, some benefits were eliminated and future increases in other benefits were scaled back.

The trust fund for old-age and survivors benefits will continue to grow and will be very large by the time the current baby boomers retire. At that time (2017) the fund will begin to decrease as the percentage of retirees grows rapidly. (Currently there are 76 million baby boomers. When they begin to retire, 50,000 will reach retirement age every day.) Projections indicate that the fund will be adequate only to the year 2041 (see figure 2-3). The fiscal strength of the old-age trust fund will be discussed later in this chapter.

ELIGIBILITY FOR BENEFITS

To be eligible for benefits under OASDI, an individual must have credit for a minimum amount of work under Social Security. This credit is based on

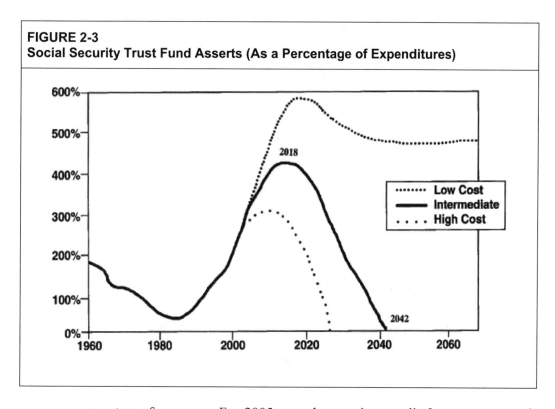

FIGURE 2-3
Social Security Trust Fund Asserts (As a Percentage of Expenditures)

quarters of coverage. For 2005 a worker receives credit for one quarter of coverage for each $920 in annual earnings on which Social Security taxes are paid. However, credit for no more than 4 quarters of coverage may be earned in any one calendar year. Consequently a worker paying Social Security taxes on as little as $3,680 (that is, $920 x 4) during the year will receive credit for the maximum 4 quarters. As in the case of the wage base, the amount of earnings necessary for a quarter of coverage is adjusted annually for changes in the national level of wages. Prior to 1978, a worker could receive credit for only one quarter of coverage in any given calendar quarter. Therefore it was necessary to be earning wages throughout the year in order to receive the maximum number of credits. Now a worker with the appropriate level of wages can receive credit for the maximum number of quarters even if all wages are earned within one calendar quarter.

quarters of coverage

fully insured

Quarters of coverage are the basis for establishing an insured status under OASDI. The three types of insured status are fully insured, currently insured, and disability insured. A person is *fully insured* if he or she has 40 quarters of coverage. Once a client acquires 40 quarters of credit, he or she is fully insured for life even if covered employment under Social Security ceases. (Please note: There are some exceptions to the 40 quarter rule for people born before 1930.)

Currently Insured

If a worker is fully insured under OASDI, there is no additional significance to being currently insured. However, if a worker is not fully insured, certain survivors' benefits are still available if a currently insured status exists. To be currently insured, it is only necessary that a worker have credit for at least 6 quarters of coverage out of the 13-quarter period ending with the quarter in which death occurs.

Disability Insured

disability insured

In order to receive disability benefits under OASDI, it is necessary to be *disability insured.* At the minimum, a disability-insured status requires that a worker (1) be fully insured and (2) have a minimum amount of work under Social Security within a recent time period. In connection with the latter requirement, workers aged 31 or older must have credit for at least 20 of the last 40 quarters ending with the quarter in which disability occurs; workers between the ages of 24 and 30, inclusively, must have credit for at least half the quarters of coverage from the time they turned 21 and the quarter in which disability begins; and workers under age 24 must have credit for 6 out of the last 12 quarters, ending with the quarter in which disability begins.

A special rule for the blind states that they are exempt from the recent-work rules and are considered disability insured as long as they are fully insured.

TYPES OF BENEFITS CLIENTS RECEIVE

As its name implies, the OASDI portion of Social Security provides three principal types of benefits:

- retirement (old-age) benefits
- survivors benefits
- disability benefits

Retirement Benefits

full retirement age

A worker who is fully insured under OASDI is eligible to receive monthly retirement benefits as early as age 62. However, the election to receive benefits prior to attainment of *full retirement age* results in a permanently reduced benefit. In 2005, the full retirement age (sometimes called normal retirement age) is age 65 years and 6 months. Planners should note that this represents a change from the long-standing practice of full benefits being paid at age 65. Table 2-3 indicates a client's full retirement age, depending on their year of birth. In addition, the following dependents of persons receiving retirement benefits are eligible for monthly benefits:

TABLE 2-3	
Social Security Normal Retirement Age	
Year of Birth	Retirement Age
1937 and earlier	65 years
1938	65 and 2 months
1939	65 and 4 months
1940	65 and 6 months
1941	65 and 8 months
1942	65 and 10 months
1943–54	66 years
1955	66 and 2 months
1956	66 and 4 months
1957	66 and 6 months
1958	66 and 8 months
1959	66 and 10 months
1960 and after	67 years

- a spouse aged 62 or older. However, benefits are permanently reduced if this benefit is elected prior to the spouse's reaching full retirement age. This benefit is also available to an unmarried divorced spouse if the marriage lasted at least 10 years. The benefit is not payable to a divorced spouse who has remarried unless the marriage is to a person receiving Social Security benefits as a widow, widower, parent, or disabled child.

- a spouse of any age if the spouse is caring for at least one child of the retired worker, and the child is (1) under age 16 or (2) disabled and entitled to a child's benefit as described below. This benefit is commonly referred to as a mother's or father's benefit.

- dependent, unmarried children under 18. This child's benefit will continue until age 19 as long as a child is a full-time student in elementary or secondary school. In addition, disabled children of any age are eligible for benefits as long as they were disabled before reaching age 22.

It is important to note that retirement benefits, as well as all other benefits under Social Security, are not automatically paid upon eligibility but must be applied for.

Survivors Benefits

All categories of survivors benefits are payable if a worker is fully insured at the time of death. However, three types of benefits are also payable if a worker is only currently insured. The first is a lump-sum death benefit of $255, payable to a surviving spouse living with a deceased worker at the time of death or, if there is no such spouse, to children eligible for monthly benefits. If neither category exists, the benefit is not paid.

There are two categories of persons who are eligible for income benefits as survivors if a deceased worker was either fully or currently insured at the time of death:

- dependent, unmarried children under the same conditions as previously described for retirement benefits
- a spouse (including a divorced spouse) caring for a child or children under the same conditions as previously described for retirement benefits

The following categories of persons are also eligible for benefits, but only if the deceased worker was fully insured:

- a widow or widower at age 60. However, benefits are reduced if taken prior to age 65. This benefit is also payable to a divorced spouse if the marriage lasted at least 10 years. In addition, the widow's or widower's benefit is payable to a disabled spouse at age 50 as long as the disability commenced no more than 7 years after (1) the worker's death or (2) the end of the year in which entitlement to a mother's or father's benefit ceased.
- a parent aged 62 or over who was dependent on the deceased worker at the time of death

Disability Benefits

A disabled worker under the full retirement age is eligible to receive benefits under OASDI as long as he or she is disability insured and meets the definition of disability under the law. The definition of disability is very rigid and requires a mental or physical impairment that prevents the worker from engaging in any substantial gainful employment. The disability must also have lasted (or be expected to last) at least 12 months or be expected to result in death. A more liberal definition of disability applies to blind workers who are aged 55 or older. They are considered disabled if they are unable to perform work that requires skills or abilities comparable to those required by the work they regularly performed before reaching age 55 or becoming blind, if later.

Disability benefits are subject to a waiting period and are payable beginning with the sixth full calendar month of disability. Besides the benefit paid to the worker, other categories of benefits—the same as those described under retirement benefits—are available to the spouse and dependents of the worker.

As previously mentioned, certain family members not otherwise eligible for OASDI benefits may be eligible if they are disabled. Disabled children are subject to the same definition of disability as workers. However, disabled widows or widowers must be unable to engage in any gainful (rather than substantial gainful) employment.

Eligibility for Dual Benefits

In many cases, a person is eligible for more than one type of OASDI benefit. Probably the most common situation occurs when a person is eligible for both a spouse's benefit and a worker's retirement benefit based on his or her own Social Security record. In this case and in any other case when a person is eligible for dual benefits, only an amount equal to the highest benefit is paid.

Termination of Benefits

Monthly benefits to any Social Security recipient cease upon death. When a retired or disabled worker dies, the family members' benefits that are based on the worker's retirement or disability benefits also cease, but the family members are then eligible for survivors benefits.

Disability benefits for a worker technically terminate at the full retirement age for that worker but are then replaced by comparable retirement benefits. In addition, any benefits payable because of disability cease if the definition of disability is no longer satisfied. However, the disability benefits continue during a readjustment period that consists of the month of recovery and 2 additional months.

As long as children are not disabled, benefits will usually terminate at age 18 but may continue until age 19 if the child is a full-time student in elementary or secondary school.

The benefit of a surviving spouse terminates upon remarriage unless remarriage takes place at age 60 or later.

AMOUNT OF BENEFITS CLIENTS CAN EXPECT

PIA

AIME

With the exception of the $255 lump-sum death benefit, the amount of all OASDI benefits is based on a worker's primary insurance amount (PIA). The *PIA,* in turn, is a function of the worker's average indexed monthly earnings *(AIME),* on which Social Security taxes have been paid.

Calculation of AIME

Even though calculation of the AIME is rather complex and somewhat unnecessary (the Social Security Administration will do it for the client or the client can use the Social Security Web site [ssa.gov] to do it for himself or herself), planners should still be aware how the system works. A rough understanding of how to calculate the AIME will enable an adviser to maximize planning opportunities. The list below sketches how the process works, as well as pointing out planning issues.

- First, list the earnings on which Social Security taxes were paid for each year up to and including the year of death or the year prior to disability or retirement. This list includes all applicable years even if there were no wages subject to Social Security tax, in which case zero is used for covered wages. Also note that in any given year someone earning in excess of the taxable wage base for the year will be credited only up to the taxable wage base that year and not his or her actual salary. *Planning Note:* "Zero years" can really hurt a client's benefit. This is one reason that women who took time off to have children often have lower benefits than their male counterparts.

- Second, index these earnings by multiplying them by an indexing factor that reflects changing wage levels. The only years that are indexed are those prior to the indexing year, which is the year a worker turned 60 for retirement purposes or 2 years preceding the year of death or disability for purposes of survivors or disability benefits. Therefore, the indexing factor for the indexing year and subsequent years is one. For years prior to the indexing year, the indexing factor for each year is equal to the average annual covered wages in the indexing year divided by the average annual covered wages in the year in which earnings are to be indexed. Average annual covered wages are the average wages on which Social Security taxes were paid. Each year the government makes the figure for the previous year available. *Planning Note:* Earnings after age 61 (which are not indexed) can be substituted for earnings in earlier years if they result in a higher benefit.

- Third, determine the number of years to be included in the calculation. For retirement and survivors benefits, the number of years is typically 35 (5 less than the minimum number of quarters necessary to be fully insured). Disability benefits, too, may be calculated by subtracting a certain number from the minimum number of quarters necessary for fully insured status. This number is five for workers aged 47 or over, four for workers aged 42 through 46, three for workers aged 37 through 41, two for workers aged 32 through 36, one for workers aged 27 through 31, and zero for workers under age 27. However, for survivors or disability benefits, at least 2 years must remain for purposes of calculating benefits. (Note: Up to 3 additional years may be dropped from the calculation if the worker had no income during the year and had a child under the age of 3 living in his or her household during the entire year.) *Planning Note:* Since only 35 years are used, a client who has earned the taxable wage figure or more for 35 years will typically get the maximum benefit. Consequently, working longer will typically not help the client to optimize his or her benefit because it is already at the maximum.

- Fourth, determine the years to be excluded from the calculation. These will be the years with the lowest indexed earnings. Of course, the number of years determined in the previous step must remain. *Planning Note:* Typically the lowest 5 years are dropped, including years with zeros.
- Fifth, add the indexed earnings for the years to be included in the AIME calculation and divide the result by the number of months in these years.

As mentioned earlier, the calculation of the AIME for retirement or disability benefits excludes the year in which retirement or disability takes place. However, the indexed earning for that year can be substituted for the lowest year in the calculation if the result will be a larger AIME.

Determination of PIA and Monthly Benefits

Once a worker's AIME has been calculated, his or her PIA is determined by applying a formula to the AIME. The 2005 formula is as follows:

- 90 percent of the first $627 of AIME
- plus 32 percent of the AIME in excess of $627 and less than $3,779
- plus 15 percent of the AIME in excess of $3,779

The dollar figures in this formula are adjusted annually for changes in the national level of wages.

The formula used to determine a worker's retirement benefit is the formula for the year in which the worker turned age 62. Therefore, a worker retiring at age 65 and 6 months in 2005 would use the 2003 formula rather than the 2005 formula. The formula used to determine survivors and disability benefits is the formula in existence for the year in which death or disability occurs, even if application for benefits is made in a later year.

The PIA is the amount a worker will receive if he or she retires at normal retirement age or becomes disabled, and it is the amount on which benefits for family members are based.

In 2005, a worker who has had average earnings during his or her lifetime can expect an average monthly retirement benefit of $955 ($11,460 per year). A worker who has continually earned the maximum income subject to Social Security taxes can expect a benefit of about $1,939 a month ($23,268 annually) for retirement purposes and a lower benefit for purposes of disability and survivors benefits. If a worker is retired or disabled, the following benefits are paid to family members:

Category	Percentage of Worker's PIA
Spouse at full retirement age	50%
Spouse caring for disabled child or	
child under 16	50%
Child under 18 or disabled	50% each

If the worker dies, survivors benefits are as follows:

Category	Percentage of Worker's PIA
Spouse at full retirement age	100%
Spouse caring for disabled child or	
child under 16	75%
Child under 18 or disabled	75% each
Dependent parent	82.5% for one,
	75% each for two

family maximum

However, the full benefits described above may not be payable because of a limitation imposed on the total benefits that may be paid to a family. This *family maximum* will usually be reached if three or more family members (including a retired or disabled worker) are eligible for benefits. The family maximum for purposes of retirement and survivors benefits can be determined for 2005 from the following formula, which, like the PIA formula, is adjusted annually based on changing wage levels:

> 150 percent of the first $801 of PIA
> plus 272 percent of the PIA in excess of $801 through $1,156
> plus 134 percent of the PIA in excess of $1,156 through $1,508
> plus 175 percent of the PIA in excess of $1,508

The family maximum for purposes of disability benefits is limited to 85 percent of the worker's AIME or 150 percent of the worker's PIA, whichever is lower. However, in no case can the maximum be reduced below the worker's PIA.

If the total amount of benefits payable to family members exceeds the family maximum, the worker's benefit (in the case of retirement and disability) is not affected, but the benefits of other family members are reduced proportionately.

When the first child loses benefits at age 18, the other family members will each have benefits increased. When a second family member loses eligibility, the remaining two family members will each receive the full benefit because the total benefits received by the family will now be less than the family maximum.

Other Factors Affecting Benefits

Benefits Taken Early

Persons can retire as early as age 62, but the monthly benefit is permanently reduced. The reduction is 5/9 of 1 percent for each of the first 36 months of entitlement immediately preceding the age at which 100 percent of PIA is payable (scheduled to increase to age 67 by the year 2022), plus 5/12 of 1 percent for each of up to 24 earlier months.

For example, a person aged 62 in 2005 (born in 1943) has a full retirement age of 66. If she retires in 2005 and it is 48 months prior to her full retirement age, she would multiply 36 months by 5/9 of 1 percent (a 20 percent reduction) and 12 months by 5/12 of 1 percent (a 5 percent reduction) and would therefore receive a 25 percent reduction of their full retirement benefit.

A spouse who elects retirement benefits prior to a full retirement age of 65 will have benefits reduced by 25/36 of one percent per month, and a widow or widower will have benefits reduced by 19/40 of one percent per month.

Delayed Retirement

Workers who delay applying for retirement benefits until after attainment of normal retirement age are eligible for an increased benefit. For persons born between 1917 and 1924, the increase is 3 percent for each year of delay up to age 70. The increase is 3.5 percent per year for persons born in 1925 or 1926 and 4 percent for persons born in 1927 or 1928. To encourage delayed retirement, the percentage will gradually increase to 8 percent for those born in 1943 or later. (See table 2-4 for a summary of the early and delayed retirement percentages.)

Earnings Test

earnings test

Benefits are reduced for Social Security beneficiaries under the full retirement age if their work wages exceed a specified level. The rationale behind having a reduction tied to wages, referred to as an *earnings test,* is that Social Security benefits are intended to replace lost wages but not other income such as dividends or interest. In 2005, Social Security beneficiaries under full retirement age (65 years and 6 months) are allowed earnings of $12,000 ($1,000/month). This figure is adjusted annually on the basis of national wage levels. If a beneficiary earns in excess of the allowable amount, his or her Social Security benefit is reduced. For persons under age 65 years, and 6 months, the reduction is $1 for every $2 of excess earnings. A different formula applies for the calendar year in which an individual attains the full retirement age. For that year, the reduction is only $1 for every $3 of excess earnings and counts only earnings before the month the individual reaches

TABLE 2-4
Social Security Retirement Ages—Reductions and Delayed Retirement Credit

Birth Year	Year Age 62	Delayed Retirement Credit	Normal Retirement Age	Earliest Eligibility Age	For Commencement at Age				
					62	65	66	67	70
1933	1995	5.5%	65	62	−20	0	5 1/2	11	27 1/2
1934	1996	5.5%	65	62	−20	0	5 1/2	11	27 1/2
1935	1997	6%	65	62	−20	0	6	12	30
1936	1998	6%	65	62	−20	0	6	12	30
1937	1999	6.5%	65	62	−20	0	6 1/2	13	32 1/2
1938	**2000**	6.5%	65 2/12	62	−20 5/6	−1 1/9	5 2/5	12	31 2/5
1939	2001	7%	65 4/12	62	−21 2/3	−2 2/9	4 2/3	11 2/3	32 2/3
1940	2002	7%	65 6/12	62	−22 1/2	−3 1/3	3 1/2	10 1/2	31 1/2
1941	2003	7.5%	65 8/12	62	−23 1/3	−4 4/9	2 1/2	10	32 1/2
1942	2004	7.5%	65 10/12	62	−24 1/6	−5 5/9	1 1/4	8 3/4	31 1/4
1943–1954	**2005–2016**	**8%**	**66**	**62**	**−25**	−6 2/3	0	8	32
1955	2017	8%	66 2/12	62	−25 5/6	−7 7/9	−1 1/9	6 2/3	30 2/3
1956	2018	8%	66 4/12	62	−26 2/3	−8 8/9	−2 2/9	5 1/3	29 1/3
1957	2019	8%	66 6/12	62	−27 1/2	−10	−3 1/3	4	28
1958	2020	8%	66 8/12	62	−28 1/3	−11 1/9	−4 4/9	2 2/3	26 2/3
1959	2021	8%	66 10/12	62	−29 1/6	−12 2/9	−5 5/9	1 1/3	25 1/3
1960 & later	2022 & later	8%	67	62	−30	−13 1/3	−6 2/3	0	24

full retirement age. Also, for that year the threshold is higher: $31,800 ($2,650/month) in 2005. Once an individual attains the full retirement age, he or she can earn any amount of wages without a reduction of benefits.

The reduction in a retired worker's benefits resulting from excess earnings is applied to all benefits paid to the family. If large enough, this reduction may totally eliminate all benefits otherwise payable to the worker and family members. In contrast, excess earnings of family members are charged against their individual benefits only. For example, a widowed mother who holds a job outside the home may lose her mother's benefit, but any benefits received by her children will be unaffected.

Cost-of-Living Adjustments

COLA

OASDI benefits are increased automatically each January as long as there has been an increase in the CPI for the one-year period ending in the third quarter of the prior year. This is known as a cost-of-living adjustment or *COLA*. The increase is the same as the increase in the CPI since the last COLA, rounded to the nearest 0.1 percent.

Social Security COLAs			
1999	1.3%	2002	2.6%
2000	2.4%	2003	1.4%
2001	3.5%	2004	2.7%

There is one exception to this adjustment. In any year that the combined reserves of the OASDI trust funds drop below 20 percent of expected benefits, the COLA will be limited to the lesser of the increase in the CPI or the increase in national wages used to adjust the wage base for Social Security taxes. When benefit increases have been based on wage levels, future cost-of-living increases can be larger than changes in the CPI to make up for the lower benefit increases in those years when the CPI was not used. However, this extra cost-of-living increase can be made only in years when the reserve is equal to at least 32 percent of expected benefits.

Offset for Other Benefits

Disabled workers under full retirement age who are also receiving workers' compensation benefits or disability benefits from certain other federal, state, or local disability programs will have their OASDI benefits reduced to the extent that the total benefits received (including family benefits) exceed 80 percent of their average current earnings at the time of disability. In addition, the monthly benefit of a spouse or surviving spouse is reduced by two-thirds of any federal, state, or local government pension that is based on earnings not covered under OASDI.

REQUESTING INFORMATION AND FILING FOR BENEFITS

Earnings and Benefit Estimate Statement

Beginning in 1999 the Social Security Administration began to send an annual *Earnings and Benefit Estimate Statement* to each worker who is not currently receiving benefits and who is over age 25. The statements are mailed automatically to clients 3 months prior to their birthday. In addition, clients seeking a revised version or more detail can use the primary insurance amount calculators on the Social Security website (www.socialsecurity.gov).

When clients receive their statements, they should be instructed to check if the earnings history is correct. If the Social Security Administration has underestimated your clients' yearly earnings, they will get less Society Security than they are entitled to. Have clients' W-2s or tax returns available for the affected years. What's more, you can try to have the return corrected even if you don't have old tax returns.

The statements also contain important information for both planner and client, including:

**YOUR FINANCIAL SERVICES PRACTICE:
THE EARNINGS TEST IN THE YEAR OF RETIREMENT**

As we have seen the earnings test can have a significant impact on a client because Social Security benefits are reduced by $1 for every $2 over the threshold level ($12,000 in 2005). Many clients who retire in mid-year may have already earned more than the yearly earnings limit. Under a special rule, a client can receive a full Social Security check for any whole month he or she is retired regardless of yearly earnings. In 2005, a person is considered "retired" if he or she earns under $1,000 per month (1/12 of $12,000) and thus will not be subject to the harsh treatment of the earnings test.

Example: John Smith retires at age 63 on August 30, 2005. He will make $45,000 through August. In September, he takes a part-time job earning $500 per month. Although his earnings for the year exceed the 2005 limit ($12,000), he gets his regular Social Security benefit from September through December because his earnings in those months are under $1,000. If John earns over $1,000 for any of those months (September to December), he will not receive a benefit for the month(s) he goes over the limit. In 2006, only the yearly limits apply to John.

One final point: Clients who are about to retire will often be able to negotiate their consulting pay, severance pay, and final months' salary all in one package. The planner should make the client aware of the earnings test and recommend negotiated solutions that avoid exceeding applicable thresholds in the year of retirement and in subsequent years.

Example: Suzanne Walsh, aged 62, will retire this year from her job as a professor at the university. She will, however, continue to teach part-time for several years. If she negotiates her final salary to be somewhat higher than the norm and her adjunct teaching salaries to be somewhat lower than the norm—and under the applicable earnings test threshold—she can restructure her affairs to avoid earnings test implications even though she is paid the same amount.

- the estimated Social Security retirement benefit the client will receive—the Social Security Administration calculates its estimated benefits by assuming that the client will make about the same as his or her latest earnings. If your client's earnings are likely to increase or decrease from present levels, then the benefit will change accordingly. *Planning Note:* Your client can request a statement with his or her own assumptions being used (online at www.ssa.gov or use Form SSA-7004).

  The Social Security benefit estimates given are in current dollars. Let the client know that each subsequent year's statement will be adjusted for cost of living increases. What's more, depending on the accumulation model (calculation of client needs) that you use, you may have to estimate adjustments to the projected benefit in "retirement time" dollars.

- the estimated disability and survivors benefits that your client will get from Social Security

- the full retirement age of the client—according to the Retirement Confidence Survey, 59 percent of workers in the nation expect to reach full eligibility sooner than they actually are scheduled to reach it.

Obtaining additional information about the Social Security system generally or getting specific information about benefits is easy—simply a telephone call away. The Social Security Administration can be reached at (800) 772-1213. Forms, brochures, and even applications for benefits can be obtained by calling this number; in fact, applications can even be made by phone or online at www.socialsecurity.gov.

OASDI benefits will not begin until an application for benefits is made. Most applications can be taken by phone at the number mentioned above or on the Internet. To ensure timely commencement, clients should be encouraged to apply for benefits 3 months in advance. However, benefit claims can technically be filed up to 6 months after benefits are due to commence because benefits can be paid retroactively for 6 months (longer in the case of a disability). If a client believes that he or she is entitled to a benefit, encourage him or her to file an application. A simple information request will not be given the same attention as a benefit application. Another important reason for filing an application is that if benefits are erroneously denied, they will be paid retroactively as of the application date once the snafu is straightened out. Also if, after benefits begin, an individual becomes aware that he or she is eligible for a second, larger benefit (for example, a spousal benefit), he or she must file an application in order to ensure receipt of the correct benefit.

TAXATION OF SOCIAL SECURITY BENEFITS

Until 1984, all Social Security benefits were received free of federal income taxation. Since that time, however, the rules have required individuals with substantial additional income to pay tax on a portion of their benefits. Until 1994, the maximum amount of Social Security benefits subject to tax was 50 percent. However, in 1994 the maximum percentage increased to 85 percent for certain taxpayers.

provisional income

The portion of the OASDI benefit that is subject to tax is based on what is referred to as the individual's *provisional income.* Provisional income is the sum of the following:

- the taxpayer's adjusted gross income
- the taxpayer's tax-exempt interest for the year
- half of the taxpayer's Social Security benefits for the year

If the provisional income is less than what is referred to as the *base amount*—$25,000 for a single taxpayer and $32,000 or less for a married taxpayer filing jointly—Social Security benefits are not taxable. If the provisional income is between the base amount and $34,000 ($44,000 for a married taxpayer filing jointly), up to 50 percent of the Social Security benefit will be includible in taxable income. If the provisional amount exceeds $34,000 ($44,000 for a married taxpayer filing jointly), up to 85 percent of the Social Security benefit will be includible in taxable income. To summarize, table 2-5 identifies the various cutoff points.

TABLE 2-5
Portion of OASDI Benefits Subject to Federal Income Tax

Taxpayer Filing Status	Provisional Income Threshold	Amount of Benefits Subject to Federal Income Tax
Single	under $25,000	0 percent
Single	$25,000–$33,999	up to 50 percent
Single	$34,000 or more	up to 85 percent
Married filing jointly	under $32,000	0 percent
Married filing jointly	$32,000–$43,999	up to 50 percent
Married filing jointly	$44,000 or more	up to 85 percent
Married filing separately (and living in the same household)	$0	up to 85 percent

---

The general description of how much is included and the various cutoffs is often sufficient for planning purposes. However, the planner may have occasion to actually calculate the specific amount of benefits that are includible as taxable income. The following explanation and example can be used to make this determination.

Step 1: Calculate provisional income.

Step 2: Determine appropriate thresholds based on the individual's tax filing status.

Step 3: The amount of Social Security benefits included as taxable income is the smallest number obtained from performing the following three calculations:

    (a) 50 percent of any provisional income that exceeds the base threshold plus 35 percent of any amount in excess of the second threshold

    (b) 85 percent of the benefits

    (c) 50 percent of the benefits, plus 85 percent of any amount in excess of the second threshold

Example:	Peggy and Larry Novenstern are married and file jointly. They have an adjusted gross income of $40,000 (not considering Social Security benefits) plus $5,000 of tax-free bond interest, and are entitled to a $15,000 Social Security benefit.

Step 1: Provisional income equals:

preliminary adjusted gross income	$40,000
tax-free bond interest	5,000
50 percent of Social Security benefits	7,500
provisional income	$52,500

Step 2: Determine income in excess of the applicable thresholds.

Excess over base threshold:
    ($52,500 – $32,000) $20,500
Excess over second threshold:
    ($52,500 – $44,000) $8,500

Step 3: Amount includible in taxable income is the lowest of the following three amounts:

(a) 50 percent of excess over base threshold plus
      35 percent of excess over second threshold
      (.5 x $20,500 + .35 x 8,500)   = $13,225
(b) 85 percent of $15,000   = $12,750
(c) 50 percent of $15,000 +
      85 percent of 8,500   = $14,725

In this case, the $12,750 (85 percent of the benefit) is included as adjusted gross income.

WHEN TO TAKE EARLY RETIREMENT BENEFITS

One of the questions most frequently asked by clients considering early retirement is whether they should begin taking Social Security retirement benefits prior to the date that full benefits are payable. In 2005, a worker may retire at age 65 years and 6 months and receive full benefits or begin receiving reduced benefits as early as age 62. (Note that currently nearly 50 percent of males and 60 percent of females begin benefits at this age.) After the client looks at some threshold issues, the decision often rests on the economic issue: Are the additional benefits received in the years before full retirement age sufficient to offset the benefits that will be forfeited after full retirement age if retirement benefits begin early? This section will review the relevant considerations and provide a mathematical model to assist in the decision making. A table is included that is based on the model and that can be used as a guideline for determining whether clients should elect reduced early Social Security retirement benefits based on their expected longevity.

Note that for some clients the solution will not be provided by the mathematical model. Other considerations, such as whether the individual is contemplating going back to work or whether he or she can really afford to retire are often more relevant. These issues are covered in more depth in "Threshold Issues" below.

Early Retirement Benefit Reduction Formulas

As described above, Social Security provides retirement benefits to four classes of persons. They are as follows:

- retiring employees who are fully insured and at least aged 62
- spouses, aged 62 or older, of retired workers who are receiving Social Security retirement benefits
- healthy surviving spouses, aged 60 or older, of deceased workers covered under Social Security
- disabled surviving spouses, aged 50 or older, of deceased workers covered under Social Security

The time that benefits can begin and the applicable benefit reductions for early commencement are different under each category. The rules for each category are summarized below.

Retiring Worker

Retirement benefits are based on a PIA. The PIA for retiring workers is the amount payable at full retirement age. The PIA is based on a person's earnings history under Social Security. If retirement benefits commence before full retirement age, the retirement benefit is reduced by five-ninths of one percent for the first 36 months that the retiring worker receives benefits before full retirement age and 5/12 of one percent for any months beyond the first 36. Note: Benefit reductions due to early payout are generally permanent.

For example, if a person with a full retirement age of 66 (anyone born from 1943–1954) begins receiving retirement benefits when he or she is aged 63 years 9 months, the retirement benefit is 85 percent of the PIA. Since the person is receiving benefits 27 months before age 65, the PIA will be permanently reduced by 15 percent (5/9 x .01 x 27). The benefit is recalculated in only one situation—when a retired person goes back to work prior to full retirement age and earns more than allowed under the earnings test. In this case, benefits will be recalculated at normal retirement age, which will make up for some of the reduction.

Spousal Retirement Benefits

At full retirement age, a spouse is entitled to a benefit equal to 50 percent of the surviving retired spouse's PIA. However, if a spouse has worked and earned a benefit that is larger than 50 percent of the other spouse's PIA, he or she will receive the larger amount. A person whose benefit is based on a surviving retired spouse's PIA may begin receiving benefits as early as age 62. However, the benefit is reduced by 25/36 of one percent (0.69444) for the first 36 months before full retirement age and 5/12 of one percent (0.41666) for any months after the first 36 months. For example, in 2005, a spouse electing to receive benefits beginning at age 62 and 4 months, who has a full retirement age of 65 years and 6 months, will only receive 37.0835 percent of his or her retired spouse's PIA. (The reduction factor is 25/36 x .01 x 36 = 25 percent plus 5/12 of .01 x 2 = .833 percent for a total of a .25833 reduction. Therefore, the person would receive only 74.167 percent of the full spouse's benefit, or 37.0835 percent of the PIA.)

Spousal Benefits of Deceased Worker

The amount a surviving spouse receives after his or her spouse's death is based on the deceased spouse's PIA at the time of his or her death, unless the survivor's own PIA, based on his or her own earnings history, is higher. At normal retirement age a surviving spouse is entitled to 100 percent of the deceased spouse's PIA. However, if the deceased spouse retired early and received a reduced benefit starting before he or she reached full retirement age, the surviving spouse cannot receive more than the reduced benefit of the deceased spouse (or 82.9 percent of the deceased spouse's PIA if this is larger than such reduced benefit).

Note that the spousal early retirement reduction is somewhat higher than the reduction for the participant. The reason for this is that the early retirement reduction ceases at the worker's death. For example, assume a worker with a full retirement age of 65 retires at age 65 and the spouse begins receiving the spousal benefit at age 62. The worker is entitled to 100 percent of his or her PIA while the spouse is entitled to 37.5 percent of the worker's PIA. At the worker's death, the spouse is entitled to 100 percent of the worker's benefit.

Disabled Spousal Benefits of Deceased Worker

A surviving spouse may elect reduced benefits beginning at age 60 if he or she is not disabled; these benefits may begin at or after age 50 if the surviving spouse is disabled. If benefits start early, the benefit is reduced by 19/40 of one percent (0.475 percent) for each month before full retirement age that benefits are received if the person is not disabled.

Table 2-6 summarizes these early benefit reduction rules.

TABLE 2-6
Social Security Early Benefit Reduction Formulas

	Classification			
	Retiring Worker	Spouse of Surviving Retired Worker	Healthy Surviving Spouse	Disabled Surviving Spouse Aged 50 to 60
1. Benefit at Full Retirement Age	PIA	50% of spouse's PIA	100% of spouse's PIA*	100% of spouse's PIA*
2. Minimum Early Retirement Age	62	62	60	50
3. Reduction Formula/ Age 65 Full Retirement Age	0.55556% x PIA x number of months early	0.34722% x PIA x number of months early	0.475% x PIA* x number of months early	28.5% of PIA* until age 60, then regular surviving spouse amount
4. Reduced Benefit Amount	PIA minus amount in Step 3	50% x PIA minus amount in Step 3	PIA* minus amount in Step 3	PIA* minus amount in Step 3

*If the deceased spouse received reduced early benefits, the surviving spouse's benefit is based on the deceased spouse's reduced benefit or, if greater, 82.9 percent of the deceased spouse's PIA.

Threshold Issues

The decision of whether an individual should elect to receive benefits early comes up in different contexts. For the retiring worker, it generally arises in three situations: as part of the decision regarding at what age to retire, as an issue of need for the individual who has been involuntarily terminated, and as an economic issue for the individual who has other potential sources of income in the early years of retirement. For this third category, the primary issue is an economic one, which is discussed in depth below. However, even for this group, one threshold issue must be addressed: Is the individual considering returning to work at any time prior to full retirement age? If so, then the individual may lose benefits due to the substantial employment rules. See the next section, "Returning to Work: The Postretirement Employment Dilemma," to understand the full effect of going back to work after retirement.

For those individuals currently contemplating early retirement, the early retirement reduction factor may affect the decision to elect early retirement; more central to this decision, however, is whether the individual will have sufficient pension benefits and/or personal savings to meet retirement needs. When advising these clients, be aware that they (1) generally are not fully aware of the financial impact of having a longer retirement period, (2) do not fully understand the impact on their pension benefits when they choose to retire early, and (3) do not understand that early commencement may (or may not) substantially lower Social Security benefits (due to factors other than the early retirement reduction factor).

Social Security benefits will be most affected when the individual has a short working history or has recently seen a drastic upswing in wages. In order to determine whether early retirement will have a substantial effect on benefits, an individual can request benefit information from the Social Security Administration. Two separate information requests should be made, one indicating that early retirement will occur, and the other indicating that benefits will begin at full retirement age. Assuming—after considering all relevant information—that an individual can afford to retire, then he or she will still have to decide whether taking early Social Security benefits makes economic sense.

Another troublesome situation involves early retirees who have been involuntarily terminated. Many in this group may feel that they do not have a choice—they need Social Security benefits to meet expenses. These individuals should still consider carefully whether or not to begin benefits early. Their major consideration is future employment possibilities. If they expect to go back to work, then taking benefits now means that Social Security benefits may be reduced or will cease during employment. As mentioned above, an individual who starts receiving benefits before full retirement age and then goes back to work will have benefits recalculated at full retirement age. At full retirement age, the early retirement reduction will be applied proportionately by the number of months in which benefits are curtailed by the substantial employment. Because there is a loss of benefits, however, an individual who is temporarily laid off will have to grapple with the difficult issue of how long the period will last and what his or her long-term employment prospects are likely to be. There is no easy answer for these individuals; the best an adviser can do is ensure that these clients are fully informed of the law.

When to Elect Early Benefits: The Economic Issue

As mentioned in the previous section, the primary factor in determining whether to elect reduced early benefits will be an economic one. Clients will be better off receiving early retirement benefits if the present value of the additional benefits received before full retirement age exceeds the present value of the higher benefits that are forgone after full retirement age and worse off if the opposite is true. Clearly if a person does not survive to full retirement age, electing to receive early retirement benefits is the better choice. But in most situations, a person will live past full retirement age, and a mathematical comparison of the two options will reveal the answer. The essential factors for computing these present values are (1) the assumed real (inflation-adjusted) discount (interest) rate (which depends on both the assumed nominal discount rate and the assumed growth (inflation) rate for Social Security benefits), (2) the number of months before full retirement age that early benefit payments will begin, and (3) the assumed life expectancy of the recipient (and sometimes that of the recipient's spouse).

The first two factors are somewhat easier to estimate with reasonable accuracy than the third one is. By equating the present value of the early benefits with the present value of the benefits forfeited after full retirement age, one can solve for the break-even life expectancy.

The break-even life expectancy can be used as a guideline when deciding whether to elect early retirement benefits. Table 2-6 presents break-even life expectancies for the four principal Social Security retirement beneficiary classifications for various early retirement ages and assumed real discount rates. An age 65 full retirement date was assumed for each circumstance. If a person (and/or a spouse in the case of a retiring worker) is likely to live beyond the break-even age, deferring retirement benefits until the full retirement age is optimal. Conversely, if a person is unlikely to survive beyond the break-even age, electing to receive early retirement benefits is best. Armed with this information a person can decide, based on his or her own health and history of family longevity, whether he or she is likely to survive until that age and, consequently, whether to elect early benefits.

For example, assume your client, a fully insured worker, plans to begin early retirement benefits at age 62—36 months before his or her full retirement age of 65. Assuming a real (inflation-adjusted) discount factor of 4 percent, the break-even life expectancy is approximately age 82 years 8 months.

Analysis and Planning Guidelines

As table 2-7 shows, the break-even life expectancy increases as the assumed real discount rate rises. Figure 2-4 illustrates the increasing rate at which the break-even age rises as the assumed real discount rate increases; this is especially helpful for persons who are considering receiving reduced early retirement benefits beginning at age 62. For assumed real discount rates exceeding about 7 percent, the break-even life expectancy for retiring workers is infinite. (The same is true at discount rates of 10 percent for spouses and 6 percent for surviving spouses.) In other words, at these levels of assumed real discount rates, electing to receive reduced early Social Security retirement benefits is always optimal.

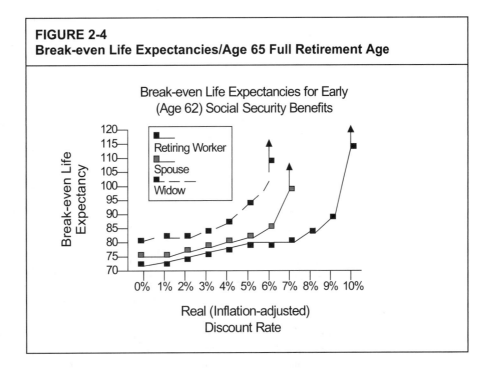

FIGURE 2-4
Break-even Life Expectancies/Age 65 Full Retirement Age

The Discount Rate

The discount rate is a measure of a person's preference for current benefits versus benefits in the future. In order to give up a dollar today, most people require more than a dollar in repayment next year. Several factors affect how much additional benefit a person requires next year for deferring a benefit today.

The first and most objective factor affecting a person's personal discount rate is the currently available market rate of interest. If a person can invest at a 6 percent secure rate of return, he or she would never accept less than $1.06 next year to defer $1 of benefits today. However, market rates of interest may not be sufficient to entice a person to defer benefits. Other, more subjective factors—such as a person's current opportunities to use the benefits today versus what he or she may perceive as more limited opportunities tomorrow; the state of a person's health and the anticipated future quality of his or her life; a person's expectations regarding his or her ability to survive and enjoy future benefits; and how willing a person is to take risks—may cause him or her to discount future benefits at more than current interest rates.

Another factor that affects discount rates is inflation. If inflation reduces the purchasing power of a dollar by 3 percent, for instance, a person would need about a 3 percent higher benefit the next year just to break even. Interest rates generally incorporate the market's expectations of inflation in the level at which the interest rates are set. However, Social Security retirement

TABLE 2-7
Break-even Life Expectancy for Early Social Security Benefits[1]

Benefit Class	Age Early Benefits Begin	Real (Inflation-Adjusted) Discount Rate[2]			
		0%	1%	2%	3%
Retiring	62	77.00	78.00	79.02	80.08
Worker	63	78.00	79.01	80.05	82.01
	64	79.00	80.02	81.07	83.05
Spouse	62	74.00	74.07	75.03	76.00
	63	75.00	75.08	76.05	77.03
	64	76.00	76.09	77.07	78.07
Healthy	60	77.07	78.09	80.03	82.03
Surviving	61	78.07	79.10	81.06	83.09
Spouse	62	79.07	81.00	82.09	85.02
	63	80.07	82.01	84.00	86.08
	64	81.07	83.02	85.03	88.02
Disabled	50	102.08	117.00	167.02	N/A
Surviving	55	90.01	95.07	105.03	132.02
Spouse	60	77.07	78.09	80.03	82.03

1. The break-even life expectancies are expressed in a format of years and months. For example, 79.02 is age 79 years 2 months. An age 65 full retirement age is assumed.
2. The real (inflation-adjusted) discount rate is derived by the following formula: real discount rate = (nominal discount rate − inflation rate)/(1 + inflation rate). For planning purposes, subtracting the assumed growth rate of Social Security benefits from the nominal discount rate is sufficient.

benefits are indexed for inflation. Consequently, when current Social Security benefits are being compared with future Social Security benefits, the discount factor must be adjusted for inflation to derive the real discount rate. Although the real interest rate may not be a perfect measure of an individual's personal real discount rate, real interest rates can serve as a starting point for estimating a person's real discount rate.

The real (inflation-adjusted) interest rate is computed by subtracting the anticipated inflation rate from the nominal (not inflation-adjusted) interest rate and dividing the result by the sum of one plus the inflation rate. In general, acceptable estimates of the real interest rate can be computed by subtracting the anticipated inflation rate from the nominal interest rate.

For many retirees, the real rate of return on long-term corporate bonds, long-term government bonds, or Treasury bills may provide a feasible starting point for estimating their real discount rates. The real (inflation-adjusted)

TABLE 2-7 (continued)
Break-even Life Expectancy for Early Social Security Benefits[1]

| | Real (Inflation-Adjusted) Discount Rate | | | | | |
4%	5%	6%	7%	8%	9%	10%
82.08	85.05	89.09	99.01	N/A[3]	N/A	N/A
84.03	87.06	92.11	107.01	N/A	N/A	N/A
85.11	89.08	96.05	122.10	N/A	N/A	N/A
77.00	78.01	79.07	81.07	84.07	90.01	117.01
78.04	70.09	81.06	84.01	88.02	97.09	N/A
79.09	81.04	83.06	86.09	92.07	118.05	N/A
85.00	89.03	97.05	N/A	N/A	N/A	N/A
86.10	91.10	102.08	N/A	N/A	N/A	N/A
88.08	94.07	109.08	N/A	N/A	N/A	N/A
90.08	97.98	120.00	N/A	N/A	N/A	N/A
92.08	100.12	149.03	N/A	N/A	N/A	N/A
N/A	N/A	N/A	N/A	N/A	N/A	N/A
N/A	N/A	N/A	N/A	N/A	N/A	N/A
85.00	89.03	97.05	N/A	N/A	N/A	N/A

3. N/A means the break-even life expectancy for the given assumed real discount rate is infinite. Electing to receive reduced early benefits at this discount rate is always optimal.

rate of return on a diversified portfolio of high-quality long-term corporate bonds over the period from 1926 through 1986 was 1.887 percent per year. For long-term government bonds the rate was lower—1.269 percent per year. The rate for Treasury bills, often used as an estimate of the "risk-free" rate of return, was only 0.377 percent per year, or barely above zero in real terms. Although nominal returns have often been quite high, these figures indicate that real interest rates have historically been quite low—less than 2 percent per year for any high-quality fixed-interest investment. In contrast, real compound annual returns on the S&P 500 stock portfolio, which is often cited as the best measure of the performance of the overall stock market, have averaged just under 7 percent per year. The particular characteristics of each client must be evaluated when estimating his or her real discount rate. However, based on the history, appropriate discount rates should generally lie somewhere in the range of zero to 7 percent. Using a mixed portfolio of stocks and bonds as a benchmark for the real rate of return, 3 to 4 percent often would be an appropriate real rate of return to use as the starting point when estimating your client's real discount rate.

Planning Guidelines

Based on the values found in table 2-7, disabled surviving spouses should virtually always elect reduced early benefits since it is highly unlikely that they will live beyond the break-even age, even if one assumes a zero percent real discount factor.

Whether healthy surviving spouses should elect reduced early benefits will depend on both the assumed real discount rate and expected longevity. IRS unisex mortality factors (Table V of IRS Reg. Sec. 1.72-9) for persons aged 60 through 65 in normal health may provide a benchmark for evaluating your clients' life expectancies. According to this table, persons aged 60 through 65 can expect to live to the ages of 84.2, 84.3, 84.5, 84.6, 84.8, and 85 years, respectively. However, women still have longer life expectancies for any given age than men have. Consequently, a woman in normal health can expect to survive to an age somewhat beyond these ages; a man can expect to survive to an age somewhat less than these ages. Also, in each individual case, examine family history to see whether there is a pattern of long or short lives, and adjust expectations accordingly.

Using the IRS mortality factors as a benchmark, the values in table 2-6 suggest that surviving spouses in normal health will generally be in a break-even position if their assumed real discount rate is between 2.5 percent and 3.5 percent, depending on the age at which they plan to take early retirement benefits. For discount factors above this range, taking reduced early retirement benefits generally will be the better choice; for discount factors below this range, deferring retirement benefits until age 65 generally will be the better choice.

The ages of married retiring workers and their spouses must be considered when deciding on early benefits. If a married retiring worker elects reduced early benefits, the spouse generally will receive the worker's reduced benefit after the worker's death rather than his or her full PIA. Consequently, the critical benchmark life expectancy is the husband and wife's joint and last survivor life expectancy, not the worker's single life expectancy.

Joint and last survivor life expectancies depend on the ages of both the husband and wife. Each case should be evaluated using the joint and last survivor expectancy for the actual age of each spouse. These expectancies should be adjusted for the health and family longevity history of each spouse. However, we can use the IRS joint and last survivor mortality factors (from Table VI of IRS Reg. Sec. 1.72-9) for a husband and wife of the same age as a benchmark for discussion. The IRS joint and last survivor expectancies of couples of the same age for ages 62 through 65 are 89.8, 89.9, 89.9, and 90, respectively.

Based on table 2-7, couples who are the same age and are in normal health—and consequently a joint and last survivor life expectancy of almost 90 years—usually will be better off deferring the retiring worker's retirement benefits until age 65 if their real discount rate is about 5 to 6 percent (about 6 percent at age 62, declining to about 5 percent at age 64).

Single retiring workers must base the early retirement decision on their own life expectancy and assumed real discount rate. Using the IRS single life mortality factors for surviving spouses described above as a benchmark (84.5, 84.6, 84.8, and 85 years, respectively, for ages 62 through 65), single retiring workers in normal health generally will be better off deferring retirement benefits until age 65 if their assumed real discount rate is less than about 4.5 percent. In cases of real discount rates above 4.5 percent, electing reduced early benefits typically will be the better choice.

Break-even life expectancies for spouses of surviving workers who are receiving Social Security retirement benefits are lower than those for the other beneficiary classifications. Consequently, based solely on the life expectancy of the nonworking spouse, deferral of spousal retirement benefits until age 65 appears optimal more often for spouses of surviving workers than for surviving spouses. Once again using the IRS single life mortality factors as a benchmark, a healthy spouse with normal life expectancy appears to be better off electing to defer benefits until age 65 if his or her assumed real discount rate is less than about 8 percent at age 62, declining to about 6 percent at age 64.

However, the spousal early benefit decision does not exclusively depend on the life expectancy of the nonworking spouse. The retired working spouse's life expectancy also must be considered. Under the rules, the benefit for the surviving nonworking spouse increases to the worker's benefit after the worker dies, even when the spouse had elected to receive benefits before age 65 and was subject to the early retirement reduction. In many cases, especially when the spouse is younger than the retired worker upon whom the nonworking spouse's benefits are based, the retired worker will die before the spouse attains his or her life expectancy. Consequently a nonworking spouse who elects early spousal benefits may collect the added benefits and forfeit nothing if the retired working spouse dies before the nonworking spouse reaches his or her break-even life expectancy. Therefore, the retired working spouse's life expectancy at the time the early spousal benefit will start, as well as the non-working spouse's life expectancy, are critical values. If either spouse is likely to die before the nonworking spouse reaches his or her break-even life expec-tancy for their assumed real discount rate, the nonworking spouse will be better off electing to receive early benefits. Only if neither spouse is likely to die before the nonworking spouse reaches his or her break-even life expectancy should spousal benefits be deferred until the nonworking spouse is aged 65.

Simplifying somewhat, there is a 50 percent chance that any given person will die before reaching the life expectancy for his or her age and, correspondingly, a 50 percent chance that he or she will survive beyond that life expectancy. The probability that two people will both live beyond the life expectancy for their ages is about one in four, or 25 percent. Therefore the probability that one or the other or both will die before reaching their life expectancy is about three in four, or 75 percent.

IRS tables include mortality factors for the first death of two lives (IRS Reg. Sec. 1.72-9 Table VIA—Annuities for Joint Life Only—Two Lives—Expected Return Multiples), which can be used as benchmark life expectancies when evaluating whether a spouse of a surviving retired worker should take early benefits. For example, assume that your client is retiring at age 65, that his nonworking wife is 62 years old, and that both are in good health with normal life expectancies. Should the wife elect to begin early spousal retirement benefits at age 62 when her husband begins receiving normal retirement benefits?

The IRS benchmark first-death life expectancy for these current ages is 15.9 years. Therefore the spouse's "adjusted" life expectancy for use in table 2-7 is 77 years 8 months (62 plus 15.9 years). Based on this life expectancy, if your clients' real discount rate is less than about 4.75 percent, electing to defer spousal benefits is the better choice. If their real discount rate is greater than about 4.75 percent, they will probably be better off if the nonworking spouse elects to receive early benefits.

Conclusion

Whether to take reduced early Social Security retirement benefits is a critical decision for many retirees. Once certain threshold issues are considered, the decision is often an economic one. Will I receive more benefits (over the long run) if I begin benefits now or wait until normal retirement age? The essential factors involved in this decision are a person's life expectancy, the assumed real (inflation-adjusted) discount rate, and the number of months before normal retirement age at which the benefits will begin. Table 2-7 presents guideline break-even life expectancies based on these essential factors to assist planners in advising their clients when and when not to take reduced early retirement benefits.

THE POSTRETIREMENT EMPLOYMENT DILEMMA

In many cases, a client finds that retirement does not meet his or her expectations. Such clients often reenter the workforce through part-time employment. In other cases, a client may feel the economic pressure of retirement and seek reemployment to add to his or her nest egg.

This section presents an example of such an individual reentering the workforce. The example illustrates the devastating tax penalties that await the unwary. It also illustrates many of the concepts discussed in this chapter. Finally, it offers strategies for effective planning for the client who ends up in this predicament.

Example:

Patty Shombert is aged 63 and single. Patty pays federal taxes, state taxes, and local taxes at the combined 33 percent marginal rate. Prior to going back to work, Patty had an adjusted gross income of $23,000 and Social Security benefits of $14,000. Then, in 2005, Patty decided to take a part-time job at the local college. The job pays $18,000 per year. Patty will be disheartened to find out that she only gets to keep $4,581 of her $18,000 salary. That represents approximately slightly over 25 percent of what she worked for.[1] Here's why:

Patty will pay the normal payroll taxes that apply to all workers:

FICA tax on $18,000 salary at 7.65%	$1,377
Federal, state, and local tax on	
$18,000 salary at 33%	6,000
Total payroll taxes	$7,377

In addition, due to Patty's higher income, a larger portion of her Social Security benefits will be taxable (table 2-8). Without the job, Patty would have paid tax of $825 on Social Security benefits. With the job, Patty will pay tax on Social Security of $3,927. The increase in tax based on Social Security is therefore $3,927 − $825 or $3,102. In other words, she increased her federal taxes by $3,102 because more of her Social Security income was subject to tax.

Patty will also be subject to the earnings test. Because Patty is aged 63, she will lose one dollar for every $2 earned over the threshold (in 2005, the threshold is $12,000 for a person under full retirement age). To determine the loss of Social Security, use the following equation. (Note: The fact that Patty's full retirement age is greater than 65 has been ignored here for the sake of simplicity. However, the results will be similar regardless of the actual full retirement age.)

Earnings	$18,000
Minus threshold	− 12,000
Excess	6,000
(lose one dollar for every 2)	
Lost Social Security[2]	$ 3,000

Postretirement Employment Losses

Salary	$18,000
Total payroll taxes	7,317
Extra tax on Social Security	3,102
Earnings test penalty	3,000
Total kept	4,581

Note that if Patty is aware that her Social Security benefits will be reduced due to the earnings test, she should notify the Social Security Administration to reduce her benefits prospectively. This will soften the blow somewhat because she is not taxed on the higher level of benefits this year.

TABLE 2-8
Additional Tax on Social Security Benefits

	No Job	Job $18,000/Year
1. Enter one-half of Social Security benefits	$ 7,000	$ 7,000
2. Adjusted gross income plus tax-exempt interest	23,000	41,000
3. Subtotal—provisional income	30,000	48,000
4. Less exemption for single Social Security recipient	25,000	25,000
5. Earnings in excess of exemption level	5,000	23,000
6. Line 5 divided by 2	2,500	11,500
7. Enter the smaller of line 1 or line 6	2,500	7,000
8. Enter the smaller amount of line 7 or $4,500 (single)		4,500
9. Enter the amount from line 3 above		48,000
10. Enter $34,000 (exemption) if single		34,000
11. Subtract line 10 from line 11		14,000
12. Multiply line 11 by 85%		11,900
13. Add line 8 and line 12		16,400
14. Multiply total Social Security benefits by 85%		11,900
15. Enter the smaller of line 13 or 14. This is the amount of taxable Social Security income		11,900
16. Tax on Social Security income (@33%)	2,500	3,972
17. Net tax increase on Social Security benefits ($3,927 – $825)	825	3,102

Planning for Returning to Work

Clearly, this example demonstrates the importance of careful planning. The retirement planner needs to emphasize to the client the impact of the decision to retire early, both economically and psychologically. If Patty had spent more time thinking through both issues, maybe she would have decided either not to retire, or at least to try it before she committed to begin receiving Social Security benefits. If she had not started Social Security, Patty would have been able to keep more of her wages when she went back to work; also she would not have been subject to the full retirement age reduction in Social Security benefits.

Note that one mitigating factor for the individual going back to work before full retirement age and earning more than the earnings test allows is that lost benefits may be partially made up. Social Security recalculates benefits at full retirement age in this case, increasing the benefit based on how much of the pre-full retirement age benefits were lost due to the reemployment. If you have a client in this situation, check with the Social Security Administration on how the increase will be calculated.

Other planning advice that is relevant to individuals who, like Patty, decide to go back to work includes the following:

- Keep income below the earnings test limit so that Social Security benefits are not reduced. Sometimes current earnings can be lowered by agreeing to receive partial payment as deferred compensation (after the earnings test no longer applies).
- The retiring worker returning to work after full retirement age is not subject to a reduction in Social Security benefits, regardless of the amount of earnings.
- Minimize the portion of Social Security benefits subject to income tax by lowering nonemployment income.
- If wages will exceed the earnings test amount, notify the Social Security Administration in advance, so benefits can be reduced in the current year. This reduction will effectively lower taxes for the current year.

THE FUTURE OF OLD-AGE SOCIAL SECURITY BENEFITS: ALTERNATIVES AND PERSPECTIVES

Given all the popular press that Social Security retirement benefits receive, it seems a good time to sort out the various alternatives under discussion and to put the probable solutions into perspective. Perhaps the best place to start is with a review of the system's history.

YOUR FINANCIAL SERVICES PRACTICE:
REPRESENTING CLIENTS WEB SITE

The Social Security Administration has a Web site for those who represent clients (www.socialsecurity.gov/representation). The site contains information on SSA regulations and operating procedures as well as links to the Social Security Handbook and other primary research sources.

Specific information about the claimant representation process is provided by topic:

- Fee Petitions
- Fee Agreements
- Exceptions to the Fee Agreement Procedure
- Model Fee Agreement
- Standards of Conduct for Representatives
- Code of Federal Regulations
- Form SSA–1696 Appointment of Representative
- Form SSA–1560 Petition to Obtain Approval of Fees

Finally, a "frequently asked questions" section provides answers to commonly asked questions about representing clients.

In addition to the adviser website, the traditional website (www.ssa.gov) is also an excellent resource. At this site you and your client can

- apply for Social Security retirement benefits on-line
- request a replacement Medicare card on-line
- use retirement, disability, or survivors planners and calculators to help with financial decisions
- replace, correct, or change the name on the Social Security card
- download publications about benefits
- request a Social Security statement
- individually tailor the Social Security statement

Historical Perspective

The Social Security old-age system has typically been funded by current workers paying taxes that are used to pay current benefits for those who are already retired. This so-called pay-as-you-go system worked well in the 1940s when the ratio of workers to retirees was 15 to 1. It even worked well in the 1960s when the ratio was 5 to 1. But today there are 152 million workers and 46 million retirees (a little over 3 to 1); an even greater concern is that by 2030 the ratio will fall to 2 to 1. (Consider that by 2020, Social Security expects to significantly increase the amount of beneficiaries from slightly over 50 million to about 83 million.)

To account for changing demographics, the Social Security law was changed in 1983 so that a surplus of assets would accrue (something like storing nuts for the winter). Currently, excess earnings are "invested" in Treasury securities, which have a long-run rate of return of about 4 percent (compared with 10 percent for common stocks). Both the investment and interest are owned by the Social Security trust fund and are legally required to be available whenever they are needed to pay promised benefits.

Some individuals worry because the "invested" amounts are really Treasury IOUs and the actual money is used for current government consumption. Others argue that the invested capital is no different from any bond; they postulate that these obligations are backed up by the full faith and credit of the U.S. government. They further point out that Social Security is a self-funded contributory program that has not contributed, does not contribute, and will not contribute to the deficit.

One final point: The surplus trust fund will not be dipped into until after the baby boomers start to retire in 2017. Because so many people will reach retirement age at once, that the principal of the trust fund will be exhausted by approximately 2041.

Dispelling the Great Myth

It seems that the 2041 prediction has sent out the wrong message. Perhaps the greatest myth being spread about Social Security retirement benefits is summed up in a survey showing that a greater number of younger people believe in UFOs than in their chances of receiving Social Security benefits. In actuality, however, without any changes, in 2041 the system will be able to pay about 73 percent of promised benefits. What's more, under the low-cost assumption, the system will not run out of money in the next 75 years. Planners should know that an increase in the payroll by just slightly over one percent will solve the entire problem. In short, only modest fixing is necessary. Ironically, the recent recommendation to privatize the system (discussed later) has less to do with the fiscal soundness of the system and more to do with intergenerational equity. In other words, a driving force of privatization is to give younger workers a "reasonable money's worth" return on their contributions.

THE ONGOING DEBATE

At the time this book was being written, an ongoing debate was taking place concerning how to fix the Social Security system. To better understand the issues involved, it is important to have a historical perspective. To properly do this, we need to examine the following:

- the Advisory Council's recommendations
- the thinking of the Boskin Commission and the Commission to Save Social Security
- other possible issues

Let's start by backing up to the late 1990s and the findings of the Social Security Advisory Council.

The Advisory Council's Recommendation

Every 4 years, a Social Security Advisory Council is scheduled to meet and look at a different area of Social Security. In the late 1990s, the problem examined was the system's long-term solvency. The Advisory Council was split on how to solve the problem and came up with three proposals. One of these was referred to as the Maintenance-of-Benefit Plan, which recommended the following:

- starting in the year 2000, redirecting $25 billion a year from Treasury bonds to the stock market. (This amount represents less than one percent of the market.) To illustrate how big the stock market really is, in March 1996 alone, investors put $20.53 billion into equity mutual funds).
- by 2015, having the federal government invest 40 percent of the old-age trust fund in the stock market (this amount would be $800 billion in 1996 dollars—which would represent less than 10 percent of the market). The majority of the money would go into corporate bonds and equity index funds.
- having the current tax rate (6.2 percent for the employer and 6.2 percent for the employee) remain unchanged under this proposal until 2045, then putting an additional 1.6 percent (split between employer and employee) into place

A second proposal was referred to as the Individual Accounts Plan. It recommended the following:

- an additional 1.6 percent deduction from each worker's pay to fund mandatory individual retirement accounts (with after-tax contributions being tax free at distribution time)
- workers choosing their own investments from a limited number of stock or bond index funds (based on the federal thrift savings plan)
- a moderate cut in guaranteed benefits for middle- and higher-income workers
- raising the age for full benefits to 67 by 2011, at which point it would be indexed to changes in life expectancy
- an expected annual stock market investment amount of $20 billion to $25 billion ($500 billion by 2015 in 1996 dollars)

A third and final proposal was referred to as the Personal Security Account Plan. It recommended the following:

- creating individual accounts that would replace a portion of Social Security. For workers under age 55 in 1998, 5 percent of the current 12.4 percent would be put into a personal security account (PSA) that would be privately invested by individuals or their designated broker. After-tax contributions would be tax free at retirement.

- having the remaining portion of Social Security tax (7.4 percent) fund a modified Social Security retirement program providing a benefit of approximately one-half of that offered by the existing system, or $410 a month, which represents two-thirds of the poverty level

- accelerating the age for full benefits, beginning in the year 2000. The new normal retirement age would be age 67 for those reaching age 62 in the year 2011. When the benefit age reaches 67, it would be indexed to reflect changes in life expectancy.

- gradually increasing the age to receive early retirement benefits from 62 to 65 (although 62 would be the age at which workers would be able to withdraw benefits from PSAs)

- incurring additional federal debt to finance the transition to the new system

- investing an expected amount of $75 billion annually in the stock market

Public Reaction

An AARP poll released a week after the Advisory Council's recommendation showed that six in ten workers were confident that they would have more money during retirement if they invested their Social Security taxes themselves. However, 90 percent of the respondents said that they wanted Social Security to be there in case they needed it during retirement. Other polls have shown that given a choice between cutting Social Security benefits or raising Social Security taxes, people would rather pay the taxes. In addition, much more has been speculated concerning the effect of any of the proposals on stock prices, interest rates, and inflation—without any definitive answer. Much has been written about the windfall for Wall Street brokers and the financial services industry if the Personal Security Account Plan was adopted. Finally, it is unclear whether the public understands investments enough to take on the additional responsibility of investing their own taxes.

The Boskin Commission

At about the same time as the Advisory Council's recommendations, the Boskin Commission also rocked the Social Security boat. This commission, which consisted of top economists appointed by the Senate Finance Committee, reported that the consumer price index (CPI) overstates inflation by 1.1 percent per year.

The Boskin Commission found that a valid CPI should account for the ways in which consumers adjust for rising prices. For example, consumers switch to lower-cost items if their normal purchases have become too expensive, and failure to account for such shifts introduces an "upward bias" in the CPI. The commission also criticized the CPI's failure to account for the value of quality improvements in goods and services or to consider the quality-of-life gains from the introduction of new products.

The Boskin Commission report was taken very seriously, and in the spring of 1998 the CPI calculation was changed to account for about one-half of the Boskin recommendations.

The Commission to Save Social Security

In December 2001, a bipartisan panel of experts which had been put together by President Bush issued a final report concerning potential changes to fix the Social Security system. Once again three models were offered. Under model one, workers could voluntarily divert 2 percentage points of their Social Security taxes to a personal account. Traditional Social Security benefits would be reduced by the amount of the personal account contributions compounded at an interest rate of 3.5 percent above inflation. However, no other changes would be made to traditional Social Security. Under model two, workers could voluntarily redirect 4 percentage points of their payroll taxes (up to $1,000 annually) to a personal account. Traditional Social Security benefits would be reduced by the amount of the personal account contributions compounded at an interest rate of 2 percent above inflation. In addition, benefits in the traditional Social Security system would be indexed to price inflation (not wage growth) beginning in 2009. What's more, a new minimum benefit of 120 percent of the poverty line would be established. In model three, workers would have the option of contributing one percent of wages into a personal account up to $1,000 annually. The contribution would be matched by 2.5 percent of payroll taxes. The add-on contribution would be partially subsidized for workers in a refundable tax credit. Traditional Social Security benefits would be reduced by the amount of the personal account contributions compounded at an interest rate of 2.5 percent above inflation. A new minimum benefit of 100 percent of the poverty line would be established. The plan calls for a payroll tax increase of 0.6 percent. Finally, traditional Social Security benefits would be reduced by taking into account future changes in life expectancy and decreasing the benefits for early retirement. Under all three systems, the privatized funds would be invested in mutual funds.

INCREASED BILATERAL ATTENTION

At the time of this writing, Social Security reform was getting increased political attention from the President and many in Congress. Shortly after his reelection, President Bush noted that the 2001 Commission Report was a good place to start for reform. (Many believe any privatized accounts may have similar investments to the federal pension fund, which has a limited number of investment choices). Agreements are also being formed concerning the fate of the estimated $2 trillion in transition costs required to convert to partial privatization. (One suggestion is to significantly increase the wage base.) Most experts believe that the traditional Social Security system will remain intact for those already retired and those about to retire. What's more, the heart of the traditional system will remain even if partial privatization occurs.

Other Changes

means testing

In addition to the committees appointed by the federal government, other changes to the old-age benefit system of Social Security have been recommended from time to time. One of these is *means testing,* which is sometimes called affluence or income testing. This solution would eliminate, reduce, or phase out benefits for individuals with a certain amount of income and assets. The premise behind this is that government aid should be targeted to the truly needy. Conventional wisdom says that Social Security's progressive benefits formula (higher replacement ratios for lower-income workers), the tax structure—which increases taxes based on provisional income—and the earnings test are existing forms of means testing. One perceived advantage of means testing is that it would save the system big money. Currently 4.4 million people with incomes of greater than $50,000 a year receive Social Security. One perceived disadvantage of means testing is that it breaks an implied contract with people who paid into the system. According to one study, if a couple with retirement income of $60,000 would lose 30 percent of their Social Security benefit and a couple with over $110,000 would lose 85 percent of their Social Security benefit, the Social Security problem shortfall would be nearly fixed. Other proposals have called for setting much higher cutoffs for means testing.

A second alternative is raising the Social Security full retirement age more quickly than planned. The full retirement age is scheduled to be gradually changed from age 65 to 67 by the year 2027. This situation focuses on either accelerating the change to age 67 or increasing full retirement age to 68, 69, or 70. The conventional wisdom is that people are living longer. Age 65 was selected in 1935, although life expectancy at birth at that time was only 61 years. Today, life expectancy at birth is age 72 for men and age 79 for women. One perceived advantage of changing the full retirement age is that it would save money and that the fairness of the savings could be rationalized because benefits are "relatively unaffected" owing to a longer life. According to one study, if the full retirement age is raised to 70 by 2030, the Social Security shortfall will be fixed by 68 percent.

One perceived disadvantage of changing the normal retirement age is that it would allow the baby boom generation and generations following it to shoulder the cost of the solution without having the current generation of retirees share in the sacrifice. It should be noted that increasing full retirement age in a minor fashion was recommended in two of the three Advisory Council proposals.

A third alternative that is postulated from time to time is to temporarily freeze cost-of-living adjustments (also referred to as "frozen COLAs"). One advantage of freezing COLAs would be to save the system money. One disadvantage would be that it would take money away from the elderly poor who need every penny. According to a study, reducing COLAs by half a percentage point would fix the Social Security shortfall by 37 percent. (However, frozen COLAs may be politically untenable because of AARP's lobbying power.)

A fourth change that is being discussed is altering the formula for determining a person's primary insurance amount (PIA). The average indexed monthly earnings (AIME) calculation could be changed to increase the number of years considered and, consequently, incorporate years with lower earnings, reduce the AIME indexing calculation, and/or eliminate the "drop-out years." These changes would result in lower Social Security benefits. Some sources theorize that women would suffer the most from the proposed increase in the number of years (from 35 to 38) because they take time off from work to raise children, and thus often do not work as many years. Men might see an average decrease of 3 percent because more low-earnings years would be counted. One advantage of changing the formula would be saving the system money without an uproar of political chest-beating. One disadvantage would be to lower replacement ratios in such a way as to put the nation's seniors closer to the poverty level.

price indexing

A fifth alternative is *price indexing.* Under price indexing, the first-year benefits for retirees would be calculated using inflation rates instead of the increase in wages and a worker's lifetime. Because wages tend to rise considerably faster than inflation, price indexing would stunt the growth of benefits. This would occur slowly at first and gain speed toward the middle of the century. According to the Social Security Administration, price indexing would reduce benefits by 9.9 percent for someone retiring in 2022, 18.2 percent for someone retiring in 2032, 25.7 percent for someone retiring in 2041, and 32.5 percent for someone retiring in 2052. (This assumes a medium earning retiree at age 65 and the numbers were in 2001 dollars when the study was released.) Price indexing is often talked about in conjunction with personal saving accounts and is thought to be offset by the higher gains possible through individual investments.

Other solutions being talked about include the following:

- raising the early retirement age. Will this help if the reduced benefit is an actuarial equivalent of the total amount received when the worker retires at the normal retirement age?

- covering new state and local government employees. With its "the more the merrier" attitude, this solution is similar to the proposal suggesting the inclusion of post-1983 federal hires.
- raising taxes on benefits. This raises revenues but not for the Social Security trust fund.
- reducing spousal benefits. The reduction or elimination of spousal benefits would be a blow to family values and may not bring about a huge savings because many families have two wage earners.
- redirecting Social Security tax revenues from Medicaid Part A hospital insurance (HI) to the Social Security trust fund. At present a portion of Old-Age, Survivors, and Disability tax revenue is allocated to finance Part A of Medicare. But doesn't the Medicare trust fund have enough trouble? This won't raise any significant revenue but otherwise seems equitable.

Conclusion

Planners may find it interesting to see what the official stance of the Social Security Administration is on reform. Appendix 1A has a series of questions and answers on the topic. In addition, Federal Reserve chairman Greenspan has indicated that he fears Social Security and Medicare have promised more benefits than can be delivered as a result of the aging of the population. He warns that in choosing among the various tax and spending options, policyholders will need to pay careful attention to the economic effects.

The most likely change to the old-age Social Security system is a combination of many of the current solutions under discussion. Just which alternatives will be chosen? This is the key—and unanswerable—question. The only thing that can be said with certainty at this point is that political pressures and perceived fairness will drive the decision. In other words, those groups whose lobbies perform effectively and who are able to spin their story to the American public in the most favorable light are likely to shape reform. Finally, everyone agrees that the sooner we act, the better, because less sacrifice will be needed if we are weaned from the existing system.

NOTES

1. This example assumes that Patty does not notify the Social Security Administration to reduce her benefits prospectively.
2. Next year's Social Security will be reduced by this amount.

3

Sources of Retirement Income: Tax-Advantaged Retirement Plans

David A. Littell

Chapter Outline

The goal of chapters 3 and 4 is to provide a better understanding of the types of retirement benefits that employees are entitled to receive from their employers. This chapter reviews the types of retirement plans that receive special tax treatment, which include qualified plans, SEPs, SIMPLEs, and 403(b) plans. Chapter 4 covers nonqualified deferred-compensation plans and other types of employer-provided incentive pay programs such as stock option programs as well as individual retirement plans.

This chapter reviews the basic features of tax-advantaged retirement plans and the typical choices that a participant has under such plans. It also discusses retirement planning concerns that are relevant for each type of plan as well as common concerns for all types of plans.

There is a brief discussion about choosing the appropriate retirement planning vehicle for the small business. This is appropriate for those working with business owners and others who are in a position to have control over the design of the retirement program. This is a complex area, and these materials are just a beginning for those intending to get involved in pension consulting.

Finally, note that when advising a client about his or her rights under a specific retirement program, all relevant contracts, summary plan descriptions, and other descriptive documents should be reviewed. The end of the chapter explains how to obtain information about a participant's benefits under the plan.

QUALIFIED RETIREMENT PLANS

qualified retirement plan

Qualified retirement plans are subject to the qualification requirements contained in IRC Sec. 401(a). There are seven types of qualified plans commonly used today. These include

- profit-sharing plans
- money-purchase pension plans
- 401(k) plans
- defined-benefit pension plans
- cash-balance plans
- stock bonus plans
- ESOPs

In exchange for satisfying specified qualification requirements, these plans are eligible for the following special tax treatment:

- The employer receives a tax deduction at the time contributions are made to the plan's funding vehicle (generally a trust).

- The trust is a tax-exempt entity, which means that earnings are not taxed until they are paid out as benefits to participants.
- The participants pay taxes on the amount of benefits received from the plan.
- A participant can generally roll a pension benefit over into an IRA or other tax-advantaged plan at termination of employment to further delay the payment of taxes on the benefits.

These tax benefits are essentially the same as the benefits for SEPs, SIMPLEs, and 403(b) plans (discussed in the following section). However, these other tax-advantaged retirement plans are subject to somewhat different qualification requirements.

Qualification Requirements

For a retirement plan subject to Code Sec. 401(a) to be eligible for special tax treatment, the plan must satisfy a number of qualification requirements. The most important are summarized in table 3-1, and several are discussed more fully below.

TABLE 3-1
Major Qualification Rules for Qualified Retirement Plans

1. The plan must be in writing.
2. The plan must be permanent. (Note: Even though the intention of permanency is required, a plan can be amended or terminated.)
3. The plan must be communicated to the participants according to statutory guidelines including distribution of a summary plan description.
4. The plan must be operated for the exclusive benefit of the employees or their beneficiaries.
5. The plan must cover enough nonhighly compensated employees to satisfy the minimum-coverage requirements.
6. Plan participants must become vested in their benefits within a specified period of time. (Benefits cannot be forfeited upon termination of employment.)
7. The plan cannot provide disproportionate benefits to the highly compensated employees.
8. The plan must meet specified funding requirements.
9. The plan's funds cannot be recaptured by the employer except when the plan is terminated and all plan liabilities are satisfied.
10. The plan must satisfy certain limitations concerning the amount of contributions or benefits provided to participants.
11. The plan must incorporate top-heavy rules, which apply when more than 60 percent of the contributions are for the benefit of key employees.
12. The plan can provide only "incidental" death benefits, meaning that if life insurance is purchased in the plan the death benefit cannot exceed certain limits.
13. Spouses are entitled to certain rights in the pension under the qualified joint and survivor annuity requirements.

The rules are complex and the regulatory scheme affects every aspect of the plan's installation, administration, and even termination. Clearly the plan's design has to take into consideration all of these rules, and the plan document must be carefully drafted to include them. With qualified plans, the plan sponsor may ask the IRS for a determination letter that specifies that the plan document has been appropriately drafted and complies with the law. Of course, the plan has to operate in conformance with the rules, and this is the job of the plan administrator. Most plans have to file an annual Form 5500 with the IRS and the DOL, which helps those agencies determine whether the plan is in compliance. Both the IRS and the DOL periodically audit plans.

If a plan fails to conform to the law, the IRS could disqualify the plan, which could have adverse consequences on both the employer's tax return (reducing or shifting tax deductions to different years) and, more importantly, on the participant's return as well. In the worst case scenario, tax deferral is lost and all benefits are taxed at one time to the participants. Fortunately the IRS rarely imposes these drastic measures. It more often negotiates an alternative solution with the plan sponsor (typically a penalty fee).

Below is a discussion of some of the rules that have the greatest effect on plan design and on determining a participant's rights and benefits under the plan.

Coverage and Eligibility

In order to benefit certain highly compensated employees (5 percent owners in the current or previous year and those earning more than $95,000 [as indexed for 2005] in the previous year), the plan must cover a certain percentage of the nonhighly compensated workforce. The rules are quite flexible, which means that the number of nonhighly compensated that must be covered depends in part on the number of highly compensated employees who are covered under the plan. The plan can satisfy one of several coverage tests, but the most relevant one for the small plan market is the ratio test.

The ratio test requires a plan to benefit a percentage of nonhighly compensated employees equal to at least 70 percent of the percentage of highly compensated employees covered under the plan. Certain classes of employees can be excluded from testing, such as collectively bargained employees, employees who have worked less than one year, certain part-time employees (working less than 1,000 hours per year), and employees younger than age 21.

| *Example:* | The Thunder Company has 120 employees on its payroll. Because 20 of these have not yet met the plan's minimum age and service requirements, the ratio test would apply to only 100 employees. Thirty of the remaining employees are highly |

compensated, but only 15 of the 30 highly compensated employees actually participate in the plan. Seventy of the remaining employees are nonhighly compensated, and 40 of 70 nonhighly compensated employees participate in the plan.

Because 50 percent (15 out of 30) of the highly compensated employees participate in the plan, the ratio test requires that at least 35 percent of the nonhighly compensated employees (70% x 50% = 35%) must benefit under the plan. In this case, at least 25 (35% x 70% = 24.5%) nonhighly compensated employees must benefit under the plan. Because Thunder Company has 40 nonhighly compensated employees benefiting under the plan, the plan satisfies the ratio test.

The rules allow employers to exclude a significant number of employees, and some will do so to limit costs. Most employers will limit eligibility to those who have met the minimum age and service requirements to avoid the administrative expense of including short-term employees.

minimum-participation rule

Defined-benefit plans must satisfy a second coverage requirement under Code Sec. 401(a)(26) referred to as the *minimum-participation rule*. Under this rule, an employer's plan will not be qualified unless it covers (1) 50 employees or (2) 40 percent of the employer's employees, *whichever is less*. However, a special rule applies when there are two employees; in this case, both employees must be covered.

The flexible coverage rules permit the plan sponsor to limit costs by excluding some of the employees. If an employer has more than one business location, the rules may allow the sponsor to cover one location but not the other (as long as the rules are satisfied).

Aggregation Rules

controlled group rules

affiliated service group rules

When testing whether a plan satisfies the coverage requirements, the definition of employer could actually include other related companies. These aggregation rules were intended to ensure that a plan sponsor could not avoid covering employees by segregating them into a separate entity. To close this loophole, the Code contains what are referred to as the *controlled group rules* that require aggregation of employers that have a sufficient amount of common ownership, and the *affiliated service group rules* for other situations in which related businesses work together to provide goods or services to the public. Aggregated companies are treated as one entity when testing under the coverage requirements.

There are two types of *controlled groups*. A parent-subsidiary controlled group exists whenever one entity (referred to as the *parent company*) owns at least 80 percent of one (or more) of the other entities. Additional entities may be brought into the group if a chain of common ownership exists. A brother-sister controlled group exists whenever the same five (or fewer) owners of two or more entities own 80 percent or more of each entity, and more than 50 percent of each entity when counting only *identical ownership*. Identical ownership is tested by counting each person's ownership to the extent that it is identical in each entity. For example, if an individual owns 10 percent of Corporation A and 20 percent of Corporation B, he or she has a 10 percent identical ownership interest with respect to each corporation. The identical ownership interests of each of the five (or fewer) individuals is added together to determine whether the 50 percent test has been satisfied.

Describing an affiliated service group is beyond the scope of this book. However, when working with clients, there are several threshold issues that help advisers to identify when affiliation problems might be present. Except for management services affiliation (discussed below), affiliated groups exist only when all three of the following elements are present:

- when two or more business entities work together to provide one service or product to the public
- when at least one of the entities is a service organization, which is an organization for which capital is not a material income-producing factor. Organizations in the fields of health, law, engineering, actuarial science, consulting, and insurance are automatically deemed service organizations.
- when at least some common ownership exists between the two entities

---

YOUR FINANCIAL SERVICES PRACTICE:
AVOIDING HIDDEN AGGREGATION PROBLEMS

One common problem the financial service professional faces when setting up a retirement plan is finding out important information at the last minute or after the fact. For example, an employer who is interested in setting up a plan for the ABC Company may also own the XYZ Company but fails to give you this important information. Because it is possible that the employees of both ABC and XYZ must be considered for the purposes of the coverage requirements, it is important to question the employer about additional holdings, other key employees' additional holdings, and the corporation's additional holdings. In the small-company context, the minimum-coverage rules are unforgiving, and an employer who misses a controlled group issue may very well end up with one or more disqualified plans. This is a complex area of the law, and the role of the pension advisor should be to identify affiliation issues and then encourage the client to pursue a final determination from a qualified tax attorney.

Management services affiliation is defined by a much broader rule, which essentially prohibits an executive of any size company from separating from the company for the purpose of establishing his or her own retirement plan.

When either a controlled group or an affiliated service group exists, the employers are treated as one employer for virtually all the qualified plan rules. Both rules apply to both corporations and "trades and businesses," including partnerships, proprietorships, estates, and trusts. Regulations provide guidance for determining ownership interests in these kinds of entities.

A different type of affiliation relates to situations where individuals are "leased" on a long-term, full-time basis. In some cases, such individuals will be treated as working for the recipient for purposes of the coverage requirements.

The affiliation rules are complex. If a financial services professional identifies a possible problem, the client's tax accountant and/or attorney should be brought in to help determine whether affiliation exists between two or more entities. The issue is extremely important because in many cases if a plan is established for one entity and the second organization that is affiliated is not covered under the plan, the plan may fail to satisfy the minimum-coverage requirements.

Nondiscriminatory Benefits

Code Sec. 401(a)(4)

When designing the benefit structure in a qualified plan, the plan has to satisfy *Code Sec. 401(a)(4),* which provides that benefits cannot discriminate in favor of highly compensated employees. In this context, the definition of highly compensated is the same as described previously. Again, like the coverage rules, the nondiscrimination rules are complicated but do allow a significant amount of design flexibility.

The nondiscrimination regulations allow a plan to choose one of the safe-harbor design formulas or test the plan's formula for discrimination each year. Most plans choose one of the design safe harbors, which allows either a formula that results in a benefit accrual that is a level percentage of pay or one that is integrated with Social Security. Social Security integration allows the employer to give slightly larger benefits to those who earn more than the Social Security taxable wage base. If the employer wants to provide significantly larger benefits to one group of employees over another, the sponsor must use the general nondiscrimination test to demonstrate that the formula complies with the rules. The general nondiscrimination test is a mathematical test performed annually. The sponsor can create any benefit structure as long as the test can be satisfied each year. This allows the employer to provide a number of different benefit structures within one plan, which in turn permits the sponsor to meet a number of different benefit objectives within a single plan.

Vesting

An employer is required to choose a *vesting schedule* that is at least as favorable as one of two statutory schedules: the 5-year cliff vesting or the 3-through-7-year graded vesting. The 5-year cliff vesting is a schedule under which an employee who terminates employment prior to the completion of 5 years of service will be entitled to no benefit (zero percent vested). After 5 years of service, the employee becomes fully entitled to (100 percent vested in) the benefit that has accrued on his or her behalf. The other statutory vesting schedule, known as the 3-through-7-year graded schedule, requires no vesting until the third year of service has been completed; at that point the vested portion of the accrued benefit increases 20 percent for each additional year of service.

While these two schedules constitute the legally mandated requirements, more liberal vesting schedules can be employed if desired. For example, an employer could establish a 2-year cliff vesting schedule or a 4-year graded schedule where the participant earns an additional 25 percent vesting for each year of service.

Note that the vesting schedules just described apply primarily in the case of an individual who terminates employment (on a voluntary or involuntary basis) prior to reaching a plan's normal retirement age—or some other stated event that triggers a benefit under the plan. Under the law, an individual who reaches the plan's normal retirement age must become 100 percent vested regardless of the number of years of service earned.

Also it is typical for a plan to fully vest participants—regardless of the years of service performed—at attainment of an early retirement age, upon disability, or at death. These decisions are voluntary and are based on the plan's objectives.

There is another important consideration. The participant's benefit attributable to employee after-tax contributions or employee pretax salary deferral elections in a 401(k) plan must be 100 percent vested at all times. This rule applies both to contributions and to investment experience thereon. For this reason, any plan that has either type of employee contributions must keep separate accounts for employer and employee contributions.

In addition, the vesting schedules discussed above must be modified in two situations. First, if the plan is top-heavy it must use a vesting schedule that is as favorable as 3-year cliff vesting (fully vested after 3 years) or a 6-year graded vesting schedule. Under the 6-year schedule, the participant must earn 20 percent vesting after 2 years of service and an additional 20 percent for each additional year of service (fully vested after 6 years). The same vesting schedules that are used for top-heavy vesting must also be used for employer matching contributions in 401(k) plans.

Top-Heavy Plans

top-heavy plan

When more than 60 percent of a plan's benefits are for certain key employees (which is often the case in a small plan), the plan is referred to as a *top-heavy plan* and special rules apply. As discussed above, shorter vesting schedules are required and minimum benefits have to be provided to nonkey employees. For a defined-contribution plan, the minimum employer contribution must be no less than 3 percent of each nonkey employee's compensation (provided the key employees receive at least 3 percent). For defined-benefit plans, the minimum benefit for each nonkey employee must be at least 2 percent of compensation multiplied by the number of the employee's years of service in which the plan is top-heavy up to a maximum of 10 years.

Participant Loans

All qualified plans are permitted to have participant loan programs. If a plan sponsor wants to include a loan program, loans must be available to all participants on a reasonably equivalent basis and must not be available to highly compensated employees in an amount greater than the amount made available to other employees. In addition, loans must

- be adequately secured
- be made in accordance with specific plan provisions
- bear a reasonable (market) rate of interest

Almost all plans use the participant's accrued benefit as security. Other property can be used as security but most plans avoid using other property because of administrative complexities.

A loan to a participant does not result in any taxable income to the participant as long as the loan fits within certain parameters. A loan cannot exceed the lesser of $50,000 or one-half of the vested account balance. Also a participant's loan must be repayable by its terms within 5 years. The one exception to the 5-year rule is if a loan is used to acquire a participant's principal residence. Loans must be repaid at least quarterly using a level amortization schedule.

From a participant's point of view, a loan is better than a distribution because it avoids income tax and the 10 percent penalty tax that generally applies to distributions prior to age 59 ½. Loans are most commonly found in 401(k) plans, since the loan feature gives participants the sense that they have access to their contributions in case of emergency.

Funding a Plan

The financial services professional must be acquainted with funding and investing rules that apply to qualified plans. For all types of plans, contributions must be made periodically into the plan's funding instrument, which is generally a trust account but can also be an insurance contract or a custodial account. It is important for the employer and the participants to understand that once contributions are made to the plan, they are the property of the trust and not the sponsoring organization. This means that the assets are now beyond the reach of the employer or the employer's creditors and will be used to pay promised benefits unless they are stolen or are invested badly.

What must be contributed depends on the kind of plan and the terms of the plan document. For example, in a defined-benefit plan, contributions are made in accordance with the minimum funding requirements. In a profit-sharing plan or SEP, employer contributions are generally at the employer's discretion.

When the funding instrument is a trust, the trustees are responsible for investing employer contributions, providing accounting to the plan sponsor, and paying out benefits. The trustees have a fiduciary relationship to plan participants, and the fiduciaries must act in the best interests of the plan participants. Thus, a business owner who is also a plan trustee cannot act in his or her own self-interest.

Most plans are subject to the fiduciary rules of ERISA. These rules require trustees to discharge their duties solely in the interest of the plan's participants and beneficiaries for the exclusive purpose of providing benefits and defraying reasonable expenses. This exclusive benefit requirement means that the fiduciary must act in the plan participant's interest first and foremost. In addition, trustees must exercise prudence, which means acting with the care, skill, discernment, and diligence (under prevailing circumstances) that a prudent person acting in a like capacity and familiar with such matters would use in the conduct of an enterprise of a like character and with like aims.

Trustees must also diversify the plan's investments to minimize the risk of large losses unless it is clearly prudent not to do so. Finally, fiduciaries are required to operate the plan in accordance with the document and instruments governing it. Trust instruments spell out the types of investments that are allowed, whether any investments are prohibited, and who is responsible for making investing decisions. Problems in this area arise when trustees and others make investment decisions without carefully consulting relevant documents. If the plan has a funding policy, an investment policy, or both (discussed further below), these documents must be carefully followed as well.

Because qualified plans of the defined-contribution type allocate dollars to the separate accounts of participants, the sponsoring employer has the option either to direct the trustees to invest plan assets or to give participants some choice over the investment of individual accounts. Because SEPs and SIMPLEs are funded with individual IRAs, participants almost always have investment options. Similarly, 403(b) plans usually give participants investment choices.

ERISA Sec. 404(c)

If a defined-contribution plan, SEP, SIMPLE, or 403(b) plan gives individual participants options with regard to the investment of their own plan benefits, it makes sense that the fiduciaries should not be responsible for the participant's investment decisions. *ERISA Sec. 404(c)* grants such fiduciary relief by providing that, in the case of a participant exercising independent investment direction over his or her own account, no fiduciary will be liable for losses that arise from such participant direction.

In order to qualify for this relief, the plan must conform to strict DOL requirements. The DOL's general rule is that the plan must provide an opportunity for a participant or beneficiary to exercise control over the assets in his or her account and offer the individual an opportunity to choose from a broad range of investment alternatives.

Still, 404(c) does not get the fiduciary completely off the hook. Fiduciaries are obligated to ensure that participant investment choices do not constitute *prohibited transactions*. Furthermore, investment choices must conform with other fiduciary obligations, such as compliance with plan documents. Most important, fiduciaries are never granted relief from the obligation to prudently select the available options.

Pension versus Profit-Sharing Plans

The rules described above apply to all qualified plans. Certain rules apply based on whether the plan is categorized as a pension or a profit-sharing plan. As shown in table 3-2, the pension category includes both types of defined-benefit plans and money-purchase plans. Profit-sharing, 401(k), stock bonus, and ESOP plans fall within the profit-sharing category.

pension plan

profit-sharing-type plan

The most important difference between a plan in the pension plan category and one in the profit-sharing category concerns the employer's commitment to contributions to the plan. Under a *pension plan,* the organization is legally required to make annual payments to the plan because the plan's main purpose is to provide a retirement benefit. Under a *profit-sharing-type plan,* however,

---

TABLE 3-2
Qualified Plan Categories

Pension Plans	Profit-Sharing Plans
• Defined-benefit pension plan • Cash-balance pension plan • Money-purchase pension plan	• Profit-sharing plan • 401(k) plan • Stock bonus plan • ESOP

**YOUR FINANCIAL SERVICES PRACTICE:
ESTIMATING RETIREMENT BENEFITS**

Because profit-sharing contributions are discretionary, be cautious when estimating benefits to be provided. When updating a retirement plan, be sure to review the assumptions made about the profit-sharing plan.

---

an organization is not required to make annual contributions. The reasoning here seems to be that profit-sharing plans are not necessarily intended to provide retirement benefits, but rather to enable a sharing of profits on a tax-deferred basis.

Consistent with this rationale, the law generally provides that profit-sharing-type plans may be written to allow distributions during employment, while pension plans cannot make distributions until the participant terminates employment. The law allows a profit-sharing-type plan to make in-service distributions on amounts that have accumulated in the plan for a stated number of years. The IRS has interpreted this to mean that distributions can be made on contributions that were made to the plan 2 or more years ago. Also, anyone who has 5 years of plan participation can receive a distribution of his or her entire account balance. In-service distributions can also be made after a stated event, such as a financial hardship. Note that one type of profit-sharing plan, the 401(k) plan, is subject to special, more restrictive in-service withdrawal constraints. Also note that this is voluntary and many profit-sharing plans do not allow for in-service withdrawals.

**YOUR FINANCIAL SERVICES PRACTICE:
IN-SERVICE WITHDRAWALS**

The opportunity for in-service distributions opens up interesting planning opportunities. Early distributions allow the participant to reposition assets, to take advantage of a specific investment, or to meet other needs—such as purchasing life insurance as part of the client's estate plan.

A final distinction between pension and profit-sharing plans concerns the ability of these plans to invest in company stock. Plans in the pension category can invest only up to 10 percent of plan assets in employer stock. Plans in the profit-sharing category, on the other hand, have no restrictions; all plan assets can be used to purchase employer stock (although this is seldom the case).

Defined-Benefit and Defined-Contribution Plans

defined-benefit plan
Qualified plans are also categorized as either defined-benefit plans or defined-contribution plans. There are two types of *defined-benefit plans:* the

traditional defined-benefit plan and the newer cash-balance arrangement. In both types, the plan specifies the benefits that an employee receives, and it is the employer's responsibility to fund the plan sufficiently to pay the promised benefits. Most plans are sufficiently funded to pay promised benefits because of the minimum funding requirements. However, occasionally a company can go out of business with the plan having insufficient assets. Because of this possibility, the program insures benefits up to a monthly maximum of approximately $3,800 (as indexed in 2005). All privately sponsored defined-benefit plans are required to participate in the PBGC insurance program except for plans sponsored by professional services organizations that have less than 25 participants.

The rules limit the maximum annual benefit that can be paid from a defined-benefit plan. The maximum benefit for any participant is the lesser of $170,000 (as indexed for 2005) or 100 percent of the employee's average compensation payable as early as age 62. However, compensation is limited to a maximum of $210,000 each year (as indexed for 2005).

The maximum deductible contribution in a defined-benefit plan is not limited to a specified percentage of payroll. It is a complicated calculation determined by the plan's actuary and is based on contributing amounts necessary to ensure sufficient assets to pay promised benefits.

defined-contribution plan

A *defined-contribution plan,* on the other hand, allocates employer contributions to the accounts of individual employees. The account grows as contributions are made and the plan's investment experience is allocated to each account. Money-purchase plans, profit-sharing plans, 401(k) plans, stock bonus plans, and ESOPs all are categorized as defined-contribution plans.

In defined-contribution plans, the maximum deductible contribution is 25 percent of aggregate compensation of all covered participants. Contributions for any one participant cannot exceed the lesser of 100 percent of compensation or $42,000 (as indexed for 2005).

One way to look at these dissimilar approaches is to say that defined-benefit plans provide a fixed predetermined benefit that has an uncertain cost to the employer, whereas defined-contribution plans have a predetermined cost to the employer and provide a variable benefit to employees (based on the rate of return). Now let's turn to a more specific discussion of each type of plan.

Traditional Defined-Benefit Plans

The traditional defined-benefit plan has all the characteristics of defined-benefit and pension categories discussed above. In the traditional arrangement, the plan promises a specified monthly benefit for life starting at some specified retirement age. However, its distinctive element is its benefit formula. Most defined-benefit plans use a formula referred to as a unit-benefit formula that takes into consideration both service and salary in determining the participant's promised benefit. For example, a unit-benefit formula might read as follows:

Example:	ABC Company's defined-benefit pension plan specifies that each plan participant will receive a monthly pension commencing at normal retirement date (the later of age 65 or 5 years of service) and paid in the form of a life annuity equal to 1.5 percent of final average monthly salary multiplied by years of service. Service is limited to a maximum of 30 years. The definition of *salary* only includes base pay, and final average salary is the average of the highest 36 months of salary. *Service* includes all years in which the individual works 1,000 hours of service.

To understand how this formula works in operation, let's calculate a benefit for Larry Novenstern, who is retiring at age 65 after being a full-time employee of ABC for 30 years. Taking Larry's base pay over the highest 36 months (his last 3 years in this case) and dividing by 36, Larry's final average monthly salary is $5,000. To determine Larry's benefit, multiply 1.5 percent by the $5,000 final average monthly salary by 30 (the number of years of service). Larry's monthly retirement benefit will be equal to $2,250. This is the benefit if Larry elects a single life annuity payable at his normal retirement age (65 in this case).

Each element of the benefit formula is meaningful and affects the value of the benefit. For example, in this formula compensation only includes base pay. If Larry has earned significant bonuses or commissions, he may not understand that these are not included in the calculation of his benefit. Similarly, the definition of final average salary and the definition of service can also affect the benefit. Also note that if Larry had decided to stay with his employer, he would have effectively stopped increasing the percentage of his final salary to be recovered at 45 percent (1.5 x 30-year cap).

In many plans, Larry can choose from a number of benefit options. If a different annuity form is chosen, an actuarial adjustment is made to the benefit amount to account for any survivor benefits or guaranteed benefits provided under the different annuity form. The timing of payment is significant. If Larry retires before age 65, the plan may provide for payment under an early retirement provision, but the benefit most likely will be reduced to reflect the longer payment period. Similarly, if he stays after age 65, benefits will increase for a shorter payout period.

There are other types of benefit formulas that a retirement planner will occasionally see. The first is the flat-percentage-of-earnings formula. This formula relates solely to a participant's salary and does not reflect his or her service in the benefit calculation. For example, the formula could read that each plan participant will receive a monthly pension benefit commencing at normal retirement date and paid in the form of a life annuity equal to 40 percent of the final average monthly salary the participant was paid.

This type of formula provides a disproportionate benefit to those employees entering the plan later in their careers. Therefore, these plans have been popular for owners establishing a plan for the first time later in life. However, IRS regulations have limited the effectiveness of this type of plan design by generally requiring that under a flat-percentage-of-earnings formula, any employee with less than 25 years of service will have his or her benefit proportionately reduced.

Two other formulas are commonly found in union-sponsored plans. With a flat amount formula, all participants receive the same benefit, such as $400 a month. With a flat-amount-per-year-of-service formula, a flat amount is multiplied by the number of years of service with the employer. The formula might read, "Each plan participant will receive a monthly pension benefit commencing at normal retirement date and paid in the form of a life annuity equal to $10 for every year of service worked."

Retirement Planning Considerations

A traditional defined-benefit plan is quite different from any other type of retirement plan that employers sponsor. In most formulas, the benefit reflects a percentage of the participant's wages, making it a predictable and valuable benefit that can be a vital piece of the retirement planning puzzle.

However, even though a defined-benefit plan can result in an excellent benefit for the long-term participant, an early termination of the benefit— because either the plan is terminated or the participant terminates employment—will significantly reduce the participant's benefit. This is because the benefit is tied to final average compensation and consequently accrues faster at the end of the career when salary and years of service are both increasing. This factor is why defined-contribution plans are considered more portable. Benefits accrue more evenly and a change in employers (each with similar defined-contribution plans) will not change the total benefit. This is an important concept to pass on to the client contemplating a job change or an early retirement. The following example demonstrates the effect of changing jobs with companies that sponsor defined-benefit plans.

Example:	Assume that a plan provides that a participant will receive a benefit at age 65 of 1.5 percent of final average compensation times years of service. At age 50, Joe has 15 years of service and a final average salary of $3,300 a month. If Joe terminates employment now, at age 65 he would be entitled to a benefit of $742 a month. If he stays until age 65 with

30 years of service and has a final average salary of $6,000 a month (the result of compensation increases of 4 percent a year), his benefit will be $2,700 a month. At age 50 and after 15 years of service, his benefit is much less than half of what it will be if he stays until age 65. If Joe transfers to another company with exactly the same defined-benefit plan and works there for 15 years, his benefit would be $1,350 a month ($6,000 x .015 x 15). The combined benefit from both companies ($742 + $1,350 = $2,092) is almost $600 a month less than if Joe stays with the same company.

Defined-benefit plan participants often have a difficult time understanding and appreciating their benefits under the plan. The retirement planner can help the participant fully understand his or her benefit and the effect of decisions made under the plan. The participant will receive periodic benefit statements that will project a retirement benefit, but this will be based on current salary and an assumption that the participant will work until the plan's normal retirement age. The retirement planner can help by taking the following three steps:

- Understand the client. Discuss the projected time of retirement or if the client is expecting to leave for a new job or career prior to that date. Also discuss the expected salary situation at the company—specifically any large increases or decreases based on a job status change.
- Understand the plan. Carefully review the plan's benefit formula, especially noting such elements as years of service, compensation, final average compensation, normal retirement age, and normal form of benefit payments. Give careful consideration to the impact of early or late retirement on the amount of the benefit formula.
- Review alternatives with the client. Based on the information above, calculate numbers that fully illustrate the effects of various courses of action that the client should consider.

Cash-Balance Pension Plans

The cash-balance concept is a relatively new idea in pension plan design, with the first plan introduced in 1984. In its short history it has been used primarily by large, and in some cases midsize, corporations as an alternative to the traditional defined-benefit plan. In fact, most of the cash-balance plans in existence today started as traditional plans that were later amended.

cash-balance pension plan

The heart of a *cash-balance pension plan* is its benefit structure. Unlike a traditional defined-benefit plan, the cash-balance plan's benefits resemble a single sum account balance, which is similar to the defined-contribution plan. Also, as in the defined-contribution plan, the benefit is stated as an account balance that increases with contributions and investment experience.

Example:　　Under the DEF Cash-Balance Plan, a participant is entitled to a single-sum benefit that is based on a credit of 5 percent of compensation each year. The credited amounts will accumulate with interest. Interest will be credited annually using the 30-year Treasury rate on that date. Actual investment experience will not affect the value of the benefit.

Unlike a defined-contribution plan, the account is fictitious. Contributions are a bookkeeping credit only—no actual contributions are allocated to participants' accounts. Investment credits are also hypothetical and are based either on a rate specified in the plan or on an external index.

It is not unusual for the benefit formula to also consider both salary and years of service to reward those with longer service. For example, a formula can assign credits of 3 percent of salary for those with less than 5 years of service, 6 percent for those with 10 or more years of service, and 9 percent for 20-year veterans. Credits given for investment experience can be stated as a fixed, predetermined rate, a floating rate (based on some external index outside the employer's control), or a combination of a fixed and floating rate, such as the rate of one-year Treasury bills. The contribution and interest credits can be treated as though they are made annually or more often, if the employer prefers. Also, since this is a defined-benefit plan, contribution and interest credits can be made for past years of service.

When an employer converts a traditional defined-benefit plan to a cash-balance arrangement, older workers will often lose benefits in the transition if a grandfathering rule is not in place. This is because with the traditional defined-benefit approach, benefits accrue more quickly at the end of the career; with the defined-contribution approach, benefits accrue more evenly. Most of the bad press that cash-balance plans received in the late 1990s was due to older workers ending up with lower benefits under the new arrangement without this being communicated to them. It is now more typical for a company converting a defined-benefit plan to a cash-balance arrangement to include a grandfathering provision that prevents older workers being penalized. Recent law changes also require full disclosure of the effect the amendment from a defined-benefit plan to a cash-balance arrangement will have on the benefits of individual plan participants.

Nevertheless, the IRS, the courts, and Congress continue to have problems with cash-balance plans—especially conversions, whose viability is still in question.

Retirement Planning Considerations

From the employee's perspective, the cash-balance design operates like a defined-contribution plan. Like defined-contribution plans, the benefit accrues more evenly, meaning that benefits are more portable and a participant working for several employers will not be penalized for participating in a number of defined-contribution plans.

However, it is important to understand that defined-contribution and cash-balance plans are not exactly the same. Instead of receiving the cash-balance plan's actual investment experience, the participant usually receives a conservative (but always positive) rate of return, such as the 30-year Treasury bond rate. Because of this, it may be appropriate to consider a cash-balance benefit as a conservative fixed-income component of the participant's entire retirement portfolio. The total dollar amount that will be received is relatively predictable, assuming that the plan is not amended by the employer and the employee works until the anticipated retirement age.

In the past, if a traditional defined-benefit plan was amended into a cash-balance arrangement, it was difficult for the employee to understand the impact of the change on his or her benefits. In some cases—especially for older workers—the benefit structure may be less favorable after the change than under the old formula. Today, plan sponsors are required to notify participants if benefits are reduced under the new arrangement and to fully explain the differences between the old and new formulas.

Money-Purchase Pension Plans

money-purchase pension plan

A *money-purchase pension plan*, like other plans in the pension category, requires annual contributions. The plan has a stated contribution formula that is usually a designated percentage of a participant's compensation.

Example:	GHI Company's money-purchase pension plan specifies that a contribution in the amount of 10 percent of compensation will be made for each eligible participant. Compensation is W2 income; the participant must work 1,000 hours of service and be employed on the last day of the plan year in order to be eligible for contribution. A terminating participant will receive the accumulated vested account balance, which includes employer investment earnings and forfeitures credited to the participant's account.

Using the formula in the example, if employee Karen Lamb earns $40,000, the annual contribution placed in her account is $4,000. If Karen worked for 20 years and her salary remained at $40,000, she would have $80,000 plus accumulated interest of $58,876 (assuming a 5 percent annual rate) at retirement.

Retirement Planning Considerations

From the participant's perspective, one major drawback of a money-purchase plan (or any defined-contribution plan) is that contributions are based on the participant's salary for each year of his or her career rather than on the participant's salary at retirement. Given a stable inflationary environment, this may not have a negative effect on the adequacy of retirement income. If inflation spirals in the years prior to retirement, however, the chances of achieving an adequate income-replacement ratio are diminished.

A second drawback is the inability to provide an adequate retirement program for participants who enter the plan at an older age. Those who enter money-purchase pension plans later in their careers have less time to accumulate sufficient assets.

Note that even though a money-purchase plan can look quite secure from the participant's perspective (the sponsor is required to make the stated annual contribution), the sponsor is allowed to amend the plan in the future. This means that a promised contribution can be reduced for subsequent plan years.

Profit-Sharing Plans

profit-sharing plan

A *profit-sharing plan* is an extremely versatile retirement plan. As already mentioned, the employer's contribution is discretionary. Most plans are written specifying that the board of directors decides each year whether to make contributions or how much to contribute. Since 1987, an employer can make a contribution to a plan whether or not there are actually profits. Whether a company actually contributes more in a good financial year is a business decision. However, if the employer is trying to use the plan to motivate participants, there should be a clear relationship between the company's performance and contributions made to the plan.

Even though contributions can be skipped for a period of time, they must be "substantial and recurring" or the IRS could determine that the plan has been terminated. If the IRS makes this determination, any employees who had left the company after the deemed termination date (typically the date of the last contribution to the plan) would have to be fully vested. To avoid this problem, the sponsor should make contributions periodically.

The heart of a profit-sharing plan is the method of allocating the employer contribution among the participants. This formula must be definite

allocation formula

and predetermined. Historically, the most common *allocation formula* has been one that allocates the total contribution so that each participant receives the same percentage of compensation—for example, 3 percent or 5 percent. This allocation formula in the plan document would read something like this:

"Employer contributions made for the year will be allocated, as of the last day of each plan year, to each participant's account in the proportion that the participant's compensation bears to the total compensation of all eligible participants for the plan year."

Example:	Under this type of allocation formula, if the employer contributed $10,000, total payroll was $100,000, and Alexander, a participant, earned $25,000, he would have an allocation of $2,500 ($10,000 x $25,000/$100,000). If Barbara, also a participant, earned $30,000, her allocation would be $3,000 ($10,000 x $30,000/$100,000). As you can see, the employer contributed 10 percent of payroll, and each participant received an allocation of 10 percent of his or her compensation.

However, a profit-sharing plan may be used to allocate a higher level of contributions for certain key employees as long as the nondiscrimination of benefits requirement is satisfied. One way to do this is to integrate the allocation formula with Social Security. With this approach, the sponsor can contribute a maximum of 5.7 percent of compensation earned in excess of the taxable wage base in addition to the amount contributed based on total compensation. At one time integration was quite effective. However, the compensation cap, which now limits compensation that can be taken into account under a qualified plan to $210,000 a year (as indexed for 2005), significantly reduces the effectiveness of the integration approach.

Regulations also offer a nondiscrimination testing methodology referred to as cross-testing (also known as new comparability), which allows the employer to test whether an allocation formula is nondiscriminatory by converting the contributions into equivalent benefit accruals and then testing the benefits provided under a nondiscrimination test. If the formula satisfies the mathematical test, the plan satisfies the regulation. This testing method gives the employer the opportunity to create virtually any allocation method as long as the test is satisfied. The employer also can make larger contributions for older employees because these convert to a smaller benefit than contributions made for younger employees. In fact, in cases where the average age of the highly compensated employees is 10 or more years older than the average age of the nonhighly compensated employees, the plan could allow for contributions of $42,000 (as indexed for 2005) for highly compensated and 5 percent of compensation for rank-and-file employees. Even though the details of cross-testing are beyond the scope of this text, it is important to understand that this approach is quite powerful and should be of interest to any employer looking for a flexible defined-contribution plan that directs a large part of the employer's contribution to the targeted group.

Stock Plans

stock bonus plan
employee stock
  ownership plan
  (ESOP)

Stock bonus plans and *employee stock ownership plans (ESOPs)* are derived from profit-sharing plans and are therefore similar to them in many ways. For example, stock bonus plans, ESOPs, and profit-sharing plans are all forms of defined-contribution plans—contributions need not be fixed or made every year, and contribution levels to any one employee (even owner-employees) typically will not exceed 15 percent (the amount of the business's deduction). However, stock bonus plans and ESOPs differ from profit-sharing plans in that they typically invest plan assets primarily in employer stock, whereas profit-sharing plans are usually structured to diversify investments. From a retirement planning standpoint, this can be disastrous because without any diversity of investment, participants are exposed to potential disaster if the employer stock drops in value.

There is, however, some relief available for ESOP participants. The law requires that once an ESOP participant attains age 55 and completes at least 10 years of participation, the participant may elect (between the ages of 55 and 60) to diversify the retirement benefit by moving up to 50 percent of his or her account balance into other investments. Planners should recommend that their clients take advantage of this in all but a few cases where the stability of the employer stock is unquestioned. There is a trade-off for diversification, however, in the loss of the tax-timing strategy (discussed next).

Tax-Timing Strategy for Stock Plans

Stock bonus plans and ESOPs allow distributions to participants in the form of employer stock. Stock distributed as part of a lump-sum distribution (see chapter 10) is eligible for special tax deferral. When stock is distributed, the tax on the distribution is determined based on the stock's value at the time it was purchased by the plan, not on the value at the time of distribution. This unrealized appreciation is not subject to tax until the stock is later sold by the participant.

Example:	Steve Gilchrist has 10,000 shares of his company's stock, each with a basis of $5 a share. The basis is the cost of the stock when it was allocated to

Steve's account. When Steve retires in 2001, the stock is worth $12 a share. Steve elects to take the ESOP distribution in stock and he does not roll the benefit into an IRA account. Steve's tax liability will be determined on the plan's cost of $50,000 (10,000 shares x $5 per share), not on the current market value of $120,000. When Steve sells the stock in 2005 at $15 a share, he then pays taxes on the $100,000 appreciation ($150,000 market value reduced by the $50,000 on which he's already paid taxes). A valuable part of this rule states that the portion of the distribution that represents the increase from the cost basis to the market value at the time of the distribution ($120,000 − $50,000 = $70,000) is always treated as long-term capital gains. The remaining gain ($30,000) is long-term or short-term capital gain depending on how long the stock is held after the options were exercised.

Put Options for Stock Plans

put option

One potential disadvantage of stock plans is the lack of liquidity of stock from a closely held business. In a stock plan, however, the employer is required to offer a repurchase option (also known as a *put option*). This option must be available for a minimum of 60 days following the distribution of the stock and, if the option is not exercised in that period, for an additional 60-day period in the following year. The repurchase option creates an administrative and cash-flow problem for business owners but significant protection for employees.

401(k) Plans

cash or deferred arrangement (CODA) 401(k) plan

A profit-sharing plan that offers a *cash or deferred arrangement (CODA)* is usually referred to as a *401(k) plan*. A 401(k) plan allows plan participants to defer taxation on a portion of regular salary or bonuses simply by electing to have such amounts contributed to the plan instead of receiving them in cash. Participants enjoy abundant tax savings. For example, if Simms is in the 28 percent marginal tax bracket and elects to reduce his salary by $6,000, he will save $1,680 in taxes. That's like having Uncle Sam as a contributing partner in Simms's retirement savings. What's more, the money Simms puts in the plan earns tax-deferred interest until retirement.

Today almost all large private employers and many midsize companies sponsor such plans (often in addition to sponsoring more traditional plans such as a defined-benefit or money-purchase pension plan). The 401(k) plan is starting to expand into the small plan market as well, and today it is the most popular new plan to install.

The maximum salary deferral amount in a 401(k) plan cannot exceed a specified limit. The limit for 2005 is $14,000. It is scheduled to increase to $15,000 in 2006; after 2006, the maximum dollar amount will increase for inflation in increments of $500. In addition, a 401(k) plan may also allow participants aged 50 and older to make a special catch-up election. For 2005, the additional allowable contribution is $4,000. The additional amount becomes $5,000 for 2006. Table 3-3 shows the maximum contribution, including the new catch-up election, for 2005 and 2006.

TABLE 3-3
Scheduled Increases to the Maximum Salary Deferral Amount

Year	Maximum for All Participants	Participants over 50	Total for Those over 50
2005	$14,000	$4,000	$18,000
2006	$15,000	$5,000	$20,000

Note that this maximum salary deferral limit to a 401(k) plan applies to the individual. This means that all salary deferral contributions made by that individual to any 401(k) plan, Code Sec. 403(b) annuity, simplified employee pension (SEP), or savings incentive match plan for employees (SIMPLE) will be treated as one plan under the rules. This is even true for an individual working for a number of unrelated employers.

The 401(k) salary deferral part of the profit-sharing plan is subject to a number of special rules:

- The 401(k) salary reductions are immediately 100 percent vested and cannot be forfeited.
- In-service withdrawals are to be made only if an individual has attained age 59 1/2 or has a financial hardship.
- An extra nondiscrimination test, called the actual deferral percentage (ADP) test, applies to salary deferrals.

The ADP nondiscrimination test compares the deferral percentages of highly compensated employees and nonhighly compensated employees. If the test is not satisfied, and then the amounts deferred by the highly compensated employees may have to be reduced or even returned. To simplify administration and to eliminate testing problems, a sponsor can avoid the ADP test by making a safe-harbor contribution. This is either a nonelective contribution of 3 percent of compensation for all eligible participants (regardless of whether they make salary deferral elections or not) or a matching contribution for those who make salary deferrals of 100 percent on the first 3 percent of salary deferred and 50 percent of the next 2 percent of salary deferred. A safe-harbor contribution (either a matching or nonelective contribution) must be fully vested and subject to the hardship withdrawal restrictions that apply to salary deferral accounts.

A 401(k) plan can have up to four different types of contributions (actually more if a safe-harbor contribution is made). In addition to salary deferrals, employers often make matching contributions to encourage employee participation in the plan. For example, the sponsor might contribute 50 cents to the plan for each dollar that the employee contributes up to the first 6 percent of compensation that the participant saves. The matching contribution could be more complicated than that, such as a graded formula in which the matching contribution rate varies for different levels of salary deferrals. Matching contributions are subject to special vesting requirements. They also must satisfy a nondiscrimination test similar to the ADP test that applies to salary deferrals.

The employer can make additional profit-sharing-type contributions as well, meaning that all eligible participants (regardless of whether they choose to make salary deferral contributions) will receive an allocation of the employer's contribution. When the 401(k) plan is the only plan sponsored by the employer, it is not uncommon (in a good year) for the sponsor to make both matching contributions and profit-sharing-type contributions.

A 401(k) plan can include employee after-tax contributions in addition to employee pretax salary deferrals. This feature occasionally included in current plans primarily because employees like the withdrawal flexibility of after-tax contributions. It is more likely in older plans that were converted from after-tax thrift plans.

To give participants access to their funds, 401(k) plans typically allow participant loans. Under the law, the maximum allowable loan is the lesser of 50 percent of the participant's vested account balance or $50,000. Also, unlike other plans, 401(k) plans almost always give participants control over the investment direction of their accounts.

Retirement Planning Considerations

A retirement planner working with participants in 401(k) plans should be aware of the following:

- Encourage participants to take advantage of saving on a pre-tax basis—especially if the contribution is matched by an employer contribution.
- Understand the company match.
- Limit borrowing to hardship withdrawals only.

- Roll the 401(k) over into another plan if changing jobs.
- Participants typically have some control over the investment of plan assets. Their investment decisions should be considered when designing the appropriate asset allocation for their entire portfolio.
- Be careful of investing in employer securities.
- The increasing maximum contribution limits and the catch-up election should allow older workers to increase saving to make up for lost time.

OTHER TAX-ADVANTAGED RETIREMENT PLANS

403(b) Plans

403(b) plan

A *403(b) plan*—sometimes referred to as a tax-sheltered annuity (TSA) or tax-deferred annuity (TDA)—is similar to a 401(k) plan in many respects. Both plans permit an employee to defer taxes on income by allowing before-tax contributions to the employee's individual account, by allowing deferrals in the form of salary reduction, and by allowing the plan's use in conjunction with, or in lieu of, most other retirement plans. The maximum salary deferral limits are the same for 403(b) plans as for 401(k) plans ($14,000 for 2005). However, 403(b) plans are distinguishable from 401(k) plans in several ways:

- The 403(b) market includes only 501(c)(3) tax-exempt organizations and public schools.
- The 403(b) plan can be funded only through annuity contracts or mutual funds.
- The 403(b) plan is not subject to a nondiscrimination test, meaning that highly compensated employees can elect to defer the maximum dollar amount without regard to the amount deferred by nonhighly compensated employees.

The 403(b) plan can be used as a stand-alone benefit (salary deferral contributions only) or as a means of providing additional retirement benefits for employees. Including employer contributions drastically changes the nature of the plan. When the plan only contains salary deferral contributions, the participant's primary relationship is with the service provider. The plan is not subject to ERISA's fiduciary rules, and the plan sponsor is not required to do annual reporting. When the plan includes employer contributions, it operates much more like a qualified plan. The plan is then subject both to ERISA and to a significant number of additional tax rules.

As in a 401(k) plan, employer contributions can be made as matching contributions based on employee elections to defer compensation. Another alternative is to make contributions on a nonelective basis as in a profit-sharing plan or a money-purchase pension plan. Typically, such plans provide contributions as a uniform percentage of compensation; however, some flexibility is available in determining the allocation formula.

Simplified Employee Pension Plans (SEPs)

simplified employee pension plan (SEP)

A *simplified employee pension plan (SEP)* is a type of retirement plan that from the participant's perspective is quite similar to the profit-sharing plan. Each year the employer has the discretion to choose the amount of contribution. Contributions are allocated to the participant's accounts based on the plan's allocation formula. However, the options for the allocation formula are more restricted than in a profit-sharing plan. Contributions must either be allocated based on the relationship of individual compensation to total compensation (which results in a level percentage of compensation for each participant) or be integrated with Social Security using the same method as in other defined-contribution plans.

The maximum contribution limits are essentially the same as a profit-sharing plan. The maximum deductible contribution to the plan is 25 percent of aggregate employee compensation and no more than the lesser of $42,000 (as indexed for 2005) or 100 percent of pay can be allocated to each participant's account.

The major advantage the SEP has over the qualified plan is that the documentation, reporting, and disclosure requirements are less cumbersome. The plan can be adopted with a simple IRS form or a short prototype document offered by a financial institution. The document itself generally serves as the summary plan description. SEPs are generally not required to file an annual Form 5500 each year.

Another reason that SEPs are easier to administer is that separate IRAs are established for each participant, and all contributions are made directly to each participant's IRA. This eliminates the need for trust accounting. Also contributions must be nonforfeitable, which means that the participant's benefit at any time is simply the IRA account balance.

As with other IRAs, participants have instant access to their benefits at any time. This is different from qualified plans where access to benefits is limited by both the terms of the plan and legal restraints. The only limitation in a SEP IRA is that the distribution will be taxable and may also be subject to the 10 percent early distribution penalty tax.

Other rules that apply to IRAs apply to SEP IRAs as well. For example, the IRA investment limitations that prohibit investment in life insurance and collectibles apply to SEP IRAs. Also the plan cannot maintain a participant loan program.

SEPs are subject to a very different set of participation requirements than those for qualified retirement plans. The rules require that contributions be made for all employees who have met all three of the following requirements:

- attained age 21
- performed services for the employer for at least 3 of the immediately preceding 5 years
- received a minimum of $450 of compensation for the year (indexed limit for 2005)

Before 1997, an employer could establish a SEP (often referred to as a SARSEP) that allowed employees to make pretax contributions in the same way as in a 401(k) plan. In 1996, the Small Business Job Protection Act replaced the SARSEP with the SIMPLE and prohibited new SARSEPs. However, employers were allowed to continue to sponsor plans that were in effect as of December 31, 1996. The SARSEP was never a very popular plan, but there are still a few remaining SARSEPs in existence today. In a SARSEP, employees can elect to defer up to the same deferral amount allowed in a 401(k) plan. Like the 401(k) plan, the SARSEP is subject to a nondiscrimination rule similar to the ADP test. SARSEPs also are subject to several requirements that do not apply to 401(k) plans, each of which makes the plan less attractive than a 401(k) plan:

- Only an employer with 25 or fewer employees can sponsor a SARSEP.
- At least 50 percent of all eligible employees must participate in the SARSEP.
- The employer may not make matching contributions to encourage employees to contribute to the plan.

SIMPLEs

Savings Incentive Match Plan for Employees (SIMPLE)

The *Savings Incentive Match Plan for Employees (SIMPLE)* is an alternative to a 401(k) that (like the acronym implies) is truly easy for the sponsor and administrator. In exchange for simplicity, the plan is subject to very rigid plan design restrictions.

Like a SEP, the SIMPLE plan is funded with individual retirement accounts, which means that the following requirements apply to the SIMPLE:

- Participants must be fully vested in all benefits at all times.
- Assets cannot be invested in life insurance or collectibles.
- No participant loans are allowed.

Any type of business entity can establish a SIMPLE; however, the business cannot have more than 100 employees (counting only those employees who earn $5,000 or more per year). Also note that to be eligible, the sponsoring employer cannot maintain any other qualified plan, 403(b), or SEP at the same time that it maintains a SIMPLE.

In a SIMPLE, all eligible employees can make elective pretax contributions of up to $10,000 (as indexed for 2005). Unlike the 401(k) plan, there is no nondiscrimination testing, meaning that highly compensated employees can make contributions without regard to the salary deferral elections of the nonhighly compensated employees.

However, in exchange for this opportunity, the SIMPLE has a mandatory employer contribution requirement. This contribution can be made in one of two ways:

- The employer can make a dollar-for-dollar matching contribution on the first 3 percent of compensation that the individual elects to defer.
- Alternatively, the employer can make a 2 percent nonelective contribution for all eligible employees.

If the employer elects the matching contribution, it has one other option. Periodically the employer can elect a lower match as long as

- the matching contribution is not less than one percent of compensation
- participants are notified of the lower contribution reasonably well in advance of the 60-day election period before the beginning of the year

The employer can elect the lower percentage for up to 2 years in any 5-year period, which can even include the first 2 years that the plan is in force.

The employer contribution amount just described is both the minimum required and the maximum employer contribution allowed. In other words, if the employer elects the matching contribution, 3 percent is the maximum match and nonelective contributions are not allowed. If the employer elects the nonelective contribution, then the 2 percent contribution is the maximum and matching contributions are not allowed.

The SIMPLE has eligibility requirements that are different from those for both the SEP and the qualified plan. The plan must cover any employee who earned $5,000 in any 2 previous years and is reasonably expected to earn $5,000 again in the current year. Employees subject to a collectively bargained agreement can be excluded.

Like SEPs, SIMPLEs cannot put any limitations on participant withdrawals. This means that participants have access to funds at any time—whether to spend them or roll them over into another IRA. However, to discourage participants from spending their SIMPLE accounts, a special tax rule assesses a 25 percent penalty tax (in addition to ordinary income taxes) for amounts withdrawn within 2 years of the date of participation.

ADDITIONAL RETIREMENT PLANNING CONSIDERATIONS

Regardless of the type of plan involved, there are a number of retirement planning issues that are relevant to many of your clients. Every retirement planner must be aware of the following issues in order to best serve the clients' retirement needs.

Plan Termination

If your client's plan is terminated after he or she is retired and receiving a monthly benefit, no change will generally occur. Plan assets will be used to purchase an annuity that will continue to pay the promised benefit.

If your client's qualified plan is terminated while he or she is still employed, the participant is entitled to receive the current account balance in a defined-contribution plan or the accrued benefit in a defined-benefit plan. If the participant was not fully vested in the benefit, he or she becomes fully vested at the time the plan is terminated.

In a defined-contribution plan, the plan will always have sufficient assets to pay the account balances (unless the trustees have absconded with plan assets). Participants will be given the option to receive a single-sum distribution or, if the plan so provides, a deferred annuity. Most will choose the lump-sum option and roll it into an IRA. If the single sum is elected, the plan is required to give your client the option to have the amount transferred directly to another qualified plan or an IRA account. As discussed further in chapters 10 and 11, the direct transfer is the best choice to avoid income tax withholding. Some participants will want to use the distribution for current needs. This both drains their retirement assets and results in current income taxes on the distribution and, for an individual under age 59 1/2, it imposes the 10 percent early distribution excise tax. For further discussion and an illustration, see chapter 11.

In a defined-benefit plan, the participant may not have a single-sum option, in which case the employer purchases annuity certificates from an insurance carrier. Under this option the insurer assumes the employer's liability and guarantees payment of the vested benefit under an annuity certificate. The annuity certificate your client will receive will contain information regarding the annuity's starting date (typically the date your client would have been eligible to retire under the plan), the amount of the annuity, and the annuity options available.

In a defined-benefit plan covered by the PBGC program, if the plan does not have sufficient assets to pay promised benefits, then the PBGC will guarantee the payment of certain benefits known as basic benefits (special or unusual benefits are generally not covered). Most notably, basic benefits do not include those benefits that become vested due to the plan termination. The PBGC insurance covers only up to a maximum benefit level. The maximum insured benefit equals the lesser of

- approximately $3,800 a month, adjusted upward each year to reflect changes in the Social Security wage base, or
- 100 percent of average monthly wages during the participant's 5 highest-paid consecutive years

Early Retirement

In addition to focusing on your client's benefit at normal retirement age, the following factors should be considered with regard to his or her benefit at an early retirement age:

- Eligibility for early retirement (especially in defined-benefit plans) may require both attainment of a specified age (for example, 55) and completion of a specified period of service (for example, 10 years).
- Early retirement benefits may end up being very costly to your client. While it is true that retirement benefits will be paid out over a longer period of time (the difference between early retirement age and normal retirement age), there are several mitigating factors.
  - For clients in a defined-benefit plan, early retirement generally reduces benefits in three ways: (1) benefits are actuarially reduced to reflect the longer payout period; (2) the number of years of service used in the benefit formula is cut short; and (3) compensation used for determining the benefit is lower than if the participant had continued working to normal retirement.
  - In some defined-benefit plans, these reductions are somewhat modified. For example, the participant may have accrued enough service to earn the maximum plan benefit. Also in some plans it is common to subsidize the early retirement benefit, which simply means that the benefit is not fully reduced to reflect the longer payout period.
  - For clients in a defined-contribution plan, early retirement causes them to lose several years of contributions based on a higher salary. By cutting out what could have been the 5 to 10 years of highest salary that a client would have earned, the shortfall in contributions may be dramatic. Also the client starts to spend down the benefit instead of letting it continue to accumulate.
  - Clients who take early retirement lose the inflation protection offered by increasing salaries and thus extend their inflation exposure during retirement.

The following items should be reviewed with a client who is considering early retirement:

- What is the earliest age at which early retirement is possible?
- What is the plan's service requirement for early retirement?
- Have lost earnings from early retirement been considered?
- What is the actuarial reduction for early retirement benefits?
- Is the actuarial reduction reflective of a true reduction for time value of money, or is early retirement partially subsidized by the employer?
- Has lost purchasing power occurring during early retirement been considered?
- Has lost income from a reduction in final average salary been considered?
- Is there a cap on years of service in the benefit formula?
- Are any early retirement incentives (such as golden handshakes) available?

Deferred Retirement

Keep the following facts in mind when dealing with a client who chooses to defer retirement:

- Clients in a defined-contribution plan will continue to receive contributions to their individual accounts until actual retirement.
- Clients in a defined-benefit plan may or may not continue to accrue benefits under the plan. If the plan specifies full accrual after a certain period of service (30 years of service is the maximum amount in which accruals are permitted), accruals for clients will cease based on service at that point. If, however, no service accrual cap applies, a client will continue to accrue benefits even after normal retirement age.
- For clients in a defined-benefit plan, the employer may actuarially increase the benefit payout to reflect the shorter payout period.
- The longer a client continues to work the shorter his or her exposure will be to postretirement inflation problems.

Changing Jobs

When a participant changes jobs, he or she will often (but not always) have the opportunity to take a distribution from the plan. As discussed elsewhere in this text, the primary concern is that distributed pension benefits are saved for retirement. The best way to do this is to elect a direct rollover into an IRA or other company-sponsored plan. This approach allows the continued deferral of taxes until the participant needs to start spending assets in retirement.

Investing Plan Assets

In any defined-contribution retirement plan, the participant's benefit is based on the total account balance. A crucial factor in determining the total benefit is the investment return earned on plan assets. In most profit-sharing plans and money-purchase pension plans, the trustees make investment decisions. And as discussed above, trustees are held to a standard of fiduciary care.

Defined-contribution plans also give participants the right to make investment choices themselves. Most 401(k) plans give participants this right as do 403(b) plans and SIMPLEs. However, participants need to make their investment decisions very carefully. This is a very complex issue, but the following considerations may help to clarify it:

- Participants need a complete understanding of each investment alternative the plan allows. Some plans offer a very limited choice (for example, a small number of mutual funds) while other plans allow as much discretion as an individual brokerage account.
- In addition to the investment alternatives, the participant will want to know two facts: how often investment changes can be made and whether there are any direct or indirect expenses associated with making investment changes.
- Investment decisions in a plan should consider tax implications. In a tax-deferred plan, sales and exchanges are not taxed and benefits are not taxed until distribution.
- The success of any investment program must be based on specified goals. The planning process should start with determining the participant's retirement needs and then looking at all sources of retirement income. Only after this examination can the participant determine how much is needed and consequently calculate the risk that is involved to achieve it.
- When making asset allocation and other investment decisions, the participant should look at the retirement portfolio as a whole. This means taking into consideration other assets such as IRAs and other outside investments.

CHOOSING A PLAN FOR THE SMALL BUSINESS OWNER

Another aspect of retirement planning is helping the small-business owner choose an appropriate retirement plan. As mentioned earlier, this is a complicated matter, but we will list some basic strategies. However, before discussing these strategies, there is one more factor to consider: whether the organization is a corporation or an unincorporated sole proprietorship or partnership.

Plans of Unincorporated Businesses

Plans sponsored by an unincorporated organization are subject to essentially the same rules as plans sponsored by corporations. Furthermore, the considerations for choosing the appropriate plan are generally the same as for other small businesses (see the discussion that follows). There is one difference, however. The maximum deductible contribution for a self-employed person is based on net earnings instead of salary. This creates some complications because net earnings can be determined only after taking into account all appropriate business deductions including the retirement plan contribution. Thus the amount of net earnings and the amount of the deduction are dependent on each other. In addition, the deduction for one-half of the Social Security taxes paid must be taken into account.

If a defined-benefit plan is used, an actuary is needed to straighten out this confusion and to determine the plan contribution amount itself. However, if a defined-contribution plan is used, the retirement planner may be called on to calculate the maximum deduction for his or her client (see the worksheet in table 3-4).

Example:	Julie is a sole proprietor. Her qualified profit-sharing plan provides that she can contribute up to 25 percent of earned income. Julie's self-employment contribution rate is 20 percent (see example in rate worksheet). Julie's net earnings from Schedule C are $100,000. Julie's deduction for self-employment tax (Form 1040) is $7,030. Julie's deduction for the tax year will be determined as follows:

(1) Enter the self-employment rate from Line 3 of Step I of table 3-4.   <u>.20</u>

(2) Enter the amount of net earnings from Schedule C (Form 1040) or from Schedule F (Form 1040). $ <u>100,000</u>

(3) Enter the deduction for the self-employment tax from Form 1040. $ <u>7,030</u>

(4) Subtract Line 3 from Line 2 and enter the amount. $ <u>92,970</u>

(5) Multiply Line 4 by Line 1 and enter the amount. This amount may be deducted by the business owner $ <u>18,594</u>

TABLE 3-4 **Self-Employed Deduction Worksheet**	
Step I: Self-employed person's worksheet	
1. Plan contribution as a decimal (for example, 25% would be 0.25)	_____
2. Rate in Line 1 plus 1, shown as a decimal (for example, 0.25 plus 1 would be 1.25)	_____
3. Divide Line 1 by Line 2. This is the self-employed contribution rate. (For example, 0.25 ÷ 1.25 = .20)	_____
Step II: Figure the deduction	
1. Enter the self-employed contribution rate from Line 3 of Step 1.	_____
2. Enter the amount of net earnings that the business owner has from Schedule C (Form 1040) or Schedule F (Form 1040).	$_____
3. Enter the deduction for self-employment tax from the front page of Form 1040.	$_____
4. Subtract Line 3 from Line 2 and enter the amount.	$_____
5. Multiply Line 4 by Line 1. This is the amount that may be deducted by the business owner.*	$_____

*Note that this amount is subject to two additional limitations. First, the amount cannot exceed the $42,000 Code Sec. 415 limit. Also, the participant's compensation cannot exceed the $210,000 maximum compensation cap (for 2005).

Start with a SEP

A SEP is an excellent place to start when considering a retirement plan for a small business with either a few employees or no employees other than the owner. The SEP is flexible because contributions are discretionary and the employer can choose how much to contribute each year. A SEP is much easier to set up and administer than a qualified plan. The documentation is simple, and no annual reports have to be filed. Also, distributions to participants require much less paperwork than with a qualified plan distribution. Even terminating the plan is easier. The SEP became more attractive beginning in 2002 when the maximum deductible contribution for all employees was increased from 15 percent of compensation to 25 percent of compensation.

For the small-business owner there are three other limits that are a concern. First, no more than the lesser of 100 percent of compensation or $42,000 (as indexed for 2005) can be contributed for each employee. Second, if the organization is unincorporated, the maximum deduction is limited to 20 percent of net earnings after taking the Social Security deduction (as discussed above) and not the 25 percent of compensation that applies to a corporation. Third, compensation cannot exceed the $210,000 compensation cap (as indexed for 2005). Note, however, that these same limits apply to a qualified profit-sharing plan.

Example: Sylvia operates her business as a sole proprietorship. She has no employees, and for 2005 she has $100,000 of net earnings after taking the Social Security deduction. The maximum contribution on her behalf for 2005 is $20,000 (20 percent of $100,000). Assume that her net earnings were $210,000. The maximum contribution would then be $42,000. Even if her net earnings were higher, the contribution made on Sylvia's behalf can never exceed $42,000.

The downside to the SEP can be the cost of providing benefits for other employees. Some employers will only set up a tax-advantaged plan when a large percentage of the total contribution is for the owner-employee (while others see the benefits provided as a means to attract and retain quality employees). With a SEP the cost can be significant for a number of reasons. First, contributions must be fully vested at all times. Second, the plan's allocation formula must either be allocated to participants as a level percentage of compensation or be a formula integrated with Social Security. This means that if a large contribution is made for the owner, a comparable contribution must be made for each participant. Third, the employer can eliminate short-term employees (those with less than 3 years of service), but even part-time employees who have met the service requirements must be covered under the plan. With rigid coverage rules, the SEP is generally not a good option for a larger company or an employer with several different related companies.

Choosing the Profit-Sharing Plan

SEPs and profit-sharing plans are quite similar in many ways. The ability to make discretionary contributions and the plans' maximum contribution limits are essentially the same. The profit-sharing plan is more expensive to administer and has many more reporting requirements. Therefore, small-business owners should probably think SEP first and only choose the profit-sharing plan when there is a good reason to do so.

Small-business owners may choose a profit-sharing plan instead of a SEP for a number of reasons—the primary one being the opportunity to allocate contributions on a cross-tested basis so as to limit the cost of providing benefits for the employees. As discussed previously, with the right employee census it may be possible to get a $42,000 contribution (limit as indexed for 2005) for the business owner while limiting the contribution for rank-and-file employees to 5 percent of compensation. The more flexible coverage requirements for qualified plans can also limit the number of employees covered under the plan (also limiting cost). The opportunities to use a deferred vesting schedule and to limit withdrawals from the plan are other reasons to elect a profit-sharing plan instead of a SEP.

401(k) Plan

An employer that has a profit-sharing plan may want to add a 401(k) feature to enable participants to save more for retirement. From the perspective of the owner looking to limit the cost of benefits for other employees, the owner can add a salary deferral benefit of $14,000 without having to make contributions for the other participants. This is not entirely true, since in order to make the contribution for the owner, the plan must satisfy the ADP nondiscrimination test. This will typically require that a matching contribution be made to encourage the nonhighly compensated to make salary deferral contributions. As an alternative, the employer can elect to make a safe-harbor contribution, which eliminates the need to perform the ADP test.

Some small-business owners with a smaller budget may choose not to make profit-sharing contributions but may want instead to allow salary deferrals and make additional matching contributions. In this way, the limited contributions of the employer are only made for those employees who choose to make salary deferral contributions as well.

Example:	Ryan and Susan are physical therapists who each earn $100,000 per year. They run a practice with six other young employees who are not that concerned about pension benefits. Ryan and Susan establish a 401(k) profit-sharing plan. Each makes salary deferral contributions of $14,000 (the maximum for 2005). In order to avoid problems with the ADP test, they decide to make a matching safe-harbor contribution of a 100 percent match on the first 3 percent of salary deferred and a 50 percent match on the next 2 percent of salary deferred. This means that they contribute an additional 4 percent of compensation ($4,000) for each of them and only make contributions for other employees who choose to participate. As their practice and their available budget grow, they may choose to add profit-sharing contributions for all eligible employees.

Choosing the SIMPLE

The employer with a small benefit budget that wants to allow employee salary deferrals may want to establish a SIMPLE instead of the 401(k) plan.

Establishing and maintaining a SIMPLE is considerably less complicated than a 401(k) plan. This fact not only lowers the cost of maintaining the plan, it also lessens the time spent by the small company's owner and reduces legal problems related to noncompliance. The other advantage is on the distribution side: participants have immediate access to their retirement accounts. This means that these funds can be rolled into other, more appropriate tax-sheltered investments or accessed in an emergency.

The SIMPLE is also preferable if the employer expects to have difficulty satisfying the ADP nondiscrimination test. For example, a retail chain of stores would like a salary deferral plan, but only the highly compensated managers are interested in participating in the plan. In this case, the plan sponsor can choose the matching contribution option in which contributions are made only for those employees interested in making salary deferral contributions.

Of course, the 401(k) plan is much more versatile. The 401(k) plan is better for maximizing contributions and directing employer contributions to a targeted group of employees—which are typically two common goals of small plan sponsors. In addition, a 401(k) plan is much more flexible than a SIMPLE. The 401(k) plan can be limited to part of the workforce as long as the minimum-coverage requirements are met, and matching and profit-sharing contributions can be designed to meet a variety of goals. Finally, employer contributions can increase or decrease over time.

The result is that the SIMPLE is a great plan for that vast number of small employers who haven't previously sponsored a retirement plan. The barriers to entry are much lower, the administrative expense and burden is minimal, and the employer contribution amount by law is modest. Also, due to recent law changes, the maximum amount that can be contributed for an employee is increasing over the next several years.

Example: Ryan and Susan in the example above may decide to establish a SIMPLE. Remember they earn $100,000 each and their other six young employees are not that concerned about pension benefits. Assuming that Ryan and Susan don't have that much to put away, they can establish a SIMPLE and each can make salary deferral contributions of up to $10,000 (in 2005). They can also make the 3 percent matching contribution for themselves and anyone else who chooses to participate. If they later want the flexibility of the 401(k) plan, they can simply stop making contributions to the SIMPLE and set up a 401(k) plan.

Reduced Need for a Money-Purchase Pension Plan

In the past, many small-business owners would choose to establish a profit-sharing plan, and if the employer wanted to contribute more than 15 percent of compensation, then add on a money-purchase pension plan. With a money-purchase and profit-sharing combination, the maximum deductible contribution was (and still is) 25 percent of covered compensation. Beginning in 2002, the maximum deductible contribution to a profit-sharing plan became 25 percent of compensation.

This leaves little reason to establish a money-purchase plan for the small business, and many small businesses may choose to eliminate current money-purchase plans to save administrative costs.

Defined-Benefit Plans

Small businesses do not typically choose defined-benefit plans because of the administrative expense and complexity. However, there is definitely a niche for the defined-benefit plan in the small plan market. When a business owner wants to contribute more than the maximum $42,000 defined-contribution limit to a plan (as indexed for 2005), the only option is the defined-benefit plan. How much can be contributed is based on the participant's age, the benefit formula, and the actuarial assumptions used. The small-business owner who is in his or her 40s or 50s, who has not accumulated enough pension assets, who currently has the ability to make large contributions, and who is looking for a significant tax deduction may be a candidate for a defined-benefit plan. If you know someone in this situation, the best strategy will be to involve a consulting actuary to provide a study on the costs and benefits of establishing a defined-benefit plan as compared with other approaches.

QUALIFIED PLANS: WHERE TO FIND OUT MORE

Employers provide many sources of information that are essential tools for the retirement planner. Let's take a closer look.

The Summary Plan Description

summary plan description (SPD)

A *summary plan description (SPD)* is an easy-to-read booklet that explains your client's pension and other employer benefit plans. An SPD bridges the gap between the legalese of the pension plan and the understanding of the average participant by effectively communicating how a plan works, what benefits are available, and how to get these benefits.

A well-drafted SPD will be fair and even-handed—that is, it won't be a sales or promotional tool. However, some SPDs spend more time "selling" the employer's benefit package than explaining the employees' rights. This type of SPD is specifically prohibited by regulations mandating that an SPD cannot downplay the negative consequences of involvement—for example, it cannot gloss over plan terms that may cause a participant to lose benefits or fail to qualify for them. Any limitations, exceptions, reductions, or other restrictions on plan benefits must also be duly noted. The SPD, however, is not prescreened to assure compliance.

If there is a conflict between the plan and the SPD, disclaimers in the SPD will typically indicate that the plan provisions will be controlling. Despite these disclaimers, however, courts could rule that the SPD's provisions are binding on the employer, given certain facts and circumstances. If an important conflict arises, the advice of an attorney should be sought.

Here is a list of the most important information you can learn about your client's retirement plan from his or her SPD:

- the plan administrator's name and address
- the plan's benefit or contribution formula
- an explanation of the plan's eligibility requirements for participation and benefits
- an explanation of any joint and survivor benefits
- an explanation of any terms that could result in a participant's losing benefits
- a description and explanation of plan provisions for determining years of service for eligibility, vesting, breaks in service, and benefit accrual
- the investment options available under the plan
- procedures for presenting claims for benefits under the plan and remedies for benefits denied under the plan
- a statement of ERISA rights (this statement is standard text promulgated by the Department of Labor)
- whether the plan is protected by PBGC insurance

Other Information Resources

In addition to the SPD, the employer will supply the following resources:

- *annual benefit statements*—Under most circumstances, employers provide these statements annually as a matter of course. However, if this is not the case, upon written request each plan participant or beneficiary is entitled to receive a statement of the individual's own accrued benefit or account balance under the qualified plan. This statement need not be furnished more than once in any 12-month period but must be furnished upon a participant's termination of employment.
- *1099R Forms*—These forms are filed with the IRS and sent to any participant or participant's beneficiary who receives a distribution.

- *plan document*—Plan participants have a right to request a copy of the plan document. This can be helpful if the SPD is at all unclear. The administrator can charge a copying fee for the plan document.

The following checklist should to help you in your fact-finding process:

Employer-Provided Documents Used for Retirement Planning
Name of Plan Administrator _____   Phone Number _____
1. Summary Plan Description   2. Annual Benefit Statements   3. 1099R Form   4. Withholding Form

Sources of Retirement Income: Nonqualified Plans and IRAs

David A. Littell

Chapter Outline

NONQUALIFIED PLANS—OVERVIEW

Nonqualified deferred-compensation plans are not subject to the same design restrictions as qualified plans and other tax-advantaged retirement plans. However, as a trade-off for design flexibility, the employer is not eligible for the special tax rules that apply to such tax-advantaged plans. In a nonqualified plan, the employer is only entitled to a deduction when the employee receives taxable income. Plans are generally designed to defer taxation until the employee receives a benefit. However, this means that the employer does not receive a deduction until the time the benefits are paid.

Nonqualified plans are found most often among executives in large and medium-sized corporations, but many small closely held businesses also use them. Nonqualified plans are often used for the following reasons:

- to bring executive retirement benefits up to desired levels by adding a second tier of benefits to the qualified plan
- to circumvent the nondiscrimination requirements for a qualified plan
- to provide a stand-alone benefit that allows highly compensated employees to defer current income as a means of supplementing retirement income
- to shift income to later years
- to encourage long service

There are two basic types of nonqualified plans: the salary reduction plan and the supplemental executive retirement plan.

Salary Reduction Plans

salary reduction plan

Under a nonqualified *salary reduction plan,* your client has the option to forgo receipt of currently earned salary, bonuses, or commissions for retirement purposes. You may run into situations where a salary reduction plan is offered as part of a package of perks to selected managers or highly compensated employees, or you may want to consider having your client negotiate with his or her employer during contract negotiations to institute such a plan. This type of plan is most beneficial when the employee's income is currently taxed at the highest marginal rates and he or she anticipates being in a lower tax bracket after retirement, but it is often employed as a means of income leveling for highly compensated employees whose income would otherwise drop sharply after retirement.

When establishing a salary reduction plan or, for that matter, a SERP (discussed below), the employer will want to be sure that the plan is exempt from the requirements of ERISA. To do this, the employer must limit participation to a select group of management and/or highly compensated employees. This exception is referred to as the top-hat exception, and a plan that satisfies these conditions is often referred to as a *top-hat plan*. Unfortunately, the ERISA rules do not define the terms "highly compensated" or "management" employees, and determining appropriate coverage under these plans involves some level of uncertainty. It is clear, however, that the Tax Code's definition of highly compensated (5 percent owners and those earning more than $95,000) is not determinative here.

Supplemental Executive Retirement Plans (SERPs)

supplemental executive retirement plan (SERP)

Perhaps the most popular type of nonqualified plan is the *supplemental executive retirement plan (SERP)*. A supplemental executive retirement plan satisfies the employer objective of complementing an existing qualified plan that is not already stretched to the maximum limits by bringing executive retirement benefits up to desired levels.

SERPs are generally dovetailed into an underlying qualified defined-contribution or defined-benefit plan. Like the salary reduction plan, the SERP must be maintained only for a select group of management or highly compensated employees in order to satisfy the top-hat exception to ERISA. A SERP can use either a defined-benefit or defined-contribution approach.

Deferring Income Tax

With nonqualified plans, the employer receives a deduction at the time that the participant has taxable income. In almost all cases, the plan is designed to defer income tax to the participants until distributions are made. Tax can generally be deferred as long as the deferred compensation is subject to a substantial risk of forfeiture.

A substantial risk of forfeiture is a significant limitation or duty that requires the fulfillment of a meaningful effort by the executive, and there must be a definite possibility that the event that will cause the forfeiture could occur. A traditional vesting provision is clearly a substantial risk of forfeiture. Requiring that an executive continue to provide consulting services to a company after retirement may or may not be a substantial risk of forfeiture, depending upon the specific facts and circumstances.

Economic Benefit Doctrine

If the benefit is not subject to a risk of forfeiture, taxes can still be deferred as long as the distribution doesn't run afoul of the economic benefit doctrine or the constructive receipt doctrine now codified in Code Sec. 409A. Under the economic-benefit doctrine an *economic* (or financial) *benefit* conferred on an executive as compensation should be included in the person's income to the extent that the benefit has an ascertainable fair market value. In other words, if a compensation arrangement provides a current economic benefit to an executive, that person must report the value of the benefit even if he or she has no current right to receive the benefit.

The economic benefit doctrine means that if a contribution is made to an irrevocable trust for a participant and the benefit is nonforfeitable, the amount will be subject to income tax. This is one reason that nonqualified plan benefits are not as secure as under a qualified plan. To avoid current income tax, any assets held to pay benefits must remain the property of the sponsor, or be placed in a trust that can be accessed by claims of the sponsor's creditors (typically called a rabbi trust).

Code Section 409A

Another concern is the constructive receipt doctrine. Code Sec. 409A has codified the constructive receipt rules. Technically, the Code provision states that deferral amounts that are not subject to a substantial risk of forfeiture are currently includible in gross income and are subject to an additional 20 percent penalty tax unless they meet certain distribution, acceleration of distribution, and deferral election rules. These requirements must be contained in the plan document governing the nonqualified plan.

Distribution Rules. Under the plan, distributions may not be made earlier than one of the following events:

- Separation from service. If the employee is a "key employee" of a publicly traded company, as defined under the top-heavy rules of Section 416(i), a distribution upon separation from service may not begin until 6 months after separation.
- Disability. Disability is defined as either the strict Social Security definition of total and permanent disability, or disability under an

accident and health plan covering employees of the employer, under certain conditions.

- Death of the employee.
- A time specified under the plan.
- A change in ownership or control, to be further defined in forthcoming regulations.
- Occurrence of an unforeseeable emergency.

Occurrence of an unforeseeable emergency includes a severe financial hardship to the participant resulting from an illness or accident, and loss of the participant's property due to casualty or other similar extraordinary and unforeseeable circumstances beyond the participant's control. The amount cannot exceed the amount necessary for the emergency plus taxes on the distribution, and distributions are not allowed to the extent that the hardship may be relieved through reimbursement or by liquidation of the participant's assets.

Acceleration of Distributions. A nonqualified deferred-compensation plan may not permit the acceleration of the time payments under the plan, except as allowed by regulatory guidance. The IRS has created a number of exceptions including:

- Payments made to meet the requirements of a domestic relations order.
- Payments that are necessary to satisfy the conflict of interest divestiture requirements.
- A *de minimus* cashout rule allowing the cashing out of the remaining interest in a plan as long the amount does not exceed $10,000. The cashout must be made before the later of 2½ months after termination of employment or December 31 of the year of termination of employment.
- Payments for FICA taxes.

Employees' Elections to Defer. An election to defer compensation for a particular year must be made not later than the close of the preceding taxable year (or other time to be provided in forthcoming regulations). For the first year of eligibility, the election may be made with respect to services to be performed beginning within 30 days after eligibility for participation. For performance-based compensation based on services performed over a period of at least 12 months, the election may be made no later than 6 months before the end of the period.

According to the Conference Report, these election rules require that the time and form of distributions must be specified at the time of initial deferral. The plan can either specify the form and timing or give participants a choice. A limited exception allows a participant to further delay payment of an existing benefit as long as the election is made at least 12 months before it is effective.

Benefit Security and Retirement Planning Concerns

In a salary deferral plan (in which the executive chooses to make salary deferral elections), the executive needs to carefully evaluate whether participation is an appropriate choice. Reasons that weigh in favor of participation include:

- The salary deferral plan provides for a method of systematic savings. Limitations on the ability to withdraw funds means the money is likely to be available at retirement.
- The plan may, like a 401(k) plan, have an employer matching contribution.
- The plan may have investment alternatives or a promised rate of return that is attractive to participants.
- Generally the participant will accumulate more with tax deferral than with saving on an after-tax basis. That equation depends upon the current and future tax rates and the rate of return earned inside the plan versus outside the plan.

On the other hand, nonqualified plans do have drawbacks that are not encountered in qualified plans. These need to be carefully considered as well before choosing the nonqualified salary deferral election.

- Nonqualified salary deferral benefits have some element of risk. Because plan assets have to be available to the claims of creditors, there is the risk that benefits would not be fully paid if the company encounters financial difficulty.
- There is also the concern that if control of the company changes that the new management may be hostile to the compensation agreement. A rabbi trust can guard against this risk, but many plans are not funded with rabbi trusts.
- Under the Sec. 409A rules, the time and form of distribution must be determined at the time of the salary deferral election—years before the participant is aware of his or her retirement needs.
- The advantage of deferring taxes is diminished if the tax rate increases at the time of withdrawal. The participant has to anticipate tax rates to make this determination.

These pros and cons should be weighed carefully by each individual. A salary deferral plan can look the same as a 401(k) plan to the participant, but as we just discussed, there are important differences.

Even when the plan is a SERP paid for by the employer, participants should be aware of these concerns. Unlike qualified plans, many of the provisions are negotiated between the employer and the executive and the executive can negotiate to mitigate some of these concerns. For example, the executive can request funding with a rabbi trust or lobby for more flexibility in the payout provisions by requesting payouts upon change in control or in the case of a financial hardship.

EXECUTIVE BONUS LIFE INSURANCE PLANS

Sec. 162 plan

An alternative that can be used in combination with, or in lieu of, the previously discussed deferred-compensation plans is the executive bonus life insurance plan (commonly known as a *Sec. 162 plan*). Like a deferred-compensation plan, a Sec. 162 plan can be provided on a discriminatory basis to help business owners and selected executives save for retirement. The Sec. 162 plan, however, does not provide for the deferral of income. Under a Sec. 162 plan, the corporation pays a bonus to the executive for the purpose of purchasing cash-value life insurance. The executive is the policyowner, the insured, and the person who makes the beneficiary designation. The corporation's only connection (albeit a major one) is to fund premium payments and, in a few cases, to secure the application for insurance. Bonused amounts can be paid out by the corporation in one of two ways: The corporation can pay the premiums for the policy directly to the insurer, or the bonus can be paid to the employee, who then pays the policy premiums. In either case, the corporation deducts the contribution from corporate taxes and includes the amount of the payment in the executive's W-2 (taxable) income.

Concern over the receipt of additional taxable income from executive bonus life insurance plans has caused many employers to provide a second bonus to alleviate any tax that the business owner or executive may pay.

EXECUTIVE INCENTIVE OR BONUS PLANS

In addition to the various qualified and nonqualified plans already described, many of your clients—especially highly paid executives—may participate in executive incentive or bonus plans. These plans reward the executive based on the performance of the company stock or, in some cases, on the basis of certain financial objectives, such as cumulative growth and earnings per share or improvement in return on investment. There is typically no tax to the executive at the time the rights to future stock appreciation or future benefits are granted; in most cases, the executive has considerable flexibility as to when benefits will be realized and subject to tax. Consequently, for executives who hold these rights as they approach retirement, one of the more important planning issues is the timing of the exercise of these rights. In particular, planners should recognize that the tax rate in the year before, the year of, and the year after retirement can vary dramatically. Let's look at the characteristics of some of the more commonly used forms of executive incentive plans.

Nonqualified Stock Options (NQSOs)

nonqualified stock option (NQSO)

Nonqualified stock options (NQSOs) are options to purchase shares of company stock at a stated price over a given period of time (frequently 10 years). The option price normally equals 100 percent of the stock's fair market value on the date the option is granted, but it may be set below this level. Typically the executive may exercise the options by paying a cash amount that is equal to the exercise price or by tendering previously owned shares of stock. Clearly these options will be valuable to the executive only if the stock price has risen since the date the option was issued, but there is a possibility of large gains if the price is increased substantially.

At the time the option is exercised, the excess of the fair market value of the stock over the option price is taxed as ordinary income and is subject to income tax withholding. The company receives a tax deduction in the amount of the executive's income from the exercise of the option in the year the executive is taxed as long as the withholding requirements are met.

Example: The employer grants Ellie Executive the right purchase 500 shares of common stock at the market price at the time of issuance ($20) at any time over the next 10 years. After 3 years, the market price has risen to $60 per share. Ellie purchases all 500 shares at $20 per share ($10,000). She now has $20,000 ($40 x 500) of ordinary income, which is the difference between the purchase price ($10,000) and the current market value ($30,000). The employer receives a deduction for $20,000.

The exercise period is subject to limitations for executives who are considered "insiders" under SEC rules. Essentially, an insider is any executive who would have access to information that is not available to the general public. Insiders are subject to an insider-trading rule that limits the executive's sale of stocks to within 6 months of the time when the option was issued. Therefore the 6-month period begins when the option is issued and ends when the stock is sold.

To understand the value of the option program, the participant and his or her advisor need to fully understand the terms and features of the program. One important feature is *vesting*. Many options are not exercisable for a period of time after the options are granted. Sometimes all options granted at a specific time become vested at once (referred to as *cliff vesting*) after a specified number of years. For example, the company grants 500 options that become exercisable 3 years from the date of the grant as long as the participant is still employed on that date. Another option is to vest a portion of the options each year (referred to as *graded vesting*). For example, one third are vested after one year, two thirds after 2 years, and full vesting after 3 years. It is also possible to have accelerated vesting upon the occurrence of a change in control of the company or the participant's death or disability. Also, be aware that the vesting provisions (even with the same company) can be different for options granted at different times.

Several newer vesting approaches are being used today. In some cases vesting is subject to the company (or executive) satisfying certain performance goals. Another approach offered in some pre-IPO (prior to the initial public offering) companies is referred to as *early exercise*. Under this arrangement, the participant is allowed to immediately exercise options when they are granted, but the stock remains restricted (forfeitable if the participant doesn't complete a specified period of service). Because the participant could forfeit the stock, there is generally no income tax treatment until the vesting restrictions lapse. As an alternative, the participant can use a Sec. 83(b) election and pay tax at the time of exercise. Once exercised, the program is really a restricted stock plan (discussed below).

The duration of the exercise period is most often 10 years, but early termination can shorten the duration. It is common for a terminating employee to have the options lapse between 60 and 180 days after termination of employment, and even possible for the options to lapse at termination of employment if the participant is terminated for cause or violates a *do not compete* clause.

In order to exercise the options, the executive needs cash to pay the option price for the stock. Although this will often require borrowing, once the options are exercised, the executive may sell a sufficient number of the shares to repay the loan. Many (but not all) stock option programs today offer cashless transactions where a designated broker will exercise the options and sell some or all of the stock to cover the cost of the options at the same time.

If the executive prefers to hold the shares for their potential future appreciation, devising a method to raise the cash necessary to purchase shares becomes an important part of retirement planning. In addition, if employer stock constitutes a disproportionate share of a retiring executive's investment portfolio, planning for the systematic repositioning of the portfolio is another consideration for the practitioner.

Incentive Stock Options (ISOs)

incentive stock option (ISO)

An *incentive stock option (ISO)* is an option to purchase shares of the company stock at 100 percent or more of the stock's fair market value on the date that the option is granted for a period of up to 10 years. ISOs are taxed more favorably to the participant than nonqualified stock options but are less flexible. There are certain limits on the value of options that can become exercisable annually, and there are certain holding period requirements before sale. In addition, any option granted to a shareholder of 10 percent or more of a company's voting stock must be priced at 110 percent or more of the stock's fair market value, with an option term of no more than 5 years. As in the case of nonqualified stock options, the options may be exercised by paying cash or by tendering previously owned shares of stock.

When the executive exercises the ISO, there is no regular income tax owed. However, the excess of the stock's fair market value at the time of exercise over the option exercise price—that is, the "spread"—is a tax preference item that may trigger an alternative minimum tax obligation. If the shares are held for at least 2 years from the date the option was granted and at least one year from exercise, the tax on sale is payable at a long-term capital-gains rate on the increase in the stock's value from the date of the grant of the option to the date of sale of the stock. If the holding period requirements are not met, the gain to the extent realized from the time the option is granted to the time of exercise of the option is taxed as ordinary income; the remainder is taxed as capital gain.

Because capital gains rates can be significantly lower than ordinary income tax rates, satisfying the holding requirements will be quite important. In addition to the lower rate, capital gains on the sale of stocks acquired through incentive stock options can be used to offset capital losses from the sale of other securities. Still, the participant will need to consider the alternative minimum tax implications of holding stock after exercise.

As with NQSOs, ISOs provide the executive with the possibility of large gains. Within limits, the executive can choose the timing of exercise of the options to maximize gains; however, options granted prior to December 31, 1986, must be exercised in the order in which they were granted. Also, as with NQSOs, the participant needs to have a full appreciation of the terms of the program, including the vesting and duration provisions, before any liquidation strategy can be conceived.

Choosing to Exercise NQSOs and ISOs

Choosing the optimal timing strategy for stock options is a difficult matter and there are no rules of thumb that apply to every situation. Because there is a risk to every alternative, in some ways choosing the right option is more of an art than a science. Given this, there can still be a structure to the decision making process that will help lead to an appropriate decision. Here are a number of considerations.

Set Goals

Starting with financial goals can go a long way in helping to decide how to address stock options as part of an individual's portfolio. Knowing what the proceeds will be used for, such as buying a home in 2 years or retiring in 10 years, will bring the right decision into focus.

Know the Program

Good decisions cannot be made without a complete understanding of the option program. Here's a fairly comprehensive list of questions to help clarify both the value of the options involved and choices that the participant has. Remember that the most serious problems often result from simple oversights—for example, letting valuable options lapse because of a misunderstanding or failing to monitor the options.

- Are the options nonqualified or ISOs subject to special tax treatment?
- How many years of service are required before options are vested, and does vesting occur at once (cliff vesting) or over time (graded vesting)?
- Will the options become vested earlier if the participant dies, becomes disabled, or if there is a change in ownership?
- Are the options exercisable before they become vested?
- What is the duration of the option period once they become exercisable?
- How long are options exercisable after termination of employment due to (a) death, (b) disability, (c) retirement, (d) voluntary termination, or (e) involuntary termination of employment?
- Do vested options lapse if the participant goes to work for a competitor?
- Does the company intend to grant additional options in the future?

Know the Tax Implications of the Program

Of course this question cannot be answered without knowing whether the options are nonqualified or ISOs. Some executives will have both types of options granted to them. Once the type is determined, the client needs to have a full appreciation of the tax timing issues. A participant will not really know the value of the options until he or she knows the value after the exercise price and all taxes have been paid. With ISOs, the alternative minimum tax is a real issue for those participants who choose to hold the stock to take advantage of the lower capital gains rate.

Devise a Long-Term Plan

Developing a long-term plan can be facilitated by asking questions such as:

- How many additional options are likely to be granted?
- How much wealth should be tied into the employer's stock?
- How long will employment with the company continue?

Because many executives acquire sizable blocks of stock in their company through various incentive plans, one important planning consideration is often the systematic liquidation of this stock and the purchase of other securities to better diversify the executive's investment portfolio at his or her retirement. The plan should also include a strategy for which stock to liquidate first.

The financial advisor can be a very important part of the process because the professional is typically better suited than the participant to help model asset allocation, long-term projections, and tax analysis.

Have an Action Plan

The plan should also have an action strategy. For example, who will notify heirs if the participant dies and still has stock options? What steps are in place to ensure that valuable options don't lapse? How often will the plan be reevaluated and adjusted for changing conditions?

Liquidation Considerations and Strategies

When devising a long-term plan, in addition to taking the above steps, the participant will need to consider a number of options.

- Because stock prices historically rise over time, the strategy of holding the options until the end of the exercise period is a good place to start when formulating a strategy.
- Countervailing considerations such as diversifying the portfolio, exercising the options to meet a specific financial goal, or a realistic assessment that the stock price is unlikely to continue to increase can be good reasons to sell sooner.
- An argument can be made for the position that participant options should be seen as a bonus for increasing stock prices, and liquidating the position (selling the stock) at the time the options are exercised ensures a positive cash position—and does not tie up the participant's assets.
- An argument can also be made that if further stock appreciation is relatively certain, a participant in a high tax bracket (who can afford to take some risk) should exercise early and hold the stock to change the tax treatment from ordinary income (up to 39.9 percent tax rate) to long-term capital gains (20 percent tax rate). This position poses significant risks, however. First, there is an economic cost in having to come up with the cash to purchase the stock earlier. Also, the increase may not materialize, or there even could be a loss.

- When choosing which options to sell, first consider selling the oldest options even if they aren't the lowest priced.
- Get to know and pay attention to the price behavior of the company's stock.
- When considering a decision to exercise, look at recent high and low trading prices and the length of the remaining exercise period.
- Consider exercising the options and selling the stock (cashless transactions) over a period of time instead of all at once. For example, exercise options monthly or quarterly over a 2-year period. This allows the price to be averaged and reduces the risk of receiving a low price for all the options. This strategy also allows the participant to invest the proceeds into new investments over time, also reducing risk.

YOUR FINANCIAL SERVICES PRACTICE:
LEARNING MORE ABOUT STOCK OPTIONS

Here are some useful Web sites for further exploring stock options.

- The National Association of Stock Plan Professionals (www.naspp.com) has information of interest to financial services professionals.
- Several informative sites for professionals and plan participants alike include www.mystockoptions.com and www.optionwealth.com.

Phantom Stock

phantom stock

Phantom stock is the name given to what is essentially just a bookkeeping entry on behalf of the executive as if the executive had been given stock in the company. Units analogous to company shares are granted to executives, and the value of the units generally equals the appreciation and market value of the stock underlying the units. Phantom units are valued at a fixed date, typically at retirement or 5 to 15 years after the grant of the phantom stock. When the phantom stock "matures" (that is, at its valuation date), the company may pay the executive in cash, stock, or some combination of both. In many cases, dividend equivalents may be credited to the units just as dividends would be paid to the underlying stock.

Example: Employer grants Executive A 100 shares of phantom stock valued at $5,000 ($50 per share). The phantom stock matures, and 5 years later its value has increased to $7,500 ($75 per share). At that time, the employer pays the employee $2,500, the difference between the value at the time of the grant and the value at the time of maturity.

On the payment date, the value of the units is taxed to the executive as ordinary income and is subject to withholding. The company takes a tax deduction in the amount of the executive's taxable income from the units.

As with other incentive plans, the executive has the possibility of large gains. Although one advantage of phantom stock over stock options is that the executive avoids the financing cost associated with exercise of the options, in some cases gains may be capped by company-imposed maximums designed to limit the company's potential payment, and, since payment is typically triggered by retirement, the executive generally has no flexibility in choosing when to value the award. In cases where the executive can control the form or timing of the unit's valuation or settlement, trading restrictions similar to those applying to stock options will apply to insiders.

Restricted Stock

restricted stock plan

In a *restricted stock plan,* the participant is given (usually at no cost) shares of company stock. The shares are actually stamped with specific restrictions, which require that the participant give the shares back to the company upon a specified event. Most commonly, the restriction is that if the employee stops working prior to some specified date, he or she will have to forfeit the shares. Another common restriction is a clause that would require forfeiture if the individual terminated employment and went to work with the competitor (commonly called a noncompete clause). Dividends on the stock are usually paid to the participant during the entire period in which he or she holds the stock.

Example: Company grants to Billy Bigshot 200 shares of stock worth $10,000. The stock will be forfeited unless Billy works until age 65, at which time the stock becomes freely transferable by Billy. At age 65, Billy retires and decides to hold the stock, which is now valued at $8,000.

For the employer, restricted stock plans are another way to tie the employee to the company (through the vesting provision), and to tie the benefit to the performance of the company stock. From the employee's perspective, this type of deferred compensation is relatively secure because the stock is titled in the executive's name, meaning that creditors cannot get to this asset if the company performs badly. Another advantage is that the employee does not have to pay anything in order to get stock ownership, unlike stock option plans. The biggest limitation, from the employee's perspective, is the possibility of forfeiture.

From a tax perspective, the shares of stock are generally not taxed until the substantial limitations on the stock lapse. At that time, the value of the stock will be treated as ordinary income to the participant and will be deductible as compensation expense to the employer. Any dividends paid to the participant will also be treated as compensation income—both includible as income to the participant and deductible as compensation by the employer.

Participants under a restricted stock plan can make an election, within 30 days of the time of the stock grant, to be taxed sooner—at the time of the grant. Making this election is a big gamble because the stock could be forfeited later, and the taxpayer would not be able to recoup the taxes paid. However, an individual who (1) does not expect to lose the stock, (2) has the money to pay taxes at the time of the grant, and (3) expects the stock to greatly appreciate in value may want to consider the election. When the participant later sells the stock, he or she will be concerned about whether the sale will be eligible for the long-term capital-gains rate. Under the rules, the one-year holding period begins at the time taxes are paid; paying taxes earlier starts the clock ticking and gives the participant a better chance of being eligible for long-term capital gains when the restrictions lapse.

INTRODUCTION TO IRAs AND ROTH IRAs

Individual retirement plans are a vital part of the financial planning business. They are important both to the financial security of clients and to the business efforts of financial services professionals. Even though the best opportunities are for lower- and middle-class workers (these plans have been called "the little guy's tax shelter"), wealthy individuals often have plans with large sums that have been rolled over from employer-sponsored tax-advantaged retirement plans.

Over the years, Congress has changed the IRA rules numerous times. The changes in the last few years have all been favorable. The Taxpayer Relief Act of 1997 added the Roth IRA and made the deductible IRA available to more taxpayers. The Economic Growth and Tax Relief Reconciliation Act of 2001 (EGTRRA) increased the maximum allowable contribution limits and added a catch-up contribution for older participants. As a result, proper use of traditional IRAs, Roth IRAs, and rollover IRAs can go a long way toward providing retirement security. Financial service professionals can help their clients achieve their goals by explaining the IRA rules, encouraging saving for retirement, and marketing IRA investments.

IRA
Roth IRA

The introduction of the Roth IRA means that there are now two types of savings vehicles that are called *IRAs*. The traditional plan is still referred to as an *IRA*, while the newer plan is referred to as a *Roth IRA*. In many ways, traditional IRAs are similar to employer-sponsored tax-sheltered retirement plans. Both are tax-favored savings plans that encourage the accumulation of savings for retirement because they allow contributions to be made with pretax dollars (if the taxpayer is eligible) and earnings to be tax deferred until retirement. With Roth IRAs, contributions are made on an after-tax basis, but earnings are not taxed and qualifying distributions are tax-free.

The funding vehicles and types of allowable investments are the same for both traditional IRAs and Roth IRAs. Both types of IRAs can use a trust or custodial account (individual retirement account) or an annuity contract (individual retirement annuity) as funding instruments. With either type of funding vehicle, a wide array of traditional investment strategies can be used.

Contribution Limits

The maximum allowable contribution to an IRA or Roth IRA is the lesser of $4,000 (the limit for years 2005 through 2007) or 100 percent of compensation. The $4,000 limit applies to all traditional IRAs and Roth IRAs to which a taxpayer contributes for the year. For example, if the taxpayer makes a $4,000 contribution to a traditional IRA, no contributions can be made to a Roth IRA for the year. The maximum allowable contribution limit is scheduled to increase to $5,000 in 2008. (See table 4-1 below.)

It is important to remember that a contribution cannot exceed a person's compensation. *Compensation* is earnings from wages, salaries, tips, professional fees, bonuses, and any other amount a taxpayer receives for providing personal services. In addition, alimony and separate-maintenance payments are also considered compensation for IRA purposes. Compensation does not include earnings and profits from property, such as rental and dividend income, or amounts received as a pension or annuity. As a general rule, if it is income the taxpayer worked for in a given year, the contribution can be made; if it is derived from investments or retirement income, it is not eligible.

For self-employeds, compensation includes earned income from personal services, reduced by any contributions to a qualified plan on behalf of the individual. Self-employeds with a net loss from self-employment cannot make IRA contributions unless they also have salary or wage income. In this case, they don't have to reduce the amount of salary income by the net loss from self-employment. If there are both salary or wage income and net income from self-employment, the two amounts are combined to determine the amount that can be contributed.

Example:	In his first year in business, Don, a self-employed creator of computer software, has a net loss of $17,000, largely because of start-up costs. However, he received $4,000 from part-time teaching. Don may contribute up to $4,000 to an IRA because his salary will not be reduced by his self-employment loss.

Spousal IRAs

If a married person does not work or has limited compensation, his or her spouse can contribute up to $4,000 (the limit for years 2005 through 2007) to a spousal IRA—which can be either a traditional IRA or a Roth IRA—as long as the following conditions are satisfied:

- The taxpayer is married at the end of the year and files a joint tax return.
- The spouse earns less than the taxpayer.
- The couple has compensation that equals or exceeds contributions to the IRAs of both persons ($8,000 if $4,000 is contributed for each).

spousal IRA

Spousal IRAs can be set up even if the taxpayer does not contribute to his or her own account, or contributions can be made for both spouses, or the taxpayer can make contributions just to the taxpayer's IRA even though a spousal IRA already exists. However, no more than $4,000 can be placed in either IRA for any year.

Catch-up Election

An individual who has attained age 50 before the end of the taxable year can contribute an additional $500 (the limit for 2005). For example, in 2005 a 55-year-old individual could contribute up to $4,500 to an IRA or Roth IRA (assuming that he or she is otherwise eligible under the phaseout limits discussed below). The catch-up amount is also scheduled to increase to $1,000 in 2006. (See table 4-1.)

Example:	In 2005, John and Sarah are married, file jointly, and have an AGI of $120,000. They are each eligible to make Roth IRA contributions. Because they are both over 50 years old, the maximum contribution for each is $4,500 or $9,000 in total.

Timing of Contributions

Contributions to an IRA or Roth IRA must be made in cash (except for rollovers). Contributions can be made at any time during the tax year for which the contribution relates or up to April 15 of the following year. Contributions for the year can be made at once or over time.

If an amount is contributed between January 1 and April 15, the sponsor should be notified for which year the contributions are being made. If the sponsor is not notified the sponsor can assume, and report to the IRS, that the contribution is for the current year (the year the sponsor received it).

TABLE 4-1
Increasing IRA Contribution Limits 2005–2008

Year	General Limit	Catch-up for Those over Age 50	Total for Those over Age 50
2005	$4,000	$500	$4,500
2006	$4,000	$1,000	$5,000
2007	$4,000	$1,000	$5,000
2008	$5,000	$1,000	$6,000

The taxpayer can file his or her tax return claiming a traditional IRA contribution before the contribution is actually made. However, the contribution must be made by the due date of the return, not including extensions.

Excess Contributions

An *excess contribution* is any amount contributed to an IRA or Roth IRA that exceeds the maximum contribution limit. Excess contributions will result in an excise tax of 6 percent on the excess. If the excess amount (plus interest) is withdrawn by the tax deadline in the year (including extensions) the excess contribution is made, the taxpayer does not have to pay the penalty. If the excess remains in the plan, the 6 percent excise tax will apply to each and every year that the excess remains. The excess can typically be used up in the following year, since it can be treated as part of the contribution for the following year.

With traditional IRAs, excess contributions are relatively rare because most taxpayers can contribute the maximum amount—even though only a portion of the contribution may be deductible. However, excess contributions may be more common in the Roth IRA because the maximum allowable contribution is reduced when the taxpayer's adjusted gross income (AGI) exceeds a specified amount.

TRADITIONAL IRAs

All individuals who have not yet attained age 70 1/2 (at any time during the calendar year) and who satisfy the compensation requirement described above can make IRA contributions. These contributions may or may not be eligible for a deduction. Earnings on both deductible and nondeductible contributions are not subject to tax as long as the assets are held in the IRA (and the contribution limits are not exceeded). The earnings are taxed as ordinary income only when they are distributed to the participant. A nondeductible contribution will not be subject to tax when it is withdrawn (see chapter 10 for a discussion of recovering the cost basis of nondeductible contributions to an IRA).

Example:	Jerry, a single taxpayer, contributes $4,000 to an IRA this year. Jerry determines that he is not entitled to a deduction for the contributions. Over the next several years, the account grows to $10,000 and Jerry takes a distribution of the whole amount. No tax is due until the benefit is distributed. Assuming that Jerry has no other IRA accounts, he will only have to pay taxes on the $6,000 of growth at the time of distribution. If the IRA contributions are deductible, Jerry pays tax on the entire distribution.

Eligibility for a Deductible Contribution

active participant

An IRA contribution will be deductible if neither the taxpayer nor the taxpayer's spouse is an *active participant* in an employer-maintained retirement plan.

Example:	Jerry, a single taxpayer who earns $250,000 as an employee of X Corporation, is not an active participant in an employer-sponsored retirement plan for the year. Because he is not an active participant, he can make the maximum IRA contribution on a deductible basis regardless of the level of his income.

If the taxpayer is an active participant, then the contribution is deductible only if his or her adjusted gross income falls below prescribed limits (designed to approximate a middle-class income). If an individual is not an active participant, but his or her spouse is, then the contribution is deductible (for the nonparticipant) if the couple's income is less than a different higher income threshold.

Active Participant Status

Qualified plans, 403(b) tax-sheltered annuity plans, SEPs, and SIMPLEs are considered employer-sponsored retirement plans for determining active participant status. Also, federal, state, and local government plans are also taken into account. However, nonqualified retirement arrangements are not treated as employer-sponsored retirement plans.

Example: As of the end of the current year, Arjun, an executive at Small Company, participates in a nonqualified deferred-compensation program, but is not a participant in a qualified plan or other tax-sheltered retirement plan. Arjun will not be an active participant in an employer-sponsored retirement plan for the current year.

Determining active participant status requires an evaluation of the type of plan involved. An individual is an active participant in a defined-benefit plan unless excluded under the eligibility provision of the plan for the entire year. This means that all eligible participants (even those who voluntarily decline participation) are active participants regardless of whether they earn a benefit accrual for the year. The only exception is when the plan benefit formula has been frozen for all participants—meaning that no additional benefits are accruing for any participant.

An individual is an active participant in a defined-contribution plan if employer contributions, employee contributions, or forfeitures are allocated to the individual's account with respect to a plan year that ends with or within the individual's tax year. SEPs, 403(b) plans, and SIMPLEs are treated as defined-contribution plans.

Example: Rachel becomes eligible for her company's 401(k) plan on November 1. The plan is maintained on a calendar year. Rachel makes salary deferral contributions for November and December but is not eligible for any employer matching or profit-sharing contributions for this period. Rachel is still an active participant because any type of contributions, even employee contributions, count toward determining active participant status.

A special rule applies when contributions are discretionary (for example, in most profit-sharing plans). In this case, if contributions are not made until after the end of the plan year (ending with or within the employee's tax year in question), then the employer's contribution is attributable to the following year. This exception is to address the concern that the participant needs to know whether he or she is an "active participant" by the time the IRA contribution deadline arrives.

Example: | Sally first becomes eligible for XYZ Corporation's profit-sharing plan for the plan year ending December 31, 2004. The company is on a calendar fiscal year and does not decide to make a contribution for the 2004 plan year until June 1, 2005. Sally is not considered an active participant in the plan for the 2004 plan year. However, due to the contribution made in 2005, she is an active participant for the 2005 plan year.

When the plan year of the employer's plan (regardless of whether the plan is a defined-benefit or defined-contribution plan) is not the calendar year, an individual's active participant status is dependent upon whether he or she is an active participant for the plan year ending with or within the particular calendar year in question.

Example: | Susan first becomes eligible for the ABC money-purchase pension plan for the plan year June 1, 2004 to May 30, 2005. Susan is an active participant for 2005 (but not 2004) because the plan year ended "with or within" the calendar year 2005.

Finally, note that in determining active participant status, participation for any part of the plan year counts as participation for the whole plan year, and that whether or not the participant is vested in his or her benefit has no bearing on the determination.

Income Level

If an individual is an active participant in an employer-sponsored retirement plan for the year, then the eligible deduction will be reduced or eliminated entirely if modified adjusted gross income (AGI) exceeds a specified schedule. Table 4-2 shows the deduction limits for 2005. The phaseout limits are scheduled to increase each subsequent year up to 2007. Table 4-3 shows the phaseout deduction limits for future years.

The level for unreduced contributions depends on the taxpayer's filing status. In 2005, married couples filing a joint return will get a full IRA deduction if their AGI is $70,000 or less (special rules apply to marrieds filing separately—see table 4-3). In 2005, individual taxpayers will get a full IRA deduction if their AGI is $50,000 or less. The maximum level for deductible contributions is $79,999.99 for marrieds filing jointly and $59,999.99 for individuals. If an active participant's AGI exceeds these levels, no part of an IRA contribution can be deducted.

TABLE 4-2			
2005 Limits for Deductible IRA Contributions			
Filing Status	Full IRA Deduction	Reduced IRA Deduction	No IRA Deduction
Individual	$50,000 or less	$50,000.01–$59,999.99	$60,000 or more
Married filing jointly	$70,000 or less	$70,000.01–$79,999.99	$80,000 or more

TABLE 4-3			
IRA Active Participant AGI Phaseout Ranges from Years 2005 through 2007			
	Single	Married Filing Jointly	Married Filing Jointly
2005	$50,000–$60,000	$70,000–$80,000	$0–$10,000
2006	$50,000–$60,000	$75,000–$85,000	$0–$10,000
2007	$50,000–$60,000	$80,000–$100,000	$0–$10,000

When applying the phaseout limits, calculation of the AGI is somewhat modified. AGI is determined without regard to the exclusion for foreign earned income, but Social Security benefits includible in gross income and losses or gains on passive investments are taken into account. Also, contributions to an IRA or Roth IRA are not deducted.

For taxpayers whose AGI falls between the no-deduction level and the full-deduction level, their deduction is reduced pro rata. To compute the reduction, use the following formula:

$$\text{Deductible amount} = \text{max. contribution} - \left(\text{max. contribution} \times \frac{\text{AGI - filing status floor}}{\text{phaseout range}}\right)$$

Example: Bob and Rita Dufus (a married couple under age 50 filing jointly) are both working, are both active participants, and have a combined adjusted gross income of $75,000 for 2005. Bob and Rita can each make the full IRA contribution of $4,000 (total $8,000). However, only a portion of each contribution is deductible. Because their AGI is $5,000 more than the lower limit for married couples ($70,000) they each lose one half (totally phased out over $10,000) of the deductible contribution. Each can deduct $2,000 (total $4,000). Using the formula

$$\$4,000 - \left(\$4,000 \times \frac{\$75,000 - \$70,000}{\$10,000} \right) = \$2,000$$

Therefore, of the $8,000 contributed to an IRA, $4,000 will be nondeductible. As discussed later, it is also possible that, instead of the nondeductible contribution, Bob and Rita may make the $4,000 contribution to Roth IRAs.

Married Taxpayers with Spouses Who Are Active Participants

If a married taxpayer and his or her spouse are both active participants, then the deduction rules just described apply to both IRAs. However, the rules are different when only one spouse is an active participant. In this case, the maximum allowable deductible IRA contribution ($4,000 for 2005) is allowed for the nonactive participant spouse as long as the couple's AGI does not exceed $150,000. The deduction is phased out if the couple's joint AGI exceeds $150,000 and will be gone entirely if their AGI is $160,000 or more.

These phaseout rules apply in the same way as the other deductible IRA phaseout rules. A deductible contribution is not available for the nonactive participant spouse if the couple files separate tax returns.

Example:	Joe and Jane Morgan are considering establishing IRAs for themselves and ask you whether contributions are deductible. Joe has AGI of $110,000 and Jane does not have any income because she stays home with the children. Joe is an active participant in a retirement plan and Jane, of course, is not. Joe cannot make a deductible IRA contribution on his own behalf because their AGI exceeds $80,000. However, he can make a $4,000 deductible IRA contribution to Jane's spousal IRA because their AGI is less than $150,000.

ROTH IRAs

Contributions to a Roth IRA are not deductible but distributions are tax free as long as certain eligibility requirements are satisfied. The maximum contribution to a Roth IRA is phased out for single taxpayers with an AGI between $95,000 and $110,000 (pro rata reduction over $15,000 income spread) and for married joint filers with an AGI between $150,000 and $160,000 (pro rata reduction over $10,000 income spread). For purposes of this calculation, the AGI is modified in the same way as for traditional IRAs.

Unlike traditional IRAs, contributions can even be made after attainment of age 70 1/2 and the minimum distribution rules that require distributions from IRAs beginning at age 70 1/2 do not apply. However, the IRA minimum distribution requirement that applies to payments after the death of the participant does apply to Roth IRAs.

For distributions to be tax free, they must be made after the 5-tax-year period beginning with the first tax year for which a contribution was made to an individual's Roth IRA. In addition, only distributions that are made under one of the following circumstances are tax free:

- The participant has attained age 59 1/2.
- The distribution is paid to a beneficiary because of the participant's death.
- The participant has become disabled.
- The withdrawal is made to pay for qualified first-time homebuyer expenses.

Qualified first-time homebuyer expenses include acquisition costs of a first home (paid within 120 days of the distribution) for the participant, the participant's spouse, or any child, grandchild, or ancestor of the participant or spouse. This exception, however, has a $10,000 lifetime limit per IRA (or Roth IRA) participant.

If a nonqualifying distribution is made, amounts representing earnings are subject to both income tax and the 10 percent penalty tax that currently applies to early distributions from regular IRAs and other qualified retirement plans. However, Roth IRA contributions can be withdrawn first, without tax consequences.

ROLLOVER CONTRIBUTIONS

The ability to roll benefits from an employer-sponsored tax-sheltered retirement plan to an IRA is a powerful concept. It gives participants the opportunity to defer income taxes and to continue to accrue tax-deferred interest until distributions are needed for retirement. It also gives the participant complete control over the investment direction of retirement funds as well as the timing of distributions.

The IRA rollover also permits the financial services professional to manage large asset accumulations. This opportunity continues to grow as more company pension plans today offer their participants a lump-sum option and as workers continue to accumulate large sums in their company's 401(k) plan.

Traditional IRAs

To facilitate portability of pensions and transferability when a taxpayer changes jobs, distributions from a qualified plan (except life insurance distribuions), 403(b) plan, 457 plan, or from an individual retirement arrangement can be made on a tax-free basis if the distribution is reinvested within 60 days in an individual retirement arrangement. This transaction is known as a *rollover*—the tax-free transfer from one retirement program to another.

There are several types of rollovers involving individual retirement arrangements:

- *Rollover from one individual retirement arrangement to another individual retirement arrangement.* Taxpayers can withdraw all or part of the balance in an IRA and reinvest it within 60 days in another IRA. The reasons for doing this include changing trusts or custodial accounts (because of dissatisfaction with investment performance or service) or temporarily boosting cash flow. To ensure that participants cannot borrow funds for 60 days on a continuous basis, rollovers are permitted only once a year. One way around this one-year rule is to make a *trustee-to-trustee transfer*—a transfer of IRA funds from one trustee directly to another trustee. However, a trustee-to-trustee transfer does not constitute a rollover because the money is never distributed.
- *Rollover from an employer-sponsored retirement plan to an IRA.* Under the rules applicable today, most distributions made from a qualified plan, 403(b) plan, or 457 plan can be rolled over (in full or in part) into a new or existing IRA. The rollover is not allowed when the distribution is part of a series of periodic payments over the life expectancy of the participant or over a period of 10 years or more or if the distribution is a hardship withdrawal from a 401(k) plan. A participant wanting to make such a rollover should generally choose what is referred to as a direct rollover from the plan to the IRA. This allows the participant to avoid the 20 percent income tax withholding requirements on a distribution paid directly to the participant. Electing the direct rollover is relatively easy to accomplish because the law now requires that qualified plans, 403(b) plans, and 457 plans give participants the option to make the direct rollover to an IRA.

Roth IRAs

Roth IRA conversion

Distributions from one Roth IRA can be rolled over tax free to another Roth IRA. Also, amounts in a traditional IRA can be rolled over to a Roth IRA if the individual's AGI for the tax year does not exceed $100,000. This type of rollover is called a *Roth IRA conversion*. The dollar limit is the same for both single taxpayers and married couples filing jointly—marrieds filing separately are not eligible for the rollover. Rollovers from Roth IRAs and conversions from traditional IRAs are subject to the 60-day rollover rules. The once-a-year rollover rule also applies to Roth IRAs but not to conversions from traditional to Roth IRAs. The 60-day rollover means that an individual can convert to a Roth IRA in 2005 by withdrawing the funds from the traditional IRA up to December 31, 2005, and then rolling the amount into the Roth IRA as late as the end of February 2006. Under the rules, this is treated as a Roth IRA conversion for 2005.

Because a conversion has to occur before the end of the year, it is quite possible that the individual's AGI is not yet known at the time of the conversion. For example, Sally, who is single, expects to have AGI of $95,000. On December 1, 2004, she converts a $10,000 IRA. After the year ends and she calculates her taxes, she realizes that she had AGI of $102,000 for 2004. The law allows an undoing of the Roth IRA conversion without penalty as long as the amount is transferred back to a traditional IRA by the due date of the tax return (plus extensions) for the year, and that any earnings on the account are also returned.

When an amount is rolled over from a traditional IRA, the distribution is subject to income tax (taxed as ordinary income), but is not subject to the 10 percent early distribution excise tax. However, because this could result in the avoidance of the 10 percent early distribution tax, individuals who withdraw converted amounts from a Roth IRA within 5 tax years of the conversion will be subject to the 10 percent penalty on early withdrawals.

Once in the Roth IRA, future growth is not taxed as long as distributions qualify for the income exclusion and as long as the distribution is a qualifying distribution as discussed above. With a converted Roth IRA, the 5-year measuring period begins for the first year that contributions to any Roth IRA were made. This means that if an individual made a contribution to a Roth IRA for 1998 and then in the year 2002 converted a $50,000 IRA to another Roth IRA, the 5-year measuring period for the Roth IRA would start in 1998.

DISTRIBUTIONS

Other materials in this course cover the taxation of qualified plan and IRA distributions in-depth. Here we will summarize the rules that apply to both traditional and Roth IRAs.

Traditional IRAs

Taxpayers can withdraw all or part of their IRAs any time they wish. Unless the participant has made nondeductible contributions, distributions from IRAs are treated as ordinary income and are subject to federal income tax. Nondeductible contributions are withdrawn tax free on a pro rata basis. If the participant dies, payments to beneficiaries are still subject to income tax. However, the income is treated as "income in respect to a decedent," which means that income taxes are reduced by the amount of estate taxes paid as a result of the IRA.

If distributions are made prior to age 59 1/2, the Sec. 72(t) excise tax imposes an additional 10 percent tax unless an exception applies. Exceptions are made for payments on account of death, disability, or for the payment of certain medical expenses. Another exception allows substantially equal periodic payments over the remaining life of the participant and a chosen beneficiary. Another allows payments for qualified higher education expenses for education furnished to the taxpayer, the taxpayer's spouse, or any child or grandchild of the taxpayer or taxpayer's spouse at an eligible educational institution. A final exception is for distributions to pay for acquisition costs of a first home for the participant, spouse, or any child, grandchild, or ancestor of the participant or spouse. This exception, however, has a $10,000 lifetime exception per IRA participant.

IRAs are also subject to rules that control the maximum length of the tax-deferral period. These are the minimum-distribution rules that generally require that distributions begin when the participant attains age 70 1/2 and also require specified payments at the participant's death.

Roth IRAs

What makes Roth IRAs unique is that qualifying distributions are tax free. As described above, in order to qualify, distributions must be made more than 5 years after the Roth IRA was established; they also must be distributed after the participant attains age 59 1/2 or dies or becomes disabled. Furthermore, up to $10,000 of homebuying expenses can be distributed tax free as well, provided the 5-year rule is satisfied.

If a nonqualifying distribution is made, the situation is somewhat more complicated. Generally an individual can withdraw his or her Roth IRA contributions (or converted contributions) without income tax consequences. Once all contributions have been withdrawn, amounts representing earnings are subject to both income tax and the 10 percent Sec. 72(t) excise tax.

Example: Thomas Veltchild, age 35, has maintained a Roth IRA for 8 years. Thomas is planning to go back to school and wants to make a withdrawal from his Roth IRA to cover those expenses. His account balance is $37,000, total contributions are $18,000, and he has not taken any previous distributions. In the first year Thomas withdraws $10,000. Because Thomas has not satisfied one of the triggering events, the distribution is a non-qualifying distribution. It is not subject to income tax, however, since the withdrawal does not exceed total contributions to the plan. Assume that in year 2, when the account balance is $28,000, he wants to withdraw an additional $10,000. The first $8,000 is not subject to tax because it represents a return of his contributions. However, the remaining $2,000 will be subject to income tax. It is also subject to the 10 percent Sec. 72(t) early withdrawal tax. However, since the withdrawal is to pay higher education expenses, an exception applies and no 10 percent penalty tax applies.

A special rule applies to converted Roth IRAs. The 10 percent Sec.72(t) early withdrawal tax continues to apply for 5 years after the conversion—even if no income tax is due. Remember, however, that all of the exceptions to the premature distributions penalty that apply to traditional IRAs will apply to distributions from Roth IRAs as well.

Example: Hope Adler, age 50, converted a $100,000 IRA to a Roth IRA last year. This year she wants to withdraw $10,000 help her child purchase a car. The $10,000 is not subject to income taxes but is subject to the 10 percent Sec. 72(t) early withdrawal penalty tax.

FUNDING VEHICLES

In addition to the legal and tax implications concerning IRAs, there are also several financial implications. Note that both traditional IRAs and Roth IRAs are subject to the same investment rules. Let's take a closer look. Individual retirement plans can be established with one of two different funding vehicles:

- individual retirement accounts
- individual retirement annuities

Individual Retirement Accounts (IRAs)

Individual retirement accounts (IRAs) are the most popular type of individual retirement arrangement. The IRA document itself is a written trust or a custodial account whose trustee or custodian must be a bank, a federally insured credit union, a savings and loan association, or a person or organization that receives IRS permission to act as the trustee or custodian (for example, an insurance company). No one will receive IRS permission to be the trustee of his or her own IRA because the IRS mandates arm's-length dealing between the beneficiary of the IRA trust and those in charge of enforcing IRA rules. IRA funds may not be commingled with other assets.

Individual Retirement Annuities (IRA Annuities)

An *individual retirement annuity (IRA annuity)* is an annuity contract typically issued by insurance companies. IRA annuities are similar to IRAs except that the following additional rules apply because of their annuity investment feature:

- The IRA annuity is nontransferable. Proceeds must be received by either the taxpayer or a beneficiary. Individuals cannot set up an IRA annuity and then pledge the annuity to another party or put the annuity up as a security for a loan. For example, if loans were made under an automatic premium-loan provision, the plan would be disqualified.
- IRA annuities may not have fixed annual premiums. It is allowable, however, to charge an annual fee for each premium or to have a level annual premium for a supplementary benefit, such as a waiver of premium in case of disability.

There are several features that make IRA annuities different than IRA accounts. First, most policies have a waiver-of-premium in case of disability. This is especially important for those relying on individual-retirement-arrangement funds as a major source of retirement income. In fact, for some people the waiver of premium in case of disability may be the only assurance of retirement income (aside from Social Security). The opportunity to elect a life annuity form of payment is another difference. This distribution option allows the individual to share the risk of a longer-than-average life with the annuity provider.

INVESTMENTS

IRAs can be invested in a multitude of vehicles running the gamut from mutual funds to limited partnerships, from investments with minimal risk and modest returns to speculative investments with promises of greater return. IRAs are typically invested in certificates of deposit, money market funds, mutual funds, limited partnerships, income bond funds, corporate bond funds, and common stocks and other equities. Self-directed IRAs (IRAs in which the taxpayer is able to shift investments between general investment vehicles offered by the trustee) are also popular because they give the investor flexibility and the ability to anticipate or react to interest-rate directions and market trends.

Choosing the best investment for an individual retirement arrangement is similar to choosing any other investment lifestyle. Other financial resources, as well as the client's degree of risk aversion, must be considered. There is, however, one hitch with an IRA investment: The *R* stands for *retirement.* The client's retirement goals must be considered to make the proper IRA investment. In rendering IRA advice, the job of a financial services professional is to induce the client to generate a retirement strategy first and an investment strategy second.

However, investing in tax-sheltered vehicles such as municipal bonds is generally not a good idea because the tax shelter is not necessary. Because an IRA provides for tax deferral already, the overkill of investing in a tax-free bond won't make it worthwhile for an investor to take the lower yield that municipal bonds offer.

Investment Restrictions

Investment of IRAs is generally open to all the investment vehicles available outside IRAs. There are, however, a few exceptions:

- life insurance
- collectibles
- prohibited transactions

Life Insurance

Investment in life insurance is not allowed for an IRA even though defined-benefit and defined-contribution retirement plans allow an "incidental" amount of life insurance. IRAs, however, are not subject to the same rules (or underlying logic) and are considered to be strictly for retirement purposes. Therefore no incidental insurance is available. But there is an interesting method for linking the sale of life insurance with an IRA.

Collectibles

If an IRA is invested in collectibles, the amount invested in collectibles is considered a distribution in the year invested. This means that the tax advantages of IRAs have been eliminated, and if the investment is made prior to age 59 1/2, a 10 percent excise tax will be applicable unless the payment is made in the form of a life annuity or its equivalent. Collectibles include works of art, Oriental rugs, antiques, rare coins, stamps, rare wines, and certain other tangible property.

There are two exceptions to the prohibition on investments in collectibles. First, specified gold, silver, and platinum coins issued by the United States and coins issued under state law can be bought with IRA funds. However, gold and silver coins of other countries are still prohibited. In addition, investments in gold, silver, platinum, or palladium bullion are also allowed. This provision allows individuals to invest in precious metals within their IRA accounts. However, these types of investments are allowed only when the IRA trustee has "physical possession" of the bullion.

Prohibited Transactions

For an IRA, prohibited transactions include borrowing money from the account or annuity, selling property to the account, borrowing from the account, or using the account or annuity as security for a loan. If a nonexempt prohibited transaction occurs, the IRA will be "disqualified" and the taxpayer must include the fair market value of part or all of the IRA assets in his or her gross income for tax purposes in the year in which the prohibited transaction occurs. There also will be a 10 percent premature distribution penalty (if prior to age 59 1/2). In effect, prohibited transactions are treated as distributions from the plan.

IRA PLANNING

For the financial services professional, understanding IRAs requires more than just knowing the various rules, restraints, and tax implications associated with IRAs. The financial services professional must also analyze whether a current client's interests are best served by making IRA contributions and must identify potential clients who need IRA assistance.

The first step in determining whether a client should use IRAs is to determine their eligibility for the various options. Tables 4-4 and 4-5 summarize the available options for both single and married (filing jointly) taxpayers in 2005.

The last several years have seen important favorable changes for IRAs. Even though IRA planning has become considerably more complicated, it has also opened up opportunities for your clients. Looking at IRAs under the current playing field, here are some general observations for your clients:

- The maximum contribution to IRAs is rising. For 2005, the limit is $4,000, and it increases $1,000 in 2008 ($5,000). Those aged 50 or older can make an additional $500 contribution each year through 2005; after 2005 they can make an additional contribution of $1,000.

TABLE 4-4
IRA Options for Singles in 2005

Type of Contribution	Tax Benefit	Availability
Nondeductible	After-tax contributions with tax deferral on earnings. Distributions of earnings taxed as ordinary income.	Individuals under age 70 1/2 with compensation from personal services (does not include investment income).
Deductible	Tax deduction on contributions with tax deferral on earnings. All distributions taxed as ordinary income.	Individuals under age 70 1/2 with compensation who are not active participants in an employer-sponsored retirement plan. Deduction phased out for individuals who are active participants with AGI between $50,000 and $60,000.
Roth	After-tax contributions. No tax on qualifying distributions.	Individuals with compensation. Ability to make contribution phased out with AGI between $95,000 and $110,000 threshold amounts.
Converting an IRA to a Roth IRA	Income tax is paid at the time the IRA is converted to the Roth IRA.	Cannot make conversion if AGI exceeds $100,000 for the year.

- The special spousal rule provides that for a married couple filing jointly with AGI of less than $150,000 and only one spouse covered in an employer-sponsored retirement plan, the other spouse can contribute the maximum amount on a deductible basis to a traditional IRA.
- The ability to make withdrawals from IRAs without penalty for family educational expenses and first homebuying expenses takes away one of the major reasons not to use an IRA.
- The Roth IRA offers a significant tax benefit that is available to a lot of taxpayers who cannot make deductible IRA contributions. For example, a single taxpayer earning $75,000 who is a 401(k) plan participant cannot make a deductible IRA contribution but can make a $4,000 contribution to a Roth IRA.
- Choosing between the Roth IRA and a deductible IRA (or other pretax savings vehicle like a 401(k) plan) can be a difficult choice (see below). However, do not forget that both are great ways to save for retirement.
- Many taxpayers will resist converting traditional IRAs to Roth IRAs. Doing so creates a current tax liability. However, conversions can accomplish a number of objectives and can be the appropriate economic choice for many individuals.

TABLE 4-5
IRA Options for Marrieds Filing Jointly in 2005

Type of Contribution	Tax Benefit	Availability
Nondeductible	After-tax contributions with tax deferral on earnings. Distributions of earnings taxed as ordinary income.	Couples under age 70 1/2 with compensation from personal services (does not include investment income).
Deductible	Tax deduction on contributions with tax deferral on earnings. All distributions taxed as ordinary income.	Couples under age 70 1/2 with compensation who are not active participants in an employer-sponsored retirement plan. If one spouse is an active participant, then the deduction is phased out (for the spouse who is not an active participant) for AGI between $150,000 and $160,000. Deduction phased out for individuals who are active participants with AGI between $70,000 and $80,000.
Roth	After-tax contributions. No tax on qualifying distributions.	Couples with compensation. Ability to make contribution phased out with AGI between $150,000 and $160,000.
Converting an IRA to a Roth IRA	Income tax is paid at the time the IRA is converted to the Roth IRA.	Cannot make conversion if AGI exceeds $100,000 for the year.

- The IRA rules offer little for taxpayers with high-end income. However, older, more affluent individuals can provide encouragement—and funds—to their children and grandchildren so they can take advantage of these opportunities.
- Likewise, the IRA rules offer little to those at the lower end of the earnings scale. These individuals are the least likely to have sufficient income to afford a contribution and are the most likely to need emergency withdrawals that will not qualify for special tax treatment.

Let's look at several of these points in greater depth.

Reasons for Using Traditional IRAs

Sometimes it is difficult to convince your clients of the importance of saving for retirement. With younger clients, it can be helpful to point out that by making just nine $3,000 contributions from age 18 to age 26—and no contributions thereafter—an IRA at age 65 will be larger than an IRA funded with a $3,000 contribution each year from age 27 to age 65 (see table 4-6). For clients who think their company-sponsored retirement plan is sufficient, point out to them that if postretirement inflation is 4 percent per year, a $1 loaf of bread at age 65 will cost $2.19 at age 85.

Another concern of clients is the effect of the 10 percent premature excise tax. If money is withdrawn too soon, the tax will reduce the client's savings. For some, this is good news because it acts as an incentive to keep

TABLE 4-6
IRA Funding Plans*

Plan One			Plan Two		
Age start	18		Age start	27	
Age end	26		Age end	65	
Amount per year	$3,000		Amount per year	$3,000	
Rate of return	8%		Rate of return	8%	
Value at age 65	$753,572		Value at age 65	$713,823	
Total amount			Total amount		
contributed	$27,000		contributed	$114,000	
Age	**Amount**	**Value**	**Age**	**Amount**	**Value**
18	$3,000	$ 3,240	18	0	0
19	3,000	6,739	19	0	0
20	3,000	10,518	20	0	0
21	3,000	14,600	21	0	0
22	3,000	19,008	22	0	0
23	3,000	23,768	23	0	0
24	3,000	28,910	24	0	0
25	3,000	34,463	25	0	0
26	3,000	40,459	26	0	0
27	0	43,696	27	$3,000	$ 3,240
28	0	47,192	28	3,000	6,739
29	0	50,967	29	3,000	10,518
30	0	55,044	30	3,000	14,600
.	.	.	.	.	.
.	.	.	.	.	.
.	.	.	.	.	.
60	0	512,869	60	3,000	472,880
61	0	553,898	61	3,000	513,950
62	0	598,210	62	3,000	558,306
63	0	646,067	63	3,000	606,211
64	0	697,752	64	3,000	657,947
65	0	753,572	65	3,000	713,823

*This comparison is hypothetical; no guarantees are implied for specific investments. The interest rate is assumed to remain unchanged for the entire period.

the money in the plan. For others, the answer is that if the withdrawals are needed to pay for educational expenses or to purchase a home, the withdrawals may be eligible for one of the exceptions to the penalty tax.

The excise tax is a real concern, however, and it would also be irresponsible to advise a client to make IRA contributions if he or she couldn't leave the money in the plan for a significant period of time. Still, there is a point at which it benefits a taxpayer to make IRA contributions even when a premature withdrawal is the taxpayer's intention. The break-even or get-ahead date depends on the tax bracket of the employee when contributions are made, the interest earned under the IRA, the tax bracket of the person when distributions are withdrawn, and the ratio of nondeductible contributions to the total IRA balance at the time of withdrawal. If the taxpayer's tax bracket is lower at the time of withdrawal, the break-even point will be shorter. (The converse is also true: a higher tax bracket at distribution time will mean a longer break-even point.)

Choosing the Roth IRA over the Nondeductible IRA

Many taxpayers who do not have the option to make deductible IRA contributions will, however, have the opportunity to make Roth IRA contributions. The ability to contribute to Roth IRAs is phased out for single taxpayers with AGI between $95,000 and $110,000 and married couples filing jointly with AGI between $150,000 and $160,000. Individuals who have the choice between nondeductible IRA contributions and Roth IRA contributions should almost always choose the Roth IRA. Tax-free distributions are clearly better than tax deferral.

In fact, it's difficult to argue for nondeductible contributions at all today because the price of tax deferral is turning investment gain into ordinary income. Arguably, investing directly in securities (outside of the IRA context) may be more attractive, since capital gains can be deferred until the sale and qualifying sales will be taxed at a maximum 15 percent tax rate. Also, securities left to heirs avoid income taxes on the growth over the participant's life.

In contrast, the tax advantages of the Roth IRA are clear. As long as distributions satisfy the eligibility requirements, the entire distribution avoids income tax—even distributions to death beneficiaries. The Roth IRA can even be used to save (up to $10,000) as a down payment for a first home. Like other IRAs, Roth IRA funds can be invested in stocks, bonds, or other investment vehicles. Even the Roth IRA participant who needs early withdrawals is taxed favorably. The participant can withdraw contributions without any income tax consequences, and because the penalty tax applies in the same manner as to traditional IRAs, additional amounts (subject to income tax) can be withdrawn (for example, for educational expenses) without having to pay 10 percent penalty tax.

A good candidate for the Roth IRA would be the a 401(k) participant who has maximized his or her contribution to the 401(k) plan, is not eligible for a deductible IRA contribution, and still wants to save more for retirement. In this case, the next place to save is definitely the Roth IRA. The harder question to answer would be, "Should the 401(k) participant who has been putting away 6 percent of compensation each year and who wants to save more contribute more to the 401(k) plan or contribute to a Roth IRA?" This individual is now choosing between the deductible savings and the tax-free saving alternatives. The issues involved in this decision are discussed below.

Choosing the Roth IRA over the Deductible IRA

Some taxpayers will be in a position to choose between a deductible IRA contribution or the Roth IRA. Similarly, many employees may be choosing between making additional contributions to a 401(k) plan or the Roth IRA. In the 401(k) setting, if the employer will match the contribution, the advantage usually goes to the 401(k) plan, because the employer match is like an instant return on the participant's contribution. However, if the contribution is not matched, then the 401(k) to Roth IRA comparison is essentially the same as the deductible IRA to Roth IRA comparison.

Comparing the financial effect of the two options is difficult, partially because it involves assumptions about rates of return in the future, tax rates in the future, and the timing of withdrawals. Numerous computer software programs are available to help with this comparison, and they can be quite valuable in helping to make choices.

Even though individual analysis is best, here are some general considerations. It is clearest that when the individual expects to be in a higher tax bracket in retirement than at the time of the contribution, the Roth IRA is the more appropriate vehicle. For example, take the young person in the 17 percent (15 percent federal and 2 percent state) bracket today who expects to be in the 42 percent bracket at the time of distribution. Table 4-7 gives an example of such an individual, who has $2,000 to contribute at age 25 and withdraws this amount at age 70. If $2,000 is contributed to the traditional IRA, after taxes are paid at age 70 she will have $37,042. However, if $1,660 is contributed to a Roth IRA ($2,000 less taxes), at age 70 she will have $53,006. This is a significant difference. As seen in table 4-8, this trend is consistent when contributions are made at age 45.

Looking at the columns in tables 4-7 and 4-8 showing the individual's tax rates to be the same (30 percent) at the time of contribution and distribution, it may appear at first glance that the Roth IRA is *not* more effective for taxpayers who will have the same or lower tax rates at the time of withdrawal. However, this will not always be the case. In our example, the participant withdraws all of the Roth IRA at age 70, but one of the Roth

TABLE 4-7
Comparing Deductible IRAs to Roth IRA Accumulations

Age	30%/30%*		17%/42%*		30%/42%*	
	Roth	Deductible	Roth	Deductible	Roth	Deductible
25	$ 1,400	$ 2,000	$ 1,660	$ 2,000	$ 1,400	$ 2,000
70	$44,691	$44,706**	$53,006	$37,042**	$44,691	$37,042**

*The first number represents the combined federal and state income tax rate at the time of contribution and the second number represents the tax rate at the time of distribution.

**Assumes that the entire accumulation is distributed and taxed at age 70. Assumes growth at 8%.

TABLE 4-8
Comparing Deductible IRAs to Roth IRA Accumulations

Age	30%/30%*		17%/42%*		30%/42%*	
	Roth	Deductible	Roth	Deductible	Roth	Deductible
45	$1,400	$2,000	$ 1,660	$2,000	$1,400	$2,000
70	$9,589	$9,591**	$11,372	$7,947**	$9,589	$7,947**

*The first number represents the combined federal and state income tax rate at the time of contribution and the second number represents the tax rate at the time of distribution.

**Assumes that the entire accumulation is distributed and taxed at age 70. Assumes growth at 8%.

IRA's powerful features is that distributions are not required during the participant's lifetime. If the beneficiary is the spouse, distributions can be delayed even further to the death of the spouse. After that, distributions can be made over the expected lifetime of the beneficiary or beneficiaries. This tax deferral can be quite powerful, and makes the Roth IRA a good way to pass on wealth to the next generation.

Also, there is another strength to the Roth IRA. The tax-free source of income gives the participant more flexibility in how and when to liquidate other taxable assets in retirement. The tax-free funds in a Roth IRA can be used in retirement to

- minimize taxable withdrawals from traditional IRAs or qualified plans
- minimize taxable income to stay in a lower tax bracket
- fund life insurance premiums for estate planning purposes
- provide liquidity for estate taxes
- minimize liquidation of other taxable investments such as stocks and mutual funds—which receive a step-up if left intact to heirs

Because of the many strengths of the Roth IRA, the following types of clients should consider the Roth IRA over the deductible IRA:

- individuals in the 15 percent federal income tax bracket
- individuals in the 25 and 28 percent federal income tax brackets who expect to be in a higher bracket at retirement
- individuals who have already accumulated significant assets for retirement on a tax-deferred basis and may want to use the Roth IRA as a way to create a more balanced portfolio
- individuals who are more concerned about estate planning than retirement planning

IRA-to-Roth-IRA Conversions

The IRA-to-Roth-IRA conversion means paying taxes now to avoid taxes later. Some taxpayers simply will not be willing to make this bargain, while others who are interested will not be eligible because of the $100,000 earnings limit. Still, it appears the Roth IRA conversion can result in greater after-tax accumulations in many cases. It is a good idea to run computer simulations so that clients can see the effect of a conversion. Consider the following when evaluating the conversion decision:

- Conversions work for young persons because there will be a long accumulation period over which the Roth IRA is growing tax free.
- Individuals who have most of their retirement savings in IRAs and Roth IRAs should consider converting at least some of those amounts to Roth IRAs. As discussed above, a nontaxable source of income in retirement can be used for a number of retirement or estate planning purposes.
- If taxes are paid out of the IRA at its conversion to a Roth IRA, the 10 percent premature excise tax may apply. This lessens the value of the conversion. If possible, other sources should be used to pay the taxes.

Even though it may appear at first glance that older persons should not convert, conversion can have significant estate planning implications. Remember that if the taxpayer does not need to make withdrawals for living expenses, the law does not require any withdrawals until after the participant's death. If the spouse is the beneficiary, no withdrawals are required over his or her life either. This means that the tax-free accumulation period for even an older person can be quite long. In addition, after death, the Roth IRA can be distributed over the entire lifetime of the beneficiary. Even if the older participant dies shortly after the conversion, the income taxes paid at the conversion reduce the value of the estate, offsetting the Roth IRA accumulation period.

5

Determining the Amount a Client Needs for Retirement

Kenn Beam Tacchino

Chapter Outline

Arguably the most important part of any comprehensive plan for retirement is the estimate of the client's retirement income needs, along with the calculation of the savings rate necessary to meet those needs. *Retirement income needs* are typically defined as the total amount of savings that allows a client to sustain the standard of living enjoyed just prior to retirement throughout the retirement period. Generating the needed savings requires accumulation of a sufficient retirement fund—the bankroll for the retirement years. Stockpiling sufficient savings requires an adequate savings rate, which is the percentage of salary that a person must put aside during his or her working years to accumulate a sufficient bankroll.

The methods used for calculating a needs and savings analysis can vary considerably. There is a variety of privately and commercially available worksheets and computer models that accomplish this objective. Some are available for free at a variety of financial services Web sites; others are sophisticated models provided by financial service companies to their agents. No matter what their origin, most worksheets and computer models leave room for the planner to insert his or her unique perspective. It is the purpose of this chapter to provide you with an understanding of the process involved in arriving at the bottom-line figure needed. While it would be impossible to review each worksheet and computer model individually, it is possible to focus on common characteristics of the process. An understanding of the process distinguishes a professional planner from the crowd and allows for a more accurate prediction to be made. To foster insight into the needs and savings analysis, this chapter will

- examine the assumptions that must be made in order to arrive at a skillful prediction regarding a client's unique circumstances
- probe into the common features of the myriad worksheets and computer models by looking at three different methods for determining the retirement income need

One caveat is in order before we begin. All too often clients and planners alike hold the retirement target generated from a worksheet or computer package as gospel. The amount needed to maintain a client's preretirement standard of living is not etched in stone, however. Successful planners realize that the number generated is an approximation that is only as valid as its underlying assumptions and methodology. Therefore the target set should be tempered with common sense and realistic expectations. After all, it is more prudent to motivate a client to action (albeit inadequate) than to scare a client into inaction or apathy.

ASSUMPTIONS REQUIRED IN WORKSHEETS AND COMPUTER MODELS

Many worksheets and computer models enable the planner to tailor the retirement prediction to a client's unique situation by choosing assumptions for future contingencies. Others make the assumption for the planner and lock out the ability to fine-tune a prediction. Since retirement planning is an art form, not a science, the better models allow the most flexibility by giving the planner control over assumptions. However, planners must be up to the complex task of effectively choosing assumptions. A thorough understanding of the details underlying the assumptions can make the difference between a child's finger painting and a master's portrait.

Assumptions that are typically required in most worksheets and computer models include the

- rate of inflation the client will experience
- age at which the client will retire
- age at which the client will die
- replacement ratio that the client will need
- tax rate applicable now and in the future
- investment return the client can expect
- step-up rate (the rate at which the client will increase annual savings allocations)

Each worksheet and computer model may treat these assumptions differently. For example, many worksheets break down inflation into two categories: preretirement and postretirement. Others are content to make one inflation assumption for both periods, and still others brush back inflation by focusing on the real rate of return (actual rate of return less inflation). Regardless of how the assumptions are treated, however, the planner and the client must be comfortable with the numbers to be plugged in if they want a realistic projection. Let's take a closer look at how to choose the best numbers for your client's situation.

Inflation Assumption

One of the most critical assumptions that a planner must make concerns the inflation rate that will apply to the client. Inflation erodes the client's purchasing power over time, making it difficult to maintain economic self-sufficiency during retirement. The effects of this erosion are dramatically illustrated when different inflation assumptions are plugged into worksheets and computer models. Consider this: By changing the inflation rate from 4 percent to 6 percent in one model, the client's target increases from $825,000 to $1,008,000—a $183,000 (20 percent) difference. The same change (4 percent to 6 percent) in another model almost doubled the amount the client needed to save (from 28 percent to 54 percent of salary!). For this reason it is essential to be as accurate as possible when forecasting the rate of inflation that will apply to your client.

Forecasting Inflation

Forecasting inflation for your client would not be an easy task even if you had a crystal ball. The reason for this is that even if an accurate prediction of the national inflation rate could be made, other factors come into play. For example:

- A decision would have to be made concerning whether the CPI (consumer price index) or the PPI (producer price index) would be a better proxy for your client.
- No matter what statistical data is chosen, a retiree's personal buying habits will affect his or her actual inflation rate.
- Retirees buy more services than goods. Historically, services have inflated at a higher rate than goods. Thus, even if a national average of inflation is accurate, it may be understated for retirees.
- There are significant regional variations in inflation from the national rate.
- Long-term inflation is the appropriate variable, but published statistical data focuses on the annual inflation rate (for example, 1.4 percent in 2004), not the long-term rate.
- Medical inflation is twice the national average. Certain retirees (generally people who fall into what demographers call the "old-old" category) will have extensive medical expenses, whereas others (the "young-old" category) do not use as many medical services.
- Inflation accounts heavily for housing costs. For many retirees this may be a moot point because they own their houses outright or live under rent control. In addition, the average market basket of goods and services that comprises the consumer price index may not be the *average* goods and services used by a retiree.
- Planning for the younger client (late 20s to early 30s) can be troublesome because inflation over 60 years or more must be considered.

Planners should not despair, however; despite uncertainty and disagreement over the best estimate for inflation, some concrete thinking exists. For one thing, most planners feel comfortable using a long-term view of inflation because preretirement and postretirement planning can encompass a long period of time. For example, for the period from 1970 to 1999, the inflation index was 4.294 percent. Successful planners are not getting caught up in today's relatively low inflation rates, nor were they overly concerned with the double-digit inflation of the late '70s and early '80s. Planners therefore help their clients prepare for the financial troubles that lie ahead by having them focus on a long-term rate.

A second issue that is generally agreed on is that a client's tolerance tendencies should be factored in. A risk-averse client will probably want a more conservative figure projected, whereas a risk taker may feel comfortable with a relatively low inflation assumption.

A third factor to consider is that the proxy used for inflation can be changed over time to reflect changes in the long-term rate and the client's actual experience. This is not to say that each year the planner should reinvent the wheel, but it does provide flexibility in planning because the retirement model is constantly evolving.

YOUR FINANCIAL SERVICES PRACTICE:
MONITORING ASSUMPTIONS

Planners cannot take a once-and-done attitude toward clients when it comes to sculpting a client's retirement plan. The plan should be revisited periodically to check the accuracy of assumptions and the effectiveness of meeting the client's goals.

Which Rate Is Best?

Most planners use inflation assumptions between 3 and 4 percent. The actual rate chosen for a client will vary depending on spending habits, current age, and risk-tolerance tendencies. Four percent is a common choice. In addition, some current economic literature indicates that 3.5 percent may be a good proxy for long-term inflation. One prudent way to operate is to ask your client about the "raise" he or she wants each year in retirement. In other words, by what percentage does the client want to increase his or her income each year? The higher the inflation rate (raise), the greater the percentage of salary that your client needs to save. Clients who choose the lowest realistic rate will have the least amount of sacrifice now. They should be warned, however, that their future behavior will be affected. According to the Bureau of Labor Statistics inflation calculator, a person who retired in 1975 and needed $2,000 a month to live will need around $6,500 a month today just to have the same buying power he or she had in 1975. (The inflation calculator and other important data about the rate of inflation and the consumer price index can be found at the Bureau of Labor Statistics home page: www.bls.gov.)

Retirement Age Assumption

Many planners automatically pencil in age 65 as the starting date for retirement despite the fact that the average retirement age in the United States is 62. Consider that only 67 percent of men 55 to 65 years old were still in the workforce in 1987 compared to 90 percent in 1947, and you get a fairly good picture of a growing trend—clients are retiring early (see also figure 5-1).

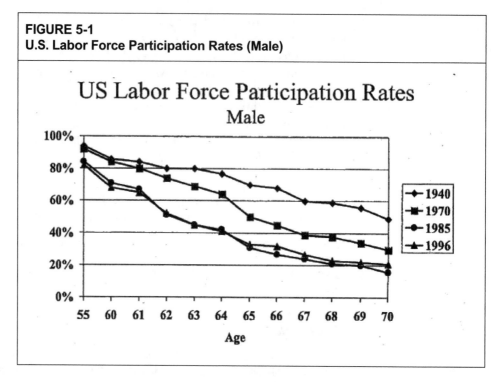

FIGURE 5-1
U.S. Labor Force Participation Rates (Male)

In fact, one Life Insurance Marketing and Research Association (LIMRA) survey showed that roughly 80 percent of people in large companies with pension plans retired before age 65. Another important statistic: 51 percent of all 64-year-olds are retired.

Reasons for Early Retirement

Some clients approach retirement planning as financial independence planning. For these people the assumption of retirement age turns into the goal for financial independence. For example, these clients approach the problem as, "What percentage of my salary do I need to save to retire at age 55?" It is generally easy to adjust computer models and worksheets to fit these clients' needs. (However, it is often difficult to acquire the needed savings by such an early age!)

In addition to retiring early for financial independence, many look at the issue of health in order to help make the early retirement decision. Some want to retire early while they are still in good health; they have perceived health issues. For example, in many instances they fear that future bad health may prevent them from accomplishing their retirement objectives. Others are forced to retire early because of actual health issues. For example, one diabetic client retired early to pursue a 10-mile-a-day walking regimen that would keep his blood sugar low. And in many cases a client is forced to retire early because of the health of his or her spouse (caregiving health issues). In other words, such a client is forced to retire early to become a caregiver to the spouse (or in some cases a parent).

Another reason for early retirement is corporate downsizing. In some cases, retirement packages known as golden handshakes are offered to cut payroll costs attributable to older employees. A *golden handshake* is an incentive offer by an employer made to an employee or group of employees to encourage early retirement. Incentives typically include lump sum payments based on service with the firm, funding for retiree health care, and/or other monetary inducements. In a recent Charles D. Spencer & Associates Survey of 71 large companies, 32 percent of early retirements during the tested year were the result of golden handshakes. No matter what the company's motivation, planners must face the fact that some people are being shown the door (pushed out?) earlier and earlier when economic conditions change and the need arises for the business to contract its workforce.

golden handshake

Other reasons that retirement prior to age 65 remains the preferred exit time for employees include the following:

- *two-wage-earner families.* In many cases normal retirement of one spouse may prompt early retirement of the younger spouse. One study showed that the profile of the individual most likely to retire was a married person whose spouse was retired.
- *death of the spouse.* Statistics show that another group likely to retire early is widows—perhaps because they received death benefits and other inheritances from their partners.
- *laborers and manual workers.* This group often retires early as well—perhaps because of the physically demanding nature of their jobs.
- *problems in the workplace.* Some people retire early because their job has grown intolerable. For example, a recent change makes the job environment a difficult one. These changes range from "I can't work with that person" to "I feel they just don't care about quality anymore and I can't work that way."
- *the desire to compromise financial goals.* The client has not yet achieved the goal of financial independence, but he or she wants to trade a lower standard of living for freedom from employment.
- *health and pension incentives.* The structure of the employer's health and pension plan may encourage early retirement. For example, a client with retiree health coverage at age 62 and a pension that provides 60 percent of salary may perceive that he or she is working for 40 cents on a dollar.

Finally, it is important to note that a recent Retirement Confidence Survey, sponsored by the Employee Benefit Research Institute and the Principal

Financial Group, revealed that 45 percent of current retirees retired earlier than they had planned. Reasons most frequently cited for earlier-than-planned retirement include health problems or disability (40 percent), downsizing or closure (14 percent), family reasons (14 percent), and other work-related reasons (12 percent). Since these reasons typically arise unexpectedly, few of these retirees had enough time to prepare adequately. They simply did not know when they would retire.

Reasons against Early Retirement

Despite the trend toward early retirement, the planner must be ready to point out the downside of leaving too early. Factors include the following:

- Social Security normal retirement age is slated to increase from 65 to 67 for some baby boomers and over 65 but before age 67 for others (see chapter 2). Clients affected by this change should be aware that the early retirement benefit will also be reduced. Typically, it had been 80 percent of the client's primary insurance amount. For those with a normal retirement age of 67, the benefit will drop to 70 percent of the client's primary insurance amount.
- The impact of early retirement on pension benefits can be devastating. In a final-average-salary defined-benefit plan, the pension is lowered because the peak earning years are shortchanged. (In other words, had the worker stayed on the job, the pension would have been higher because it would have been based on higher earnings.) The same holds true for the account balance in a defined-contribution plan.
- Pensions are often adjusted downward to reflect the longer payout that comes with early retirement.
- Early retirement means increased exposure to inflation.
- Early retirement may have to wait for the payoff of fixed long-term liabilities such as mortgage and college tuition for the kids. Many baby boomers had children later in life, exacerbating this problem.
- Early retirement may mean the loss of health insurance. In one study, only 46 percent of large companies provided some form of health coverage for early retirees. What's more, COBRA coverage lasts only 18 months for retirement.
- Early retirement may decrease the amount of Social Security benefits paid. In other words, Social Security benefits will be reduced if the 35 years of averaged indexed monthly earnings (that are used to calculate the primary insurance amount of Social Security) include some low- or zero-earning years.

What Age Is Best?

Considering that a myriad of factors must be examined, the choice of a retirement date is not the easy task that it appeared to be at first blush. The planner's role, with the aid of worksheets and computer models, is to make the retirement age as realistic as possible for the client. Often a client will seek to retire on what he or she considers to be a large amount of money. Unfortunately, it is typically not going to be enough. It is up to the planner to point out that because of inflation and longevity, delaying retirement may be the most logical situation. In other words, one of the chief functions of the planner and the retirement worksheet/printout is to foster a realistic attitude in the client. This attitude will then enable the planner to better forecast the client's intended retirement date.

Longevity Assumption

Ideally, clients would accumulate enough assets to allow them to live on the interest alone and never have to liquidate the principal. For many clients, however, this is not a viable strategy. These clients must liquidate their retirement savings throughout the retirement period. We have already discussed the uncertainty of the inauguration of retirement. Imagine our dilemma over the uncertainty concerning the end of retirement—death! As ghoulish as it may sound, the impossible task of predicting the demise of their clients is a real issue that planners face. Severe mistakes in either direction can tend to grossly overstate or understate the amount of savings needed to meet a particular retirement goal. As a case in point, consider the unlucky client who retires at age 64 and dies at age 66; for this client only a modest sum is actually needed. Had the client known that his postretirement

---

YOUR FINANCIAL SERVICES PRACTICE:
ESTIMATES VERSUS HABITS

At this point it has become clear that there is an interplay between the assumptions used in the worksheets and computer models and the current and future habits of retirees. In some instances the worksheet will help a person to "see the light" and change his or her habits to ensure financial security in the future. In other cases assumptions need to be changed, in part because retirement goals are not etched in stone and in part because clients are not willing to alter their behavior.

Astute planners will use the worksheet or computer software as a reality check for their clients—a way to show clients that decisions they make today have a direct correlation to their quality of life tomorrow. *For this reason, assumptions are part of the educational process for the client (and the planner) and subject to manipulation by both.*

life span would be short, both the planner and client would have been spared the needless headaches of trying to squeeze the most out of every penny prior to retirement. On the other hand, take Joe "Methuselah" Brown, who retired at age 64 and just sent you an invitation to his 105th birthday party. Not only have the extra years of life formed a planning problem, but Joe has had an increased exposure to inflation as well.

Notwithstanding the potential for error, planners must make their best educated guess concerning their clients' (both spouses if applicable) life expectancies in order to complete a retirement worksheet or computer model. In many cases this assumption is generated by the ages at which parents and grandparents have died. This is generally sound thinking because medical studies show a strong relationship between genetics and life expectancy. In addition to family history, factors that should be considered include

- the physical condition of the client, including the client's personal medical history
- life expectancy tables (see table 5-1). Make note, however, that insurance tables tend to understate life expectancy and annuity tables tend to overstate life expectancy. What's more, even if tables are accurate, *one-half of the people outlive the tables' projections.*
- According to the Centers for Disease Control, life expectancies for Americans have reached an all-time historical high. At the turn of the new century, men were expected to live 74.4 years (up from 68.2 in 1980 and 62.6 in 1950) and women were expected to live 79.8 years (up from 76.1 years in 1980 and 67.4 years in 1950).
- the tendency of higher socioeconomic groups to have longer life expectancies. Many believe this is due in part to easy access to medical care.
- the fact that the average number of years until the second death in a couple is longer than the individual life expectancy of either person alone. For example, based on one table of life expectancies for all races (not reproduced in this text), the husband of a married couple where each spouse is aged 65 has a life expectancy of about 14.1 years while the wife has a life expectancy of 18.3 years. However, the average number of years until the second death of a husband and wife who are each aged 65 is about 21.3 years—3 years, or over 16 percent, longer than the wife's expectancy of 18.3 years. In other words, although each spouse has less than a 50 percent chance of living an additional 21.3 years when each life is considered alone, there is about an even chance that one of the two will live at least an additional 21.3 years when you consider their joint (second-to-die) life expectancy.
- life expectancy calculators on the Internet or proprietary software that projects longevity based on family and personal health history

TABLE 5-1
Expectancies of Life at Single Years of Age, by Color and Sex:
United States: 1980*

	All Races			White			All Other					
							Total			Black		
Age	Both Sexes	Male	Female	Both Sexes	Male	Female	Both Sexes	Male	Female	Both Sexes	Male	Female
50	27.8	24.9	30.6	28.1	25.2	30.9	25.5	22.6	28.3	24.5	21.6	27.3
51	27.0	24.1	29.7	27.2	24.3	30.0	24.8	21.9	27.5	23.8	21.0	26.5
52	26.1	23.3	28.8	26.4	23.5	29.1	24.0	21.2	26.7	23.1	20.3	25.7
53	25.3	22.5	28.0	25.6	22.7	28.2	23.3	20.6	25.9	22.4	19.7	24.9
54	24.0	21.7	27.1	24.8	21.9	27.4	22.6	19.9	25.1	21.7	19.0	24.2
55	23.7	21.0	26.3	23.9	21.2	26.5	21.9	19.3	24.4	21.0	18.4	23.4
56	22.9	20.2	25.4	23.1	20.4	25.7	21.2	18.6	23.6	20.3	17.8	22.7
57	22.2	19.5	24.6	22.4	19.6	24.8	20.5	18.0	22.9	19.7	17.2	22.0
58	21.4	18.8	23.8	21.6	18.9	24.0	19.9	17.4	22.1	19.0	16.6	21.3
59	20.6	18.0	23.0	20.8	18.2	23.2	19.2	16.8	21.4	18.4	16.0	20.5
60	19.9	17.4	22.2	20.1	17.5	22.4	18.6	16.2	20.7	17.8	15.5	19.8
61	19.2	16.7	21.4	19.3	16.8	21.6	17.9	15.7	20.0	17.2	14.9	19.2
62	18.5	16.0	20.6	18.6	16.1	20.8	17.3	15.1	19.3	16.6	14.4	18.5
63	17.8	15.4	19.8	17.9	15.4	20.0	16.7	14.6	18.6	16.0	13.9	17.8
64	17.1	14.7	19.1	17.2	14.8	19.2	16.1	14.0	18.0	15.4	13.4	17.2
65	16.4	14.1	18.3	16.5	14.2	18.5	15.5	13.5	17.3	14.8	12.9	16.5
66	15.7	13.5	17.6	15.8	13.6	17.7	15.0	13.0	16.7	14.3	12.4	15.9
67	15.1	12.9	16.9	15.2	13.0	17.0	14.4	12.5	16.0	13.7	11.9	15.3
68	14.4	12.3	16.1	14.5	12.4	16.2	13.8	12.0	15.4	13.2	11.4	14.6
69	13.8	11.8	15.4	13.9	11.8	15.5	13.3	11.5	14.8	12.6	10.9	14.0
70	13.2	11.3	14.8	13.3	11.3	14.8	12.8	11.1	14.2	12.1	10.5	13.4
71	12.6	10.7	14.1	12.7	10.7	14.1	12.2	10.6	13.6	11.6	10.0	12.9
72	12.0	10.2	13.4	12.1	10.2	13.5	11.7	10.2	13.0	11.1	9.6	12.3
73	11.5	9.7	12.8	11.5	9.7	12.8	11.3	9.7	12.5	10.6	9.2	11.8
74	10.9	9.3	12.1	10.9	9.3	12.2	10.8	9.3	12.0	10.1	8.8	11.2
75	10.4	8.8	11.5	10.4	8.8	11.5	10.3	8.9	11.4	9.7	8.3	10.7
76	9.9	8.4	10.9	9.9	8.3	10.9	9.8	8.5	10.9	9.2	7.9	10.2
77	9.3	7.9	10.3	9.3	7.9	10.3	9.4	8.1	10.4	8.8	7.5	9.7
78	8.9	7.5	9.7	8.8	7.5	9.7	8.9	7.7	9.9	8.3	7.1	9.2
79	8.4	7.1	9.2	8.4	7.1	9.2	8.5	7.3	9.4	7.9	6.7	8.7
80	7.9	6.7	8.6	7.9	6.7	8.6	8.1	6.9	9.0	7.4	6.3	8.2
81	7.5	6.3	8.1	7.4	6.3	8.1	7.7	6.5	8.5	7.0	6.0	7.7
82	7.0	6.0	7.6	7.0	6.0	7.6	7.3	6.2	8.1	6.6	5.6	7.3
83	6.6	5.7	7.2	6.6	5.6	7.1	6.9	5.8	7.7	6.2	5.2	6.9
84	6.2	5.3	6.8	6.2	5.3	6.7	6.6	5.5	7.3	5.8	4.9	6.5
85	5.9	5.0	6.4	5.9	5.0	6.3	6.3	5.3	7.0	5.5	4.5	6.1

* From the Department of Health and Human Services, Public Health Service, annual report, Vital Statistics of the United States, for the year 1980.

- the probability of living from age 65 to a specified age (see figure 5-2) (This is a more accurate life expectancy table then life expectancy at birth.)

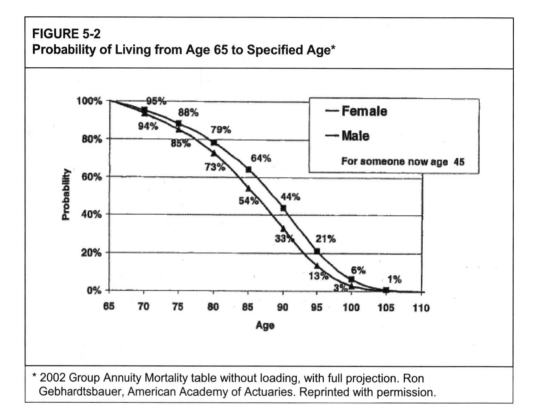

FIGURE 5-2
Probability of Living from Age 65 to Specified Age*

* 2002 Group Annuity Mortality table without loading, with full projection. Ron Gebhardtsbauer, American Academy of Actuaries. Reprinted with permission.

What's a Planner to Do?

First, identify the client's expected retirement age. Factor in statistical life expectancy information, then adjust the estimate up or down for factors such as health, lifestyle, and family history (or use life expectancy calculators). In addition, many planners feel comfortable adding a fudge factor to their life expectancy estimate. If the client lives longer than can be anticipated, the fudge factor will make up for the additional years. If the client does not live as long, some excess assets will be left for heirs (which generally is a viable planning goal anyway). At the extreme, some planners use a life expectancy assumption of age 100 because statistically very few people will live beyond this point. Using this as a conservative estimate will save the planner from the fatal (pun intended) error of understating life expectancy.

Another way to fudge this decision about life span is to divide assets into different classes. For example, X fund will be used for the normal expected life expectancy and Y fund can be reserved for heirs, but consumed if longevity necessitates it. In many cases the reserve fund will be a home's value (or equity) or the value of a vacation home.

Note, however, that whatever fudge factor is used, planners must guard against overstating the retirement need to the extent that the annual amount of savings needed is unattainable. In other words, using unrealistically high life expectancies will create unreasonably high demands on the percentage of salary a client needs to save and ultimately scare the client into inaction because of inability to meet savings schedules.

Income Requirement Assumption

**income requirement
assumption**

The *income requirement assumption* represents the planner's estimation of the level of income needed by retirees to sustain the standard of living they enjoyed just prior to retirement throughout their retired life. In some cases it can be measured as a percentage of final salary (called the *replacement-ratio approach).* In other cases it is the projected retirement budget for a client (called the *expense method).*

**replacement-ratio
approach**

Replacement-Ratio Approach

Some experts believe that between 70 and 80 percent of a person's final salary will keep him or her in the style to which he or she is accustomed throughout retirement. Note that postretirement inflation is not factored into the replacement ratio. Instead it is treated separately. In other words, the worksheets and computer models account for an inflation-protected stream of income separate from the replacement ratio that will be needed in the first year of retirement.

Factors That Influence a Replacement Ratio of Less Than 100 Percent. Support for a replacement ratio of less than 100 percent of final salary rests on the elimination of some employment-related taxes and some expected changes in spending patterns that reduce the retiree's need for income (such as expenditures that will either decrease or disappear in the retirement years).

Reductions in Taxation. In many circumstances, retirees can count on a lower percentage of their income going to pay taxes in the retirement years. Some taxes are reduced or eliminated, and retirees may enjoy special favorable tax treatment in other areas too. Let's take a closer look at the potential reductions in taxation that are granted to retirees.

Social Security Taxes. FICA contributions (old-age, survivors, disability, and hospital insurance) are levied solely on income from employment. Distributions from pensions, IRAs, retirement annuities, and other similar devices are not considered income subject to FICA or SECA taxes. Hence for the retiree who stops working entirely, Social Security taxes are no longer an expenditure.

Increased Standard Deduction. For a married taxpayer aged 65 or over, the standard deduction is increased by an additional $950 (in 2004). If the taxpayer's spouse is also 65 or older, yet another $950 increase in the standard deduction can be taken ($950 for each spouse, or $1,900 total). For a taxpayer over 65 who is not married and does not file as a surviving spouse, $1,200 is added to the standard deduction (in 2004). Note that for taxpayers who itemize deductions (using schedule A), this will be a moot point. In other words, clients have the option of doing one thing or the other—itemizing or using the standard deduction.

Social Security Benefits Exclusion. A married taxpayer can exclude all Social Security benefits from his or her income for tax purposes if the taxpayer's modified adjusted gross income (which includes interest earned on state and local government securities) plus one-half of the Social Security benefits does not exceed the base amount of $32,000 ($25,000 for single taxpayers). For others, only part of their Social Security benefit will be untaxed. See chapter 2 for a thorough discussion of how Social Security is taxed.

Some examples will help to show just what the Social Security benefits exclusion means in tax savings for a retiree.

Example 1:	Paul and Peggy are married and file jointly. They receive $20,000 in pension income and $10,000 in Social Security income. All of their Social Security income is received tax free. Because they are in the 28 percent federal and state marginal tax bracket, this amounts to a tax savings of $2,800.
Example 2:	Arthur and Ann are married filing jointly. They receive $30,000 in pension income and $20,000 in combined Social Security benefits. Arthur and Ann will pay taxes on $4,000 of their Social Security income and will receive $16,000 of their Social Security income tax free. Because they are in the 28 percent federal and state marginal tax bracket, this amounts to $4,480 in tax savings.
Example 3:	James and Julie are married filing jointly. They receive combined pensions of $200,000 and combined Social Security of $20,000. James and Julie will pay taxes on $17,000 of their Social Security benefit and receive $3,000 tax free. Because they are in the 36 percent federal and state marginal tax bracket, they will save $1,080 in taxes.

State and Local Income Taxation. In some states, Social Security benefits are fully exempt from state income taxation; in others, some taxation of these benefits might occur if the state's income tax is assessed on the taxpayer's taxable income as reported for federal income tax purposes. In addition, some states grant extra income tax relief for seniors by providing increased personal exemptions, credits, sliding scale rebates of property or other taxes (the amount or percent of which might be dependent on income), or additional tax breaks such as

- exemption of all or part of retirement pay from the state income tax base
- exemption of all or part of unreimbursed medical expenses from the state income tax base
- freezing of taxes at the level for the year the taxpayer reaches 65
- deferring real estate taxes until after the death of the retiree

Deductible Medical Expenses. Due to the reduced retirement income level and the increased medical expenses that retirees often face, it might be easier for taxpayers who itemize deductions to exceed the 7.5 percent threshold for deductibility of qualifying medical expenses.

Reduced Living Expenses. In addition to the possible reductions in taxation, certain reduced living expenses may permit retired individuals to maintain their standard of living on a lower income. Let's take a closer look at some of them.

Work-Related Expenses. The costs of proper clothing for work, commuting, and meals purchased during work hours are eliminated when a person retires. In addition, other expenses, such as membership dues in some professional or social clubs, may be reduced because of retired status or may be eliminated if no longer necessary.

Home Ownership Expenses. By the time of retirement, many homeowners have "burnt the mortgage" and no longer have this debt reduction expenditure. (*Planning Note:* It may be worthwhile for a client to pay off the mortgage at or near the date of retirement. This mortgage redemption not only eliminates the debt repayment expenditure but also reduces income from interest or dividends on assets used to pay the mortgage, thereby reducing income for federal and state tax purposes. For taxpayers of modest means, the income reduction might place them just below the threshold for taxation of Social Security benefits. Also, most of the monthly mortgage payments typically are applied to principal reduction; thus interest deductibility would be a minor tax benefit. Furthermore, the interest being paid could exceed the rate of earnings on invested funds, thereby producing real savings for the retiree.)

ILLUSTRATION 5-1
Justification of Less Than 100 Percent Replacement Ratio

Patty and Ken Tailor (both aged 64) have a combined salary of $100,000 ($50,000 each) and would like to maintain their current purchasing power when they retire next year. If their anticipated reduced nonwork expenses are offset by increased living expenses (see below), they can maintain their purchasing power by having a retirement income of 80 percent of their salary, as illustrated below.

Working salary		$100,000
Less FICA taxes[1]	$ 7,650	
Less increase in standard deduction[2]	0	
Less tax savings on tax-free part of Social Security[3]	840	
Less state and local tax reduction[4]	1,400	
Less deductible medical expenses[5]	0	
Less reduced living expenses[6]	0	
Less retirement savings[7]	10,000	
Reductions subtotal		19,890
Total purchasing power needed		$ 80,110
Percentage of final salary needed (approximate)		80%

1. Since each earns $50,000, each pays $3,825 in FICA taxes.
2. No increase in standard deduction will occur because they itemize using Schedule A.
3. Patty and Ken will get $20,000 in Social Security; $3,000 will be received tax free for a savings of $840 at the 28 percent tax bracket.
4. The Tailors will get a sliding scale rebate on their property taxes equal to $1,400.
5. They will not take a medical deduction.
6. The Tailors think any reduced living expenses in retirement from work will be offset by increased retirement expenses (see below).
7. The Tailors had been saving 10 percent of their salary in a 401(k) plan (5 percent each).

Absence of Dependent Children. The expense of supporting dependent children is usually completed by the time a client enters retirement. Be cautious, however, because retirees, especially those who married later in life, occasionally have children who are not self-supporting and will require continued financial support during some of the clients' retirement years.

Senior Citizen Discounts. Special reductions in price are given to senior citizens. Some reductions, such as certain AARP discounts, are available at age 50. Many businesses, however, require proof of age 65 (usually by having a Medicare card) to qualify for discounts on prescriptions, clothing, and restaurant meals. Discounts typically range from 5 to 15 percent of an item's cost.

No Longer Saving for Retirement. For many retirees, retirement is not a time to continue to save for retirement. Cessation of payments to contributory pension plans, lack of eligibility for IRA or Keogh plan contributions, and just the psychological fact of being retired can help to weaken retirees' motivation to save for the future. Note that a retired worker's income can fall by the amount being saved with no concurrent reduction in standard of living. Therefore a retired worker who has been saving 10 percent of income needs only to maintain an "inflation protected" 90 percent (before tax) of income to enjoy the same purchasing power.

Increased Living Expenses. Some retirement planners are rather uncomfortable with recommending a planned reduction in income in the first year of retirement. These planners believe that certain factors suggest that during the first year of retirement, at least as much if not more income will be required to maintain the preretirement standard of living. Let's take a closer look at these factors.

Medical Expenses. Without question, medical expenses will increase over time for virtually all clients. The mere act of aging and the associated health problems generate additional demands for medical services. Even if advancing age does not create an increase in an individual's demands for medical services, inflation in these costs will. Furthermore, increases in inflation are not evenly distributed in the various medical care disciplines, and those services that will potentially affect retirees have been hit hardest. For example, over the past 20 years, the cost of hospital rooms has risen 719 percent, professional medical services have risen 406 percent, and prescription drugs have risen 196 percent. This final increase does not consider the prices for some of the newer, more costly wonder drugs.

Although retirees are often covered by Medicare and other health insurance, the trend in these coverages has been toward cost containment—defined by the government and the insurance companies as that of shifting more of the medical cost to the insured by means of larger deductibles and coinsurance payments. These higher medical expenses would be in addition to the increased premiums for the insurance.

Travel, Vacations, and Other Lifestyle Changes. Many clients expect to devote considerably more time to travel and vacations upon retirement than they did during their working years. Increased leisure time, once a scarce commodity, now provides the opportunity to travel. Unfortunately, vacationing can be an expensive activity. Indeed, an increase in vacation activities represents a rise in the standard of living and will require additional income.

Dependents. As previously stated, parents usually need less income during the first year of retirement because they no longer financially support their children, who typically become self-supporting prior to parental retirement. However, many retirees still have dependents to support. Many parents have children with mental or physical problems who will require long-term custodial and financial care throughout the retirement years.

YOUR FINANCIAL SERVICES PRACTICE:
WARNING YOUR CLIENTS ABOUT THE RISKS

Whether your clients accept an 80 percent replacement ratio or feel something less is necessary, it should be stressed that there is no definitive answer to determine absolutely if the postretirement income should be less than, equal to, or greater than that of the preretirement years.

Estimating financial needs during the first year of retirement is like trying to hit a moving target when you are blindfolded: Your aim is obscured by many unknown variables and the target is hard to draw a bead on.

Because medical care, surgical techniques, and drugs are helping to prolong life, other retirees may have to provide for their aged parents who no longer possess the wherewithal to do so themselves.

Additional Services. As people age, they often need to hire others to perform services that they previously performed themselves. This can include a wide number of physically demanding activities such as cutting the lawn, working on the car, painting the house, climbing ladders to make repairs, and shoveling snow. It may also include hiring individuals for housecleaning or caring for an infirm spouse or other family member. Some physical impairment may require a change in transportation mode—such as a change from public transportation to taking taxis—which will mean an increased expense.

Expense Method

expense method

A second way planners can estimate their client's retirement needs *in the first year of retirement* is by using the *expense-method* approach. The expense method of retirement planning focuses on the projected expenses that the retiree will have in the first year of retirement. For example, if the 64-year-old near-retiree expects to have $3,000 in monthly bills ($36,000 annually), then the retirement income for that retiree should maintain $36,000 worth of purchasing power in today's dollars. If, however, a younger client is involved, more speculative estimates of retirement expenses must be made (and periodically revised).

A list of expenses that should be considered includes expenses that may be unique to the particular client as well as other, more general expenses. As noted for the replacement-ratio approach, expenses that tend to increase for retirees include the following:

- utilities and telephone
- medical, dental, drugs, health insurance
- house upkeep, repairs, maintenance, property insurance
- recreation, entertainment, travel, dining
- contributions, gifts

ILLUSTRATION 5-2
Understanding the Expense Method

Your clients, Bob and Betty Smith, both aged 64, would like to maintain their current purchasing power when they retire next year. They can do this by having an annual income of $40,860 as illustrated below. Note that the figures are estimates of their expenses during retirement (some are higher than their current expenses and some are lower than their current expenses). Also note that postretirement inflation will be accounted for later.

Estimated Retirement Living Expenses (in Current Dollars)

	Per Month x 12 = Per Year	
1. Food	$ 500	$ 6,000
2. Housing:		
a. Rent/mortgage payment	400	4,800
b. Insurance (if separate payment)	25	300
c. Property taxes (if separate payment)	150	1,800
d. Utilities	180	2,160
e. Maintenance (if owned)	100	1,200
3. Clothing and Personal Care:		
a. Wife	75	900
b. Husband	75	900
4. Medical Expenses:		
a. Doctor (HMO)	75	900
b. Dentist	20	240
c. Medicines	75	900
5. Transportation:		
a. Car payments	130	1,560
b. Gas	50	600
c. Insurance	50	600
d. Car maintenance (tires and repairs)	30	360
6. Miscellaneous Expenses:		
a. Entertainment	150	1,800
b. Travel	200	2,400
c. Hobbies	50	600
d. Other	100	1,200
e. Club fees and dues	20	240
7. Insurance	100	1,200
8. Gifts and contributions	50	600
9. State, local, and federal taxes	800	9,600
10. Total expenses (current dollars)	3,405	40,860

YOUR FINANCIAL SERVICES PRACTICE:
RATIO VERSUS EXPENSE METHOD

If your worksheet or computer model gives you a choice of whether to use a replacement ratio or expense amount, consider the following:
- The expense method usually works well for clients at or near retirement since they have a handle on their projected retirement budget.
- The replacement-ratio method usually works well for younger clients since they do not have a handle on their retirement expenses but can sometimes gauge the standard of living they want to enjoy.
- To predict final salary for the replacement ratio of a younger client, one can do the following:
  - Put a growth factor onto current salary and do a time value calculation (this is sometimes done for you by the worksheet).
  - Examine the salaries of those retiring today who hold the position the client feels he or she will attain by retirement.
  - Look at salary scales when applicable.

Conversely, some expenses tend to decrease for the retiree. These include the following:

- mortgage payments
- food
- clothing
- income taxes
- property taxes
- transportation costs (car maintenance, insurance)
- debt repayment (charge accounts, personal loans)
- child support, alimony
- household furnishings

REFINING THE EXPENSE AND REPLACEMENT RATIO ASSUMPTIONS

When we talked above about expenditures that tend to increase or decrease for retirees, we were focusing on the period immediately following retirement. But what about later retirement? For example, travel and recreation expenses tend to increase immediately after retirement, but clients in their 90s will seldom continue to spend heavily on these categories. To better account for clients' spending patterns later in retirement, there needs to be a clarification of the proper replacement ratio or expense method used. In other words, while accounting for an initial downward adjustment to expenditures, both the ratio and expense methods ignore the fact that spending patterns voluntarily decline over the retirement period and throughout the aging process (especially for those with adequate Medigap and long-term care insurance). Consider the following changes in several expenditures based on data from the Consumer Expenditure Survey. (See table 5-2.)

TABLE 5-2
Expenditure Level for 65–74 and 75+ Age Groups with $40,000+ Income (Nearly $60,000+ in 1999 dollars)

Expenditure Category	65–74	75+	Change
Food	$ 5,779	$ 3,970	–1,809
Housing	12,027	9,678	–2,349
Apparel	2,160	1,256	–904
Transportation	8,185	5,428	–2,757
Health Care	2,385	3,189	804
Entertainment	2,108	1,027	–1,081
Personal Insurance/Pensions	4,540	2,678	–1,862
Total*	$43,967	$36,825	–7,142

* Minor categories are not reported; therefore, categories do not sum to total.

Note that there is nearly a 20 percent decline in spending. Experts believe this decline is a voluntary reduction based on the fact that a constant real income level was maintained. In other words, people had the same amount of income but spent less.

In addition to the empirical data provided, we can make the following generalizations:

- Older age itself means a more sedentary existence for many clients. The timing will vary from client to client, but Mother Nature will eventually have her way. For example, some people are forced to give up their car along with commensurate payment and insurance expenses; others cut back on travel and recreation expenses because of limited mobility.
- The longer the life expectancy assumed for the client, the greater the effect on the client's replacement ratio.
- Many current models typically ignore the fact that clients may receive financial and caregiving support from children, other family members, churches and synagogues, and other support mechanisms.
- Many current models typically ignore the existence of long-term care insurance. Because financial expenditures for a nursing home may be covered in part or in whole, the money needed for the time spent in a nursing home can be reduced. (Perhaps a better way to look at this is to reduce the life expectancy assumption to accommodate the fact that some clients will have many expenses for the last 12 to 18 months of their life paid for by long-term care insurance.)
- Current models ignore the fact that some clients move to an area with a lower cost of living and can spend less to receive the same goods and services. (Perhaps a better way to deal with this is to reduce the post-retirement inflation assumption for the client.)

A Comparison of Alternative Models

Accumulation models should paint as accurate a picture of retirement as possible. Toward this end, planners and clients should account for a reduction in spending by the demographic cohort age 75 and over. Additionally, to be more precise, all available data and research indicate that there is a gradual reduction in spending starting shortly after retirement. Spending decreases are natural, voluntary, and acceptable, and they should be reflected in the client's accumulation model. The downward adjustment in spending by age 75 is approximately 20 percent of the initial spending levels during retirement that starts at age 65. Consequently, if the initial replacement ratio for age 65 is set at 80 percent of preretirement earnings, the age 75 ratio would be 64 percent (20 percent times 80 percent equals a 16-point reduction) of preretirement earnings.

There are two potential ways to correct accumulation models. The first is to use a weighted average to reflect a lower overall replacement ratio during the retirement period. This average will depend upon a client's life expectancy. For example, a client who assumes an initial replacement ratio of 80 percent with a life expectancy of 25 years after retirement should use a blended rate of 70 percent (rounded from 70.4). (See table 5-3.)

The second alternative is to account for a downward reduction in annual income for consumption at the predetermined age of 75. If this scenario is adopted, the accumulation model needs to accommodate separate replacement ratios for each time period (such as age 65–74 and 75 and older). This two-step method will generate a larger annual amount that the client needs to save when compared with the amount calculated by the blended rate method. Assuming a gradual reduction in spending, the two-step method leads to greater over-estimation of savings for the early retirement years, however.

Other Assumptions

In addition to making assumptions concerning inflation, retirement age, longevity, and the amount/percentage of final salary to be deemed the appropriate standard of living (replacement ratio), planners must predict tax

TABLE 5-3
Blended Replacement Ratios

Life Expectancy at Retirement	80%	75%	70%	65%
10	.800	.750	.700	.650
15	.750	.700	.654	.610
20	.720	.675	.630	.585
25	.704	.660	.616	.572
30	.693	.652	.608	.565

rates and investment returns. Some factors to consider that might help in this process are

- the historical return of the retirement portfolio with which a client is comfortable
- the ability of a client to use tax-sheltered qualified plans and IRAs
- the potential future income the retiree is expecting. (Note that past thinking has been to assume that a retiree's tax rate will decline because his or her income has declined; however, this will not be the case if the planner has done a good job!)
- the propensity to invest more conservatively (and consequently have a lower rate of return) as a client approaches retirement and after a client retires
- the propensity of clients to invest too conservatively in their qualified plan at work
- the inevitable federal tax law changes that are likely to occur
- the state income taxes that may be applicable to a relocated client
- the planner's investment recommendations
- the possibility of an inheritance from parents
- the possibility of a lump-sum payment for retirement

These and other considerations can help a planner to tailor his or her assumptions to a client's specific situation.

step-up rate

Many models look at savings as a percentage of income. If this is the case, the amount saved each year increases as salary increases. Some models have the added flexibility of a *step-up rate*, which is the percentage growth in the client's annual allocation to savings. The step-up rate typically corresponds to the client's projected growth rate in compensation, thus keeping the rate of savings a constant percentage. In other words, clients can increase retirement savings in a painless way by bolstering savings with future salary increases. To best predict this assumption, contracts, salary scales, and salary history should be reviewed. Such a review will tell the planner about expected increases in income.

HOW WORKSHEETS AND COMPUTER MODELS WORK

Now that we have examined the assumptions used in many worksheets and computer models, it is time to turn to an examination of the models themselves. Given the variety of packages available, each having its own unique features, we are presented with a daunting task. There is a manageable solution to this problem, however. The next few pages take a five-step approach to acquainting you with worksheets and computer models. The first step is to discuss the theory behind a generic computer model. This will demystify the process and allow you to understand the common theory that is utilized in most software. The second step is to introduce a shorthand formula that can be used to identify the retirement need. This formula will enable you to show clients a quick estimate of their need. It also can be used in conjunction with other models to give a range of possible targets (thus dispelling the myth that the numbers are etched in stone). The third step is to introduce you to a consumer worksheet. The worksheet we have chosen first appeared in *U.S. News and World Report* several years ago and is widely used. The fourth step is to introduce you to our version of a planner's worksheet. The model can be used to create a target savings amount for your client. The fifth step is to introduce you to Internet-based models and proprietary software. In steps two through four, we will use a case study approach to demonstrate how a retirement needs analysis is conducted.

The Theory Behind a Generic Computer Model

Computer software packages use many different approaches for calculating retirement fund needs. The following steps are typical of the internal workings of these models.

Step 1: Projecting Retirement Income from Existing Resources

One essential element in any retirement needs analysis is knowing where a client stands now. Planners usually use a fact finder in conjunction with their software. Information from the fact finder that must be input into the computer includes Social Security estimates (typically in current dollars), defined-benefit pension estimates (typically in current dollars), defined-contribution retirement plan estimates (the current account balance), and private savings (including IRAs, annuities, and other investment funds earmarked for retirement).

Step 2: Comparing What a Client Has to What a Client Needs

Many models determine a retirement income shortfall (RIS). Determining the RIS is a simple matter of subtracting the annual income that is projected from existing resources from the annual income that is needed at retirement (which is arrived at by either a replacement-ratio or an expense approach). To produce the income shortfall requires a "pot of money" that the planner must help the client fill.

Example :	Patty (aged 60) has a $100,000 salary. After using the replacement-ratio approach, Patty and her planner feel that an $80,000 (80 percent) target will meet her desired living standards. (Note that the $80,000 figure will have to be increased after her first year of

retirement to account for inflation.) In addition, Patty and her planner determine that her Social Security, pension, and *current* savings will provide $60,000 per year. Patty therefore has a shortfall of $20,000 ($80,000 need minus $60,000 resources). The computer software will effectively calculate the amount necessary at retirement to produce this stream of income over her projected lifetime. This amount becomes one target for which the planner and Patty must save.

Step 3: Providing Inflation Protection for Income Derived from Existing Resources

Determining this income shortfall is only one part of the picture. In addition, any computer model must take into consideration the decline in purchasing power that is the result of continued inflation. For example, a $25,000 company pension that is not increased for inflation will have significantly less purchasing power at age 75 than at age 65.

Most sources of income (other than Social Security, which is subject to an annual cost-of-living adjustment, or COLA) will be subject to a decline in purchasing power (or DIPP). To make up for this DIPP, the computer model will determine an additional amount that must be saved in order to keep up with the increasing needs during retirement. This additional "pot of money" that the planner must help to fill is sometimes called an existing-resources DIPP fund.

Example:	Patty's pension at retirement was $40,000 annually and her other savings at retirement were converted to a $10,000-a-year annuity. Due to the effects of the DIPP, her pension and annuity must be bolstered each year to maintain a level purchasing power—she must maintain her own COLA fund for these amounts. The $10,000 that she will receive from Social Security is already adjusted for inflation and need not be considered for this calculation.

Step 4: Computing the Sum Needed at Retirement

Once the RIS is calculated and all the sources of income that need DIPP protection have been identified, the program will calculate the sum the client will need to have saved by the time he or she retires. The following describes what the computer actually calculates.

- *RIS calculation.* Most programs will calculate a single sum representing the amount needed to provide the RIS stream of income over the expected lifetime of the retiree. To reflect the impact of DIPP, the program will actually calculate the amount needed to provide an increasing stream of income so as not to lose ground against inflation. Technically speaking, the number calculated is the present value (at retirement) of the inflation-protected RIS stream of income over the projected lifetime or payment period. Note that with this method, the amount that is calculated will be exhausted at the end of the expected lifetime.
- *DIPP fund calculation.* In the previous calculation the impact of DIPP was actually taken into account for determining the amount needed to meet the RIS needs. A second calculation is needed to provide an inflation-protected supplement for other sources of income that are subject to DIPP. An additional amount is needed from which to make increasing payments to supplement the fixed payment stream. Technically, the number that is calculated represents the sum of the present values (at retirement) of all the inflation adjustments needed for all existing-resource income that will not automatically adjust for inflation.

Example:	To protect against a 4 percent inflation rate, the $50,000 first-year retirement income from existing non-inflation-adjusted resources must grow to $52,000 in the second year ($50,000 x 1.04), to $54,080 in the third year ($50,000 x 1.042), and to $56,243 in the fourth year ($50,000 x 1.043), and must continue to grow at 4 percent a year. Thus the inflation adjustments above the $50,000 first-year retirement income are $2,000 in the second year, $4,080 in the third year, $6,243 in the fourth year, and so on for the projected life of the client. It is these inflation adjustments that are discounted back to the retirement year and added together to calculate the existing-resource DIPP fund.

- *Adding the RIS and DIPP numbers.* This "retirement target" amount represents the additional amount that the individual needs to save by retirement age in order to meet his or her financial objectives.

Step 5: Determining an Annual Savings Amount to Achieve the Targeted Amount

Some programs will stop after step 4. However, most will also figure out the stream of contributions (annual savings) needed to meet the target. This calculation may either provide an answer expressed as a level savings stream or as a stepped-up stream that increases with a person's salary.

Determining Retirement Needs Using a Shorthand Formula

The goal of the shorthand formula is to calculate the capital needed at retirement that will sustain a person at a constant standard of living until death. In other words, it tells a client how much he or she needs to save in order to have enough annual income each and every year of retirement to maintain his or her current standard of living. The assumptions used in the formula method are the replacement ratio needed, expected inflation, anticipated rate of return, and the duration of retirement. The formula used is

$$C_r = E_r \left[\frac{1 - a^n}{1 - a} \right]$$

where

C_r = capital needed at retirement in then-current dollars

E_r = income needed in the first year of retirment in then-current dollars

$$a = \frac{1 + i}{1 + r}$$

i = inflation rate

r = after-tax rate of return

n = duration of retirement

It is important to emphasize that E_r (income needed in the first year of retirement) and C_r (capital needed at retirement) are in then-current dollars. One approach to calculating E_r is to specify the retirement income needed in today's dollars and adjust for the inflation anticipated between today and the year of retirement. Using future value concepts,

$$E_r = E_t (1 + i)^b$$

where

E_t = target retirement income in today's dollars

b = number of years until retirement

Some examples will help to illustrate.

Example 1:	After analyzing the replacement ratio needed (using our prior discussion), the planner feels that Stan and Judy need $48,000 in then-current dollars in their first year of retirement to maintain their standard of living. In addition, the planner specifies that

- a 5 percent inflation assumption should be used
- a 7 percent rate of return assumption should be used
- retirement is projected to last 20 years

Step 1: Assign numbers to the variables.

$$E_r = \$48,000$$
$$i = 5\%$$
$$r = 7\%$$
$$n = 20 \text{ years}$$

Step 2: Solve for *a*.

$$\frac{1 + .05}{1 + .07} = .9813$$

Step 3: Solve the formula.

$$C_r = E_r \left| \frac{1 - a^n}{1 - a} \right|$$

$$= \$48,000 \left[\frac{1 - .6855}{.0187} \right]$$

$$= \$48,000 \left[\frac{.314}{.0187} \right]$$

$$= \$48,000 \times 16.813$$

$$= \$807,024$$

Stan and Judy need $807,024 for retirement.

Example 2:	Fred and Wilma also need a replacement ratio of $48,000. They are, however, more optimistic about living longer than Stan and Judy (example 1) and feel they need to use the following assumptions:

- 5 percent inflation (same as example 1)
- 7 percent rate of return (same as example 1)
- 35 years for life expectancy (15 years longer than example 1)

Step 1: Assign numbers to the variables.

$$E_r = \$48,000$$
$$i = 5\%$$
$$r = 7\%$$
$$n = 35$$

Step 2: Solve for *a*.

$$\frac{1 + .05}{1 + .07} = .9813$$

Step 3: Solve the formula.

$$C_r = E_r \left| \frac{1 - a^n}{1 - a} \right|$$

$$= \$48,000 \left| \frac{1 - (.9813^{35})}{1 - .9813} \right|$$

$$= \$48,000 \left[\frac{1 - .5165}{.0187} \right]$$

$$= \$48,000 \times 25.855$$

$$= \$1,241,040$$

Fred and Wilma need $1,241,040 for retirement. This is $434,016 more than Stan and Judy because of the 15 years of additional life expectancy.

Determining Retirement Needs Using a Consumer Worksheet

The worksheet that follows can be used to illustrate the percentage of salary a person needs to save each year. Conceptually this worksheet makes most of the assumptions for you—for example, an 80 percent replacement ratio (step 2) and a 25-year life expectancy (see line 8 explanation). While this simplicity can be a limitation for a planner (as discussed earlier), it may be a blessing for the weary client. For this reason planners may want to use this type of worksheet as an informational piece in a client mailer (with strong comments about its limitations).

Example:	The following financial information applies to Bob and Donna:

- They are 15 years from retirement.
- Their current salary is $100,000.
- They have a defined-benefit plan of $2,000 a month ($24,000 annually).
- Their combined Social Security benefits are estimated to be $18,000.
- They have $130,000 in IRAs, 401(k) plans, and mutual funds.

Using the worksheet in table 5-4, Bob and Donna can see that they need to save 25 percent of their current salary.

Determining Retirement Needs Using a Planner's Worksheet

The worksheets in tables 5-5, 5-6, 5-7, and 5-8 allow the planner to focus on tailoring a retirement needs analysis to a particular client. The first step is to list a variety of assumptions (these are discussed with the clients prior to filling out the worksheets). The second step is to list factors generated from time-value-of-money tables. An explanation of how each factor was determined follows the worksheets in the commentary for tables 5-9 through 5-16. The third step is to calculate the amount the clients need to save in the initial year.

Case Study Facts

Ann Stack (aged 44 in the current year) and Robert Stack (aged 46 in the current year) are married and have two children. Ann and Robert both plan to retire in 19 years unless their planner counsels otherwise. Robert will be 65 and Ann will be 63 when they retire.

Pertinent financial data includes the following:

- Ann earns $35,000 as a schoolteacher.
- Robert earns $140,000 as an engineer.
- Ann has $64,000 in her 403(b) retirement plan.

- Ann will receive a pension of $1,400 a month at age 63.
- Robert has a 401(k) plan with $120,000 in it.
- Robert has no defined-benefit plan at work.
- Robert will receive $1,100 a month from Social Security when he retires at age 65.

TABLE 5-4
Worksheet: Calculation of Retirement Expenses—Alternative 2

	Your Circumstances	Example
1. Current annual gross salary	$_____	$ 100,000
2. Retirement-income target (multiply line 1 by 0.8—80 percent target)	$_____	80,000
3. Estimated annual benefit from pension plan, not including IRAs, 401(k)s, 403(b)s, or profit-sharing plans[1]	$_____	24,000
4. Estimated annual Social Security benefits[1]	$_____	18,000
5. Total retirement benefits (add lines 3 and 4)	$_____	42,000
6. Income gap (subtract line 5 from line 2)[2]	$_____	38,000
7. Adjust gap to reflect inflation (multiply line 6 by factor A, below)	$_____	68,400
8. Capital needed to generate additional income and close gap (multiply line 7 by 16.3)[3]	$_____	1,114,920
9. Extra capital needed to offset inflation's impact on pension (multiply line 3 by factor B, below)	$_____	204,000
10. Total capital needed (add lines 8 and 9)	$_____	1,318,920
11. Total current retirement savings (includes balances in IRAs, 401(k)s, profit-sharing plans, mutual funds, CDs)	$_____	130,000
12. Value of savings at retirement (multiply line 11 by factor C, below)	$_____	416,000
13. Net capital gap (subtract line 12 from line 10)	$_____	902,920
14. Annual amount in current dollars to start saving now to cover the gap (divide line 13 by factor D, below)[4]	$_____	25, 578
15. Percentage of salary to be saved each year (divide line 14 by line 1)[5]	_____ %	25%

TABLE 5-4 (Continued)
Worksheet: Calculation of Retirement Expenses—Alternative 2*

Factors for Worksheet Calculations Assuming 4 Percent Inflation
and 8 Percent Rate of Return

Years to Retirement	Factor A	Factor B	Factor C	Factor D
10	1.5	7.0	2.2	17.5
15	1.8	8.5	3.2	35.3
20	2.2	10.3	4.7	63.3
25	2.7	12.6	6.9	107.0
30	3.2	15.3	10.1	174.0

[1] Lines 3 and 4: Employers can provide annual estimates of your projected retirement pay; estimates of Social Security benefits are available from the Social Security Administration at (800) 937-2000. Both figures will be stated in current dollars, not in the high amounts that you will receive if your wages keep up with inflation. The worksheet takes this into consideration.

[2] Line 6: Even if a large pension lets you avoid an income gap, proceed to line 9 to determine the assets you may need to make up for the erosion of a fixed pension payment by inflation.

[3] Line 8: This calculation includes a determination of how much capital you will need to keep up with inflation after retirement and assumes that you will *deplete the capital over a 25-year period.*

[4] Line 14: Amount includes investments earmarked for retirement and payments by employee and employer to defined-contribution retirement plans such as 401(k)s and 403(b)s. The formula assumes you will increase annual savings at the same rate as inflation.

[5] Line 15: Assuming earnings rise with inflation, you can save a set percentage of gross pay each year, and the actual amount you stash away will increase annually.

* Copyright 1989 *U.S. News & World Report*, L.P. Reprinted with permission.

- Ann will receive $800 a month from Social Security when she retires at age 63.
- Both Social Security amounts are in today's dollars and, where applicable, reflect early retirement reductions.
- They have joint savings of $50,000 earmarked for retirement.
- They have sufficient savings to meet their other long-term financial goals, including sending their children to college.
- After an initial interview with the planner, it was decided that the following assumptions will be used:

- – an inflation rate of 4 percent
- – an expected duration of retirement of 25 years. (Note that the Stacks have decided to set aside the potential gain from the sale of their home and vacation home to cover them should they live longer than the 25-year period—if not, this will be part of the legacy they leave their children.)
- – an after-tax rate of return of 7 percent after retirement
- – an 80 percent replacement ratio
- – a savings step-up rate of 6 percent. (This means that the annual allocation to savings will increase by 6 percent each year until retirement.)

TABLE 5-5
Planner's Worksheet—Step 1: List Assumptions

	ASSUMPTIONS	
A1.	Inflation rate prior to retirement	4%
A2.	Inflation rate after retirement	4%
A3.	Number of years until retirement	19 Yrs.
A4.	Expected duration of retirement	25 Yrs.
A5.	Rate of return prior to retirement	8%
A6.	Rate of return after retirement	7%
A7.	Savings step-up rate	6%

TABLE 5-6
Planner's Worksheet—Step 2: Calculate Factors

The following factors were calculated using tables 5-9 through 5-16, which follow your blank worksheet in this book. After the tables is a detailed explanation (and example) of how to extract the appropriate factor.

	FACTORS		Assumptions (from table 5-5)
F1.	Preretirement inflation factor	2.11	Table 5-9; years = A3, rate = A1
F2.	Retirement needs present value factor	17.936	Table 5-10; years = A4, rate = A6 minus A2
F3.	Current assets future value factor	4.32	Table 5-9; years = A3, rate = A5
F4.	Defined-benefit income present value factor	12.469	Table 5-10; years = A4, rate = A6
F5.	Savings rate factor	0.01435	Table 5-14; years = A3, rate = A7 minus A5

TABLE 5-7
Planner's Worksheet
Step 3: Computation of Retirement Need and Amount to Be Saved

		COMPUTATIONS		
L1.		Projected annual retirement budget	$140,000	(80% of $175,000)
L2.	–	Social Security benefit	22,800	(Ann and Robert annual total)
L3.	=	Net annual need in current dollars	$117,200	
L4.	x	F1 factor	2.11	
L5.	=	Inflation-adjusted annual retirement need	247,292	
L6.	x	F2 factor	17.936	
L7.	=	Total resources needed for retirement		$4,435,429
L8.		Total in defined-contribution plans	184,000	
L9.	+	Total private savings earmarked for retirement	50,000	
L10.	=	Current assets available for retirement	234,000	
L11.	x	F3 factor	4.32	
L12.	=	Future value of current assets		$1,010,880
L13.		Annual income from defined-benefit plan	16,800	(Ann's annual pension)
L14.	x	F1 factor	2.11	
L15.	=	Inflation-adjusted annual income from defined-benefit plan	35,448	
	x	F4 factor	12.469	
L17.	=	Lump-sum value of defined-benefit plan		442,001
L18.		Total resources available for retirement (line 12 and line 17)		1,452,801
L19.		Additional amount you need to accumulate by retirement		2,982,628
L20.	x	F5 factor		0.01435
L21.	=	Amount you need to save—first year		$42,801 (24% of salary)

(Savings in each subsequent year must increase by the savings step-up rate, 6%)

TABLE 5-8
Retirement Planning Worksheet

ASSUMPTIONS

A1.	Inflation rate prior to retirement	_____
A2.	Inflation rate after retirement	_____
A3.	Number of years until retirement	_____
A4.	Expected duration of retirement	_____
A5.	Rate of return prior to retirement	_____
A6.	Rate of return after retirement	_____
A7.	Savings step-up rate	_____

FACTORS

F1.	Preretirement inflation factor	_____
F2.	Retirement needs present value factor	_____
F3.	Current assets future value factor	_____
F4.	Defined-benefit present value factor	_____
F5.	Savings rate factor	_____

COMPUTATIONS

L1.		Projected annual retirement budget	_____
L2.	−	Social Security benefit	_____
L3.	=	Net annual need in current dollars	_____
L4.	x	F1 factor	_____
L5.	=	Inflation-adjusted annual retirement need	_____
L6.	x	F2 factor	_____
L7.	=	Total resources needed for retirement	_____
L8.		Total in defined-contribution plans	_____
L9.	+	Total private savings earmarked for retirement	_____
L10.	=	Current assets available for retirement	_____
L11.	x	F3 factor	_____
L12.	=	Future value of current assets	_____
L13.		Annual income from defined-benefit plan	_____
L14.	x	F1 factor	_____
L15.	=	Inflation-adjusted annual income from defined-benefit plan	_____
	x	F4 factor	_____
L17.	=	Lump-sum value of defined-benefit plan	_____
L18.		Total resources available for retirement (line 12 and line 17)	_____
L19.		Additional amount you need to accumulate by retirement	_____
L20.	x	F5 factor	_____
L21.	=	Amount you need to save—first year	_____

(Savings in each subsequent year must increase by the savings step-up rate, 6%)

THE INFLATION AND FUTURE VALUE FACTORS

Table 5-9 is used to select the appropriate Preretirement Inflation Factor (F1) and Current Assets Future Value Factor (F3) for use in the Retirement Planning Worksheet.

TABLE 5-9
Future Value Factors

Yrs	0%	1%	2%	3%	4%	5%	6%
1	1.00	1.01	1.02	1.03	1.04	1.05	1.06
2	1.00	1.02	1.04	1.06	1.08	1.10	1.12
3	1.00	1.03	1.06	1.09	1.12	1.16	1.19
4	1.00	1.04	1.08	1.13	1.17	1.22	1.26
5	1.00	1.05	1.10	1.16	1.22	1.28	1.34
6	1.00	1.06	1.13	1.19	1.27	1.34	1.42
7	1.00	1.07	1.15	1.23	1.32	1.41	1.50
8	1.00	1.08	1.17	1.27	1.37	1.48	1.59
9	1.00	1.09	1.20	1.30	1.42	1.55	1.69
10	1.00	1.10	1.22	1.34	1.48	1.63	1.79
11	1.00	1.12	1.24	1.38	1.54	1.71	1.90
12	1.00	1.13	1.27	1.43	1.60	1.80	2.01
13	1.00	1.14	1.29	1.47	1.67	1.89	2.13
14	1.00	1.15	1.32	1.51	1.73	1.98	2.26
15	1.00	1.16	1.35	1.56	1.80	2.08	2.40
16	1.00	1.17	1.37	1.60	1.87	2.18	2.54
17	1.00	1.18	1.40	1.65	1.95	2.29	2.69
18	1.00	1.20	1.43	1.70	2.03	2.41	**2.85**
19	1.00	1.21	1.46	1.75	**2.11**	2.53	3.03
20	1.00	1.22	1.49	1.81	2.19	2.65	3.21
21	1.00	1.23	1.52	1.86	2.28	2.79	3.40
22	1.00	1.24	1.55	1.92	2.37	2.93	3.60
23	1.00	1.26	1.58	1.97	2.46	3.07	3.82
24	1.00	1.27	1.61	2.03	2.56	3.23	4.05
25	1.00	1.28	1.64	2.09	2.67	3.39	4.29
26	1.00	1.30	1.67	2.16	2.77	3.56	4.55
27	1.00	1.31	1.71	2.22	2.88	3.73	4.82
28	1.00	1.32	1.74	2.29	3.00	3.92	5.11
29	1.00	1.33	1.78	2.36	3.12	4.12	5.42
30	1.00	1.35	1.81	2.43	3.24	4.32	5.74
31	1.00	1.36	1.85	2.50	3.37	4.54	6.09
32	1.00	1.37	1.88	2.58	3.51	4.76	6.45
33	1.00	1.39	1.92	2.65	3.65	5.00	6.84
34	1.00	1.40	1.96	2.73	3.79	5.25	7.25
35	1.00	1.42	2.00	2.81	3.95	5.52	7.69
36	1.00	1.43	2.04	2.90	4.10	5.79	8.15
37	1.00	1.45	2.08	2.99	4.27	6.08	8.64
38	1.00	1.46	2.12	3.07	4.44	6.39	9.15
39	1.00	1.47	2.16	3.17	4.62	6.70	9.70
40	1.00	1.49	2.21	3.26	4.80	7.04	10.29
41	1.00	1.50	2.25	3.36	4.99	7.39	10.90
42	1.00	1.52	2.30	3.46	5.19	7.76	11.56
43	1.00	1.53	2.34	3.56	5.40	8.15	12.25
44	1.00	1.55	2.39	3.67	5.62	8.56	12.99
45	1.00	1.56	2.44	3.78	5.84	8.99	13.76

An explanation of the use of table 5-9 appears on the page following these tables under the headings "Selecting the Preretirement Inflation Factor (F-1)" and "Selecting the Current Assets Future Value Factor (F-3)."

TABLE 5-9 (Continued)
Future Value Factors

Yrs	7%	8%	9%	10%	11%	12%	15%	20%
				Rate				
1	1.07	1.08	1.09	1.10	1.11	1.12	1.15	1.20
2	1.14	1.17	1.19	1.21	1.23	1.25	1.32	1.44
3	1.23	1.26	1.30	1.33	1.37	1.40	1.52	1.73
4	1.31	1.36	1.41	1.46	1.52	1.57	1.75	2.07
5	1.40	1.47	1.54	1.61	1.69	1.76	2.01	2.49
6	1.50	1.59	1.68	1.77	1.87	1.97	2.31	2.99
7	1.61	1.71	1.83	1.95	2.08	2.21	2.66	3.58
8	1.72	1.85	1.99	2.14	2.30	2.48	3.06	4.30
9	1.84	2.00	2.17	2.36	2.56	2.77	3.52	5.16
10	1.97	2.16	2.37	2.59	2.84	3.11	4.05	6.19
11	2.10	2.33	2.58	2.85	3.15	3.48	4.65	7.43
12	2.25	2.52	**2.81**	3.14	3.50	3.90	5.35	8.92
13	2.41	2.72	3.07	3.45	3.88	4.36	6.15	10.70
14	2.58	2.94	3.34	3.80	4.31	4.89	7.08	12.84
15	2.76	3.17	3.64	4.18	4.78	5.47	8.14	15.41
16	2.95	3.43	3.97	4.59	5.31	6.13	9.36	18.49
17	3.16	3.70	4.33	5.05	5.90	6.87	10.76	22.19
18	3.38	4.00	4.72	5.56	6.54	7.69	12.38	26.62
19	3.62	4.32	5.14	6.12	7.26	8.61	14.23	31.95
20	3.87	4.66	5.60	6.73	8.06	9.65	16.37	38.34
21	4.14	5.03	6.11	7.40	8.95	10.80	18.82	46.01
22	4.43	5.44	6.66	8.14	9.93	12.10	21.64	55.21
23	4.74	5.87	7.26	8.95	11.03	13.55	24.89	66.25
24	5.07	6.34	7.91	9.85	12.24	15.18	28.63	79.50
25	5.43	6.85	8.62	10.83	13.59	17.00	32.92	95.40
26	5.81	7.40	9.40	11.92	15.08	19.04	37.86	114.48
27	6.21	7.99	10.25	13.11	16.74	21.32	43.54	137.37
28	6.65	8.63	11.17	14.42	18.58	23.88	50.07	164.84
29	7.11	9.32	12.17	15.86	20.62	26.75	57.58	197.81
30	7.61	10.06	13.27	17.45	22.89	29.96	66.21	237.38
31	8.15	10.87	14.46	19.19	25.41	33.56	76.14	284.85
32	8.72	11.74	15.76	21.11	28.21	37.58	87.57	341.82
33	9.33	12.68	17.18	23.23	31.31	42.09	100.70	410.19
34	9.98	13.69	18.73	25.55	34.75	47.14	115.80	492.22
35	10.68	14.79	20.41	28.10	38.57	52.80	133.18	590.67
36	11.42	15.97	22.25	30.91	42.82	59.14	153.15	708.80
37	12.22	17.25	24.25	34.00	47.53	66.23	176.12	850.56
38	13.08	18.63	26.44	37.40	52.76	74.18	202.54	1020.67
39	13.99	20.12	28.82	41.14	58.56	83.08	232.92	1224.81
40	14.97	21.72	31.41	45.26	65.00	93.05	267.86	1469.77
41	16.02	23.46	34.24	49.79	72.15	104.22	308.04	1763.73
42	17.14	25.34	37.32	54.76	80.09	116.72	354.25	2116.47
43	18.34	27.37	40.68	60.24	88.90	130.73	407.39	2539.77
44	19.63	29.56	44.34	66.26	98.68	146.42	468.50	3047.72
45	21.00	31.92	48.33	72.89	109.53	163.99	538.77	3657.26

ANNUITY FACTORS

Table 5-10 is used to select the appropriate Retirement Needs Present Value Factor (F2) and Defined-Benefit Present Value Factor (F4) for use in the Retirement Planning Worksheet.

TABLE 5-10
Present Value of Annuity Factors

Yrs	Rate 0%	1%	2%	3%	4%	5%	6%
1	1.000	1.000	1.000	1.000	1.000	1.000	1.000
2	2.000	1.990	1.980	1.971	1.962	1.952	1.943
3	3.000	2.970	2.942	2.913	2.886	2.859	2.833
4	4.000	3.941	3.884	3.829	3.775	3.723	3.673
5	5.000	4.902	4.808	4.717	4.630	4.546	4.465
6	6.000	5.853	5.713	5.580	5.452	5.329	5.212
7	7.000	6.795	6.601	6.417	6.242	6.076	5.917
8	8.000	7.728	7.472	7.230	7.002	6.786	6.582
9	9.000	8.652	8.325	8.020	7.733	7.463	7.210
10	10.000	9.566	9.162	8.786	8.435	8.108	7.802
11	11.000	10.471	9.983	9.530	9.111	8.722	8.360
12	12.000	11.368	10.787	10.253	9.760	9.306	8.887
13	13.000	12.255	11.575	10.954	10.385	9.863	9.384
14	14.000	13.134	12.348	11.635	10.986	10.394	9.853
15	15.000	14.004	13.106	12.296	11.563	10.899	10.295
16	16.000	14.865	13.849	12.938	12.118	11.380	10.712
17	17.000	15.718	14.578	13.561	12.652	11.838	11.106
18	18.000	16.562	15.292	14.166	13.166	12.274	11.477
19	19.000	17.398	15.992	14.754	13.659	12.690	11.828
20	20.000	18.226	16.678	15.324	14.134	13.085	12.158
21	21.000	19.046	17.351	15.877	14.590	13.462	12.470
22	22.000	19.857	18.011	**16.415**	15.029	13.821	12.764
23	23.000	20.660	18.658	16.937	15.451	14.163	13.042
24	24.000	21.456	19.292	17.444	15.857	14.489	13.303
25	25.000	22.243	19.914	17.936	16.247	14.799	13.550
26	26.000	23.023	20.523	18.413	16.622	15.094	13.783
27	27.000	23.795	21.121	18.877	16.983	15.375	14.003
28	28.000	24.560	21.707	19.327	17.330	15.643	14.211
29	29.000	25.316	22.281	19.764	17.663	15.898	14.406
30	30.000	26.066	22.844	20.188	17.984	16.141	14.591
31	31.000	26.808	23.396	20.600	18.292	16.372	14.765
32	32.000	27.542	23.938	21.000	18.588	16.593	14.929
33	33.000	28.270	24.468	21.389	18.874	16.803	15.084
34	34.000	28.990	24.989	21.766	19.148	17.003	15.230
35	35.000	29.703	25.499	22.132	19.411	17.193	15.368
36	36.000	30.409	25.999	22.487	19.665	17.374	15.498
37	37.000	31.108	26.489	22.832	19.908	17.547	15.621
38	38.000	31.800	26.969	23.167	20.143	17.711	15.737
39	39.000	32.485	27.441	23.492	20.368	17.868	15.846
40	40.000	33.163	27.903	23.808	20.584	18.017	15.949
41	41.000	33.835	28.355	24.115	20.793	18.159	16.046
42	42.000	34.500	28.799	24.412	20.993	18.294	16.138
43	43.000	35.158	29.235	24.701	21.186	18.423	16.225
44	44.000	35.810	29.662	24.982	21.371	18.546	16.306
45	45.000	36.455	30.080	25.254	21.549	18.663	16.383

An explanation of the use of table 5-10 appears on the pages following these tables under the headings "Selecting the Retirement Needs Present Value Factor (F2)" and "Selecting the Defined-Benefit Present Value Factor (F4)."

TABLE 5-10 (Continued)
Present Value of Annuity Factors

Yrs	7%	8%	9%	10%	11%	12%	15%	20%
				Interest Rate				
1	1.000	1.000	1.000	1.000	1.000	1.000	1.000	1.000
2	1.935	1.926	1.917	1.909	1.901	1.893	1.870	1.833
3	2.808	2.783	2.759	2.736	2.713	2.690	2.626	2.528
4	3.624	3.577	3.531	3.487	3.444	3.402	3.283	3.106
5	4.387	4.312	4.240	4.170	4.102	4.037	3.855	3.589
6	5.100	4.993	4.890	4.791	4.696	4.605	4.352	3.991
7	5.767	5.623	5.486	5.355	5.231	5.111	4.784	4.326
8	6.389	6.206	6.033	5.868	5.712	5.564	5.160	4.605
9	6.971	6.747	6.535	6.335	6.146	5.968	5.487	4.837
10	7.515	7.247	6.995	6.759	6.537	6.328	5.772	5.031
11	8.024	7.710	7.418	7.145	6.889	6.650	6.019	5.192
12	8.499	8.139	7.805	7.495	7.207	6.938	6.234	5.327
13	8.943	8.536	8.161	7.814	7.492	7.194	6.421	5.439
14	9.358	8.904	8.487	8.103	7.750	7.424	6.583	5.533
15	9.745	9.244	8.786	8.367	7.982	7.628	6.724	5.611
16	10.108	9.559	9.061	8.606	8.191	7.811	6.847	5.675
17	10.447	9.851	9.313	8.824	8.379	7.974	6.954	5.730
18	10.763	10.122	9.544	9.022	8.549	8.120	7.047	5.775
19	11.059	10.372	9.756	9.201	8.702	8.250	7.128	5.812
20	11.336	10.604	9.950	9.365	8.839	8.366	7.198	5.843
21	11.594	10.818	10.129	9.514	8.963	8.469	7.259	5.870
22	11.836	11.017	10.292	9.649	9.075	8.562	7.312	5.891
23	12.061	11.201	10.442	9.772	9.176	8.645	7.359	5.909
24	12.272	11.371	10.580	9.883	9.266	8.718	7.399	5.925
25	12.469	11.529	10.707	9.985	9.348	8.784	7.434	5.937
26	12.654	11.675	10.823	10.077	9.422	8.843	7.464	5.948
27	12.826	11.810	10.929	10.161	9.488	8.896	7.491	5.956
28	12.987	11.935	11.027	10.237	9.548	8.943	7.514	5.964
29	13.137	12.051	11.116	10.307	9.602	8.984	7.534	5.970
30	13.278	12.158	11.198	10.370	9.650	9.022	7.551	5.975
31	13.409	12.258	11.274	10.427	9.694	9.055	7.566	5.979
32	13.532	12.350	11.343	10.479	9.733	9.085	7.579	5.982
33	13.647	12.435	11.406	10.526	9.769	9.112	7.591	5.985
34	13.754	12.514	11.464	10.569	9.801	9.135	7.600	5.988
35	13.854	12.587	11.518	10.609	9.829	9.157	7.609	5.990
36	13.948	12.655	11.567	10.644	9.855	9.176	7.617	5.992
37	14.035	12.717	11.612	10.677	9.879	9.192	7.623	5.993
38	14.117	12.775	11.653	10.706	9.900	9.208	7.629	5.994
39	14.193	12.829	11.691	10.733	9.919	9.221	7.634	5.995
40	14.265	12.879	11.726	10.757	9.936	9.233	7.638	5.996
41	14.332	12.925	11.757	10.779	9.951	9.244	7.642	5.997
42	14.394	12.967	11.787	10.799	9.965	9.253	7.645	5.997
43	14.452	13.007	11.813	10.817	9.977	9.262	7.648	5.998
44	14.507	13.043	11.838	10.834	9.989	9.270	7.650	5.998
45	14.558	13.077	11.861	10.849	9.999	9.276	7.652	5.998

THE SAVINGS RATE FACTOR

Tables 5-11 through 5-16 are used to select the appropriate Savings Rate Factor (F5) for use in the Retirement Planning Worksheet.

TABLE 5-11
Yearly Savings Rate Factors
0% Savings Step-up Rate (A7)

Yrs	Assumed Rate of Return (A5)						
	1%	2%	3%	4%	5%	6%	7%
1	0.99010	0.98039	0.97087	0.96154	0.95238	0.94340	0.93458
2	0.49259	0.48534	0.47826	0.47134	0.46458	0.45796	0.45149
3	0.32675	0.32035	0.31411	0.30803	0.30210	0.29633	0.29070
4	0.24384	0.23787	0.23207	0.22643	0.22096	0.21565	0.21049
5	0.19410	0.18839	0.18287	0.17753	0.17236	0.16736	0.16251
6	0.16094	0.15542	0.15009	0.14496	0.14002	0.13525	0.13065
7	0.13726	0.13187	0.12671	0.12174	0.11697	0.11239	0.10799
8	0.11950	0.11423	0.10918	0.10435	0.09974	0.09532	0.09109
9	0.10568	0.10051	0.09557	0.09086	0.08637	0.08210	0.07802
10	0.09464	0.08954	0.08469	0.08009	0.07572	0.07157	0.06764
11	0.08560	0.08057	0.07580	0.07130	0.06704	0.06301	0.05921
12	0.07807	0.07310	0.06841	0.06399	0.05983	0.05592	0.05224
13	0.07170	0.06678	0.06216	0.05783	0.05377	0.04996	0.04640
14	0.06624	0.06137	0.05682	0.05257	0.04859	0.04489	0.04144
15	0.06151	0.05669	0.05220	0.04802	0.04414	0.04053	0.03719
16	0.05737	0.05260	0.04817	0.04406	0.04026	0.03675	0.03351
17	0.05372	0.04899	0.04461	0.04058	0.03686	0.03344	0.03030
18	0.05048	0.04579	0.04146	0.03749	0.03385	0.03053	0.02749
19	0.04758	0.04292	0.03865	0.03475	0.03119	0.02794	0.02500
20	0.04497	0.04035	0.03613	0.03229	0.02880	0.02565	0.02280
21	0.04260	0.03802	0.03386	0.03008	0.02666	0.02359	0.02083
22	0.04046	0.03591	0.03179	0.02808	0.02473	0.02174	0.01907
23	0.03850	0.03399	0.02992	0.02626	0.02299	0.02007	0.01749
24	0.03671	0.03223	0.02820	0.02460	0.02140	0.01857	0.01606
25	0.03506	0.03061	0.02663	0.02309	0.01995	0.01720	0.01478
26	0.03353	0.02912	0.02518	0.02170	0.01863	0.01595	0.01361
27	0.03212	0.02774	0.02385	0.02042	0.01742	0.01481	0.01255
28	0.03082	0.02646	0.02261	0.01924	0.01631	0.01377	0.01158
29	0.02960	0.02527	0.02147	0.01815	0.01528	0.01281	0.01070
30	0.02846	0.02417	0.02041	0.01714	0.01433	0.01193	0.00989
31	0.02740	0.02313	0.01942	0.01621	0.01346	0.01112	0.00916
32	0.02641	0.02217	0.01849	0.01534	0.01265	0.01038	0.00848
33	0.02547	0.02126	0.01763	0.01452	0.01190	0.00969	0.00786
34	0.02459	0.02041	0.01682	0.01376	0.01120	0.00906	0.00729
35	0.02377	0.01961	0.01606	0.01306	0.01054	0.00847	0.00676
36	0.02298	0.01886	0.01534	0.01239	0.00994	0.00792	0.00628
37	0.02225	0.01814	0.01467	0.01177	0.00937	0.00741	0.00583
38	0.02155	0.01747	0.01404	0.01118	0.00884	0.00694	0.00542
39	0.02088	0.01683	0.01344	0.01064	0.00835	0.00650	0.00503
40	0.02025	0.01623	0.01288	0.01012	0.00788	0.00610	0.00468
41	0.01965	0.01566	0.01234	0.00963	0.00745	0.00572	0.00435
42	0.01908	0.01511	0.01184	0.00917	0.00704	0.00536	0.00405
43	0.01854	0.01460	0.01136	0.00874	0.00666	0.00503	0.00377
44	0.01802	0.01411	0.01090	0.00833	0.00630	0.00472	0.00351
45	0.01753	0.01364	0.01047	0.00794	0.00596	0.00443	0.00327

An explanation of the use of tables 5-11 through 5-16 appears on the pages following these tables under the heading "Selecting the Savings Rate Factor (F5)."

TABLE 5-11 (Continued)
Yearly Savings Rate Factors
0% Savings Step-up Rate (A7)

	Assumed Rate of Return (A5)						
Yrs	8%	9%	10%	11%	12%	15%	20%
1	0.92593	0.91743	0.90909	0.90090	0.89286	0.86957	0.83333
2	0.44516	0.43896	0.43290	0.42697	0.42116	0.40445	0.37879
3	0.28522	0.27987	0.27465	0.26956	0.26460	0.25041	0.22894
4	0.20548	0.20061	0.19588	0.19129	0.18682	0.17414	0.15524
5	0.15783	0.15330	0.14891	0.14466	0.14054	0.12897	0.11198
6	0.12622	0.12194	0.11782	0.11385	0.11002	0.09934	0.08392
7	0.10377	0.09972	0.09582	0.09209	0.08850	0.07857	0.06452
8	0.08705	0.08319	0.07949	0.07596	0.07259	0.06335	0.05051
9	0.07415	0.07046	0.06695	0.06361	0.06043	0.05180	0.04007
10	0.06392	0.06039	0.05704	0.05388	0.05088	0.04283	0.03210
11	0.05563	0.05224	0.04906	0.04605	0.04323	0.03571	0.02592
12	0.04879	0.04555	0.04251	0.03966	0.03700	0.02998	0.02105
13	0.04308	0.03997	0.03707	0.03437	0.03185	0.02531	0.01718
14	0.03824	0.03526	0.03250	0.02994	0.02756	0.02147	0.01408
15	0.03410	0.03125	0.02861	0.02618	0.02395	0.01828	0.01157
16	0.03053	0.02780	0.02529	0.02299	0.02088	0.01561	0.00953
17	0.02743	0.02481	0.02242	0.02024	0.01826	0.01336	0.00787
18	0.02472	0.02221	0.01994	0.01788	0.01602	0.01147	0.00650
19	0.02234	0.01994	0.01777	0.01582	0.01407	0.00986	0.00539
20	0.02023	0.01793	0.01587	0.01403	0.01239	0.00849	0.00446
21	0.01836	0.01616	0.01420	0.01247	0.01093	0.00732	0.00370
22	0.01670	0.01459	0.01273	0.01109	0.00965	0.00632	0.00307
23	0.01521	0.01319	0.01143	0.00988	0.00854	0.00546	0.00255
24	0.01387	0.01195	0.01027	0.00882	0.00756	0.00472	0.00212
25	0.01267	0.01083	0.00924	0.00787	0.00670	0.00409	0.00177
26	0.01158	0.00983	0.00833	0.00704	0.00594	0.00354	0.00147
27	0.01060	0.00893	0.00751	0.00630	0.00527	0.00307	0.00122
28	0.00971	0.00812	0.00677	0.00564	0.00468	0.00266	0.00102
29	0.00891	0.00739	0.00612	0.00505	0.00416	0.00231	0.00085
30	0.00817	0.00673	0.00553	0.00453	0.00370	0.00200	0.00071
31	0.00751	0.00613	0.00500	0.00406	0.00329	0.00174	0.00059
32	0.00690	0.00559	0.00452	0.00364	0.00293	0.00151	0.00049
33	0.00634	0.00510	0.00409	0.00327	0.00261	0.00131	0.00041
34	0.00584	0.00466	0.00370	0.00294	0.00232	0.00114	0.00034
35	0.00537	0.00425	0.00335	0.00264	0.00207	0.00099	0.00028
36	0.00495	0.00389	0.00304	0.00237	0.00184	0.00086	0.00024
37	0.00456	0.00355	0.00275	0.00213	0.00164	0.00074	0.00020
38	0.00420	0.00325	0.00250	0.00191	0.00146	0.00065	0.00016
39	0.00388	0.00297	0.00226	0.00172	0.00131	0.00056	0.00014
40	0.00357	0.00272	0.00205	0.00155	0.00116	0.00049	0.00011
41	0.00330	0.00248	0.00186	0.00139	0.00104	0.00042	0.00009
42	0.00304	0.00227	0.00169	0.00125	0.00093	0.00037	0.00008
43	0.00281	0.00208	0.00153	0.00113	0.00083	0.00032	0.00007
44	0.00259	0.00191	0.00139	0.00101	0.00074	0.00028	0.00005
45	0.00240	0.00174	0.00126	0.00091	0.00066	0.00024	0.00005

TABLE 5-12
Yearly Savings Rate Factors
2% Savings Step-up Rate (A7)

Yrs	Assumed Rate of Return (A5)						
	1%	2%	3%	4%	5%	6%	7%
1	0.99010	0.98039	0.97087	0.96154	0.95238	0.94340	0.93458
2	0.48773	0.48058	0.47360	0.46677	0.46009	0.45356	0.44717
3	0.32035	0.31411	0.30803	0.30210	0.29633	0.29071	0.28522
4	0.23671	0.23096	0.22538	0.21997	0.21470	0.20959	0.20463
5	0.18656	0.18115	0.17590	0.17083	0.16592	0.16116	0.15656
6	0.15317	0.14800	0.14301	0.13820	0.13355	0.12907	0.12475
7	0.12934	0.12437	0.11958	0.11498	0.11056	0.10631	0.10223
8	0.11149	0.10669	0.10208	0.09766	0.09343	0.08938	0.08550
9	0.09764	0.09297	0.08852	0.08426	0.08020	0.07633	0.07263
10	0.08657	0.08203	0.07772	0.07361	0.06970	0.06599	0.06246
11	0.07753	0.07311	0.06892	0.06495	0.06119	0.05762	0.05424
12	0.07001	0.06571	0.06164	0.05779	0.05415	0.05072	0.04749
13	0.06367	0.05946	0.05550	0.05177	0.04826	0.04496	0.04186
14	0.05824	0.05413	0.05028	0.04665	0.04326	0.04008	0.03711
15	0.05355	0.04953	0.04577	0.04226	0.03898	0.03592	0.03307
16	0.04945	0.04553	0.04186	0.03845	0.03527	0.03232	0.02959
17	0.04585	0.04201	0.03843	0.03511	0.03204	0.02920	0.02657
18	0.04266	0.03890	0.03541	0.03218	0.02920	0.02646	0.02394
19	0.03981	0.03613	0.03272	0.02958	0.02670	0.02405	0.02164
20	0.03726	0.03365	0.03032	0.02727	0.02448	0.02192	0.01960
21	0.03495	0.03142	0.02817	0.02520	0.02249	0.02003	0.01780
22	0.03286	0.02940	0.02623	0.02334	0.02071	0.01834	0.01620
23	0.03097	0.02757	0.02447	0.02166	0.01912	0.01682	0.01477
24	0.02923	0.02591	0.02288	0.02014	0.01767	0.01546	0.01349
25	0.02764	0.02438	0.02142	0.01876	0.01637	0.01423	0.01234
26	0.02618	0.02298	0.02009	0.01750	0.01518	0.01312	0.01130
27	0.02483	0.02170	0.01887	0.01635	0.01410	0.01211	0.01037
28	0.02359	0.02051	0.01775	0.01529	0.01311	0.01120	0.00952
29	0.02243	0.01942	0.01672	0.01432	0.01221	0.01036	0.00875
30	0.02136	0.01840	0.01576	0.01343	0.01138	0.00960	0.00806
31	0.02036	0.01746	0.01488	0.01261	0.01062	0.00890	0.00742
32	0.01943	0.01658	0.01406	0.01185	0.00992	0.00826	0.00684
33	0.01856	0.01576	0.01330	0.01114	0.00927	0.00767	0.00631
34	0.01774	0.01500	0.01259	0.01049	0.00868	0.00713	0.00583
35	0.01697	0.01429	0.01193	0.00988	0.00813	0.00664	0.00539
36	0.01625	0.01362	0.01131	0.00932	0.00762	0.00618	0.00498
37	0.01558	0.01299	0.01073	0.00879	0.00714	0.00576	0.00461
38	0.01494	0.01240	0.01019	0.00830	0.00670	0.00537	0.00426
39	0.01434	0.01184	0.00969	0.00784	0.00629	0.00501	0.00395
40	0.01377	0.01132	0.00921	0.00742	0.00591	0.00467	0.00366
41	0.01323	0.01083	0.00876	0.00702	0.00556	0.00436	0.00339
42	0.01272	0.01036	0.00834	0.00664	0.00523	0.00408	0.00315
43	0.01224	0.00992	0.00795	0.00629	0.00492	0.00381	0.00292
44	0.01178	0.00951	0.00758	0.00596	0.00463	0.00356	0.00271
45	0.01134	0.00912	0.00723	0.00565	0.00436	0.00333	0.00252

TABLE 5-12 (Continued)
Yearly Savings Rate Factors
2% Savings Step-up Rate (A7)

	Assumed Rate of Return (A5)						
Yrs	8%	9%	10%	11%	12%	15%	20%
1	0.92593	0.91743	0.90909	0.90090	0.89286	0.86957	0.83333
2	0.44092	0.43480	0.42882	0.42296	0.41722	0.40072	0.37538
3	0.27987	0.27466	0.26957	0.26461	0.25976	0.24592	0.22496
4	0.19980	0.19511	0.19055	0.18612	0.18181	0.16959	0.15134
5	0.15210	0.14779	0.14361	0.13956	0.13564	0.12460	0.10836
6	0.12059	0.11657	0.11269	0.10894	0.10533	0.09524	0.08065
7	0.09830	0.09453	0.09091	0.08742	0.08407	0.07480	0.06161
8	0.08179	0.07823	0.07483	0.07157	0.06845	0.05989	0.04795
9	0.06911	0.06575	0.06254	0.05949	0.05658	0.04867	0.03783
10	0.05911	0.05592	0.05290	0.05004	0.04732	0.03999	0.03016
11	0.05105	0.04803	0.04518	0.04249	0.03995	0.03316	0.02425
12	0.04445	0.04158	0.03889	0.03636	0.03398	0.02769	0.01961
13	0.03896	0.03624	0.03369	0.03131	0.02908	0.02326	0.01595
14	0.03434	0.03176	0.02935	0.02711	0.02503	0.01964	0.01302
15	0.03042	0.02796	0.02569	0.02358	0.02163	0.01665	0.01067
16	0.02706	0.02472	0.02257	0.02059	0.01877	0.01416	0.00876
17	0.02416	0.02194	0.01990	0.01804	0.01634	0.01208	0.00722
18	0.02164	0.01953	0.01760	0.01585	0.01426	0.01033	0.00595
19	0.01943	0.01743	0.01561	0.01396	0.01248	0.00885	0.00492
20	0.01750	0.01559	0.01388	0.01233	0.01094	0.00760	0.00407
21	0.01579	0.01398	0.01236	0.01091	0.00961	0.00653	0.00337
22	0.01428	0.01256	0.01103	0.00967	0.00846	0.00562	0.00280
23	0.01294	0.01130	0.00986	0.00858	0.00746	0.00485	0.00232
24	0.01174	0.01019	0.00882	0.00763	0.00658	0.00418	0.00193
25	0.01067	0.00920	0.00791	0.00679	0.00581	0.00361	0.00160
26	0.00971	0.00831	0.00710	0.00605	0.00514	0.00312	0.00133
27	0.00884	0.00752	0.00638	0.00539	0.00455	0.00270	0.00111
28	0.00807	0.00681	0.00574	0.00482	0.00403	0.00234	0.00092
29	0.00737	0.00618	0.00516	0.00430	0.00358	0.00203	0.00077
30	0.00673	0.00561	0.00465	0.00385	0.00317	0.00176	0.00064
31	0.00616	0.00509	0.00419	0.00344	0.00282	0.00152	0.00053
32	0.00564	0.00463	0.00378	0.00308	0.00250	0.00132	0.00044
33	0.00517	0.00421	0.00341	0.00276	0.00222	0.00114	0.00037
34	0.00474	0.00383	0.00308	0.00247	0.00198	0.00099	0.00031
35	0.00435	0.00349	0.00279	0.00222	0.00176	0.00086	0.00025
36	0.00399	0.00318	0.00252	0.00199	0.00156	0.00075	0.00021
37	0.00366	0.00290	0.00228	0.00178	0.00139	0.00065	0.00018
38	0.00337	0.00264	0.00206	0.00160	0.00124	0.00056	0.00015
39	0.00309	0.00241	0.00187	0.00144	0.00110	0.00049	0.00012
40	0.00285	0.00220	0.00169	0.00129	0.00098	0.00043	0.00010
41	0.00262	0.00201	0.00153	0.00116	0.00088	0.00037	0.00009
42	0.00241	0.00183	0.00139	0.00104	0.00078	0.00032	0.00007
43	0.00222	0.00168	0.00126	0.00094	0.00070	0.00028	0.00006
44	0.00205	0.00153	0.00114	0.00084	0.00062	0.00024	0.00005
45	0.00188	0.00140	0.00103	0.00076	0.00055	0.00021	0.00004

TABLE 5-13
Yearly Savings Rate Factors
4% Savings Step-up Rate (A7)

Yrs	\multicolumn{7}{c}{Assumed Rate of Return (A5)}
	1%	2%	3%	4%	5%	6%	7%
1	0.99010	0.98039	0.97087	0.96154	0.95238	0.94340	0.93458
2	0.48298	0.47592	0.46902	0.46228	0.45568	0.44924	0.44293
3	0.31411	0.30803	0.30210	0.29633	0.29071	0.28522	0.27987
4	0.22980	0.22428	0.21891	0.21370	0.20864	0.20372	0.19893
5	0.17932	0.17418	0.16920	0.16439	0.15972	0.15520	0.15082
6	0.14575	0.14090	0.13623	0.13172	0.12736	0.12316	0.11910
7	0.12184	0.11724	0.11282	0.10856	0.10446	0.10052	0.09673
8	0.10396	0.09958	0.09537	0.09134	0.08747	0.08375	0.08019
9	0.09011	0.08592	0.08190	0.07807	0.07440	0.07089	0.06754
10	0.07908	0.07505	0.07122	0.06756	0.06407	0.06075	0.05758
11	0.07009	0.06622	0.06255	0.05905	0.05573	0.05258	0.04959
12	0.06264	0.05892	0.05539	0.05205	0.04888	0.04589	0.04306
13	0.05636	0.05278	0.04940	0.04620	0.04318	0.04033	0.03765
14	0.05102	0.04757	0.04431	0.04125	0.03836	0.03565	0.03311
15	0.04641	0.04309	0.03996	0.03702	0.03426	0.03168	0.02926
16	0.04241	0.03920	0.03619	0.03337	0.03073	0.02827	0.02598
17	0.03890	0.03580	0.03291	0.03020	0.02768	0.02533	0.02315
18	0.03580	0.03281	0.03002	0.02742	0.02501	0.02277	0.02071
19	0.03305	0.03016	0.02748	0.02498	0.02267	0.02054	0.01857
20	0.03059	0.02781	0.02522	0.02282	0.02061	0.01857	0.01670
21	0.02839	0.02569	0.02320	0.02090	0.01878	0.01683	0.01506
22	0.02640	0.02380	0.02139	0.01918	0.01715	0.01529	0.01361
23	0.02460	0.02209	0.01977	0.01764	0.01569	0.01392	0.01232
24	0.02296	0.02053	0.01830	0.01626	0.01439	0.01270	0.01117
25	0.02147	0.01913	0.01697	0.01500	0.01322	0.01160	0.01015
26	0.02011	0.01784	0.01576	0.01387	0.01216	0.01062	0.00924
27	0.01886	0.01667	0.01466	0.01285	0.01120	0.00973	0.00842
28	0.01771	0.01559	0.01366	0.01191	0.01034	0.00893	0.00768
29	0.01665	0.01460	0.01274	0.01106	0.00955	0.00820	0.00702
30	0.01567	0.01369	0.01190	0.01028	0.00883	0.00755	0.00642
31	0.01476	0.01285	0.01112	0.00956	0.00818	0.00695	0.00588
32	0.01392	0.01208	0.01041	0.00891	0.00758	0.00641	0.00538
33	0.01314	0.01136	0.00975	0.00831	0.00703	0.00591	0.00494
34	0.01242	0.01069	0.00914	0.00775	0.00653	0.00546	0.00453
35	0.01174	0.01007	0.00857	0.00724	0.00607	0.00504	0.00417
36	0.01111	0.00950	0.00805	0.00677	0.00564	0.00467	0.00383
37	0.01052	0.00896	0.00757	0.00633	0.00525	0.00432	0.00352
38	0.00997	0.00846	0.00712	0.00593	0.00489	0.00400	0.00324
39	0.00945	0.00800	0.00670	0.00555	0.00456	0.00371	0.00299
40	0.00897	0.00756	0.00631	0.00521	0.00425	0.00344	0.00276
41	0.00851	0.00715	0.00594	0.00488	0.00397	0.00319	0.00254
42	0.00808	0.00677	0.00561	0.00459	0.00371	0.00296	0.00235
43	0.00768	0.00641	0.00529	0.00431	0.00346	0.00275	0.00217
44	0.00730	0.00608	0.00499	0.00405	0.00324	0.00256	0.00200
45	0.00695	0.00576	0.00471	0.00380	0.00303	0.00238	0.00185

TABLE 5-13 (Continued)
Yearly Savings Rate Factors
4% Savings Step-up Rate (A7)

Yrs	\multicolumn{7}{c}{Assumed Rate of Return (A5)}
	8%	9%	10%	11%	12%	15%	20%
1	0.92593	0.91743	0.90909	0.90090	0.89286	0.86957	0.83333
2	0.43676	0.43072	0.42481	0.41902	0.41336	0.39706	0.37202
3	0.27466	0.26957	0.26461	0.25977	0.25504	0.24154	0.22107
4	0.19429	0.18977	0.18538	0.18111	0.17695	0.16516	0.14753
5	0.14658	0.14247	0.13849	0.13463	0.13090	0.12036	0.10485
6	0.11518	0.11140	0.10775	0.10422	0.10082	0.09129	0.07749
7	0.09308	0.08957	0.08620	0.08295	0.07983	0.07117	0.05881
8	0.07678	0.07351	0.07038	0.06738	0.06450	0.05658	0.04549
9	0.06433	0.06128	0.05836	0.05558	0.05292	0.04567	0.03568
10	0.05457	0.05171	0.04899	0.04640	0.04394	0.03729	0.02830
11	0.04675	0.04407	0.04152	0.03911	0.03684	0.03073	0.02263
12	0.04038	0.03786	0.03548	0.03324	0.03112	0.02551	0.01823
13	0.03512	0.03275	0.03052	0.02843	0.02647	0.02131	0.01476
14	0.03072	0.02849	0.02640	0.02445	0.02264	0.01790	0.01200
15	0.02701	0.02491	0.02295	0.02114	0.01945	0.01510	0.00980
16	0.02385	0.02187	0.02004	0.01834	0.01678	0.01278	0.00802
17	0.02114	0.01928	0.01756	0.01598	0.01452	0.01085	0.00659
18	0.01880	0.01704	0.01543	0.01396	0.01261	0.00924	0.00542
19	0.01677	0.01512	0.01361	0.01223	0.01098	0.00789	0.00447
20	0.01500	0.01344	0.01202	0.01074	0.00958	0.00675	0.00369
21	0.01344	0.01198	0.01065	0.00945	0.00838	0.00578	0.00305
22	0.01208	0.01070	0.00945	0.00834	0.00734	0.00496	0.00252
23	0.01087	0.00957	0.00841	0.00737	0.00644	0.00427	0.00209
24	0.00980	0.00858	0.00749	0.00652	0.00566	0.00367	0.00173
25	0.00885	0.00770	0.00668	0.00578	0.00498	0.00316	0.00144
26	0.00801	0.00692	0.00596	0.00512	0.00439	0.00273	0.00119
27	0.00726	0.00623	0.00533	0.00455	0.00387	0.00235	0.00099
28	0.00658	0.00562	0.00478	0.00405	0.00342	0.00203	0.00082
29	0.00598	0.00507	0.00428	0.00360	0.00302	0.00176	0.00068
30	0.00543	0.00458	0.00384	0.00321	0.00267	0.00152	0.00057
31	0.00494	0.00414	0.00345	0.00286	0.00237	0.00131	0.00047
32	0.00450	0.00374	0.00310	0.00255	0.00210	0.00114	0.00039
33	0.00410	0.00339	0.00279	0.00228	0.00186	0.00099	0.00033
34	0.00374	0.00307	0.00251	0.00204	0.00165	0.00085	0.00027
35	0.00342	0.00279	0.00226	0.00182	0.00146	0.00074	0.00023
36	0.00312	0.00253	0.00203	0.00163	0.00130	0.00064	0.00019
37	0.00285	0.00230	0.00183	0.00146	0.00115	0.00056	0.00016
38	0.00261	0.00209	0.00165	0.00131	0.00102	0.00048	0.00013
39	0.00239	0.00190	0.00149	0.00117	0.00091	0.00042	0.00011
40	0.00219	0.00172	0.00135	0.00105	0.00081	0.00036	0.00009
41	0.00201	0.00157	0.00122	0.00094	0.00072	0.00032	0.00008
42	0.00184	0.00143	0.00110	0.00084	0.00064	0.00027	0.00006
43	0.00169	0.00130	0.00099	0.00076	0.00057	0.00024	0.00005
44	0.00155	0.00118	0.00090	0.00068	0.00051	0.00021	0.00004
45	0.00142	0.00108	0.00081	0.00061	0.00045	0.00018	0.00004

TABLE 5-14
Yearly Savings Rate Factors
6% Savings Step-up Rate (A7)

Yrs	Assumed Rate of Return (A5)						
	1%	2%	3%	4%	5%	6%	7%
1	0.99010	0.98039	0.97087	0.96154	0.95238	0.94340	0.93458
2	0.47831	0.47134	0.46453	0.45788	0.45137	0.44500	0.43877
3	0.30803	0.30211	0.29633	0.29071	0.28522	0.27987	0.27466
4	0.22312	0.21781	0.21265	0.20763	0.20276	0.19802	0.19342
5	0.17236	0.16748	0.16276	0.15818	0.15375	0.14945	0.14529
6	0.13867	0.13414	0.12976	0.12553	0.12144	0.11749	0.11368
7	0.11473	0.11048	0.10639	0.10246	0.09866	0.09501	0.09149
8	0.09688	0.09289	0.08905	0.08536	0.08182	0.07843	0.07516
9	0.08309	0.07932	0.07571	0.07225	0.06894	0.06577	0.06273
10	0.07214	0.06858	0.06517	0.06191	0.05881	0.05584	0.05301
11	0.06325	0.05988	0.05666	0.05359	0.05067	0.04789	0.04525
12	0.05591	0.05271	0.04967	0.04677	0.04402	0.04141	0.03894
13	0.04976	0.04672	0.04384	0.04110	0.03851	0.03606	0.03375
14	0.04454	0.04166	0.03892	0.03634	0.03390	0.03159	0.02942
15	0.04007	0.03732	0.03473	0.03229	0.02998	0.02782	0.02578
16	0.03619	0.03359	0.03113	0.02882	0.02664	0.02460	0.02269
17	0.03282	0.03034	0.02801	0.02582	0.02376	0.02184	0.02005
18	0.02985	0.02750	0.02529	0.02321	0.02127	0.01946	0.01778
19	0.02724	0.02500	0.02290	0.02093	0.01910	0.01740	0.01582
20	0.02492	0.02278	0.02079	0.01893	0.01720	0.01559	0.01411
21	0.02284	0.02082	0.01892	0.01716	0.01552	0.01401	0.01261
22	0.02099	0.01906	0.01726	0.01559	0.01404	0.01261	0.01130
23	0.01932	0.01748	0.01578	0.01419	0.01273	0.01138	0.01015
24	0.01781	0.01607	0.01445	0.01294	0.01156	0.01029	0.00913
25	0.01645	0.01479	0.01325	0.01183	0.01052	0.00932	0.00823
26	0.01521	0.01364	0.01217	0.01082	0.00958	0.00845	0.00743
27	0.01409	0.01259	0.01120	0.00992	0.00875	0.00768	0.00672
28	0.01306	0.01163	0.01031	0.00910	0.00799	0.00699	0.00608
29	0.01212	0.01077	0.00951	0.00836	0.00731	0.00636	0.00551
30	0.01126	0.00997	0.00878	0.00769	0.00670	0.00580	0.00500
31	0.01047	0.00925	0.00812	0.00708	0.00614	0.00530	0.00454
32	0.00975	0.00858	0.00751	0.00653	0.00564	0.00484	0.00413
33	0.00908	0.00797	0.00695	0.00602	0.00518	0.00443	0.00376
34	0.00846	0.00741	0.00645	0.00556	0.00477	0.00406	0.00343
35	0.00790	0.00690	0.00598	0.00514	0.00439	0.00372	0.00313
36	0.00737	0.00642	0.00555	0.00476	0.00404	0.00341	0.00285
37	0.00688	0.00598	0.00515	0.00440	0.00373	0.00313	0.00261
38	0.00643	0.00558	0.00479	0.00408	0.00344	0.00287	0.00238
39	0.00602	0.00520	0.00446	0.00378	0.00318	0.00264	0.00218
40	0.00563	0.00485	0.00415	0.00351	0.00293	0.00243	0.00199
41	0.00527	0.00453	0.00386	0.00325	0.00271	0.00224	0.00183
42	0.00493	0.00424	0.00360	0.00302	0.00251	0.00206	0.00167
43	0.00462	0.00396	0.00335	0.00281	0.00232	0.00190	0.00153
44	0.00433	0.00370	0.00313	0.00261	0.00215	0.00175	0.00141
45	0.00406	0.00346	0.00292	0.00243	0.00199	0.00161	0.00129

TABLE 5-14 (Continued)
Yearly Savings Rate Factors
6% Savings Step-up Rate (A7)

Yrs	Assumed Rate of Return (A5)						
	8%	9%	10%	11%	12%	15%	20%
1	0.92593	0.91743	0.90909	0.90090	0.89286	0.86957	0.83333
2	0.43268	0.42671	0.42088	0.41516	0.40957	0.39347	0.36873
3	0.26957	0.26461	0.25977	0.25505	0.25044	0.23726	0.21726
4	0.18894	0.18459	0.18035	0.17624	0.17223	0.16086	0.14383
5	0.14125	0.13734	0.13355	0.12988	0.12631	0.11626	0.10144
6	0.11000	0.10644	0.10300	0.09968	0.09647	0.08749	0.07443
7	0.08810	0.08484	0.08170	0.07868	0.07577	0.06768	0.05610
8	0.07203	0.06903	0.06615	0.06338	0.06073	0.05341	0.04311
9	0.05983	0.05705	0.05440	0.05186	0.04944	0.04280	0.03362
10	**0.05031**	0.04774	0.04529	0.04296	0.04074	0.03471	0.02651
11	0.04273	0.04035	0.03808	0.03594	0.03390	0.02842	0.02109
12	0.03660	0.03438	0.03229	0.03031	0.02844	0.02345	0.01690
13	0.03156	0.02950	0.02756	0.02573	0.02402	0.01947	0.01362
14	0.02738	0.02546	0.02367	0.02198	0.02040	0.01625	0.01103
15	0.02388	0.02209	0.02042	0.01886	0.01741	0.01363	0.00897
16	0.02091	0.01925	0.01770	0.01626	0.01492	0.01148	0.00732
17	0.01839	0.01684	0.01540	0.01407	0.01284	0.00970	0.00598
18	0.01622	0.01478	0.01344	0.01221	0.01108	0.00822	0.00491
19	0.01435	0.01301	0.01177	0.01063	0.00959	0.00698	0.00403
20	0.01274	0.01148	0.01033	0.00928	0.00832	0.00595	0.00332
21	0.01133	0.01016	0.00909	0.00812	0.00724	0.00507	0.00274
22	0.01010	0.00901	0.00802	0.00712	0.00630	0.00434	0.00226
23	0.00903	0.00801	0.00708	0.00625	0.00550	0.00371	0.00187
24	0.00808	0.00713	0.00627	0.00550	0.00481	0.00318	0.00155
25	0.00724	0.00635	0.00556	0.00485	0.00422	0.00273	0.00128
26	0.00650	0.00568	0.00493	0.00428	0.00370	0.00235	0.00106
27	0.00585	0.00508	0.00439	0.00378	0.00325	0.00202	0.00088
28	0.00527	0.00455	0.00391	0.00334	0.00285	0.00174	0.00073
29	0.00475	0.00408	0.00348	0.00296	0.00251	0.00150	0.00061
30	0.00429	0.00366	0.00311	0.00263	0.00221	0.00129	0.00050
31	0.00387	0.00329	0.00277	0.00233	0.00195	0.00112	0.00042
32	0.00350	0.00296	0.00248	0.00207	0.00172	0.00096	0.00035
33	0.00317	0.00266	0.00222	0.00184	0.00152	0.00083	0.00029
34	0.00288	0.00240	0.00199	0.00164	0.00134	0.00072	0.00024
35	0.00261	0.00216	0.00178	0.00146	0.00119	0.00062	0.00020
36	0.00237	0.00195	0.00160	0.00130	0.00105	0.00054	0.00017
37	0.00215	0.00176	0.00143	0.00116	0.00093	0.00047	0.00014
38	0.00196	0.00159	0.00129	0.00103	0.00082	0.00040	0.00012
39	0.00178	0.00144	0.00116	0.00092	0.00073	0.00035	0.00010
40	0.00162	0.00130	0.00104	0.00082	0.00065	0.00030	0.00008
41	0.00147	0.00118	0.00094	0.00074	0.00057	0.00026	0.00007
42	0.00134	0.00107	0.00084	0.00066	0.00051	0.00023	0.00006
43	0.00123	0.00097	0.00076	0.00059	0.00045	0.00020	0.00005
44	0.00112	0.00088	0.00068	0.00053	0.00040	0.00017	0.00004
45	0.00102	0.00080	0.00062	0.00047	0.00036	0.00015	0.00003

TABLE 5-15
Yearly Savings Rate Factors
8% Savings Step-up Rate (A7)

Yrs	1%	2%	3%	4%	5%	6%	7%
1	0.99010	0.98039	0.97087	0.96154	0.95238	0.94340	0.93458
2	0.47373	0.46685	0.46013	0.45356	0.44713	0.44084	0.43469
3	0.30211	0.29633	0.29071	0.28522	0.27987	0.27466	0.26957
4	0.21666	0.21155	0.20659	0.20176	0.19707	0.19251	0.18807
5	0.16568	0.16105	0.15657	0.15222	0.14800	0.14392	0.13996
6	0.13192	0.12768	0.12358	0.11961	0.11578	0.11207	0.10849
7	0.10801	0.10409	0.10031	0.09666	0.09315	0.08976	0.08650
8	0.09023	0.08660	0.08310	0.07974	0.07650	0.07339	0.07040
9	0.07656	0.07317	0.06992	0.06681	0.06382	0.06096	0.05821
10	0.06574	0.06258	0.05956	0.05667	0.05391	0.05126	0.04873
11	0.05700	0.05405	0.05124	0.04855	0.04599	0.04354	0.04121
12	0.04981	0.04706	0.04444	0.04194	0.03956	0.03729	0.03514
13	0.04382	0.04125	0.03880	0.03647	0.03426	0.03216	0.03017
14	0.03877	0.03636	0.03408	0.03190	0.02985	0.02790	0.02606
15	0.03446	0.03221	0.03007	0.02805	0.02613	0.02433	0.02262
16	0.03076	0.02865	0.02665	0.02477	0.02298	0.02131	0.01973
17	0.02755	0.02558	0.02371	0.02195	0.02029	0.01873	0.01727
18	0.02475	0.02291	0.02116	0.01952	0.01798	0.01653	0.01517
19	0.02230	0.02058	0.01895	0.01741	0.01597	0.01463	0.01337
20	0.02014	0.01853	0.01700	0.01557	0.01423	0.01298	0.01181
21	0.01823	0.01672	0.01530	0.01396	0.01271	0.01155	0.01046
22	0.01653	0.01512	0.01379	0.01254	0.01138	0.01029	0.00929
23	0.01502	0.01370	0.01245	0.01129	0.01020	0.00920	0.00826
24	0.01367	0.01243	0.01127	0.01018	0.00917	0.00823	0.00737
25	0.01245	0.01130	0.01021	0.00920	0.00825	0.00738	0.00658
26	0.01136	0.01028	0.00926	0.00832	0.00744	0.00663	0.00588
27	0.01038	0.00937	0.00842	0.00753	0.00672	0.00596	0.00527
28	0.00949	0.00854	0.00766	0.00683	0.00607	0.00537	0.00472
29	0.00868	0.00780	0.00697	0.00620	0.00549	0.00484	0.00424
30	0.00795	0.00713	0.00636	0.00564	0.00498	0.00437	0.00381
31	0.00729	0.00652	0.00580	0.00513	0.00451	0.00395	0.00343
32	0.00669	0.00597	0.00530	0.00467	0.00410	0.00357	0.00309
33	0.00614	0.00547	0.00484	0.00426	0.00372	0.00323	0.00279
34	0.00564	0.00502	0.00443	0.00389	0.00339	0.00293	0.00252
35	0.00518	0.00460	0.00405	0.00355	0.00308	0.00266	0.00227
36	0.00477	0.00422	0.00371	0.00324	0.00281	0.00241	0.00206
37	0.00439	0.00388	0.00340	0.00296	0.00256	0.00219	0.00186
38	0.00404	0.00356	0.00312	0.00271	0.00233	0.00199	0.00169
39	0.00372	0.00328	0.00286	0.00248	0.00213	0.00181	0.00153
40	0.00342	0.00301	0.00263	0.00227	0.00195	0.00165	0.00138
41	0.00316	0.00277	0.00241	0.00208	0.00178	0.00150	0.00126
42	0.00291	0.00255	0.00222	0.00191	0.00163	0.00137	0.00114
43	0.00268	0.00235	0.00204	0.00175	0.00149	0.00125	0.00104
44	0.00247	0.00217	0.00188	0.00161	0.00136	0.00114	0.00094
45	0.00228	0.00200	0.00173	0.00147	0.00125	0.00104	0.00086

TABLE 5-15 (Continued)
Yearly Savings Rate Factors
8% Savings Step-up Rate (A7)

Yrs	Assumed Rate of Return (A5)						
	8%	9%	10%	11%	12%	15%	20%
1	0.92593	0.91743	0.90909	0.90090	0.89286	0.86957	0.83333
2	0.42867	0.42278	0.41701	0.41137	0.40584	0.38994	0.36550
3	0.26461	0.25977	0.25505	0.25044	0.24594	0.23307	0.21354
4	0.18376	0.17956	0.17548	0.17151	0.16765	0.15667	0.14023
5	0.13612	0.13239	0.12878	0.12528	0.12189	0.11230	0.09814
6	0.10503	0.10168	0.09845	0.09532	0.09230	0.08382	0.07147
7	0.08336	0.08033	0.07740	0.07459	0.07188	0.06433	0.05349
8	0.06753	0.06478	0.06213	0.05958	0.05714	0.05038	0.04083
9	0.05558	0.05306	0.05065	0.04835	0.04614	0.04008	0.03164
10	0.04632	0.04401	0.04181	0.03972	0.03772	0.03226	0.02480
11	0.03899	0.03688	0.03487	0.03296	0.03114	0.02623	0.01961
12	0.03309	0.03115	0.02931	0.02757	0.02592	0.02149	0.01563
13	0.02828	0.02650	0.02482	0.02323	0.02173	0.01773	0.01253
14	0.02432	0.02268	0.02113	0.01968	0.01832	0.01471	0.01010
15	0.02102	0.01951	0.01809	0.01676	0.01552	0.01226	0.00817
16	0.01824	0.01685	0.01555	0.01434	0.01321	0.01026	0.00664
17	0.01590	0.01462	0.01342	0.01231	0.01128	0.00862	0.00541
18	0.01390	0.01272	0.01163	0.01061	0.00967	0.00726	0.00442
19	0.01220	0.01111	0.01010	0.00917	0.00831	0.00614	0.00362
20	0.01073	0.00972	0.00880	0.00795	0.00716	0.00520	0.00297
21	0.00946	0.00853	0.00768	0.00690	0.00619	0.00441	0.00244
22	0.00836	0.00751	0.00672	0.00601	0.00536	0.00376	0.00201
23	0.00741	0.00662	0.00590	0.00524	0.00465	0.00320	0.00166
24	0.00657	0.00584	0.00518	0.00458	0.00404	0.00273	0.00137
25	0.00584	0.00517	0.00456	0.00401	0.00352	0.00233	0.00113
26	0.00520	0.00458	0.00402	0.00352	0.00307	0.00200	0.00093
27	0.00464	0.00406	0.00355	0.00309	0.00268	0.00171	0.00077
28	0.00414	0.00361	0.00314	0.00272	0.00234	0.00147	0.00064
29	0.00370	0.00321	0.00278	0.00239	0.00205	0.00126	0.00053
30	0.00331	0.00286	0.00246	0.00211	0.00179	0.00108	0.00044
31	0.00297	0.00255	0.00218	0.00186	0.00157	0.00093	0.00036
32	0.00266	0.00228	0.00194	0.00164	0.00138	0.00080	0.00030
33	0.00239	0.00204	0.00172	0.00145	0.00121	0.00069	0.00025
34	0.00215	0.00182	0.00153	0.00128	0.00107	0.00060	0.00021
35	0.00193	0.00163	0.00137	0.00114	0.00094	0.00051	0.00017
36	0.00174	0.00146	0.00122	0.00101	0.00083	0.00044	0.00014
37	0.00157	0.00131	0.00108	0.00089	0.00073	0.00038	0.00012
38	0.00141	0.00117	0.00097	0.00079	0.00064	0.00033	0.00010
39	0.00127	0.00105	0.00086	0.00070	0.00057	0.00029	0.00008
40	0.00115	0.00095	0.00077	0.00062	0.00050	0.00025	0.00007
41	0.00104	0.00085	0.00069	0.00056	0.00044	0.00021	0.00006
42	0.00094	0.00077	0.00062	0.00049	0.00039	0.00019	0.00005
43	0.00085	0.00069	0.00055	0.00044	0.00035	0.00016	0.00004
44	0.00077	0.00062	0.00050	0.00039	0.00031	0.00014	0.00003
45	0.00070	0.00056	0.00044	0.00035	0.00027	0.00012	0.00003

TABLE 5-16
Yearly Savings Rate Factors
10% Savings Step-up Rate (A7)

Yrs	1%	2%	3%	4%	5%	6%	7%
			Assumed Rate of Return (A5)				
1	0.99010	0.98039	0.97087	0.96154	0.95238	0.94340	0.93458
2	0.46924	0.46245	0.45581	0.44932	0.44297	0.43676	0.43068
3	0.29634	0.29071	0.28522	0.27987	0.27466	0.26957	0.26461
4	0.21041	0.20550	0.20072	0.19607	0.19155	0.18716	0.18289
5	0.15927	0.15487	0.15061	0.14648	0.14247	0.13859	0.13482
6	0.12550	0.12152	0.11768	0.11396	0.11037	0.10689	0.10352
7	0.10165	0.09804	0.09454	0.09117	0.08792	0.08478	0.08176
8	0.08401	0.08070	0.07751	0.07444	0.07149	0.06864	0.06591
9	0.07048	0.06745	0.06453	0.06173	0.05904	0.05645	0.05397
10	0.05984	0.05705	0.05438	0.05181	0.04935	0.04700	0.04475
11	0.05129	0.04872	0.04627	0.04392	0.04167	0.03952	0.03747
12	0.04430	0.04194	0.03968	0.03753	0.03547	0.03351	0.03164
13	0.03851	0.03633	0.03426	0.03228	0.03040	0.02860	0.02690
14	0.03365	0.03165	0.02974	0.02793	0.02620	0.02456	0.02300
15	0.02954	0.02770	0.02595	0.02428	0.02269	0.02119	0.01977
16	0.02604	0.02434	0.02273	0.02119	0.01974	0.01837	0.01707
17	0.02302	0.02146	0.01998	0.01857	0.01724	0.01598	0.01479
18	0.02042	0.01898	0.01762	0.01632	0.01510	0.01395	0.01286
19	0.01816	0.01683	0.01558	0.01439	0.01327	0.01221	0.01122
20	0.01618	0.01496	0.01381	0.01272	0.01169	0.01072	0.00981
21	0.01445	0.01333	0.01227	0.01126	0.01032	0.00943	0.00860
22	0.01292	0.01189	0.01092	0.01000	0.00913	0.00832	0.00756
23	0.01158	0.01063	0.00974	0.00889	0.00809	0.00735	0.00665
24	0.01039	0.00952	0.00869	0.00792	0.00719	0.00651	0.00587
25	0.00933	0.00853	0.00778	0.00706	0.00639	0.00577	0.00519
26	0.00839	0.00766	0.00696	0.00631	0.00569	0.00512	0.00459
27	0.00755	0.00688	0.00624	0.00564	0.00508	0.00455	0.00407
28	0.00680	0.00619	0.00560	0.00505	0.00453	0.00405	0.00361
29	0.00613	0.00557	0.00503	0.00453	0.00405	0.00361	0.00320
30	0.00553	0.00502	0.00452	0.00406	0.00363	0.00322	0.00285
31	0.00500	0.00452	0.00407	0.00365	0.00325	0.00288	0.00254
32	0.00451	0.00408	0.00367	0.00328	0.00291	0.00257	0.00226
33	0.00408	0.00368	0.00330	0.00295	0.00261	0.00230	0.00202
34	0.00369	0.00333	0.00298	0.00265	0.00235	0.00206	0.00180
35	0.00334	0.00300	0.00269	0.00239	0.00211	0.00185	0.00161
36	0.00302	0.00272	0.00243	0.00215	0.00190	0.00166	0.00144
37	0.00274	0.00246	0.00219	0.00194	0.00171	0.00149	0.00129
38	0.00248	0.00222	0.00198	0.00175	0.00154	0.00134	0.00115
39	0.00225	0.00201	0.00179	0.00158	0.00138	0.00120	0.00103
40	0.00204	0.00182	0.00162	0.00143	0.00125	0.00108	0.00093
41	0.00185	0.00165	0.00146	0.00129	0.00112	0.00097	0.00083
42	0.00167	0.00149	0.00132	0.00116	0.00101	0.00087	0.00075
43	0.00152	0.00135	0.00120	0.00105	0.00091	0.00079	0.00067
44	0.00138	0.00123	0.00109	0.00095	0.00083	0.00071	0.00060
45	0.00125	0.00111	0.00098	0.00086	0.00075	0.00064	0.00054

TABLE 5-16 (Continued)
Yearly Savings Rate Factors
10% Savings Step-up Rate (A7)

Yrs	| Assumed Rate of Return (A7)						
	8%	9%	10%	11%	12%	15%	20%
1	0.92593	0.91743	0.90909	0.90090	0.89286	0.86957	0.83333
2	0.42474	0.41892	0.41322	0.40765	0.40219	0.38647	0.36232
3	0.25977	0.25505	0.25044	0.24594	0.24155	0.22898	0.20991
4	0.17873	0.17469	0.17075	0.16692	0.16320	0.15261	0.13672
5	0.13117	0.12762	0.12418	0.12085	0.11761	0.10847	0.09493
6	0.10027	0.09712	0.09408	0.09113	0.08829	0.08029	0.06862
7	0.07884	0.07602	0.07331	0.07069	0.06817	0.06112	0.05099
8	0.06328	0.06075	0.05831	0.05597	0.05373	0.04749	0.03865
9	0.05159	0.04931	0.04712	0.04502	0.04302	0.03748	0.02974
10	0.04259	0.04053	0.03855	0.03667	0.03487	0.02995	0.02316
11	0.03551	0.03364	0.03186	0.03017	0.02855	0.02416	0.01821
12	0.02986	0.02816	0.02655	0.02502	0.02357	0.01966	0.01442
13	0.02528	0.02374	0.02228	0.02090	0.01960	0.01610	0.01150
14	0.02153	0.02013	0.01881	0.01756	0.01639	0.01326	0.00922
15	0.01842	0.01716	0.01596	0.01483	0.01378	0.01098	0.00742
16	0.01584	0.01469	0.01360	0.01258	0.01163	0.00913	0.00600
17	0.01367	0.01262	0.01164	0.01072	0.00986	0.00762	0.00486
18	0.01184	0.01089	0.00999	0.00916	0.00838	0.00638	0.00396
19	0.01029	0.00942	0.00861	0.00785	0.00715	0.00536	0.00323
20	0.00896	0.00817	0.00743	0.00675	0.00612	0.00451	0.00264
21	0.00783	0.00710	0.00643	0.00582	0.00525	0.00381	0.00216
22	0.00685	0.00619	0.00558	0.00502	0.00451	0.00322	0.00177
23	0.00601	0.00541	0.00486	0.00435	0.00388	0.00273	0.00145
24	0.00528	0.00473	0.00423	0.00377	0.00335	0.00232	0.00120
25	0.00465	0.00415	0.00369	0.00328	0.00290	0.00197	0.00099
26	0.00410	0.00364	0.00323	0.00285	0.00251	0.00168	0.00081
27	0.00362	0.00320	0.00283	0.00248	0.00217	0.00143	0.00067
28	0.00320	0.00282	0.00248	0.00217	0.00189	0.00122	0.00055
29	0.00283	0.00249	0.00217	0.00189	0.00164	0.00104	0.00046
30	0.00251	0.00219	0.00191	0.00166	0.00143	0.00089	0.00038
31	0.00222	0.00194	0.00168	0.00145	0.00124	0.00076	0.00031
32	0.00197	0.00171	0.00148	0.00127	0.00108	0.00065	0.00026
33	0.00176	0.00152	0.00130	0.00111	0.00095	0.00056	0.00022
34	0.00156	0.00135	0.00115	0.00098	0.00083	0.00048	0.00018
35	0.00139	0.00119	0.00102	0.00086	0.00072	0.00041	0.00015
36	0.00124	0.00106	0.00090	0.00076	0.00063	0.00036	0.00012
37	0.00111	0.00094	0.00079	0.00067	0.00055	0.00031	0.00010
38	0.00099	0.00084	0.00070	0.00059	0.00049	0.00026	0.00008
39	0.00088	0.00074	0.00062	0.00052	0.00043	0.00023	0.00007
40	0.00079	0.00066	0.00055	0.00046	0.00037	0.00020	0.00006
41	0.00070	0.00059	0.00049	0.00040	0.00033	0.00017	0.00005
42	0.00063	0.00053	0.00043	0.00036	0.00029	0.00015	0.00004
43	0.00056	0.00047	0.00039	0.00031	0.00025	0.00013	0.00003
44	0.00050	0.00042	0.00034	0.00028	0.00022	0.00011	0.00003
45	0.00045	0.00037	0.00030	0.00025	0.00020	0.00009	0.00002

Selecting the Preretirement Inflation Factor (F1)

The appropriate F1 factor depends on the assumed annual inflation rate prior to retirement (line A1 of the Retirement Planning Worksheet) and the number of years until retirement (line A3 of the Retirement Planning Worksheet). The F1 factor is found in table 5-9 by looking in the column with the interest/inflation rate equal to the inflation rate specified in line A1 and the row with the number of years equal to that specified in line A3 of the Retirement Planning Worksheet. For example, if you assume inflation will average 6 percent per year until retirement (A1) and you expect to retire in 18 years (A3), the appropriate preretirement inflation factor (F1) is 2.85.

Selecting the Current Assets Future Value Factor (F3)

The appropriate F3 factor depends on the assumed rate of return on investment prior to retirement (line A5 of the Retirement Planning Worksheet) and the number of years until retirement (line A3 of the Retirement Planning Worksheet). The F3 factor is found in table 5-9 by looking in the column with the interest/inflation rate equal to the rate of return specified in line A5 and the row with the number of years equal to that specified in line A3 of the Retirement Planning Worksheet. For example, if you assume you can invest at a rate of 9 percent per year until retirement (A5) and you expect to retire in 12 years (A3), the appropriate current assets future value factor (F3) is 2.81.

Selecting the Retirement Needs Present Value Factor (F2)

The appropriate F2 factor depends on the assumed annual inflation rate after retirement, the expected duration of retirement, and the assumed rate of return on investment after retirement (lines A2, A4, and A6, respectively, of the Retirement Planning Worksheet [table 5-5]). The F2 factor is found using a two-step process. First, you must determine the inflation-adjusted interest rate. This is estimated by subtracting your assumed inflation rate after retirement (A2) from your assumed investment rate of return after retirement (A6). Specifically,

<u>Value from A6</u>	–	<u>Value from A2</u>	=	Inflation-Adjusted <u>Rate</u>
_____	–	_____	=	_____

Next, you can find the appropriate F2 factor by looking in table 5-10 in the column with the inflation-adjusted interest rate equal to that just computed and the row with the number of years equal to that specified in line

A4 of the Retirement Planning Worksheet. For example, if you assume inflation will average 5 percent per year after retirement (A2) and you expect to earn 8 percent on your investments after retirement (A6), your inflation-adjusted interest rate would be

Value from A6	−	Value from A2	=	Inflation-Adjusted Rate
8%	−	5%	=	3%

If your expected duration of retirement is 22 years (A4), the appropriate retirement needs present value factor (F2) is found by looking in the 3 percent column and the 22 year row of table 5-10. In this case, F2 is 16.415.

Selecting the Defined-Benefit Present Value Factor (F4)

The appropriate F4 factor depends on the assumed rate of return on investment after retirement and the expected duration of retirement (lines A6 and A4 of the Retirement Planning Worksheet, respectively). The F4 factor is found in table 5-10 by looking in the column with the interest rate equal to the rate of return specified in line A6 and the row with the number of years equal to that specified in line A4 of the Retirement Planning Worksheet. For example, if you assume you can invest at a rate of 7 percent per year after retirement (A6) and you expect your retirement needs to last 26 years (A4), the appropriate defined-benefit present value factor (F4) is 12.654.

Selecting the Savings Rate Factor (F5)

The appropriate F5 factor depends on the number of years until you plan to retire, the average annual rate of return you expect to earn on investment until retirement, and your savings step-up rate (lines A3, A5, and A7 of table 5-8, the Retirement Planning Worksheet, respectively). To find the appropriate F5 factor, you must first select the table corresponding to your savings step-up rate (A7). The tables correspond to step-up rates ranging from 0 percent to 10 percent, with the step-up rate increased by 2 percentage points in each successive table.

The savings step-up rate is the rate at which you plan to increase or step up the amount you save each year. Frequently, the step-up rate is set equal to the rate at which a person expects his or her annual earnings to grow. If the step-up rate is set equal to the earnings growth rate, the amount that must be saved each year remains a fixed proportion of those growing earnings. Therefore the "burden" of saving for retirement remains the same each year relative to your growing income. For example, if you expect your earnings to grow at an average annual rate of 6 percent per year and want your required savings each year to be constant relative to your earnings, you would use the table showing a 6 percent savings step-up rate.

Once you have selected the table corresponding to your desired step-up rate, you would find your savings rate factor (F5) in the column and row corresponding to your assumed investment rate of return prior to retirement (A5) and the number of years until you plan to retire (A3), respectively. For example, if your step-up rate is 6 percent (A7), your assumed rate of return is 8 percent (A5), and you plan to retire in 10 years, your savings rate factor (F5) is 0.05031.

Remember, line 21 of the Retirement Planning Worksheet (table 5-8) calculates the amount you need to save the first year. In each subsequent year you must increase the amount you save by your assumed savings step-up rate if you are to reach your goal. For example, assume your savings step-up rate is 5 percent and the amount calculated in line 21 of the Retirement Planning Worksheet is $1,000. In the second year you would have to save $1,050; in the third year, $1,102.50; in the fourth year, $1,157.62; and so on.

The amount you must save each year is calculated by multiplying the prior year's savings amount by (1 + the step-up rate). For example, if your savings step-up rate is 6 percent, you would compute each subsequent year's savings amount by multiplying the previous year's savings amount by 1.06.

If you specify a 0 percent savings step-up rate, you will reach your retirement accumulation goal by saving the same level amount each year as determined in line 21 of the Retirement Planning Worksheet (table 5-8), assuming your actual investment rate of return matches your assumed rate of return.

WEB CALCULATORS AND PROPRIETARY SOFTWARE

Our goal for this chapter was to provide insight into the "numbers" a client needs for retirement. We realize that many planners will have proprietary software that calculates the client's savings target and the annual savings needed for retirement. As a general rule, this software often provides an excellent way to measure a client's needs. If you do not have proprietary software available to you, or if you would like a second opinion, we recommend using the "ballpark estimate," which is found at www.ASEC.org (click on *savings tools*). The American Savings Educational Council has teamed up with, among others, the Department of Labor and Social Security Administration to provide a consumer-friendly retirement calculator. The calculator will no doubt be more simplistic than your proprietary software, but can provide an excellent check for accuracy to see if you are in the ballpark (pun intended). What's more, clients who are skeptical of your numbers may be convinced by this "quasi-official" government version.

Clients without a computer can download a noninteractive worksheet version to do a manual calculation.

CONCLUSION

The material in this chapter will help you and your client to set goals and to better understand the retirement needs analysis. Properly utilizing the tools provided and properly analyzing the assumptions needed will assist clients immeasurably. We feel it bears repetition, however, that this is an art form, not a science. The numbers are not absolute. Your best judgment should be used in conjunction with what this chapter has given you to achieve the best results for your client.

The importance of using a retirement needs analysis to motivate clients to save for retirement should be emphasized. According to the General Accounting Office (GAO), neither baby boomers nor Generation Xers have accumulated sufficient savings for retirement. In addition, according to an Employee Benefit Research Institute (ERBI) study, calculating retirement savings seems to affect savings habits regardless of age. According to a recent Employee Benefit Research Institute Retirement Confidence Survey of the 40 percent of workers who did a retirement needs calculation, 58 percent began saving more.

6

Retirement Investment Strategies: The Accumulation Period

Walt J. Woerheide

Chapter Outline

In chapter 5, we discussed how to determine the amount a client needs for retirement. This process involved looking at how much income a person would need during retirement, how much income would come from other sources, and how much would need to be provided through a person's own savings program. The process also examined the client's current investments to ascertain how much income they could be expected to provide during retirement. Finally, a calculation was made as to how much additional savings a client would need to accumulate during his or her working life to meet the desired retirement goals.

In that chapter, the rates of return a client could be expected to earn were taken as a given. In this chapter, we look at the issues of what are appropriate investments for a client saving for retirement and what are appropriate investment strategies. It is these investments and investment strategies that should clarify for a financial planner what rates of return he or she should use for a client.

We will start by reviewing modern portfolio theory to have a better understanding of what is meant by the risk-return tradeoff. We will then look at issues associated with determining a client's attitude toward risk, which is referred to as risk tolerance. Next, we will consider the topic of time diversification. Time diversification is particularly critical for retirement savings because it is the retirement savings program that has the longest time horizon for investors, and time diversification is relevant only for long time horizons. Many people mistakenly believe that because of time diversification, money that younger investors are saving for retirement should be put into the riskiest investments, regardless of an investor's risk tolerance.

We will then look at issues of strategic and tactical asset allocation, as well as issues specific to the management of portfolios with long time horizons. The final topic is that of whether a client should be encouraged to pay off his or her mortgage prior to or at the time of retirement, and some of the strategies for doing this.

MODERN PORTFOLIO THEORY: OVERVIEW AND IMPLICATIONS FOR RETIREMENT PLANNING[1]

Modern portfolio theory (MPT) starts with the idea that all investments may be characterized with two basic numbers: their expected returns and the variances (or standard deviations) of these returns. (Variance and standard deviation are defined later, but are simply measures of the variability of an asset's possible returns.) Thus, the world of all possible risky assets could be plotted on a graph that has expected return on the vertical axis and the standard deviation of return on the horizontal axis, as shown in figure 6-1.

Defining the Efficient Frontier

MPT makes the assumption that one can identify for each pair of securities the covariance of the returns for those two securities. The covariance of returns is simply a measure of the extent to which the returns of two securities

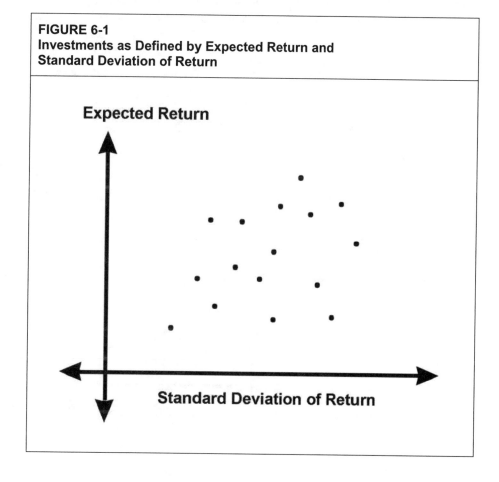

FIGURE 6-1
Investments as Defined by Expected Return and
Standard Deviation of Return

are related. A covariance between two securities that is large and positive indicates the prices of the two securities almost always move in the same direction. Thus, when the price on one security has a large jump or drop, the price of the other security would likely have a similar jump or drop. Similarly, if the covariance is a large negative number, then the prices of those two securities tend to move in opposite directions. Namely, when the price of one makes a big move, the price of the other also tends to have a big move, but in the opposite direction. Finally, when the covariance equals or is near zero, the changes in prices of the two securities tend to be unrelated. By taking advantage of knowledge of the covariances between all of the risky securities and using a mathematical tool known as quadratic programming, one can construct an efficient frontier. The *efficient frontier* can be defined in either of two ways. One is that it is the locus of portfolios that can be created which, for any given level of risk as measured by the standard deviation of return, provides the maximum expected return. The other is that it is the locus of portfolios that can be created which, for any given level of expected return, provides the minimum level of risk as measured by the standard deviation of return. An example of an efficient frontier is shown in figure 6-2.

efficient frontier

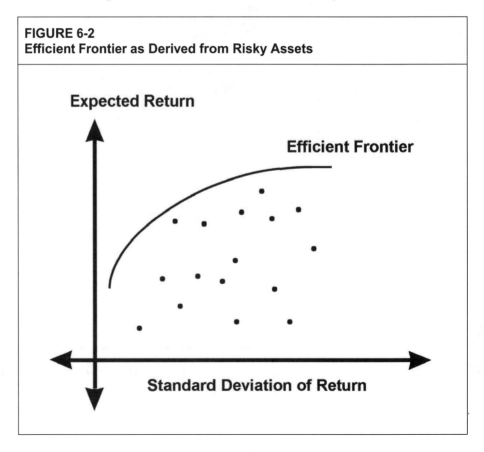

FIGURE 6-2
Efficient Frontier as Derived from Risky Assets

Defining the Capital Market Line

The next concept in MPT is the recognition of a risk-free asset. Most people think of the 90-day Treasury bill as the risk-free asset. This would be true only if one's holding period time horizon were 90 days. However, for the sake of discussion, let's assume the existence of a risk-free asset. When an investor has the opportunity to invest in a risk-free asset in addition to all of the risky assets we have previously discussed, there is a dramatic change in the efficient frontier. In fact, a new efficient frontier is created that consists of various combinations of only two assets. These two assets are the risk-free asset and a portfolio that is labeled portfolio M. This new efficient frontier is known as the *capital market line*. The relationship between the capital market line and the old efficient frontier is shown in figure 6-3. The implication here is that all investors would invest in only portfolio M and the risk-free asset; only what differs is the percentage invested in each asset. This is called the *separation theorem*.

Because the capital market line is composed of only two assets, the risk-free asset and a portfolio labeled M, the composition of portfolio M is

capital market line

separation theorem

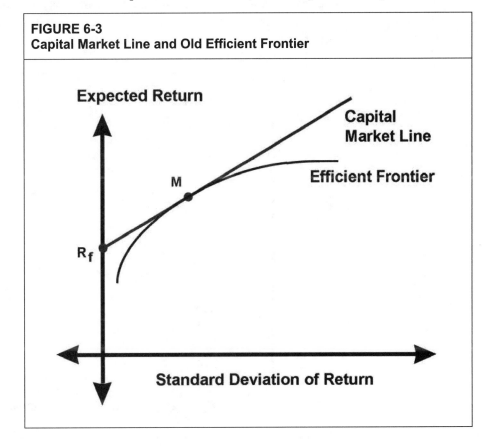

FIGURE 6-3
Capital Market Line and Old Efficient Frontier

market portfolio
obviously critical. Portfolio M must be what is known as the market portfolio. In theory, the *market portfolio* is the portfolio of all assets, where the amount invested in each asset is a function of the market value of that asset relative to the market value of all assets. A broad market index such as the Standard & Poor's 500 index is frequently used as a surrogate for portfolio M. Note that in figure 6-3, portfolios to the left of portfolio M on the capital market line are created by investing some money in the risk-free asset and the rest in portfolio M. Portfolios to the right of portfolio M are created by putting all one's money into portfolio M and also borrowing money at the risk-free rate and using that money to buy portfolio M.

Determining the Optimal Portfolio to Hold

It is important to remember that the capital market line only shows the most efficient portfolios that an investor should consider holding, but does not show which specific portfolio an investor should hold. That determination can only be made by utilizing what are known as indifference curves (shown in figure 6-4). Each investor has a unique utility for wealth.

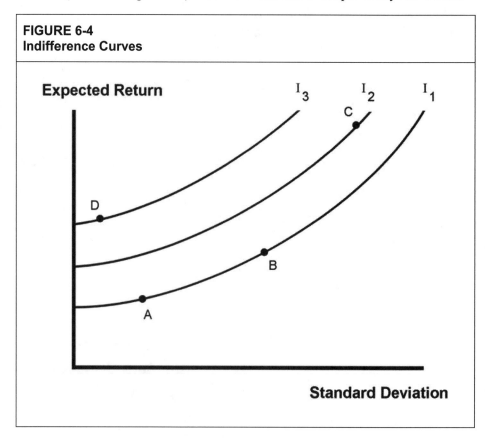

FIGURE 6-4
Indifference Curves

The utility for wealth, in turn, allows us to define indifference curves. The critical feature here is to assume that each investor seeks to obtain a portfolio on the highest possible indifference curve. It does not matter to the investor which portfolio is held on a particular indifference curve as, by definition, he or she is indifferent among all portfolios that lie on the same curve. Hence, in figure 6-4, the investor is indifferent between holding portfolios A and B.

This same investor would, naturally, prefer to hold portfolio C over either A or B because it lies on a higher indifference curve. Finally, this same investor would be even happier to hold portfolio D over C, even though D has less expected return than C. Portfolio D has so much less risk than C that the reduction of some expected return is a price the investor is willing to pay to obtain the large reduction in risk.

To obtain the portfolio an investor should hold, we only need (in theory) to impose that investor's indifference curves onto the capital market line, as shown in figure 6-5. In this figure, the indifference curves for two investors are shown. The first investor (I_1, I_2, I_3) is more risk averse than the second investor (I_4, I_5, I_6). Thus, the first investor should put a significant portion of his or her

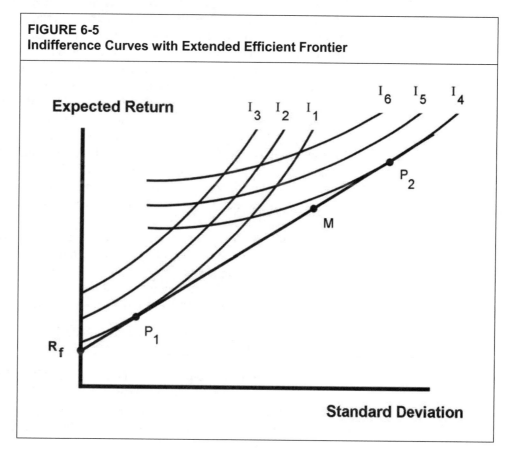

FIGURE 6-5
Indifference Curves with Extended Efficient Frontier

money into the risk-free asset and the rest into portfolio M. The second investor would actually borrow money (that is, buy on margin) and use both the borrowed money and his or her own money to buy lots of portfolio M.

This description leads to two of the most critical concepts in investment planning. The first is that it is incredibly important for a financial planner to understand a client's risk tolerance so that a portfolio with the appropriate level of risk can be created. The second is that it is equally important that the risky assets that are held in a client's portfolio constitute a diversified portfolio. That is, investors cannot actually acquire portfolio M; they must make do by acquiring a portfolio that is a reasonable surrogate of the market portfolio.

Diversification

The significant feature of the market portfolio is that it provides the ultimate in portfolio diversification. So, the relevant question for any investor is, how many securities must be held to have an adequately diversified portfolio size in 1968.[2] In their research, they started with a large database of stocks and randomly selected 60 securities. For each of these 60 securities, they computed the standard deviation of returns over a fixed time period. They then computed the arithmetic average of the 60 standard deviations. They repeated the exercise by creating 60 portfolios, each of which contained two randomly selected securities. The standard deviations of these 60 portfolios were computed and the arithmetic average again derived. This process was repeated for 60 portfolios of three randomly selected securities on up to 60 portfolios of 40 randomly selected securities. For each portfolio size, the average of the 60 standard deviations was computed. These 40 average standard deviations were graphed with the vertical axis showing the standard deviation and the horizontal axis showing the number of securities in the portfolios. Finally, Evans and Archer computed the standard deviation for the portfolio consisting of every single security in their database. This was defined as the standard deviation of the market portfolio.

This exercise has been repeated many times using different data sets, different time periods, different time horizons, and so on. The actual numerical results differ with each application, but the general principles that emerge are always the same. The typical graph that is produced is shown in figure 6-6. The general conclusions from these studies form some of the most important principles of investments today. They include:

1. On average, the total risk of a portfolio declines as additional securities are added to the portfolio.

2. The total risk of a portfolio declines at a DECREASING rate as additional securities are added. Thus, the addition of a third security to a two-security portfolio will reduce total risk by a substantially greater amount than will the addition of a 40th security to a 39-security portfolio.

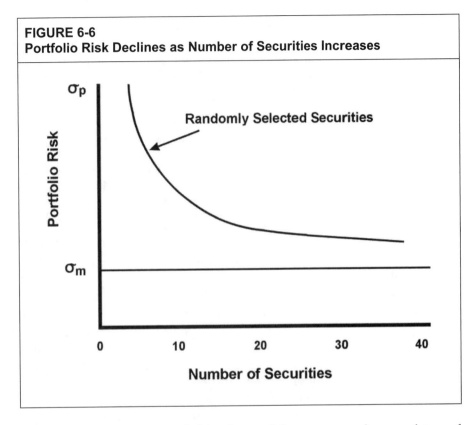

FIGURE 6-6
Portfolio Risk Declines as Number of Securities Increases

3.   On average, the total risk of a portfolio converges downward toward the total risk of the market portfolio.

4.   On average, no amount of diversification can reduce the total risk of a portfolio below that of the market portfolio.

That is, diversification does not eliminate all risk. It only eliminates nonmarket or nonsystematic risk. This means that systematic risk becomes an increasing portion of the portfolio's total risk. *Systematic risk* refers to changes in a stock's price that are the result of events that affect virtually all stocks.

systematic risk

The Evans-Archer graph brings us to the crux of the optimal portfolio size question. If we assume that there is some cost to adding a security to a portfolio, then at some point the cost of adding a security to a portfolio exceeds the value of the reduction in risk from adding that security. Certainly for most investors the commission to buy 100 shares in each of two companies is more than the commission to buy 200 shares in one company. Some people would also argue that there is a monitoring cost. That is, a portfolio manager may have to spend more time monitoring a 50-stock portfolio than a 10-stock portfolio. Hence, to the extent that each additional security necessitates additional time for monitoring, there is an implicit time cost when stocks are added to portfolios.

Let's ignore the monitoring cost issue by assuming that markets are efficient and therefore no monitoring is necessary. Let's also assume that the only transaction fee is the commission. If this were the case, then the optimal portfolio size is inversely related to the magnitude of the commission. This becomes our fifth principle:

5.   The lower the commission one pays, the larger the number of securities that would be optimal.

If one paid no commission (for example, suppose one had a wrap account in which one paid an annual fee but did not pay any commissions per se), then in theory the optimal portfolio size becomes extremely large.

The Impact of Portfolio Composition on Optimal Portfolio Size

As one might suspect, the Evans-Archer graph can be quite sensitive to the composition of the portfolio. For example, suppose the securities that made up the portfolio were all mutual funds. Thus, each security would represent a portfolio of as many as several hundred or more securities. In other words, each security would already represent a highly diversified portfolio. In this case, the curve in figure 6-6 would converge much more quickly to the market portfolio than is the case when the securities represent individual stocks. This result is shown by the drop in the risk exposure curve in figure 6-7. Hence, the optimal number of holdings would likely be a much smaller number when one limits the holdings to only mutual funds.

Furthermore, if the mutual funds were load funds, then the optimal number of funds to hold would be limited. If they were no-loads, then once again the optimal number of securities to hold would be potentially unlimited even though there is negligible risk reduction as funds are added to the portfolio.

Finally, another famous research piece looked at the effect of including securities of foreign companies in one's portfolio.[3] The stock markets in different countries appear to have a large component of independent variability. That is, a large part of the variability in their returns is unrelated to fluctuations in any other country's domestic market. A strategy of adding foreign securities to a portfolio of domestic securities can be used to reduce the impact of the home country's business cycle. The inclusion of international securities in one's portfolio will result in a risk curve that is lower than the risk curve of portfolios that consist only of domestic securities.[4]

ASSESSMENT OF RISK TOLERANCE AND ASSET ALLOCATION

As stated earlier, the first obligation of a financial planner is to assess a client's risk tolerance—that is, to asses whether the client's indifference curves are steeply sloped and the client is highly risk averse (that is, risk

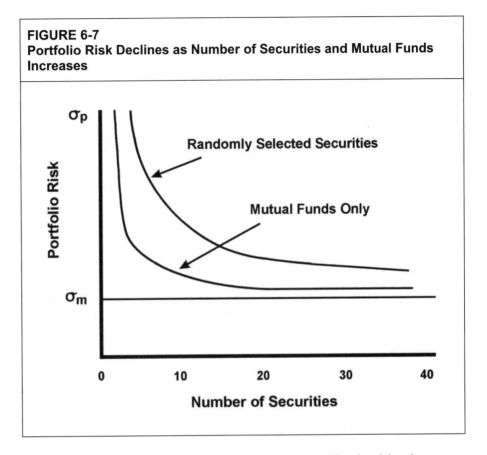

FIGURE 6-7
Portfolio Risk Declines as Number of Securities and Mutual Funds Increases

intolerant or conservative) or only mildly risk averse (that is, risk tolerant or aggressive). Once this assessment is made, the planner then needs to have a scheme to relate the degree of risk tolerance to an asset allocation recommendation. Unfortunately, there is no real research yet that allows us to tie any asset allocation strategies to general assessments of risk tolerance, or to precise numerical measures of risk tolerance where a formal quantitative scheme is used with a client. This doesn't mean that assessment of risk tolerance is not worthwhile. At the very least, it shows due diligence and thus would help protect the financial advisor in the event an unhappy client sues the planner. Many financial planning firms and financial planners give their clients risk tolerance questionnaires to try to get a sense of the client's feelings on this issue. Financial planning is problematic in the case of a couple where each has a substantially different risk tolerance than the other. For example, if the husband is an aggressive investor and the wife is a conservative investor, then there is little the planner can do that will please both parties.

Studies of risk tolerance show that clients may have different degrees of risk tolerance for different investment goals. Consider the following example:

Example: Mark Charles is a new client. He has indicated four financial goals. He wants to buy a new car in 3 years, buy a house in 5 years, pay for his kids' college educations starting in 16 years, and have a financially secure retirement starting in 35 years. Unless Mark is already independently wealthy, all of these goals will call for a substantial program of saving and investing. Nonetheless, Mark's attitude toward risk on each of these goals may well differ. Mark may want to place a near certainty on the purchase of a house and the financing of the college tuition, and at the same time be much more aggressive with regard to the purchase of the car and the financing of retirement.

Although modern portfolio theory treats financial assets as a single portfolio, it may make more sense in Mark's case to think about two, three, or even four different portfolios, where each portfolio is characterized by a different degree of risk tolerance, and thus a different asset allocation. All of these portfolios may be combined within one account. Thus, each time the financial planner meets with Mark, he or she would have to provide a breakdown on how each of the portfolios within the account is doing. Alternatively, multiple accounts could be set up, with each account dedicated to a separate goal. In fact, Mark may already have separate accounts if he is in a defined-contribution pension plan or has a traditional IRA, a Roth IRA, a Keogh account, Coverdell IRAs, and one or more non-qualified accounts between his wife and himself. The advantage of the multiple accounts is that the asset allocation for each goal is easier to see within each account, and the progress toward achieving these separate goals is also easier to see.

In this chapter, when we talk about the investment portfolio, we are talking about all of the assets that are categorized as having the primary purpose of providing income during retirement. These assets may be in one account, ten accounts, or even in accounts that are shared with assets that are dedicated to other objectives.

Time Lag from Decision to Fruition

As we will see shortly, investors should take on more risk in their retirement portfolio than they might take on investments made for other purposes. Fortunately, research has shown that a decision about a risky matter is influenced by the lag between the time of making the decision and the time the decision reaches fruition. Generally, if the consequences of the decision will be known right away, the decision maker will be relatively more risk averse than if the consequences of the decision will be unknown for some time. People often make very risk-averse decisions because they have a short-term perspective on their financial status. If these investors were to adopt a more long-term perspective, such as considering the value of their investments at retirement, they might opt for an investment with greater risk but with a higher potential payoff in the long run.

If clients learn to adopt a long-term investment perspective, then more aggressive investments become more palatable. One approach is to have the client, over time, reduce the frequency with which he or she examines the performance of the investment. Annual or biannual reviews of a client's portfolio and progress toward retirement would tend to minimize anxiety, although it will not eliminate it.

One technique to help a client become more risk tolerant is to increase his or her knowledge of financial matters. Research on risk taking shows that individuals who engage in a risky activity report a greater understanding of the risks involved as well as less fear of the risks. Unknown risks loom larger than known risks, and experience with the activity reduces this fear. Although education may not always be a substitute for experience, it is the next best thing to it.

Less Choice Equals More Action

Recent research on employees who were being offered 401(k) programs through their jobs found that the more choices the employees had, the less likely they were to participate in any program at all! In other words, too much choice appeared to produce "analysis paralysis." Thus, after the planner has ascertained the client's risk tolerance, a limited number of choices that are consistent with this risk tolerance should be provided to the client.

THE CONCEPT OF THE PORTFOLIO OF ASSETS

Many people overlook a critical issue in understanding asset allocations in portfolios: that the relevant portfolio for financial planning consists of ALL of an individual's assets and liabilities. This includes certain assets that are not a direct part of a person's investment portfolio, but are a critical part of that person's total portfolio. An analysis of the investment portfolio in isolation could lead to inappropriate or less than optimal recommendations. The major such asset is what is known as human capital. For simplicity, let's define people's wealth at any point in time as the sum of their financial assets and their human capital. In equation form:

$$\text{Wealth} = \text{Human Capital} + \text{Financial Assets}$$

There is a propensity to equate wealth with financial assets. This would be true, however, only for someone who no longer has any human capital value.

Definition of Human Capital

human capital

Human capital refers to a person's ability to generate income—primarily the ability to generate wage and salary income, but it could just as easily refer to the ability to generate income from such sources as royalties on written material and profits from sole proprietorships. To simplify the discussion, let's define human capital as the present value of future net wage income. When most people are moving out of their parents' home and starting their own lives, their wealth consists almost entirely of human capital. Of course, some young adults are fortunate enough to be given substantial financial assets early in life, and thus their financial assets may dominate their human capital, but even in these cases, their human capital is not necessarily trivial in absolute terms.

Most people's working careers can be defined as the process of moving from a position in which their wealth consists exclusively or almost exclusively of human capital to a position in which their wealth consists exclusively or almost exclusively of financial assets. This is illustrated in figure 6-8, where the vertical axis is measured in dollars and the horizontal axis in time. The origin represents a person starting his or her career. At the origin, wealth equals human capital and financial assets are zero. Three things then happen as the individual moves through his or her career. First, his or her human capital starts to rise initially. This is because he or she moves closer toward his or her higher salary years with the passage of each year. The increase in the present value of each future year's income more than offsets the loss of one year of income. Second, eventually the shorter number of remaining years of working overshadows the increase in the present value of the remaining years, and the person's human capital begins to decline. At final retirement, the person's human capital hits zero, as there is by definition no future wage income that this person will generate.

Third, the individual presumably starts setting aside money to invest. Over time, these contributions to investments, combined with the total returns on the investments, will cause the financial assets to steadily grow. At retirement, the person's wealth will consist entirely of his or her financial assets.

Example 1:   John Henry is 22 and has just graduated from college. He has accepted a position with a starting salary of $40,000. He believes his salary will grow at a rate of 3 percent over his working career of 45 years (his normal retirement age for Social Security purposes is 67). If 8 percent is arbitrarily selected as

FIGURE 6-8
Human Capital and Wealth Over Time

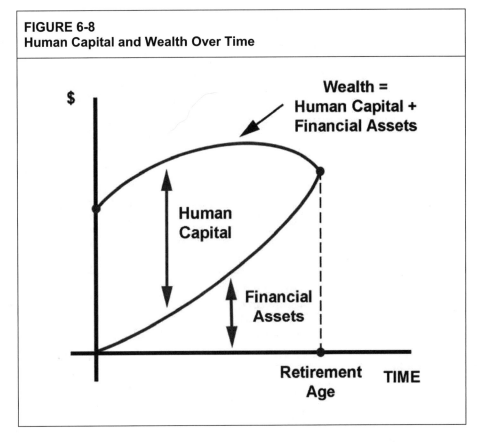

the appropriate discount rate, then the value of his human capital when he starts his job (assuming he is paid at the end of each year) is $705,224.50. (See table 6-1.) Note that this number is a pretax number, as it ignores the income taxes and Social Security taxes that John will have to pay on his income as it is earned.

If all of the assumptions are still in place 10 years later, then John's human capital value will have risen to $870,520. As indicated above, his human capital has actually grown because the increase in the present value of each remaining salary payment is more significant than the fact that his working life is shortened by 10 years. Eventually, the reduction in the number of remaining years of income exceeds the increase in the present value of the other years, and John's human capital value will begin to decline. In table 6-1, John's human capital is at its peak at age 42, and is still substantially higher at age 52 than at ages

22 and 32. By age 62, his human capital value is in rapid decline. At age 67, John retires and his human capital, as measured by the present value of his future wage income, is zero.

To complete the example, suppose that at the end of each year John Henry contributes 5 percent of his annual income to an investment account. Suppose further that he is able to earn 7 percent on his investments. His accumulation of financial assets is shown in the third column of table 6-1. To keep the computation comparable with human capital, the numbers are all shown on a pretax basis. At the end of John's 45-year career, his financial assets will have grown to $824,354.

TABLE 6-1
Valuation of Human Capital and Financial Assets at Ages 22, 32, 42, 52, 62, and 67

Age	Human Capital	Financial Assets	Total
22	$ 705,224	$ 0	$ 705,224
32	870,520	27,725	898,245
42	1,008,144	96,419	1,099,563
52	988,117	245,952	1,234,069
62	550,678	559,462	1,110,140
67	0	824,354	824,354

Relationship of Human Capital Value and Portfolio Diversification

It is important to understand that wealth consists of both human capital and the value of financial assets because this affects the question of diversification. When one is young, diversification does not matter much. Consider our example of John Henry. Suppose that at the end of his first year of working, he is able to invest $4,000 into financial assets (this includes any pension funds as well as nonqualified investments). At that time, his total wealth will equal nearly $709,000. Of this amount, $4,000 is in financial assets and $705,000 is in human capital. His financial assets are such a minor portion of his total wealth that even if he loses his entire investment (for example, by buying stock in a company that goes bankrupt) his wealth is hardly affected. Although one of the most fundamental pieces of investment advice ever provided is to diversify, John cannot really diversify because his wealth is primarily in the form of human capital. John's overriding concern should be to protect his human capital (for example, life insurance, disability income insurance, health insurance), and diversify his human capital to the extent possible (for example, acquire additional skills and/or additional education).

Although diversification is unimportant at the start of John's working career, it becomes more important with each passing year. This is because financial assets will constitute an increasingly larger percentage of John's wealth. Finally, on the day John retires, his wealth will consist completely of his financial assets. From that time forward, diversification is of paramount concern to John.

Another way to look at this issue is that during the early years of his career, John has substantial opportunity to rebuild his portfolio should he suffer any financial setbacks. His income is growing, and although no one likes to contribute more to savings at the expense of current consumption, at least John has the option to do so. Early in his career, John has the opportunity to spread out his increased contributions over many years, and he has the power of time value of money working for him. Toward the end of his career, John has a limited number of years over which to provide increased contributions to make up for losses, and the lack of time till retirement means a substantial loss in the power of time value of money.

Correlation Between Human Capital and Financial Assets

The prior discussion also emphasizes one of the most basic principles of financial planning: In a portfolio that consists of only two assets, it is desirable to minimize the correlation between the assets. This means that investors should minimize the correlation between their human capital and their financial assets.

Many investors might ask, "What does my ability to draw a salary have to do with the performance of my portfolio?" The problem arises when an employee invests in the stock of his or her employer. Although the employee may feel that he or she understands the business and sees the prospects for the business as favorable, there is always the chance that he or she may be wrong. If the company's performance declines and employees are laid off, then not only could the securities of the company decline in value, but the investor could also be laid off. Hence, there could be a substantial decline in both his or her human capital and his or her financial assets at the exact same time. Even investing in other companies in the same industry presents a similar problem. Although it is possible that an industry as a whole could be doing well while only one company within that industry is struggling, it is also possible that when one company struggles, the entire industry could be in difficulty. Hence, employees should avoid investing in both their own company and in other companies in their industry.

Some investors cannot avoid investing in their own company's stock, or are given a substantial temptation to buy their employer's stock. For example, some employees participate in employee stock purchase plans. These plans sell stock to employees at discounts of up to 15 percent from their current market values, which is a strong inducement to invest in an employer's stock! Another situation is where the employee may have substantial stock options in the employer's stock. The purpose of the stock options is usually to align the financial interests of the employee with the shareholders of the company. From the company's perspective, large stock options may be a wonderful tool for motivating managers and other key employees to make decisions that are in the best interests of shareholders. However, from the individual's perspective, this method of compensation increases the risk of simultaneous large losses in both human capital and financial assets.

The above discussion assumes that it is only the returns on the employer's stock that are highly correlated with an investor's human capital. In truth, there are many stocks whose returns are potentially highly correlated with an investor's human capital. Thus, not only should the individual avoid investing in his or her own company's stock, but he or she should have minimal to no investment in other financial assets whose returns are highly correlated with his or her human capital (that is, wage income). This observation has rather interesting implications for portfolio theory. Recall that under the separation theorem derived from modern portfolio theory, all investors would hold only some combination of the market portfolio and the risk-free assets. Once human capital is considered—as well as the fact that for different people there are different correlations between assets and their own human capital—then it becomes clear that almost no one should hold the market portfolio![5]

TIME DIVERSIFICATION

Having an investment time horizon of many years leads people to the concept of time diversification. The usual argument presented for time diversification is, unfortunately, incorrect. Nonetheless, the implications of the time diversification argument may have some validity, but for different reasons. It is important that a financial planner understand how time diversification may work in practice. To explain why time diversification is so appealing, let's begin by considering representative numbers for rates of return, and then look at a typical time diversification argument.

Historical Perspective—Nominal Rates of Return

A financial planner always has to start his or her portfolio projections with estimates of future rates of return for various types of securities. Naturally, there is no definitive statement as to what the future rates of return will be. A planner can only provide a guess. To make the guess sound more sophisticated, practitioners sometimes use the word "guesstimate." Next, the most common technique for deriving guesstimates is to look at historical data, and to assume that the expected (that is, future) rates of return and associated risk will equal the average historical rates of return and variability. Although this is one of the best and most defensible approaches for developing guesstimates of expected returns and risk, the practitioner should be aware that there are two problems associated with this process. One is resolvable with a little algebra, while the other cannot be resolved.

The first issue is to decide the asset categories for which to obtain historical data. The simplest forecasts typically use three asset categories: stocks, bonds, and Treasury bills. Many people use the database provided by Ibbotson & Associates, which provides information for five asset categories. These are: large company common stocks, small company common stocks, long-term corporate bonds, long-term government bonds, and Treasury bills.

To ascertain historical rates of return that are valid for guesstimating expected rates of return, the major question facing the practitioner is what time frame to use. This is critical because historical rates of return vary with the time frame selected. For example, if one estimates the historical rate of return for stocks ending in the year 1999, then the average (or mean) rate of return will be somewhat larger than the mean rate of return if the years 2000, 2001, and 2002 are added to the data set.

It is true that if one uses longer time periods, then the mean rates of return are more stable. For example, the database for Ibbotson & Associates goes back to December 31, 1925. Thus, by using the full database, one can compute the mean rate of return for any particular category of assets from 1926 to the most recent year for which data is available. Adding or deleting one year from this database will have a negligible impact on the statistics computed therein. However, using such a large amount of historical data creates a conceptual problem—that is, are the rates of return on securities during the 1920s, 1930s, and even the 1940s appropriate or representative data for what future rates of return might be? The nature of the United States' economy, and even the world economy, is so different from what it was even 50 years ago that these older rates of return numbers may be more misleading than they are useful. Thus, although using these older rates of return numbers may give a sense of accuracy because their revisions will not change much from year to year, this sense of accuracy is likely ill-conceived. Conceptually, it makes more sense to use a shorter time frame rather than a longer one when using historical data to develop forecasts, although shorter time frames can lead to more changes on a year-to-year basis.

Thus, rather than provide the reader with some historical rates of return numbers and encouraging the reader to use these as representative of future rates of return, let us simply consider what might be called typical rates of return numbers of various asset categories. Such typical rates of return are shown in table 6-2, along with typical numbers for the rate of inflation during recent years. The rates of return for large company common stocks are taken from the Standard & Poor's (S&P) composite index, small company stocks are intended to represent the bottom 20 percent (as ranked by capitalization) of the stocks listed on the New York Stock Exchange, and long-term corporate bonds are based on AAA-rated bonds.

TABLE 6-2
Typical Nominal Returns

Series	Geometric Mean Return	Arithmetic Mean Return	Standard Deviation
Large company stocks	10.50%	12.00%	20.00%
Small company stocks	12.50	18.00	30.00
Long-term corporate bonds	6.00	6.40	9.25
Long-term government bonds	5.50	5.80	9.00
Treasury bills	3.50	3.60	3.00
Inflation	3.00	3.20	4.25

Geometric Mean and Arithmetic Mean[6]

Table 6-2 shows the geometric and arithmetic mean rates of return, as well as the standard deviation of each series. It is important that the reader understand the statistical basis for each of these three numbers.

The computation of the arithmetic mean for a set of rates of return for n periods involves adding up the rates of return and dividing by n. For example, suppose that over the last 2 years, a stock achieved rates of return of +25 percent and –20 percent. The *arithmetic mean return (AMR)* in this example would be + 2.5 percent, computed as

$$[+25\% + (-20\%)] / 2 = 2.5\%$$

The problem with the arithmetic mean return is that it can be misleading because it shows the average rate of return over time, not the effective rate of return over time. To understand the difference, suppose a client has a portfolio worth $100,000. If in the first of two periods, this portfolio achieves a 25 percent rate of return, it would be worth $125,000. If in the second period, the value declines by 20 percent, then it would be worth $100,000. If a portfolio starts out being worth $100,000, and ends up being worth $100,000, the effective rate of return is clearly zero, not 2.5 percent.

geometric mean return (GMR)

The effective rate of return is defined by what is known as the *geometric mean return (GMR).* Computation of the GMR is a four-step process. The first step is to add one to each period's rate of return. This sum is known as the per period return relative (PPRR). When the rate of return for a period is negative, the PPRR will be less than one. Step two is to multiply together all of the PPRRs. The number thus produced is the holding period return relative (HPRR). Step three is to take the nth root of the product in step two, where n is the number of periods used in the calculation. Remember, taking the nth root is the same as taking that number to the 1/n power. The last step is to subtract one from the nth root. Stated as equations:

Step 1: $PPRR_i = 1 +$ rate of return in period i

Step 2: $HPRR = PPRR_1 \times PPRR_2 \times ... \times PPRR_n$

Step 3: $n^{th} \text{ root} = HPRR^{1/n}$

Step 4: $GMR = n^{th} \text{ root} - 1$

In the previous example where we had rates of return of +25 percent and –20 percent, the GMR would be computed as:

Step 1: $PPRR_1 = 1 + .25 = 1.25$, $PPRR_2 = 1 - .20 = .80$

Step 2: $HPRR = 1.25 \times .80 = 1.00$

Step 3: $n^{th} \text{ root} = 1.0^{1/2} = 1.0$

Step 4: $GMR = 1.0 - 1 = 0.0$

This result is exactly what we intuitively know the answer should be. Now let us consider a more complicated example.

Example: Suppose a broad-based stock market index provided the following rates of return over the last 5 years: –13 percent, 17 percent, –2 percent, 8 percent, and 18 percent. What were its geometric mean rate of return and its arithmetic mean rate of return?

The arithmetic mean is:

$(-13\% + 17\% - 2\% + 8\% + 18\%)/5 = 5.6\%$.

To compute the GMR, the first step is to compute the PPRRs, and the second step is to compute the HPRR. The HPRR is computed as:

$HPRR = .87 \times 1.17 \times .98 \times 1.08 \times 1.18 = 1.2713$

Next, we must take the nth root of the HPRR. In this instance n is 5, so the exponent (measured as 1/n) is .2.

$$\text{GMR} = 1.2713^{.2} - 1.00$$

$$= 1.0492 - 1.00 = .0492 \text{ or } 4.92\%$$

There are three points to remember about the relationship between the GMR and the arithmetic mean return.[7] First, only when all the PPRRs are identical will the GMR and arithmetic mean be equal. Second, if the PPRRs are not identical, then the GMR will always be less than the arithmetic mean return. Third, this difference increases as the variability among the PPRRs increases.

Let us now return to table 6-2. Note that the numbers in the table conform to what we know about the relationship between GMRs and AMRs. That is, for each category of securities and for inflation, the geometric mean return is less than the arithmetic mean return. In addition, the greater the standard deviation of each series, the greater the spread between these two numbers.

Standard Deviation

standard deviation

The *standard deviation* is defined as the square root of the variance. The reason is that one can only directly compute the variance. So, although it is the standard deviation in which we are interested, we have to talk first about the variance. The formula for computing variance from historical data is shown in equation 6-1.

$$\sigma^2 = \frac{1}{n-1} \sum_{t=1}^{n} \left[R_t - \overline{R} \right]^2 \qquad \text{(Equation 6-1)}$$

where σ^2 = variance

n = number of years of data

R_t = the rate of return for each year

$\overline{R}$ = the arithmetic mean of the rates of return

Thus, the standard deviation is computed as:

$$\sigma = \sqrt{\sigma^2} = \text{standard deviation}$$

Example:

$$\overline{R} = \frac{-15\% + 5\% + 10\% - 3\% + 28\%}{5} = 5\%$$

The standard deviation is derived from the variance as follows:

$$\sigma^2 = \frac{1}{5-1} \times \left[(-15-5)^2 + (5-5)^2 + (10-5)^2 + (-3-5)^2 + (28-5)^2 \right]$$

$$= \frac{1}{4} \times (400 + 0 + 25 + 64 + 529)$$

$$= 254.5$$

$$\sigma = \sqrt{254.5} = 15.95\%$$

HP-10BII keystrokes
      SHIFT, C ALL
      15, +/−, Σ+
      5, Σ+
      10, Σ+
      3, +/−, Σ+
      28, Σ+

      SHIFT, s_x, s_y (display: 15.95)

normal distribution

It is critical to understand the relationship between the mean returns and the standard deviations. Most people are familiar with what is known as a normal distribution. A *normal distribution* looks like a bell-shaped curve. (See figure 6-9.) Although the pattern of stock market returns is not normally distributed, it is close enough to a normal distribution that we may think about it as being normally distributed without any detriment to this discussion. The key point in a normal distribution is that there is approximately a 2/3 probability that an actual observation will be within one standard deviation of the mean of the distribution. There is a 95 percent probability that an actual observation will be within two standard deviations of the mean, and a 99 percent probability that an actual observation will be within three standard deviations of the mean. Hence, when we note in table 6-2 that large

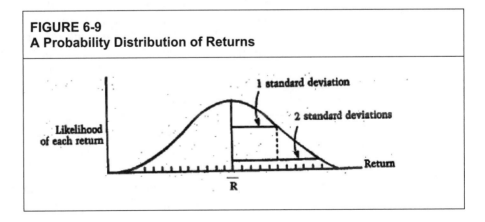

FIGURE 6-9
A Probability Distribution of Returns

company common stocks have an arithmetic mean return of 12 percent and a standard deviation of 20 percent, what we are saying is that if next year's return is based on this distribution, then there is a two-thirds probability that it will be between –8 percent (12% – 20%) and +32 percent (12% + 20%). Furthermore, there is 95 percent probability that it will be between –28 percent and +52 percent.

The Effect of Repeated Sampling on Future Returns

With this understanding of mean returns and standard deviations, let's now look at the concept of repeated sampling. Let's start with a simple proposal. Suppose someone approached you with the following bet. You can flip a coin, and if it comes up heads, this person will pay you $2. If it comes up tails, you will pay this person $1. Now, the expected value of this bet is $.50 if we assume that the coin has a 50 percent probability of coming up heads and a 50 percent probability of coming up tails (.50 x (+$2) + .50 x (–$1)). The expected value is in your favor, and the dollar magnitude of the loss under the worst-case scenario is small, so you would likely take this bet.

If we change the size of the bet from $2 and $1 to $20,000 and $10,000, most people would not take the bet. The expected value of $5,000 (.50 x (+$20,000) + .50 x (–$10,000)) is still to your favor but the pain of losing $10,000 with a single coin flip would be too much for most people to cope with (especially if they had to explain later how they lost $10,000 on the flip of a coin!). There is nothing irrational in these two examples.

Now let's make one more change to the bet. Suppose the person approaching you proposes to keep the bets at $20,000 and $10,000, but offers to repeat the coin flip 20 times. Many people who rejected the previous bet out of hand would reconsider because the prospect of making 20 such bets means that it is highly likely they would win money at this game. After all, they would lose money only if they flipped six or fewer heads out of the 20 flips.[8] The key point of this third proposal is that it has the benefit of diversification through repeated bets.

Many people view the security returns for the different asset categories as a set of repeated bets. In the case of security returns, stocks have higher expected returns than bonds or Treasury bills, but substantially larger standard deviations of returns. For this reason, if a person with a normal degree of risk aversion were planning to invest for only one year, he or she might avoid stocks in favor of bonds or Treasury bills due to the smaller amount of variability of return.

As with our coin-flipping example, suppose this investor plans to invest for not just one year, but for 20, 30, or even 40 years. Each year could be viewed as a repeated "bet" or sampling from the distribution of stock returns. As it is highly unlikely that returns substantially below the mean return will occur each and every period, these occasional positive returns will more than offset the poor returns of other periods. Put another way, the differential in average returns is sufficiently large that it is highly unlikely that over a long time horizon a person would be worse off in the riskier securities than if he or she had invested only in the least risky securities. *Time diversification is the idea of looking at each year as a new drawing from this distribution.*

Empirical Evidence in Favor of Time Diversification

The empirical evidence in favor of time diversification is impressive. Although it would be easy enough to generate data using historical returns, such numbers would vary depending on the number of years of data used and the time period selected. Therefore, let's examine a typical analysis and its associated results.

Let's consider large company stocks. Using the same data period as might have been used to construct table 6-2, we could look at all of the possible overlapping 5-year holding periods starting from the first year of our sample and ending with the last year. For example, for data spanning the period of 1951 to 2004, there would be 54 annual rates of return. The first 5-year period would be for the years 1951 to 1955. The second 5-year period would cover the years 1952 to 1956. The last 5-year period would include the years 2000 to 2004. There would be 50 different 5-year holding periods.

Next, we would compute the mean annual rate of return for each of our 50 holding periods. Finally, we could rank order these 50 mean annual rates of return. There are then three numbers that are critical to our analysis. These are the maximum annual rate of return, the minimum annual rate of return, and the average annual rate of return. This output could be shown graphically, such as seen in the first rectangle in figure 6-10. In this figure, the horizontal axis represents the holding period and the vertical axis represents the mean annual percentage rate of return. The blackened portion of the rectangle represents those mean rates of return that are less than zero. The height of the rectangle defines the maximum-minimum range. The height of the rectangle becomes an indirect measure of the standard deviation of the mean average return.

The above process could then be repeated for holding periods of 10, 20, 30, and even 40 years. There are three key points that are implied by this figure. First, note that the maximum-minimum range keeps getting smaller as the holding period gets longer. In other words, the standard deviation of the average annual return keeps getting smaller! Second, the percentage of each rectangle that is blackened (the portion of mean returns less than zero) become smaller until there are no blackened areas. Finally, the average of the mean holding period returns for each rectangle is pretty much unchanged.

These types of results were first reported by Richard McEnally in 1985[9] and revalidated by Kockman and Goodwin in 2001.[10]

Proponents of time diversification thus offer these types of graphs as evidence to support the argument that, if one's time horizon is long enough,

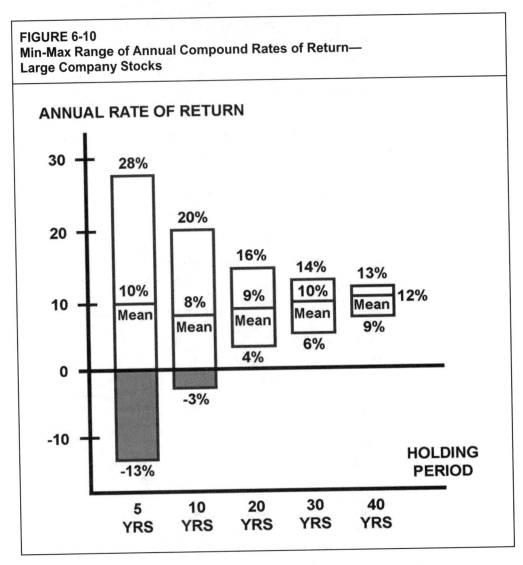

FIGURE 6-10
Min-Max Range of Annual Compound Rates of Return—
Large Company Stocks

one can be assured of achieving a satisfactory mean rate of return. They maintain that even if there is a spell of poor rates of return, there are sure to be enough good rates of return to produce satisfactory results—certainly better than if one invests in safer securities. Another way to describe this is that, as the holding period gets longer, the expected average annual return does not change much, but the standard deviation of that expected return becomes smaller. A typical proponent for time diversification would go on to make the following argument:

> The practical implication of this result is that investors with
> long-term investment objectives should be willing to invest

in what are considered higher-risk, higher-return instruments than they would tolerate for short-term objectives. Investors who can tolerate the high-risk investments for short-term objectives must understand that they may realize extraordinary results—either high returns or high losses.[11]

In other words, when investors who are in their 20s and 30s are starting to save for retirement, they have a sufficiently long time horizon that they should be able to take advantage of time diversification and thus, regardless of their risk tolerance, should initially invest in a portfolio of all common stocks.

Why the Time Diversification Argument Is Fallacious

Although the argument presented above is persuasive to many, and the empirical evidence is frequently compelling, it is also deceptive to the point of being fallacious. There are several reasons why this is the case. Let's start with the simplest argument. As longer holding periods are used in figure 6-10, there is an illusion of accuracy caused by the fact that the data overlaps. Thus, when a 40-year holding period is considered, and the database has only 54 years' worth of data, there are a maximum of 15 different unique holding periods. In our case, the first holding period would be represented by 1951–1990, and the last holding period would be for the years 1965–2004. Note that the first and the second holding periods, 1951–1990 and 1952–1991, have 39 observations in common. It is mathematically inevitable that the mean returns for these two holding periods will be almost identical. Even the first and last holding periods (1951–1990 and 1965–2004) have 26 of their 40 years in common. Although the mean returns for these two holding periods will not be identical, they will necessarily be close. So the fact that the rectangular boxes become narrower as the holding periods become longer is more a tribute to the overlapping nature of the data than to any unique feature of time diversification. This does not mean that the time diversification argument is wrong, but rather that the evidence supporting it is not as overpowering as it might appear.

One way to avoid this bias of overlapping data is to have unique 40-year holding periods. For example, let's say we wanted to have at least 10 non-overlapping holding periods of 40 years each. This would mean 400 years' worth of data. Even the most extensive databases on security returns go back only about 200 years. In addition, one has to question the relevancy of rates of return from the 19th century or earlier.

A more compelling argument for the fallacy of time diversification is to note that what matters to the investor is not the mean annual rate of return, but the aggregate holding period return. Thus, rather than looking at the mean rate of return for 5-year holding periods, we should be considering the aggregate holding period return for the 5-year period. When we do this, we see that the standard deviation of the aggregated holding period return is substantially larger than the standard deviation for the single period holding period return. In fact, it can be proven that when one takes an average of numbers drawn from the same distribution, the standard deviation of the average is equal to the standard deviation of the distribution times the square root of n, where n is the number of observations. In mathematical notation:

$$\sigma_n = \sigma_1 \times \sqrt{(n)}$$

σ_1 = standard deviation for a single year's rate of return

σ_n = standard deviation for an n-year holding period return

In our example of 5-year holding periods, n would equal 5, and thus

$$\sigma_5 = \sigma_1 \times \sqrt{5} = \sigma_1 \times 2.23$$

Hence, the standard deviation of the 5-year holding period return is more than double that of the standard deviation of the one-year holding period return. For a 40-year holding period, the standard deviation of the 40-year holding period return is 6.32 times that for a single year's standard deviation. Thus, it is just not true that longer holding periods magically mean less risk. *Longer holding periods mean more risk, just not proportionately more.*

Another way to make these points is with two more examples based on the flipping of a coin. Suppose you have flipped the coin four times in the bet described earlier (you win $2,000 for a head and lose $1,000 for a tail), and you have flipped four tails in a row. At this point, you might be discouraged! You can think about the next flip in two ways. One is to think about the probability of flipping 5 tails in a row, which is only .0312.[12] Using the time diversification argument, one would think it is a near certainty that the next flip will be a head. However, because consecutive flips are statistically unrelated events, the true probability of flipping a head is exactly 50 percent. Time diversification does not alter the probability of what any one outcome will be.

The other point is that in our coin flip example, we are assuming the bet is the exactly the same each time. When investing, one cannot usually place the same bet each time period. Thus, if an investor has a bad rate of return in the first time period, the size of his or her "bet," which is the value of the portfolio, will necessarily be smaller at the start of the next time period. The changing size of the "bet" over time potentially offsets the value of repeated bets.

Why Time Diversification Does Not Work

Having demonstrated that the basic argument of time diversification is incorrect, and that the empirical evidence to support this argument is deceptive at best, does this mean that the holding period for an individual is irrelevant in the construction of a portfolio? That is, once a client's level of risk tolerance has been determined, then the same asset allocation percentages would be recommended regardless of whether the client's holding period is one year or 40 years. Under certain circumstances, this is in fact correct!

The classic work on this subject is by Nobel Laureate Paul Samuelson. Samuelson (1963, 1969, 1989, 1990, and 1994)[13] has shown that under certain circumstances, investors will hold the same asset allocation regardless of time horizon. Samuelson has three critical assumptions. They are:

1.   investors have a constant relative risk aversion,
2.   stock returns in each period are unrelated to the prior period's returns, and
3.   wealth is limited only to the investment portfolio.

Almost everyone would agree that at least one of these assumptions is not true, most people would agree that at least two of them are not true, and a few people would even argue that none of these three assumptions are true. Let's consider each of them in turn.

Constant Relative Risk Reversion

constant relative risk aversion

Constant relative risk aversion is an academic term to describe the assumption that a person has the same risk tolerance despite the amount of wealth that he or she currently has. All empirical evidence to date indicates that this is not the case. Rather, it appears that virtually all investors could be characterized as having decreasing relative risk aversion. This means that the wealthier they are, the more willing they are to take risk. The implication of this is that the longer the time horizon, the more likely an investor is to increase the percentage invested in equities.[14]

Independent Stock Returns

The random walk theory states that the returns in each period (for example, each year) are completely independent of the prior year's returns. Hence, even if the market had gone up or down by 50 percent last year, the rate of return achieved by the market is the same as if the market had been created from scratch on January 1 of the next year. The basis for this argument is that at any point in time, market prices are based on investors' expectations about future news. As long as investors' expectations about future news are unbiased, then when news occurs, the effect of that news will take on the appearance of a random distribution. Thus, stock prices will follow a random walk. Empirical evidence suggests that the market does not follow a perfect random walk. There is evidence of overreactions to certain events, and also that the full impact of certain events is incorporated over time, rather then instantaneously. Nonetheless, most researchers would agree that for the market as a whole, stock returns are independent.

mean reversion
process

Nonetheless, if one believes stock returns are characterized by a mean reversion process, then the time diversification argument should be taken quite seriously. A *mean reversion process* means that a particularly high (low) rate of return in one time period is more likely to be followed by a low (high) rate of return in the next time period.

Alternatively, some people believe security returns are characterized by "momentum." A "momentum" process means that a particularly high (low) rate of return in one time period is more likely to be followed by another high (low) rate of return in the next time period. People who believe in the momentum process should reduce the percentage allocation in equities because the longer the time horizon, the more volatile stock returns are likely to be. Some people believe the market operates with a mean reversion process; almost no one believes it operates with a momentum process.

The Role of Human Capital

Human capital has several implications for investors with long time horizons. We have already noted how the magnitudes of the values of human capital and financial assets can affect the need for diversification among the financial assets. In addition, the presence of human capital for most investors means that they will be contributing additional capital over time, via either savings placed in nonqualified accounts, or savings placed in tax-qualified accounts such a defined-contribution pension plans. The steady flow of new monies into the investment portfolio means that poor rates of return in the earlier years can be compensated for by new monies.

In addition, as people continue to be employed, they have the ability to change their work habits. Thus, if they sustain poor rates of return in the earlier years and they have a long investment time horizon, they have the ability to reduce their consumption (that is, increase the incremental savings contributions they would have made) by a little bit over a period of several years to make up losses. For example, if a 30-year-old has a bad rate of return, he or she could probably reduce consumption expenses slightly over the next 10 or 20 years and easily make up for the loss. Thus, for investors with longer time horizons, the adverse effects can be spread over so many years as to create negligible pain in any one year.

Finally, reconsider for a moment the relationship of human capital and financial assets. For young investors with long time horizons, the percentage of wealth that they would like to have in equities far exceeds the amount of financial assets. For example, looking again at table 6-1, we saw that John Henry at age 32 has a total wealth of $898,234, and financial assets of only $27,725. Suppose John would like to have 50 percent of his wealth in equities. This would mean over $449,000 in equities. Obviously, John could only place $27,725 in equities because he cannot divert his human capital to equities. In fact, it would not be until John is about 62 that he would be able to place 50 percent of his total wealth into equities. Hence, for many years this portfolio should be 100 percent equities.

Dominance

Finally, there is one quite compelling argument for aggressive investment portfolios for people with long time horizons. This is a consideration of how the worst case that might reasonably be anticipated under the more aggressive investment strategy compares to the best and worst cases under a more conservative investment strategy. To keep the discussion simple, let's treat the aggressive portfolio as if it is a diversified stock portfolio, and the conservative portfolio as if it is strictly a bond portfolio. The analysis hinges on the expected returns and the standard deviations of the two portfolios.

Let's consider the data presented earlier in table 6-2 for large company stocks and long-term government bonds. The historical geometric mean rates of return for these two holdings are typically 10.5 percent and 5.50 percent, and the standard deviations are 20 percent and 9 percent. Based on these numbers, one could project the mean value of each portfolio into the future, as well as the 95th and 5th percentile portfolio values. Let's look at figure 6-11, which shows these two portfolios over a 30-year period. The vertical axis is the logarithm of each portfolio's value, and the horizontal axis is time. Because we are using the logarithmic function, the mean value of each portfolio over time is a straight line, rather than the upward bending curve we normally see when we project values that are growing at a constant rate.

The mean of the stock portfolio grows steadily relative to the mean of the bond portfolio. More importantly, the 5th percentile of the stock portfolio starts to do better than the mean of the bond portfolio, and in this case, eventually would do better than the 95th percentile of the bond portfolios. There are a couple of points that are critical in figure 6-11.

1. The greater the difference in the expected returns on the two portfolios, the greater the divergence in the distributions over time and the greater the likelihood that the 5th percentile of the stock portfolio will outperform the 95th percentile of the bond portfolio.
2. The smaller the standard deviation of the stock portfolio relative to the bond portfolio, the greater the likelihood that the 5th percentile of the stock portfolio will outperform the 95th percentile of the bond portfolio.

In other words, the expected returns and standard deviations of the two portfolios are critical, but no one really knows with any certainty what these values will be. As indicated above, practitioners frequently use historical values as surrogates for expected values. So, unfortunately, there is no definitive

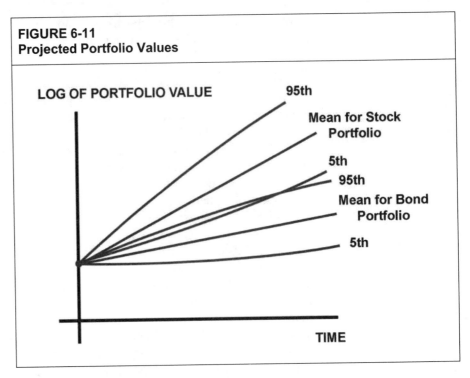

FIGURE 6-11
Projected Portfolio Values

answer to the question of whether or not one is always better off with a riskier portfolio if one's time horizon is long enough. What is clear is that a financial planner could easily provide a client with an impression one way or another by adjusting the inputs on a software package that would provide these numbers.

ASSET ALLOCATION

Invariably, a significant component of investment portfolio management involves the process known as asset allocation. That is, the financial planner needs to recommend what percentage of the portfolio should consist of certain types of assets. This has nothing to do with asset or security selection. Rather, it is the framework within which assets or security selection occurs. The planner must distinguish between strategic and tactical asset allocation because strategic and tactical asset allocation issues are major factors as additional monies are added to the client's portfolios.

Strategic Asset Allocation

A strategic asset allocation decision is normally made with reference to only a few broad asset categories. The simplest asset allocation decision might involve only three asset categories: stocks, bonds, and cash equivalents. A common asset allocation strategy would be 60 percent stocks, 30 percent bonds, and 10 percent cash equivalents. The strategic asset allocation sometimes involves a range of weights rather than a precise weight. Thus, an asset allocation strategy might read as 50 to 60 percent stocks, 40 to 50 percent bonds, and up to 10 percent cash equivalents.

Setting the strategic asset allocation is analogous to selecting a portfolio on the efficient frontier. Hence, it should be thought of as a two-step process. The first step involves the percentage breakdown between the risk-free assets (cash equivalents) and the risky assets (stocks and bonds). The second step divides up the risky asset weightings into its component categories.

Because strategic asset allocation decisions work to locate the optimal portfolio on the capital market line for the client, their purpose is to match the portfolio to the client's level of risk tolerance. They are not intended to "beat" the market; they are made with the understanding that if the asset allocation matches the market's returns and are appropriate for the client's level of risk tolerance, they are successful decisions.

When a client wants to strictly follow a strategic asset allocation approach, the planner might consider index funds. Thus, the choice for stocks would be a stock index fund, the choice for bonds would be a bond index fund, and the choice for cash equivalents would be a broadly diversified money market mutual fund. We will return to this topic of index funds versus security selection later in the chapter.

Strategic asset allocation decisions must be long-term decisions. It is acceptable to change a strategic asset allocation, but the planner should discuss why the new allocation is better with the client. A change in the strategic asset allocation for a client should reflect a change in the client's risk tolerance. This change in risk tolerance could be due to the client becoming older, a significant change in the overall level of wealth, a change in the client's family situation, or a change in the client's career opportunities. If the changes in strategic asset allocation are frequent, then these changes are actually tactical, not strategic.

Portfolio Rebalancing

One of the consequences of strategic asset allocation is that strictly adhering to it can cause the financial advisor to make recommendations that might seem foolish to the client. Remember, security prices fluctuate on a daily basis. Thus, although one's portfolio might start with a perfect asset allocation, such as 60 percent stocks, 30 percent bonds, and 10 percent cash equivalents, most likely the weights will have changed slightly at the end of one day of trading. Implicit in strategic asset allocation is the frequency of verification. That is, at what frequency is the portfolio reexamined to check for adherence to the strategic weights? Weekly? Monthly? Quarterly? Annually?

A second issue is what ranges are tolerated. If the strategic allocation is 50 to 60 percent stocks, then as long as the stock holdings are within this range, no trading is necessary. However, if during a bullish move, stocks increase to 60.1 percent of the portfolio, then should some stocks be sold?

A third issue is that rebalancing the portfolio necessarily means selling what has done well and buying what has not done well. For example, if the client starts with the 60-30-10 mix, and over the course of the year one or two stocks have done spectacularly well, then the portfolio could suddenly have weights of 70, 22.5, and 7.5. The decline in the bond and cash holdings is not because those market values have gone down but because the stocks have gone up as a percentage of the entire portfolio. The easiest way to rebalance the portfolio and to keep a diversified stockholding is to sell a good percentage of the exact stocks that have done the best and put the money into bonds and cash equivalents. This creates the dual problem of having to pay capital gains taxes as a result of selling the strong performers and having to explain to the client why you are selling off the best performing stocks to buy more securities that are not performing well.[15]

Tactical Asset Allocation

Tactical asset allocation decisions differ from strategic decisions in several ways:

- Decisions are made for the purpose of beating the market rather than setting the desired level of risk exposure.
- Decisions are made more frequently.
- Decisions typically include many more asset categories.

If the financial planner believes in the efficient market hypothesis, then he or she would not necessarily engage in tactical asset allocation decisions. Tactical asset allocation decisions tend to imply that the financial planner believes he or she has a better idea of what is going to happen in each sector of the market than most other investors.

Timing of Contributions

Research has shown that accumulation of wealth is more effectively accomplished through steady contributions of new money, rather than attempting to achieve superior security selection. This is not to say that superior security selection (for example, buying Home Depot, Wal-Mart, and Yahoo when they first came out) does not help build wealth. But as most people are not lucky enough to pick one of these big winners and hold them, the primary path to wealth accumulation is a steady stream of contributions.

Wealth Accumulation Under Perfect Certainty

When investors save through qualified plans at work, the new contributions are sent in automatically on a regular basis. It is when investors save in nonqualified accounts that a savings regimen may become inconsistent. For example, suppose an investor earns $100,000 and plans to place 5 percent ($5,000) of his or her income into a nonqualified account each year. As demands for his or her money occur, it is easy to let the commitment to contribute $5,000 slide to the end of the year. Let's consider the effect on the investor's wealth if this happens each year.

Suppose the investor intends to invest $5,000 per year for the next 30 years on January 1 of each year (ignore the fact that this is a national holiday). Let's also assume that the investor will earn an average rate of return of 8 percent (ignore taxes). At the end of the 30 years, the investor's account will be worth $611,729. (Keystrokes: SHIFT, C ALL, SHIFT BEG/END [so that BEGIN is displayed], 5000, PMT, 8, I/YR, 30, N, FV [display: −611,729.34)]). Suppose, however, that instead of making the payment on the first day of each year, the investor slips and makes the payments on the last day of each year (December 31). If the time horizon is still 30 years and the rate of return is still 8 percent, then the investor's account will be worth $566,416.06. (Keystrokes: SHIFT, C ALL, SHIFT BEG/END [so that BEGIN is not displayed], 5000, PMT, 8, I/YR, 30, N, FV [display: −566,416.06).])[16]

To understand why there is such a big difference, consider the fact that in the above two scenarios, there are 29 contributions that occur at exactly the same time. That is, in the first scenario, the second contribution occurs at the same time as the first contribution in the second scenario. Similarly, the 30th contribution of the first scenario occurs at the same time as the 29th contribution in the second scenario. The only conceptual difference in the two scenarios is that the first contribution of the first scenario is replaced by the last contribution of the second scenario. The first contribution of the first scenario contributes $50,313.29 to the final total. (Keystrokes: SHIFT, C ALL, SHIFT BEG/END [so that BEG is displayed], 5000, PV, 8, I/YR, 30, N, FV [display: −50,313.28].) In the second scenario, the last contribution contributes $5,000 to the final value because the final contribution is made at the same time as the ending value of the account is being determined. The difference in the ending value of these two contributions of $45,313.29 is also the difference in the ending value under these two scenarios. Simply put, the real difference in contributing on the first day of each year and the last day of each year is essentially the ending value of the first contribution. Hence, it is particularly critical to persuade a new client to start an investment program NOW rather than one year from now.

Wealth Accumulation with Uncertainty

The previous example makes a good point for the importance of contributing to one's investments as early as possible, but the example is based on perfect certainty as to the rate of return. Let's now reconsider the argument for early contributions in a world of uncertainty.

The market moves in a random manner on a day-to-day basis. On some days there are big moves, and on other days the movement is inconsequential. Recent research by John Stowe looks at market returns over the period of 1991 to 1998.[17] The holding period return on the market over this 8-year period was 19.87 percent. During this time period, there were 2,023 trading days. The research included an allowance for trading costs, but not the effect of taxes.

The question was then posed as to what would happen if an investor misses the 10, 20, 30, and 40 best trading days of this period. The results are dramatic. If an investor missed the 10 best days, his or her returns drop to 15.06 percent for the period (13.62 percent after expenses). Similarly, an investor who missed out on the 20, 30, and 40 best days of the period would have total returns of 11.98 percent, 9.4 percent, and 7.15 percent (9.2 percent, 5.35 percent, and 1.9 percent after expenses).

Now it is true that if an investor were able to be out of the market on the 10, 20, 30, or 40 worst trading days of the period, his or her rate of return would be substantially better. The improvements in return from liquidation and reinvestment to avoid these worst trading days amount to 25.85, 29.56, 32.76, and 35.74 percent (24.28, 26.35, 27.85, and 26.09 percent after expenses). The numbers indicate that even if an investor missed both the best and worst trading days, he or she would still be worse off. Simply put, an investor cannot afford to be out of the market during the few really dramatic price increase days that occur over a period of time.

A similar point was made by one of the most successful investors of the 20th century, Peter Lynch.[18] Lynch points out that if one had stayed fully invested in the S&P 500 index over a period of 40 years starting in 1954, one would have achieved an annual rate of return of 11.4 percent. If an investor happens to miss out on the 10, 20, and 40 best months of this period, the mean annual rate of return drops to 8.3, 6.4, and 2.7 percent. Again, the reason it is so important that investors with long-term time horizons (such as saving for retirement) should attempt to make their contributions at the earliest opportunity is that they cannot afford to miss the best trading days, weeks, or months that might occur. This is also the argument for not attempting to be a market timer.

Portfolio Adjustments over Time

As discussed earlier, many financial planners like to make projections of financial well being based on assumptions of perfectly certain rates of return over time, and to offer the erroneous concept of time diversification to support this presentation. In truth, longer time periods simply mean greater variability of portfolio values. As mentioned in chapter 5, projecting wealth accumulation for retirement is not done once and then everyone waits until the person retires to see how the assumptions turned out. Instead, a good financial planner should meet with the client at least every 1 to 2 years to monitor the plan and see if any adjustments need to be made.

There are two problems that may be noted at the time of review. The more serious is that of a client becoming underfunded. The less serious, but still important issue, is that of the client becoming overfunded. We will assume in the following discussion that the client becomes underfunded or overfunded because of worse or better than expected results in the performance of the client's portfolio.

The Underfunded Client

The client who becomes underfunded has pretty much the same options as a new client for whom a plan cannot be made to work. That is, the client can plan to retire at a later date, increase contributions to the investment account, take on a second job, increase the expected return on the portfolio, or downsize his or her expectations of lifestyle during retirement. Another possibility is that the financial planner can advise the client that he or she has had a run of bad luck in the market, and that he or she should not worry, as "time diversification means the client is due some unusually good returns in the future."

return/return tradeoff

Somehow, this last piece of advice sounds like famous last words. An alternative to this "just sit tight" recommendation is to increase the expected return on the portfolio by taking on a more aggressive posture. Nobel laureate William Sharpe refers to this strategy as the *return/return tradeoff*.[19] This is not a typo. Dr. Sharpe's point is that in revising financial plans, it is all too easy for the planner and client to focus on increasing the expected return of the portfolio, and forget that the only way to truly increase expected return is also to increase risk. Thus, a portfolio with more risk may only cause a client to fall further behind if things do not go well, rather than automatically providing the opportunity to catch up. It is analogous to a gambler doubling the bet every time he or she loses. If the gambler wins before running out of money, all will be well. If the gambler runs out of money first, then the game is over. If the financial planner had designed the original portfolio as appropriate for the client's risk tolerance, then increasing the riskiness of the portfolio to increase the expected return is clearly inappropriate.

The Overfunded Client

The client who becomes overfunded also has to make some choices, but they are much less painful. First, the client could decide to reduce his or her contributions to the retirement portfolio. This means spending more money today. An obvious alternative is to continue the same contribution level as a "risk cushion."[20] In the event the portfolio has some setbacks in subsequent years, the client will still have a good chance of meeting his or her target retirement income. If the portfolio continues to meet or exceed expectations, then the client will have a more comfortable retirement than he or she planned upon. A third possibility is to alter the strategic asset allocation to a more conservative stance to increase the likelihood that the client will meet his or her target retirement income.

A fourth possibility is to actually move the portfolio to an even more aggressive position. The argument here is that the client has a safety cushion that allows the luxury of a gamble. If the gamble does not work out, the client can take comfort in achieving the original target retirement income. If the gamble does work out, the client can, as indicated above, have a more comfortable retirement than imagined.

A fifth possibility is to keep the same plan, but encourage the client to think about more gifts or legacies to charities during retirement, or to increase the inheritances he or she would plan to give to children and grandchildren.

PORTFOLIO ISSUES

The Impact of Data Assumptions on Asset Allocation Recommendations

Many financial planners use software to derive asset allocation recommendations. The necessary inputs are the expected returns, standard deviation of returns, and the correlation coefficients among the asset categories. Naturally, many people will compute mean returns, standard deviations, and correlation coefficients using historical data. This process raises two critical issues. The first is, what time period should be used for the historical data. As discussed earlier, the Ibbotson data bank goes back to 1926. Statisticians always say more data is better for making estimates than less data. However, if the additional data is not relevant, then using more data (that is, going back further in time) may well do more harm than good.

The second issue is the appropriateness of using historical numbers without alteration. William Jahnke (2004) has recently made a persuasive argument that using unedited historical data is professionally negligent.[21,22] His argument rests on the observation, as mentioned earlier, that studies of the distributions of security returns always report the distributions to be leptokurtic rather than normal. Normal distributions are the nice, bell-shaped curves we are used to seeing. Leptokurtic distributions have "fat tails." This means there are more observations over time that are several standard deviations above and below the mean or average return than one would expect if returns were normally distributed. Jahnke attributes this to instability in the return generating process. That is, the mean return and the standard deviation of return, in fact, change over time.

The consequence of this is that when certain asset categories have had several years of favorable (or unfavorable) rates of return, asset allocation programs will increase (or decrease) the weights assigned to these categories. If future returns are not as favorable (or more favorable), the client will be poorly served.

The solution would be to use alternative sources of information to derive estimates of the statistical inputs. These could be "based on economic fundamental variables, represented by the yield curve, dividend yields, consensus long-term earnings-growth forecasts, and price/earnings ratios."[23] The net result of looking at these other sources of information would likely be estimates that are more tempered than what would result from using strictly historical inputs.

How Significant Are Inappropriate Inputs?

Having just argued that it is probably desirable to temper historical data with other sources of information to avoid inappropriate inputs, we should also consider exactly what sort of damage would be done by inappropriate inputs. Waggle and Moon (2004) have recently looked at what happens to the optimal portfolio weights if one errs on the appropriate value for the expected return on stocks and on the correlation coefficient between stocks and bonds.[24,25]

Before discussing their results, let us consider briefly the framework for their study. They started by looking at the mean returns, standard deviation of returns, and correlation coefficients for the rates of return on large company stocks, long-term government bonds, and U.S. Treasury bills for the period from 1926 to 2002. The mean rates of return were 12.2 percent, 5.8 percent, and 3.8 percent. The standard deviations of the returns were 20.5 percent, 9.4 percent, and 3.2 percent. Finally, the correlation coefficients between the stocks and bonds was .127, between the stocks and Treasury bills was −.016, and between the bonds and Treasury bills was .229. To determine the optimal asset allocation for different investors, they used one of the most common utility functions in academic research. They assumed an investor's indifference curve could be modeled as

$$U = \text{expected return} - .5 \times A \times \text{variance}$$

where the term A is a measure of the investor's risk aversion. An investor who was completely indifferent to risk would have a risk aversion value of 0 (that is, A = 0). Naturally, such investors are assumed not to exist. The more risk averse an investor is, the higher the value of A. Waggle and Moon considered values of A that ranged from 1 to 10.

The authors' first result is that, as the expected return on stocks is increased while all of the other parameters are kept the same, the optimal percentage allocated to stocks increases. In and of itself, this would not be surprising. However, the impact is more significant for more aggressive investors. Increasing the expected rate of return on stocks has much less effect on the optimal portfolios of more conservative investors.

The second result is that as the expected rate of return on stocks is increased while all of the other parameters are kept the same, then the more aggressive investors would reduce their holdings of Treasury bills more so than their bond holdings. Conversely, the more conservative investors would reduce their bond holdings rather than their Treasury holdings.

The third result is that changes in the stock-bond correlation coefficient have relatively little effect on the portfolio allocation to stocks, regardless of the investor's degree of risk aversion. However, what is significant is that as the correlation coefficient between stock returns and bond returns increases, more conservative investors should increase their holdings of Treasury bills and reduce their holdings of bonds.

In other words, changes in the inputs to portfolio optimization models will sometimes lead to changes in the optimal asset allocations, and in some cases the magnitude of change depends on the investor's level of risk tolerance.

Predicting Expected Return

When one is forecasting future rates of return based on historical rates of return, it is not immediately obvious whether such forecasts should be based on the arithmetic average rate of return or the geometric mean rate of return. For example, suppose a financial planner is reviewing a client's portfolio and notes that over the past 10 years, the arithmetic average rate of return is 10 percent, and the geometric mean rate of return is 8 percent. Which rate of return would make most sense to use in projecting the future value of the portfolio?

The traditional rule-of-thumb is that if a planner is forecasting for a single year, then the arithmetic average is the best forecast of future return. However, if a planner is forecasting for a large number of years, then the geometric mean is the best forecast of future return. Using the above example, this means that if the planner were making a 1-year forecast of the portfolio's value, he or she should use a 10 percent rate of return. If the planner were forecasting 10 years into the future, an 8 percent annual rate of return would be more appropriate. This rule of thumb obviously leaves open the question of which rate of return one should use if forecasting a limited number of years, say 2 or 3 years.

Recent research by Jacquier, Kane, and Marcus[26] shows that a weighted average of the two historical rates of returns provides the best forecast, where the weights depend on the number of time periods used to compute the historical rates of return and the number of time periods over which one is forecasting. The formula is:

Forecast = (Arithmetic mean x [1 – H/T]) + (Geometric mean x [H/T])

where T = number of time periods used in the historical computation
H = number of time periods being forecasted (that is, horizon)

Note that in the above formula, if the forecast is for a single period (H = 1), and the number of periods used in the historical computation is relatively large, then the forecasted rate of return should be primarily based on the arithmetic mean. Note also that if the number of historical periods used equals the number of periods being forecasted (H = T), then the best rate of return for forecasting is strictly the geometric mean rate of return. Conceptually, it would be highly inappropriate to forecast over a longer time horizon than was used to compute the historical rate of return. That is, it would be unprofessional to use this model in a situation where H > T.

Example: In analyzing a client's portfolio, you look at the performance over the last 5 years and compute that the annual arithmetic average rate of return has been 12 percent, and the geometric mean rate of return has been 10 percent. You want to forecast the rate of return for the next 2 years. What is the most appropriate rate of return assumption to use if you want to base the future rate of return on past performance?

Optimal forecast $= (12\% \times [1 - 2/5]) + (10\% \times [2/5])$
$= 7.2\% + 4\% = 11.2\%$

Measuring Diversification

Although we have emphasized the growing importance of the degree of diversification of a client's financial assets as he or she becomes older, we have not really defined effective ways to measure diversification. Let's consider what is meant by the concept of diversification, and how it might be measured. Unfortunately, what we will see is that there are not any really good ways to measure diversification.

Time-Based Measures of Diversification

As described in the discussion of modern portfolio theory, the benefit of diversification is that an investor reduces the risk of his or her portfolio, presumably without altering its expected return. Portfolios on the efficient frontier are defined as those offering the highest expected return for each level of risk (as measured by the standard deviation of the portfolio). To obtain diversification, it is not sufficient to merely add securities to a portfolio. Holding the stocks of two companies that are in the exact same line of business and whose rates of return are highly correlated provides little in the way of diversification. One must hold stocks whose correlation coefficients are low. Ultimate diversification occurs if one holds two stocks and their correlation coefficient equals minus one.

Based on these two observations, it would seem that there would be two obvious candidates as tools for measuring diversification. The first would be the standard deviation of the portfolio's rate of return, and the second would be to calculate the correlation coefficient between each pair of securities in the portfolio and compute the average of these correlation coefficients. The problem with computing the portfolio's standard deviation is that research has shown that the standard deviations of are not stable. For example, suppose you were looking at ten portfolios, each containing the same number of holdings of common stocks. Next, you compute the standard deviation of each portfolio over two consecutive holding periods (for example, two consecutive 5-year periods). Finally, you rank order these ten portfolios by the size of their standard deviations for each period. What you will find is that there is no consistency between the two rank orderings.

Even if there were consistency among the rank orderings, there is a second problem. It is that investment portfolios are not stationary over time for two reasons. The first reason is that people normally make trades over time. They will sell some securities and replace them with others. Also, as they add cash to their portfolio or remove cash from it, they will buy new securities or liquidate other holdings without replacement.

The second reason is that the composition of the portfolio will change over time even without trades. Some holdings will increase in value, others will decrease in value. Thus, computing the standard deviation using historical data means using data for portfolios that are different than the current portfolio.

There are two problems associated with computing the average correlation coefficient. The first is that this computation requires knowledge of the standard deviations of the various securities, which we have already seen is problematic. This could be overcome by computing the covariances of the securities, although the covariances calculation has the same problem as the standard deviations, namely that the changing nature of the portfolios renders the computation meaningless over any significant period of time.

The second problem with computing either correlation coefficients or covariances is that there is no standard of comparison. For example, suppose there are two portfolios. One had two securities, and their correlation coefficient is .25. The other has five securities, and their average correlation coefficient is .30. Which one is more diversified? The first portfolio has more efficient diversification because its correlation coefficient is lower. The second has a lot more securities in it. Without more information, one cannot render an opinion.

Some people have suggested measuring a portfolio's degree of diversification by calculating the coefficient of determination obtained by regressing the returns on the portfolio against the returns of a stock market index. This statistic has the positive attribute that the higher the value of the coefficient of determination, the more diversified the portfolio. However, it also has the drawback that its computation requires the use of rates of return from several years. Therefore, it is subject to the same uncertainty as the other statistical measures of standard deviation, correlation coefficient, and covariance.

Instantaneous Measures of Diversification

It would clearly be beneficial to the financial planner to be able to measure the degree of diversification of a portfolio without having to resort to time-based statistical measures. Such an index has been suggested in the literature. It is called the Woerheide-Persson index. The index can be developed from a simple listing of the securities in a portfolio and their market value. The first step to obtain the index is to compute the market value weight of each security in the portfolio. Thus, if the market value of a particular holding is $10,000 and the market value of the entire portfolio is $100,000, then the market value weight of this holding is .10 (10 percent), which is obtained by dividing the $10,000 value of the holding by the $100,000 value of the portfolio. The second step is to square each of these weights. The third step is to add up the squared weights. The final step is to subtract this total from one. The difference is the index value. Let's consider an example of this computation before discussing what the resulting index number means.

Example 1:   Sally Jones has brought you her monthly brokerage statement. It contains the following listing of securities and the market value of each:

ABC Company	$10,000
DEF Company	15,000
GHI Company	25,000
JKL Company	5,000
MNO Company	10,000
PQR Company	35,000

The market value of her portfolio is $100,000. Thus, the market value-based weights are .10, .15, .25, .05, .10, and .35. When these weights are squared, we get .01, .0225, .0625, .0025, .01, and .1225. The sum of these weights is .23. Finally, we subtract this sum from 1.0, to obtain an index value of .77 (1 - .23). We need to now consider how to interpret this index value.

The interpretation of this index value rests on comparing it to a table of index values that are computed for portfolios that are equally divided among all of the holdings. For example, the index value for a portfolio that contains two securities, each with a market value-based weight of 50 percent, would be .50 ($[1- (.5^2 + .5^2)]$). The index value for a portfolio that contains five securities, each with a market value based weight of 20 percent, would be .80. In general, if there are n securities in a portfolio, and they all have identical market values, the Woerheide-Persson index would equal

$$1 - 1/n$$

The index for portfolios containing one to 20 securities, all with equal weights, is shown in table 6-3.

TABLE 6-3
Index Values for the Woerheide-Persson Index

#	Index Value	#	Index Value	#	Index Value	#	Index Value
1	0.0	6	.833	11	.910	16	.938
2	.5	7	.857	12	.917	17	.941
3	.667	8	.875	13	.923	18	.944
4	.75	9	.889	14	.929	19	.947
5	.80	10	.90	15	.933	20	.950

Example 2:   We can now interpret the degree of diversification of Sally Jones' portfolio. Her index value was 77. This is closest to the index value for a portfolio that has exactly four securities, each with 25 percent of the market value. Thus, even though Sally has six stocks in her account, her diversification is the same as if she had only four stocks with equal market values.

What Is the Appropriate Degree of Diversification?

Naturally, the question would arise as to what is an adequate amount of diversification. Unfortunately, this has no clear answer. Early research suggested a minimum of 10 securities with equal market values. This would mean an index value of .90 or better is adequate diversification. Later writers argued for values of 15 to 20 securities, which means index values of .933 to .95 would be adequate.

Another issue is that the Woerheide-Persson index was developed for portfolios that were fully invested and contained only stocks. It does not take into consideration obvious factors that would affect the need for diversification such as the extent to which the stocks in the portfolio are related. Hence, if a portfolio had 25 stocks in it, all with equal weights, but all 25 companies were in the auto industry, then the index value of .96 would vastly overstate the degree of diversification of the portfolio. Portfolios with higher-quality securities (for example, blue chip stocks) and other securities such as bonds and preferred stocks might provide better diversification benefits even though they have fewer holdings. The index also does not deal with the presence of cash and cash equivalents such as Treasury bills, which substantially reduce the variability of a portfolio's return, and thus provide the benefits of diversification without the need for a large number of holdings. Finally, the index does not deal with debit balances, which are the result of buying stocks on margin or borrowing money from a broker using a portfolio as collateral. The presence of debit balances will substantially increase the variability of the portfolio's return. Hence, a portfolio that may appear diversified without a debit balance may not be as effectively diversified when a debit balance is present. The Woerheide-Persson index is not perfect, but it is a major step forward to solving the problem of how to effectively measure the quality of diversification in a portfolio.

Concentrated Portfolios

A particular problem arises when a client ends up with what is known as a concentrated portfolio, or a portfolio in which one or a few securities have disproportionate weights. There is no mathematical definition as to what constitutes a concentrated portfolio and no precise description, but a capable financial planner will recognize it when it exists. However, there is usually a price to pay to reduce the concentration.

Concentration exposes the investor to non-market risk. Unless the investor has an incredibly strong reason to believe that the security (or securities) creating the undue concentration is (are) expected to have excess return, there is no reward for the concentration to compensate for the risk exposure.

About the only time there is an easy solution to the problem of a concentrated portfolio is when the concentration occurs in a tax-deferred or tax-exempt account, and there is no restriction on selling the asset. In this case, the concentrated holding can be sold and replaced with a set of diversified holdings without any tax consequences.

In the more common scenario, the concentrated position occurs in a taxable account. The concentration sometimes comes about because one security has strongly outperformed the rest. In this case, there will be a substantial capital gain associated with the position. Selling the position creates a capital-gains tax, which will reduce the value of the account when the tax is paid. An alternative is to set up some sort of hedge with the position. Usually, options would provide the best opportunity for hedging. However, note that when options are used for hedging, the expected return on the asset is then substantially reduced.

Concentrated positions must be dealt with, and the only truly effective way to deal with them is to sell some of the holding to reduce its weight in the portfolio. Selling will usually incur capital gains taxes for the client, as well as possible emotional pain for having to dispose of something that has done so well. It is all too easy to fantasize that an investment that has done incredibly well will keep performing in that manner, leaving the client with wealth beyond his or her imagination.

Tax Efficiency in Retirement Investing

In tax-advantaged and tax-qualified accounts, such as IRAs, 401(k), and 403(b) plans, there is no taxation as long as there are no distributions from the plan, regardless of whether the invested funds generate capital gain distributions, dividends, and/or interest income. Taxes are assessed when funds are withdrawn from the account, which for most people is at retirement or during the retirement years. The exception is the Roth IRA, which allows tax-exempt withdrawals provided certain conditions are met.

The Traditional Tax-Efficient Allocation Argument

The traditional investment strategy is to hold fixed-income investments in tax-deferred accounts and equity investments in nonqualified accounts. The reasoning for this rule of thumb is simple. Fixed-income investments pay interest, which is taxed as ordinary income anyway. Holding these investments in a tax-deferred account, therefore, does not change the marginal tax rate at which this income is taxed. With Roth IRA accounts, an investor can even avoid taxation on what is otherwise taxable income.

Equity investments pay dividends and provide capital gains (assuming the investor is fortunate enough to own stocks that go up in value). Under current tax laws, most dividend income and all capital gains are taxed at lower marginal rates. Furthermore, capital gains are not taxed until the investments are sold. By placing equities in tax-deferred accounts (except for Roth IRAs), the dividend income and capital gains are eventually taxed as ordinary income (that is, a withdrawal from a tax-deferred account), rather than retaining their special tax status.

A second problem that arises if an investor buys equities in tax-deferred accounts is that most of these accounts have minimum required distributions (MRDs). Regardless of whether the investor wants to withdraw the full MRD from a tax-deferred account each year, he or she must do so; the penalty for not doing so is rather severe. Hence, if the cash for an MRD that is not needed must be obtained by selling some of the holdings in the account, the capital gain effectively becomes taxed as ordinary income at that time. Had the securities been held in an ordinary account, there would be no MRD, and the investor could continue to defer the capital gains tax. In fact, depending on the size of the estate and who the beneficiaries are, if the investor still holds the stock when he or she dies, the tax on the built-up capital gain might be completely avoided because the cost basis can still be stepped up to market value at the time of death for the beneficiaries under the tax law currently in effect. If the securities are still held in a tax-deferred account at the time of death, the decedent's beneficiaries will have to pay ordinary income taxes on the withdrawals they are required to take.

The Problem with the Traditional Argument

There is one potential problem with the traditional argument for asset allocation based on tax efficiency. Portfolio theory makes it clear that the risk of the portfolio (in this case, the combined qualified and nonqualified portfolios) should be appropriate for the investor. The investor's risk tolerance translates into some stock, bond, and cash equivalent asset allocation percentage. Most investors are limited as to how much money can be added to their tax-advantaged accounts each year. Due to early withdrawal penalties, they are certainly limited as to how much money can be withdrawn prior to retirement. Suppose that an investor puts all of his or her tax-advantaged accounts into bonds, and all of his or her nonqualified accounts into stocks and cash equivalents. If the percentage allocation matches that defined by his or her strategic asset allocation, then the investor is set.

However, as is often the case, what happens if the allocation based on tax efficiency is different than that defined by the strategic asset allocation? The investor faces two choices. He or she can live with a portfolio whose asset allocation composition is different than the desired one, or he or she can have a less than perfectly tax-efficient allocation of assets. Neither choice is necessarily beneficial. Unfortunately, there are no simple answers to this quandary. Consider the following example:

Example:	James and Jennifer Watson are new clients. They have accumulated $50,000 in their company's 401(k) plan and hold $100,000 in nonqualified assets. Their 401(k) is invested entirely in stock mutual funds, and their personal assets are 50 percent stocks, 50 percent bonds. You and the Watsons decide on a strategic asset allocation of 50 percent stocks, 40 percent bonds, and 10 percent cash equivalents. In dollars, this translates into $75,000 in stocks, $60,000 in bonds, and $15,000 in cash

equivalents. The obvious first step in executing the plan is to sell the stock funds in the 401(k) plan and replace them with bond funds. This provides $50,000 of the desired $60,000 investment in bonds, which means that the non-qualified account will hold $75,000 in stocks, $10,000 in bonds, and $15,000 in cash equivalents. Note that since the purpose of the cash equivalents is to provide cash reserves, they should not be in the 401(k) plan because this would make them inaccessible unless a steep penalty is paid. Note that in this plan the Watsons still end up with bonds in their non-qualified account!

Liquidity and Retirement Accounts

In our discussions, we have assumed that the investor has some segregation of accounts by objective. For illustrative purposes, let us assume that all of the tax-qualified and tax-advantaged accounts are part of the retirement portfolio. Any nonqualified accounts would hold the assets with different objectives. Thus, a nonqualified account might have some assets that are being held for buying a car, other assets that are being held for emergency liquidity, and yet others that are being held for retirement.

Given this scenario, one could argue that cash equivalent assets should have no role in the retirement portfolio. The reason for this is that cash equivalent assets, although quite safe, provide low returns relative to other assets. Given the long time horizon for a retirement portfolio, the investor should select assets providing higher rates of return. The only exception to this would be if the investor wanted to engage in market timing with his or her retirement assets.

Note, however, that under certain circumstances, an investor may want to use his or her tax-advantaged retirement accounts for either non-retirement objectives or as a potential source of emergency liquidity. Let's consider the circumstances under which this would make sense.

Using Retirement Accounts for Non-Retirement Purposes

This discussion will focus strictly on traditional, deductible IRA and Roth IRA accounts.[27] The general ideas of this discussion can certainly be applied to other types of retirement accounts. The basic rules for IRA accounts were discussed in chapter 4, and will not be repeated here.

There are two reasons that one would not normally think about using IRAs for non-retirement objectives or as a source of liquidity. The more significant reason is the 10 percent penalty for early withdrawals. The second

breakeven holding period (BHP)

reason is that withdrawals from traditional IRA accounts and early withdrawals from Roth IRAs are treated as ordinary income, even if they represent capital gains.

The key to when one would be better off using an IRA for non-retirement objectives lies in what could be called the *breakeven holding period (BHP)*. The BHP is the amount of time that would have to lapse before one would be indifferent between saving in a nonqualified account and saving in an IRA account. If the actual holding period is longer than the BHP, then an investor is better off using an IRA despite its drawbacks. If the actual holding period is less, then an investor is better off putting the money in a nonqualified account. The actual BHP depends on a variety of factors. It is unlikely that at the time an investor undertakes an investment that he or she will know the exact time horizon for the investment and therefore determine how this compares to the BHP. Therefore, we want to focus on those factors that influence the magnitude of the holding period so that a financial planner can better understand when using IRAs over nonqualified accounts is preferable and when it is not. The discussion assumes that the same investments would be purchased whether the investor uses a nonqualified account or an IRA.

The key variables include the investor's tax rate at the time of the contribution to a traditional IRA if it is a deductible contribution, the investor's marginal tax rates on ordinary income and on capital gains during the accumulation period, and those same tax rates at the time of withdrawal. We can make the following observations with regard to traditional IRAs:

- Higher rates of return tend to shorten the BHP because the deferral of taxation becomes more attractive.
- Higher marginal tax rates at the time of the contribution lower the BHP for deductible IRAs because the tax savings at the time of the contribution become more valuable.
- Higher marginal tax rates at the time of the withdrawal increase the BHP rather substantially.
- Lower tax rates on dividends and/or capital gains substantially increase the BHP because investments in nonqualified accounts then enjoy some of the same tax avoidance benefit as provided through the IRA account.

We can make some additional observations with regard to Roth IRAs:

- Because the withdrawals of principal from Roth IRAs are not taxable, the BHP is immaterial for these withdrawals.
- BHPs are significantly longer for Roth than for traditional, deductible IRAs because of the lack of any tax savings at the time of the contribution.

For both types of accounts, we can also make the following observations:

- If the securities purchased are non-dividend-paying common stocks, and the only tax due is a capital gains tax, then the BHP is essentially infinite because the tax deferral of unrecognized capital gains provides the same or better tax benefit than the IRA accounts and does not have the early withdrawal penalty.
- If the penalty for early withdrawal is increased to 20 percent, then there are almost no circumstances in which these IRA accounts would be used for non-retirement objectives.

Investment Companies versus Individual Securities

One of the significant choices that a financial planner has to make is how much of the client's portfolio should be in mutual funds and how much in individual securities. In some situations, mutual funds are either the only choice or the only choice that make sense. For example, if the client has some accounts with smaller amounts of assets, such as Coverdell IRAs or 529 plans, then attempting to create a diversified portfolio in each of these accounts through the selection of individual securities would be futile. If the client is in a defined-contribution pension plan at work, then the menu of investment choices usually consists only of mutual funds, although the employer's stock is frequently an option when the client works for a publicly traded company. We have already established the inappropriateness of investing in the stock of one's employer. Hence, the client is essentially forced to invest in mutual funds in these accounts.

The primary arguments for investing in investment companies in general and mutual funds in particular start with the assertion of professional portfolio management. Most investment company portfolio managers are among the most qualified individuals to decide what to buy, what to hold, and what to sell. Also, investment companies usually provide the essence of significant diversification. Each share of the investment company represents a pro rata claim on the company's entire portfolio, so even the smallest holdings in an investment company represent ample diversification. The exception would be sector funds or specialty funds.

The primary arguments against investing in investment companies in general and mutual funds in particular start with the fees. These include load fees (both front-end and back-end) for load funds, and the various fees paid to managers and for the expenses of operating the fund. Some investment companies are noteworthy for having lower fee structures than others. The reason that these fees are so important is that research has repeatedly shown that, on average, mutual funds underperform the market by an amount approximately equal to the fees charged to the investor. Hence, on average, professional portfolio managers earn market averages on their investments, but the investors in these portfolios earn less due to the fees they have to pay.

There is a second and equally significant argument against investing in mutual funds if the alternative is to build a portfolio of individually owned securities. There is more tax efficiency in direct ownership of securities. First, when one owns many securities, usually some will perform well, and others will perform poorly. If the investor needs to remove some cash from the account through the liquidation of securities, selling the ones that have gone down in price, or at least not gone up by much, will avoid or minimize the necessity of paying capital gains taxes. Second, although it is never fun to have losses in a portfolio, having losses on some securities allows the investor to recognize those losses to reduce his or her taxable income. Remember, most taxpayers can deduct up to $3,000 per year in net capital losses on their tax returns. Depending on one's marginal tax rate, this could produce tax savings of as much as $1,000 per year or more. This process is referred to as tax harvesting.

One can still engage in tax harvesting with mutual funds, but it is trickier. The potential complexities of the tax treatment of gains and losses on the sale of mutual fund shares is covered in the most recent edition of *Fundamentals of Investments for Financial Planning,* published by The American College.

Let's now consider the implication of the following assumptions and observations:

1. Financial markets are reasonably efficient. Therefore, an investor can buy and hold stocks with minimal research for each stock and be confident that he or she has paid a fair price for these stocks when they are bought and receives a fair price for them when they are sold.
2. The diversification benefits offered by mutual funds are very valuable.
3. The fees and charges of most mutual funds are significant.
4. When investors are first starting to acquire financial assets, their human capital usually dwarfs their financial assets, so the diversification of their financial assets is immaterial at this time.
5. As investors approach retirement and their human capital starts to decline, the diversification of their financial assets becomes crucial.

The implication is that the investor should build a portfolio that looks like a mutual fund. Specifically, recent research by Hsu and Wei indicates that for long-term goals such as retirement, portfolios of at least 50 securities are appropriate, and risk-averse investors should consider portfolios with even larger holdings.[28]

The most efficient way to build a diversified portfolio of 50 or more securities is to start with one, and then as monies become available to add to the portfolio, invest these monies in one or more new securities. Depending on the portfolio's initial value, the amount of monies that are being added each year, the magnitude of dividends and interest being received in the portfolio each year, and the average size of each holding selected by the financial planner, a well-diversified portfolio may be built in a period of 10 to 20 years.

Although it might seem more efficient to start the investment process with mutual funds, a significant glitch can occur. Suppose the account is extremely successful during the early years. Then, just when the client might be comfortable converting the account to individual stocks, he or she might have to pay significant capital gains taxes, thus reducing the value of the portfolio.

Retirement-Oriented Mutual Funds

For investors who still feel that mutual funds should be either a component or even the central focus of their retirement portfolio, there are some mutual fund groups that offer funds whose objective is to provide a retirement portfolio for investors planning to retire in a specific year. These funds are typically set up on a "fund of funds" basis, which means they simply invest the monies of that particular fund in other funds managed by the same manager. Over time, they adjust the asset allocation of the retirement fund to reflect the fact that the investors are presumably approaching retirement.

A review of the portfolios of the funds with common retirement dates reveals that some have substantially different asset allocations.[29] This means two things. First, they don't all agree on what is the appropriate asset allocation for an investor with a particular retirement date. Second, an investor should pay close attention to the prospectus when purchasing such a fund, and not assume that because the retirement date is appropriate, the asset allocation must be appropriate.

There is one more problem an investor in these types of funds should consider. A "fund of funds" means that an investor is paying two sets of management fees. The first set is for the fund in which he or she is directly investing; the second set is in each of the funds held in the first fund's portfolio.

Dollar Cost Averaging

One of the most obvious goals for investing is "buy low, sell high." The only problem with seeking to do this is that no one knows at the time whether the current price will later be viewed as a high price or a low price! Dollar cost averaging is a strategy that attempts to put this advice into practice. In simple terms, dollar cost averaging is the investment of a fixed amount of money at specified time intervals. For example, an investor might commit to buy $1,000 worth of a stock or mutual fund on the first day of each month for the period of one year. Investing a fixed dollar amount per period means that investors buy more shares when prices are low than when they are high. The benefit of such a strategy is that it frequently results in a lower average purchase price per share. It also helps some investors who are reluctant to invest a large sum of money in a single shot.

Unless a stock goes into a persistent decline, dollar cost averaging will accomplish its objective. It works best when the stock has an early decline and a later rise. It does not, however, protect the investor against losses in a steadily declining market.

Example:	Hernando DeSoto,[30] a new client, has just found out that he has inherited $1 million from a long-lost uncle. After a consultation, the two of you agree that his strategic asset allocation should be 80 percent stocks, 15 percent bonds, and 5 percent cash equivalents. You then present a list of 40 stocks that would represent an appealing diversified portfolio of common stocks. He immediately blanches when he realizes you are proposing to take $800,000 of his newly acquired wealth to buy stocks the next day. He says, "But suppose the market starts going down?" In this case, he would be better off waiting. You remember that many investors fear regret more than they desire success. That is, they are more concerned that they will rue rushing into an investment than they are concerned about paying more later. Of course, such an attitude could easily lead to perpetual postponement of the stock purchase.
	To overcome this fear of regret, you suggest dollar cost averaging because if stock prices fall, Hernando can buy more shares later. You propose to invest $40,000 per month over the next 20 months until the portfolio reaches it strategic asset allocation. Hernando is quite pleased with this plan and agrees to begin the investment program immediately.

The only problem with the above scenario is that research has shown that in terms of expected future wealth, Hernando would do best if he agreed to plunk down all $800,000 immediately.[31] However, encouraging investors to do what is best for them sometimes requires the use of suboptimal tactics.

Dividend Reinvestment Plans

One form of dollar cost averaging is a dividend reinvestment plan (DRIP) —a program in which stockholders can reinvest their dividends directly into the company's stock. These plans may acquire either existing or newly issued stock. The first plans to be established relied on existing stock purchases. Typically the corporation sends the dividends of participating stockholders to the managing bank's trust department, which maintains an account for each shareholder. Each participant is credited with his or her shares minus broker-age fees and administrative costs. Many DRIPs also permit additional stock purchases for cash. Large round-lot purchases by the plan tend to reduce bro-kerage fees. Some companies give discounts on their dividend reinvestments. Firms selling newly issued shares charge no brokerage fees on the transactions.

DRIPs have a number of advantages. From the firm's standpoint, such a plan adds to stockholder goodwill, increases demand for the firm's stock, saves some dividend-related expenses, and encourages small stockholders to increase ownership. In addition, plans involving new share purchases reduce the firm's debt-to-equity ratio, provide a regular source of equity capital, and permit new equity to be sold without payment of underwriting fees or other flotation costs.

There is one drawback to DRIPs, particularly for investors with larger portfolios. When investors have enough dividend income during the year, they can accumulate sufficient cash to purchase stocks in other companies. When an investor enrolls in a DRIP, he or she ends up buying more shares in the stocks held in the existing portfolio. Thus, DRIPs reduce the ability to increase portfolio diversification by acquiring stock in other companies.

Direct Purchase Plans

Many companies now also offer a direct purchase plan (DPP). With a DPP, the investor opens an account and arranges for a regular debit to a checking or savings account to purchase new shares. DPPs have the benefit of permitting investors to build a stock portfolio with what may be relatively small monthly purchases. They have the same drawback as DRIPs in that they limit diversification potential. However, DPPs are most attractive for new, younger investors who typically lack the resources to immediately build a diversified portfolio. In addition, after investors have accumulated a certain amount of shares in any one company, they can switch the DPP to other companies, thus building diversification over time.

An alternative to a DPP for one company is to set up an account with a firm such as Sharebuilder (www.sharebuilder.com), which allows the investor to create what is essentially a direct purchase plan for a variety of stocks, index funds, and even closed-end bond funds. Some brokerage firms have even set up similar programs for their clients and at times have also allowed for reinvestment of dividends in the stock paying the dividends. From the stockholder's perspective, this will create fractional shares.

Loans Against 401(k) and 403(b) Plans

In chapter 3, we touched on the fact that employees may borrow from their qualified plans if the employer has such a provision in place. Currently, about 82 percent of 401(k) plans have loan provisions, and they are becoming more common as new plans are created.[32] As the mechanics of the process were discussed in chapter 3, we will not repeat those here. Instead, we will focus on the implications of such loans as they affect one's retirement portfolio.

There appears to be a substantial misunderstanding about the portfolio effects of taking such loans. A typical argument against taking out such a loan runs as follows:

> Taking out a loan of say, $20,000, reduces the balance in your account. The money you are taking out of your account is losing the opportunity to grow. Thus, you lose the earnings potential of the loan dollars while you are repaying it. Put another way, you are losing the benefits of compounding.

To understand why this argument is fallacious, let's consider a simple, although not technically correct, comparison. Let's say that the client is considering a $20,000 loan and then decides to leave the money in the account. The money is invested to earn a 10 percent rate of return. One year later, this part of the portfolio will be worth $22,000. As an alternative, the client lends the $20,000 to himself at a 10 percent interest rate, and repays the loan one year later. At that time, this part of the portfolio will be worth $22,000. Hence, if the interest rate on the loan were identical to the rate of return on the other investments in the account, there is no effect on the value of the account from such a loan.

As a practical matter, the interest rate charged on the loan is required to be a market rate, and is usually set at prime plus one or two percentage points. If the assets in the qualified account would have been invested in equities, then the expected return on them is likely to be higher than the interest rate on the loan. The real issue here is that by taking such a loan, the individual is changing the asset allocation of his or her retirement portfolio by increasing the percentage that is invested in debt instruments and reducing the percentage invested in stocks. For younger clients with long time horizons, this is not a good strategy. However, for older clients who are nearing retirement and would like to alter the composition of their retirement portfolio, taking out a loan against a qualified plan would accomplish this objective.

Is It the Best Source of Money?

The real issue to consider is whether or not this loan is the best source of money for the person with a financial need. The drawback to the loan is that the interest is not tax deductible. If the borrower has a choice between a tax-deductible loan such as a home equity line of credit (HELOC), a home equity loan, a margin loan in a nonqualified account, or a nondeductible loan, then he or she is always better off with the tax-deductible loan. However, this last statement is true only if the borrower can deduct all of the incremental interest. If the borrower is unable to deduct any of the interest on these other loans, then the analysis becomes more complex.[33]

A HELOC or home equity loan carries the risk that if a person defaults, then the borrower could lose his or her home. However, if one were about to default, then one could borrow from one's qualified account and use the proceeds to pay off the HELOC or home equity loan. In other words, one is no worse off taking out a tax-deductible loan first, and then resorting to a nondeductible loan later to pay off the former. Even if there is a significant default risk, one cannot be turned down for a loan from one's own retirement account. In the meantime, the borrower would presumably have saved money on his or her income taxes from the deduction of the interest payments.

Inflation Issues

As investors plan for retirement, one concern is the effect of inflation on their cost of living during retirement. This is a major issue that we will deal with in the next chapter when we discuss the role of inflation protection in asset allocation choices. During the accumulation period, securities designed to provide inflation protection are normally a poor choice. This is for the simple reason that the returns are limited. Inflation rates are incorporated into the rates of returns on all securities over time. Thus, an investor with a long time horizon will implicitly and eventually receive rates of return that will adequately compensate for inflation.

THE MORTGAGE AS A COMPONENT OF ONE'S PORTFOLIO

It is easy to overlook the fact that one's mortgage is a part of one's portfolio of financial assets. There are several aspects of having a mortgage that need to be integrated with one's savings plan for retirement.

The Mortgage for Clients in their 20s, 30s, and 40s

As part of the large selection of mortgages that are available to home-buyers and homeowners who are refinancing, many people can now choose an interest-only mortgage.[34] Although a few mortgage lenders offer 30-year term interest-only mortgages, most interest-only mortgages are either 5/1 or 10/1 (ARMs). This means the interest rate is fixed during the first 5 or 10 years, which is also the interest-only period After 5 or 10 years, the mortgages convert to where the interest rate is adjusted to an index on an annual basis, and the mortgage is amortized over the remaining 25 or 20 years.

There are two reasons why people take out interest-only mortgages. The first is so that they can afford a larger home. Remember, one of the key rules that nearly all lenders follow in approving mortgages is that the monthly PITI cannot exceed 28 percent of the borrower's gross monthly income. PITI stands for the Principal and Interest payment for the month (that is, the mortgage payment) and the prorated monthly payments due on property Taxes and the homeowner's Insurance premium. An interest-only mortgage would mean no principal payments are included in the mortgage payment, which means the buyer could take out a larger loan and still qualify under the 28 percent rule. A good financial planner would discourage a client from this strategy.

The other reason a person would take out an interest only mortgage is to increase the amount of money available for new investments. A person attempting to save for retirement can build his or her portfolio by putting payments that would have gone to principal into an investment portfolio.

What Principal Payments Represent

There are two crucial features to understand about principal payments on a mortgage (or any loan for that matter). The first feature is that payments of principal are the same as investing that money in a savings account that pays the same interest rate as the mortgage. Thus, if a homeowner has a fixed-rate, 6 percent mortgage, then all principal payments have the same effect on the homeowner's wealth as if this money were used to purchase an investment that paid a fixed rate of 6 percent. From an asset allocation perspective, principal payments on a mortgage are the same as increasing the fixed return portion of one's portfolio.

The second feature of principal payments is, if the mortgage is a fixed-rate mortgage, then the rate of return achieved is risk-free. That is, there is no default risk associated with this investment and no interest rate risk. If the mortgage is a variable rate mortgage, then the prepayments do have some risk associated with them as the future interest savings are now somewhat uncertain. However, there is no default risk associated with the mortgage.[35]

Thus, for clients who want an all-equity or nearly all-equity investment portfolio, interest-only mortgages provide a tremendous opportunity.

The Mortgage for Clients in their 50s, 60s, and 70s

When most clients retire, it usually makes sense for them to have their mortgage paid off and to own their home on a free and clear basis. There is a psychological benefit to a retired person living in a home that is fully paid for; however, there also can be substantial financial benefits. The interest payments on a mortgage are useful only for people who have income to shelter from taxation, and itemized deductions are a good sheltering mechanism. However, as retirees usually have less income, their marginal tax brackets are lower, and their need for tax sheltering is reduced.

A complicating factor is that retirees with mortgage payments may have to sell assets or take additional withdrawals from their retirement accounts. Selling assets usually creates capital gains, and the additional withdrawals from retirement accounts usually mean more taxable income. Remember, most retirees will also have Social Security income. The amount of Social Security income that is taxable depends on a retiree's total income. Hence, creating taxable income to make mortgage payments will only increase the amount of income taxes that are owed, which will create the need to generate more taxable income![36]

Unless a homeowner is lucky enough to have lived in a home long enough so that the mortgage would be paid off by the time he or she retires, then there are essentially only two strategies for paying off the mortgage early. The first is to make additional payments of principal over time. Some people make an extra mortgage payment once or twice a year; others add a fixed amount, such as $100, to each mortgage payment. The particular strategy does not matter because the conceptual issues remain the same as described earlier—namely, the extra payments are equivalent to investing in a fixed return security whose rate of interest is the mortgage interest rate, and the investment is essentially risk-free. By making extra payments on the principal, the homeowner is slowly but effectively rebalancing his or her portfolio to have more debt and less equity.

The alternative strategy to making prepayments is for the homeowner to take what would have been the prepayments and invest them to earn a rate of return greater than the mortgage interest rate. This is the same idea that was discussed above with interest-only mortgages. As long as the homeowner is able to achieve a mean average annual rate of return greater than the mortgage rate, then the value of these investments will be greater than the incremental reduction in the mortgage that would have resulted from the mortgage prepayments. At some point in time, the value of these investments would equal the value of the mortgage. The homeowner could then liquidate the investments and pay off the mortgage a lot sooner than if he or she had simply made the prepayments directly. In fact, depending on the spread between the mortgage rate and the mean annual rate of return on the investments, the benefits from the acceleration in paying off the mortgage could be substantial.

Example:	Juan Valdez has just taken out a 30-year, 6 percent mortgage for $200,000. His monthly payment is $1,199.10. Juan indicates to you, his financial planner, that he plans to add an extra $200.90 to each payment to bring the monthly payment to $1,400.00. The loan officer has told him that there are no prepayment penalties, and if he does this, he will end up paying off

his mortgage in 253 months (21 years and 1 month) instead of the full 360 months.

Point out to Juan that if instead he were to put the $200.90 each month into an investment that paid a 9 percent annual rate, then at the end of 185 months (15 years and 5 months) he would have accumulated $79,181.75. At that time, his mortgage balance would be $78,715.00. Hence, he could liquidate his investments, pay off the mortgage, and still have nearly $460 left over. More importantly, he would have saved an additional 6 years' worth of mortgage payments.

The above discussion has omitted taxes. Taxes would have minimal effect on the concepts presented herein, and under certain conditions the numbers would favor an even earlier payoff for the mortgage with the alternative investment. These conditions include that the investment chosen is taxed at a capital gains tax rate rather than as ordinary income, and that sometimes not all of the mortgage interest is utilized in the homeowner's itemized deductions.

All of this is not to say that the financial planner should advise the homeowner to place prepayment monies in alternative investments. The expected rate of return on the alternative investment may not be large enough to offset the fact that the prepayments are providing a risk-free rate of return. In our example with Juan Valdez, the 6 percent rate of return with perfect certainty may be more appropriate for his level of risk tolerance than the 9 percent risky rate of return. The key point here is that if the client has a mortgage outstanding, prepayments on that mortgage should be a consideration of the client's retirement portfolio.

SUMMARY

Modern portfolio theory presents the idea that an efficient frontier exists. Based on the intersection of this efficient frontier and the indifference curves of individuals, each investor would hold some combination of the risk-free asset and the market portfolio. As no one can actually hold the market portfolio, it is clear that one should hold a portfolio as diversified as possible. Larger numbers of securities provide the desired risk reduction.

It is critical that a financial planner assess the risk tolerance of each client to ensure that a reasonable asset allocation distribution is recommended. Longer intervals between making decisions and seeing the results of those decisions encourage more risk tolerance. Also, people are more inclined to make decisions when there are fewer decisions to make.

To understand the construction of a retirement portfolio, it is critical to understand that people's wealth equals the sum of their human capital and financial assets. For most people, the value of their human capital exceeds the value of their financial assets for most of their lives. Diversification of financial assets is not critical initially, but then it becomes incredibly important as the investor approaches retirement. It is important to minimize the covariance between the value of one's human capital and the value of one's financial assets.

Many people promote the benefits of time diversification when discussing long time horizons for investments. Unfortunately, time diversification is a misleading concept. The longer the holding period, the greater the variability of returns for that holding period. Time diversification is a valid argument only if an investor is willing to assume constant relative risk aversion, independent stock returns, and no value to human capital. Nonetheless, the longer the time horizon, the greater the likelihood that the poor performance of an all-stock performance *will* exceed the best performance of an all-bond portfolio.

Strategic asset allocation is critical for setting a portfolio's overall risk level. Tactical asset allocation is for the primary purpose of beating the market. It is better to make contributions to a retirement portfolio sooner rather than later, as this allows the value of the holdings to start growing sooner. It also reduces the chance of an investor missing one of the best performing days or months of the intended holding period. Early investing also means a client will have more opportunity to make up for any poor performance. Clients who have become overfunded need to alter their risk exposure, increase their objectives, or simply divert more cash to current consumption.

Erroneous estimates of future rates of return, variances, and covariances will tend to have a greater effect on the portfolio recommendations for aggressive investors than for conservative investors. When defining rates of return to use for projecting portfolio recommendations and results, the planner should avoid using strictly historical averages, and consider the current economic environment. Most techniques suggested for measuring the degree of diversification in a portfolio require data measured over time, and thus may be misleading. The Woerheide-Persson Index avoids these problems by using only the current weights of the assets in the portfolio, although it has its own set of deficiencies.

Tax efficiency is important in investing, but it should not drive the strategic asset allocation. Depending on the break-even holding period, retirement accounts may be effective vehicles for non-retirement investing. Otherwise, the retirement portfolio should not have any need for liquidity.

In general, the most efficient strategy for constructing a retirement portfolio is the accumulation of individual securities over time, rather than mutual funds. Retirement-oriented mutual funds can vary substantially in terms of asset allocation and types of securities selected. Dollar cost averaging can provide an effective way to build a portfolio, but runs the risk of creating concentrated portfolios. Loans from 401(k) and 403(b) plans may make sense as people approach retirement and want to increase the percentage of debt in their portfolio. Nonetheless, loans from these plans should only be considered as one option against other sources of loans. A retirement portfolio should probably not focus on securities that emphasize inflation adjustments.

During the first part of investors' careers, it may make sense to utilize interest-only mortgages to allow more money to be directed into the retirement portfolio. In later years, paying off the mortgage prior to retirement may make sense where a risk-free rate of return at the mortgage rate is attractive relative to potential risky rates of return.

NOTES

1. Most of the material in this section is a review of material that was presented in The American College's HS 328 course (Investments), and is included in most college courses on investments. Students who have had an investments course may lightly skim this section as a review, or skip it altogether.
2. John Evans and Stephen Archer, "Diversification and the Reduction of Dispersion: An Empirical Analysis," *Journal of Finance*, 1968, XXIV: 761–769.
3. Bruno Solnik, "Why Not Diversify Internationally Rather Than Domestically?," *Financial Analysts Journal*, 1974, 30: 48–54.
4. Recent research suggests that markets in different countries are becoming much more similar than before. Hence, the benefit of international diversification may be diminishing.
5. Stephen J. Davis and Paul Willen, "Income Shocks, Asset Returns, and Portfolio Choice," in *Innovations in Retirement Financing,* edited by Olivia S. Mitchell, Zvi Bodie, P. Brett Hammond, and Stephen Zeldes, Pension Research Council, University of Pennsylvania Press, Philadelphia, 2002.
6. Students who have taken The American College's HS 328 course may skip both this section and the next section, as all of the following concepts are covered therein.
7. These three observations can be proven mathematically, but for simplicity they are stated here without mathematical proof.
8. If six heads are flipped, then you would win $120,000 (6 heads x $20,000 per head), but lose $140,000 (14 tails x $10,000 per tail). If seven heads are flipped, you win $140,000 for the heads and lose only $130,000 for the tails, thus coming out ahead by $10,000.
9. Richard McEnally, "Time Diversification: Surest Route to Lower Risk?," *Journal of Portfolio Management,* Summer 1985, 24–26.
10. Ladd Kockman and Randy Goodwin, "Updating the Case Against Time Diversification: A Note," *The Mid-Atlantic Journal of Business,* (Vol. 37, issue 2/3, Jun/Sep 2001), 139–141.
11. This is not a direct quotation from any particular source, but a paraphrase developed from several sources.
12. The probability of five tails in a row is $.5^5$.
13. "Risk and Uncertainty: A Fallacy of Large Numbers," *Scientia,* April-May 1963, 1–6; "Lifetime Portfolio Selection by Dynamic Stochastic Programming," *Review of Economic Studies,* Vol. 36, 1969, 239–46; "The Judgment of Economic Science on Rational Portfolio Management: Indexing, Timing, and Long-Horizon Effects," *Journal of Portfolio Management,* Vol. 16, 1989, 4–12; "Asset Allocation Could Be Dangerous to Your Health," *Journal of Portfolio Management,* Vol. 17, 1990, 5–8; and "The Long-term Case for Equities," *Journal of Portfolio Management,* Vol. 21, 15–24.
14. Unfortunately, the proof as to why decreasing relative risk aversion means a higher equity allocation with a longer time horizon is mathematically complex and not intuitively obvious.

The reader will have to take the word of the many brilliant researchers who have looked at this issue.

15. The payment of capital gains taxes is a point only with nonqualified accounts. With qualified accounts, this is not a relevant point. However, as we will see later, investors are usually encouraged to hold equities primarily in their nonqualified accounts.

16. If no additional entries have been made since the prior computation, then the following keystrokes are sufficient: SHIFT, BEG/END, FV.

17. John Stowe, "A Market Timing Myth," *The Journal of Investing,* Winter 2000.

18. Peter Lynch, *Worth,* September 1995.

19. "Financial Planning in "Fantasyland," http://www.stanford.edu/~wfsharpe/art/fantasy/fantasy. htm, October 26, 2004.

20. For another discussion on this topic, see "Retirement Planning and the Asset/Salary Ratio," by Martin L. Leibowitz, J. Benson Durham, P. Brett Hammond, and Michael Heller in *Innovations in Retirement Financing,* edited by Olivia S. Mitchell, Zvi Bodie, P. Brett Hammond, and Stephen Zeldes, Pension Research Council, University of Pennsylvania Press, Philadelphia, 2002.

21. William Jahnke, "It's Time to Dump Static Asset Allocation," *Journal of Financial Planning,* June 2004, 26, 28–29.

22. William Janke, "Corrupted Investment Solutions." *Journal of Financial Planning,* October 2004, 26, 28.

23. Jahnke, June 2004, op cit., 28.

24. Doug Waggle and Gesung Moon, "Expected Returns, Correlations, and Optimal Asset Allocations," paper presented at the 2004 annual meeting of the Academy of Financial Services, New Orleans, LA.

25. This paper by Waggle and Moon received The American College's Best Paper Prize for the above conference.

26. Eric Jacquier, Alex Kane, and Alan Marcus, "Geometric or Arithmetic Mean: A Reconsideration," *Financial Analysts Journal,* November/December 2003, 46–53.

27. For additional discussion on this topic, see "Breakeven Holding Periods for Tax-Advantaged Savings Accounts with Early Withdrawal Penalties," by Stephen M. Horan, a paper presented at the Academy of Financial Services 2004 Annual Meeting in New Orleans, LA. Forthcoming in *Financial Services Review,* 13(4).

28. H. Christine Hsu and H. Jeffrey Wei, "Stock Diversification in the U.S. Equity Market," www.westga.edu/~bquest/2003/research03.htm.

29. "Targeted Retirement Funds Are a Simple Solution, but May Not Fit Everyone," *The New York Times,* Feb. 24, 2004.

30. On April 1, 2004, Hernando de Soto, the Peruvian economist who has devoted his life to bringing real property rights to the world's poor, became the second winner of the Milton Friedman Prize for Advancing Liberty. See, "The Man Who Really Helped the Poor," http://www.foxnews.com/story/ 0,2933, 117126,00.html, April 14, 2004.

31. Richard E. Williams and Peter W. Bacon, "Lump Sum Beats Dollar-Cost Averaging," *Journal of Financial Planning,* June 2004, 92–95.

32. http://www.smartmoney.com/retirement/401k/index.cfm?story=4; October 20, 2004.

33. The interest may not be deductible because the total of the borrower's itemized deductions are less than the standard deduction.

34. Shaun Aghili, "Advantages and Caveats of Interest-Only Adjustable Mortgages for Clients," *Journal of Financial Planning,* October 2004, 64–72.

35. One could argue that there is some remote chance of default risk associated with prepayments. Suppose a homeowner started out with a $200,000 mortgage on a house purchased for $250,000. Suppose further that between the obligatory mortgage payments and the voluntary principal payments, the balance due on the mortgage is down to $190,000. Finally, suppose the homeowner has to move and due to a decline in housing values, the market price of the

house is only $150,000. Legally, the homeowner would still owe the mortgage lender the full balance of $190,000. Some people simply default and sometimes are able to avoid having to pay the full $190,000. It would be in this rare circumstance that there is some default risk associated with prepayments on a mortgage.

36. Jonathan Clements, "Forget the Deduction: Why You Should Pay Off Your Mortgage Before You Retire," *Wall Street Journal,* October 6, 2004, D1.

7

Retirement Investment Strategies: The Distribution Period

Walt J. Woerheide

Chapter Outline

In the previous two chapters, we discussed how to project the amount a client needs for retirement and we considered various issues in managing the client's portfolio during the accumulation process. We will now examine portfolio strategies that should be in place when the client retires. Thus, wealth accumulation is no longer an issue. The client has exceeded, met, or fallen short of his or her portfolio wealth objective. Whatever the client has in his or her portfolio at this point in time, the issue now becomes one of how the client can live most effectively off of this portfolio during retirement. Thus, the primary focus of this chapter is how much the client should plan on withdrawing from his or her portfolio during the retirement years.

The vast majority of research in the field of investments and portfolio management has focused on wealth accumulation issues. It is only in the last few years that a handful of people have started seriously looking at strategies for managing a portfolio that is being liquidated. This creates a "good news/bad news" scenario. The "good news" is that this initial research provides guidelines and ideas that suggest appropriate professional standards for managing a retirement portfolio. The "bad news" is that there are still many, many questions that need to be resolved, and can be resolved only through a complex research process. Thus, the objectives in this chapter are to define and clarify the commonly agreed upon issues and practices in managing a retirement portfolio, as well as to indicate those areas in which we need more research to establish what are appropriate professional standards.

A NEW RISK-RETURN PARADIGM

The traditional risk-expected return paradigm as defined by modern portfolio theory (MPT) was described in the last chapter. In the basic MPT paradigm, the financial planner first identifies the optimal portfolios on the efficient frontier and then ascertains the client's degree of risk tolerance to select the one portfolio on the efficient frontier that lies on the client's highest possible indifference curve. Risk and return take on a completely different meaning when one is managing a portfolio that is being liquidated. To emphasize this distinction, we will refer to a portfolio where the objective is retirement income with the possibility of steady erosion in the value of the portfolio as a *retirement portfolio*.

In this case, return refers to the amount of cash that can be withdrawn from the portfolio each year. Risk refers to the probability that the portfolio will be exhausted before the portfolio's owner dies. Thus, we now move from a risk-return paradigm that is defined in terms of expected return (standard deviation of return) to one of cash withdrawal (probability of not outliving the cash withdrawals).

Example:	Many investors confuse the concepts of income and cash withdrawals. A prospective client may approach a financial planner and say something like, "I have a portfolio worth $500,000 and I want to generate an income of $30,000 per year." If this statement were taken literally, then the implication (particularly at today's historically low interest rates) is that the planner should put virtually the entire portfolio into moderately risky bonds as it is the only way to generate this much annual income on a portfolio of this size.
	However, what the individual probably means is that he or she wants $30,000 in cash that can be withdrawn from the portfolio each year. Cash can be obtained from a variety of investments, including bonds that are maturing, the liquidation of some of the shares of stocks that have appreciated, or even taking out margin loans. Thus, the removal of $30,000 in cash from a portfolio may be associated with the generation of substantially less than $30,000 worth of investment income. In addition, to the extent that some or all of the cash withdrawn is tax exempt, the client may not need the full $30,000 each year.

The Withdrawal Rate

The amount of cash that can be withdrawn from the portfolio is referred to as the withdrawal rate. For simplicity, the *withdrawal rate* is always defined as the amount of cash withdrawn from the portfolio during (or at the end of) the first year of liquidation as a percentage of the portfolio's value at the start of the liquidation period. In the above example, the desire to withdraw $30,000 per year in cash given an initial portfolio value of $500,000 means a withdrawal rate of 6 percent.

withdrawal strategy   Once the withdrawal rate is defined, the next task is to select a withdrawal strategy. A *withdrawal strategy* is defined as the process by which withdrawals will be adjusted once the withdrawal process has started.

There are three basic withdrawal strategies from which to choose, and many variations on these three. These are:

- *Flat annuity.* In a flat annuity, cash withdrawals are set at a fixed dollar amount per year, and the goal is to maintain this amount each year until the client dies.
- *Inflation-adjusted annuity.* In an inflation-adjusted annuity, the objective is to have the cash withdrawals grow each year at the rate of inflation. Because the increase in withdrawals from year to year is based on the inflation rate for the prior year, the growth rate would also vary from year to year. In fact, if we were to experience a year of deflation, the annual withdrawal would actually be reduced!
- *Performance-based annuity.* In a performance-based annuity, the withdrawal each year is based on the performance of the portfolio during the prior year. The simplest example of a performance-based annuity is that the withdrawal rate each year is a fixed percentage of the value of the portfolio at the end of the previous year. Thus, in the above example, suppose that the value of the portfolio at the end of the first year (after the $30,000 withdrawal) was $520,000. The withdrawal for the second year would then be $31,200, which is 6 percent of $520,000. If the year-end value instead had been $480,000 after the $30,000 withdrawal, then the second year's withdrawal would be only $28,800.[1]

An example of a variation would be a combination of the second and third strategies. For example, the withdrawal strategy could be to increase the annual withdrawal by the rate of inflation if and only if the value of the portfolio has increased during the year. Otherwise, take the same annual withdrawal is taken as in the prior year.[2]

Frequency and Timing of Withdrawals

So far, we have implied that annual withdrawals occur at the end of the year. For most of this chapter, we will use this description of the withdrawal process, despite the fact that it would be a rather absurd procedure to follow. The reason for using this concept is that most of the research that has examined determining the optimal withdrawal rate uses this model. Thus, treating withdrawals as if they are single payments at the end of each year facilitates a convenient discussion in terms of published research.

A slightly more practical view of taking withdrawals would be to maintain an annual withdrawal, but to think of it as occurring at the start of each year rather than at the end of each year. This means the client would have money to live on during the first year! It is easy enough to convert the discussion and examples to just such a process by assuming that the client has already withheld the cash for the first year's withdrawal when the portfolio strategy process is initiated. In the above example, we could say that the prospective client has already taken out $30,000 for the first year's living expenses, and the portfolio to be managed is still worth $500,000. At the end of the first year, when the next annual withdrawal is made, that withdrawal will cover living expenses for the second year, rather than the first year.

The most practical way to think about the withdrawal process is in monthly payments. As with annual payments, one can simply convert end-of-month payments to beginning-of-month payments by assuming the cash for the first month has already been removed when the initial value of the portfolio is specified. Some of the research in this field has considered the issue of monthly withdrawals, and we will discuss those results later in the chapter.

When the withdrawal strategy involves monthly payments, then the three basic strategies need clarification. The flat annuity strategy would simply mean that the monthly withdrawal is defined as the annual withdrawal divided by 12. The inflation-adjusted annuity could be defined as being adjusted either once per year or each month. Most discussions of inflation-adjusted annuities involve adjusting the monthly payment only once per year. The mechanics of doing this will be discussed later. Similarly, the performance-based annuity could also be defined as being adjusted either once per year or each month.

The New Risk-Return Tradeoff

As with MPT, the financial planner and the client need to make a serious decision involving the risk-return tradeoff. The simplest way to describe this tradeoff is that the higher the withdrawal rate, the higher the probability of **portfolio failure**. *Portfolio failure* is defined as having the value of the portfolio be less than or equal to an intended withdrawal, thus creating a final withdrawal that would zero out the portfolio. This relationship is graphically represented in figure 7-1.

The exact nature of the curve in figure 7-1 depends on the composition of the portfolio and the withdrawal strategy being employed. The **risk-free withdrawal rate** *withdrawal rate* in this figure is a withdrawal rate based only on net investment income. However, the basic points are these:

- If the withdrawal rate is set equal to the risk-free rate of return, then there is absolutely no chance of portfolio failure.
- The higher the withdrawal rate, the greater the probability of portfolio failure.
- The upper point of the curve would be where a 100 percent withdrawal rate provides a 100 percent probability of portfolio failure.

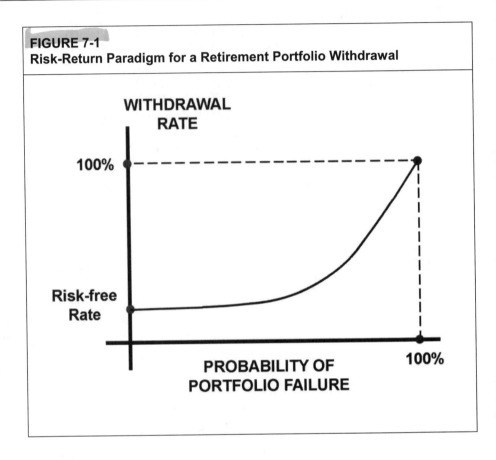

FIGURE 7-1
Risk-Return Paradigm for a Retirement Portfolio Withdrawal

The Influence of the Beneficiaries

Unfortunately, there is a third component to this model of the retirement portfolio risk-return paradigm. This third element is the value of the estate upon the death of the client. In cases where there are no beneficiaries and the client truly does not care what happens to his or her estate upon death, then the above paradigm is sufficient. However, many people do have beneficiaries to whom they would like to provide a significant bequest. Thus, they look not only at the trade-off between the withdrawal rate and the probability of portfolio failure, but also at the trade-off between the withdrawal rate and the expected size of the estate.

Although these two separate tradeoff functions may appear to be the same tradeoff, this is not necessarily the case. As we will see shortly, if one starts with a portfolio that is invested in all bonds, and then one considers substituting some equity investments for some of the bond holdings, the curve in figure 7-1 changes, as shown in figure 7-2. The risk-free rate is lower because dividend yields on stock are lower than current yields on bonds, but the curve is steeper, resulting in higher withdrawal rates for most

FIGURE 7-2
Risk-Return Paradigm with a Mixed Portfolio

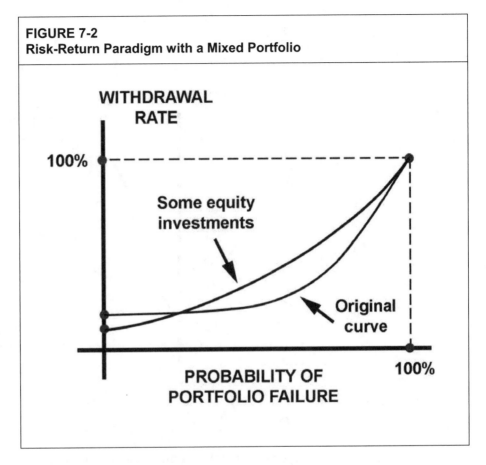

of the probabilities of failure. That is, one can establish a higher withdrawal rate without increasing the probability of portfolio failure. However, as one continues to substitute equity investments for bonds, the curve eventually reaches its highest location and then starts to shift back down. In other words, a portfolio that has too much equity in it actually means a lower withdrawal rate for a given probability of portfolio failure. It appears there is some optimal combination of debt and equity that an investor should hold.

Now, when it comes to the case of the tradeoff between the withdrawal rate and the expected size of the estate at the client's death, there is no optimal debt-equity mix. The greater the percentage of equity in the portfolio, the larger will be the expected size of the estate at the client's death. This is shown graphically in figure 7-3.

We see in the above figure that the moderate debt-equity portfolio has a lower expected value for the estate, but that relatively little of the distribution falls below zero. (Although as a practical matter, an estate cannot be worth less than zero, the graph is built on the assumption that if the portfolio is wiped out, the client would borrow money on which to live, and the part of

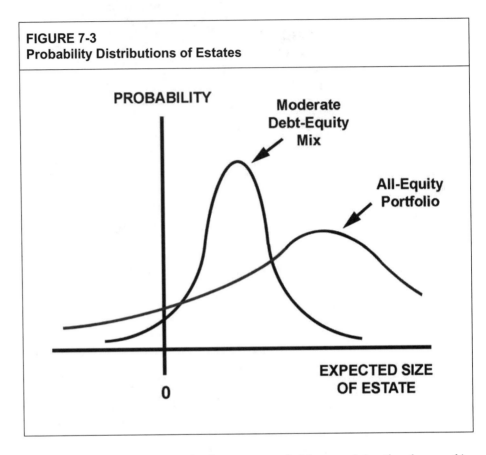

FIGURE 7-3
Probability Distributions of Estates

the distribution below zero is the amount of debt owed by the deceased.) With the all-equity portfolio, the expected value of the estate is much larger, but a significant part of the distribution lies below zero.

Capital Preservation and Purchasing Power Preservation Models

capital preservation model

Two models are sometimes referred to in setting a withdrawal rate, the capital preservation model and the purchasing power preservation model. The *capital preservation model* is defined as "a capital needs analysis method that assumes that at life expectancy, the client has exactly the same account balance as he did at retirement."[3] This model builds conservatism into setting the withdrawal rate, but it also provides for beneficiaries. A capital preservation model is easily accomplished by limiting withdrawals to the risk-free rate of return earned on the portfolio (that is, living only off of the income). This model can also be constructed to incorporate an annual inflation adjustment, but the calculation of the withdrawal rate under this assumption is more complex.

The *purchasing power preservation model* attempts to have the purchasing power of the portfolio at life expectancy equal the purchasing power of the portfolio at the time of retirement.[4] This means that the principal value of the portfolio would have to grow at the rate of inflation. As an approximation, this is accomplished by setting the withdrawal rate equal to the rate of return on the portfolio minus the inflation rate. Hence, if the portfolio achieves a 6 percent rate of return and the inflation rate is 2 percent, then the client would have to reinvest 2 percent each year, and could then establish a 4 percent withdrawal rate. As we will see shortly, none of the research in the field of managing retirement portfolios focuses on either of these models as a management strategy.

The Task of the Financial Planner

The financial planner must first determine the portfolio composition that will provide the client with the highest possible trade-off function in figure 7-1. These decisions will be influenced by the size of the estate that the client would like to provide his or her beneficiaries. Next, it is up to the financial planner to help the client to choose the withdrawal rate and associated probability of portfolio failure with which the client is most comfortable.

One aspect of the management of retirement portfolios for which research data are scarce is that of the maximum allowable probability of portfolio failure that a client should be allowed to undertake. There are at least three schools of thought on this subject. They are:

- Any risk is permissible, as long as there is full disclosure. This is more of a straw man argument, as most writers on this topic do suggest some maximum probability of failure that any client should be allowed to undertake. The selection of a maximum probability of failure that is advocated should also protect the planner against potential lawsuits if a client exhausts his or her portfolio and then decides to blame the planner.
- Maximum probability should be in the 5 to 25 percent range. This is probably the most common recommendation. Such probabilities allow for potentially large estates at the time of death because they accommodate portfolios with significant amounts of equity. The assumption is probably implicit in numbers such as these that the client could simply reduce the amount of the annual withdrawal if the portfolio declines precipitously in value.
- Maximum probability should be no more than one or two percent. Planners suggesting this maximum feel that the horror of even one client suffering portfolio failure is sufficiently grim that all clients should forgo the opportunity to substantially grow their estates. Such

a low percentage implies that any reduction in the annual withdrawal is tantamount to portfolio failure.

DETERMINING THE WITHDRAWAL RATE

As discussed in chapter 5, determining the withdrawal rate would be a relatively simple matter if all of the following conditions were met:

- The individual knew the exact date of his or her death,
- The individual knew the exact amount of withdrawals from his or her portfolio that would be needed each year, and
- The individual knew the exact rate of return that would be achieved on the portfolio.

Because none of these conditions can be met, managing the retirement portfolio and selecting a withdrawal rate is a matter of professional opinion. To fully understand what we know about this process, let's take a look at some of the more significant papers that have been published on this topic. Keep in mind as we review the literature that different articles will give different, and in some cases, conflicting results. This arises from the fact that they are using different databases, different methodologies, and/or different time periods. Thus, there is no correct answer about the optimal portfolio composition or the optimal withdrawal rate. Nonetheless, the financial planner needs to understand the basis upon which he or she is making his or her recommendations. Also, keep in mind that the portfolio composition and the withdrawal rate are really a joint decision process. Decisions on one have a tremendous effect on the other.

Ho, Milevsky, and Robinson (1994)

Ho, Milevsky, and Robinson develop a two-asset model to ascertain the portfolio composition to fund a desired withdrawal figure relative to current wealth.[5] The two assets are equities (for example, an index fund) and Treasury bills. The model is based on real rates of return, rather than nominal, and thus implicitly is assuming an inflation-adjusted withdrawal strategy. The specific rates of return are 8 percent and 2 percent, and the associated standard deviations are 17.5 percent and 3.5 percent. Two sets of empirical results are generated, one that is based on the life expectancies for men and the other that is based on the life expectancies of women. All of the empirical data are based on Canadian experience, although there is no reason not to believe that nearly identical results would be obtained if one used data based on the experience in the United States.

The major conclusions of the authors are that

1.   The equity requirement is greater for women than for men. Women should invest in an all-equity portfolio until they are about 5 years older than men with the same wealth-to-consumption ratios.
2.   Women with quite low wealth to consumption ratios should invest in an all-equity portfolio until as late as 80 years of age.
3.   Virtually all women should invest in an all-equity portfolio at age 65 or earlier.
4.   Men with low wealth should invest in an all-equity portfolio as late as 75 years of age.
5.   Virtually all men should invest in an equity portfolio at least through age 60.

Bengen (1994)

Bengen starts by considering a portfolio that has an asset allocation mix of 50 percent stocks and 50 percent bonds and looking at how such a portfolio would have performed assuming a person retired on January 1 of each year, beginning in 1926.[6] The rates of return data were drawn from Ibbotson Associates' *Stocks, Bonds, Bills and Inflation: 1992 Yearbook*. The rates of return for the bond portion of the portfolio are based on intermediate-term Treasuries, and the stock returns are based on the large cap series. It appears that he rebalances the portfolio at the time of each withdrawal and the withdrawals are made annually at the end of each year. Bengen found the following results:

1.   Regardless of the year in which a person would have started retirement during the period from January 1, 1926, to January 1, 1976, if he or she had established a 3 percent withdrawal rate, and adjusted the withdrawals for the rate of inflation thereafter, every single start date would have provided a minimum of 50 years worth of withdrawals.[7]
2.   When the withdrawal rate was increased to 4 percent, only 10 of the start dates provided less than 50 years' worth of withdrawals, but the worst case was 35 years' worth of withdrawals.
3.   At a 5 percent withdrawal rate, a significant number of retirees would have had less than 50 years worth of withdrawals, with the worst case being only 20 years worth of withdrawals (the worst cases belong to people retiring in the mid to late 1960s).

He next explored the issue of whether a different asset allocation would have allowed a higher withdrawal rate without an increase in the risk of portfolio failure. In doing so, he made these additional observations:

1. Portfolios that had 0 percent and 25 percent stock allocation performed much worse than the 50 percent stock portfolio.
2. A portfolio with 75 percent stock performed slightly better than the one containing only 50 percent stock in terms of the number of start years that achieved 50 years' worth of withdrawals. However, there are a few start years in which a 75 percent stock allocation provided substantially fewer years' worth of withdrawals.
3. When the values of the portfolios are computed 20 years after the start dates, those portfolios with 75 percent stock allocation were, on average, 123 percent greater than those portfolios that have a 50 percent stock allocation.
4. When the stock allocation is increased beyond 50 percent, the number of start dates that would have achieved more than 50 years' worth of withdrawals declines dramatically, and the worst-case scenarios become even worse. The only positive feature to higher stock allocations is that the average ending value of the portfolios grows substantially.

Next, Bengen considers three strategies that could have been utilized by retirees whose portfolios performed poorly in the early years of retirement. The first was to shift to 100 percent bonds. This strategy turns out to be worse than just maintaining the original asset allocation. The second strategy is to increase the allocation to stocks. This strategy would have produced incredible results, but is one that few clients would be willing to do. The third strategy would be simply to reduce the annual withdrawal to 95 percent of what it otherwise would have been. This strategy also serves the client well.

Bengen's concluding recommendations are that:

•   Retirement portfolios should have no less than a 50 percent stock allocation and no more than a 75 percent stock allocation.
•   Although the safe withdrawal rates must be identified through discussions with the client, a rate of 4 percent for a client in the 60 to 65 age range certainly seems appropriate.

Bengen (1996)

In his second article on retirement portfolios, Bengen extends the concepts of his first article to create some rules of thumb for the management of retirement portfolios.[8] The key point is the presentation of two simple, three-part rules for the appropriate percentage of a client's portfolio that should be allocated to stocks. The balance of the portfolio would be placed in intermediate-term government bonds. The recommendations are for tax-deferred and nonqualified portfolios, and are shown in table 7-1.[9]

TABLE 7-1
Bengen's Rules For Stock Allocation

Investor Risk Tolerance	Tax-Deferred Portfolio	Nonqualified Portfolio
Conservative	115 – client's age	125 – client's age
Moderate	128 – client's age	138 – client's age
Aggressive	140 – client's age	150 – client's age

In addition to the suggestions in table 7-1 for asset allocation guidelines, Bengen also suggests that the withdrawal rate for nonqualified portfolios be at least one-half percent less than what the withdrawal rate would have been on a tax-deferred portfolio. Although he emphasizes that the ultimate withdrawal rates depend on how much risk of portfolio failure a client is willing to accept, he encourages withdrawal rates of 4 percent and 3.5 percent for the tax-deferred and the nonqualified portfolios. As another way to look at the withdrawal issue, Bengen suggests that clients in a combined 20 percent marginal tax bracket should withdraw 7 percent less than they otherwise would, and clients in a combined 35 percent marginal tax bracket should withdraw 20 percent less[10] than they otherwise would. Naturally, higher tax brackets would suggest even greater reductions in the withdrawal rate.

Bengen assumes that the investor would be paying taxes each year on the investment income and the net capital gains in the nonqualified portfolio. He also notes that the half-percent differential in withdrawal rates is not really significant because withdrawals from the tax-deferred portfolio are fully taxable and those from the nonqualified portfolio are minimally taxable.

Notice that the asset allocation for a 65-year-old in a tax-deferred portfolio, according to these formulas, ranges from 50 percent for a conservative client to 75 percent for an aggressive client. This is exactly the range specified by Bengen in his earlier article. The other key point is that this model implies that in addition to cash withdrawals each year, there also would likely be a need to rebalance the portfolio. Remember, in the majority of years, the return on stocks will exceed that on bonds. Hence, the need to reduce the percentage allocated to stocks by one percent, combined with the more common scenario of superior stock performance, would mean that in most years there would be a need to sell stocks and put some of the proceeds in bonds.

With regard to the probability of portfolio failure, Bengen suggests a maximum probability of portfolio failure of 15 percent. The number of years of withdrawal that he seeks to guarantee is to age 95.

Bengen (1997)

In his third article, Bengen extends his earlier work by considering "the effects of adding small cap stocks and Treasury bills to the asset mix. . . . (and) retirement scenarios are expanded to include retirement beginning on the first day of any quarter, rather than just on January 1, as in earlier research."[11] With one exception, Bengen finds that looking at quarterly retirement dates rather than annual retirement dates does not alter any of the conclusions from his earlier work, other than to emphasize that stock allocations above 75 percent can result in even higher probabilities of portfolio failure than the data previously showed. The one exception is for someone who retired on October 1, 1929. Bengen suggests that because this is only one sample observation out of 201 observations in his data set, and because accommodating this one possibility would substantially increase the likelihood of setting too low of a standard of living during retirement than is necessary, he opts to disregard it although clients should be advised of this situation.

In order to study the effect of including small-cap stocks in a client's portfolio, Bengen looked at various percentage splits in the stock holdings, ranging from 100 percent large cap (which is his results from the earlier articles) to 100 percent small cap. He concludes that the optimal split is to have from 30 to 40 percent of the stock holdings be in small caps. He goes on to note that there is a debate in the literature regarding stock returns in the latter half of the 20th century. Some people believe that the higher rates of return we have observed historically on small cap stocks were due to a unique sequence of returns that is unlikely to be repeated, and because of the omission of direct and indirect transaction costs may not have truly been achievable. Others hold that small-cap stocks should still be expected to outperform large-cap stocks. Bengen concludes that there is no evidence that splitting the stock portion of the portfolio between small-cap and large-cap stocks would do any harm, and may be beneficial.

Bengen next considers allocating some of the portfolio to Treasury bills (T-bills). He finds that when the T-bills replace some of the intermediate-term Treasuries, there is substantial harm to the potential withdrawal rate unless the T-bills are kept to 10 percent or less of the bond portion of the portfolio. At this level, there is little effect on the overall results, and such a strategy may facilitate the cash withdrawal and balancing process of the portfolio. Next, consideration is given to adding T-bills to the portfolio by substituting them for some of the stock holdings. In all cases, this causes great harm to the portfolio.

Bengen next looks at the issue of the ending value of the portfolios as a function of the asset allocation. He finds that portfolios with 75 percent stock allocations ended up being worth substantially more than those portfolios with only 50 percent stock allocation. He concludes that "clients interested in growth of wealth should consider stock allocation near the upper end of the recommended range."[12] Finally, the issue of what could be done for clients who picked the worst possible times to retire (that is, just before a major market crash). He finds an immediate adjustment of the withdrawal rate can restore the portfolio to its former ability to support withdrawals until age 95. When done promptly, the reduction in the withdrawal rate ranged from 11 to 27 percent, and that was for people with a 5 percent (that is, aggressive) initial withdrawal rate.

Cooley, Hubbard, and Walz (1998)

portfolio success rate

In the first of four studies, Cooley, Hubbard, and Walz (CHW) looked at the *portfolio success rate* (which could be defined as 100 percent minus the portfolio failure rate) as a function of portfolio composition and withdrawals rates.[13] They considered the following combinations:

- withdrawal rates that ranged from 3 to 9 percent
- payout periods of 15, 20, 25, and 30 years
- portfolios that ranged from 100 percent stocks to 100 percent bonds, in increments of 25 percent

Based on these combinations of parameters, CHW were able to calculate 200 portfolio success rates (10 withdrawal rates x 5 portfolio allocation schemes x 4 payout periods).

They tested all possible overlapping payout periods starting with January 1, 1926, to December 31, 1995. The first portfolio tested was for a 3 percent withdrawal rate from a portfolio composed of 100 percent stocks, where the payout period started on January 1, 1926, and ended on December 31, 1940. The second portfolio tested started on January 1, 1927, and ended on December 31, 1941. CHW used the Standard & Poor's 500 Index to represent stock returns, and the index provided by Ibbotson for long-term, high-grade corporate bonds over this same period. They did not adjust for taxes or transaction fees, and assumed annual withdrawals at the end of each year. In their first pass at the data, they also treated the withdrawals as a flat annuity. Hence, there was no inflation adjustment. The following observations can be made about their flat annuity results:

- Portfolio success rates declined as the withdrawal period grew longer or the withdrawal rate became larger (which is the obvious conclusion).
- Based on a withdrawal rate of 3 percent, all combinations of holding periods and portfolio composition were successful.
- Based on a withdrawal rate of 4 percent, the 100 percent stock portfolio had only a 98 percent success rate for holding periods of 20

years or more. However, all other combinations of withdrawal rates and portfolio composition were 100 percent successful.

- In the 5, 6, and 7 percent withdrawal range, the optimal portfolio composition depended on the withdrawal period. But overall, the 50 percent stock, 50 percent bond portfolio seemed to perform the best.
- In the 8 to 12 percent withdrawal range, there was no universally superior portfolio combination, but the 100 percent stock portfolio tended to do a little better than the others.

CHW conclude from this table that:

> If history is any guide for the future, then withdrawal rates of 3 percent and 4 percent are extremely unlikely to exhaust any portfolio of stocks and bonds during any of the payout periods shown in [their] table 1. In those cases, portfolio success seems close to being assured. For planning purposes, where should an investor draw the line between acceptable and unacceptable portfolio success rates? The answer will vary from investor to investor, but it seems clear that some investors will choose withdrawal rates exceeding the highly conservative 3 percent and 4 percent rates.[14]

CHW then repeat the above analysis in two ways. First, they limit the data to the 1946 to 1995 period. When this is done, they find that the portfolios dominated by stocks can sustain withdrawal rates of 7 percent to 8 percent. Naturally, they leave the issue of whether the 1926 starting date or the 1946 starting date is the more relevant for an investor who is attempting to use historical rates of return as a guide for future market movements.

The second repetition of the computations involved the adjustment of the withdrawals for the annual rate of inflation. When this is done, CHW find that even a 3 percent withdrawal rate with a 100 percent bond portfolio has only an 80 percent success rate for a 30-year withdrawal period. At a 4 percent withdrawal rate, none of the portfolios has a 100 percent success rate for the 30-year withdrawal period. As the withdrawal rate is increased, all of the portfolio combinations start to perform poorly, although the more stock in the portfolio, the less rapid the deterioration in the success rate.

Finally, CHW look at the issue of what the terminal value of the portfolio is likely to be. The results are what one would expect: the lower the withdrawal rate and the higher the percentage of the portfolio allocated to stocks, the higher the average and median ending values of the portfolios.

Based on all of their results, CHW provide the following general conclusions:

- Most retirees would benefit from allocating at least 50 percent to common stocks.
- For retirees with significant fixed costs and for those who tend to spend less as they age, CPI adjustments will likely cause a suboptimal exchange of present consumption for future consumption.
- For stock-dominated portfolios, withdrawal rates of 3 percent and 4 percent represent exceedingly conservative behavior. At these rates, retirees who wish to bequeath large estates to their heirs will probably be successful. Ironically even those retirees who adopt higher withdrawal rates and who have little or no desire to leave large estates may end up doing so if they act reasonably prudent in protecting themselves from prematurely exhausting their portfolios.
- For short payout periods (15 years or less), withdrawal rates of 8 percent or 9 percent from stock-dominated portfolios appear to be sustainable.

Cooley, Hubbard, and Walz (1999)

In this paper, CHW extend their earlier work by making the withdrawals monthly instead of annually, and incorporating 2 more years worth of data (that is, to the end of 1997).[15] They also look at one scenario involving the addition of T-bills to the retirement portfolio.

CHW found that the use of monthly rather than annual withdrawals has no effect on the portfolio success rates for annual withdrawal rates of 3 percent to 7 percent. However, when the annual withdrawal rates are 8 percent or higher, the monthly withdrawals lead to a noticeable reduction in portfolio success rates.

CHW also find that a portfolio that was 60 percent stocks, 30 percent bonds, and 10 percent T-bills performed fairly comparably to portfolios that were 50 percent stocks and 50 percent bonds. For rates of return on the T-bills, they used the 30-day returns reported by Ibbotson Associates.

As an alternative approach to the question of what is an appropriate withdrawal rate, CHW computed the annual withdrawal rate for each time period in their study that would exactly exhaust the portfolio at the end of the intended withdrawal period. For all of the 30-year overlapping payout periods encompassing the years 1926–1997, they found a mean annual withdrawal rate of 8.4 percent for a regular annuity, with minimum and maximum values of 5.2 and 10.9 percent. When they considered inflation-adjusted payouts, they found a mean initial withdrawal rate of 6.2 percent, with minimum and maximum values of 4.0 and 8.9 percent.

Their major conclusion is as follows:

Investors who plan to inflation adjust withdrawals should choose lower withdrawal rates and invest at least 50 percent of the portfolio in stocks. Finally, the lower withdrawal rates of 3 percent and 4 percent recommended by some analysts appear to be excessively conservative for portfolios with at least 50 percent stock, unless the investor wishes to leave a substantial portion of the portfolio retirement portfolio to his/her heirs.[16]

Cooley, Hubbard, and Walz (2003a)

One of the drawbacks of the above cited studies, and one alluded to by Bengen, is that the portfolios used in these historical studies have consisted primarily of common stocks and corporate or government bonds, although there has been some consideration of the inclusion of T-bills. The risk-reduction benefits of international diversification have been widely cited in the literature, although recent research suggests that the risk-reduction value of international diversification is disappearing. Therefore, CHW take the next logical step in the analysis by reconsidering the sustainability of withdrawal rates when the portfolio includes international equities.[17]

Rather than following the traditional pattern of using overlapping periods of historical data for their study, they use Monte Carlo simulation. For each withdrawal rate, withdrawal period, and portfolio composition, 1,000 simulations were performed. Thus, the success rates reported were as a percentage of 1,000. The authors considered only the case of monthly withdrawals, but they evaluated both fixed withdrawals and inflation-adjusted withdrawals.

To gauge the effects of international diversification, CHW compared portfolio success rates for various combinations of withdrawal rates and withdrawal periods for four sets of portfolios. These included:

- 100 percent S&P 500 versus 75 percent S&P 500/25 percent EAFE
- 75 percent S&P 500/25 percent high-grade corporate bonds versus 50 percent S&P 500/25 percent EAFE/25 percent bonds
- 50 percent S&P 500/50 percent high-grade corporate bonds versus 25 percent S&P 500/25 percent EAFE/25 percent bonds
- 25 percent S&P 500/75 percent high-grade corporate bonds versus 25 percent EAFE/75 percent bonds

Note that in each case, the comparison involves moving 25 percent of the portfolio from the S&P 500 to the EAFE holdings.

Their major conclusion is that:

The results of the simulations of fixed monthly withdrawals and inflation-adjusted monthly withdrawals suggest that retirees who prefer portfolios of at least 50 percent equities benefit modestly from including EAFE stocks as 25 percent of the market value of their portfolio in spite of the inferior performance of the EAFE Index in the 1990s.[18]

Cooley, Hubbard, and Walz (2003b)

Whether one is researching the subject of the optimal withdrawal and associated portfolio composition or presenting evidence to clients as to what the choices and associated benefits and risk are, there are really only two methodologies to consider: historical analysis and Monte Carlo simulation. The vast majority of the research has been in the form of historical analysis. Although we are not aware of empirical evidence as to what percentage of financial planners use each (or both) of these methods to present information to clients, it is clear that at many of the conferences for financial planners, the software packages and many of the presentations involving retirement portfolios focus on Monte Carlo simulations.

Each method has a significant deficiency. With historical data, there is no guarantee that the patterns that have prevailed in the past are representative of what will occur in the future. Is a 1987-style market correction repeatable? Is a 1990s-style bull market something that can happen again? No one knows. Thus, the use of historical data may be interesting, but that does not mean it is necessarily a valid basis for evaluating withdrawal strategies.

Monte Carlo simulations have the benefit of permitting the investor to specify what the mean returns, standard deviations of returns, and correlation coefficients among asset returns in the future will be. If one is omniscient, then there should be substantial value to such an analysis. However, because it is unlikely that anyone is omniscient, then a Monte Carlo simulation suffers the risk of being a GIGO (garbage in, garbage out) analysis.

In their most recent work, CHW pose the simple question, "Would Monte Carlo simulations provide the same results as the overlapping periods methodology if the former used statistics based on the latter?"[19] The answer may seem obvious, but it is an important point as we consider evidence from both types of research, as well as the standard for a professional presentation to a client. The reason that the two methodologies may not produce the same results is that Monte Carlo simulation is built on the assumption that the distribution of returns is a stationary, independent process—that is, that the mean return for each asset category and the standard deviation of returns are the same for each and every time period, and the returns each period are completely independent of those for the prior period. If this is not the case, then a historical based analysis is strongly preferred. If the distribution of returns is a stationary, independent process, then the Monte Carlo simulation is preferred because it would provide a much clearer picture of the likely consequence of any particular strategy.

In this study, CHW use data only from 1946–2001. Their annualized rates of return for equities and bonds were 13.2 and 10 percent, with standard deviations of 14.4 and 7.6 percent. Their mean inflation rate was 4 percent, with a standard deviation of 1.6 percent. CHW note that:

> On average, the Monte Carlo simulation success rates are higher than the overlapping periods' success rates when monthly withdrawals are fixed throughout the payout periods. The larger differences occur in the longer payout periods, and when bonds are included in the portfolios.[20]

CHW go on to note that there is a significant reason for the differences that do occur. It is because the overlapping periods methodology does not weight all observations equally. For example, the rates of return for 1946 appear in only those withdrawal periods that start on January 1, 1946. The rates of return for 1947 appear in both the withdrawal periods that start on January 1, 1946 and those that start on January 1, 1947. Hence, they appear twice as many times as the 1946 numbers. It turns out that the 1970 to 1981 numbers appear in a disproportionate number of samples. It is also the case that this is a time period during which stocks performed particularly poorly relative to bonds. Hence, it is not really surprising that Monte Carlo simulation provides slightly higher success rates.

CHW conclude this study with the observation that:

> Despite some differences in findings, simulation and the overlapping periods methodology imply sustainability of a fixed annual 7 percent withdrawal rate for 30 years from portfolios with at least 50 percent stock. When withdrawals are adjusted for inflation, both methodologies imply sustainability of the 4 percent (plus) withdrawal rate for the 50 percent stock-50 percent bond portfolio over 30 years. These implications are drawn assuming that 75 percent is the lowest acceptable portfolio success rate. . . . Individuals who require more assurance and demand a 90 percent success rate must lower their withdrawal rates by at least one percentage point.[21]

CHW also recommend to financial planners that when they are making recommendations using long withdrawal periods, they should probably use a simulation methodology. However, when making recommendations involving shorter withdrawal periods, the overlapping periods methodology might be better because it produces the same results as simulation, and it would be easier for clients to understand.[22]

Terry (2003)

Not all of the research published on withdrawal rates agrees that having a significant portion of the retirement portfolio in equity is beneficial. Rory Terry argues for an inverse relation between the percentage of equity in the portfolio and the sustainable withdrawal rate.[23]

Terry notes the variety of opinions offered in the literature as to what is a maximum acceptable probability of portfolio failure (or conversely, what is a minimum probability of portfolio success). He suggests a probability of portfolio failure of *less than one percent* is the most that clients would find acceptable.

Terry uses Monte Carlo simulation to ascertain the probability of portfolio failure over a 30-year withdrawal period, with a 4.5 percent inflation-adjusted annual withdrawal. His simulation involves 100,000 iterations, mean returns of 12 percent for equities and 10 percent for bonds, with standard deviations of 10 percent and 0 percent, and an inflation rate of 3 percent with perfect certainty. A standard deviation of zero means, of course, a risk-free rate of return. Such a scenario is possible with bonds, if the bond portfolio is immunized.[24] Terry argues that the bond portfolio can be immunized. Immunization is not possible for the equity portfolio.

Eleven different portfolios are then considered, which change in increments of 10 percent and go from 100 percent debt to 100 percent equity. Terry reports that the portfolio failure rates monotonically increased at a decreasing rate, starting at 0 percent for the all-debt portfolio and rising to 25.18 percent for an all-equity portfolio.

Although Terry argues that the results are not driven by the 10 percent risk-free rate of returns on the bonds, it appears to this author that in fact they are. If the risk-free rate of return is reduced to 4.9 percent, a $100,000 portfolio has a terminal value of $120 after 30 years. A 4.8 percent rate of return results in portfolio failure after 29 years. Hence, the crux of the study is that with a 30-year withdrawal period, the safest portfolio is all debt as long as the rate of return is risk-free and the rate of return is at least 1.9 percent higher than the perfect certain 3 percent rate of inflation. If there is any variation in either the rate of return on the bond portfolio or in the rate of inflation, then there would be some risk of portfolio failure even with an all-debt portfolio.

The key point about this article is that it introduces the concept that the bond portion of the portfolio may be immunized to some extent. Such immunization would mean that the standard deviations for the bond portfolios used in other Monte Carlo simulations that are based on historical bond indices may be greatly overstating the risk of the bond component in a portfolio. *As a result, these other studies may be understating the optimal amount of debt that should be included in a retirement portfolio.*

Guyton (2004)

In most of the literature on the portfolio withdrawal rate, the authors focus on an inflation-adjusted withdrawal rate. CHW do report results for fixed annuities, but they place as much or more emphasis on their inflation-adjusted withdrawals. Guyton considers the effect of skipping or limiting some of the withdrawals on the sustainability of withdrawals.[25] He defines the safe initial withdrawal rate as the maximum rate that can achieve these conditions:

1. Never requires a reduction in withdrawals from any previous year
2. Allows for systematic increases in withdrawals to offset inflation
3. Maintains the portfolio's ability to satisfy the first two conditions for at least 40 years[26]

Guyton starts his analysis by expanding his portfolio to include holdings in the following categories: U.S. Large Cap Value, U.S. Large Cap Growth, U.S. Small Cap Value, U.S. Small Cap Growth, International Equities, and REITs. Most other studies considered either a single equity holding (either the S&P 500 index or Ibbotson's large cap index) or a limited equity holding. Guyton considers only two portfolios, the first with a 65 percent equity allocation and the second with an 80 percent equity allocation. He finds the above conditions alone increase the withdrawal rate from 4.3 percent to 4.7 percent with the 65 percent equity portfolio and 5.0 percent with the 80 percent equity portfolio.

Guyton then proceeds to test some additional rules regarding the computation of the withdrawal amount. One of them is as follows:

- There is no increase in withdrawals following a year in which the portfolio's total investment return is negative.
- There is no make-up for a missed increase in any subsequent year.

He finds that for the 65 percent equity portfolio, the initial withdrawal rate is substantially higher, and that total withdrawals after 30 years were essentially the same as if the withdrawals were based strictly on the inflation rate. Because initial withdrawals were higher and total withdrawals were the same, the time value of money makes this rule superior to not having it at all.

Guyton then turns to another rule for defining the withdrawal amount. This rule is:

- The maximum inflationary increase in any given year is 6 percent.
- There is no make-up for a capped inflation adjustment in any subsequent year.[27]

This rule allowed an increase in the "safe initial withdrawal rate from 4.4 to 5.1 percent with the 65 equity portfolio, and from 4.7 percent to 5.4 percent with the 80 percent equity portfolio."[28]

Finally, Guyton considers the effect of implementing both sets of the above decision rules on the safe initial withdrawal rate. In this case, the rate for the 65 percent equity portfolio becomes 5.8 percent, and for the 80 percent equity portfolio becomes 6.2 percent.

Although Guyton explores a lot of new ideas with regard to portfolio withdrawal rates, including a broader definition of what should be in the equity portfolio and a consideration of a withdrawal strategy that lies between an inflation-adjusted annuity and a performance-based annuity, his results are limited for several reasons. The most significant is that he tests his models only during a single period, namely the January 1, 1973 to December 31, 2002 period. This was a particularly difficult stretch for any portfolio, but it nonetheless means the ideas suggested in the article were tested with only a single (albeit 30-year) observation.

Why Most Research Overstates the Probability of Portfolio Failure

Much of the research discussed above, and nearly all of the other research on the topic of optimal withdrawal rates seen by this author, almost certainly overstate the amount of money one needs at retirement and/or what would constitute a reasonable withdrawal rate. There are several reasons for this. Let us consider each of them.

Underestimate Flexibility of Retirees to Adjust to Income Reductions

The research on the subject of an optimal withdrawal rate tends to assume (with the exception of Guyton) that retirees will continue to adhere to the initial withdrawal pattern regardless what happens to the portfolio. This means that if there is a dramatic decline in portfolio values, the research assumes the retiree will continue the same planned withdrawals, even if such a strategy means a guaranteed portfolio failure prior to any reasonable expected date of death. In fact, retirees, like everyone else, would most likely be realistic enough to understand that they may need to scale back their standard of living when they have been hit by adversity.

Example:	Jim and Sally Fontaine had a portfolio of $1.6 million that was providing the desired level of cash flow. This last year, they took out $90,000 from their portfolio. Unfortunately, during this last year, the market suffered a serious setback, and their

portfolio is now worth only $1.2 million. Another withdrawal of $90,000 would mean a withdrawal rate of 7.5 percent, and would start the Fontaines down the path of a significant probability of portfolio failure. They had been planning a month-long trip to Europe this summer, and a reduction of income would mean they would have to skip this trip. Should they skip the trip?

If during his working career, Jim had been planning a similar trip and then suddenly lost his job, he and Sally would not think twice about the appropriateness of foregoing the trip until such time as his job situation had improved. Asking them to make a similar accommodation during retirement is no greater a burden then making this adjustment during their working years.

Omission of Normal Reduction in Living Expenses

As was shown in table 5-2 of chapter 5, there is strong evidence that as people continue to age, they voluntarily make reductions in their consumption expenditures. The reasons for these reductions were enumerated in chapter 5, and will not be repeated here. None of the withdrawal strategies discussed heretofore indicated a plan for an actual reduction in the level of income. The closest possibility is the flat annuity concept, which implies a declining value in purchasing power if one assumes that inflation is a more likely scenario than deflation.

To understand the potential effects of this omission, let us consider the following two scenarios:

- Scenario #1: John and Rafaella Rodriguez are new clients. Rafaella is a full-time homemaker, and John plans to retire today at age 65. They want to withdraw $100,000 from the portfolio at the end of the first year, and want to have this grow at a rate of 3 percent per year. You expect they will live another 25 years (let's assume simultaneous death to keep the scenario simple). If you are able to earn a 10 percent rate of return on the portfolio, how much would you need today to fund these withdrawals? The answer is $1,707,175, and the derivation of this is shown in table 7-2.
- Scenario #2: You point out to the couple that after they take their cash withdrawal at age 75, they would probably be able to live just as comfortably with a withdrawal that is reduced by 20 percent thereafter. Thus, the withdrawal at age 76 is 80 percent of what it would have been

TABLE 7-2
Projection of Portfolio Requirements Under Two Strategies

	Strategy #1			Strategy #2	
Age	Withdrawal	PV of Withdrawal	Withdrawal		PV of Withdrawal
66	$100,000	$ 94,340	$100,000		$ 94,340
67	$103,000	$ 91,670	$103,000		$ 91,670
68	$106,090	$ 89,075	$106,090		$ 89,075
69	$109,273	$ 86,554	$109,273		$ 86,554
70	$112,551	$ 84,105	$112,551		$ 84,105
71	$115,927	$ 81,724	$115,927		$ 81,724
72	$119,405	$ 79,411	$119,405		$ 79,411
73	$122,987	$ 77,164	$122,987		$ 77,164
74	$126,677	$ 74,980	$126,677		$ 74,980
75	$130,477	$ 72,858	$130,477		$ 72,858
76	$134,392	$ 70,796	$107,513		$ 56,637
77	$138,423	$ 68,792	$110,739		$ 55,034
78	$142,576	$ 66,845	$114,061		$ 53,476
79	$146,853	$ 64,953	$117,483		$ 51,963
80	$151,259	$ 63,115	$121,007		$ 50,492
81	$155,797	$ 61,329	$124,637		$ 49,063
82	$160,471	$ 59,593	$128,377		$ 47,674
83	$165,285	$ 57,906	$132,228		$ 46,325
84	$170,243	$ 56,268	$136,195		$ 45,014
85	$175,351	$ 54,675	$140,280		$ 43,740
86	$180,611	$ 53,128	$144,489		$ 42,502
87	$186,029	$ 51,624	$148,824		$ 41,299
88	$191,610	$ 50,163	$153,288		$ 40,130
89	$197,359	$ 48,743	$157,887		$ 38,995
90	$203,279	$ 47,364	$162,624		$ 37,891
		$ 1,707,175			$1,532,116

under the first strategy. The result is that the client would need a portfolio of only $1,532,116 today to fund these withdrawals. This means a reduction in the initial portfolio value of approximately $175,000, without any effect on the withdrawals during the first 10 years.

Death of a Spouse

Most discussions of the withdrawal rate assume one client and one date of death. Many clients come in pairs, usually a husband and wife. Although it is not a pleasant topic to bring up, one of the spouses will likely die sooner than the other (the majority of the time the husband dies first). As one person can usually live somewhat cheaper than two, there would be an expectation of a reduced need for withdrawals at this time.

Unfortunately, this author knows of no research that has looked at the interaction of withdrawal rates, volatility of portfolio withdrawal rates, and joint life expectancies, although some researchers recognize this as an appropriate issue.[29]

Why Research Understates the Probability of Portfolio Failure

Omission of Bond Immunization

Most of the research that examines the role of bonds in a retirement portfolio (with the exception of Terry) treats the rates of return as if the investor were holding bond index funds—that is, mutual funds that invested in selected bonds to match the performance of a particular bond index. This creates additional volatility in the total return of the complete portfolio. Given that the cash withdrawals from the portfolio are fairly well known in advance, one could certainly immunize the bonds in the portfolio to match a significant number of the cash withdrawals.[30] This means that the volatility of returns on this part of the portfolio are much closer to zero than to the standard deviation associated with a typical bond index. The implication of this is that a given withdrawal rate could likely be supported with a higher percentage of the portfolio in bonds than would have otherwise been the case.

Omission of Transaction Fees and Taxes

All of the research reviewed by this author, and all of the studies discussed above, omitted transaction fees. With the steady decline in commission rates in recent years, this omission may not have been terribly significant, but at some point research will be done to validate the amount of trading activity that would likely accompany some of the these portfolio liquidation strategies.

Only Bengen gave consideration to tax issues in analyzing withdrawal rates. It makes a significant difference in the value of the income if the money is coming from a tax-deferred account such as a 401(k), in which case it is fully taxable; a tax-free account (such as a Roth IRA if all of the conditions are met); or a nonqualified account, in which case some of the cash is tax free as return of principal and some of it is taxed at the capital gains tax rate rather than the higher tax rates attached to ordinary income. When a client is choosing among risk-return options, he or she needs to understand how much of the withdrawals would be subject to taxation.

Inability to Match the Performance of Indexes

Over time, it is nearly impossible to match the performance of an index. There are two ways to try to match the performance of an index. One is to buy an index fund (either an open-end or a closed-end fund). The problem here is that there may be a load fee, commission, or 12b-1 fees; also, there will definitely be a management fee. Hence index funds over time may track the index to which they are tied, but they will usually underperform it by a slight amount. The alternative way to match the performance of an index is to build a portfolio that contains the same securities as the index. In the case of most indices, this would require a large portfolio, as well as an effort to monitor the portfolio to make sure it continues to match the index. Most investors would end up holding fewer securities than the index contains. Fewer securities would mean that the standard deviation of the returns of one's portfolio would be larger than the standard deviation of the index's returns.

DOES THE HARVESTING SEQUENCE MATTER?[31]

So far, we have discussed the withdrawal rate/portfolio composition issue as if clients hold only one portfolio. If a client's financial assets are all in one portfolio account, then the presence of taxes might affect the decision of what the withdrawal rate should be, but all of the withdrawals will be taken from that one account. Most clients will have their retirement monies in multiple portfolios rather than one portfolio, and these accounts will likely have different tax treatments. In this case, there may be significant implications in terms of which accounts one takes the withdrawals from initially.

The concept of harvesting sequence is subject to one obvious constraint. Some of the accounts have minimum required distributions (MRDs). Nothing that is said here is meant to override the obligation to take the MRDs. The context for the following discussion assumes that all MRDs are taken, and the financial planner must take some additional monies from one of the accounts. Thus, the question is, does it matter from which account the monies are withdrawn that are in excess of the MRDs?

For discussion purposes, let's assume a client has three types of accounts. The first is a Roth IRA in which the withdrawals are all tax exempt. The second is a 401(k) in which the withdrawals are all taxable as ordinary income. The third is a nonqualified account in which interest and dividend income is taxed each year as earned, but withdrawals are taxed only to the extent they exceed the cost basis.

Our goal here is to identify some guidelines that the financial planner can use in deciding from which account to take any withdrawals that are in excess of the MRDs. We also would like to comment on guidelines for the harvesting sequence when rates of return fluctuate from period to period, but we are not aware of any such research that has been published to date on this topic. Finally, note that in the following discussion, our focus is strictly on the harvesting sequence, not withdrawal rate issues.

Case I: Tax-Exempt versus Tax-Deferred, All-Bond Portfolio

Let's start with the simple case of all accounts containing identical bond portfolios. Consider the situation of Larry Baker. Larry has $100,000 in a 401(k) account and another $100,000 in a Roth IRA account. Let's further assume the accounts are fully invested in bonds that have a current yield of 5 percent. Let's assume that Larry is able to reinvest all interest income at the 5 percent rate. Finally, let's assume that Larry wants to withdraw $14,000 per year on an after-tax basis and that his marginal tax rate (federal and state) is 30 percent. That is, we are using the flat annuity withdrawal strategy to keep the computations simple.

Larry has two choices: he can take all his voluntary withdrawals initially from his 401(k) account and then start on his Roth IRA when that account is exhausted, or he can take all his voluntary withdrawals initially from his Roth IRA account and then start on his 401(k) when that account is exhausted. Let's look at how long his withdrawals will last under each strategy.

Strategy #1: Start with 401(k) Account

In order to obtain an after-tax withdrawal of $14,000, Larry will have to withdraw $20,000 from his account. This is derived by dividing the $14,000 by the complement of his tax rate, or $14,000 / (1 − .30). The next question is how long will this account last, assuming an annual rate of return of 5 percent and an annual withdrawal of $20,000? It turns out that this account will last 5.90 years. The keystrokes[32] are as follows:

> SHIFT, C ALL
> 14000, ÷, .7, =, PMT
> 100000, +/-, PV
> 5, I/YR
> N (display: 5.90)

During these 5.90 years, the value of the Roth account will continue to grow. At the end of the 5.90 years, it will be worth $133,357.32. The keystrokes are as follows:

SHIFT, C ALL
5.90, N
5, I/YR
100000, +/-, PV
FV (display: 133,357.32)

Finally, as the withdrawals from this account are tax free, Larry need only withdraw exactly $14,000 per year to maintain his annuity on an after-tax basis. These withdrawals will then last for another 13.26 years, computed as:

SHIFT, C ALL
14000, PMT
133,357.32, +/-, PV
5, I/YR
N (display: 13.26 years)

Thus, between the two accounts, Larry will be able to generate his $14,000 annuity for 19.16 years (5.90 years + 13.26 years).

Strategy #2: Start with Roth Account

If Larry starts taking withdrawals from his Roth IRA account, then he need only take exactly $14,000 each year. He will exhaust this account after 9.06 years. The keystrokes are:

SHIFT, C ALL
14000, PMT
100000, +/-, PV
5, I/YR
N (display: 9.06 years)

During this time, the value of the 401(k) account will grow to $155,587.62. The keystrokes are:

SHIFT, C ALL
9.06, N
5, I/YR
100000, +/-, PV
FV (display: 155,587.62)

At this point in time, Larry will then start taking his $20,000 withdrawals from his 401(k) account. This account will provide payments for 10.10 years, where the keystrokes are:

> SHIFT, C ALL
> 20000, PMT
> 155,587.62, +/-, PV
> 5, I/YR
> N (display: 10.10 years)

Between the two accounts, Larry will be able to generate his $14,000 annuity for 19.16 years (9.06 years +10.10 years).

Comparison of Strategies #1 and #2

The critical point in this example is that the harvesting order does not matter. Regardless of the sequence, Larry's annuity will last for 19.16 years, assuming the interest rate and the tax rate do not change. However, if the financial planner has concerns that either interest rates or marginal tax rates might change in later years, then the harvesting sequence might in fact matter. Let's consider each of these possibilities.

Impact of an Increase in Interest Rates. For simplicity, let's assume that interest rates increase from 5 percent to 10 percent exactly 5.90 years from today. Under the first strategy in which the 401(k) is harvested first, the longevity of the withdrawals increases to 37.88 years. The longevity of the 401(k) account is still 5.90 years, as the interest rate increase does not take effect until this account is exhausted (again, the 5.90 is selected for purposes of simplicity). The withdrawals from the Roth IRA will now last 31.98 years [keystrokes: SHIFT, C ALL; 14000, PMT; 133357.32, +/-, PV; 10, I/YR; N (display: 31.98 years)]. The combined longevity is now 37.88 years (31.98 + 5.90).

The longevity under the second strategy is slightly more complicated to compute. If we start the withdrawals from the Roth IRA, then after 5.90 years, there will still be money left in that account. The amount remaining will be $39,956.82 [keystrokes: SHIFT, C ALL; 14000, PMT; 100000, +/-, PV; 5, I/YR; 5.90, N; FV (display: 39,956.82)]. Thus, we need to compute how much longer this account will last if interest rates then jump to 10 percent at this time. It turns out that the payments will last another 3.53 years [keystrokes: SHIFT, C ALL; 14000, PMT; 39956.82, +/-, PV; 10, I/YR; N (display: 3.53)]. This means that the payments from the Roth IRA will now last 9.43 years (5.90 + 3.53) rather than the 9.06 years we computed when we assumed interest rates would remain constant at 5 percent.

Next, we need to determine the value of the 401(k) account after 9.43 years, when the interest rate is 5 percent for the first 5.90 years and 10 percent for the remaining 3.53 years. This requires two future value calculations. The ending value is $186,695.15. The keystrokes are: SHIFT, C ALL; 100000, +/-, PV; 5, I/YR; 5.90, N; FV (display: 133,357.32); and SHIFT, C ALL; 133357.32, +/-, PV; 10, I/YR; 3.53, N; FV (display: 186,695.15). The final step is to compute how many years Larry can take withdrawals from the 401(k) plan. This number turns out to be 28.44 years [keystrokes: SHIFT, C ALL; 20000, PMT; 186695.15, +/-, PV; 10, I/YR; N (display: 28.44)]. The combined longevity in this case totals 37.87 years (9.43 years + 28.44 years). As this difference of .01 year (37.88 versus 37.87) is well within the margin of rounding error, it is arguably the case that a change in interest rates would have no effect on the preference of one strategy over the other.

Impact of an Increase in Income Tax Rates. A change in tax rates makes the comparison more interesting. Suppose that Larry's marginal tax rate were to jump from 30 percent to 50 percent after the first portfolio is exhausted. Under strategy #1, Larry's annuity will still last 19.16 years because the withdrawals from the Roth are unaffected by his marginal tax rate. However, if he starts taking the withdrawals from his Roth first and his marginal tax rate rises, then the longevity of his annuity declines because he has to take out larger withdrawals ($28,000 rather than $20,000) from his 401(k) to achieve his $14,000 per year after-tax annuity. Conversely, if his marginal tax rate were to decline in later years, then Larry would be better off to start his withdrawals from his Roth. Thus, the harvesting order does matter if one believes that the client's marginal tax rate will change in later years. Simply put, the harvesting sequence in this case boils down to nothing more than the expectation of the direction of change in the client's marginal tax rates. If the planner has no reason to expect a particular change, then he or she would truly be indifferent. In this case, taking one-half of the desired withdrawals from each account would minimize the harm from guessing wrong with respect to the direction of future changes in tax rates.

Case II: Tax-Deferred versus Taxable, All-Bond Portfolio

Now let's consider the harvesting question when the two portfolios that are available are a tax-deferred account (again, we'll use a 401(k) account as our example) and a nonqualified account. As before, we will assume $100,000 in each account, that both portfolios are 100 percent in bonds, that both portfolios have a 5 percent current yield that does not change, and that Larry wants to withdraw $14,000 per year on an after-tax basis and that his marginal tax rate (federal and state) is 30 percent. The question again is does the sequence of harvesting affect the longevity of his annuity.

Strategy #3: Start with the 401(k) Account

As before, if Larry starts his withdrawals from the 401(k) account, the account will be exhausted after 5.90 years. What is different in this example is that the taxable account will only grow at a 3.5 percent rate during these years. That is, if Larry's marginal tax rate is 30 percent, and the account is providing 5 percent in interest income that is taxable as ordinary income, then Larry will have to pay the equivalent of 1.5 percent in taxes on this account (5 percent current yield x .30 tax rate), which would leave him with 3.5 percent after taxes. After 5.90 years, this account will be worth $122,503.38 [keystrokes: SHIFT, C ALL; 5.90, N; 3.5, I/YR; 100000, +/-, PV; FV (display: 122,503.38)].

The one advantage of this nonqualified, all-bond portfolio is that the withdrawals would consist of principal only. The withdrawals from this portfolio would last 10.63 years [keystrokes: SHIFT, C ALL; 14000, PMT; 122503.38, +/-, PV; 3.5, I/YR; N (display: 10.63 years)]. Thus, the longevity of the $14,000 annuity will be 16.53 years (5.90 years + 10.63 years).

Strategy #4: Start with the Nonqualified Account

As before, let's switch the sequence and start the withdrawals from the nonqualified account first. In this case, the nonqualified account will provide withdrawals for 8.36 years [keystrokes: SHIFT, C ALL; 14000, PMT; 100000, +/-, PV; 3.5, I/YR; N (display: 8.36 years)]. During this time, the 401(k) account will grow to a value of $150,363.54 [keystrokes: SHIFT, C ALL; 100000 +/-, PV; 5, I/YR; 8.36, N; FV (display: 150,363.54)]. This amount will then provide withdrawals for 9.66 years [keystrokes: SHIFT, C ALL; 20000, PMT; 150363.54, +/-, PV; 5, I/YR; N (display: 9.66 years)]. Hence, the total longevity of the payments is 18.02 years (8.36 years + 9.66 years).

Comparison of Strategies #3 and #4

In this case, the harvesting sequence makes a substantial difference as it adds about 1 1/2 years to the longevity (18.02 versus 16.53 years) if one starts with the nonqualified account first. The reason for the differential is the fact that the effective rate of return on the nonqualified account is lower (3.5 percent versus 5 percent). Hence, it is far more beneficial to leave the 401(k) account untouched as long as possible.

Impact of an Increase in Interest Rates. Let's now consider the impact of a change in interest rates over the life of the holdings. As before, let's start with the assumption that interest rates change from 5 percent to 10 percent after 5.90 years. This means that when we start harvesting the 401(k) account, this account will be exhausted exactly at the time of the change in interest rates. As before, the nonqualified account will have grown to $122,503.38 over this time period. At a 10 percent interest rate, the after-tax return on the nonqualified account increases to 7 percent ([10% x (1 − .30]) at exactly the time we would start harvesting from this account.[33] At this rate, the nonqualified account will last for 14.01 years [keystrokes: SHIFT, C ALL; 14000, PMT; 122,503.38, +/-, PV; 7, I/YR; N (display: 14.01 years)]. Hence, the combined longevity is 19.91 years (5.90 years + 14.01 years).

If we start our withdrawals from the nonqualified account, then after 5.90 years, we will still have $32,489.87 left in the account [keystrokes: SHIFT, C ALL; 14000, PMT; 100000, +/-, PV; 3.5, I/YR; 5.90, N; FV (display: 32,489.87)]. If we assume an increase in interest rates to 10 percent, then this account will provide withdrawals for another 2.62 years [keystrokes: SHIFT, C ALL; 14000, PMT; 32489.87, +/-, PV; 7, I/YR; N (display: 2.62)]. Hence, the nonqualified account will provide payments for a total of 8.52 years (an increase of .16 years from when there was no change in interest rates).

The 401(k) plan will grow at 5 percent for 5.90 years, 10 percent for 2.62 years, and 10 percent during the time period it is being harvested. The 401(k) account will then provide payments for a total of 20.33 years [keystrokes: SHIFT, C ALL; 100000, +/-, PV; 5, I/YR; 5.90, N; FV (display: 133,357.32); SHIFT, C ALL; 133,357.32, +/-, PV; 10, I/YR; 2.62, N; FV (display: 171,184.99); SHIFT, C ALL; 20000, PMT; 171184.99, +/-, PV; 10, I/YR; N (display: 20.33)]. Thus, the shift in interest rates provides withdrawals for 28.85 years (5.90 + 2.62 + 20.33), a substantial increase from the 18.02 years of withdrawals when there was no increase in interest rates.

Simply put, under the strategy in which the 401(k) plan is harvested first, the increase in interest rates after 5.90 years increases the longevity of withdrawals from 16.53 years to 19.91 years, an increase of 3.38 years. However, under the strategy in which the nonqualified account is harvested first, the increase in interest rates after 5.90 years increases the longevity of withdrawals from 18.02 years to 28.85 years, an increase of 10.83 years. Clearly, the expectation of an increase in interest rates would favor even more the harvesting of the nonqualified assets first. Conversely, the expectation of a decline in interest rates would reduce the relative attractiveness of this strategy.

Impact of an Increase in Income Tax Rates. Finally, let's consider the effect of an increase in the client's marginal tax rates. Again, for simplicity, let's assume that marginal tax rates were to increase from 30 percent to 50 percent after 5.90 years. In strategy #3, the 401(k) account would still last for exactly 5.90 years and the nonqualified account would still be worth $122,503.38 at this time. However, the nonqualified account would last only 10.00 years [keystrokes: SHIFT, C ALL; 2.5, I/YR; 122503.38, +/-, PV; 14000, PMT; N (display: 10.00)]. Hence the combined longevity of this approach is 15.90 years.

Under strategy #4, the computations are again much more complex. First, we have to determine how much money is left in the nonqualified account after 5.90 years. This turns out to be $32,489.87 [keystrokes: SHIFT, C ALL; 3.5, I/YR; 100000, +/-, PV; 14000, PMT; 5.90, N; FV (display: 32,489.87)]. Next, we need to determine how much longer this money will last. The answer turns out to be 2.42 years [keystrokes: SHIFT, C ALL; 32489.87, +/-, PV; 2.5, I/YR; 14000, PMT; N (display: 2.42)]. Hence, the nonqualified portfolio will last a total of 8.32 years (5.90 years + 2.42 years).

Next, we need to determine the value of the 401(k) account at the time that the nonqualified account is exhausted. As the growth in the account is unaffected by the increase in tax rates, this turns out to be $150,070.38 [keystrokes: SHIFT, C ALL; 100000 +/-, PV; 5, I/YR; 8.32, N; FV (display: 150,070.38)]. To generate $14,000 in an after-tax withdrawal when the marginal tax rate is 50 percent would require a $28,000 withdrawal ([$14,000 / [1 −.50]). Based on this withdrawal rate, the account will provide withdrawals for 6.39 years [keystrokes: SHIFT, C ALL; 28000, PMT; 150070.38, +/-, PV; 5, I/YR; N (display: 6.39 years)]. The combined longevity of payments is now 14.71 years (8.32 years + 6.39 years).

Notice that not only does the increase in the marginal tax rate reduce the longevity by 3.31 years (from 18.02 years to 14.71 years), but it also makes the longevity less than strategy #3 (14.71 years versus 15.90 years). This means that the financial planner must make some complicated choices when choosing the harvesting order between a 401(k) plan and a nonqualified plan. Nonetheless, we can make the following observations.

- If neither interest rates nor marginal tax rates are expected to change, then the nonqualified plan should be liquidated first.
- If interest rates are expected to rise, then liquidating the nonqualified plan first is even more attractive. However, if interest rates are expected to fall, then the sequence of liquidation may depend upon the magnitude of the expected fall in rates.
- If marginal tax rates are expected to fall, then liquidation of the nonqualified account first is, again, the more attractive choice. However, if marginal tax rates are expected to rise, especially by a lot, then it is not as clear as to which account should be liquidated first.

Case III: Tax-Exempt versus Taxable, All-Bond Portfolio

To complete the analysis of these three types of accounts, let's consider the third comparison of which should be harvested first when the two portfolios that are available are a tax-exempt (again, we'll use a Roth IRA account as our example) and a nonqualified account. Again, we will assume $100,000 in each account, that both portfolios are 100 percent in bonds, both portfolios have a 5 percent current yield that does not change, and that Larry wants to withdraw $14,000 per year on an after-tax basis and that his marginal tax rate is 30 percent.

Strategy #5: Start with the Roth Account

If Larry starts his withdrawals from the Roth account, the account will be exhausted after 9.06 years, as we saw in strategy #2. As the taxable account will grow at the after-tax rate of 3.5 percent rate during these years, it will be worth $136,571.34 [keystrokes: SHIFT, C ALL; 9.06, N; 3.5, I/YR; 100000, +/-, PV; FV (display: 136,571.34)]. The withdrawals from the nonqualified account would then last another 12.44 years [keystrokes: SHIFT, C ALL; 3.5, I/YR; 136,571.34, +/-, PV; 14000, PMT; N (display: 12.14 years)]. Thus, the longevity of the $14,000 annuity under strategy #5 will be 21.20 years (9.06 years + 12.14 years).

Strategy #6: Start with the Nonqualified Account

As we saw in strategy #4, if Larry starts the withdrawals from the nonqualified account first, this account will be exhausted after 8.36 years. The Roth account, like the 401(k) account in strategy #4, will grow to a value of $150,363.54. Finally, because the withdrawals from this account are tax-exempt, this account will provide withdrawals for 15.78 years [keystrokes: SHIFT, C ALL; 5, I/YR; 150363.54, +/-, PV; 14000, PMT; N (display: 15.78 years)]. Thus, the combined total will be 24.14 years (8.36 years + 15.78 years).

Comparison of Strategies #5 and #6

The above results are really a statement of the obvious. The difference in the longevity (21.20 years versus 24.14 years) is a direct result of the benefit of leaving as much money in the tax-free growth account as long as possible, and the value of disposing of taxable income as soon as possible. We will note without example that neither a subsequent change in interest rates nor a subsequent change in tax rates will affect this outcome.

Case IV: Tax-Exempt versus Tax-Deferred, All-Stock Portfolio

Let's now revisit our pair wise considerations except we now want to consider the implications if the portfolios are all stock rather than all bond holdings. The difference, of course, is the tax treatment of the capital gains. With a tax-exempt account, the capital gains are tax exempt by definition. With a tax-deferred account, the capital gains are taxed as ordinary income at such time as a cash withdrawal is made. With a nonqualified account, a capital gains tax is paid at the time the stocks are sold, which presumably is at the time the cash withdrawal is taken, but the capital gains tax rate is 5 or 15 percent, depending on one's marginal tax rate. In either case, it is substantially less than the tax rate on ordinary income.

In this first comparison, the analysis would be exactly the same as in Case I. That is, it would not matter which account was harvested first, as the longevity of the payments would be the same. Similarly, a change in the rate of return would not affect the result, but a change in the marginal tax rate would make a substantial difference in which was harvested first.

Case V: Tax-Deferred versus Taxable, All-Stock Portfolio

In this comparison, let's assume that all assets in the taxable account are non-dividend-paying common stocks. For the 401(k) account, the cost basis does not matter. For the nonqualified account, the cost basis is significant. We will assume a cost basis of $100,000, a 30 percent marginal tax rate for ordinary income, and a 15 percent marginal tax rate for capital gains. Next, whereas we assumed a 5 percent current yield on bonds, let's assume an 8 percent rate of return on stocks. Finally, we will continue the assumptions that Larry wants to withdraw $14,000 on an after-tax basis each year. This means a pre-tax withdrawal of $20,000 from the 401(k) account, but the amount of stocks to be sold will depend each year on the cost basis.

Strategy #7: Start with the 401(k) Account

The only difference between the longevity of the all-stock portfolio and the all-bond portfolio is the higher rate of return being earned on the stocks. In this case, the $20,000 withdrawals from the 401(k) account will last 6.64 years [keystrokes: SHIFT, C ALL; 20000, PMT; 100000, +/-, PV; 8, I/YR; N (display: 6.64)]. After 6.64 years, the nonqualified account will be worth $166,699.28 [keystrokes: SHIFT, C ALL; 6.64, N; 8, I/YR; 100000, +/-, PV; FV (display: 166,699.28)]. Unlike the all-bond portfolio analysis, the rate of return on the nonqualified account during this period is unaffected by tax based on the assumptions that there are no dividends and none of the securities are sold, and thus there is no capital gains tax due. Once the 401(k) account is exhausted, then the withdrawals will start from the nonqualified account.

Unfortunately, the longevity of these payments cannot be computed on a calculator because the amount of stock that has to be sold to generate $14,000 in after-tax withdrawals will change each period. For example, after the 401(k) plan is exhausted, the nonqualified account will have one more year to grow in value and will grow to be worth $180,035.20.[34] At this point in time, the cost basis is still $100,000, so it is 55.5447 percent ($100,000 / $180,035.20) of any stock sold. To obtain a $14,000 after-tax withdrawal, it turns out that $15,000 worth of stock would have to be sold. Of this, 55.5447 percent ($8,331) is a tax-free return of capital. The remainder, $6,668, is taxed at the 15 percent capital gains tax rate. This means a tax payment of $1,000 (.15 x 6668). Thus, the sale of $15,000 worth of securities less the $1,000 payment of the capital gains tax leaves an after-tax withdrawal of $14,000. For the next year, the cost basis of the portfolio is then reduced by $8,331 to $91,669. It is as a result of this adjustment in the cost basis that the necessary sale of stock each year to provide $14,000 in an after-tax withdrawal will actually increase.[35] Hence, the longevity of the remaining payments can only be projected on an Excel spreadsheet. In this case, the portfolio will support payments for approximately another 25.2 years. The combined longevity of withdrawals if one starts with the 401(k) account is 31.84 years (6.64 + 25.2).

Strategy #8: Start with the Nonqualified Account

If the client starts taking the withdrawals from the nonqualified account first, these withdrawals will last 11.2 years[36]. During this time, the 401(k) account will grow to a value of $236,780.57 [keystrokes: SHIFT, C ALL; 11.2, N; 8, I/YR; 100000, +/-, PV; FV (display: 236,780.57)]. The withdrawals from this 401(k) account would then last another 12.44 years [keystrokes: SHIFT, C ALL; 8, I/YR; 236780.57, +/-, PV; 20000, PMT; N (display: 38.20 years)]. Thus, the longevity of the $14,000 annuity under strategy #8 will be 49.4 years (11.2 years + 38.2 years).

Comparison of Strategies #7 and #8

Just as in the case of the bonds-only portfolio, the client is substantially better off in terms of longevity if the withdrawals are initially taken from the nonqualified portfolio. However, in this case, the difference in longevity produced by the harvesting sequence is dramatic (49.4 versus 31.84 years). Thus, when both portfolios hold stock portfolios with the same expected rates of return, it is crucial that the planner start withdrawals from the nonqualified account first.

Case VI: Tax-Exempt versus Taxable, All-Stock Portfolio

Finally, we note without a detailed example that when the planner has to choose between a tax-exempt account and a nonqualified account, the greater longevity will derive from harvesting the nonqualified account first.

Additional Observations About the Order of Harvesting

The above discussion has focused on the issue of the sequence of harvesting from different types of accounts only from the perspective of maximizing the longevity of withdrawals when rates of return are known with certainty. The principles established are relevant only when the security one is considering selling is the same in each account. Thus, if one has stocks in a nonqualified account and bonds in a 401(k) account, then the decision of which to harvest first must include a consideration of the effect on the overall asset allocation and attendant riskiness of the portfolio, as well as the associated tax issues. It becomes a much more complex decision.

Another issue is that the nonqualified portfolio provides more liquidity to an investor. Suppose your client needs an extra $20,000 for 6 months, and then wants to reinvest the money. With a 401(k) or a Roth IRA account, once the money is taken out, it cannot be put back. In addition, taking the money from the 401(k) generates a tax liability. With a nonqualified account, one could potentially take the $20,000 as a loan from the margin account. Also, one could sell those securities which are trading at less than their cost basis and/or sell those securities which are trading at their cost basis or at a minimal capital appreciation. Either way, little or no tax is due, and thus the withdrawal is a tax-free source of funds.

WHAT SHOULD A FINANCIAL PLANNER DO?

All of the foregoing may leave a financial planner somewhat confused. That is, what should he or she tell a client? The most critical observation is that because the selections of the portfolio composition and the withdrawal rate involve risk-return tradeoffs, there is no "one size fits all" solution. A planner is expected to make different recommendations for different clients.

There is clearly a lot more research that needs to be done to determine what is appropriate advice about portfolio composition and withdrawal rates. There is a somewhat broad range as to what a financial planner could propose.

If a client is ultraconservative and wants absolutely zero risk of outliving his or her principal, but also wants some inflation protection, the financial planner could suggest putting 100 percent of the portfolio into T-bills or TIPS and having the client live off of the interest income only. The client is at risk of a drop in income if real interest rates drop, but he or she is guaranteed to not outlive his or her principal and has no default risk.

The real question a financial planner needs to ask a client is NOT what is the maximum probability of portfolio failure the client will accept. The real question is how willing the client would be to trade off a higher withdrawal rate today for the risk that he or she may not be able to adjust his or her income for inflation adjustments in later years.

THE ROLE OF OTHER INCOME

In chapter 5, we discussed the process whereby an investor computes his or her other sources of retirement income and then looks to see how much income he or she needs to derive from a retirement portfolio in order to achieve a specified standard of living. Heretofore in this chapter, we have focused on the retirement portfolio as if it were an investor's only source of income. We now need to consider the issue of the interaction of other sources of income with the retirement portfolio.

Virtually all clients will have Social Security retirement income, pension income, or both. Although the Social Security income is indexed to inflation, it functions for all practical purposes as a fixed annuity. If the clients have a defined-benefit annuity, then that also functions as a fixed annuity. A defined-contribution pension could also be annuitized.

Although the next two chapters will discuss annuities in detail, there are several basic characteristics to keep in mind about them. A basic annuity promises the annuitant a fixed dollar payment forever.[37] However, there is no residual cash benefit at the death of the annuitant unless one has selected a policy feature to accept a lower payment in exchange for the guarantee of a fixed number of payments. There are other characteristics to an annuity, but for purposes of our discussion, these are the key features.

The purchase of an annuity is analogous to the purchase of a fully immunized bond investment. Thus, to the extent that the client has Social Security retirement income, fixed pension payments, and/or has already established an annuity, his or her complete portfolio has a significant bond component to it. Consider the following example:

Example:

Winston Anderson is a new client. Upon reviewing her (Winston was named for her father, who wanted a son) assets and income, you note the following annual income:

Social Security retirement Income	$20,000
Pension benefits	$30,000
Investment portfolio:	
Dividends	$2,000
Interest	$15,000

The investment portfolio consists of $200,000 invested in stocks (1 percent average dividend yield), and $300,000 invested in bonds (5 percent average current yield).

There are two ways to think about her portfolio. One is to say that Winston has $50,000 in base income and the financial planning goal is to figure out the optimal allocation of the $500,000 in her investment portfolio. The objective in this allocation, as discussed earlier, is to select the asset allocation and withdrawal rate that provides the highest level of current income with appropriate consideration for the risk of portfolio failure.

The other way to think about her retirement portfolio is to capitalize her Social Security and pension income. The easiest way to do this is to divide the annual income by the appropriate interest rate. In this case, 5 percent would seem to be an appropriate rate, as it is the rate she is already getting on her other bonds. This means we could think of Social Security as a bond investment worth $400,000 ($20,000 / .05) and the pension as a bond investment worth $600,000 ($30,000 / .05). Thus, Winston's retirement portfolio could be thought of as worth $1.5 million. Of this, $1 million is permanently locked into bonds. However, there is perfect certainty as to the returns on this bond portfolio. Thus, to be consistent with the research results discussed earlier, it would be reasonable to consider putting all $500,000 in the investment portfolio into equities, and then to select a withdrawal rate based on the knowledge that two-thirds of the portfolio is already locked into fixed return instruments, some of which have an inflation adjustment to them.

In addition to the fact that most clients will already have ownership of some de facto annuities, it is also reasonable to consider the direct purchase of annuities as part of the bond component of a client's portfolio. Annuities are not a popular vehicle because of the one disadvantage mentioned above, there is no residual value to the estate, unless an option for a guaranteed number of payments were chosen. There are three factors that would influence the purchase of annuities.[38]

The first factor is one's life prospects. The longer one lives, the greater the return on the annuity. Hence, anyone who believes he or she will not live at least to their life expectancy at the time of the annuity purchase should not buy the annuity. Annuities are easier to purchase for people who are in good health and have a family history of a longer-than-normal life expectancy.

The second factor is the presence of family who will provide additional funds. If family members are willing to step up and help the older person if his or her assets get depleted, then there is less need for an annuity. One way to view this is as a risk-return proposition by the family members. If no annuity is purchased, then more of the client's assets go into financial assets which have significant likelihood of providing a residual estate. If there is no portfolio failure, then the family members, who are presumably the beneficiaries, would stand to inherit what might be a reasonable estate. However, if no annuity is purchased, and there is portfolio failure, then taking care of the client could be a substantive expense to these family members. Whether or not the family members want to be involved in the client's financial affairs, they may have a significant stake in the selection of assets.

The third factor in the purchase of an annuity is the extent to which the client has fixed return income. It may not be appropriate to purchase an annuity for clients with substantial pension income.

One aspect of annuitization to remember is that it is essentially an irreversible decision. Thus, an annuity should not be purchased if the financial planner only thinks it is probably a good idea. An annuity should be purchased when the planner knows for a fact that it is a good idea. Remember, if one postpones the purchase of an annuity, then one can always wait one year and revisit the decision. If one buys today, then there is no decision to be made a year from now. By putting off the purchase of an annuity, one of three things might happen. Interest rates could go up, stay the same, or go down. As the amount of income an annuity purchase will provide is dependent on the age of the buyer and the level of interest rates at the time of purchase, if interest rates go up or stay the same, then the client is no worse off by waiting a year and may be better off. The improvement would be due to the fact that the client is a year older and his or her life expectancy is approximately one year less. The only harm from waiting is if interest rates were to fall substantially during the one-year time period.

It is possible to partially hedge this risk of a decline in interest rates by purchasing long-term bonds. If interest rates decline, then the prices of the bonds will rise, allowing more money to be used to purchase the annuity. The drawback to this hedge is that if interest rates rise, the prices of the bonds will fall, and there is less money available to purchase the annuity. However, not as large a premium is necessary to get the same payment as before because of the rise in interest rates.

SELLING A CLIENT ON A PLAN

One of the problems with all of the above discussion about portfolio composition, withdrawal rates, withdrawal strategies, and the probability of portfolio failure is that for many clients, this comes across as "black-box" gibberish. The client is looking for a plan that he or she can understand in tangible ways. There are several strategies that have great intuitive appeal to them, and may make it easier to convince a client to do what he or she should do. Let's consider some of these.

The 5-Year Safety Stock Plan

You are discussing strategic asset allocation with a newly retired client, Anne Cliff. She has $1 million in assets and wants to withdraw $50,000 in cash each year. You know one of the greatest fears of retired clients is the concept of "liquidating the principal." You also know that, given the strong chance that this client may live for at least another 20 years or so, she must have a significant holding in equities or face substantial exposure to purchasing power risk.

You propose the following plan. Put $250,000 into cash equivalents and $750,000 into equities. If the stock market goes up, sell enough shares to withdraw $50,000. For example, if the portfolio goes up 10 percent during the year, then at the end of the year it will be worth $825,000 ($750,000 x [(1 + .10)]). Sell enough stocks to take out $50,000 in cash and start the next year with an equity portfolio worth $775,000. However, if the market goes down, take the $50,000 out of the cash equivalents. If the market goes up the second year, sell enough stock to take out the $50,000 cash and replenish the cash equivalents holdings. If the market goes down the second year in a row, then again take the cash withdrawal from the cash equivalents and plan to replenish this account in the third year. The only way that the entire cash equivalents holdings would be eliminated is if the market went down 5 years in a row, an event that has never occurred in our modern era. This approach allows the planner to adopt a 75 percent stock, 25 percent cash portfolio strategy. It would also mean dramatic fluctuations in the asset allocation percentage.

It should be noted that the actual application of a strategy as suggested above would also require the financial advisor to incorporate the effect of dividends and interest into the cash that will be available at the end of the year. For example, if the average dividend yield for the stocks in the portfolio was one percent and the average current yield on the cash equivalents was 3 percent, then the portfolio would generate about $7,500 in dividends and $7,500 in interest during the year for a total of $15,000 in income. Hence, the planner only needs to come up with an additional $35,000 at the end of the year. In addition, there would likely be some tinkering to the portfolio that would be necessary to stay on target with the strategic asset allocation of 75 percent stock and 25 percent cash.

Disadvantages to this Plan

The major disadvantage to this plan is that the rate of return on the cash equivalents is typically quite low compared to what can be obtained in other investments. Although this plan gives the appearance of a high degree of certainty with regard to withdrawals, unpublished research by this author and others indicates that when the overlapping periods methodology is utilized to test this strategy against other portfolio combinations, this portfolio allocation performs much worse than alternative portfolios. The problem here is that the opportunity loss of income that results from having 5 year's worth of withdrawals in cash equivalents can be viewed as an insurance premium against the market dropping for 5 years. Market returns for the last 80+ years would suggest that the probability of having such a string of bad returns is incredibly unlikely. In our modern era, the market has never gone down 5 or more years in a row, and it has only gone down 4 years in a row once. Hence, it would appear that the likelihood of such an event is so remote that the insurance premium that is being paid is much too large. The insurance premium eventually takes the form of an increased likelihood of portfolio failure.

The Laddered Portfolio Strategy

A variation of the above scenario would allow a planner to put the client into a bonds and stocks portfolio. Let's assume again a $1 million portfolio and a desire to generate an "income" of $50,000 per year. In this case, the planner could invest $50,000 in each of five categories of bonds. The bonds range in annual maturities from 1 year to 5 years. The remaining assets are invested in stocks. The strategy for the generation of cash is then much the same as before. If the market goes up the first year, the investor can take the cash by selling shares of stock. In addition, he or she would take the proceeds from the bonds that have matured and buy a new set of 5-year bonds since each set of bonds would move up in maturity one year. Let's consider an example of how this process would work.

Example 1:	Ann Cliff has a retirement portfolio worth $1 million and wants a first-year withdrawal of 5 percent. You have recommended the laddered portfolio strategy that is 25 percent fixed return and 75 percent equities. The bond portfolio is evenly distributed in annual maturities of 1 to 5 years. Let's assume the bonds have a current yield of 4 percent and the stocks have a dividend yield of 2 percent. At the end of the first year, Ann's account will have generated $10,000 in interest income, and $15,000 in dividend income. A total of $25,000 needs to be taken from the principal. Let's assume the stock portfolio has gone up by 10 percent, so that the value of the stock is $825,000. Because the market has gone up, the $25,000 is taken from the sale of equities, leaving a total of $800,000 in the portfolio. In the meantime, the $50,000 that had been invested in one-year bonds

has matured. The bonds with maturities of 2 through 5 years now have maturities of 1 through 4 years. The $50,000 in maturity value is then used to buy a new set of 5-year bonds.

If the market goes down, the investor can take the cash from the maturing bonds (less whatever dividends and interest income have been generated). Each set of bonds will have moved up in maturity by one year. At such time as the market goes up again, the bond holdings can be replenished. Let's look at an example.

Example 2:   Same scenario as in example one, except let's assume that the stock portfolio goes down by 10 percent, so that the value of the stock is $675,000. Because the market has gone down, the $25,000 that is needed on top of the interest and dividend income is taken from the bonds that are maturing. The remainder of the maturity value ($25,000) is used to buy new 5-year bonds.

If the market goes up the next year, the necessary principal for the annual withdrawal is taken from the sale of stocks and the bond holdings are rounded up to equal their original values. Consider the following example.

Example 3:   Assume the scenario in example two occurs, and then during the second year the stock portfolio increases by 5 percent. Its value is now $708,750. The dividend income for the year is $14,175 (2 percent dividend yield), and the interest income is $9,000 (4 percent current yield). Thus, interest and dividends provide $23,175 in cash, and $26,825 is needed from principal. Because the equity markets went up, the money is taken from the equity, bringing that value down to $681,925 ($708,750 − $26,825). In addition, another $25,000 is taken out of equities and used to replenish what are now 4-year bonds to a value of $50,000. This reduces the equity holdings to $656,925 ($681,925 − $25,000). Finally, the maturing bonds are rolled into new 5-year bonds.

Disadvantages to this Plan

A laddered portfolio strategy is more beneficial for a client than a 5-year safety stock plan for two reasons. First, the use of bonds with maturities of 1 to 5 years will almost always provide a higher current yield than cash equivalents (the exception would be when there is a downward-sloping yield curve). Second, although holding bonds whose maturities match the dates of the intended cash withdrawals is not an immunization process unless the bonds are all zero-coupon bonds, they nonetheless provide a close approximation of immunization. However, this strategy still has the disadvantage, as shown in example 3, that one can end up selling equities when prices are lower than they were at the start of retirement and thus creating a portfolio that is more bond dominated than would be desirable.

PRACTICAL ISSUES

As we noted above, most of the research on withdrawal rates has focused on the process in which annual withdrawals are made at the end of each year. Cash for the first year is presumably derived from an amount that is held out from the retirement portfolio. Only CHW explicitly looked at the issue of monthly withdrawals, and they ascertained that such withdrawals would result in a slightly lower withdrawal rate than would otherwise be the case. As a practical matter, most people live off of monthly income, not annual income. Handing a large once-a-year payment to a client would seem rather foolish. In this section, let's consider some of the processes that could be used to generate monthly income. Let's also look at the practical problem of how one determines an inflation adjustment.

The Mechanics of Taking Out the Cash

The easiest process for taking out cash on a monthly basis is to liquidate the amount of principal needed in excess of dividend and interest income. Such liquidation would also provide the opportunity to rebalance the portfolio to the desired debt-equity distribution. If the client is invested entirely in mutual funds, then this strategy may work effectively provided that no back-end load charges are triggered. However, if the investor has direct ownership of securities, then there are two potential problems. The first problem is that it would generate monthly transaction fees. Some of these fees would have been avoidable by simply waiting another month or two. The second problem is that bonds have minimum transaction amounts that may make small adjustments difficult to process.

If the client has at least one account that is nonqualified, then one alternative is to set this account up as a margin account and each month transfer the monthly withdrawal from this account into the client's checking account by increasing the debit balance. This means the client will accrue some interest charges on the loan being created. Under some situations, these charges may be tax-deductible. More importantly, this gives the financial planner the flexibility to rebalance the account on an as needed and as appropriate basis. Then on a once-a-year basis, or as the opportunity arises, the necessary securities could be sold to rebalance the portfolio and pay off the debit balance.

An alternative to using a margin account is a home-equity line of credit. This strategy requires that the client own his or her own home with enough equity built up to allow a line of credit of the necessary magnitude. The advantage here is that it is more likely that the interest charges would be tax-deductible. Once again, a monthly transfer can be made from this account to the client's checking account, and when appropriate, the necessary securities sold and the cash transferred to bring the loan balance back to zero and to rebalance the portfolio.

The Mechanics of Adjusting for Inflation

As we have seen, most discussions on withdrawals from retirement portfolios assume that clients would want inflation-adjusted withdrawals. Although the inflation adjustments could be made on a monthly basis, most clients would probably prefer to think in terms of annual adjustments. In fact, there would be a lot of work associated with monthly adjustments for each client, with meaningless changes occurring in most months.

Inflation adjustments require an estimate of the inflation rate. The easiest way to obtain this is from the Bureau of Labor Statistics (BLS). The accompanying box provides the current series of clicks on the BLS Web site that will allow the planner to access this information. The description of the sequence of clicks beginning with the home page is provided in the event that subsequent to the publication of this book, the BLS changes the structure of its Web site. The step-by-step sequence should allow the planner to ascertain how to get to this information under any structure.

Web Clicks: Start at **www.bls.gov,** click on the link *Consumer Price Index* under the general category of *Inflation and Consumer Spending*. Next, look for the link labeled *Get Detailed CPI Statistics*. Then click on Consumer Price Index-*All Urban Consumers (Current Series)*. Finally, check the box labeled **U.S. All items, 1982-84=100,** and then go to the bottom of the page and click on *Retrieve Data*. This should bring up a table similar to the one shown in table 7-3.

TABLE 7-3
Consumer Price Index—All Urban Consumers

Year	Jan	Feb	March	April	May	June	July	Aug	Sep	Oct	Nov	Dec	Annual
1995	150.3	150.9	151.4	151.9	152.2	152.5	152.5	152.9	153.2	153.7	153.6	153.5	152.4
1996	154.4	154.9	155.7	156.3	156.6	156.7	157.0	157.3	157.8	158.3	158.6	158.6	156.9
1997	159.1	159.6	160.0	160.2	160.1	160.3	160.5	160.8	161.2	161.6	161.5	161.3	160.5
1998	161.6	161.9	162.2	162.5	162.8	163.0	163.2	163.4	163.6	164.0	164.0	163.9	163.0
1999	164.3	164.5	165.0	166.2	166.2	166.2	166.7	167.1	167.9	168.2	168.3	168.3	166.6
2000	168.8	169.8	171.2	171.3	171.5	172.4	172.8	172.8	173.7	174.0	174.1	174.0	172.2
2001	175.1	175.8	176.2	176.9	177.7	178.0	177.5	177.5	178.3	177.7	177.4	176.7	177.1
2002	177.1	177.8	178.8	179.8	179.8	179.9	180.1	180.7	181.0	181.3	181.3	180.9	179.9
2003	181.7	183.1	184.2	183.8	183.5	183.7	183.9	184.6	185.2	185.0	184.5	184.3	184.0
2004	185.2	186.2	187.4	188.0	189.1	189.7	189.4	189.5	189.9	190.9	191.0		

Source: http://data.bls.gov/cgi-bin/surveymost; January 12, 2005

Because this figure was downloaded in January 2005, the Consumer Price Index for December 2004 was not available. In fact, this points out one slight problem in inflation adjustments. If the client wants his or her monthly payment on the first of each month, and if the client wants the inflation adjustment in January of each year, then the necessary data will not be available to compute the inflation rate for the prior calendar year. In this case, the most convenient substitute is to base the inflation rate on a November to November basis. Let's consider the following example.

Example:

Your client Ann Hayes has been taking a $10,820 monthly payment during 2004. She takes her payment on the first of each month, and likes the inflation adjustment to occur with the January payment. To compute an appropriate inflation adjustment, simply divide the Consumer Price Index for November 2004 by the corresponding figure for November 2003, and multiply this ratio with 2004's monthly payment. In this case, the new monthly payment would be computed as:

$10,820 x (191.0 / 184.5) = $10,820 x 1.0352 = $11,201

The actual answer is $11,201.19, but it would be convenient to all to round to the nearest dollar. It would probably be even easier to round to the nearest $10, making $11,200 the monthly payment for 2004.

Note that in the above calculation, the ratio of the two indices is 1.0352. If one is subtracted from this number, then the remainder is the annual inflation rate. Thus, the annual inflation rate in this example, on a November to November basis, is 3.52 percent.

Let's now consider an easier scenario. Assume the client is happy to take the payment on the last day of each month. The planner can then use the December to December computation.

Finally, if the client wants each monthly payment adjusted for inflation, the planner can use the table to compute the inflation rate for each month as it would apply to each month. However, be aware that during some months there is deflation. For example, for June of 2004 the CPI was 189.7, and for July it was 189.4. Thus, a person who had previously drawn $10,000 as a monthly payment would now be able to draw only 9,984.19 ($10,000 x 189.4 / 189.7).

NOTES

1. This strategy is discussed in Jonathan Clements, "Squeezing out Cash in Retirement," *The Wall Street Journal Online,* October 12, 2003.
2. This strategy is part of a more elaborate strategy described by Jonathan Guyton in "Decision Rules and Portfolio Management for Retirees: Is the 'Safe' Initial Withdrawal Rate Too Safe?," *The Journal of Financial Planning*, October 2004. The full strategy will be discussed later in this chapter.
3. Dalton and Dalton, *Personal Financial Planning Theory and Practice,* Dalton Publishing LLC, St. Rose, LA, 653–54.
4. Ibid.
5. Kwok Ho, Moshe Ayre Milevsky, and Chris Robinson, "Asset Allocation, Life Expectancy, and Shortfall," *Financial Services Review,* 3(2), 109–126.
6. William P. Bengen, "Determining Withdrawal Rates Using Historical Data," *Journal of Financial Planning,* 7(1), 171–180. This article was reprinted in the March 2004 edition of the same journal as part of its series of the best articles to appear during its first 25 years.
7. He actually found that a person could go as high as a 3.5 percent withdrawal rate and still be good for 50 years.
8. William P. Bengen, "Asset Allocation for a Lifetime," *Journal of Financial Planning,* 9(3), 58–67.
9. The numbers presented in the original article for the nonqualified portfolio are 120, 133, and 145. However, in his follow-up publication (1997), Bengen indicates he had found an error in his spreadsheets, and provides these corrected numbers.

10. The number presented in the article is actually 12 percent. However, in his follow-up publication (1997), Bengen indicates he had found an error in his spreadsheets; the number should have been 20 percent.

11. William P. Bengen, "Conserving Client Portfolios During Retirement, Part III," *Journal of Financial Planning,* December 23, 2004, 84.

12. Bengen (1997), op cit., 93.

13. Phillip L. Cooley, Carl M. Hubbard, and Daniel T. Walz, "Retirement Savings: Choosing a Withdrawal Rate That is Sustainable," *AAII Journal,* 20 (1998), 16–21.

14. Ibid., 18.

15. Phillip L. Cooley, Carl M. Hubbard, and Daniel T. Walz, "Sustainable Withdrawal Rates From Your Retirement Portfolio," *Financial Counseling and Planning,* Volume 10(1), 1999, 39–47.

16. Ibid., 45.

17. Phillip L. Cooley, Carl M. Hubbard, and Daniel T. Walz, "Does International Diversification Increase the Sustainable Withdrawal Rates from Retirement Portfolios?," *Journal of Financial Planning,* 16(1), 74–80.

18. Ibid., p. 79.

19. Phillip L. Cooley, Carl M. Hubbard, and Daniel T. Walz, "A Comparative Analysis of Retirement Portfolio Success Rates: Simulation Versus Overlapping Periods," *Financial Services Review,* 12 (2003), 115–128.

20. Ibid., 124–25.

21. Ibid., 127.

22. Ibid., 128.

23. Rory L. Terry, "The Relation Between Portfolio Composition and Sustainable Withdrawal Rates," *Journal of Financial Planning,* May 2003, 64–71.

24. For a complete discussion of bond immunization, see chapter 9 in Walt J. Woerheide and David M. Cordell, *Fundamentals of Investments for Financial Planning,* 4th edition, The American College Press, Bryn Mawr, PA, 2004.

25. Jonathan T. Guyton, "Decision Rules and Portfolio Management for Retirees: Is the 'Safe' Initial Withdrawal Rate Too Safe?," *Journal of Financial Planning,* October 2004, 54–62.

26. Ibid., 54.

27. Ibid., 60.

28. Ibid., 60.

29. See, for example, Ho, et al., op. cit., 119.

30. For a discussion of immunization, see chapter 9 in Walt J. Woerheide and David M. Cordell, *Fundamentals of Investments for Financial Planning,* 4th edition, The American College Press, Bryn Mawr, PA., 2004.

31. Several of the ideas expressed in this section are based on the paper, "Withdrawals During Retirement" by John J. Spitzer and Sandeep Singh, presented at the 2004 Academy of Financial Services annual meeting, New Orleans, LA.

32. If the student is using the HP10BII calculator, be sure that the compounding frequency is set to once per year, and the display is set to two decimal points.

33. If market rates were to jump from 5 percent to 10 percent, one would normally expect the market value of these bonds to decline. To keep the example focused, let's add the assumption that the entire bond portfolio matured just as the rates changed, and the proceeds are reinvested at the higher rate with the lower market value.

34. For simplicity of programming, we are assuming that the first withdrawal from the nonqualified account will be one year after the 401(k) plan is exhausted, rather than having the first withdrawal continue on the exact one-year anniversary of the previous withdrawals. The impact on the results is believed to be trivial.

35. We are assuming that all stocks appreciate at the same rate, and that the percentage of each withdrawal that is tax free equals the ratio of the cost basis to the market value of the portfolio.
36. Again, this calculation is made on the Excel spreadsheet.
37. There are, of course, variable-rate annuities, but rather than complicate this discussion further, we will focus on fixed-rate annuities.
38. William Reichenstein, "Allocation During Retirement: Adding Annuities to the Mix," *AAII Journal*, November 2003, 3–9.

8

Annuities—Part I

Richard A. Dulisse

Chapter Outline

INTRODUCTION

annuity

The American Heritage Dictionary and *Webster's Third New International Dictionary* define the word *annuity* as follows:

- the annual payment of an allowance or income
- the right to receive this payment or the obligation to make this payment
- an investment on which a person receives fixed payments for a lifetime or a specified number of years. Derivation: Latin; annus, year[1]
- a contract or agreement under which one or more persons receive periodic payments in return for prior set payments made by themselves or another (as an employer)[2]
- a series of periodic payments that begin at a specific date and continue throughout a fixed period or for the duration of a designated life or lives

These definitions focus on how money is paid from an annuity contract. Annuities that provide current payments to an annuitant are commonly called "immediate annuities" or "payout annuities." Normally, immediate annuities are purchased with a single deposit and income payments begin within one year; the insurance and financial services industry commonly refers to these annuities as single-premium immediate annuities or SPIAs.

The above definitions do not focus on the more common type of annuity, which is one where the income payments are not paid until some time well in the future. These contracts are referred to as deferred annuities because the income payments are deferred until an indefinite time. Today, purchasers of deferred annuity contracts generally focus on the accumulating values of their annuities, not the future income.

This chapter and the next will concentrate on both types of annuity contracts—immediate annuities for paying income, and deferred annuities for accumulation and growth. Annuities will be referred to throughout these chapters as annuity contracts or annuity policies. Either term is correct. The owner of the annuity will be referred to interchangeably as the annuity owner, the policyowner, or the contract owner.

Parties to an Annuity Contract

The parties to the annuity contract include the insurance company that issues the annuity, the owner of the annuity, the annuitant, and the beneficiary. Each of the parties has a different set of obligations, rights, and responsibilities.

Insurance Company

The insurance company who issues an annuity contract assumes a number of financial obligations to the owner, annuitant, and beneficiary. These can be summarized in two basic promises, as follows:

- to invest the owner's premium payments responsibly and credit earnings on interest to the funds placed in the annuity, depending on the particular type of contract
- to pay benefits according to the contract

Even though the Internal Revenue Service Code requires all annuity contracts to contain certain provisions to be eligible for federal income tax benefits, there is considerable variation among contracts from different companies. Therefore, it is a good business practice to obtain sample contracts of the annuity products offered by the insurers with whom you work to be certain that you understand them completely and can explain them to senior clients.

Owner

owner

The annuity contract *owner* is a person, or legal entity, who enters into the contract with the insurance company to purchase the annuity. The owner of the contract is the person or entity with all the legal rights to the contract and whose Social Security number or tax identification number is shown in the contract. The IRS uses the term "holder" and, although it does not specifically define the term, it generally means whoever is holding the income tax liability, no matter what other title that holder might have.

This is an important distinction from the annuitant. The owner is the person who pays the premiums, chooses which optional policy features or riders are to be included in the contract, and has the right to withdraw or surrender the annuity.

Furthermore, the policyowner is the person with the authority to communicate with the insurance company about the annuity's values and to determine who will receive the annual or quarterly statements from the company.

Entity/Nonnatural Person Owner. It also is possible to have an entity or a nonnatural person, as opposed to a natural person, own an annuity. However, if an irrevocable trust, corporation, or other nonnatural person is not simply acting as an agent for a natural person, all tax deferral in the annuity contract will be lost and current earnings will be taxable.[3]

Annuitant

annuitant

The *annuitant* is the person whose life is the measuring life for the annuity. The annuitant must be a living person. It cannot be a legal entity because a legal entity has no measuring life. For example, a corporation cannot be an annuitant because a corporation has no age and has no death. The annuitant has no legal rights in the contract. Therefore, the annuitant has no right to surrender or withdraw funds from the annuity or to change the beneficiary.

The contract owner may also choose to add, if allowed, contingent annuitants, such as a spouse, to become the annuitant should the primary annuitant die.

The insurance company's promise to pay annuity payments is based on the age and sex of the annuitant.

Joint Annuitants. Some policies may also allow joint annuitants. Normally, joint annuitants are named when joint owners are named and generally should be restricted to use for spouses only. The effect of naming joint annuitants is to allow the annuity policy to continue to stay in force and not pay a death benefit until the death of both annuitants.

Beneficiary

beneficiary

The *beneficiary* is the person, or legal entity, who normally inherits the annuity proceeds at the death of the annuitant. There can virtually be any number of beneficiaries listed in the policy that can be living people or entities, such as trusts, businesses, or other entities. In addition, a revocable beneficiary designation can be changed as frequently as the owner wishes, as long as the insurance company receives the necessary paperwork to properly record the transaction.

The annuitant and the beneficiary should not be the same person because the beneficiary is to receive the funds at the annuitant's death. It would not be sensible to name the beneficiary as the same person whose death triggers the distribution.

The beneficiary, like the annuitant, has no legal right in the contract before the annuitant's death. Once the annuitant has died, the beneficiary does have a legal right to receive the death proceeds. However, the owner may generally change the beneficiary at any time prior to the death of the annuitant—even right up until the time of the annuitant's death. This is why the beneficiary is presumed to have only an "expectancy" in the annuity, but no legal rights arise until the annuitant's death.

Types of Annuities

Annuities may be classified in several different categories. Table 8-1 shows the various classifications of annuities based on the following:

- single-premium or flexible-premium annuities
- immediate or deferred-payment annuities
- qualified or nonqualified annuities
- fixed-interest, indexed, or variable deferred annuities

TABLE 8-1
Annuity Classifications

	Single-Premium Deferred Annuity	Flexible-Premium Deferred Annuity	Single-Premium Immediate Annuity
Qualified Annuity	Fixed-interest annuities Indexed annuities Variable annuities	Fixed-interest annuities Indexed annuities Variable annuities	Fixed payments Variable payments
Nonqualified Annuity	Fixed-interest annuities Indexed annuities Variable annuities	Fixed-interest annuities Indexed annuities Variable annuities	Fixed payments Variable payments

Single-Premium or Flexible-Premium Annuities

single-premium annuity

flexible-premium annuity

First, annuities can be classified by how many deposits the consumer pays into the annuity. For example, annuities are classified as either single-premium or flexible-premium annuities. A *single-premium annuity* is structured to allow only one contribution in the contract. Subsequent contributions are usually not allowed with these types of policies. If the policyowner envisions making additional contributions into an annuity contract, the policyowner should consider purchasing a flexible-premium annuity. A *flexible-premium annuity* allows additional contributions at any time from the policyowner.

Note that immediate annuities generally fall only under the category of single-premium annuities. This is due to the nature of the contract, in which a policyowner will give one deposit into the immediate annuity in return for a fixed amount of income. Immediate annuities, by their very nature, do not accept additional deposits. To purchase a second income stream, the policyowner will need to buy a second immediate-annuity contract. Whether the policyowner foresees making additional contributions later into a deferred annuity is a question both the financial advisor and the policyowner should discuss prior to the purchase of the annuity to make sure that the proper annuity is chosen.

Immediate or Deferred Annuities

immediate annuity

An annuity is a contract between a purchaser and an insurance company in which the insurance company promises to make periodic payments to the purchaser starting immediately or at some time in the future. This definition gives us our next classification of annuities, immediate or deferred, regardless of whether they contain qualified or nonqualified money. An *immediate annuity* is a contract with an immediate payment or one with

deferred annuity

payments that begin within one year of the contract date. A *deferred annuity* is a future-pay contract with payments to begin at some later date beyond the first contract year.

These two basic types of annuities will be discussed in greater detail in this and the next chapter. Immediate annuities will be discussed in the latter section of this chapter, and the three types of deferred annuities, introduced below, will be discussed in greater detail in the next chapter.

Qualified or Nonqualified Annuities

Annuities are also classified based on the type of money placed in the annuity contract. The annuity may be funded with monies accumulated within employer-provided qualified retirement plans—such as pensions, profit-sharing plans, 401(k)s, 403(b)s, Keogh or HR-10 plans, SEP IRAs, and SIMPLE IRAs—or other plans that allow the investor to put pretax money into the plan, such as a traditional IRA. Because each of these plans is designed to meet regulatory qualifications in order to allow pretax investments and tax deferral on earnings, the plans are referred to as qualified plans. An annuity that accepts these types of funds is referred to as a *qualified annuity.*

qualified annuity

Obviously, the tax-deferral feature that is a part of all annuity contracts is redundant when dealing with qualified money that already enjoys the advantage of tax deferral. As a result, when the decision is made to invest qualified money into annuities, it should be because of the features that annuity contracts offer, rather than for the redundant tax deferral.

nonqualified annuity

If the money placed in the annuity has already been subject to income tax, the annuity is classified as a *nonqualified annuity.* The benefit of tax deferral in nonqualified annuities can be a great value for nonqualified money that does not enjoy tax deferral in the vehicle in which it is currently invested. Tax deferral allows money that would otherwise be paid out in income taxes to remain invested in the annuity contract and to continue to earn a return. This increases the size of the annuity that one day will be used to generate income.

However, because annuity contracts, whether qualified or nonqualified, are virtually identical in contract language, classifications, features, and associated costs and regulation, the chapters that deal with those issues will not generally distinguish between qualified and nonqualified annuities.

Fixed-Interest, Indexed, and Variable Deferred Annuities

Deferred annuities are classified by the method the insurance company uses to determine how interest is credited to the annuity contract (that is, fixed-interest annuity, indexed annuity, or variable annuity).

fixed-interest annuity

A *fixed-interest annuity* is the simplest type of deferred annuity. They generally offer the annuity owner a guaranteed interest rate for a certain period of time. That time frame may be one year or 5 to 7 years, depending on the annuity contract. Once the initial guarantee period for the interest rate is over, companies generally set renewal interest rates in conjunction with the interest rate environment at the time of the renewal. Therefore, annuity purchasers will have no idea when they buy the annuity what level of interest the annuity will earn once the guarantee period is over.

However, fixed annuities do have a guaranteed minimum interest rate by which the company must abide. This guaranteed minimum serves to provide some level of comfort to the annuity purchaser. Fixed-interest deferred annuities are covered in detail later in this chapter.

Indexed annuities, which are rather new to the industry and generally became popular in the 1990s, are another type of deferred annuity. They were developed as a response to the rising equity markets and the need for insurance advisors who were not licensed to sell variable annuities to have a product to offer their clients that could generate higher returns than a traditional fixed annuity.

indexed annuity

An *indexed annuity* ties the earnings in the annuity contract to an outside index. Therefore, the true earnings of the insurance company are not an indicator of the earnings for the annuity contract. The most popular type of indexed annuity is one tied to the Standard and Poor's (S&P) 500 Index. This type of annuity is meant to assist clients who want more growth potential than a fixed annuity can offer but who may not be ready for the full risk of a variable annuity.

variable annuity

A *variable annuity* is a deferred annuity that allows the annuity purchaser to participate in the investment of the annuity funds by determining how much of the contribution will be invested in a series of accounts. These accounts range from a general account to a series of sub-accounts tied to various financial markets.

Variable annuities are the most regulated of the three types of deferred annuities.

Primary Objective of an Annuity Contract

The primary objective of an annuity contract is to pay financial benefits to the persons who receive the annuity payments during their lifetimes. Its primary objective is not to pay a death benefit, like its cousin, the life insurance contract.

There are three important distinctions between an annuity contract and a life insurance contract:

• An annuity contract has no significant mortality charges. In other words, the insurance company does not have to build a cost into the annuity to protect itself against the early death of the annuitant. No medical underwriting is required. The insurance company is not insuring against early death.

- An annuity has no net amount at risk, whereas life insurance does. The death benefit that is payable is nothing more than the value of the annuity. The insurance company does not suffer a financial loss at the death of the annuitant.

- An annuity contract is not tax efficient in paying benefits at the annuitant's death. The beneficiary of an annuity will have to pay income taxes on any gain in the value of the annuity over the principal paid by the annuity owner. Life insurance, on the other hand, is almost always 100 percent income tax free to the beneficiary.

Why Individuals Purchase Annuities

One of the most prevalent reasons individuals purchase annuity contracts is to accumulate funds for retirement and then, once in retirement, to manage distributions of those funds. Annuities compete for investment funds that would otherwise be in currently taxable investments. Fixed-interest deferred annuities, which guarantee principal and some level of interest earnings, compete for money that would otherwise be in such vehicles as savings accounts or certificates of deposit. Variable annuities compete for money that might otherwise be in taxable mutual funds. Investments in which earnings are subject to income taxes each year may be placed in nonqualified annuities and enjoy tax-deferred growth until withdrawal.

The deferred annuity contract is used to accumulate money for some future date. It is most efficiently used to accumulate money to be used in the future either as a lump sum or as a stream of payments. Annuitization is the surest way to provide systematic payments from a specific sum of money over a specified period, or for the duration of a single life or the lives of two people, because the payments are guaranteed by the insurance company.

This brings up the distinction between qualified and nonqualified annuities. Nonqualified annuities are annuity contracts into which investors put their after-tax funds. For example, an individual takes $1,000 from his or her savings account at the local bank and deposits it into an annuity contract. Because the $1,000 had already been taxed to the individual (we will assume it was money from his or her employer's paycheck), it is considered nonqualified money. For that reason, nonqualified annuities are also referred to as after-tax annuities.

Qualified annuities are funded with pretax (or before-tax) funds. To illustrate, an annuity purchaser who recently changed employment decides to use funds from his or her previous employer's 401(k) account to purchase a rollover IRA annuity. Because the employee has never paid income tax on the funds inside the 401(k) account, it is considered funded with pretax or qualified money.

Annuities in Retirement Planning

By 2011, the leading edge of the baby boomer generation of 77 million individuals will turn 65. This unique group of people, characterized by their self-reliance, independence, and indulgence, will undoubtedly reflect these traits in their retirement-related choices and lifestyles. But will they have adequate savings to fund their desired lifestyle during retirement? Will they acquire a state of financial independence where decisions are made based on choice and not on economic necessity? Will this generation, which hopes to retire earlier and will probably live longer in an environment of reduced Social Security benefits and diminished pension plan guarantees, be able to live comfortably in a retirement that may last another 20 to 30 years?[4]

Financial and Emotional Retirement Needs

For your clients to achieve financial success in retirement, it has to be planned. The decision to retire does not mean that people should stop planning. Retirement planning is a continual process that can be facilitated by the use of annuities. While the planning strategies after retirement may differ from those that you suggest to your prospects and clients who are planning and saving for retirement, they are no less important. However, an individual's planning perspective usually changes in the years before and after retirement occurs. Nevertheless, the older a person gets, the greater the probability that he or she will need annuities as a financial vehicle either to accumulate tax-deferred dollars for future use in retirement or as a source of guaranteed income that provides unique financial security features during retirement. In retirement planning, there are not only financial considerations but also dynamic psychosocial factors involved.

Preretirement. When preretirees in their 20s and 30s are just starting out in their careers, they tend to see retirement as a far-off, elusive concept that they will probably have to deal with someday. These workers are too busy climbing corporate ladders, establishing their own businesses, and starting their families to give retirement too much thought or too many financial resources.

However, as people enter their 40s and 50s, retirement takes on a much higher priority. The picture of retirement begins to crystallize in their minds as the possibility of living to old age becomes an increasing reality to them. It is during these decades of life (usually ages 45 to 64) that workers are demographically classified as "preretirees." They develop a growing concern about their well-being beyond their working years. Many people become obsessed with the need to accumulate enough money to maintain and enjoy their lifestyle during their golden years. Accordingly, they begin to allot greater resources into their qualified and nonqualified retirement plans, despite their contemporary financial obligations concerning education funding for their children, long-term care for their parents, and their own personal living expenses. Their sense of urgency regarding retirement funding is typically at its peak during their middle years.

This "preretirement mentality" is evidenced by anxiety about ensuring a comfortable retirement. Financial planning goals are geared toward amassing a large sum of money. Preretirement mentality is greatly focused on building and accumulating money in an effort to allay the increasing fear of financial destitution in old age.

Deferred annuities that are inherently tax deferred are ideal to help accomplish this financial goal of the preretiree. This is because deferred annuities offer flexibility in making contributions into them, and non-qualified deferred annuities allow virtually unlimited deposits. Furthermore, there is a choice of three types of deferred products (fixed interest, indexed, and variable) that accommodate any individual's risk tolerance and investment objectives.

We will examine each of the three basic types of deferred annuities for the remainder of this chapter. In the next chapter we will explore the product characteristics of immediate annuities. We will also discuss the appropriate uses of both deferred and immediate annuities within the overall context of retirement planning.

FIXED-INTEREST DEFERRED ANNUITIES

Annuity contracts that guarantee principal and some amount of interest are referred to as fixed-interest deferred annuities. The client basically buys the quality of the insurance company's guarantee of principal and the interest rate over the period selected.

Fixed-interest deferred annuities may be purchased with single investments as single-premium deferred annuities (SPDAs) or with flexible investments in contracts referred to as flexible-premium deferred annuities (FPDAs). The insurance company's profit over time is the difference between what the company earns on the invested money and what it pays out to the policyowner. The company's objective is to earn at least 1.5 percent—preferably 2 percent—more than it passes on to the consumer. The company can usually do this if the policyowner holds the contract for a long enough period of time. If the policyowner chooses to terminate the contract early, the insurance company protects itself from the lost income by imposing surrender charges.

Typically, fixed-interest deferred annuities are marketed with guaranteed interest rates from one to 10 years. Higher credited interest rates, longer surrender charge periods, and higher surrender charge percentages can be found in even longer-term contracts or bonus annuities. Longer-term contracts also may incorporate a market value adjustment in addition to, or in lieu of, the contractual surrender charge.

Single-Premium Deferred Annuities

The single-premium deferred annuity is a fixed-interest annuity contract that competes for the client's investment by offering competitive current interest rates and tax deferral on the interest earnings within the contract. Typically, this type of annuity is attractive to those who have invested in certificates of deposit or those who seek high-interest-rate investments. Like a certificate of deposit, it accepts a single deposit with a current interest rate that is guaranteed to some future date. At that time, the insurance company will offer a new interest rate for the next period of time. The policy's maturity may be at a date after the end of the interest guarantee period, such as age 90.

Flexible-Premium Deferred Annuities

A flexible-premium deferred annuity is a tax-deferred fixed-interest annuity contract that accepts periodic premiums and typically offers a minimum guaranteed interest plus excess interest, reflecting the general interest rate marketplace for shorter periods of time. Because the insurance company has the ability to adjust interest rates, it can allow individuals to make additional contributions to the contract without unacceptable interest rate risk. An important client concern in these flexible-premium contracts is the measurement period for any surrender charge. The time period for the surrender charge may be measured from the original date of the contract or from the date of each deposit, referred to as a rolling surrender charge. This will be explained in more detail when we cover contract provisions. However, the existence of a rolling surrender charge means that the contract owner has to consider the risk this puts on each future deposit into the annuity contract. The policy's maturity may be at a future retirement or postretirement date, such as age 65 or 90.

Insurance Company Financial Strength

Annuities are guaranteed by the insurance company that issues the contract, making the financial strength of the insurance company a fundamental issue the client must consider.

It is particularly important for purchasers of annuities to choose a company that will last as long as they will. As a result of increasing longevity among both males and females in the United States and the long period of time an annuity contract needs to be productive for contract owners, it is prudent for individuals to purchase annuities from financially stable insurance companies.

Benefits of Tax Deferral

tax deferral

Tax deferral for money in an annuity contract is granted by the government under tax law. This concept allows for the accumulation of money in a deferred annuity contract to be free of taxation until the funds within it are withdrawn. Tax deferral is the first feature that most people think of when they consider deferred annuities. It is a crucial aspect of nonqualified annuities. However, when annuity contracts are used for qualified plan money that already has the benefit of this feature, tax deferral is redundant as a result of the qualified plan structure.

The government encourages people to leave the money in the deferred annuity until their retirement by making preretirement, nonperiodic distributions less tax efficient. The bottom line is that the income tax deferral on money inside annuities is granted by the federal government and can be changed or taken away by the federal government.

The good news about income tax deferral in deferred annuities is that the downside of paying income taxes on the earnings does not happen every year; nor does it reduce the funds that a contract owner otherwise would have available to invest.

The bad news is that income taxes eventually will have to be paid. Deferring taxes during an individual's high-income-earning preretirement tax years and paying taxes in lower post–age 59 1/2 tax years is profitable. Doing otherwise is less tax efficient. Deferred annuities are usually purchased for the purpose of accumulating money for retirement. To accomplish this, the client needs time for compound interest to multiply the retirement money that will be used as an income generator during retirement.

The deferral of income taxes on money available within qualified plans and nonqualified annuities gives people time to accumulate a block of money that is intended to be used to provide income in the future. The larger the retirement fund base, the greater the income.

Annuity Contract Provisions

Insurance companies develop and sell annuity contracts. The contract between the insurer and the client describes what happens during the accumulation and distribution phases of the contract. It sets forth the rights and obligations of the contracting parties. Generally speaking, the client agrees to be a purchaser and to place money into an annuity contract in order to have the rights offered under the contract. The insurance company agrees to the obligations because it has the capacity to meet those obligations and is in the business of doing so as a for-profit enterprise. Although insurance companies are regulated by the individual states and contract forms have to be acceptable to each state, in the interest of efficiency, there is a great deal of standardization in all annuity contracts.

The annuity contract's general provisions include a statement defining the document as a contract between the insurance company and the contract owner. The documentation of the agreement is the contract, the application, and any riders or endorsements attached to it. The application identifies the contract owner and successive owners (if named), the beneficiary and any successive beneficiaries, and the annuitant or annuitants. The general provisions also include the premium payment arrangement—such as single or flexible—and define the accumulation value of the contract.

Annual Fees

Some deferred annuities may charge a nominal annual contract maintenance fee, such as one percent of the cash value not to exceed $20 to $50. These fees are usually deducted from the annuity cash values, and they will often expire when the contract accrues a certain amount of cash value, such as $5,000 or $10,000. Recent competition among annuity products, however, has made this contract provision less common in newly issued annuity contracts.

Minimum Initial Premium

Each annuity contract will designate a minimum premium that the policyowner must pay to purchase an annuity. Normally these amounts are in the $5,000 to $10,000 range for single-premium policies and $25 to $50 per month for flexible-premium policies. Insurance companies may designate a different minimum amount, depending on the type of funds the client places inside the annuity. For example, a policy might show a minimum premium of $1,000 for a qualified single-premium annuity but still keep the nonqualified annuity minimum premium at $5,000. Lower premium amounts are common for qualified contracts so that the annuity can accept small annual IRA contributions.

Issue-Age Requirements

Each annuity contract will have a provision for the minimum and maximum age of the owner or the annuitant who can purchase the contract. Generally, the insurance company is more interested in the age of the annuitant for purposes of mortality. But the issue age of the owner is also important because of legal issues related to minors who purchase a contract.

Normally, an insurance company does not want a minor to own one of its policies because of the minor's legal right, upon reaching the age of 18, to rescind a purchase made while he or she was a minor. For our purposes, we will consider the issue age of the annuitant. Usually, annuity contracts allow annuitants between the ages of 18 and 85. Some companies may stop issuing annuities at age 70 or 75; other companies will issue annuities up to age 90.

In addition, the insurance company may limit the issue age based on the type of funds in the annuity. Qualified annuity contracts typically carry a maximum issue age of 70, while nonqualified annuities will be issued to age 85 or 90. The reason for the qualified funds' limitation is based on the minimum distribution requirements for qualified annuity contracts. The tax code stipulates that qualified plans distribute a certain percentage of the account after the owner reaches age 70 1/2. The insurance company does not want to accept new policies with these types of funds at the same time the policyowner will be forced to take immediate distributions. This tax code distribution requirement goes against the fundamental principle of the insurance company's desire to have a long-term investment from the policyowner.

Crediting Interest

The amount of interest the annuity product earns is of primary importance to the owner of the policy. In addition, because the initial interest rate is guaranteed for some period of time, the length of the guarantee period is critical. Furthermore, the owner needs to know how the insurance carrier has typically treated its policyowners in terms of renewal interest rates—that is, the interest rates declared once the initial guaranteed interest rate period has expired.

Interest Rates and Guarantee Periods

When individuals consider purchasing a deferred annuity, they are most interested in two areas: (1) What is the current interest rate available, and (2) what length of time is that interest rate guaranteed? Is it for one year only, for 2 years, for 5 years, or longer? The length of time the annuity will pay the initial interest rate is important. Policyowners need to know how long they can count on the insurance company to pay the specified interest rate. Often, the *interest rate guarantee period* is tied to the length of the annuity's surrender charge period.

interest rate guarantee period

Minimum Interest Guarantees

Fixed-interest deferred annuity contracts will also provide a minimum interest rate, and the insurance company guarantees that it will never credit an interest rate less than this percentage to the annuity. This rate has typically been 3 percent. Even if the economy or market is at an all-time low, this provision allows policyowners to feel comfortable, knowing that they will earn at least 3 percent per year, no matter what the economy is doing.

These guaranteed minimum interest rates were basically ignored and of little importance for many years, but in 2003, with money market and CD interest rates at one and 2 percent, the guarantees became highly valued. In early 2003, however, many annuity contracts were paying only their guaranteed minimum interest rates because of the extremely low interest rate environment. It is highly likely that future contracts will not offer the 3 and 4 percent minimums found in old annuity contracts. The National Association of Insurance Commissioners (NAIC) met in San Diego in December 2002 and worked on model legislation that would allow a minimum interest rate as low as 1 percent, which may float above that rate during the life of a contract, depending on market conditions.[5]

Bonus Interest Rates

bonus interest rates

Bonus interest rates are extra amounts of interest granted to new purchasers of fixed-interest deferred annuities that are paid in addition to the normal stated current interest rate. These amounts are usually based on the total dollars contained in the contract during its first year. Bonus-plan annuities are designed to attract money from existing annuity contracts, which still may be subject to a surrender charge, by paying extra interest in the first year. This extra interest (the bonus) is designed to offset some of the loss caused by the termination of the old policy. Clients must understand that these bonuses have an indirect cost behind them. Thus, the financial advisor must be sure to tell prospects of any circumstance in which the bonus will not be paid, such as early termination or surrender.

Both the client and advisor should be well informed regarding any bonus interest rates. Bonus rates are enticements to get the individuals to purchase an annuity. Bigger enticements usually mean bigger constraints on when that bonus will be applied or earned. Any forfeiture and possibly even a withdrawal prior to the end of the surrender charge period could void the bonus.

Unfortunately, interest rate bonuses often encourage replacement of annuities. The policyowner is lured by the high interest rate and a bonus above the normal current interest rate; the annuity owner may feel that the bonus will help to offset any surrender penalties he or she may incur. Bonus annuities will bear much higher surrender charges than a nonbonus product, putting the policyowner at a still greater disadvantage if withdrawals are needed during the surrender charge period.

When interest rate bonuses are used, the bonus is usually offered for one year to 5 years, after which the interest rate may be reduced. Clients need to understand this and to know that the insurance company will seek to keep their money for a longer period of time with surrender charges or penalties so that these products remain profitable.

Deferred credits, a variation of a bonus, may not be paid unless the contract is still in force for periods of time up to 10 to 12 years. A typical example might be an insurance company offering a 5 percent bonus interest rate that is not guaranteed until the policyowner keeps the annuity in force at the insurance company for the specified period of years.

premium bonus

Premium Bonus. A *premium bonus* is similar to an interest rate bonus incentive found in deferred annuities except that the percentage of bonus interest granted by the issuing insurance company is applied to the premium when it goes into the contract, not added later to the current interest rate paid on total dollars accrued after they were deposited into the contract. For example, a 3 percent premium bonus would pay $300 (.03 x $10,000), and this amount would be immediately added to the client's policy. Check the contract provisions to determine how much, if any, of this premium bonus is actually guaranteed and what the additional surrender charges are to have a premium bonus applied to the policy.

Renewal Interest Rates

A critical area for a prospective purchaser to consider is how the company treats its policyowners regarding the interest rate it declares it will pay when the guarantee period is over. For example, if an annuity owner purchases a policy with a one-year interest rate guarantee period of 5 percent, at the end of the first year the insurance company will declare what interest rate the company will credit for the second policy year. The prospect should know if the rate for the second year will be competitive with what other annuities are paying at that time. Will the renewal interest rate equal the same rate the insurance company is giving to newly issued policies? Will the renewal rate drop to the guaranteed policy minimum?

A problem that can crop up in fixed-interest deferred annuities is that their renewal interest rate, especially in times of decreasing interest rates, may be less than what most people desire. This is not very different from what happens with certificates of deposit with banks. However, it often feels to individuals that insurance companies and banks attract their attention with higher first-year teaser interest rates in which companies may give up some of their spread or profit. Later, when the rates are up for renewal, the companies lower renewal rates to increase their spread.

Whether true or not, this feeling is most prevalent during times of falling interest rates and is most annoying to clients if their annuity contracts have surrender charges that prevent them from moving their money to a more profitable place. Purchasers are put in the position of having to trust that the insurance company will not take advantage of them by providing exceedingly low interest rates during the period in which they are locked into the contract by a surrender charge.

Liquidity

Deferred annuities are purchased with long-term accumulation in mind and particularly as retirement savings tools. In accordance with those goals, annuities are not structured to be liquid investments. Nevertheless, policyowners need to know how they can access the funds, if needed, in the annuity product they are buying.

Withdrawals or Surrenders

Deferred annuities are retirement planning financial tools. Because the goal is to have an annuity as a long-term investment, the insurance companies design deferred annuities to be illiquid investments during the early years of the policy. The length of the period of illiquidity is concurrent with the period of time the company needs the policy to stay on the books to be profitable.

withdrawal
partial surrender

In the event the policyowner needs to access funds prior to maturity, the owner has the option of requesting a *withdrawal,* also called a *partial surrender*. Withdrawal provisions in deferred annuity contracts allow the policyowner limited withdrawal of funds prior to maturity of the contract.

surrender

If the owner needs to access all of his or her annuity values, the owner can request a full *surrender* of the policy. A full surrender provision in a deferred annuity contract allows the policyowner total withdrawal of funds prior to maturity of the contract, which results in termination of the contract.

surrender charge period

The surrender or withdrawal, if made during the *surrender charge period,* is normally subject to a surrender charge. If the withdrawal is requested after the policy is beyond its surrender charge period, the policyowner should be able to access the withdrawal without any charges imposed by the insurance company. Withdrawals are not expected to be repaid to the annuity contract. In fact, with single-premium deferred annuities, the policyowner cannot reinvest the withdrawn funds even if he or she is able to. With flexible-premium policies, the withdrawal can later be paid into the annuity policy as new premiums, but the policyowner should make sure the policy does not inflict a new set of surrender charges on those funds.

Annuity policies do not generally have loan provisions available to the policyowner due to the adverse tax consequences. Therefore, in terms of access to annuity values, our discussion will be in the context of withdrawals or surrenders.

surrender charges

Surrender Charges

Surrender charges are used by the insurance company to encourage purchasers to make long-term commitments. If contract owners want to take money out of their annuity contracts prior to the end of the period to which they committed when they invested in the contract, the insurer imposes a charge. In fixed annuities, the period during which the insurer can impose a surrender charge typically lasts 5 to 10 years, depending on the company that issues it.

A surrender charge is paid from the annuity values. It is usually highest within the first years of the contract or within the first years after money is put into the contract, and it decreases and is eliminated over the years.

Example:	A 7 percent, 7-year surrender charge decreasing 1 percent per year means that any amount withdrawn is subject to a 7 percent charge in year one, a 6 percent charge in year 2, and so on until the money has been in the contract for a full 7 years. Money that has been in this contract for 8 years can be entirely withdrawn without a surrender charge. See table 8-2 for a comparison of two different surrender charge schedules that both start with 7 percent and end in 7 years. As the table shows, one schedule is much more liquid than the other.

accumulation value
surrender value

The annuity value before any surrender charges is usually called the *accumulation value*; the account value after surrender charges have been deducted is called the *surrender value*. The surrender value is the actual amount the owner would receive upon a complete and total surrender of the policy.

TABLE 8-2
Annuity Surrender Charges

Policy Year	Company A Surrender Charge Percentage	Company B Surrender Charge Percentage
1	7%	7%
2	6	7
3	5	7
4	4	5
5	3	5
6	2	3
7	1	1
8	0	0

A "rolling" surrender charge begins with each additional investment into the contract. This means that the surrender charge is applicable to each contribution to the contract for the full surrender charge period from the date money is put into the contract. In the example above, if the surrender charge was a rolling one, any money added to this contract in the eighth year would have to remain in the contract for 8 more years before it would be free of surrender charges. Typically, the older money, which is free of surrender charges, plus the free-corridor amount (described below) would be withdrawn first to avoid the surrender charge on the new money in this contract.

Rolling surrender charges can sometimes be a source of client confusion and complaints. In our example, it would be understandable that after the first 8 years the contract owner would remember only that there was an 8-year surrender charge but not remember that putting more money into the policy would create constraints on that amount of new money for another 8 years. It is possible that the contract owner could lodge a complaint merely because he or she did not understand what rolling surrender charges entail. Such charges may also influence clients not to put additional funds into their contracts. For those reasons, rolling surrender charges can be counter-productive.

Waiving Surrender Charges. Almost all fixed annuities waive surrender charges or market value adjustments at the death of either the contract owner or the annuitant—but not both. In addition, some, but not all, annuities will waive the surrender charges if the policyowner wants to annuitize his or her values into a guaranteed income stream.

In some cases, there are waivers of surrender charges for withdrawals or full surrenders due to admittance to a long-term care facility, terminal illness, and even unemployment of either the contract owner or the annuitant. Owners of contracts in which the annuitant and the contract owner are different individuals need to know whether these waivers-of-surrender-charge provisions apply to the annuitant's or the contract owner's condition.

One important issue with respect to penalty-free withdrawals that must be examined for any contract issued with qualified funds is whether the insurance company will waive surrender charges for any required minimum distributions that must begin to be taken by individuals at age 70 1/2. Clients and advisors need to fully understand the consequences of minimum distributions and how they interact with the particular policy's surrender charges. Minimum distribution rules will be discussed later in this text.

Free-Corridor Amount

free-corridor amount

To accommodate a contract owner's unforeseen need for money, practically all companies provide a free withdrawal corridor. A *free-corridor amount* is some maximum amount of money that a contract owner can withdraw from the contract each year before the end of the surrender charge period without incurring a surrender charge.

Normally, this amount is about 10 percent of the last year's accumulation value or 10 percent of the initial premium paid. However, some contracts do not allow any withdrawals without charge; the most generous allow withdrawals of up to 15 percent per contract year without charge. Amounts in excess of the free corridor amount are subject to proportional surrender charges.

Examine surrender charges and free-corridor provisions carefully. A client should be confident that there are no foreseeable situations that will result in withdrawing funds prematurely and incurring a surrender charge. If the client makes a withdrawal and incurs a surrender charge for a situation that he or she should have foreseen, nobody wins.

Income Taxation of Withdrawals and Surrenders

Nonqualified deferred annuities purchased after August 13, 1982, are taxed on a last-in, first-out basis (LIFO). Withdrawals are taxed first to the extent that there is any gain in the annuity. This is referred to as the "interest first" rule. The purpose of the "interest first" rule applicable to investments in contracts after August 13, 1982, is to limit the tax advantages of deferred annuity contracts to long-term investment goals, such as retirement income security, and to prevent the use of tax-deferred inside build-up as a method of sheltering income on freely withdrawable short-term investments. Once all the gain has been withdrawn, any further withdrawal is not taxable income to the annuity owner but is considered a tax-free withdrawal of the cost basis.

Withdrawals from policies issued before August 14, 1982, are taxed differently from the LIFO method. This rule applies only to contributions made prior to August 14, 1982, and the accompanying growth on those contributions. Withdrawals are first considered a return of premium, and second as interest earnings—the first dollars in are the first dollars out (FIFO). The first dollars withdrawn from the policy are tax free to the extent that they are considered a return of the policyowner's premiums. Once all the premium dollars have been withdrawn tax free, any remaining amounts withdrawn are taxed to the policyowner as ordinary income. This is called the "cost recovery rule."

If the deferred annuity has income from both pre–August 14, 1982, and post–August 13, 1982, premiums, the taxation of withdrawals is more complex. Withdrawals are first considered a tax-free return of pre–August 14, 1982, premiums; then interest income on pre–August 14, 1982, premiums; then interest income on post–August 13, 1982, premiums; and finally, a tax-free return of post–August 13, 1982, premiums.

pre–59 1/2 IRS penalty tax

Penalty Tax. The general rule of thumb with nonqualified deferred annuities is that premature distributions taken from these accounts prior to the policyowner's age 59 1/2 will cause the taxable amount of the withdrawal to be subject to a 10 percent penalty tax levied by the IRS. The policyowner pays the *pre–59 1/2 IRS penalty tax*, not the insurance company. It is paid to the IRS with the taxpayer's IRS Form 1040 by April 15, the usual tax filing deadline.

Misconception about Penalty Tax. A misconception sometimes occurs about the surrender charge the insurance company imposes against the policyowner and the penalty tax the Internal Revenue Service imposes against the withdrawn annuity cash value. The surrender charge is paid by the policyowner from the annuity cash value. The 10 percent penalty tax for premature distributions is a tax the policyowner pays on his or her annual income tax return, along with any income tax owed on the gain in the annuity proceeds.

Example: A policyowner aged 52 withdraws $10,000 from an annuity with an accumulation value of $82,000, all of which is considered taxable income. The policyowner will be subject to a surrender charge of 6 percent, or $600 ($10,000 x .06). Therefore, the policyowner will actually receive $9,400 ($10,000 – $600).

Because the policyowner is under age 59 1/2, the withdrawal is subject to a 10 percent penalty tax against the $10,000. The tax is equal to $1,000 ($10,000 x .10). And the full $10,000 is subject to income tax that is payable at the owner's marginal tax bracket.

The annuity owner receives $9,400, and the insurance company keeps $600. The penalty tax of $1,000 is paid by the annuity owner to the IRS on his income tax return, and he may use part of $9,400 to pay the penalty, as well as the income tax on the $10,000.

IRC Sec. 1035 Exchanges

When a contract owner purchases a new annuity contract to replace an existing one, the new contract is referred to as a replacement contract. Replacement contracts usually occur in connection with a tax-free exchange of nonqualified contracts under IRC Sec. 1035, or because of a rollover or direct transfer of a qualified plan contract, such as an individual retirement annuity (IRA), from one insurance company to another. The reasons for the exchange may include the following:

- The owner has a fixed annuity that has a substantially lower interest rate or investment performance than other contracts currently available.
- The company that issued the current contract is not as financially strong as it once was.
- The new contract may include substantially better contract features.
- The new contract may have lower fees and contract charges.

Sec. 1035 exchange

The IRS provides tax relief to the purchasers of nonqualified deferred annuities, life insurance, and endowment policies, if the purchaser wants to move funds from one insurance company to another. The tax code allows this transaction, a *Sec. 1035 exchange*, to occur without making it a taxable event.

The tax-free exchange rules under IRC Sec. 1035 state that a life insurance policy can be exchanged for a life insurance policy, an annuity policy can be exchanged for an annuity policy, and a life insurance policy can be exchanged for an annuity policy. It does not matter what type of annuity is under consideration. It can be variable, fixed, equity indexed, and so on. The same is true for life insurance.

A deferred annuity policy, however, cannot be transferred through a tax-free exchange into a life insurance policy. This is partly because the IRS does not want a taxpayer to exchange a taxable asset—such as an annuity—for a potentially tax-free asset—such as life insurance. It does, however, allow the taxpayer to move from a potentially tax-free asset to a taxable asset.

These rules apply to nonqualified annuities. Qualified annuities are subject to a different set of rules.

A tax-free exchange is important because it allows the policyowner to exchange one deferred annuity for another without having to recognize any taxable gain in the annuity policy upon transfer. Instead, the policyowner is allowed to carry over the cost basis from the old annuity into the new annuity and defer recognition of gain.

Example: A policyowner has a deferred annuity worth $100,000 and a cost basis of $25,000. If the owner decides to purchase a new deferred annuity, he can transfer the cash value of $100,000 into a new deferred annuity policy, and that new policy will have the cost basis of $25,000 from the old policy.

To have a valid Sec. 1035 exchange, the owner of the deferred annuity must be the same on the old and the new policy. In addition, the annuitant must also be the same person on the old and the new policy. The beneficiary designation, however, does not have to be the same on both policies.

Market Value Adjustments

**market value
adjustment (MVA)**

Market value adjustments are features added to some deferred annuities to discourage surrenders prior to their contractual maturity date. If, during the contract period and before the maturity date, money in excess of any free-corridor amount is withdrawn, it is subject to a *market value adjustment (MVA)*. The MVA is an increase or decrease in the annuity's value, depending on the level of the general economy's interest rates relative to the interest rates of the contract from which the withdrawal is taken. Annuities with MVA features often offer a slightly higher interest rate than a comparable fixed annuity without MVA features.

The MVA works in the annuity contract in a manner similar to the way individual bond prices fluctuate. For example, if a contract owner has an annuity with a contractual interest rate of 8 percent with 5 years left prior to its maturity date, and similar contracts are being issued with 4 percent interest rates, the contract owner can expect some gain upon early surrender. This is because the surrender will relieve the insurance company from its 8 percent obligation in a market where interest rates have decreased to 4 percent. On the other hand, if the opposite occurred and the old contractual obligation was for 4 percent in a current interest rate market of 8 percent, the contract owner can expect a negative MVA and therefore will receive a smaller surrender value.

Death Benefits

Deferred annuities are traditionally purchased to build retirement nest eggs for the policyowner. However, if the entire annuity value is not consumed during retirement, when the annuitant dies, the annuity will still be in force. Therefore, deferred annuities must have provisions for a beneficiary or some other party to legally receive the values at the annuitant's death.

Nonqualified deferred annuity death benefits are typically not income tax free to the beneficiary like the proceeds of a typical life insurance policy. The gain in the deferred annuity policy is taxed to the beneficiary as ordinary income. Unless the beneficiary is a valid charitable organization, the taxable gain in the policy cannot be avoided. The tax liability just moves from owner to beneficiary at death.

death benefit

Deferred annuity contracts can be classified in one of two ways depending on how the *death benefit* is payable in the policy: Policies are either annuitant driven or owner driven. In an annuitant-driven contract, the death of the annuitant causes the payment of the death benefit. However, if the annuity contract specifies a death benefit free of surrender charges at the death of an owner, it is referred to as an owner-driven contract. Regardless of the distinction, depending on the contract, the insurance company may still apply surrender charges at death.

The majority of annuity contracts are annuitant driven. That is, the death-benefit provisions become effective when the annuitant dies, and other provisions become effective based on the annuitant's age, health, and so on. If the contract owner and the annuitant are the same person, the only question to be resolved is the best legal way to distribute the money to the beneficiary.

If the death occurs prior to the time that annuitization payments have begun and an individual who is not a spouse is the beneficiary, the contract proceeds payable to that nonspouse beneficiary must either be distributed (1) within 5 years of the death of the annuitant/owner or (2) as an annuity based on the life expectancy of the beneficiary, as long as payments begin within one year of the date of the owner's death (or such later date as the Secretary of the Treasury may, by regulations, prescribe).[6]

Spousal Beneficiary Options

Under the tax code, the spouse as the beneficiary of an annuity contract may choose not to accept the death benefit and instead may choose to continue the annuity contract with the insurance company. The insurance company will change the owner from the deceased person's name to that of the surviving spouse. The surviving spouse now has the right as the owner to name a new beneficiary. This right exists whether the policy is a nonqualified annuity contract or a qualified annuity contract.

Example: Suppose Larry purchases an annuity and is the owner and annuitant, and he names his wife, Laura, as the beneficiary. Upon Larry's death, Laura has two choices: She can either keep the policy in force in her own name (the insurance company will then change the owner and annuitant designation to Laura's name, and she will need to name a new beneficiary), or she can accept the proceeds as a death benefit.

Settlement Options

Deferred annuity contracts also include provisions for taking the money out of the contract at some future contract-owner-determined date—called annuitization—or at the insurance company's designated maximum age at which distributions must begin—also known as the *maturity date*.

maturity date

These optional modes of settlement may be taking a lump-sum withdrawal, leaving the proceeds in the contract at interest, choosing fixed-period or fixed-amount payments, or selecting the various life-contingent or joint-life-contingent options. The immediate annuity settlement options are described in the next chapter.

The minimum payout rates for settlement options are listed in the annuity policy. Therefore, it is important for the owner to look at the guaranteed settlement option rates in the policy and compare those rates to the current offerings from the insurance company to be sure to obtain the best rates available.

Annuity Riders

Annuity policies can have riders attached to them to add various features to the annuity. Some of the more common annuity riders are described below.

Terminal Illness Rider

terminal illness rider

A *terminal illness rider* generally makes annuity values available to the policyowner if the annuitant becomes "terminally ill." Terminally ill is commonly defined as having 12 months or less life expectancy as determined by the annuitant's doctor. The rider usually allows the owner to access up to 75 percent of annuity values without a surrender charge. Generally, the owner and annuitant are the same person, but in a situation where they are two different people, it is important to check the policy to determine if the terminal illness provision is applicable to the owner or the annuitant.

The rider should specify the definition of terminally ill and what evidence the annuitant/owner must provide to the insurance company for this option to be activated. Also, the insurance company may have a provision that if the annuitant becomes terminally ill in the first 12 months of the insurance contract, the owner will not be able to activate this provision. Therefore, this type of provision is usually not helpful to those who are already ill at policy issue.

Long-Term Care Benefit

long-term care benefit rider

A *long-term care benefit rider* generally provides the owner of the contract access to cash values if the annuitant has to enter a long-term care facility. This rider usually allows the owner to access up to 50 percent of annuity values without a surrender charge. The purpose of the rider is to provide peace of mind so that if annuity owners have to go to long-term care facilities, they will have access to funds to pay for these costs without incurring high surrender charges.

Most riders will state at policy issue a maximum age the annuitant can be and still have this rider made available to the owner. It is important when a policy is replaced to be sure the policy being exchanged does not contain significant benefits, such as a long-term care benefit rider, that could be lost if the new policy does not make the same features available to the owner, or if the annuitant is too old to have this rider on the new policy.

Qualified Plan Riders

Depending on how the annuity policy is drafted by the particular insurance company, it may provide for the acceptance of qualified funds through the addition of riders to the policy. Riders are normally provided to allow IRA funds, 403(b)/tax-sheltered annuity funds, and IRC Sec. 457 funds into otherwise nonqualified annuity policies. Alternatively, the annuity policy may have specific versions drafted for each of the qualified plan types. It is important that the financial advisor knows how the specific company handles the qualified plan provisions to ensure that he or she applies for the correct type of annuity.

Disability Rider

Lastly, a disability rider will waive surrender charges if the owner is totally disabled and unable to work due to injury or illness. There is a waiting period required, such as 3 to 6 months, before this liberal access to cash values is allowed.

INDEXED ANNUITIES

An indexed annuity (or as it is frequently referred to, an equity-indexed annuity) is a unique form of a deferred annuity that offers a middle ground between a fixed-interest deferred annuity and a variable deferred annuity. It pays interest not on what the insurance company declares but on what the outside index actually does. It also provides a minimum guaranteed return.

The idea of tying an annuity's interest to an index outside the insurance company's control accomplishes two things: (1) It eliminates the "trust me" objection clients feel regarding the insurance company's interest-crediting practices because the interest rates credited to their policies are tied to an index, and (2) it addresses annuity owners' frustrations. Their frustrations arose from fixed-interest deferred annuities during the period from 1982 to 1999 when annuity owners were earning competitive interest rates while their neighbors were bragging about the huge returns they were experiencing in the stock market. Indexed annuities or equity-indexed annuities were first designed to tackle these two problems.

Equity-indexed annuities and other indexed annuities emerged in the insurance industry in 1995. At that time, the stock market was doing very well, and many clients were purchasing variable deferred annuities. Nonregistered representatives could sell only traditional fixed-interest and immediate annuities. But fixed-interest deferred annuities were not looking

competitive next to their cousin, the variable annuity. Because only registered representatives can sell variable deferred annuities, the nonregistered
representatives were asking insurance companies to build a product that
would capture some of the stock market's upside potential.

In response, the insurance industry designed a product that would offer the
upside of the variable deferred annuity but would avoid SEC registration so
that nonregistered representatives would have an attractive product to offer.

From this product development effort, the indexed annuity appeared.
Sales of this product have increased each year since 1995 reaching $12.6
billion in 2003, which was 14 percent of all fixed annuity sales.

Most indexed annuities are tied to an "equity" index, meaning a stock
index. Some are tied to a nonequity index—for example, a bond index.
Although this section will mainly use the phrase equity-indexed annuity, bear
in mind that not all indexed annuities are actually tied to an equity index.

Product Design

The equity-indexed annuity is unique among annuity products. New
product features and terms were created to design this new and innovative
product. This section will help the financial advisor understand the various
product designs available and become familiar with the terminology
associated with the equity-indexed annuity market. The section will
demonstrate how the different product features work together to provide
indexed-linked interest to annuity clients.

Equity and Bond Indexes

index

Indexing is a strategy insurance companies use to match the performance
of the annuity to an outside group of securities. The outside group of
securities forms an *index*. The index is a measure of the group's performance.
The index's performance is then the measure of the indexed annuity's
performance, which the insurance company uses as a basis for the current
rates of interest that it passes on to owners of its indexed annuity products.

A 2003 review of the indexed annuity marketplace shows the following
indexes are used for interest crediting purposes:

- S&P 500 Index
- S&P Midcap 400
- Dow Jones Industrial Average
- Lehman Brothers U.S. Treasury Index
- Lehman Brothers Aggregate Bond Index
- Merrill Lynch All Convertibles Index
- NASDAQ 100 Index
- various international indexes

Indexing Methods

To understand how the indexing methods in indexed annuities work, it helps to become familiar with the following three key terms:

contract term
- *contract term.* Interest credited to an equity-indexed annuity is based on the increases in the index that occur over a defined period of time, which is called the contract term. The term can be from one year to 7 or even 10 years. The term is an important concept for a prospect to understand because once the term is selected, it will usually limit the owner's free access to the funds during the term. Therefore, if funds are withdrawn before the end of the term, they will usually be subject to an early surrender penalty imposed by the issuing company.

free window period
- *free window period.* The owner usually has several options at the end of the contract term, which is called the free window period or window period. Those options include the following:
  - The equity-indexed annuity can be renewed for another contract term.
  - It can be exchanged for another type of annuity, such as a fixed-interest deferred or variable deferred annuity.
  - The contract can be annuitized, and the annuitant can begin to receive the benefits under one of the available settlement options.
  - The contract's indexed account value can be partially or completely surrendered without incurring company surrender charges, and the owner will pay any income taxes that are due.

percentage change
- *percentage change.* The percentage change is the change in the index from the beginning of the contract term to the end of the contract term expressed as a percentage. For example, if the S&P 500 Index stands at 1,000 at the beginning of the term and it rises to 1,150, there is a 15 percent change.

Various methods can be used to measure the performance of the index from the starting point (the date the contract was originally put in force) to the end of the contract term. The three principal methods of index measurement for crediting interest to an equity-indexed annuity are the annual reset design, point-to-point design, and high-water mark design.

There are many variations of each of these basic designs. We will examine how the three different indexing methods affect the performance of three equity-indexed annuities by comparing the cash value growth of the three policies when applying hypothetical percentage changes in the S&P 500 Index using the three basic indexing methods to credit interest within each of them. We will assume that an investor deposits $100,000 into each equity-indexed annuity, and we will track the results of the cash value growth over a 5-year interest-crediting period. For simplicity's sake, the three scenarios ignore any cap rates, participation rates, or asset fees, which are discussed in detail later in this chapter.

To begin, look at figure 8-1, which represents the S&P 500 Index for a 5-year period. When our investor buys the three annuities, the S&P 500 Index level, upon which the annuities' performance will be based, stands at 1,000. At the end of year 1, the index has risen 15 percent to the 1,150 level. By the end of year 2, the index has fallen back to 1,100 (a 4.35 percent decline). By the end of year 3, the index has fallen again to 1,050 (a 4.55 percent decline). By the end of year 4, the index has fallen a third time to 1,000 (a 4.7 percent decline). By the end of year 5, the index has increased to 1,100, which is a 10 percent increase.

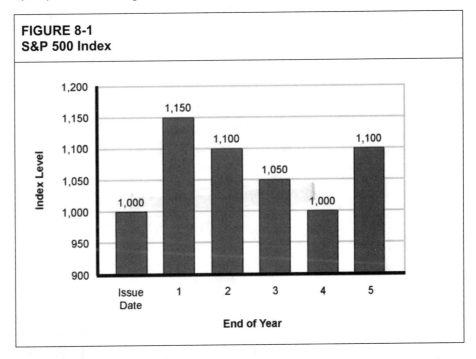

FIGURE 8-1
S&P 500 Index

We will compare how $100,000 deposited into three separate equity-indexed annuities performs when linked to the S&P 500 Index according to the changing levels in the index over a 5-year period. The three annuities will use the annual reset, point-to-point, and high-water mark indexing methods respectively.

Annual Reset Design

annual reset indexed annuity

An *annual reset indexed annuity* compares the positive change in the index from the beginning of the policy year to the end of the policy year. The annual reset method provides incremental protection on growth by locking in the previous year's anniversary value. Locking in the positive index returns and ignoring negative index returns preserves the contract's principal and past positive earnings. This process of building on the past positive returns is sometimes referred to as *ratcheting*. Annual resets will perform well when the index experiences moderate consistent growth; they will also perform well in choppy markets.

As figure 8-2 shows, the annual reset design will credit growth as follows: from the issue date to the end of year 1, and from the end of year 4 to the end of year 5. However, no losses are subtracted or lost in the negative years from the end of year 1 to the end of year 2, from the end of year 2 to the end of year 3, and from the end of year 3 to the end of year 4. The starting point for one year is the end of the year value from the year before; hence the term annual reset.

Therefore, in this scenario, the first annuity's contract value increased by 15 percent from the issue date ($100,000) to the end of year 1 ($115,000), then by another 10 percent from the end of year 4 ($115,000) to the end of year 5 ($126,500).

Averaging. Another strategy to bring up the value of returns in negatively moving indexes and bring down the value of returns in positively moving indexes is averaging. Some indexed annuities average an index's value either

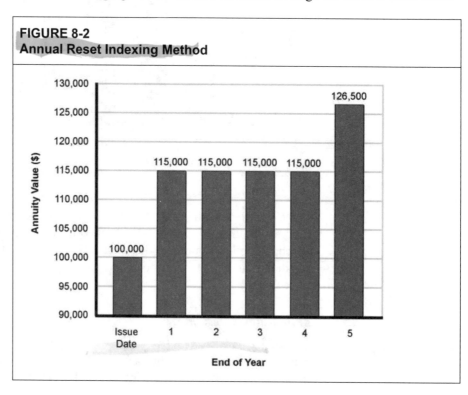

FIGURE 8-2
Annual Reset Indexing Method

daily or monthly, rather than using the actual value of the index on a specified date. Because averaging can reduce the amount of index-linked interest, it reduces the insurance company's risk and, therefore, its cost.

Table 8-3 shows the negative effect that monthly averaging can have in a constantly rising market. The table shows a straight 7 percent increase in the index. Note the monthly average increase compared to 7 percent.

TABLE 8-3
S&P 500 Index Growth Using Monthly Averaging Assuming a Constantly Increasing Index over the 12-Month Period

Purchase Date: December 1
December 1 Index = 900

Index Date	Index Value	Index Date	Index Value
January	900	July	935
February	910	August	940
March	915	September	945
April	920	October	950
May	925	November	960
June	930	December	963
		Total Index Values	11,193

The following formula is used to calculate the index average:

$$\text{Total index values} \div 12 \text{ months} = \text{Monthly index average}$$

$$\frac{11,193}{12} = 933$$

$$\frac{\text{Monthly index average} - \text{starting index}}{\text{Starting index}} = \text{Monthly average index earnings}$$

$$\frac{933 - 900}{900} = 3.7\%$$

Therefore, the monthly average index earnings for the year are 3.7 percent, which is roughly one-half the straight line increase of 7 percent.

Had the annuity policy used the annual reset method without monthly averaging, the policy would credit:

$$\frac{\text{End-of-year index value} - \text{beginning-of-year value}}{\text{Beginning-of-year index value}} = \text{Index growth}$$

$$\frac{963 - 900}{900} = 7.0\% \text{ Index growth}$$

These two calculations show that while the actual index using the annual reset method increased at 7.0 percent for the year, with averaging, the index credits only 3.7 percent. This is a large difference in interest earnings based on the same index, simply by using different methods to calculate the interest. Clients need to understand how interest is credited on their policies to be satisfied with their annuity's performance and not be surprised by the numbers on their annual statement. The importance of having the policyowner and the financial advisor understand equity-indexed annuities and how they credit interest is critical to maintaining satisfied and happy clients.

Point-to-Point Design

point-to-point indexed annuity

A *point-to-point indexed* annuity does not lock in positive growth in the index each year. Instead, it compares the change in the index at the beginning and at the ending dates of the contract term. For example, if an S&P 500–indexed, 5-year, point-to-point contract was purchased in January 2002, the contract owner will not know if he or she will receive any indexed interest until January 2007. Therefore, the client risks losing previous gains if the index declines near the end of the term. The primary benefit of the point-to-point design is that it offers the highest return to the client during constantly rising markets.

Figure 8-3 shows the hypothetical performance of the second equity-indexed annuity using a 5-year point-to-point indexing method. This annuity will credit interest based on the difference between the issue date and the end of year 5 only, which is also the value at the end of the 5-year contract term. In a 5-year point-to-point annuity, the annual changes in the index are not relevant. Thus, the points between the issue date and years 1, 2, 3, and 4 are of no consequence because the only two points used in the calculations are the issue date and the end of year 5. Therefore, the annuity's cash value increases from $100,000 at the issue date to $110,000 at the end of the 5-year contract term, which is a 10 percent gain in value.

Some policies will also use the concept of averaging with point-to-point policies. With point-to-point products, this concept works slightly differently. The policy may choose to average the last policy year's monthly indexes and compare that year's monthly average to the policy issue index. Another alternative is to average the last 6 months instead of the last year. For example, the policy may take the index value 4 years and 6 months into the contract term and average that index value with the index as of the end of the contract term. By averaging these two index points, the annuity owner has a better chance of receiving interest earnings if the market has dropped in the last year.

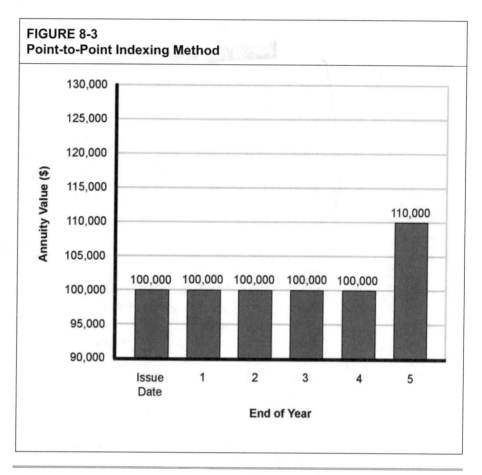

FIGURE 8-3
Point-to-Point Indexing Method

Example: Assume the index as of the policy issue date is 1,000, the index at 4 1/2 years is 1,050, and the year 5 index value is 980. With a pure 5-year point- to-point the policy issue index of 1,000, no interest is credited for the 5-year period.

However, by averaging the last 6 months, the interest earnings is calculated as follows:

$$980 + 1050 = 2030/2 = 1015$$

$$1015/1000 = 1.5\% \text{ increase}$$

This calculation shows the difference that averaging can make in how much interest is credited to the policy. Clearly, without averaging the client would receive no interest earnings for the 5-year period. By averaging the last 6 months' indexes, the annuity would earn 1.5 percent interest.

High-Water Mark Design

high-water mark
indexed annuity

The *high-water mark indexed annuity* crediting method typically assesses the index value at each prior anniversary of the contract during the measuring period and uses the highest of these anniversary index values. The index level at the start of the contract is then compared to the highest point during the measuring period. Each year that a new high-water mark value is achieved for the index, the value of the equity-indexed annuity grows. If the index level at the end of the year is below the previous high-water mark, the account value does not grow, but previous gains are not lost. During periods of volatility, the index must recover to its previous highs before further gains are recorded.

In figure 8-4, from the issue date to the end of year 1, the contract will earn 15 percent interest because the S&P 500 Index level of 1,150 is 15 percent higher than the level at the issue date, which was 1,000. However, at the end of year 2 no interest earnings will be credited because the index level has dropped to 1,100, and it is not the highest mark so far in the policy's first 2 years. At the end of year 3, no interest earnings will be credited because the index level has dropped to 1,050, and it is not the highest mark so far in the policy's first 3 years. Again, at the end of year 4, no interest earnings will be credited because the index level has dropped to 1,000 and is not the highest mark in the policy's first 4 years. Finally, although the index increases from the end of year 4 at the 1,000 level to the 1,100 level at the end of year 5, no interest is credited to the policy because the index has not exceeded the high-water mark within the 5-year contract term, which was 1,150 at the end of year 1. Therefore, this annuity contract receives the 15 percent gain the S&P 500 Index experienced from the issue date to the end of year 1, then remains constant at a $115,000 cash value for the remainder of the 5-year contract term.

With each crediting method, it is crucial to know when earnings will be credited to the policy as well as when those credited earnings will be available for the client to withdraw. Some product designs may not credit interest annually, and some still might not allow the client to withdraw funds even if they are credited annually. In addition, it is important to determine how withdrawals from the policy affect interest already credited. The policyowner might forfeit any earnings if he or she withdraws funds before the end of the contract term, which can sometimes be as long as 10 to 15 years.

Note that during a prolonged bear market, none of these methods will offer positive results, and the contract will provide only its underlying guarantees. Generally speaking, if we could expect a fixed annuity to provide approximately a 5 percent return and a diversified equity-based variable deferred annuity to provide a 9 percent return, we should not expect more than 7 percent from an S&P 500–indexed annuity. The reason that clients will accept less is that they want to eliminate any downside risk.

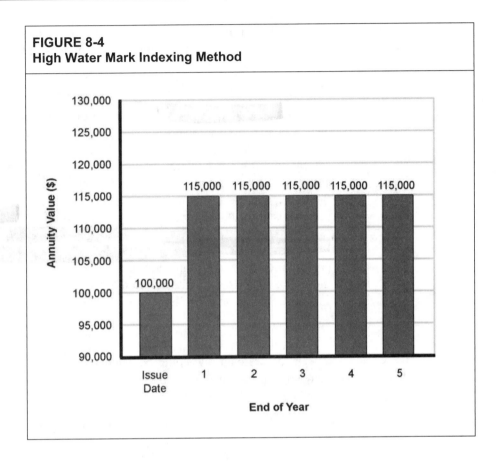

FIGURE 8-4
High Water Mark Indexing Method

Crediting Interest

The uniqueness of the equity-indexed annuity is based on the method the insurance company uses to calculate the annuity's interest earnings. This method is what sets equity-indexed annuities apart from all other annuity products. Various concepts, such as asset fees, participation rates, and caps, all fit together like a puzzle when calculating interest earnings.

Asset Fees

asset fee
spread
margin

Some indexed annuities use an *asset fee* (also called a *spread* or a *margin*) to reduce the amount of interest credited to the policy. The asset fee is the company's profit on the annuity policy. This fee is stated as a percentage, such as 2 percent or 3 percent. The asset fee is subtracted from any gain in the index. For example, if the index gained 16 percent and the asset fee is 2 percent, then the credited interest will be 14 percent.

Typically, assets fees are adjustable every year by the insurance company. The policy should state a maximum that the asset fee will never exceed. For example, the current asset fee charged by the insurance company might be 2 percent, but the contract may state a maximum asset fee of 5 percent.

Participation Rates

participation rate

The *participation rate* is the proportionate amount of the percentage change that is used to determine the actual interest rate that will be credited to an equity-indexed annuity for the contract term. The participation rate is set by the insurance company and stated in the equity-indexed annuity contract. Insurance companies offer various percentages of participation in the index, such as 100 percent, 80 percent, or 70 percent. A participation rate may be used in addition to, or in lieu of, an asset fee. The insurance company may set the participation rate at 80 percent, which means the annuity will be credited with only 80 percent of the gain experienced by the index. If the participation rate is used in addition to a hypothetical 2 percent asset fee, and the index rises 16 percent, the credited interest rate could be calculated as 11.2 percent, as shown below:

$$16\% - 2\% = 14\% \times 80\% = 11.2\%$$

Or the credited rate could be calculated as 10.8 percent if the insurance company applies the participation rate of 80 percent before it applies the 2 percent asset fee, as shown below:

$$16\% \times 80\% = 12.8\% - 2\% = 10.8\%$$

Participation rates are adjustable by the insurance company; they are usually adjustable on each policy anniversary. However, some policies may guarantee the participation rate for the length of the contract term.

Cap Rates

cap rate

The insurance company may place a *cap rate* or upper limit on the amount of interest the annuity can earn. The cap rate is usually expressed as a percentage. For example, in the case above, assume the cap rate is 10 percent. We do not have to worry about whether the company applies the 80 percent participation rate or the 2 percent asset fee first. Because both credited rates are over 10 percent, the cap rate will prevail, and 10 percent will be the maximum amount of interest credited to the annuity.

Like asset fees and participation rates, caps are adjustable by the insurance company. They are normally adjusted on each policy anniversary.

Example: Assume the S&P 500 Index has grown 13 percent over the year and the annuity has

- 100 percent participation
- 11 percent cap
- 3.5 percent asset fee

If the insurance company applies the cap before the asset fee is subtracted, the annuity's growth is calculated by comparing the actual index earnings of 13 percent to the current cap rate of 11 percent. Because the current cap is less than the actual index earnings, the annuity formula will use the lesser of the two figures—11 percent. Next, the asset fee is subtracted from the above figure:

$$11\% - 3.5\% = 7.5\% \text{ credited interest}$$

Alternatively, if the annuity policy's formula requires the asset fee to be deducted from the indexed earnings before the cap is applied, then thecalculation used is as follows:

$$13\% - 3.5\% \text{ asset fee} = 9.5\% \text{ growth}$$

Compare 9.5 percent to the cap of 11 percent. The lower of the two figures is used to credit interest earnings to the policy. Because 9.5 percent is less than 11 percent, the company will credit 9.5 percent interest earnings to the annuity policy.

Note that not all product designs will have a cap. Caps are frequently used with annual reset methods but not with long-term point-to-point or high-water mark designs.

Financial advisors might ask the question, "What happens to the profit if the index earns 13 percent and the cap is 11 percent? Does the insurance company keep the profit earned above the cap?" The answer is that normally the insurance company will buy only enough options to reach the cap. In this example, the insurance company would only cover the index up to 11 percent and not 13 percent. Therefore, there would not be any profit for the company to keep.

All these examples show the importance of understanding how insurance companies credit interest and how the participation rate, cap, and asset fee are applied to the formula. Each of these factors in the interest-crediting formula is established by the insurance company to control the amount of profit the company earns and the amount of interest earnings it must credit to its indexed policies. Bear in mind that just knowing one of the elements—for example, knowing the participation rate is 100 percent—does not give the financial advisor the whole picture. Participation rates, caps, and asset fees are all part of the total package. A product could be competitive and still have a low participation rate. Likewise, a product could be uncompetitive and still have a low asset fee. The bottom line is to know all the features of the indexed annuity you are recommending and how they work together.

Minimum Interest Guarantees

guaranteed minimum interest rate

The *guaranteed minimum interest rate* is the contractually stated percentage rate that will be credited to an indexed annuity during a year or over the term of the contract. This guaranteed minimum interest rate is what allows the equity-indexed annuity to be considered a fixed annuity rather than a securities product.

To address decreasing profits from equity-indexed annuities partially due to the decreasing spreads from interest rates, companies have revised their policies. Revisions include decreasing the 3 percent guaranteed minimum interest rate. When indexed annuities first came to the market, the minimum guarantee was 3 percent on 100 percent of the premium. Now some policies guarantee only 3 percent on 90 percent of the premium.

Another method to reduce interest rates—while trying to make the lower rate sound not quite so bad—is to describe it as a guaranteed minimum return of 115 percent of premium at the end of a 10-year term, which comes out to be less than a 1 percent return on 90 percent of premium paid.

A large misconception with equity-indexed annuities is that many advisors, as well as clients, believe that during a down year in the index, the indexed account value will earn the minimum interest rate. Unfortunately, that is not how equity-indexed annuities are designed. This is easily explained by the use of two separate and distinct calculations: the indexed account value and the guaranteed account value.

The indexed account value is based solely on the earnings of the index, and the guaranteed account value is based solely on guaranteed minimum interest rates. Neither calculation crosses over into the other. The indexed account value will grow based only on the indexed earnings, subject to the participation rates, caps, and asset fees. If the index has a down year, the indexed account value just stays constant, meaning it does not grow for the year but it also does not decrease. The guaranteed interest of 3 percent is not applied to the indexed account value.

The guaranteed account value might start at only 80 percent or 90 percent of the premium and earn 3 percent from that figure. An important distinction is that asset fees normally are deducted from only the indexed account value and never from the guaranteed account value. This answers a commonly asked question: "If the guarantee is only 3 percent and the asset fee is 3.5 percent, how can the client earn any interest?" The answer is that these two parts of the indexed annuity do not function together. The asset fee is deductible only against index earnings, not guaranteed interest.

When a policyowner decides to surrender the policy, generally the insurance company determines which of the two account values is the higher. Usually, that is what the client receives, minus any applicable surrender charges. However, note that not all indexed policies will credit guaranteed interest if the client surrenders the policy before the end of the contract term.

Table 8-4 shows a hypothetical indexed annuity with a $100,000 single premium and a 3 percent guaranteed account value based on 100 percent of the premium. If the policy credits guaranteed interest earnings at the end of each policy year, and does not wait until the end of the contract term, the client will receive the higher of column A or column B at surrender. (During years in which the index falls, the indexed account value remains constant and does not decrease.)

TABLE 8-4
Indexed Account Values and Guaranteed Account Values

End of Year	S&P 500 Index Annual Earnings	Indexed Account Value* (Column A)	Guaranteed Account Value Based on 3% on 100% of Premium (Column B)
Year 1	5%	$105,000	$103,000
Year 2	0%	$105,000	$106,090
Year 3	–2.0%	$105,000	$109,273
Year 4	4.0%	$109,200	$112,551
Year 5	8.0%	$117,936	$115,928
Year 6	6.0%	$125,012	$119,406
Year 7	2.0%	$127,512	$122,988
Year 8	–2.0%	$127,512	$126,678
Year 9	4.0%	$132,612	$130,478
Year 10	–1.0%	$132,612	$134,392

*After the participation rate, cap, and asset fees have been applied

Withdrawals and Surrenders

Indexed annuity surrender charges are more complicated than those for fixed-interest deferred annuities. The free withdrawal corridors are also more complicated. Depending on how the interest is calculated, both potential interest from the underlying guarantee and index-calculated interest can be forfeited. In addition, surrender charges are typically higher than in fixed-interest deferred annuities—up to 17 percent in the first year—and last longer, ranging from 7 to 16 years; 12 years is typical. The variety of surrender charges makes the decision to purchase more difficult for the client and the advisor.

If, at the time of purchase, a client's time horizon for taking money out of the annuity (in excess of the free corridor) is shorter than the surrender charge period, the product by definition is unsuitable. However, life events can happen after purchase that unexpectedly cause people to withdraw money from their contracts. It is for this reason that companies provide a free corridor and waivers of the surrender charge for nursing home stays, terminal illness, and even unemployment in some cases.

The good news about surrender charges is that they allow insurance companies to pay a higher rate of interest than they would be able to pay if people could freely withdraw from their contracts. The existence of the surrender charge allows the insurance company to invest in longer-duration, higher-interest-paying bonds to provide better returns. Just as is typical in certificates of deposit, the longer the restricted period, the higher the interest.

Death Benefits

Death benefit provisions in equity-indexed annuity contracts have some similarities to those of declared-rate fixed-interest deferred annuities, but there also are some differences. In some equity-indexed annuities, the death benefit will be the greater of the guaranteed account value or the indexed account value. In others, it will be the return of premium or the return of premium plus a minimum interest rate, regardless of index interest growth. In a very few situations, it will be the guaranteed account value only.

The second aspect of death benefits has to do with equity-indexed annuities that pay the indexed account value at death. In these contracts, the interest rate calculation method used by the particular equity-indexed annuity can affect how much index interest there is. When looking at an equity-indexed annuity that credits the total index interest rate, it is important to know how that total interest rate is determined at the time of death. Sometimes the index level at the time of death is used; at other times, the calculation is based on the value at the last anniversary of the policy. This difference can cause great variations under certain economic conditions that may affect the index being used. It is also important to know whether a pro rata portion of the participation rate or asset fees is applied if interest is calculated as of the date of death.

There are many considerations to look at regarding death benefits. Clients and their families must have a clear understanding of what the death benefit will be at any given time. It is critical that you communicate as clearly as possible how the death benefit in an equity-indexed annuity is calculated so that your clients readily understand it.

Annuitization

Some equity-indexed annuities provide full access to the indexed account value and also waive surrender charges during the index period if the account values are annuitized. If there is not full access and waiver of surrender charges, there is often a minimum length of time that must pass before annuitization is permitted. Typically, this is the first few contract years. In many cases, there is also a minimum time period over which the values are to be paid out. These provisions tend to work similarly to their counterparts in fixed-interest deferred annuities. Clients should carefully explore contractual options and limitations on annuitization when considering various equity-indexed annuities.

Generally, account values may be distributed over a period of years or for the life of the annuitant either on a single-life or joint-life basis. There are various payment options available if annuitization is chosen. These life income options and the tax advantages of annuitization are discussed in chapter 9.

VARIABLE DEFERRED ANNUITIES

Variable deferred annuities are contractually similar to fixed-interest deferred annuities. They have the same policy forms, general provisions, and nonforfeiture rights. The settlement options and option tables, actuarial principles, and mortality and expense assumptions are the same. Variable deferred annuities are subject to similar income tax treatment. The major difference between the variable deferred annuity and fixed-interest deferred annuity is the underlying investment vehicle.

Variable deferred annuities typically offer two major categories of investment selection: a general account and a separate account. The general account selection provides a guarantee of principal and interest. The separate account offers an array of diversified subaccounts that operate in a manner similar to mutual funds.

Unlike fixed-interest deferred annuities, variable deferred annuities are considered securities and are registered products. They may be sold only by salespeople who are properly licensed by the state and are registered representatives with the National Association of Securities Dealers (NASD). Any potential buyer of a variable deferred annuity must be given a

prospectus

prospectus, (a document that provides the complete details of the product including its investment features, options, fees, other costs, death benefits, and payout options).

A major difference between variable deferred annuities and fixed-interest deferred annuities is which party to the annuity policy assumes the investment risk. With the fixed-interest deferred annuity, the insurance company declares in advance what level of interest will be credited to the annuity policy for the year. If the insurance company declares that it will pay 5.5 percent interest for the year, the company will need to earn at least 7.5 percent on its invested assets to cover both the promised interest of 5.5 percent plus its profit spread of 2 percent.

On the other hand, with a variable deferred annuity, the investment risk lies with the policyowner, not the insurance company. The policyowner chooses the investment options into which his or her premiums are allocated. The insurance company does not promise any returns except, of course, the minimum interest rate guarantee on assets within the general account. Therefore, how the subaccounts perform is a risk to the policyowner, not the insurance company.

Because the investment responsibility lies with the policyowner, insurance companies generally provide the following investment features and benefits to assist policyowners with their investment responsibilities:

- professional money management, as with mutual funds
- an array of subaccount choices that offer the opportunity for investment diversification among companies of various sizes and investment management styles
- economy of investing and reasonableness of asset-based fees
- flexibility to make deposits at the contract owner's convenience, including the opportunity to dollar cost average with small deposits at minimum expense
- a variety of payout options to match future withdrawals to future needs

Product Design

The features and costs of variable deferred annuities are unique. Many policies have varying features and benefits, as well as special names and terms for the features. It is imperative that both the policyowner and the advisor consult the prospectus and the annuity contract itself for the specific features, costs, and design of the variable deferred annuity policies under consideration.

General Account

general account

The foundation of the typical variable deferred annuity is a *general account,* which guarantees principal and some minimum fixed amount of interest—usually 3 or 4 percent under most state insurance laws. Although efforts are being made to lower the guaranteed interest in newly issued policies, this will have no impact on policies already in force. Most insurance companies did not have difficulty paying more interest than the minimum guarantee while still maintaining their 2 percent margin for profit. During 2003, however, company margins were under pressure from generally low interest rates; this caused some companies to withdraw the general account option.

Other companies use a sliding scale approach to the minimum interest guarantee. This approach gives the company the flexibility to set the minimum guarantee anywhere from 2 percent to 3 percent for newly issued policies.

Separate Account and Subaccounts

separate account
subaccounts

In addition to the general account, a *separate account* is an option for the policyowner. It is composed of various *subaccounts* from which the contract owner can select investment options that match his or her investment objectives and risk tolerance. Contract owners can continually adjust their investment choices as their circumstances change.

The general account offering is spread based, and it is priced within the normal 2 percent spread. The costs of the subaccounts within the separate account are paid for by asset-based fees, much like mutual funds. Because these subaccounts are similar to mutual funds and are priced in the same fashion, the marketplace compares mutual fund costs to variable deferred annuity costs to determine relative value. See the "Mutual Fund versus Variable Deferred Annuity" section in chapter 9 for a discussion of variable annuities compared to mutual funds.

Variable deferred annuity subaccounts offer investment funds from large, medium, and small company common stock accounts. There are a range of professional investment manager styles, from value to growth, including the aggressive, blue-chip, and balanced varieties. These subaccounts also offer quality and high-yield bond funds, zero-coupon bond funds, and Ginnie Mae and real estate accounts. Contract owners have the option of moving among these funds, switching their contributions and accumulations from one fund to the other, and managing the funds in accordance with their particular objectives.

The insurance company then invests premium dollars in the variable annuity policy according to the policyowner's choices. Those choices are in two main categories: the general account, which provides fixed-interest earnings, and the separate account, which is made up of the many various subaccounts.

However, these subaccounts may contain restrictions on the ability to transfer funds, such as limiting the number of transfers from one account to another during a particular time period, or charging a fee for making a transfer from one account to another.

People who fear the stock market can still appreciate the variable annuity. They often put their money into the general account and then just transfer their interest earnings into the subaccounts each month. This strategy ensures that they will have no loss to their principal investment, and they can still participate in the stock market.

Variable Deferred Annuity Accumulation Units

A policyowner purchases accumulation units with the money invested in a variable deferred annuity subaccount. The purchase of an accumulation unit is similar to the purchase of a share in a mutual fund. Money arrives at the insurance company, and the company calculates the value of the account accumulation unit at the "closing price" on the day the money is received or the next business day of the New York Stock Exchange. The money purchases units of the fund based on that unit value. This procedure is referred to as "forward pricing" to distinguish it from the procedure used to purchase stock based on a quoted price prior to the receipt of payment.

Although the number of accumulation units will stay the same for a given amount of premium paid by the policyowner, the value of the units will vary depending on the investment performance of the underlying subaccount.

Example:	A client purchases a variable annuity with a $30,000 single premium and receives 3,000 units. The cost of each unit is $10 ($30,000/3,000). The client allocates 50 percent of his premium to the fixed-income subaccount and 50 percent to the large-cap subaccount. If the fixed-income subaccount grows by 6 percent ($15,000 x 1.06 = $15,900) and the large-cap account fund grows by 15 percent ($15,000 x 1.15 = $17,250), the account value is then worth $33,150 ($15,900 + $17,250). However, the annuity owner still has 3,000 units. Each unit has now increased in value to $11.05 ($33,150/3,000).

A hypothetical accumulation is shown in table 8-5. In this example, the initial purchase is made at age 35 with a premium high enough to cover a $200 purchase of units each month after paying insurer expenses. The assumptions behind the table 8-5 numbers are that the accumulation units change value once each year and that a full $200 is available each month to acquire more units. The units in this example grow at approximately 7.5 percent in most years but fluctuate more or less than that in other years as stock prices are prone to do over short intervals. In this case, there is an accumulation of $258,459.62 at the end of the 30th year (end of age 64 or beginning of age 65) consisting of 31,751.80 accumulation units.

Morningstar publishes its *Principia Pro* for variable annuity subaccounts. This service provides information about the performance, features, and expenses of mutual funds and variable annuities. In mid-2003, its database consisted of more than 15,110 mutual funds and 19,368 subaccounts in variable annuities. Financial advisors can use Morningstar data

TABLE 8-5
Variable Annuity Accumulation Units
Deferred Annuity Purchased at Age 35 at $200 per Month

Year	Age	Unit Value	New Units	Total Units	Total Value
1	35	$ 1.00	2,400.00	2,400.00	$ 2,400.00
2	36	1.08	2,232.56	4,632.56	4,980.00
3	37	1.16	2,076.80	6,709.36	7,753.50
4	38	1.24	1,931.91	8,641.26	10,735.01
5	39	1.34	1,797.12	10,438.38	13,940.14
6	40	1.07	2,242.99	12,681.37	13,569.07
7	41	1.15	2,086.50	14,767.88	16,986.75
8	42	1.24	1,940.93	16,708.81	20,660.76
9	43	1.88	1,276.60	17,985.41	33,812.56
10	44	2.12	1,132.08	19,117.48	40,529.06
11	45	2.28	1,053.09	20,170.57	45,968.74
12	46	2.45	979.62	21,150.20	51,816.39
13	47	2.63	911.28	22,061.47	58,102.62
14	48	2.83	847.70	22,909.17	64,860.32
15	49	3.04	788.56	23,697.73	72,124.84
16	50	3.27	733.54	24,431.27	79,934.21
17	51	3.52	682.36	25,113.63	88,329.27
18	52	3.78	634.76	25,748.39	97,353.97
19	53	3.50	685.71	26,434.10	92,519.37
20	54	3.25	738.46	27,172.57	88,310.84
21	55	3.00	800.00	27,972.56	83,917.70
22	56	3.60	666.67	28,639.23	103,101.24
23	57	4.01	598.50	29,237.74	117,243.32
24	58	4.97	482.90	29,720.63	147,711.55
25	59	5.76	416.67	30,137.70	173,590.85
26	60	6.25	384.00	30,521.30	190,758.13
27	61	7.16	335.20	30,856.50	220,932.51
28	62	7.90	303.80	31,160.29	246,166.32
29	63	8.09	296.66	31,456.96	254,486.78
30	64	8.14	294.84	31,751.80	258,459.62

to evaluate the costs of annuity contracts, including the costs of the sub-accounts inside variable deferred annuities. Advisors can also use the Morningstar data on mutual funds to compare the costs of mutual funds to annuities. Morningstar can be located on the Web at www.morningstar.com.

Annuity Units

annuity units

At the beginning of the liquidation period, the accumulation units are exchanged for *annuity units.* The number of annuity units that the annuitant will acquire depends on the company's assumptions as to mortality, dividend rates, and expenses as well as the market value of the assets underlying the annuity units. In essence, the number of annuity units is determined by dividing the dollar value of the accumulation units ($258,459.62 in our example) by the present value of a life annuity at the participant's attained age in an amount equal to the current value of one annuity unit (assumed to be $35 in this case). Although the number of accumulation units of a particular person increases with each premium payment and each allocation of dividends, the number of annuity units remains constant throughout the liquidation period (7,384.6 annuity units in this case). The units are revalued each year, however, reflecting the current market price of the common stock, and the mortality, investment, and expense experience for the preceding year.[7] The dollar income payable to the annuitant each month is determined by multiplying the number of annuity units by the current value of each unit. During the annuitization—or liquidation—period, the higher the market price of the stock and the greater the dividends, the greater the annuitant's dollar income. During the accumulation stage, however, it is to the annuitant's advantage for stock prices to be relatively low because he or she will thus be able to acquire a larger number of accumulation units for each premium payment.

Distributions

When it is time to begin the distribution phase of the variable annuity, the contract owner must decide which portion of the payment he or she wishes to receive, respectively, from the separate account and from the general account.

General Account Annuity Payout. The owner of the contract may transfer all or part of the value of the contract to the general account and elect to take one of the payout options available under the contract. Funds annuitized from the general account produce a guaranteed income that will not change from period to period.

Separate Account Annuity Payout. The contract owner may transfer all or part of the value of the contract to one or more of the subaccounts that are available in the separate account. Funds annuitized from the separate account produce an income that changes from period to period based on the performance of the subaccount in which the funds are placed.

Investment Features

Professional Management

Although registered representatives typically select just one or two mutual fund families when managing client funds in their taxable portfolios, insurance companies usually select a number of money managers other than the insurer itself for their annuity policies. It is not unusual for a variable annuity contract to have proprietary or insurance-issuer managed subaccounts and 15 or more outside money managers. Early in the development of variable annuity contracts, all subaccounts were managed by the issuing insurance company. Many competitors, however, disparaged this proprietary management, claiming that insurance companies could not manage money as well as "professional" money managers. Because perception is often more important than reality, companies began to hire professional money managers. Initially, insurers hired only highly visible money managers. This strategy of hiring a well-known money manager created favorable publicity and enhanced credibility for their variable annuity contracts; it also attracted investment capital.

In the 1990s, insurance companies were doing what most people were doing—chasing last year's performance numbers—which resulted in a high number of large capitalization growth fund managers. As insurers learned that this strategy was counterproductive to wealth retention, the public's respect for diversification returned. Insurance companies now hire and fire managers based on their performance and competency. Companies want to provide variable annuities that offer credible investments within the equity categories of large, medium, and small companies (both domestic and international) and growth, value, and blend styles of management, adding real estate investment trusts and even hedge funds if they enhance diversification. Insurers also draw bond managers with experience managing quality to high-yield portfolios as well as short to long duration, in addition to money market and guaranteed-interest, guaranteed-principal bond accounts.

Tax-Free Transfers among Subaccounts

Some accounts may contain restrictions on the contract owner's ability to transfer funds. There can be limitations on the number of transfers that can be made during a particular time period or charges for making transfers from subaccount to subaccount. People's risk tolerance does change, depending on what is going on in their lives and what is going on in the markets. The ability to put money into a guaranteed-interest account can, at times, be a valuable and comforting alternative and protect some or all of the money in a variable contract from downside risk. The subaccounts have all of the upside and downside risk of their respective asset classes.

Diversification is essential to and possibly the single most important tool for managing risk. In effect, diversification means that the investor does not put all of his or her money into one investment. Instead, he or she invests across asset categories to take advantage of the relationships among investments and to minimize risk. Diversification works because different investments tend to have highly opposite fluctuation sensitivities.

The transfer of funds within a variable deferred annuity contract will not trigger taxable income to the policyowner. The variable annuity may, however, charge a fee for transfers among subaccounts, depending on the policy. The ability to transfer funds among subaccounts enables policyowners to adjust the investments within the policy to meet their needs. They may also adopt any of the investment strategies without concerns over tracking their cost basis or triggering taxable gain and, therefore, taxable income.

Most variable annuity contracts do, however, limit transfers that are part of market timing activity that the insurance company considers disruptive to the operation of its investment funds. For example, the company may limit an individual or group of contract owners if it sees repeated transfers in and out of the same investment fund within a period of 5 days. It will also limit the transfer of money out of the principal account to protect itself against policyowners' trying to outinvest the insurance company.

Dollar Cost Averaging

Dollar cost averaging is the consistent investment of equal periodic payments into a diversified equity-based investment over an extended period of time. With variable deferred annuities, this concept means depositing regularly scheduled additional premium payments into a flexible-premium variable deferred annuity. Another example of the dollar cost averaging concept with variable deferred annuities is making a large contribution into the general account and then regularly moving funds into the various subaccounts. Regardless of which approach is used, the point is to invest the same amount on a regularly scheduled basis. With each consistent investment, the number of shares or units purchased will vary with the share price. In some months, the investor will purchase more shares or units than in other months. The goal is to achieve a lower average cost per unit over time than the average price per unit.

Most variable annuity contracts facilitate dollar cost averaging by providing a guaranteed-interest, guaranteed-principal account that usually offers an interest rate that is above current market interest rates. A lump sum of money may be put into this guaranteed-interest account and then directions given to the insurance company to transfer money monthly from that account into client-selected subaccounts.

If this were done in a taxable account, the interest from the interest-bearing account would be taxable, and each purchase would create a cost-basis issue and possible purchase expense, which would have to be tracked until sale. At sale time, any gain or loss would be a taxable event.

The annuity contract eliminates all of this because its cost basis is whatever money the policyowner has put into it. All gain is taxable as ordinary income when withdrawn or surrendered from the annuity contract.

The cost for this feature is built into the basic cost of the annuity contract as part of the mortality and expense cost (see "Mortality and Expense Charges [M&E]" later in this chapter), and in most cases, the contract owner incurs no additional expense.

asset allocation

Asset-Allocation Services

Asset allocation is the process of developing a diversification strategy that allocates premium payments to the various asset classes to build an overall portfolio consistent with the investor's risk tolerance and long-term investment objectives. Properly used, it gives the investor an excellent opportunity to protect assets and to experience consistently favorable overall investment returns.

Most insurance companies offer asset-allocation subaccounts and asset-allocation assistance to registered representatives and their broker-dealers to help policyowners allocate the assets in their annuity policies. Allocation among the subaccounts should be accomplished in a manner that is appropriate to that client's personal investment objectives.

Automatic Rebalancing

Once an asset-allocation plan is decided and the policyowner determines the diversification among the asset classes to be appropriate, it is inevitable that the market will cause the asset-allocation percentages to change and thus necessitate rebalancing. Rebalancing is readjusting the investment portfolio back to the asset-allocation percentages that were originally chosen among subaccounts after growth in them has occurred.

Example:	Suppose a policyowner allocates 60 percent of her premium to a balanced subaccount and 40 percent to the international stock subaccount. The balanced subaccount performs so well that now the ratio between the two accounts is no longer 60%/40% but is 70%/30%. Automatic rebalancing would then sell off enough of the balanced subaccount and put the proceeds into the international subaccount to pull the ratio back to a 60%/40% split.

Rebalancing is selling winning asset classes and repositioning the proceeds in less favorable categories. Some investors like this strategy. Many investors find it to be counterproductive in taxable portfolios, however, because it can create current expenses and taxes. Most investors also find rebalancing difficult to do because they hate selling winners and buying losers even if they know intellectually that selling high and buying low makes sense.

Many variable deferred annuities offer automatic rebalancing, which makes it easy for the investor. Once the investor decides on the appropriate strategy, all he or she has to do is identify the subaccounts to use, determine the percentages of the total to be allocated to each, and tell the insurance company at what interval to rebalance the accounts.

Charges and Expenses

One aspect of the variable deferred annuity that sets it apart from the fixed-interest deferred annuity is the fee structure. Although a fixed-interest annuity may assess a nominal yearly fee against the accumulation value, variable deferred annuities have a much more complex fee and expense structure. The detailed fee structure of the variable deferred annuity arises from its sophisticated investment structure. Charges, fees, and expenses are outlined in the variable deferred annuity prospectus.

Front-End and Back-End Loads

Among approximately 600 variable deferred annuity contracts that can be found in the Morningstar database, only 13 annuities charge a front-end load. Of those 13, only two also charge a back-end load. One of these funds charges 6 percent on incoming money and 6 percent for 6 years on outgoing money. The other fund charges 8.5 percent on incoming money and 8 percent for 8 years on outgoing money.

front-end load

The *front-end load* is deducted as a percentage from money coming into the contract. Front-end loads range from a high of 8.5 percent to a low of 2.5 percent; 5.75 percent is typical. The front-end load is often seen as a disadvantage to the client because less of the contract owner's money is put to work in the contract.

back-end load

The *back-end load* is also called a surrender charge or contingent deferred sales charge. This charge is assessed at the time of a withdrawal from a variable deferred annuity as a percentage of the amount withdrawn, according to a contractually defined schedule. Nearly every variable deferred annuity policy has surrender charges. These policies have surrender charge periods, surrender charge schedules, and free-corridor amounts just like fixed-interest deferred annuities.

When the variable deferred annuity is sold as an individual contract, surrender privileges are made available but on a more restricted basis than in connection with ordinary annuities. When the variable deferred annuity is used as part of a pension plan, surrender values are generally not made available.

Annual Contract Charges

annual contract charges

Annual contract charges are designed to offset some of the insurance company's administrative costs for servicing these contracts. Charges range from $10 to $50, with an average of about $30 per year. There are 25 contracts that list no annual contract charge. Most of the rest of the contracts waive this administrative charge for contracts with fund values above some minimum amount, such as $10,000 or $20,000. Administrative charges, which are applied as specific dollar amounts, are not a major consideration in most contracts.

A very small number of policies, however, may impose an administrative charge as a percentage of funds in the contract. This type of charge can be more significant and costly than the flat annual fee noted above. Both financial advisors and their clients must be aware that some contracts do impose these asset-based administrative charges, and thus they should make sure that such charges do not make the total expense ratio (see "Total Expense Ratio" below) for the contract unacceptable.

Mortality and Expense Charges (M&E)

mortality and expense charges (M&E)

Insurance expenses, often referred to as *mortality and expense charges (M&E),* are asset-based charges against the investment subaccounts in a variable deferred annuity. The insurance company assesses these charges to cover its costs for the guarantees it provides (such as a minimum guaranteed interest rate in the general account) and for the guaranteed annuity factors for annuitization calculations. These charges also cover the guarantee that, in the event of death, the beneficiary will receive the greater of the deposits made into the contract or the account value—a protection against adverse investment results.

Typically, the M&E is the same percentage charge in all subaccounts within a variable annuity contract. In some contracts, however, M&E charges vary according to which subaccounts the policyowner has chosen. This M&E method is called layered or multiple.

Note that the M&E is not charged against the guaranteed-interest account. All charges in that account are taken from the spread between what the insurance company expects to earn on the contract owner's money and what it pays out to the contract owner. The guaranteed-interest account typically specifies the net amount of interest it pays the contract owner. To the extent that funds raised by the M&E are not needed to provide for these minimum guarantees, they serve as a source of profit to the insurance company.

The average annual M&E in variable deferred annuity subaccounts as tracked in Morningstar's *Principia Pro* for VA/VL (variable annuity/variable life) subaccounts as of 2003 is 1.3 percent, and it ranges from 0 percent to 2.1 percent.

Fund Expense

fund expense

The *fund expense* is an asset-based fee for management operations of the various subaccounts. It is the expense charged against the subaccounts for paying the fund managers and the fund's operating expenses. The fund expense may not include the brokerage costs.

As a percentage of assets under management, the fund expenses are expected to go down as a fund gets bigger and gains some economies of scale. However, this is not always the case. Fund expenses do change, and clients need to realize that an increasing expense ratio will lower their return.

The average annual fund expense in variable deferred annuity subaccounts, as tracked in Morningstar's *Principia Pro* for VA/VL subaccounts as of 2003 is .974 percent, and it ranges from 0 percent to 6.15 percent.

A number of companies seem to be reporting fund expense ratios of zero. This does not mean that they are providing fund management for free but that they are lumping all of their asset-based charges into the M&E. As a result, the most meaningful number for comparison purposes may be the total expense ratio.

Total Expense Ratio

total expense ratio

The *total expense ratio* combines both the M&E and the fund expense; it is commonly used to compare the expenses for variable deferred annuities to those for regular mutual funds. The average total annual expense ratio in the 19,386 variable deferred annuity subaccounts as tracked in Morningstar's *Principia Pro* for VA/VL subaccounts as of 2003 is 2.31 percent, and it ranges from 0.33 percent to 8.99 percent.

The average annual asset-based charge in a mutual fund is 1.45 percent. Compare that to the average asset-based charge in a variable deferred annuity of 2.31 percent. The extra cost to manage assets inside, rather than outside, a variable annuity contract is about .86 percent (2.31 percent – 1.45 percent), or about $86 extra per year per $100,000 of invested assets. However, if a client is making a selection among the 621 variable annuity contracts, as opposed to a specific mutual fund family, a direct comparison of actual costs is a much better way to make a choice than relying on averages.

Guaranteed Living Benefits

When applying for a variable deferred annuity, the contract owner can purchase additional benefits that will provide protection against market losses while both the contract owner and the annuitant are living. Companies impose a conservative charge for these benefits, which is designed to cover the risk and provide a margin of profit.

Guaranteed Minimum Income Benefit

guaranteed minimum income benefit

The *guaranteed minimum income benefit* increases the contract owner's investment in a variable deferred annuity by some compounded percentage amount—typically between 3 percent and 6 percent. After a period of time, such as 7 to 10 years, this increased amount may be used on any contract anniversary to change the contract to an immediate annuity using guaranteed annuity factors. Basically, by purchasing this benefit, the policyowner is making sure he or she will receive a minimum level of income, regardless of how much money was actually in the account value at the time of annuitization.

Guaranteed Minimum Return of Premium Benefit

guaranteed minimum return of premium benefit

This *guaranteed minimum return of premium benefit* guarantees that contract owners may take back their premium after a specified number of years if the investment is more than the variable deferred annuity account value. When this benefit is offered, it can be costly, depending on its design. For example, after 10 years, a contract owner can immediately withdraw his or her premium of $50,000 even if the account value is only $43,000. This is possible even if during those 10 years, the owner has been able to pick and choose and transfer among the equity accounts.

Guaranteed Minimum Accumulation Benefit

guaranteed minimum accumulation benefit (GMAB)

The *guaranteed minimum accumulation benefit (GMAB)* guarantees the contract owner that the value will be at least equal to a certain minimum amount after a specified number of years. The GMAB is a guarantee that the value of the variable deferred annuity account can be stepped up to a certain amount on a specified date if the actual account value is lower than the guaranteed minimum accumulation amount, whether or not the contract owner annuitizes. Also, at the end of the specified holding period, if the value is higher than the guaranteed accumulation amount, the owner is entitled to walk away with the profits. Many GMABs guarantee a return of premium over a 10-year period. This guarantee eliminates the forced annuitization of the guaranteed minimum income benefit.

To minimize their own risk, some carriers' contracts require buyers to diversify risk into several subaccounts according to prescribed asset-allocation models.

Guaranteed Minimum Withdrawal Benefit

A guaranteed minimum withdrawal benefit (GMWB) guarantees the systematic withdrawal of a certain percentage (usually 5 percent to 7 percent) of premiums annually until premiums are completely recovered, regardless of market performance. This guarantee feature offers distinct tax advantages in that the portion of the guaranteed income stream apportioned to the principal (as opposed to income derived only from investment gains) may be withdrawn tax free. In addition, some carriers offer step-up provisions, enabling the annuity holder to participate in future investment gains.

Guaranteed Payout Annuity Floor

The guaranteed payout annuity floor (GPAF) contract feature guarantees that future annuity payments will never be less than a certain percentage of the first payment (typically 85 percent to 100 percent). In some cases, the GPAF is tied to the stock market. Payments increase as the market goes up, but they can never go lower than the guaranteed floor. GPAFs are often a feature of variable immediate annuities, although they are also found in some variable deferred annuity products with required holding periods before annuitization.

Each insurance company tries to design its own variation of these types of living benefits to be unique and in some cases derive a competitive marketing advantage by obtaining patents for these product innovations.

Guaranteed Death Benefits

The most basic form of death benefit in a variable deferred annuity is payment of the account value upon death. A death benefit equal to the account value will pay whatever the account value happens to be on the date it becomes payable, and it involves no insurance company minimum guarantee or subsidy.

When the death benefit in a variable deferred annuity is equal only to the account value, there is no insurance against a declining account value. This death benefit may be referred to as an accumulated value or account value death benefit. There is no charge for this because it provides no real additional benefit to the contract owner.

It is important that policyowners clearly understand the death benefit provisions in the policy. Some policies pay death benefits when the owner dies; other policies pay death benefits when the annuitant dies. Furthermore, depending on who is the owner and who is the annuitant, the death benefit might not be paid, but instead, the "surrender value" might be forced out as a payment to the policyowner and not the beneficiary. In addition, it is important to understand if the policy allows surrender charges to be deducted from the death proceeds.

With other types of death benefits, the contract owner can request, and pay an additional cost for, a death benefit that provides greater protection. The insurance company offers some minimum guaranteed death benefit at the death of the contract owner or at the death of the annuitant—possibly even both. Because the owner and annuitant are the same individual in most annuity contracts, many people do not concern themselves about whether the death benefit is paid out as a result of the annuitant's death or the owner's death. The minute that one party is the owner and another party is the annuitant, this distinction becomes critical. If the owner has paid extra for an increased death benefit, that owner needs to understand whose death will and will not cause that extra benefit to be paid.

Guaranteed minimum death benefits that provide a death benefit equal to more than the account value come in several basic varieties:

- a guarantee of the return of premium or account value, whichever is greater
- a guarantee of the return of premium plus some amount of interest
- a guarantee of the stepped-up or ratcheted death benefit
- a guarantee of a death benefit that is an extra percentage of the gain in the contract

Account Value or Premiums Paid Death Benefit

The vast majority of variable deferred annuity policies will state that at the owner's or annuitant's death, the death benefit will equal the larger of

- the contract value on the date that the required proof of death is received. (By SEC regulation, contract value is determined on the date that the required proof of death is received.) Note the need to submit the proof of death promptly with this type of contract to guard against market conditions that cause an erosion of value.
- the sum of the net premiums, minus partial withdrawals

This type of guaranteed death benefit is a standard feature in most variable deferred annuities, and it is funded by the M&E.

Example: A policyholder paid $24,000 in premiums into a variable annuity; upon death, the contract value is $52,000. With this type of death benefit in the policy, the death benefit equals the higher of the two amounts, or $52,000.

Rising Floor Death Benefit

rising floor death benefit

The *rising floor death benefit* is a minimum guaranteed death benefit equal to the larger of the variable deferred annuity account value or the premiums paid plus compounding interest. The death benefit will be equal to the larger of

- the contract value on the date the required proof of death is received. Note the need to submit the proof of death promptly in this type of contract to guard against market conditions that cause an erosion of value.
- the sum of the net premiums, minus partial withdrawals, plus interest at a stated percentage from date of issue until the earlier of the annuitant's age 80 or date of death

Death benefits that apply compound interest to the owner's premiums have offered interest rates between 4 percent and 6 percent for premium invested in the equity subaccounts, and interest rates of 3 percent to 4 percent for premium in the quality bond, money market, and guaranteed-interest accounts. This interest rate differential encourages policyowners not only to select equity accounts but also to hold them for the long term.

The annual cost of this death benefit option is between 40 and 50 basis points.

Stepped-up or Ratcheted Death Benefit

stepped-up death benefit

A *stepped-up death benefit* means that the minimum death benefit (total premiums minus withdrawals) will be replaced on the specific policy anniversary dates by the policy value as of that date, if it is higher. Stepped-up dates can occur at every anniversary of the policy up to the annuitant's age 80 or 85. Or the stepped-up dates can occur at intervals anywhere between every second to tenth policy anniversary.

Expect stepped-up death benefits to cost about 20 to 30 basis points of the policy's accumulation value per year. This is less than the rising floor death benefit and beneficial to insurance companies because policyowners must pay for the benefit even during falling markets, when the benefit provides no real value.

Example: Suppose the minimum death benefit for a policy is $40,000, and on the policy anniversary, the death benefit steps up to the account value, which is $47,000. The death benefit remains at $47,000 until the next step-up trigger date in the policy. This feature allows the policyowner to have a higher death benefit, to lock in gains in the account value, and to allow the locked-in gains to be available to the heirs if the policyowner dies during the year.

Some policies offer a death benefit equal to the higher of a stepped-up benefit or the rising floor death benefit. The cost of this combination benefit has increased from about 45 to about 60 basis points.

Increases to Offset Beneficiary Income Taxes

One of the objections to putting money into a deferred annuity has been that death benefits from deferred annuities do not receive a step-up in cost basis. (In deceased persons' estates, the beneficiaries usually receive most types of inherited assets with a cost basis equal to the value of the asset as of the date of death.) Therefore, the beneficiary receives the annuity proceeds with the same cost basis as the policyowner had at death. The beneficiary is liable for income taxes on the gain over the inherited cost basis.

To deal with this objection, insurance companies created a death benefit option that increases the death benefit from 25 percent to 40 percent of the policy gain, which would give the beneficiary enough extra to pay 25 percent to 40 percent income taxes on the gain in the policy. When available, this benefit costs around 35 basis points of the policy's accumulation value per year. The benefit is ineffective when the policy's market value provides no gain.

Example: Assume a policyowner purchases a variable annuity with a $20,000 single premium that grows to $80,000 at the time of death. The policyowner's beneficiary will receive $80,000 from the insurance company, but the beneficiary will have to pay income taxes on $60,000 in taxable income from the gain in the annuity ($80,000 − $20,000).

On the other hand, assume the beneficiary does not inherit an annuity but instead inherits IBM stock worth $80,000. The stock was originally purchased by the deceased for $20,000. The beneficiary inherits $80,000 in stock income tax free and with an $80,000 cost basis. The beneficiary will not have any income taxes to pay.

This difference in taxation to the beneficiary, depending on what kind of asset he or she inherits, led to the creation of the increased death benefit. With the additional death benefit option, the $80,000 annuity might pay $100,000 at death. Assume the benefit in the example above is used to increase the death benefit by one-third of the gain. If the gain is $60,000, one-third of $60,000 is $20,000. The total death benefit, therefore, is increased from $80,000 to $100,000.

If the beneficiary has to pay income tax on $80,000 ($100,000 – $20,000) and assuming a 25 percent income tax bracket, the taxes the beneficiary owes will equal $20,000 ($80,000 x 0.25). The beneficiary receives $100,000 minus $20,000 in taxes, which means a net of $80,000 (the original value of the annuity). Therefore, this benefit is the equivalent of receiving an income-tax-free inheritance.

Withdrawals Affect Death Benefits

Another aspect that policyowners and advisors need to understand about variable deferred annuities is what happens to the death benefit in the policy if the owner takes a withdrawal prior to death. Death benefits are decreased if withdrawals are taken. The issue is how much the decrease is. Generally, decreases are either a dollar-for-dollar reduction or a pro rata reduction.

A dollar-for-dollar reduction of the death benefit is just that: When the policyowner withdraws $10,000 from a variable deferred annuity policy, the death benefit is reduced by $10,000.

The alternative to a dollar-for-dollar reduction is a pro rata reduction. A pro rata reduction causes a decrease in the death benefit equal to the percentage of the withdrawal to the account value.

Example: Suppose a policy started out with a premium of $100,000, but the death benefit has now grown to $300,000 even though the policy value has tumbled back to $100,000. At this point, the policyowner chooses to withdraw $50,000. A dollar-for-dollar reduction would reduce the death benefit to $250,000 ($300,000 – $50,000).

A pro rata reduction, which is determined by the ratio of the withdrawal to the account value ($50,000 over $100,000), would drop the death benefit by 50 percent (0.50 x $300,000) to $150,000.

The difference in the death benefits paid in this example is significant, illustrating the importance of knowing which reduction method is used when a withdrawal is made.

NOTES

1. *The American Heritage Dictionary*, 2d College ed., 1985, Houghton Mifflin Company.
2. *Webster's Third New International Dictionary*, 1971, G&C Merriam Co.

3. Title 26, Internal Revenue Code Sec. 72(u), Letter Ruling 199905015.
4. *2003 Annuity Fact Book*, 2d ed., p. 9, © National Association for Variable Annuities (CAVA).
5. "NAIC Advances Model to Deal with Annuity Interest Rate Squeeze," Jim Connolly, *National Underwriter Life & Health/Financial Services Edition*, vol. 106, no. 50, December 16, 2002, p. 24.
6. Letter Ruling 200307095.
7. More precisely, the value of an annuity unit at the end of each fiscal year is obtained by dividing the current market value of the funds supporting the annuity units by the total number of annuity units expected to be paid over the future lifetimes of all participants then receiving annuity payments, in accordance with the assumptions as to mortality, investment earnings, and expense rates for the future.

9

Annuities—Part II

Richard A. Dulisse

Chapter Outline

INTRODUCTION TO IMMEDIATE ANNUITIES

This section covers the topic most people in the United States think of when they hear the word "annuity"—that is, a series of payments made to the annuity owner over the annuitant's lifetime. Even though the three most popular types of annuities sold today are the fixed-interest deferred, indexed, and variable deferred annuities, the type of annuity that most commonly comes to our minds is the immediate annuity.

People buy an immediate annuity for one of two main reasons: to protect against the risk of running out of income during life or to ensure the receipt of a series of payments for a fixed period of time.

In the payout mode, an annuity can protect against the risk of running out of income during life by lifetime annuitization rather than periodic withdrawals. The economic risk of living too long is a growing concern because our life spans are increasing so rapidly. A generation of preretirees is becoming more concerned with the possibility that their parents may run out of money, or have a severely diminished standard of living, as a result of the dramatic increases in the cost of living during their retirement years. Many people who retired with Social Security and pension income felt much more secure the day they retired than they do now. With 20-20 hindsight, we can see that they might have been better off than they are today if they had used a portion of their money to purchase an immediate annuity. As retirees quickly learn, it is not the size of one's net worth that makes a person rich; it is the amount of replaceable, steady, guaranteed income that arrives every month. We must all keep in mind that one of the most devastating risks we face is outliving our income.

Individuals have a choice between fixed and variable immediate annuities. The basic contract structures of both are similar. Fixed immediate annuities generally provide level guaranteed payments. However, a variable immediate annuity provides fluctuating income payments, and this fluctuation makes its use more limited than a fixed immediate annuity. The variable immediate annuity purchaser is concerned with the long-term effects of inflation on a fixed income and is willing to accept volatility of income, both up and down, in the hope that the income stream over the long term will offset the effects of inflation. Therefore, variable immediate annuities are primarily life-contingent contracts, while fixed immediate annuities have many fixed-amount and fixed-period, as well as life-contingent, applications. To distinguish between fixed and variable immediate annuities throughout this chapter, we will refer to "fixed" immediate annuities as immediate annuities and refer to variable immediate annuities as variable immediate annuities. First, we will discuss fixed immediate annuities.

TYPES OF IMMEDIATE ANNUITIES

An individual can purchase an immediate annuity by giving an amount of money to the insurance company; the company will begin to make periodic payments in accordance with the contract owner's instructions. To be classified as an immediate annuity, payments must begin within a period of time, usually ranging from one month after deposit to no longer than one year after deposit. Income is typically paid to the policyowner, but some contracts may specify that income will be paid to the annuitant.

Purchasers of immediate annuities generally have the funds originate from one of two sources. The first, and more common, source is a lump sum of money that the annuity purchaser has obtained from other investments like certificates of deposit, a recent inheritance, or the sale of an asset. Purchasers bring their lump sums to the insurance company in exchange for a series of payments made back to the annuity owner.

The second source of funds for the immediate annuity originates when the owner of either a life insurance policy or a deferred annuity policy wants to "annuitize" policy cash values. The insurance company will take the policy values and exchange them for a series of payments it will make over time for the policyowner. If the original policy is a life insurance policy, the life policy is then terminated and a new contract is established (an immediate annuity contract). If the original policy is a deferred annuity, it is also normally terminated in exchange for the immediate annuity contract. In either of these two situations, the annuity may be called a "settlement option" instead of an immediate annuity. Both terms mean the same thing. The settlement option is distinguishable because, as its name suggests, the funds to purchase the immediate annuity come from an underlying annuity or life insurance policy already established at that insurance company. At present, however, it has been reported that less than one percent of annuity owners ever annuitize their policies. The other 99 percent merely ask for periodic or nonperiodic withdrawals from their deferred annuity cash values on an as-needed basis.

Non-Life-Contingent Immediate Annuities

The payment of either the fixed-period or fixed-amount immediate annuity is issued to the annuity owner in a level dollar amount for the duration of the payout period. The payout period is determined by the contract owner, who requests either the period of time during which the checks are distributed or the specific amount and interval of each check.

Fixed Period

fixed-period annuity

With a *fixed-period annuity,* the purchaser pays a premium and selects the period of time the insurance company is to make the periodic payments. The company calculates the payment amount and informs the client what that amount will be. The period chosen could be as little as 2 months or as long as desired (payments must satisfy the company's minimum payment rules—for example, no less than $20 per payment). This is not a life-contingent option, which means that whether the annuitant lives beyond or dies during the distribution period, payments continue to the annuitant or the annuitant's beneficiary, respectively, until the end of the distribution period.

Fixed Amount

fixed-amount annuity

With a *fixed-amount annuity,* the purchaser pays a premium and selects the periodic payment amount the insurance company is to pay. The company informs the purchaser how long it will be able to pay the stipulated amount. Like the fixed-period option, this is not a life-contingent option, which makes it useful for distributing lump sums over time in situations when lifetime payments are not needed or when there is a shortened life expectancy for the annuitant. If the annuitant dies before the funds in the annuity have been paid, the remainder is generally paid to the annuitant's beneficiary.

Life-Contingent Immediate Annuities

The immediate annuity is like an insurance policy that protects annuitants from the economic consequences of living too long. Just as buying any insurance creates a pool of money from which claims can be paid to those who experience losses, life-contingent annuities pay the claims of those who live exceedingly long lives.

The typical reason for the purchase of an immediate life annuity is the concern that the annuity owner's money will be exhausted before he or she dies. The solution is to purchase an annuity with payments based on the annuitant's life or on the lives of the annuitant and spouse.

Life-contingent annuities can be purchased by targeting either (1) an amount of income desired or (2) the amount available to invest. For example, an annuity buyer might say to the financial advisor, "How much would it cost for me to receive a $5,000 check each year for my lifetime?" Or "I have $30,000 to purchase a lifetime annuity. How much income will this provide me each year?"

For the insurance company to provide a quote, it needs to know the date of birth and gender of the annuitant or annuitants.

Life Annuity (Straight Life/Life Only)

life-only annuity

A life annuity, commonly called a straight life annuity or *life-only annuity,* is the least expensive type of life-contingent annuity. It provides the largest possible payment for a given deposit. It is low in cost because there is a high risk of loss of money. The risk in a life annuity is that if the annuitant dies prior to the time that an amount equal to the original deposit in the annuity has been repaid to the annuitant, the balance of the deposit is forfeited to the insurance company. Thus, at the annuitant's death, the annuity payments cease, regardless of how many payments have been made since the annuity contract was issued. This would occur even if only one check had been paid prior to death. The reason for this forfeiture is that there is no beneficiary in a straight life annuity.

Most buyers of immediate annuities consider that the possibility of losing all their money after receiving only one annuity check is too great a risk. They want more safety and assurance that the payout stream will continue in some fashion in the event of an early death. To ensure some degree of safety, the following five immediate annuity payout options are available in addition to the life-only option:

- life with period certain
- life with installment or cash refund
- joint and survivor life annuity
- joint and survivor life annuity with period certain
- joint and survivor life annuity with installment or cash refund

We will first discuss the individual annuity payout options, followed by payout options for joint and survivor life annuities.

Life-Contingent Individual Annuity with Payment Guarantees

Life with Period Certain (5, 10, 15, 20, 25, and 30 Years)

life annuity with period certain

Life annuity with period certain is a life-contingent annuity in which the purchaser requests that if the annuitant's death occurs before a certain number of years have passed, payments are to continue until they reach the end of the specified period. Payments continue for life, however, if the annuitant survives longer than the specified period. Choosing this type of annuity ensures the purchaser that someone other than the insurance company, such as a named beneficiary, will benefit if the annuitant dies early.

Life Annuity with Installment or Cash Refund

life annuity with installment refund

life annuity with cash refund

This life-contingent annuity assures the purchaser that if the annuitant dies prior to payout of a total dollar amount that is equivalent to the contract's initial deposit, installment payments will continue until a full refund of the deposit has been paid. This is known *as life annuity with installment refund.* If cash refund is the option selected, the payment is likely to be a lump sum equal to the discounted present value of the beneficiary's remaining payments. This is known as *life annuity with cash refund.*

Joint and Survivor Life Annuities

Joint and Survivor Life Annuity

joint and survivor life annuity

A *joint and survivor life annuity* pays income for the lives of two individuals. After the death of the first annuitant, the insurance company continues to make full payments until the death of the second annuitant. Variations of this form of payout can provide for higher payments while both annuitants are living with reduced income payments of, for example, 75 percent, 66 percent, or 50 percent to the survivor. Some insurance companies offer joint life annuities for more than two lives.

Joint and Survivor Life Annuity with Period Certain

joint and survivor life annuity with period certain

The *joint and survivor life annuity with period certain* protects against the early termination of payments if both of the annuitants die early. The insurance company is instructed to continue payments until the death of the last to die, with a guaranteed minimum payout period, generally 5, 10, 15, 20, 25, or 30 years.

Joint and Survivor Life Annuity with Installment or Cash Refund

joint and survivor life annuity with installment or cash refund

The *joint and survivor life annuity with installment or cash refund* protects against the early termination of payments due to the death of both or all annuitants. Under the installment refund option, the insurance company is instructed to refund the remaining balance of the deposit by continuing payments to the named beneficiary after the death of all annuitants until the full deposit is returned. If the cash refund option is selected, the lump-sum payout will be the discounted present value of the remaining payments.

Annuitization and Exclusion Ratios

exclusion ratio

Once an annuity owner decides to use an annuity to provide a guaranteed income stream, the insurance company will give the owner the guaranteed dollar amount of the payments. In addition, the insurance company will provide the owner with an *exclusion ratio.* The exclusion ratio is the percentage of each payment that is receivable on an income-tax-free basis. The remaining amount of each payment is subject to ordinary income taxes.

expected return

The purpose of the exclusion ratio is to allow the policyowner to receive back over time the amount of premium dollars he or she paid in. The premium is returned in the form of payments without being subject to income tax. The exclusion ratio is determined by dividing the total investment in the annuity by the *expected return.* In other words, it is roughly equivalent to the premiums paid divided by the amount of income the annuitant should receive back over the specific period of time.

$$\frac{\text{Total investment}}{\text{Expected return}} = \text{Exclusion ratio}$$

Fixed-Period, Fixed-Amount, and Straight Life Annuities

With fixed-period or fixed-amount annuities, the expected return is the sum of the guaranteed payments. With life expectancy annuities, it is the number of years until the annuitant reaches his or life expectancy multiplied by the annual payment.

Life expectancies are found in IRS Annuity Tables, contained in IRS Publication 939, which is available on the Internet at www.irs.gov. Single life expectancy tables are listed in Tables I and V. Joint and survivor life expectancies are listed in Tables II, IIA, VI and VIA. Sex-distinct life expectancies are listed in Tables I through IV. These tables apply if investments in the annuities were made before June 30, 1986. Unisex life expectancies are listed in Tables V through VIII. Unisex tables are applicable to investments made after June 30, 1986.

Example: Sharon buys an immediate annuity from an insurance company. Her total investment is $119,714.16. She will receive $12,000 per year paid in monthly installments of $1,000 for the rest of her life. Sharon is aged 72, and her life expectancy is 14.6 years according to Table V.

The exclusion ratio for her payment is 68.3 percent. This means that 68.3 percent, or $683.00, of each $1,000 monthly payment is income tax free to Sharon.

$$\frac{\$119,714.16}{\$12,000 \times 14.6} = \frac{\$119,714.16}{\$175,200} = 68.3\%$$

$$\$12,000 \times .683 = \$8,196$$

The balance, $3,804 ($12,000 − $8,196 = $3,804), will be taxed to her as ordinary income. The insurance company gives Sharon the income tax information (IRS Form 1099) at the end of each year so she can account for the income on her annual tax return.

TABLE V—Ordinary Life Annuities—One Life— Expected Return Multiple (IRS)	
Age	Multiple
70	16.0
71	15.3
72	**14.6**
73	13.9
74	13.2
75	12.5

The exclusion ratio will remain constant each year until Sharon reaches her life expectancy. At that point she has recovered her investment in the contract. Once she reaches her life expectancy, the full $1,000 monthly payment will be taxable to her as ordinary income and the exclusion ratio will no longer be applicable. This rule applies to annuities purchased after December 31, 1986.

Policies issued before January 1, 1987, do not lose the exclusion ratio once the annuitant reaches life expectancy. Therefore, those annuitants can receive partially tax-free income for their entire lives.

Life Annuity with Refund or Period Certain Guarantee

The computation above is for a straight life annuity (without refund or period-certain guarantee). The exclusion ratio for a single life refund or period-certain guarantee is determined in the same way, but the investment in the contract must first be adjusted by subtracting the actuarial value of the refund or period-certain guarantee.

Thus, the formula for calculating the exclusion ratio for a life annuity with a refund or period certain guarantee would appear as:

$$\frac{\text{Total investment} - \text{Value of refund or period-certain}}{\text{Expected return}} = \text{Exclusion ratio}$$

The actuarial value of the refund or period-certain guarantee is computed by the following steps:

1. Determine the duration of the guaranteed amount (number of years necessary for the total guaranteed return to be fully paid). In the case of a period-certain life annuity, the duration of the guaranteed amount, in years, is known (for example, 10, 15, or 20 "years certain"). To find the duration of the guaranteed amount, in years, for a cash or installment refund life annuity, divide the total guaranteed amount by the amount of one year's annuity payments, and round the quotient to the nearest whole number of years.

2. Find the factor in Table III or VII (whichever is applicable, depending when the investment is made in the contract) under the whole number of years (as determined in step one) and the age and (if applicable) the sex of the annuitant. This factor is the percentage value of the refund or period-certain guarantee.

3. Apply the applicable Table III or Table VII percentage to the SMALLER of (a) the investment in the contract or (b) the total guaranteed return under the contract. The result is the present value of the refund or period-certain guarantee.

4. Subtract the present value of the refund or period-certain guarantee from the investment in the contract. The remainder is the adjusted investment in the contract to be used in the exclusion ratio. (See Treas. Reg. §1.72-7(b).)

We will illustrate the purchase of an installment refund annuity only, to describe how the steps in the computation are applied. The steps in the computation that apply to a period-certain annuity are very similar.

Example: If Sharon in the example shown above purchases an installment refund annuity in 2005 for $119,714.16 that pays her $900 per month, her investment in the contract is adjusted for the purpose of determining the exclusion ratio as follows:

1.	Unadjusted investment in the contract	$119,714.16
	Amount to be received annually	$ 10,800
	Duration of guaranteed period ($119,714.16 ÷ $10,800)	11.08 yrs.
	Rounded to the nearest whole number of years	11
2.	Percentage value of guaranteed refund (Table VII for age 72 and 11 yrs.)	15%

3. Value of refund feature (rounded
   to nearest dollar)
   (15% of $119,741.16) $17,957
4. Adjusted investment in the contract
   ($119,714 – $17,957) $101,757

TABLE VII—Present Value of Refund Features Duration of Guaranteed Amount (IRS)				
Age	Years			
Unisex	1	6	11	16
70	1%	7%	12%	20%
71	1	8	13	22
72	1	8	15	24
73	1	9	16	26
74	1	10	18	28
75	1	11	19	31

Once the investment in the contract has been adjusted by subtracting the value of the refund (or period-certain guarantee), an exclusion ratio is determined in the same way as for a straight life annuity. That is, expected return is computed; then the adjusted investment in the contract is divided by the expected return.

Continuing the refund annuity example for Sharon above:

Investment in the contract (adjusted for
   refund guarantee) $101,757
One year's guaranteed annuity payments
   (12 x $900) $10,800
Life expectancy from Table V for a
   post-1986 annuity for a 72-year old   14.6 years
Expected return (14.6 x $10,800) $157,680
Exclusion ratio ($101,757 ÷ $157,680)   64.6%
Amount excludible from income each year
   (annualized) (64.6% of $10,800)* $6,976.80
Amount includible in gross income
   ($10,800 – $6,976.80) $3,823.20

---

* Since the annuity starting date is after December 31, 1986, the total amount excludible is limited to the investment in the contract; after that has been recovered, the remaining amounts received are includible in income.

However, if the annuity has a refund or guaranteed feature, the value of the refund or guarantee feature is not subtracted when calculating the unrecovered investment (IRC Sec. 72(b)(4)). Therefore, the annuity exclusion ratio would apply to each of Sharon's payments for this refund annuity contract until her tax-free payments exceed a total of $119,714.

Variable Immediate Annuities

Variable immediate annuities (discussed in detail later in this chapter) do not necessarily have an expected return because the dollar amount of the income benefit is unknown. Therefore, for variable immediate annuities, the calculation is a little different. Because the expected return under a variable annuity is unknown, it is considered to be the investment in the contract. A fixed portion of each annuity payment is excludible from gross income as a tax-free recovery of the annuity purchaser's investment. The amount of tax-free payments is determined by simply dividing the investment in the contract (adjusted for any period-certain or refund guarantee) by the number of years over which it is anticipated the annuity will be paid.

$$\frac{\text{Total investment (adjusted if necessary)}}{\text{Number of years payments will be made}} = \text{Tax-free portion of each payment}$$

If payments are to be made for a fixed number of years without regard to life expectancy, the divisor is the fixed number of years. If payments are to be made for a single life, the divisor is the appropriate life expectancy multiple as determined by IRS Table I for pre-January 1, 1987 premiums or Table V, for premiums paid into the policy after December 31, 1986. If payments are to be made for a joint and survivor basis, the divisor is the appropriate life expectancy multiple as determined by IRS Table II for pre-January 1, 1987 premiums or Table VI, for premiums paid into the policy after December 31, 1986.

To illustrate, assume that a male age 65 elects an immediate variable life annuity and his investment in the deferred variable annuity is $100,000, made after January 1, 1987. His annual variable annuity payments are initially $8,000. IRS Table V indicates his life expectancy is 20 years. One hundred thousand dollars divided by 20 years is $5,000, which is the portion of each payment that is excluded from income. During each of the first 20 years, $5,000 of the annual payments are excluded from income, and the balance will be included in income. Whether the variable annual payments increase to $10,000 or decrease to $6,000 for any given year, the tax-free portion remains at $5,000 per year. After 20 years, assuming the man is still alive, the cost basis of $100,000 will have been returned to him tax free, and any future annual payments to him would be fully taxable.

The financial advisor should have a working knowledge of how the exclusion ratio is derived in order to communicate it to clients. However, the financial advisor does not usually calculate this ratio for the policyowner. It is normally provided by the insurance company's home office or from its computerized illustration system.

IMMEDIATE ANNUITY COSTS

The cost of an immediate annuity depends primarily on the prevailing level of interest rates at the time it is purchased and the age(s) and gender(s) of the annuitant(s).

The insurance company invests the purchaser's deposit to guarantee the payments promised by the contract. The company expects to pay out the deposit and the interest earned on the deposit over the annuitant's lifetime.

Within the insurance company's total "life only" annuity business, certain annuitants will die before their deposit is expended, which, in actuarial terms, will make up for annuitants who live beyond their life expectancy. Those annuity funds assure annuitants who live an exceedingly long time that their income will last as long as they do. The insurance company spreads its risk by having a large book of business and many annuitants. In the actuarial pricing model that insurance companies use to price their immediate annuities, the forfeitures of those who die early are available in the large pool for payments to those who live a very long time. The company also factors into the formula costs associated with issuing the contract and an allowance for profit.

The state in which the purchaser lives can also influence what he or she must pay for an annuity. Each state may have different rules regarding what annuities can be offered to its residents and the costs of those annuities. Purchasers may find the annuity they want is not available in their state of residence, or it costs more or less than it does in another state.

For instance, some states levy a tax on the purchase price of immediate annuity contracts, as shown in table 9-1. An advisor should check with each of the insurance companies with which he or she writes annuity contracts to determine if the insurance company passes along the premium taxes to the annuity owner or if the company absorbs them. Depending on how the company handles the costs of premium taxes, the consumer may find much more competitive annuities at one insurance company than another.

ANNUITY VARIATIONS

This chapter has discussed the various types of immediate annuities available to individuals through traditional life insurance companies. Several variations from the traditional annuity exist. One of them combines a deferred

TABLE 9-1 State Premium Taxes (Percentage of Cost) on the Purchase of an Immediate Annuity		
State	Nonqualified Annuity	Qualified Immediate Annuity
Alabama	1.00%	1.00%
California	2.35	.50
District of Columbia	2.25	2.25
Kansas	2.00	0
Kentucky	2.00	2.00
Maine	2.00	0
Nevada	3.50	0
South Dakota	1.25	0
West Virginia	1.00	1.00
Wyoming	1.00	0

annuity with long-term care insurance (LTCI), the other is an immediate annuity that is designed to help pay long-term care (LTC) expenses.

Annuity/LTCI Combinations

annuity/LTCI combination

Annuity/LTCI combinations are a relatively new innovation, and although few such products exist today, future growth is expected. With this type of product, asset accumulation can be combined with asset protection and preservation.

For example, an annuity/LTCI combination product may be funded by a single deposit that creates a separate benefit for both needs. The deposit buys an amount of LTC protection equal to twice the value of the annuity account. The policyowner, in effect, triples his or her protection for LTC by purchasing the annuity. The annuity account grows tax-deferred to accumulate funds at a fixed rate of interest, with all the usual annuity options available. In the event of a need for LTC benefits, the first benefit payments are considered a liquidation of the annuity account. After the annuity account is liquidated, the remaining LTC benefits come from the LTCI portion of the contract. Because the policyowner is, in effect, paying for LTC expenses with his or her own money from the annuity account before any LTCI benefits start, the insurer has time before its liability begins, thus lowering costs and the underwriting time needed to issue the contract. If the insured dies before receiving any benefits from the contract, a death benefit equal to the original deposit is paid to the beneficiary.

Another annuity combination product design that addresses LTC needs has two accounts: one that pays a regular fixed interest rate and another that pays a significantly higher interest rate. The first account works like a traditional annuity, while the second allows withdrawals only if the person needs assistance with at least two activities of daily living (ADLs) or has cognitive impairment.

Under the combination product of another insurer, the insured purchases a deferred variable annuity. The initial deposit is split between two accounts, one for the annuity and the other to fund the LTC benefits. The insured has the choice of several options for each account, and the final annuity and LTC benefit amounts depend on investment results. This insurer's product provides two totally separate benefits. If the insured withdraws annuity benefits, there is no effect on the LTC benefits. Similarly, if the insured uses LTC benefits, the annuity account remains unaffected. There is a guaranteed death benefit under the contract, so that the insured's beneficiary always receives an amount at least equal to the initial deposit.

Substandard (Impaired Risk) Annuities

substandard (impaired risk) annuity

Substandard (impaired risk) annuities are a special type of immediate annuity in which the insurance company requires the annuitant to undergo medical underwriting. The underwriting process is similar to the process used for applying for life insurance. Through the underwriting process, the annuitants show the insurance company that their life expectancy is less than normal. Evidence of ill health that is likely to reduce life expectancy may increase the amount of income provided in medically underwritten annuities. The substandard annuity pays higher income because the insurance company will not be making the annuity payments for as long as normally expected. Not all insurance companies offer medically underwritten, or substandard, annuities. The financial advisor should check to determine which companies offer substandard annuities.

DEALING WITH INFLATION

The purchaser's risk with an immediate annuity is the never increasing, constant amount of the check that the annuity owner will receive for the duration of the annuity period. If inflation increases at 5 percent per year, the dollars received from an annuity, although fixed in amount, will purchase 5 percent less each year. This decrease in purchasing power will mean a reduction in the standard of living.

Assuming 5 percent inflation, a check that purchased $1,000 worth of goods in 1997 will purchase an equivalent of only $340.56 worth of goods 21 years later in 2018. The annuitant's standard of living will have been cut to one-third of what it was in 1997. To deal with this risk, and avoid the volatility of variable annuities, cost-of-living adjustment riders are available in some fixed immediate annuities that can provide, at the contract owner's option, a one percent to a 6 percent cost-of-living adjustment (COLA). Innovations in annuity products are constantly being made to offset the effects of inflation on an annuitant's standard of living. It would be wise for advisors to be familiar with the latest innovations in annuities in order to tailor a contract to a specific annuitant's needs.

For a comparable lump-sum investment of $100,000 by the annuity owner, the insurance company prices this COLA feature by reducing the payments that would be available from a corresponding level-payout annuity so that the income not paid early in the contract years can be used to increase the income in later years. For example, the above $100,000 deposit purchases $700 per month on a 20-year fixed-period annuity. A comparable annuity providing income that would increase by 3 percent per year would have an initial payment of about $550 per month. See table 9-2 comparing a $100,000 lump sum for a male aged 55.

TABLE 9-2
Level Payments: Cost of Living Comparison

100,000 Lump Sum Male Age 55	Level Payments	Payments with 3% COLA
Year 1	$700	$550
Year 2	$700	$567
Year 3	$700	$584
Year 4	$700	$602
Year 5	$700	$620
Year 6	$700	$639
Year 7	$700	$658
Year 8	$700	$678
Year 9	$700	$698
Year 10	$700	$719
Year 11	$700	$741
Year 12	$700	$763
Year 13	$700	$786
Year 14	$700	$810
Year 15	$700	$834

POSTANNUITIZATION LIQUIDITY

annuitization

Annuitization may be defined as contracting for a series of payments from a deferred annuity or from life insurance cash values. There are risks to the annuity owner with annuitizing. First, as we have discussed, the annuity owner carries the risk that the annuitant will die too early, or that he or she will select the wrong guarantee and not receive back from the insurance company what could have been received under another payout arrangement.

The second risk is that once the insurance company has issued the annuity, if the annuity owner suddenly needs to have the money, there is no turning back. Immediate annuities do not have account balances that the owner can access. There are usually no surrender or withdrawal provisions. The annuity owner has purchased a right to receive a stipulated income at future intervals.

Example:	The purchaser deposits $65,000 for an immediate annuity that pays $1,000 per month for life. The owner now owns the right to receive $1,000 per month for life. The owner does not own an account with a $65,000 balance.

Several companies have recently begun to market immediate annuities that do offer limited access to lump-sum cash withdrawals under certain contingencies and with various restrictions. This is accompanied by a downward adjustment in the amount of future periodic annuity payments within the contract. These contracts, however, are the exception and not the rule regarding immediate annuities. The vast majority of contracts do not contain lump-sum liquidity provisions once annuitization has begun.

This customary lack of access to the principal deposit is the downside of purchasing an immediate annuity. This is one of the obstacles that prospective buyers must understand in order to feel comfortable about purchasing an immediate annuity.

The annuity owner's alternative to annuitizing the policy is to keep the deferred annuity intact but to take partial surrenders or withdrawals as needed from the annuity policy. Taking partial withdrawals leaves the principal balance available to the policyowner, but it does not guarantee that he or she will not run out of money.

ANNUITIZATION: PORTFOLIO STRESS RELIEVER

A retirement portfolio intended to provide financial security gets in trouble when market conditions make it impossible to generate enough income, and principal has to be liquidated just to make ends meet. Losses that occur at that point may be losses from which the retiree may never recover. One solution to this problem could be to relieve the stress on the portfolio during these difficult periods by using an immediate annuity.

For example, in mid-2003, it would have taken approximately $58,893 to purchase an immediate annuity to pay $1,000 per month for 5 years. By using a portion of the principal to purchase an immediate annuity, the portfolio is relieved of having to generate $1,000 per month in income. These payments may have to be liquidated from excellently performing investments without which the owner would lose future growth opportunities. However, if the premium to fund an immediate annuity that generates $1,000 per month is taken from low-yielding investments, future losses can be minimized.

This technique allows the balance of the portfolio to be managed for growth during the 5-year period. It is important to note that all annuity payments rely upon the full faith and credit of the insurance company making the payments; therefore, the insurance company's financial strength is extremely important.

COMPETITION

A common approach when selling deferred annuities is to check which insurance company is paying the highest guaranteed interest rate for a given period of time. Unfortunately, this same approach is actually a mistake if used to determine the most competitive immediate annuity rates. When determining the most competitive immediate annuity policies, the financial advisor must focus not on what interest rate the insurance company used in the actuarial formula to ascertain the guaranteed payout rates, but on the actual dollar amount of income.

The advisor and the potential purchaser need to look at two issues when shopping for immediate annuity rates. The first issue is the strength and financial stability of the insurance company that is guaranteeing the payments. Because the annuity purchaser is buying a contractual right to receive these payments guaranteed by the insurance company, the contract will not be worth much if the insurance company is financially unstable and it cannot stand behind a lifetime of guaranteed payments.

Second, the purchaser must compare the dollar amount of the payments among companies. If the purchaser is aged 65 and has $45,000 to purchase an immediate annuity for life with 10 years certain, the most competitive quote is determined by which stable insurance company offers the highest payment. It will not help the advisor or potential purchaser to know what the interest rate is inside the actuarial formula that calculated the actual payment. Mortality costs and expenses are other factors used to determine the payment. Because these costs could be relatively higher or lower than another company's, it is useless to learn what the interest factor is when the other factors in the formula remain unknown and therefore can skew the payment. See table 9-3 for a comparison of immediate annuity quotes and how the highest interest rate does not accurately reflect the competitiveness of the annuity.

When comparing immediate annuity quotes, the advisor must make sure to have equivalent quotes from the competing insurance companies. The quotes must be examined to ascertain whether the date of birth, gender of annuitant, payment guarantee, and amount of dollars deposited are the same for each

TABLE 9-3 Comparison: $100,000 Immediate Annuity Female Aged 72, Monthly Payments			
	Company A	Company B	Company C
Interest rate	6.7%	7.0%	6.0%
Expenses	6.1%	5.0%	3.7%
Monthly income	$988.72	$1,004.12	$1,010.99

quote. Each quote must also accurately state whether the funds are qualified or nonqualified, the time of the first payment, and the state in which the contract will be written.

VARIABLE IMMEDIATE ANNUITIES

variable immediate annuity

A *variable immediate annuity* is one in which the periodic payments received from the contract vary with the investment experience of the underlying investment vehicle. The variable immediate annuity was developed to answer the problem of a fixed-payment immediate annuity's purchasing power being eroded by inflation. The variable annuity is designed to adjust its payments to reflect the current purchasing power and offset the eroding effects of inflation on annuity income. The variable immediate annuity can accomplish this objective, but not without risk. The risk to the annuity owner is that the payments can decrease as well as increase.

With fixed immediate annuities, the insurance company accepts the mortality risk, the expense risk, and the interest rate risk. The contract owner accepts the liquidity and the purchasing power risks. With the variable annuity, the contract owner trades guarantees and unwavering income for variable payments. The mortality and expense risks stay with the insurance company.

Currently, the market for variable immediate annuities is small, but it is expected to increase as the baby boomers deal with retirement. Trying to live for several decades on money from a 401(k) plan can be stressful and difficult. It is likely that those with extreme longevity in their families will opt to have some portion of their income guaranteed for life while still being able to withstand inflation. The baby boomers have watched their parents live a lot longer than they expected and have seen their parents' pensions, which seemed sufficient when they retired, become insufficient to maintain their standard of living. That lesson will not be lost. It will cause more and more people to purchase variable immediate annuities to provide a portion of their retirement income.

Assumed Investment Return (AIR)

In the process of implementing a variable immediate annuity, the annuity owner selects from among the various subaccounts offered in the contract to create a diversified portfolio and a suitable asset allocation. In most cases, this asset allocation can be changed among the subaccounts offered within the contract. However, exchanging one contract for another will not be possible after annuitization has begun. The annuity owner may also select automatic rebalancing within most variable immediate annuity contracts. The proceeds to be immediately annuitized buy units of the selected subaccounts on the date of purchase; future changes in value of the selected subaccounts will determine the amount of the future annuity payments.

assumed investment return (AIR)

The amount of the two initial monthly annuity checks will be determined by the insurance-company-offered and contract-owner-accepted *assumed investment return (AIR)*. Once the assumed base rate of investment return is applied to the money, with the other assumptions of expenses and mortality—life expectancy in this case—the amount of the initial two checks is determined. If the contract owner is given a choice of AIRs, such as 3 percent, 5 percent, and 7 percent, the two initial checks will be calculated using the chosen AIR. However, after the two initial checks, the underlying investment accounts have to exceed the AIR to increase the amount of future checks. If the subaccount performance is below the chosen AIR, future checks will decrease. Accepting a low AIR increases the chances of having higher future checks, whereas accepting a high AIR increases the chances of receiving lower future checks.

Variable Immediate Annuity Costs

The prospectus for a variable immediate annuity itemizes expenses, so cost identification and quantification should not be a problem. Typically, individuals considering a variable immediate annuity purchase compare initial income with that provided by a comparable fixed immediate annuity. The amount of initial income a variable immediate annuity provides will be less than the income offered by a fixed immediate annuity with comparable guarantees. Also, some insurance companies' variable immediate annuities do not offer the refund-certain guarantee or the provision in a joint life annuity for a higher income level while both annuitants are living with a lower income level to the survivor.

The AIR may assume that the market earns a steady return of 5 percent throughout the year. However, only the first two checks of this particular contract are guaranteed to be the same. For the rest of the year, the income checks will reflect the level of the underlying investment account. If the underlying investment account earns nothing but remains level at a zero percent rate of return, income for the year will be down by 5 percent. In addition, a 2 percent expense charge will be levied against the underlying investment account.

It is important for advisors and purchasers to understand that the AIR is a net number. It is not the final number, however. Underlying fund expenses need to be added to it. The underlying investment in the contract must gross 7 percent to net 5 percent. If a purchaser wants positive income surprises in the future, it would be wise to select the lowest AIR available.

ANNUITIES AND RETIREMENT

As you will see in this section, annuities can be a valuable tool to help seniors succeed in achieving many of their retirement income planning goals.

The Problem

When you do fact-finding interviews and analyze the financial future of your senior clients and prospects, you often discover a disturbing problem people face is that they can outlive their retirement income. There are three basic reasons why this might happen:

- inadequate savings
- increasing life expectancy
- inflation

Inadequate Savings

Traditionally, Americans have relied on three sources of retirement income:

- Social Security
- employer pension plans
- personal savings and investments

Over time, people are relying more and more on their own assets in retirement. Unfortunately, major studies have confirmed that Americans are saving, at most, one-third of the amount they should be saving to retire comfortably. Despite the urgent need for individuals to plan and save for their own retirement, the savings rate in our nation continues to decline. One recent study from the U.S. Department of Commerce, Bureau of Economic Analysis indicated that the savings rate in the United States fell from a high of 10.6 percent of disposable income in 1975 to 3.7 percent in 2002.[1]

Increasing Life Expectancy

As cited elsewhere in this book, statistics reflect steady progress toward longer, healthier lives for the majority of Americans. A child born today can expect to live beyond age 77. This is a dramatic change from 1900, when life expectancy was age 47. The United States Census Bureau projects that life expectancy will continue to increase. For many people, this translates into a greater number of years in retirement and thus more years that need to be funded by their retirement income.

Inflation

A third reason why people might outlive their retirement income is inflation, which was discussed previously in this chapter. Inflation can best be described as the rise in the price of goods and services, and it is equated with money's loss of purchasing power. For example, during the period between 1966 and 2000, prices generally went up an average of 5 percent a year. The net effect was the reduced purchasing power of the dollar. Goods worth $1 in 1966 cost $4.47 in 2000. Suppose you are working on a retirement plan with a client who is 50 years old and considers $50,000 a year in today's dollars to be an adequate retirement income. Even if inflation continues at a modest 4 percent, the client will need $87,450 per year by the time he or she reaches 65 and $152,950 by age 80 to maintain the same lifestyle. Of course, lower rates of inflation, such as those enjoyed in recent years, would lower the amount of required income.

THE ANNUITY SOLUTION

You may have talked to retirees who have solved the problem of outliving their retirement income by choosing a strategy of living off of the earnings from their investments without touching the underlying principal. As a result of this decision, many of these people will leave their principal for their heirs but will never have enjoyed as much income as they might have liked. Had they been able to spend their principal and interest and been guaranteed that it would last until their death, they would have been able to do much more during their retirement.

Annuities offer a practical way for these people to enjoy not only earnings on their principal but also the principal itself without the risk of running out of money before they die.

With annuities, accumulating funds for retirement is only one side of the coin. Positioning assets to provide sufficient income during retirement is also critical because inflation does not stop at the time someone retires. Therefore, products such as equity-indexed annuities or variable annuities, which were discussed previously in this book, allow the annuitant to receive payments based on the growth of the financial markets and may be ideal choices as hedges against inflation. Even with modest investment returns, the payments from an equity-indexed annuity or variable annuity can gradually increase over the years as long as an individual lives. However, these products contain the risk that payments can also decrease during periods of poor market returns, and this needs to be disclosed to senior clients.

Relationship to the Fact Finder

An annuity plan solution for the clients must be customized according to the information you gathered by means of establishing their financial/ retirement goals.

If you use a comprehensive retirement planning fact finder in its entirety, you can then determine the annual retirement income gap the prospect needs to fill and develop potential annuity plan recommendations according to his or her premium commitment, risk tolerance, and investment objectives.

If, on the other hand, you use a dominant need approach, you would probably complete only the pages of the fact finder regarding personal data, along with selected retirement planning assumptions, and then perhaps an abbreviated income statement, along with selected questions regarding risk tolerance and investment objectives. (More comprehensive risk profile analysis would always be required by your company whenever variable annuity products are proposed.) Finally, only selected portions of the section of a fact finder dealing with retirement income sources, such as the current investments and/or future distribution options or deposits and earnings, may need to be completed, depending on the prospect's dominant need situation.

The analysis of the prospect's information involves taking the relevant data gathered from the fact finder and designing a plan that reflects the prospect's needs, preferences, and either premium or lump-sum investment commitment. Creating a solution to meet the prospect's individual needs depends heavily on the quality of the information gathered during the fact-finding process. The solution must be based on the prospect's own circumstances and preferences. Thus, the importance of a thorough fact finder cannot be overemphasized.

Because fact finding affects your analysis of the prospect's situation, you can apply information from the fact finder to questions that are related to the possible inclusion of annuity product features in the type of plan you recommend. For example, you can ask the prospect if he or she is concerned about reducing taxes on his or her savings. Such a concern would mean that he or she might be receptive to the concept of tax deferral. Alternatively, you could ask how the prospect feels about taking investment risks or into what risk category any additional products purchased would be included. Answers to these two questions that express a willingness to take investment risks and show that the prospect considers himself or herself to be an aggressive investor may indicate interest in a variable annuity. Understanding the prospect's preferences and priorities will dictate which features and riders to include in your recommended annuity policy options.

DESIGNING THE PLAN

Your objective is to help the prospect get the best value for his or her money through an effective plan design. Plan design is a balancing act between the prospect's prioritized retirement or financial needs and his or her premium or lump-sum investment commitment. One way to approach this task is to start with the basic plan design, which is a deferred or immediate annuity, depending on whether the prospect requires tax-favored wealth accumulation or income. Next, formulate choices of several possible product types according to the prospect's risk tolerance and investment objectives. Then, using the premium or investment commitment and the prospect's planning priorities, begin to adjust and fine-tune the plan to create an optimal solution that will best meet his or her financial goals within the specified premium or investment commitment.

Using the following policy classification criteria, you can then develop an annuity recommendation according to the prospect's financial goals:

- how premiums are paid—single- or flexible-premium annuity
- when annuity payments begin—deferred or immediate annuity
- how annuity funds are invested—fixed, indexed, or variable annuity

Below is a brief discussion of when each annuity product type may be applicable based on the prospect's financial circumstances.

How Premiums Are Paid

Reasons to Recommend a Single-Premium Annuity

A single-premium deferred annuity (SPDA) often makes good financial sense for a person who has received a large sum of money and would like to set it aside for a retirement nest egg. A retiree may want to invest a lump sum from a pension plan or a certificate of deposit into an SPDA. Perhaps a widow or widower who has just received the lump-sum death proceeds from a spouse's life insurance policy might be advised to invest these funds in a single-premium immediate annuity that will pay a monthly income for life. Another potential client for a single-premium deferred annuity might be a business owner who has sold all or a portion of his or her company. This can be particularly important to a business owner or self-employed person who has not been able to set up a qualified plan.

Reasons to Recommend a Flexible-Premium Annuity

A flexible-premium annuity is useful as a tool to gradually accumulate retirement benefits. The initial deposit may be as little as $25, and the contract owner can determine the schedule and amount of additional deposits. When discussing a flexible-premium annuity with a working client, point out the long-term benefits of saving a portion of each paycheck by making regular contributions to the annuity.

As you design a flexible-premium annuity policy, it is important to work within a prospect's retirement planning premium commitment as determined in the fact-finding interview. Develop some alternative policy designs that reflect the prospect's risk tolerance and investment objectives and fall within his or her premium commitment. You should limit the choices to just a few so that you do not confuse the prospect. You can always customize a policy further by using a few basic illustrations as the starting point and introducing several interest rate assumptions or policy variations within reasonable parameters. You can also enrich the selling/planning process by interjecting your personal experiences and/or making more sophisticated sales illustrations if appropriate.

When Annuity Payments Begin

Reasons to Recommend a Deferred Annuity

Most people purchase a deferred annuity because they want their money to grow tax deferred. They are attracted to deferred annuities because they provide premium flexibility and several options for the growth of funds over long periods of time. Deferred annuities can be fixed, equity-indexed, or variable, and they offer a range of annuity payout options. Later, if annuity owners choose, they can receive income from the annuity either through occasional or regularly scheduled payments.

However, a feature of nonqualified deferred annuities that may be attractive to retirees is the fact that in most cases they can remain tax-deferred financial vehicles throughout the owner's retirement period. Although a deferred annuity when purchased has a "retirement date" specified in the contract that will guarantee its owner an immediate income at a certain age, such as 65, conversion of a deferred annuity into an immediate annuity can be postponed via a written request to the insurance company. In this way, the owner continues to enjoy tax-deferred growth of the cash value in the contract and can still make ad hoc withdrawals of cash from it when and if desired. Furthermore, there are no adverse income tax penalties incurred by keeping the funds in a nonqualified tax-deferred annuity beyond age 70 ½ like there are in traditional IRAs or some other tax-qualified retirement plans. Like the insurance company, the IRS allows tax-deferred annuities to maintain their tax-deferred status until their owner's death (and beyond in the case of those contracts with a named spouse beneficiary).

In comprehensive retirement planning situations, the reason for buying deferred annuities is to accumulate funds for later use in retirement. This can also include situations where a retiring employee transfers funds from an employer-sponsored qualified retirement plan into a fixed-interest or equity-indexed deferred annuity that maintains its qualified status so there is no income taxation at the time of the transfer, and provides for continued tax-deferral of the accumulated funds, safety of principal, and modest growth potential.

However, in dominant needs sales situations, a prospect may have a variety of other uses for deferred annuity products. Some examples include

- the retiree who buys a nonqualified deferred annuity in order to reduce the interest received from other investments, such as CDs, and thus reduce his or her total income tax bill, as well as the taxation on Social Security benefits (see example below)
- a prospect who has recently sold a business or who sells his or her house when retirement begins and uses the deferred annuity as a tax-favored vehicle for depositing the substantial nonqualified funds acquired
- the couple who uses a nonqualified deferred annuity as part of a charitable giving strategy or as a component of a charitable remainder trust
- a grandparent who uses a nonqualified deferred annuity to help fund a college education for a grandchild

For the Financial Service Practice: Using an Annuity to Reduce Taxation of Social Security Benefits. Generally, Social Security benefits are received tax free for federal income tax purposes, but they can be taxed for seniors with high income. The amount of a senior client's Social Security benefits that is taxable depends on whether the person is receiving income from sources in addition to Social Security. To find out if any of your client's benefits are taxable, begin by totaling the following items:

- the individual's adjusted gross income
- one-half of the client's Social Security benefits
- tax-exempt interest such as interest on municipal bonds
- exclusions such as tax-free foreign earned income and foreign housing

Compare the total to the applicable threshold to calculate the portion of Social Security benefits that will be taxed. The thresholds for determining the potential taxation of Social Security retirement benefits are shown in table 9-4.

One way that seniors may reduce their taxes is to transfer some investments that are producing taxable income into a tax-deferred annuity product. The cash accumulation inside a tax-deferred annuity does not count toward the provisional income used in determining the potential taxation of Social Security retirement benefits.

TABLE 9-4		
Thresholds for Taxation of Social Security Retirement Benefits		
Single Filer	**Amount Taxable**	**Married Filing Jointly**
$25,000	Taxation of up to 50% of Social Security benefits	$32,000
$34,000	Taxation of up to 85% of Social Security benefits	$44,000

Also, deferred annuity products can help to reduce the overall amount of current income that these seniors pay.

Example: Retiree Mr. Johnson is over age 65, collecting Social Security retirement benefits, and married filing a joint federal income tax return. He and his wife take a standard deduction of $11,400 and personal exemptions that total $6,100. Mr. Johnson is currently earning $10,000 in taxable interest income that he really does not need. What if he transfers those funds that generate this current income into a tax-deferred annuity? The exposure of his Social Security benefits to income taxation—as well as his total tax liability—is significantly reduced.

As shown in table 9-5, the transfer of funds from taxable vehicles that generate $10,000 in currently taxable interest into taxed-deferred funds yields a total federal income tax savings of $2,625 (or 26.25 percent) even though Mr. Johnson is in only a 15 percent tax bracket. This consists of $1,500 in direct income tax savings and an additional $1,125 in indirect income tax savings that result from the reduction in the amount of taxable Social Security benefits. Details of the calculations of taxable Social Security benefits under Mr. Johnson's "current" and "what-if" scenarios are shown in table 9-6.

Although decisions about retirement should not be based solely on their tax impact, income tax ramifications should be considered. When planning, it is necessary to examine all the alternatives. The best choice may be the one that minimizes seniors' taxes.

Reasons to Recommend an Immediate Annuity

Immediate annuity contracts can be purchased only with a single lump-sum premium. Immediate annuities can be either fixed or variable. They also

TABLE 9-5
What-If Tax Calculation Program Prepared for Retiree Mr. Johnson
Summary Based on Tax Return for Recent Tax Year

	Current	What If	Difference
8a. Taxable interest	$10,000.00	$ 0.00	$10,000.00
9. Dividend income	5,000.00	5,000.00	0.00
16a. Total pensions and annuities	30,000.00	30,000.00	0.00
20a. Total Social Security benefits	15,000.00	15,000.00	0.00
Total income from all sources	**$60,000.00**	**$50,000.00**	**$10,000.00**
Federal income tax	**(5,338.00)**	**(2,713.00)**	**(2,625.00)**
Net income after federal tax	**$54,662.00**	**$47,287.00**	**$ 7,375.00**
Federal tax bracket	15.0%	15.0%	
Total Social Security benefits	$15,000.00	$15,000.00	$ 0.00
Taxable Social Security benefits	12,750.00	5,250.00	7,500.00
Federal tax paid on Social Security	1,913.00	788.00	1,125.00

TABLE 9-6
Calculating Your Taxable Social Security Amount

Retiree Mr. Johnson	Current	What If
1. Social Security Benefit amount	$15,000	$15,000
2. Adjusted gross income (excluding Social Security)	45,000	35,000
3. Tax-exempt interest (and other excluded income)	0	0
4. One-half of Social Security benefits (from line 1)	7,500	7,500
5. Add lines 2, 3, and 4 to get provisional income	52,500	42,500
6. Threshold amounts: $32,000 (married); $25,000 (single)	32,000	32,000
7. Subtract line 6 from line 5	20,500	10,500
8. 50% of line 7	10,250	5,250
9. Smaller of lines 4 and 8	7,500	5,250
10. Enter $6,000 (married); $4,500 (single)	6,000	6,000
11. Smaller of lines 9 and 10	6,000	5,250
12. 85% of (line 5 minus $44,000 if married) 85% of (line 5 minus $34,000 if single)	7,225	0
13. Sum of lines 11 and 12	13,225	5,250
14. 85% of Social Security benefits (line 1)	12,750	12,750
15. Lesser of lines 13 or 14 = taxable benefits	12,750	5,250

provide a range of annuity payout options, which were discussed previously in this chapter.

An immediate annuity can be useful to a senior client who has received a large sum of money and must count on these funds for income over a long period of time—for example, a senior prospect who has received a lump-sum distribution from an employer qualified retirement plan, the proceeds from a matured CD, life insurance proceeds, or the proceeds from the sale of a business. An annuity buyer study conducted by LIMRA International, Inc., revealed that the number one reason people buy immediate annuities is for the guaranteed income they provide during retirement. A modest percentage of a retiree's liquid assets allocated into a fixed-payment immediate life annuity, within the context of a diversified portfolio of investments, can provide guaranteed periodic payments that will not change for as long as the annuitant lives.

YOUR FINANCIAL SERVICES PRACTICE:
USING ANNUITIES TO FUND LONG-TERM CARE INSURANCE (LTCI)

Fixed annuities only: Because most of one advisor's LTCI clients are in their 60s and 70s—and at this age, they usually should scale back some percentage of their asset allocation from variable products into more fixed products—he suggests a deferred annuity to fund their LTCI.

First, the advisor determines the premium the couple needs for LTCI, which in this case is $3,500. Then the advisor divides the premium by .05, which is the conservative interest rate that can be earned on the capital needed to deposit into the deferred annuity. Therefore, $70,000 is needed to fund the LTCI, which is put into a deferred annuity:

$$\$3,500 \div .05 = \$70,000$$

Thus, the couple never dips into the principal, and the interest from the annuity funds the LTCI. In this example, a couple is using the average cost of a nursing home for one person for one year ($70,000) to fund LTCI forever for both of them. Also, the principal of $70,000 then goes to the heirs at the couple's death, rather than being consumed many times over if used personally to fund long-term care facility costs directly.

An alternative: "If $70,000 is too much, you could use a life-income immediate annuity to fund the LTCI with a lot less than $70,000—maybe only $45,000, depending on age. Or maybe a joint life with 50 percent survivor benefit is a possibility, so that if one spouse dies, only half the income from the annuity is needed for LTCI. This may only cost $30,000. There are solutions right on down the line, depending on affordability."

A second alternative: Using a medically underwritten (substandard) immediate annuity is an ethical answer to the unethical practice of unscrupulously using an immediate annuity payable to the community spouse to hide a lump sum. A medically underwritten immediate annuity is recommended by some advisors so that the sick spouse can qualify for Medicaid. If a person is ill and needs long-term care in a facility, this annuity product will base payments on a rated-up age with the assumption that life expectancy is greatly reduced, and thus the payments the annuitant receives are much higher. Such an approach to LTC funding is both legal and ethical.

Immediate annuities can also be used to provide a reliable periodic stream of funds that can be applied to pay for other financial products, such as long-term care or life insurance. By internally directing specifically earmarked payments into these other products, a senior retired policyowner can be relieved of the worry of where the funds will come from to pay for them, as well as the responsibility of having to submit the payments by writing checks. This concept is demonstrated in the Financial Services Practices box titled "Using Annuities to Fund Long-Term Care Insurance (LTCI)."

Another possible use for leveraging annuities under the appropriate set of circumstances is to combine them with a reverse mortgage in order to provide the senior homeowner with increased income compared to that available from a reverse mortgage alone.

A reverse mortgage is a loan against an individual's home that requires no repayment for as long as the individual continues to live in the home. In other words, a reverse mortgage is a strategy that allows a client to live in his or her home and extract substantial amounts of money from the home's equity that can be used for current needs without repayments being due. Reverse mortgages will be discussed in detail in chapter 12 of this book. However, for now, consider the following example of combining a HUD Home Equity Conversion Mortgage (HECM) reverse mortgage with a fixed-interest deferred and an immediate life annuity.

YOUR FINANCIAL SERVICES PRACTICE: COMBINING A REVERSE MORTGAGE WITH AN ANNUITY

A senior client (age 62 or older) may apply for a reverse mortgage, electing to draw on a portion of the equity on a monthly basis for several years. At the same time, he or she may invest another portion of the loan in the form of a lump sum in a fixed-interest annuity and allow it to grow untouched for the same time period. At the end of the elected period, the monthly reverse mortgage payments will stop, and the funds in a deferred annuity are used to begin providing monthly immediate annuity payments.

Suppose Mr. Stephens is the 65-year-old owner of a home worth $150,000. He is interested in using a reverse mortgage program to provide extra monthly income. A basic HUD HECM loan gives him $447.26 of monthly income.

Alternatively, he can combine a HUD credit line with a fixed-interest deferred annuity. In this situation, Mr. Stephens receives $538.08, or an additional $90.82 per month, for 9 years from the credit line. A lump-sum loan of $31,641 is put into a deferred annuity. (See note below.) At the end of the 9 years, Mr. Stephens stops receiving payments from the credit line and relies on the commercial annuity to provide the $538.08 of monthly income for life.

The result is that Mr. Stephens achieves both a consistent monthly income and asset diversification.

Note: The risk is that the deferred annuity will have to earn a sufficient interest rate during the 9-year period in order to grow to a lump sum of $60,000 that could then be used to purchase an immediate annuity that pays $538.08 monthly for life.

Postretirement Mentality Syndrome—Not all seniors will be emotionally comfortable with their financial outlook during retirement. As a matter of fact, there is some concern on the part of retirees that no matter how much money they have accumulated over their lifetimes for use in retirement, they cannot properly enjoy its use because they fear that they may exhaust it before they die. This concept can be referred to as the "postretirement mentality syndrome." Prior to retirement, the objective for many people is to save as much money as possible to ensure a comfortable retirement. However, the main focus in postretirement is not how much money the retiree has accumulated but, rather, that the money never runs out. This paradigm shift often evidences itself in behavior that results from the natural insecurity associated with becoming poor. This fear, like many others, may have little rational basis. Nonetheless, after 40 working years of conditioning themselves to be thrifty and put something away for tomorrow, retirees often never abandon this tendency. They may deprive themselves of modest luxuries and reasonable indulgences, even if they truly can afford them. This, in part, accounts for some retirees whom we might consider well-to-do taking part-time jobs to bolster their incomes. Although we as advisors can attempt to alleviate their feeling of financial insecurity during retirement, we also need to be sensitive to its reality.

This is where immediate annuities can help. Immediate-annuity buyers generally purchase for one obvious financial reason: to provide guaranteed income in retirement. However, the reasons for purchasing annuities are not strictly financial. For instance, some of the more common reasons for purchase other than income are to cover specific expenses, to avoid becoming a financial burden on their children, to benefit from a variety of income and estate tax reasons, and to ensure the payment of life and long-term insurance premiums.[2] Thus, the motivation to purchase immediate annuities depends on how the prospects perceive both the financial and the emotional aspects of what the product can do for them.

Fixed Immediate Annuity Distributions—Distributions from a fixed immediate annuity can give the annuitant the assurance of knowing that the income stream will remain constant for the duration of the chosen payout period. The guaranteed income stream can be used to provide a degree of investment portfolio balance in comparison to other sources of retirement income that may fluctuate. The trade-off is that these fixed-income payments will lose their purchasing power when exposed to the effects of inflation.

Variable Immediate Annuity Distributions—Using the separate account for annuitization offers the variable annuity owner the opportunity for benefit amounts to increase sufficiently to keep up with inflation. If the annuitant is not comfortable with the risk and the variable aspect of the separate account, he or she can put all or a portion of the accumulated funds in the general account.

How Annuity Funds Are Invested

Reasons to Recommend a Fixed-Interest Annuity

Because of the guaranteed principal and interest, a fixed-interest annuity is for conservative investors—people who want assurances about the safety of their principal and who want to know exactly what they can expect in interest on their annuity cash value. Fixed-interest annuities can provide balance to an overall investment portfolio for moderate to aggressive investors. No matter what happens to stocks, bonds, gold, or mutual funds, all investors in fixed-interest annuities know that at least one part of their holdings is low risk and guaranteed.

The amount of the benefit that is paid out during the distribution phase is fixed. If the annuitant chooses a life annuity option, the amount of the check he or she receives each month will be the same without any investment decisions or risk.

The downside of the fixed-interest annuity is that, over time, such an approach may fall behind the cumulative effect of inflation.

Reasons to Recommend an Equity-Indexed Annuity

You should consider recommending an equity-indexed annuity to prospects who do not want to put money into a product where there is risk of loss but who do want to take advantage of the potential gains to be made in the stock market. Seniors in their late 50s and early 60s, including those who intend to work beyond retirement, may find an equity-indexed annuity to be particularly well suited to their need to accumulate funds over time to build their retirement nest egg. A single-premium equity-indexed annuity might be the ideal place to move funds from a CD when it matures in the hope of benefiting from future market increases without assuming the risk of losing principal.

Be sure to remind clients with equity-indexed annuities not to miss the window periods at the end of the policy terms when they can choose to continue the contract and lock it in for another term, annuitize it, or exchange it for another type of annuity. Clients coming to the end of a term who plan to retire relatively soon can usually exchange an equity-indexed annuity for either a fixed-interest or variable annuity. These two types of annuities offer greater flexibility to an individual who will retire soon because they do not have a contract term.

Market Criticisms of Equity-Indexed Annuities—Equity-indexed annuities have been subject to criticism since their introduction in 1995. Criticism stems from the complexity of the product and misunderstandings from clients. Some individuals assumed they were buying a product that operated and credited interest one way and then later found out it operated and paid interest quite differently.

The complexity of the equity-indexed annuity results from the way the annuity is designed. The annuity policy does not credit a flat amount of annual interest like its cousin, the fixed-interest deferred annuity. Instead, the insurance company must look to some event that happens outside the insurance industry, outside the insurance company, and outside the annuity policy itself just to credit interest. This leads to confusion.

Second, the formula for determining the amount of interest can be complex to an average consumer. Furthermore, instead of directly connecting the interest to the index, the policy also compares the index earnings to yet another number (that is, the cap) before the client can figure out how much the annuity is really worth. Add the concept of "averaging" index values, and the client can become glassy-eyed.

The lack of SEC registration is another area of strong criticism against equity-indexed annuities. Critics would like to see these annuities registered with the NASD and SEC so that consumers are given more disclosures in the sales process and also so that the product is regulated more heavily than fixed annuities.

The relatively high commissions paid to the advisor to sell some, but not all, equity-indexed annuities have also brought criticism to the industry. Whereas traditional fixed-interest deferred annuity commissions are in the 4 percent range, equity-indexed annuities pay up to 15 percent.

Critics contend that insurance companies that have not provided the level of detailed training on the product, the crediting methods, and the link to indexes have caused the industry to come under scrutiny.

The financial services industry was criticized for the unjustified use of replacements and for subjecting the policyowner to a brand-new set of surrender charges. Equity-indexed annuities have been heavily criticized for having surrender charges that are longer than fixed-interest deferred annuity policies. Some equity-indexed annuities have surrender charges up to 15 years. When these annuities are sold to individuals whose actuarial life expectancy is shorter than the surrender charge period, it compounds the criticism.

To put an end to the complaints over this product, financial advisors should determine that the client falls within all the following categories before recommending an equity-indexed annuity product. The client

- does not want a fixed-interest deferred annuity because the interest earnings are too low
- does not want a variable deferred annuity because of the possible loss of principal
- wants the possibility of higher interest than fixed-interest deferred annuities offer and will accept substantially less than the potential return of variable deferred annuities to avoid downside risk

- understands the indexed annuity structure and will not need the funds committed to the contract until after the surrender charge period
- understands and accepts the maturity date, index, and crediting method and finds them suitable
- understands and accepts the limitations on interest earnings from participation rates, spreads, and caps and finds them suitable
- understands and accepts the minimum guarantee as a trade-off for the potential interest that may be earned if the index's performance is poor
- knows what the commission is and considers it acceptable and well earned

Reasons to Recommend a Variable Annuity

Whether or not you recommend a variable deferred annuity depends on the prospect's risk tolerance and how long the money will be invested before it must be withdrawn. People with short investment time horizons and low investment risk tolerance will generally be happier with a fixed-interest annuity. If they have long time horizons and moderate risk tolerance, you might recommend an equity-indexed annuity. The advantage of both the variable deferred annuity and the equity-indexed annuity over the fixed-interest annuity is that they are more likely to keep up with inflation because of their link to the financial markets.

The variable deferred annuity is for the prospect who realizes that gains and losses may occur, but who wants the investment flexibility that comes from being able to move funds among subaccounts within the separate account. This flexibility allows annuity owners to change their investment focus in response to changes in the financial markets or changes in their personal situation at the different stages of their retirement.

Because of the separate accounts, variable annuities are considered securities under federal law. This means you must have a life insurance license and be registered with the National Association of Securities Dealers to sell variable annuities. You must also obtain state licensing powers or authorization to sell variable annuities within each jurisdiction where you transact business. Also, any potential buyer of a variable annuity must be given a prospectus, and you must take steps to determine that a variable annuity is a suitable product choice for the purchaser. Suitability involves assessing a potential investor's investment objectives, time horizon, and risk tolerance.

MUTUAL FUND VERSUS VARIABLE DEFERRED ANNUITY

Another difference between variable deferred annuities and fixed-interest deferred annuities lies in their competing investments. While fixed-interest deferred annuities often compete against certificates of deposit, the nearest competitor to the subaccounts of a variable deferred annuity is mutual finds.

Mutual funds have an average total expense ratio of 1.41 percent and have no insurance features. The average total asset charge in variable annuities is 2.26 percent. Therefore, clients who wish to avoid insurance charges can do so and save an average of 85 basis points by using taxable mutual funds.

However, no individual can make a personal decision based on these averages. A better process is for the client to determine which mutual fund alternative he or she wants to compare. It may be the elusive low-cost, tax-efficient fund or a mutual fund family. The best approach is to identify the actual costs in the mutual fund choice, and compare the cost difference with a variable annuity.

Product Feature Differences

Besides costs, the potential purchaser should know and understand the differences in the operation and design of variable deferred annuities versus mutual funds. Table 9-7 compares the features of a nonqualified variable deferred annuity and a nonqualified mutual fund.

Each product offers features that may be advantageous for the purchaser of these products. For example, the death proceeds of mutual funds receive a stepped-up or stepped-down cost basis at the owner's death that is equivalent to the fair market value of the shares at death. Thus, assuming the share value has appreciated, the increase in cost basis results in no income tax payment being immediately due when the beneficiary receives the mutual fund at the owner's death. Furthermore, less income tax will be due when the beneficiary subsequently sells those inherited mutual fund shares because of their step-up in cost basis. Also, the income tax due at the time of subsequent sale will be calculated using the lower capital gains rate as long as the beneficiary maintains ownership for one year or longer.

If a mutual fund's value has declined at the time of the owner's death, a decrease in cost basis results. This lower cost basis will be the cost basis that the beneficiary of the fund assumes. Any capital gain or loss resulting from the beneficiary's future sale of the fund shares will be calculated using the fund's value at the time he or she took ownership.

On the other hand, under current tax law, the investment earnings that accrue in nonqualified variable deferred annuities while the owner is alive are totally tax deferred until the funds are withdrawn, distributed, or the owner/annuitant dies. At the annuity owner's death, the previously tax-deferred accumulation of gain in the cash value is then taxable as ordinary income and payable by the named beneficiary at his or her respective marginal income tax bracket. However, the beneficiary will not be taxed on the gain in the year of the annuitant's death if he or she elects, within 60 days

TABLE 9-7
Mutual Fund versus Variable Deferred Annuity (Nonqualified)

Product Feature	Variable Deferred Annuity	Mutual Fund
Guaranteed death benefit	Yes	Not available
Death benefit	Higher of account value or premium	Account value
Guaranteed lifetime income at annuitization or other payout option guarantees	Numerous	None
Transfers	Among available subaccounts without taxes and often without expenses	Within fund family are free, but each is a taxable event
Ability to purchase enhanced death benefits rider	Yes	Not available
Stepped-up cost basis at death	Not available	Yes
Ability to purchase guaranteed living benefits riders	Yes	Not available
Taxation of gains	100% tax deferred until withdrawal or death, then taxed as ordinary income	Capital gains based on increase in net asset value of fund shares when fund is sold while owner is living, but annual dividend income and distributions of capital gain income are realized by shareholders
Withdrawals	Company surrender charges during any surrender charge period or IRS penalties prior to owner's age 59 1/2	Company withdrawal constraints depending on class of shares; no IRS penalties prior to age 59 1/2
Excise tax on investment	A few states impose a state premium tax	None
Guaranteed minimum interest account	Available	Not available

after the annuitant's death, to apply the proceeds under a life-income or installment-payment option. These periodic payments will then be taxable to the beneficiary under the regular taxation for annuity payment rules discussed previously in this chapter.

The owner of a variable deferred annuity can also purchase the enhanced death benefits rider discussed in the previous chapter that will increase the death benefit in order to cushion the potential income taxation of death proceeds to the beneficiary of the contract.

Furthermore, if a variable deferred annuity experiences a loss in value at the time of the owner's death, because the death benefit is guaranteed at least to equal the premiums paid into the contract, the beneficiary will receive this amount as a death benefit payment. Thus, there is no taxable loss (or gain) to him or her that results from the receipt of the proceeds. By contrast, there is no death benefit guarantee whatsoever with a mutual fund.

Some other features available in variable deferred annuities that are not found in mutual funds include

- guaranteed lifetime income options at annuitization
- availability of a guaranteed minimum interest account
- ability to purchase one of several guaranteed living benefits riders

The real downside with variable deferred annuities occurs when they are purchased or sold inappropriately or when they are subject to excessive expenses. All charges, especially those that are asset based, must be disclosed and evaluated in light of other investment alternatives. The prospective purchaser must understand the features of the policy, understand all the fees and expenses, understand the tax implications, and intend to remain in the policy long enough to avoid surrender charges.

VARIABLE ANNUITIES REGULATION

All variable products must be suitable to the client, while fixed-interest annuities do not require the determination of the product's suitability to the client.

Also, prospects must be given a prospectus in the sales process for variable annuities. Fixed-interest products do not have prospectuses. The regulatory environment is also different between variable and fixed annuities. Both the NASD and the Securities and Exchange Commission (SEC) are involved in variable annuity sales regulation. Neither the NASD nor the SEC is involved in the sale of fixed annuities.

In a landmark decision, the United States Supreme Court held that an individual variable annuity contract is a security within the meaning of the Securities Act of 1933 and that any organization offering such a contract is an investment company subject to the Investment Company Act of 1940. Any company that offers individual variable annuity contracts is subject to dual supervision by the SEC and the various state insurance departments. Persons selling variable annuities must pass the NASD's Series 6 licensing exam.

As part of its regulatory nature, the SEC developed the following list of questions for potential clients to consider before purchasing a variable annuity policy (see http://www.sec.gov/investor/pubs/varannty.htm) Before you decide to buy a variable annuity, consider the following questions:

- Will you use the variable annuity primarily to save for retirement or a similar long-term goal?
- Are you investing in the variable annuity through a retirement plan or IRA (which would mean that you are not receiving any additional tax-deferral benefit from the variable annuity)?
- Are you willing to take the risk that your account value may decrease if the underlying mutual fund investment options perform badly?
- Do you understand the features of the variable annuity? Do you understand all of the fees and expenses that the variable annuity charges?
- Do you intend to remain in the variable annuity long enough to avoid paying any surrender charges if you have to withdraw money?
- If a variable annuity offers a bonus credit, will the bonus outweigh any higher fees and charges that the product may include?
- Are there features of the variable annuity, such as long-term care insurance, that you could purchase more cheaply separately?
- Have you consulted with a tax advisor and considered all the tax consequences of purchasing an annuity, including the effect of annuity payments on your tax status in retirement?
- If you are exchanging one annuity for another one, do the benefits of the exchange outweigh the costs, such as any surrender charges you will have to pay if you withdraw your money before the end of the surrender charge period for the new annuity?

SENIOR PROTECTION IN ANNUITY TRANSACTIONS MODEL REGULATION

suitability

Until 2003, determining the *suitability* of a product offered to the consumer had not been a requirement in the sale of fixed annuities. Suitability, however, has been an element in variable annuity sales in which registered representatives are required to complete an investor profile form that asks a prospective client questions about risk tolerance, time horizon, and investment objectives when applying for a policy. In 2003, the NAIC adopted a model regulation to deal with the increasing criticisms against the insurance industry for inappropriate sales of annuity products to senior citizens. This model regulation protects senior citizens against abusive annuity sales. It is anticipated that each of the states will quickly take action and adopt the model regulation beginning in early 2005. The key points of the model regulation are as follows:

- The regulation helps protect senior citizens either at the point of purchase or upon the surrender of an annuity.
- It ensures that the insurance needs of seniors are appropriately addressed.
- It establishes standards and procedures for both insurance companies and financial advisors.
- The regulation applies to both variable and fixed annuities.
- It requires that financial advisors obtain financial information from prospective clients and determine whether or not the annuity products are suitable for those clients.
- It directs that the advisor must have reasonable grounds for believing the annuity product is appropriate for the senior.
- It provides that insurance companies set standards for compliance, guidelines, education, and monitoring devices.

Purpose

Senior Protection in Annuity Transactions Model Regulation

The *Senior Protection in Annuity Transactions Model Regulation* sets standards and procedures for recommendations of annuity products to senior citizens. The purpose is to make sure seniors' insurance needs and financial objectives are appropriately addressed at the time the financial advisor makes the recommendation to purchase the annuity. The model regulation includes these definitions:

- An annuity is defined as any fixed or variable annuity that is individually solicited, whether classified as an individual or group annuity.
- Recommendation is defined as the advice provided by an insurance producer to an individual senior consumer that results in a purchase or exchange of an annuity product based on that advice.
- A senior consumer is defined as any person aged 65 or older.

Scope

The model regulation applies to any recommendation the financial advisor makes to purchase or exchange an annuity, resulting in the purchase or exchange of an annuity product. Compliance with the NASD Conduct Rules regarding suitability will satisfy the requirements for variable annuities. However, this does not limit the insurance commissioner's ability to enforce the provision of the new regulation.

There are several exemptions from the suitability requirement, including the following:

- direct response annuity solicitations
- employee pension or welfare plans covered by ERISA
- 401(a), 401(k), 403(b), 408(k), or 408(p) plans if established or maintained by an employer
- government or church plans under IRC Sec. 414
- IRC Sec. 457 plans
- nonqualified deferred-compensation arrangements
- structured settlement annuities
- prepaid funeral contracts

Duties of Insurer and Producers

In making a recommendation, the advisor must have reasonable grounds to believe that the recommendation is suitable on the basis of facts the senior consumer disclosed about his or her investments and other insurance products and about his or her financial situation and needs.

Prior to completing a transaction, the advisor must make a reasonable effort to obtain information concerning the client's

- financial status
- tax status
- investment objectives
- other information used or considered reasonable in making recommendations

The recommendation must be reasonable under all circumstances actually known to the advisor at the time of the recommendation. The advisor does not have an obligation to a senior consumer concerning any recommendation, if that consumer

- refuses to provide relevant information requested
- fails to provide accurate or complete information
- decides to enter into a transaction not based on the advisor's recommendation

Insurers have to establish and maintain a system to supervise advisors' recommendations that is reasonably designed to achieve compliance, including

- written procedures
- periodic reviews of its records aimed at detecting and preventing violations of the regulation
- other processes as necessary

Insurance companies are not required to

- review all producer-solicited transactions
- include recommendations to senior consumers for insurance products that are not that insurer's annuities

Record Keeping

Records of the information collected from the consumer or other information collected and used in making recommendations must be kept. The length of time for keeping these records is up to each individual state, but the expectation is that it will be for at least 5 years after the annuity ceases to exist, or for 5 years after the date of any other such transaction based on the recommendation.

ASSET PROTECTION

One important feature of annuities that is often overlooked is that they can be used to protect the owner's assets from creditors, depending on the type of annuity chosen and applicable state law. This protection is unique to life insurance products, and it cannot be provided by stocks, bonds, mutual funds, or any other investment.

In most states, the person who invests money in an annuity is usually assured that those funds within the contract are protected from creditors. This protection may not exist in all situations. Be sure to check with your company before mentioning this feature; be sure to check also with your client's attorney.

ETHICAL CONSIDERATIONS IN SELLING ANNUITIES

The ethical considerations in selling annuities can be broken down into three categories:

- appropriateness
- prospect and client education
- due care considerations

Appropriateness

As you have discovered, annuities are complex products with many possible variations. For the seniors market, your challenge will be to match annuity product design features with the retirement income investment objectives of each senior prospect to determine the best possible solutions to their needs. One size does not fit all.

There are two sides of the coin in providing the best possible solutions: (1) Know the senior prospect's problems and (2) know how your products can work to solve those problems. On one side, you must complete a fact-finding interview, analyze the information, and communicate your observations effectively to the senior prospect. Know the senior prospect's objectives, identify the shortfalls in his or her current financial plan for reaching those objectives, and define the problems in a way that he or she can understand before making your recommendations. On the other side, strive to understand the planning applications for annuities. Acquire the knowledge to put the options into an annuity package with the right owner, beneficiary, and annuitant so that the result exactly matches your senior prospect's needs.

Prospect and Client Education

Client education is a key factor in helping the owner get full benefit from annuities. Clients should understand their contracts. They should know when and how the annuity goes from the accumulation phase to the distribution phase and which distribution option best meets their needs. They should know the rules about, and possible charges for, full and partial surrenders. Potential owners of equity-indexed annuities and variable annuities particularly need to know how their contracts work and understand the investment risks.

Before buying an equity-indexed annuity, the prospect should understand the workings of the indexing method of the product—including the length of the policy terms, the participation rate, and the cap. They should be aware of the window periods at the ends of the policy terms at which they can make the decision to continue the contract for another term, annuitize it, or exchange it for another type of annuity. At the end of equity-indexed annuity terms, you may want to be on hand to guide them through these decisions.

With variable annuities, prospects should be educated about the risks involved before investing. Gains may occur, but there can also be losses. You should discuss the various subaccounts in the separate account so that prospects understand the risks and possible gains from investing in each.

Due Care Considerations

Financial advisors need to remember that in selling annuities they are usually recommending investments for the senior clients' "safe money," not their speculative or emergency funds. Investors in annuities must know about the safety of the companies in which you are recommending they put their money. You should bring this up with them rather than wait for them to ask.

Many advisors recommend that you use insurance companies with at least two high-quality ratings from the various rating agencies. For example, the rating can be an A or better from A.M. Best Company and an AA or better from Standard & Poor's. High ratings represent the capacity of the company to meet its financial obligations.

To practice due care in a reasonable and prudent manner, after consulting the ratings of the life insurance company issuing the annuities you hope to use, go to the company itself and inquire about its financial strength. Find out whether it has adequate financial resources to pay claims. Does the company have its assets invested wisely? Does the company earn a reasonable rate of return on invested assets to support competitive interest and dividend payments on its permanent life insurance plans and annuities from the general account?

CONCLUSION

There is a tremendous opportunity for financial advisors to shape millions of Americans' retirement security through the annuity products discussed in this book. The need for both deferred and immediate annuities is evident based on the increased longevity of the American population in general and the baby boom generation in particular.

There are two sides of the coin in providing the best possible annuity solutions: Know the prospect's problems, and know how your products can work to solve those problems. On the one side, do a complete fact-finding interview, analyze the information, and communicate your observations effectively to the prospect. Know the prospect's objectives, identify the shortfalls in his or her current financial plan for reaching those objectives, and define the problems in a way that he or she can understand before making your recommendations. On the other side, strive to understand the planning applications for annuities. Acquire the knowledge necessary to put the appropriate annuity options into a plan so that the result addresses your prospect's needs.

The more you work with your annuity products, the more knowledge you will accrue about them. Sometimes you may work with annuity contracts that are so similar in design or policy features that they confuse prospects. For example, a long-term care benefit rider and terminal illness rider found in many deferred annuities may seem like the same thing to your prospect. It is your job to simplify these two riders so that the prospect can easily distinguish between them.

Finally, the design of a policy and its sale to a prospect should not be considered a one-time event. The retirement planning process should be ongoing even after the sale because the client's personal situation and needs will most likely change over time. Besides, many changes could occur in the often lengthy time lapse between when an annuity policy is purchased and when an individual retires.

Now you have a basic idea of what annuities are, what they do, and why people buy them. In the next two chapters, concepts related to retirees' planning for pension distributions will be explored.

NOTES

1. *2004 Annuity Fact Book,* © 2004 National Association for Variable Annuities (NAVA).
2. *Immediate Annuity Buyer Study: Profiles and Attitudes, A 2000 Report.* © 2000, LIMRA International, Inc.

Planning for Pension Distributions—Part I

David A. Littell

Chapter Outline

Planning for the distribution of funds from employer-sponsored retirement plans and IRAs can be one of the most challenging aspects of retirement planning. Any strategy selected must account for the following factors:

- the client's needs and goals
- the variety of distribution options that are available in your client's particular situation
- the implications of choosing one option over another from a tax perspective
- the implications of choosing one option over another from a cash-flow perspective
- the implications of choosing one option over another from a death benefit and estate tax perspective

- the ability to delay the receipt and taxation of a distribution by rolling the distribution over into an IRA or another tax-advantaged retirement plan

This chapter will examine the tax implications of the withdrawal. The following chapter will discuss the nontax rules, typical distribution options, and planning considerations for selecting the appropriate distribution option.

TAX TREATMENT

General

From the employee's perspective, the advantage of tax-sheltered retirement plans (qualified plans, 403(b) plans, IRAs, SEPs, and SIMPLEs) is that taxes are deferred until benefits are distributed—the day of reckoning. Generally the entire value of a distribution will be included as ordinary income in the year of the distribution. If the individual has made after-tax contributions or receives an insurance policy and has paid PS 58 costs, he or she will have a "cost basis" that can generally be recovered. Taxable distributions from tax-sheltered retirement plans made prior to age 59 1/2 will also be subject to the 10 percent Sec. 72(t) penalty tax, unless the distribution satisfies one of several exceptions.

If the benefit is distributed in a single sum, the taxable portion may be eligible for one of several special tax benefits, although only if the distribution is from a qualified plan and satisfies certain lump-sum distribution requirements. Persons born before 1936 may be eligible for 10-year forward averaging or special capital-gains treatment. Any participant who receives employer securities as part of a lump-sum distribution can defer tax on the unrealized appreciation until the stock is later sold.

In many cases, all taxes, including the Sec. 72(t) penalty tax, can be avoided by rolling—or directly transferring—the benefit into an IRA or other tax-advantaged retirement plan. Today most distributions are eligible for rollover treatment. Taxes cannot be deferred indefinitely, however. Under the minimum-distribution rules, distributions usually have to begin at age 70 1/2.

Estate Taxation of Pension Accumulations

Qualified plan and other tax-sheltered benefits payable to a beneficiary at the death of the participant will be included in the participant's taxable estate. Benefits payable to beneficiaries will still be subject to income tax, although the benefit amount is treated as income in respect to a decedent, meaning that the income taxes will be reduced by the estate taxes paid as a result of the pension benefit.

**YOUR FINANCIAL SERVICES PRACTICE:
ASKING THE RIGHT QUESTIONS**

In most cases, the taxation of a distribution from a pension plan or IRA is simple. The distribution is fully taxable as ordinary income. However, there are a number of critical exceptions. (This whole chapter is about the exceptions.) Here are a series of questions to ask your client to see if any of the special rules apply.

1. Is a portion of the distribution attributable to amounts that have already been taxed?

    After-tax employee contributions or PS 58 costs in a qualified plan or nondeductible contributions to an IRA are treated as cost basis and will not be taxed twice. The methodology for recovering the basis is complicated and depends on the type of plan involved. Form 1099R, which is provided to the recipient, will reveal such amounts.

2. Is the benefit payable to an individual who has not attained age 59 1/2?

    If the answer is yes, then in addition to income taxes, a 10 percent penalty tax may apply if the recipient is not eligible for one of the exceptions.

3. Is the distribution to a plan participant or to a beneficiary receiving a death benefit?

    If it is a distribution to the death beneficiary, the beneficiary still pays income taxes, but he or she might be entitled to a deduction if the participant had paid federal estate taxes on the value of the pension.

4. Is some or all of the distribution attributable to stock of the sponsoring entity?

    If the distribution is from a qualified plan and it qualifies as a lump-sum distribution, the taxpayer may be entitled to deferral of gain on the unrealized appreciation on the employer stock.

5. Is the distribution from a qualified plan payable as a lump sum to an individual born before 1936?

    If the distribution is from a qualified plan, the recipient may be entitled to a special tax rate using grandfathered 10-year averaging or the grandfathered capital gains rule.

Sec. 72(t) Penalty Tax

Sec. 72(t) penalty tax

Distributions prior to age 59 1/2 from all types of tax-advantaged retirement plans are subject to the 10 percent *Sec. 72(t) penalty tax* (unless an exception applies). The 10 percent penalty applies to distributions that are made from a qualified plan, a Sec. 403(b) plan, an IRA, or a SEP. The rule also applies to SIMPLEs, with a modification: During the first 2 years of plan participation, the early withdrawal penalty is 25 percent instead of 10 percent.

The 10 percent tax applies only to the portion of the distribution subject to income tax. This means the tax does not apply when a benefit is rolled over from one tax-deferred plan into another. It also does not apply to the nontaxable portion of a distribution (which may occur with a distribution of after-tax contributions).

However, a distribution made prior to age 59 1/2 can escape the 10 percent penalty if it qualifies under one of several exceptions. To avoid the 10 percent penalty, the distributions must be

- to a beneficiary or an employee's estate on or after the employee's death
- attributable to disability
- part of a series of substantially equal periodic payments made at least annually over the life or life expectancy of the employee or the joint lives or life expectancies of the employee and beneficiary. (If the distribution is from a qualified plan, the employee must separate from service.)
- made to cover medical expenses deductible for the year under Sec. 213 (medical expenses that exceed 7.5 percent of adjusted gross income)
- after a separation from service for early retirement after age 55 (not applicable to IRAs, SEPs or SIMPLEs)

Several additional exceptions apply to IRAs (which include SEPs and SIMPLEs). Distributions from IRAs escape the penalty if the distribution is for

- the purpose of paying health insurance premiums by an individual who is collecting unemployment insurance
- the payment of acquisition costs (paid within 120 days of the distribution) of a first home for the participant, spouse, or any child, grandchild, or ancestor of the participant or spouse (with a lifetime limit of $10,000 per IRA participant)
- the payment for qualified higher education expenses for education furnished to the taxpayer, the taxpayer's spouse, or any child or grandchild of the taxpayer or taxpayer's spouse at an eligible postsecondary educational institution

Qualified home acquisition expenses are those used to buy, build, or rebuild a first home. To be a first-time homebuyer, the individual (and spouse, if married) must not have had an ownership interest in a principal residence during a 2-year period ending on the date the new home is acquired. Qualified education expenses include tuition, fees, books, supplies, and equipment required for enrollment in a postsecondary education institution. For at least half-time students, room and board are also qualified education expenses.

The following examples should help to illustrate when the Sec. 72(t) 10 percent penalty applies and when it does not.

Example 1:   Greg Murphy, aged 57, takes a $50,000 distribution from his profit-sharing plan. If Greg terminated employment after age 55 and before receiving the benefit, the tax does not apply. If Greg is still employed at the time of the distribution, then the $50,000-sum distribution will be subject to a $5,000 (10 percent) penalty.

Example 2:	Jane Goodall, aged 45, takes a life annuity from Biological Researchers, Inc., when she quits and goes to work for The Primate Institute. Jane's distribution is not subject to penalty because of the substantially equal periodic payments exception.
Example 3:	Ed Miller, aged 35, takes a $10,000 distribution from his 401(k) plan as a downpayment on his first home. Ed's distribution is subject to the 10 percent penalty.
Example 4:	Sandra Smalley, aged 45, takes a distribution from her IRA to pay for her child's college education. Sandra's distribution is not subject to the 10 percent penalty.
Example 5:	Catherine Thegrate, aged 45, withdraws $10,000 from her IRA to make the downpayment on her first home. The distribution is exempt from the 10 percent penalty; however, no additional withdrawals from any of Catherine's IRAs (or Roth IRAs) can qualify for the exception.

Avoiding the Sec. 72(t) Penalty Tax

Clients may need to make withdrawals prior to age 59 1/2 to pay personal or business expenses. Voluntary early retirement, involuntary retirement followed by a period of not working, or leaving a job to start a business are common scenarios. Within the list of exceptions to the Sec. 72(t) penalty tax, some planning opportunities do exist.

Age 55 Exception. Distributions from a qualified plan or 403(b) plan to a participant who retires after attaining age 55 are exempt from the penalty tax. This exception is useful if the participant wants to take a portion of the

---

YOUR FINANCIAL SERVICES PRACTICE:
TAX FORMS REQUIRED WITH EARLY WITHDRAWALS

When a participant receives a distribution from a pension plan or IRA, the payor must report the distribution on Form 1099-R. If the recipient has not yet attained age 59 1/2, the payor will identify in box 7 of the form whether an exception to the Sec. 72(t) tax applies (in this case they identify "2", "3", or "4" in the box.) If the payor writes "1" in the box for "no known exception," then the recipient is required to file Form 5329 with his or her tax return. On Form 5329, the taxpayer identifies the taxable amount but also has the opportunity to identify the applicable exception to the penalty tax.

distribution into income now and roll over the rest to an IRA. It also works when the participant elects a stream of installment distributions or an annuity payment from the plan. However, if the participant wants more discretion over the timing of the withdrawal then the plan allows, the only option is a rollover into an IRA. Once the distribution is in the IRA, it is no longer eligible for the exception.

Education Expenses. For IRA participants (this includes SEPs and SIMPLEs too), the exception for educational expenses can also be useful. The education expense exception requires that the taxpayer pay qualified education expenses for the family member, but the expenses do not have to be paid directly from the IRA. The actual education payments can be paid from employment income, loans, a gift, or an inheritance. However, education expenses paid with tax-free distribution from a Coverdell education account, tax-free scholarships, Pell grants, employer-provided educational assistance, or Veterans' Administration educational assistance do not qualify.

Qualified education expenses include tuition, fees, books, supplies, and equipment required for enrollment in a postsecondary education institution. Room and board is also included for students attending school at least half time. An eligible educational institution is any college, university, or vocational school eligible to participant in the student aid programs administered by the Department of Education. It includes virtually all accredited, public, nonprofit, and proprietary postsecondary institutions.

Example: Randolph, age 56, withdraws $50,000 during the year from his IRA to pay for a new boat (before calling his financial advisor). It turns out that he also took out a second mortgage to pay $25,000 of tuition, $1,000 for books, and $12,000 for room and board for his daughter, a full-time student at Private University. Because Randolph incurred $38,000 of qualified education expenses for his daughter, he only has to pay the 10 percent penalty on $12,000 of the $50,000 withdrawal.

substantially equal periodic payment exception

Substantially Equal Periodic Payments. The most helpful exception is the *substantially equal periodic payment exception*. Although the exception applies to all types of plans, with qualified plans, the participant must separate from service before distributions begin in order to be eligible. Payments can begin at any age as long as the stream of distributions is set up to last for the life of the participant or the joint lives of the participant and his or her beneficiary. For the individual who needs the withdrawals for ongoing financial needs, periodic distributions may be just right. If, on the other hand, a large single-sum amount is needed, this strategy could still work. The individual can borrow the sum needed and repay the loan from the periodic distributions. The borrower, however, is not allowed to use a pension or IRA account as collateral for the loan.

Under this exception, there is quite a bit of flexibility in calculating the annual withdrawal amount. Withdrawals must be made at least annually (or more often) and the stream of withdrawals can be calculated under one of three IRS-approved methods. The first is the required minimum-distribution method. Under this approach, the annual payment for each year is determined by dividing the account balance for that year by the number from the chosen life expectancy table for that year. The account balance, the number from the chosen life expectancy table, and the resulting annual payments are redetermined for each year.

The second method is the fixed-amortization method. The annual payment for each year is determined by amortizing, in level amounts, the account balance over a specified number of years (determined using the chosen life expectancy table) and the chosen interest rate. Under this method, the account balance, the number from the chosen life expectancy table, and the resulting annual payment are determined once for the first distribution year, and the annual payment is the same amount in each succeeding year.

The third method is the fixed-annuitization method. The annual payment for each year is determined by dividing the account balance by an annuity factor that is the present value of an annuity of one dollar per year beginning at the taxpayer's age and continuing for the life of the taxpayer (or the joint lives of the individual and beneficiary). The annuity factor is derived by using the mortality table in appendix B of Rev. Rul. 2002-62 and by using the chosen interest rate. Under this method, the account balance, the annuity factor, the chosen interest rate, and the resulting annual payment are determined once for the first distribution year and then the annual payment is the same amount in each succeeding year.

The life expectancy tables that can be used to determine distribution periods are the uniform lifetime table (found in Rev. Rul. 2002-62, a portion of which can be found in the minimum-distribution materials in the next chapter), the single-life table or the joint and survivor table (found in appendix 1). These are the same tables used for determining the required minimum distribution. The number that is used for a distribution year is the number shown from the table for the participant's age on his or her birthday in that year. If the joint and survivor table is being used, the age of the beneficiary on the beneficiary's birthday in the year is also used. In the case of the required minimum-distribution method, the same life expectancy table that is used for the first distribution year must be used in each following year. Thus, if the taxpayer uses the single-life expectancy table for the required

> ## YOUR FINANCIAL SERVICES PRACTICE:
> ## THE SUBSTANTIALLY EQUAL PAYMENT EXCEPTION
> ## IN A DOWN MARKET
>
> The biggest limitation of the substantially equal periodic payment exception is the inability to change the calculation methodology once payments have begun. With the amortization and annuitization approaches, the amount withdrawn in each and every year must remain the same for the prescribed period. This can cause problems in a down market when the value of the account can drop suddenly. A participant who is concerned about this issue should consider using the required minimum-distribution approach. Interestingly, in Rev. Rul. 2002-62, the IRS has indicated that anyone who chooses either the amortization or annuitization methods can, after the first year, make a one-time election to change the method to the required minimum-distribution approach. This gives taxpayers a safety net if the value of the account suddenly drops.

minimum-distribution method in the first distribution year, the same table must be used in subsequent distribution years.

The interest rate that may be used is any interest rate that is not more than 120 percent of the federal mid-term rate for either of the 2 months immediately preceding the month in which the distribution begins. For example, the mid-term rate was 3.55 percent for November of 2004.

Even though the distribution amount is calculated based on lifetime payments, fortunately the rules do not actually require that payments continue for life. Payments can be stopped without penalty after the later of 5 years after the first payment or age 59 1/2. For example, an individual who began distributions in substantially equal payments at age 56 in January 2000 must continue taking the distributions until January 2005. Or, in the case of an individual beginning withdrawals at age 47, the payments must continue until he or she attains age 59 1/2, which is a period of 12 1/2 years.

A client who uses the substantially equal payment exception needs to be aware of potential potholes. The largest is that once payments have begun, they must continue for the minimum period in order to avoid the tax. Failure to make the required number of payments means the 10 percent penalty will be due on all distributions made before age 59 1/2, as well as interest on the tax obligation that was avoided during the years in which distributions were made.

Nontaxable Distributions

Most distributions made from qualified plans, IRA accounts, and 403(b) annuities are fully taxable as ordinary income. However, if some of the participant's benefit under the plan is attributable to dollars in the plan that have already been subject to taxation—for example, employee after-tax contributions and amounts attributable to term insurance premiums (PS 58 costs)—then a portion of a distribution may be exempt from tax until the total nontaxable amount has been distributed.

Calculating the appropriate tax treatment for periodic payments can become quite complex. The rules differ depending on the type of plan and type of distribution involved. At the same time, fewer participant benefits contain nontaxable basis. This is true in part because of law changes that almost eliminated all new after-tax contributions to qualified plans beginning in 1987 (with the exception of a few large 401(k) plans that still allow after-tax contributions). Also, life insurance benefits in qualified plans have become more uncommon, reducing the amount of recoverable PS 58 costs. One additional complicating factor is that today participants are allowed to roll nontaxable contributions into an IRA. The tax treatment of withdrawals from the IRA is different than withdrawals from a qualified plan, meaning that the decision to roll over the after-tax dollars should be made carefully. Even though these situations are not that common, they still come up and the financial service professional does need to have a basic understanding of the rules. A summary of the rules follows.

IRA Distributions

Let's begin with the simplest case, the traditional IRA. A participant can accumulate nontaxable amounts (referred to as cost basis) from either nondeductible contributions to the IRA or nontaxable amounts that have been rolled over from qualified plans. The rule is simply that if an individual has unrecovered cost basis, then a portion of each IRA distribution is tax free. The amount excluded from income is

$$\frac{\text{Unrecovered cost basis}}{\underset{\text{account}}{\text{Total IRA}} + \underset{\text{distribution}}{\text{Current year's}}} \times \underset{\text{amount}}{\text{Distribution}} = \underset{\text{portion}}{\text{Tax-free}}$$

This calculation is made looking at all of the IRAs an individual owns—which can have quite a negative impact on the recovery of cost basis if the participant has both nondeductible and deductible IRA contributions. This method applies until the individual has recovered all of his or her nondeductible contributions. After that, any distribution is fully taxable. If the IRA owner dies prior to recovering all nondeductible contributions, the remaining amount can be deducted on the individual's final income tax return.

PS 58 Costs

The cost of the "pure amount at risk" in a life insurance contract held in a qualified plan or 403(b) annuity is taxable to the participant. Historically, the amount included in income is based on the cost of providing the life insurance protection under the PS 58 table—and accumulated taxable amounts are typically referred to as PS 58 costs. Note that recently the IRS changed the methodology for calculating the taxable amount and issued a new table (referred to as table 2001).

At the time a participant receives a distribution of the insurance policy, the accumulated PS 58 costs are not subject to income tax. The policy must be distributed to the participant in order to recover the PS 58 costs. However, a participant who does not want to continue the policy could request that the trustee strip the cash value of the policy (by borrowing) to reduce the cash value to the accumulated PS 58 costs and then receive both the stripped contract and the cash. Also note that self-employed persons (sole proprietors and partners) do not technically accumulate PS 58 costs (even though they do have to pay tax on the pure amount at risk), and they are not permitted to recover them upon distribution of the contract.

Rollovers from Qualified Plans

When a participant receives a distribution from a qualified plan that is eligible to be rolled into an IRA, the whole distribution (including after-tax contributions) may be rolled into an IRA. However, if the after-tax amount is rolled over, it is subject to the IRA recovery rules. As described above, these rules are not very favorable, especially with large rollover accounts. A participant may want to choose instead to roll over all but the nontaxable amount. In *IRS Publication 575, Pension and Annuity Income,* the IRS states that if only a portion of the distribution is rolled over, the amount rolled over is treated as coming first from the taxable part of the distribution. This means the participant is not required to pay any income taxes if he or she rolls over all of the distribution except for the amount of after-tax contributions.

As mentioned above, when a participant receives a life insurance policy from a qualified plan, the PS 58 costs may be recovered tax free if the policy is distributed. Special consideration must be made when the participant wants to receive the policy but minimize the tax consequences by rolling over as much of the benefit into an IRA as possible. Because a life insurance policy may not be rolled into an IRA, the tax consequences of this transaction can be minimized by having the trustee strip the cash value of the policy (by borrowing) to reduce the cash value to the accumulated PS 58 costs. Then the extra cash is distributed as part of the benefit and may be rolled over.

Single-Sum Distributions

If a participant receives the entire benefit and does not roll it into an IRA or other tax-sheltered retirement plan, recovery of basis occurs at the time of the distribution.

Distribution of After-tax Contributions Prior to the Annuity Starting Date

Prior to 1987, an amount up to the participant's cash basis could be withdrawn before the annuity starting date (the time when periodic retirement benefits begin) without income tax consequences. The Tax Reform Act of 1986 changed this rule significantly. A grandfather provision still allows a participant to withdraw an amount equal to the pre-1987 cash basis as long as the plan provided for in-service distributions on May 5, 1986. Post-1986 amounts attributable to the cash basis, however, are now subject to a pro rata rule. The general rule is that the amount of the distribution that is excluded from tax is based on a ratio, with the numerator being cash basis and the denominator being the total account balance at the time of the distribution. However, when determining the ratio, an individual may treat employee after-tax contributions and the investment experience thereon separately from the rest of the participant's benefit. This rule still allows a participant to withdraw after-tax contributions with limited tax liability. This principle can be best illustrated with an example.

Example:	Joe has an account balance of $1,000, $200 of which is attributable to post-1986 employee contributions and $50 of which is attributable to investment earnings on $200. Joe takes an in-service distribution of $100. The exclusion ratio is $200/$250 or 80 percent. Therefore, Joe will receive $80 income tax free and will owe tax on $20.

**YOUR FINANCIAL SERVICES PRACTICE:
AFTER-TAX CONTRIBUTIONS**

It's not uncommon for a business owner to have made after-tax contributions prior to 1987. These amounts can be withdrawn tax free, making them an excellent source of funds if the owner has a life insurance need or has some other reason to need cash. After 1986, typically 401(k) plans are the only plans that may still have an after-tax contribution feature.

Periodic Distributions from Qualified Plans and 403(b) Annuities

Again the rules have changed significantly over time. Today (for any distributions that began after November 18, 1996), the amount is determined by dividing the cash basis by the number of expected monthly annuity payments. When the annuity is on the life of the participant only, the number of months is as described in table 10-1. For a joint and survivor annuity, use the number of months described in table 10-2.

The cash basis is the aggregate amount of after-tax contributions to the plan (plus other after-tax amounts such as PS 58 costs and repayments of loans previously taxed as distributions) minus the aggregate amount received before the annuity starting date that was excluded from income.

TABLE 10-1
Number of Months—Single Life Annuity

Age of Distributee	Number of Payments
55 and under	360
56–60	310
61–65	260
66–70	210
71 and over	160

TABLE 10-2
Number of Months—Joint Annuity

Combined Age of Annuitants	Number of Payments
Not more than 110	410
More than 110 but not more than 120	360
More than 120 but not more than 130	310
More than 130 but not more than 140	260
More than 140	210

The distributee recovers his or her cash basis in level amounts over the number of monthly payments determined in the tables above. The amount excluded from each payment is calculated by dividing the investment by the set number of monthly payments determined as follows:

$$\frac{\text{Investment}}{\text{Number of monthly payments}} = \frac{\text{Tax-free portion}}{\text{of monthly annuity}}$$

The dollar amount determined will be excluded from each monthly annuity payment, even where the amount of the annuity payment changes. For example, the amount to be excluded as determined at the annuity starting date remains constant, even if the amount of the annuity payment rises due to cost-of-living increases or decreases (in the case of a reduced survivor benefit annuity). If the amount to be excluded from each monthly payment is greater than the amount of the monthly annuity (as might be the case with decreased survivor payments), then each monthly annuity payment will be completely excluded from gross income until the entire investment is recovered. Once the entire investment is recovered, each monthly payment is fully taxable.

Example: John Thomas is about to begin a retirement benefit in the form of a single life annuity. His investment in the contract is $40,000. John is aged 65 at the time benefit payments begin. The set number of months used to compute the exclusion amount is 260 (for age 65 from table 10-1). Because his cash basis is $40,000, the amount excluded from each payment is $154 ($40,000 ÷ 260).

ROLLOVERS

When a plan participant retires, changes jobs, or wants to change service providers (in the case of an IRA), in most cases a plan benefit can be rolled out of one plan and into another tax-deferred vehicle without any income tax consequences. Even though the rollover rules are relatively straightforward today, that doesn't mean that things don't go wrong, and a mistake could result in one of the biggest tax problems that an individual will ever encounter.

Distributions From Qualified, Governmental 457, and 403(b) Plans

The regulatory scheme is virtually the same for distributions from qualified plans, 403(b) annuities, and 457 plans sponsored by a governmental agency. A participant receiving "an eligible rollover distribution" can defer tax on the distribution by rolling it over in total or in part to a qualified plan, 403(b) annuity, 457 governmental plan, or to a traditional IRA. Most distributions qualify as eligible rollover distributions with a few limited exceptions. The most common distributions that do not qualify are as follows:

- minimum required distributions
- hardship withdrawals from a 401(k) plan
- distributions of substantially equal periodic payments made
  - over the participant's remaining life (or life expectancy)
  - over the joint lives (or life expectancies) of the participant and a beneficiary
  - over a period of more than 10 years

In addition, certain corrective distributions, loans treated as distributions, dividends on employer securities, and the cost of life insurance coverage are not eligible rollover distributions.

Example: Your client, Jean Jones, calls you to say she is receiving a life annuity from her former employer's defined-benefit plan. This month, Jean doesn't need the money. Jean wants to know whether she should roll the benefit into an IRA account. The answer is no. Because it is part of a stream of life annuity payments, it is not an eligible rollover amount.

Rollover

rollover

The term *rollover* is used to describe the situation in which the participant physically receives the distribution and subsequently deposits the amount into an eligible plan. A distribution must be rolled over by the 60th day after the day it is received, or the entire distribution is subject to income tax and, if applicable, the 10 percent Sec. 72(t) penalty tax. The IRS can waive the 60-day requirement when the failure to satisfy the requirement is beyond the reasonable control of the individual (discussed further below).

Direct Rollover

eligible rollover
distribution

Rollovers are problematic because *eligible rollover distributions* from qualified plans, 403(b) annuities, or 457 governmental plans are subject to 20 percent mandatory income tax withholding. This means that a participant who wants to roll over the benefit only receives 80 percent of the total benefit. The entire benefit could be rolled over, but the other 20 percent would have to be contributed from other funds.

direct rollover

Mandatory withholding is not required if the participant elects a *direct rollover*. Qualified plans, 403(b) plans, and 457 governmental plans are required to give participants the option to elect a direct rollover for eligible distributions to an IRA or other employer-sponsored retirement plan. When a participant elects the direct rollover, instead of receiving the distribution directly, the funds are paid to the trustee of the new plan.

Planning Considerations

For many retiring plan participants, the best strategic decision is to elect a direct rollover of the entire benefit into an IRA. The direct rollover bypasses the 20 percent withholding rules, and once the benefit is in the IRA, the participant has maximum investment and withdrawal flexibility. As discussed in the next chapter, in some cases (especially defined-benefit plans) it might be economically beneficial to take the distribution directly from the employer's retirement plan. As discussed later in this chapter, there is also the occasional situation in which a participant receiving a lump sum distribution from a qualified plan will want to consider electing one of the special tax rules that applies to lump sum distributions.

There may also be several good reasons not to elect to roll over the entire distribution. As discussed earlier, the portion of the benefit that represents after-tax contributions should not be rolled over in most cases. Second, if the distribution includes the sponsoring company's stock, then the participant needs to carefully evaluate whether the net unrealized appreciation rules make it advantageous to take the stock portion of the distribution into income.

A participant over age 55 (but not yet age 59 ½) who needs funds might consider withdrawing the amount of the current need and rolling over the rest to avoid the 10 percent early withdrawal tax.

If the participant is changing jobs, the new employer's qualified plan, 403(b) annuity, or 457 governmental plan may (but is not required) to permit rollovers. Most individuals prefer the investment and withdrawal flexibility of an IRA. Also, if a participant dies while the money is held in the qualified plan (or 403(b) annuity or 457 plan), the beneficiary will be limited by the distribution options offered by the plan. The plan may require a single sum distribution or limited installment payments. If the benefit was in an IRA, the beneficiary typically can withdraw the funds over his or her entire life expectancy as allowed under the minimum distribution rules. Stretching out the payments defers income taxes, resulting in additional tax-deferred growth and a larger after-tax benefit for the heirs.

On the other hand, the ability to borrow from the employer's plan, or specialized investment options like a guaranteed investment contract, may create an incentive to choose the new employer's plan. If the participant is approaching or has attained age 70 1/2 and is continuing to work, the rollover can potentially delay the timing of required minimum distributions. Maybe the best reason to consider the employer's plan is that most employer-sponsored retirement plans are eligible for protection against claims of creditors in bankruptcy while assets in an IRA may not be. Whether IRAs enjoy asset protection is determined on a state-by-state basis.

Distributions from IRAs

Rollovers from SEPs and SIMPLEs (as well as traditional IRAs) are somewhat easier because the 20 percent mandatory withholding rules do not apply. SIMPLE distributions have the most limitations. They can be rolled into another SIMPLE or, 2 years after the SIMPLE was established, into a traditional IRA. Once in a traditional IRA, in most cases, the entire IRA amount can be rolled to another IRA or, for that matter, a qualified plan, 403(b) annuity, or 457 governmental plan. One exception is that required minimum distributions for the year cannot be rolled over. Also, nontaxable amounts cannot be rolled to a qualified plan, 403(b) annuity, or 457 plan.

trustee-to-trustee transfer

Even though the mandatory withholding rules do not apply, a participant wishing to roll over a distribution from a SEP, SIMPLE, or IRA should have the assets transferred directly from one trustee to the other. This transaction, referred to as a *trustee-to-trustee transfer*, ensures that the participant does not violate the 60-day rollover rule. This is an important consideration because failure to meet the 60-day requirement means the entire distribution is subject to income tax and, if applicable, the 10 percent Sec. 72(t) penalty on the entire taxable portion of the distribution.

YOUR FINANCIAL SERVICES PRACTICE:
CLIENT QUERY

Question: Your client Rudolph, aged 50, has found out that he is eligible to receive a hardship withdrawal from his profit-sharing plan in the amount of $5,000. The withdrawal is to pay the college education expenses for his daughter. He wants to know the withholding rules and income tax consequences of this distribution.

Solution: Because a hardship withdrawal is not an eligible rollover amount, he can receive the entire $5,000—the plan administrator is not required to withhold 20 percent for payment of income taxes. However, at the end of the year, Rudolph will have significant tax consequences. He will have to pay ordinary income taxes and the Sec. 72(t) 10 percent penalty tax. If the withdrawal was from an IRA account instead, the 10 percent penalty would not apply because the withdrawal is to pay for college education expenses of a family member.

Even considering the potential for a tax problem, there will be some occasions in which the participant will want short-term access to an IRA account. It is possible to withdraw some or all of the assets from a plan for 60 days. If a withdrawal is made and then returned within the 60 days, this is considered a rollover, and no additional rollover can occur in that plan for one year from the time of the withdrawal. However, this requirement applies to each IRA separately, so a participant with multiple IRAs could have one rollover in each plan each year. For purposes of the one-year rule, trustee-to-trustee transfers and direct transfers from a qualified plan to an IRA are not counted as a rollover.

Rollovers by Beneficiaries

Up until this point, we have been discussing rollovers by participants. There are several situations in which other recipients are permitted the rollover option. A beneficiary who is the surviving spouse receiving "an eligible rollover distribution" from a qualified plan, 403(b) annuity, or 457 governmental plan may roll it over in total or in part to a qualified plan, 403(b) annuity, 457 plan, or to a traditional IRA. Similarly, a spouse or former spouse entitled to a payout of benefits under a qualified domestic relations order (QDRO) is also entitled to a rollover.

Distributions in these cases are also subject to the direct rollover requirement as well as the 20 percent mandatory withholding requirements. When a spouse (or former spouse) rolls the benefit into an IRA or other plan, the spouse is treated as if he or she were the participant. This characterization has a significant effect on the requirement minimum distribution provisions discussed in the next chapter.

A spousal death beneficiary inheriting an IRA can leave the IRA account in the decedent's name or roll the benefit into an IRA in his or her own name. Technically, the account can be retitled without even changing the IRA vehicle.

The decision whether or not to retitle the account into the spouse's name has an effect on several related tax rules. If the spouse has not yet attained age 59 1/2, changing the title could result in penalty taxes if withdrawals are made prior to age 59 1/2. If the account is left in the participant's name, any payments to the spouse are death benefits exempt from the 10 percent penalty tax. On the other hand, retitling typically has advantages under the minimum distribution rules. Fortunately there is no time limit on the ability to retitle the IRA, so the spousal beneficiary could leave the benefit in the name of the participant until the spouse attains age 59 1/2 and then retitle it in his or her own name.

Death beneficiaries other than the spouse (and QDRO distributees other than spouses and former spouses) are not allowed to rollover distributions from any type of plan. When the benefit is in a qualified plan, 403(b) plan, or 457 plan, the beneficiary will have to take benefit distributions directly from the plan under one of the allowed distribution options. If the death benefit is already in an IRA, then the IRA is treated as an inherited IRA. The IRA is the more flexible vehicle because most IRAs allow the death beneficiary to take withdrawals as slowly as required under the minimum distribution rules. As discussed in the minimum distribution materials in the next chapter, when there are multiple beneficiaries, it may even be possible to divide the inherited IRA into separate accounts to facilitate separate investing and withdrawal plans by the beneficiaries.

Waivers for the 60-Day Rollover Requirement

Code Sec. 402(c)(3) provides that the IRS may waive the 60- day rollover requirement when the failure to waive such requirement "would be against equity or good conscience, including casualty, disaster, or other events beyond the reasonable control of the individual subject to such requirement."

When the 60-day rule has been violated, Rev. Proc. 2003-16 clarifies the conditions in which a waiver can be granted. The waiver is automatic (no application to the IRS is required) if a financial institution receives funds prior to the expiration of the 60-day rollover period, the taxpayer follows all procedures for depositing the funds into an eligible retirement plan within the 60-day period, and, solely due to an error on the part of the financial institution, the funds are not deposited into an eligible retirement plan within the 60-day rollover period. Automatic approval is granted only: (1) if the funds are deposited into an eligible retirement plan within 1 year from the beginning of the 60-day rollover period; and (2) if the rollover would have been valid if the financial institution had deposited the funds as instructed.

If an automatic waiver is not available, the taxpayer can file for a waiver using the same procedures for a private letter ruling described in Rev. Proc. 2003-4 and paying the user fee described in Rev. Proc. 2003-8 (generally $90). Rev. Proc. 2003-16 provides that in determining whether to grant a waiver of the 60-day rollover requirement, the IRS will consider all relevant facts and circumstances, including: (1) errors committed by a financial institution; (2) inability to complete a rollover due to death, disability, hospitalization, incarceration, restrictions imposed by a foreign country, or postal error, (3) the use of the amount distributed (for example, in the case of payment by check, whether the check was cashed); and (4) the time elapsed since the distribution occurred.

A review of the Private Letter Rulings that have been granted show that the IRS has been quite generous in granting a waiver of the 60-day requirement. Typically, a waiver has been grated when

- the facts and circumstances consisted of an error by the financial institution
- erroneous investment advice was given
- plan administrator errors were made
- the client's medical condition made it difficult to comply with the rules
- client errors occurred which ran contrary to the client's intention to make a rollover
- there was an existence of intervening causes such as the death of a spouse, weather conditions, or fraud by the taxpayer's child

Typically the waiver has been denied in situations where the taxpayer intended to use the amount for personal purposes and could not return it to the IRA before the 60-day time limit.

LUMP-SUM DISTRIBUTIONS

Instead of taking periodic payments from a qualified plan, employees are frequently permitted to receive their retirement benefit in a lump-sum distribution. In the past, participants receiving a lump sum from a qualified plan had the opportunity to take advantage of several special tax rules. Most of these rules have been repealed, but several are still grandfathered for certain taxpayers. One rule that continues to be broadly available defers the net unrealized appreciation of distributed employer securities. Grandfather rules include 10-year income averaging and a special capital-gains rate available for distributions attributable to pre-1974 participation. These rules are only available to individuals born before 1936.

Unrealized Appreciation

net unrealized appreciation (NUA)

Whenever a recipient receives a lump-sum distribution from a qualified plan, he or she may elect to defer paying tax on the *net unrealized appreciation (NUA)* in qualifying employer securities. If the distribution is not a lump-sum distribution, NUA is excludible only to the extent that the appreciation is attributable to nondeductible employee contributions.

lump-sum distribution

To qualify as a *lump-sum distribution,* the participant's entire benefit (referred to as balance to the credit) must be distributed in one tax year on account of death, disability, termination of employment, or attainment of age 59 1/2. For purposes of 10-year forward averaging (but not the NUA rules), the participant also needs 5 years of plan participation to qualify. Under the balance-to-the-credit rules, all pension plans of a single sponsor (defined-benefit, money-purchase, target-benefit, or cash-balance plan) are treated as a single plan; all profit-sharing plans (including 401(k)) are treated as a single plan; and all stock-bonus plans are treated as a single plan. This means, for example, that a participant in both a defined-benefit plan and a money-purchase plan would have to receive both benefits in the same year to receive the balance to the credit.

The NUA in the employer's stock that is included in a lump-sum distribution is excluded when computing the income tax on the distribution. NUA is the difference between the value of the stock when credited to the participant's account and its fair market value on the date of distribution. The plan provides the participant with the value of the stock when it was credited to the account (referred to as the stock's cost basis). The plan can choose one of several methods for valuing the cost basis as found in Treas. Reg.1.402(a)-1(b)(2)(i).

This NUA is taxable as long-term capital gain to the recipient when the shares are sold, even if they are sold immediately. If the recipient holds the shares for a period of time after distribution, any additional gain (above the NUA) is taxed as long- or short-term capital gain, depending on the holding period (long term if held for one year or more).

At the time of the distribution, the participant can elect to pay tax on the NUA (versus taking advantage of the opportunity to defer taxes). The only reason do this is if the effective tax rate using one of the other special averaging rules is less than the capital-gains rate (15 percent in most cases). However, it is unlikely that this will be the case.

To ensure that the participant's unrealized appreciation is taxed at some point, if the stock is left to an heir, the unrealized appreciation is not entitled to a step up in basis. It is treated as income in respect of a decedent (IRD). The IRD amount retains its character as long-term capital gain, and as with other IRD, the beneficiary is entitled to a deduction for the amount of estate taxes paid on the IRD amount.

Taking Advantage of the NUA Rule

Recently, the NUA rule has been receiving more attention in the press. First, it is one of the only remaining special tax rules that apply to qualified plan distributions. Second, with the proliferation of the 401(k) plan, many plan participants are accumulating large employer stock accounts. Many mid-size and large companies provide employer securities as an investment alternative or even make employer matching contributions in employer stock. Third, the current long-term capital-gains rate of 15 percent (10 percent in some cases) is less than half the top marginal tax rate (35 percent) for ordinary income. Participants receiving lump sums that include a distribution of employer securities should seriously consider taking advantage of this rule versus simply rolling the entire benefit into an IRA or other tax-sheltered retirement plan. Once the benefit is rolled over, future distributions will be subject to ordinary income tax.

The IRS has issued several private letter rulings that allow participants significant choice concerning this rule. In Private Letter Ruling 9721036, the IRS allowed a taxpayer who received both cash and stock as part of a lump-sum distribution to roll over the cash into an IRA and treat the stock as taxable income subject to the NUA rule. In Private Letter Ruling 200243052, the IRS allowed taxpayers to elect to roll over a portion of the company stock into an IRA while taxing a portion of the company stock using the NUA rule. If the IRS continues ruling in a similar manner, it means that a participant in a 401(k) plan with an employer securities account can elect NUA treatment on all or a portion of the employer stock account and roll over any other investments tax free into an IRA.

Example:	Joe retires at age 62 and receives a lump-sum distribution with a current market value of $700,000. The market value of employer securities is $200,000, but the cost basis is $50,000. Joe should consider rolling the cash (worth $500,000) into an IRA but not rolling over the $200,000. At the time of the distribution, Joe will have to pay tax on the $50,000 cost basis. When he sells the stock, he will pay long-term capital gains on the $150,000 NUA, and he will pay long-term gain on any subsequent appreciation (as long as he holds the stock for at least one year). If Joe is in the 35 percent federal income tax bracket, he pays 35 percent on the $50,000 distribution, but he pays only 15 percent on the rest of the gain. If he rolls the employer securities into an IRA, all subsequent distributions will be taxed as ordinary income (35 percent). If Joe wants to sell a portion of his stock account so he can diversify his retirement portfolio, he could also consider rolling over a portion of the stock account into the IRA.

This example illustrates the importance of considering NUA tax treatment. It is the type of situation in which the election may well be the right choice. However, in each individual case, determining whether or not to roll the benefit into an IRA or to take the employer stock into income will not be an easy decision. Here are some factors that will influence the decision.

- Clearly, this rule only has a positive impact when the cost basis of the securities is significantly lower than the current market value.
- If the participant needs cash in the near future, then taking the stock into income is probably a good idea since it results in a conversion of a portion of the taxable income from ordinary income to capital gains. Also, if the individual is under age 59 1/2, the Section 72(t) tax will only apply to the portion of the income subject to ordinary income tax.
- A younger person receiving a distribution that includes company stock will generally want to sell the stock to diversify his or her retirement portfolio. Because the sale will result in current taxation, the individual is giving up what could be significant income tax deferral if he or she decides not to roll the stock into an IRA. Deferral is very valuable, even if the tax rate in the future is somewhat higher than the rate today.

In the end, there is probably no right decision for any particular taxpayer. In addition to the above considerations, the participant's attitude about paying taxes and projections about future tax rates will be important considerations. The planner's main objective should be to help lay out all the alternatives clearly, so that the participant can make the right election for himself or herself.

Grandfathered Special Tax Rules

Individuals born before 1936 who receive lump-sum distributions from qualified plans (these rules never applied to IRAs, SEPs, SIMPLEs, or 403(b) plans), may still be eligible for several grandfathered tax rules. Since these rules effect only a small portion of the pension population, they are covered here briefly.

Ten-Year Averaging

ten-year averaging

Ten-year averaging may still be available for individuals born prior to January 1, 1936, if the following conditions are met:

- The distribution qualifies as a lump-sum distribution.
- The election for 10-year averaging has not been made before (only one election per taxpayer).

The tax rate on a lump sum eligible for 10-year averaging depends on the amount of the lump sum. Even though most will go directly to a tax table (table 10-3) to calculate the tax, to understand the concept, it is helpful to review the steps of the actual calculation. To determine the tax,

- calculate one-tenth of the distribution (after taking into consideration a minimum distribution allowance on distributions under $70,000)
- calculate the tax on that amount using 1986 tax rates considering the lump-sum distribution as the taxpayer's only income
- multiply the result by 10

Because tax rates in 1986 were highly bracketed, the tax rate is generally favorable only when the distribution amount is relatively low. Table 10-3 can be used to determine the tax on a specific distribution. Assume your client receives a lump-sum distribution of $150,000. For simplicity, assume that the entire distribution is taxable and that there are no plan accumulations attributable to pre-1974 service. Looking at the table, the $150,000 distribution

TABLE 10-3
Ten-Year Averaging (Using 1986 Tax Rates)*

If the adjusted total taxable amount is		the separate tax is	plus this %	of the excess over
at least	but not more than			
. . .	$ 20,000	0	5.5	0
$ 20,000	21,583	$ 1,100	13.2	$ 20,000
21,583	30,583	1,309	14.4	21,583
30,583	49,417	2,605	16.8	30,583
49,417	67,417	5,769	18.0	49,417
67,417	70,000	9,009	19.2	67,417
70,000	91,700	9,505	16.0	70,000
91,700	114,400	12,977	18.0	91,700
114,400	137,100	17,063	20.0	114,400
137,100	171,600	21,603	23.0	137,100
171,600	228,800	29,538	26.0	171,600
228,800	286,000	44,410	30.0	228,800
286,000	343,200	61,570	34.0	286,000
343,200	423,000	81,018	38.0	343,200
423,000	571,900	111,342	42.0	423,000
571,900	857,900	173,880	48.0	571,900
857,900	. . .	311,160	50.0	857,900

*Persons electing 10-year averaging must use the 1986 single tax rate schedule regardless of the year in which they actually receive the distribution.

falls in the range between $137,100 and $171,600. Therefore, the tax on the $150,000 distribution is equal to $21,603 plus 23 percent of the excess over $137,100. The excess over $137,100 is $12,900; 23 percent of $12,900 is $2,967. Thus the total 10-year averaging tax on a $150,000 distribution is equal to $21,603 plus $2,967, or $24,570.

The taxpayer reports the tax on Form 4972, which is filed with the tax return for the year. Form 4972 is quite useful because it includes detailed instructions and a worksheet for making the calculation. (See appendix 2.)

Capital-Gains Election

Clients born before January 1, 1936, can elect to treat the portion of a lump-sum distribution attributable to pre-1974 plan participation as capital gain. If this election is made, the amount subject to capital gain is taxed at a special grandfathered rate of 20 percent. A recipient may make only one such election.

capital-gain provision

If the *capital-gain provision* is elected, the capital-gain portion of a lump-sum distribution is then excluded when the person calculates the 10-year averaging tax. Therefore, the total tax payable on a lump-sum distribution when a person elects capital-gain treatment for pre-1974 plan accruals is equal to 20 percent of the portion of the distribution attributable to the pre-1974 plan accruals plus the averaging tax on the remainder. For example, assume that a lump-sum distribution is equal to $150,000, and the capital-gain portion is $33,000. If your client elects capital-gain treatment, only the portion of the distribution not attributable to the capital-gain portion (in this case, $117,000) is included in the adjusted total taxable amount when computing the averaging tax.

Clearly, a client born before January 1, 1936, should elect the capital-gain provision for pre-1974 plan accruals whenever the adjusted total taxable amount after subtracting the capital-gain portion is taxed at an effective rate of more than 20 percent. If we look at table 10-3, we can see that a person who elects 10-year averaging will always benefit by electing the capital-gain treatment for pre-1974 plan accruals if the adjusted total taxable amount after subtracting the capital-gain portion is equal to or greater than $137,100. At that level, each additional dollar of adjusted total taxable amount is taxed at a rate of 23 percent or higher.

Choosing Ten-Year Averaging and the Capital-Gain Treatment

When should clients who are still eligible for these grandfathered special tax rules elect to receive lump-sum distributions, rather than periodic payouts from their plans (or from IRA rollover accounts)? First, tax rates in 1986 were quite high and the tax rate with special averaging will not be very attractive unless the distribution is approximately $300,000 or less. If this is the case, it is generally appropriate to explore the decision at least to the point of calculating the tax under the special rules.

Once the special tax rate is determined, then the client needs to consider whether the tax rate looks attractive or not. This will depend on factors including

- the length of the potential period of additional tax deferral
- the current investment environment
- expected increases (or decreases) in the income tax rates

Estate planning considerations are also crucial in the equation. Sometimes deferring income taxes as long as possible is the best way to pass on wealth to the next generation (see discussion in the following chapter). Other times, concerns about liquidity will weigh in favor of taking a lump sum. In estate planning, the liquidity can be needed for funding a gifting program, retitling assets in the name of the spouse, or funding the purchase of life insurance.

Even when the special tax rate seems quite low, it is appropriate to maintain a healthy skepticism regarding the advantages to paying tax on the lump sum. Tax deferral is hard to beat, especially when the potential distribution stream is going to be 20 years or more—which is the case for most clients.

Ultimately, the decision generally needs to be made only after a lot of fact finding and consideration of the factors mentioned above. Only then can it be determined whether special averaging treatment makes sense for a specific client.

11

Planning for Pension Distributions—Part II

David A. Littell

Chapter Outline

MINIMUM-DISTRIBUTION RULES

The minimum-distribution rules contained in IRC Sec. 401(a)(9) are designed to limit the deferral of taxation on plan benefits. The primary reason for allowing the deferral of taxes is to encourage savings for retirement. This tax-preferred item comes at a great cost to the government; therefore, the minimum-distribution rules have been designed both to ensure that a significant portion of a participant's benefit is paid out during retirement and to limit the period for benefits paid after death.

General

The rules of 401(a)(9) apply in essentially the same way (with a few exceptions) to all tax-preferred retirement plans including qualified plans, IRAs (including SEPs and SIMPLEs), 403(b) annuity plans, and even IRC Sec. 457 plans. Roth IRAs are not subject to the rules governing lifetime distributions to the participant but are required to make distributions to a death beneficiary.

It is important to understand that there are actually two separate minimum-distribution rules. One rule applies to those individuals who live until the required beginning date (generally the April 1 following the year the participant attained age 70 1/2), and a separate rule applies when the participant dies before the required beginning date.

Another complicating factor is that Code Sec. 402 allows a spouse the option to roll over a benefit received at the death of the participant into an IRA in his or her own name. The rollover is treated as a complete distribution from the participant's plan, meaning that the minimum-distribution rules will have to be satisfied, treating the spouse as the participant. This rule provides planning opportunities, but can also be confusing.

Failing to satisfy the minimum-distribution rules results in an extremely harsh penalty. Under IRC Sec. 4974, if the minimum distributions are not made in a timely manner, the plan participant is required to pay a 50 percent excise tax on the amount of the shortfall between the amount actually distributed and the amount required to be distributed under the minimum-distribution rules. In addition, if the plan is a qualified plan, it may lose its tax-favored status if the minimum-distribution rules are not satisfied.

To help enforce the minimum distribution rules, IRA trustees are required to report participants that have a required minimum distribution on Form 5498. At the same time, IRA trustees are also required to notify participants by January 31 that a required distribution is due for that year. The trustee can either provide a calculation of the required minimum distribution or offer to make the calculation at the participant's request. At the present time, there are no similar reporting requirements for qualified plans.

Minimum Distributions at the Required Beginning Date

The next several pages describe the minimum-distribution rules that apply when the individual has lived until the required beginning date (generally April 1 of the year following attainment of age 70 1/2). The rules for determining the minimum distribution are different depending upon whether the distribution is from an individual account plan or is payable as an annuity—either from a defined-benefit plan or from a commercial annuity. The account plan rules apply to all IRAs, 403(b) plans, SEPs, SIMPLEs, Sec. 457 plans, and qualified plans of the defined-contribution type, unless a commercial annuity is purchased prior to the required beginning date. The account plan rules are reviewed below, followed by a discussion of the annuity distribution rules.

Required Beginning Date

required beginning date

The date benefit payments must begin is called the *required beginning date.* This date is generally April 1 of the year following the calendar year in which the participant attains age 70 1/2. However, there are two important exceptions:

- Any participant in a government or church plan who remains an employee after reaching age 70 1/2 will not have to begin distributions until the April 1 following the later of either the calendar year in which the participant reaches age 70 1/2 or the calendar year in which he or she retires.
- Any qualified plan participant who reaches 70 1/2 and who is not considered a 5 percent owner of the entity sponsoring the plan will not have to begin distributions until the April 1 following the later of either the year of attainment of age 70 1/2 or the year in which the participant retires. This exception also applies to 403(b) plans without regard to the 5 percent owner rule.

Note that there are no exceptions to the required beginning date for IRAs—which also includes SEPs and SIMPLEs. For these plans, the required beginning date is always the April 1 of the year following the calendar year in which the covered participant attains age 70 1/2.

YOUR FINANCIAL SERVICES PRACTICE:
CLIENT QUERY

Question: Your client Emma calls to say that her husband Ed is self-employed and maintains a Keogh profit-sharing plan. Ed is turning 70 1/2 this year. Because he is still working, she is not sure whether or not he has to start taking minimum distributions.

Solution: Because he is the 100-percent owner of the entity, he is not eligible for the exception to the age 70 1/2 rule. He will have to start taking distributions from the plan by the April 1 following attainment of age 70 1/2.

---

first distribution year

The required beginning date is somewhat of a misnomer since a minimum distribution is required for the year in which the participant attains age 70 1/2 or, if one of the exceptions applies, the year in which the participant retires. Because a distribution must be made for this year, it is referred to as the *first distribution year.* The distribution for the first distribution year can be delayed until the following April 1, but required distributions for all subsequent distribution years must be made by December 31 of the applicable year.

Example:	Shelley, who has an IRA, turned 70 on March 15, 2005. On September 15, 2005, she turned 70 1/2. The first required distribution from Shelley's IRA is for the year ending December 31, 2005, but she has the option to take the distribution any time in 2005 or delay it up to the required beginning date of April 1, 2006. However, if she delays the distribution into 2006, she will still have to take a minimum distribution for the second distribution year by December 31, 2006.

As you can see, delaying the first distribution into the second year doubles up the required distribution for that year and increases taxes for that year—not a desirable result in some cases.

Account Plan Distributions during the Participant's Life

applicable distribution period

Once the participant attains the required beginning date, a minimum distribution is required for each and every distribution year (and no credit is given for larger distributions in prior years) through the year of the participant's death. The required distribution is calculated by dividing the account balance by the *applicable distribution period*. The participant's benefit in a defined-contribution plan, 403(b) plan, or IRA is based on the participant's account balance. In an IRA account, the benefit for a distribution year is the IRA account balance at the end of the previous calendar year. For qualified plans and 403(b) plans, the employee's benefit is his or her individual account balance as of the last valuation date in the calendar year immediately preceding the distribution year.

The distribution period comes from the Uniform Lifetime Table (table 11-1) and is determined based on the age of the participant at the end of the distribution year. The same methodology is used for every year that the participant is alive. Each year, the applicable distribution period is determined by simply looking at the uniform table based on the age of the participant during that year.

Example:	Sally, an IRA participant, is aged 71 at the last day of the first distribution year (the year she attains age 70 1/2). Her IRA balance at the end of the preceding year is $200,000. The first year's required distribution is $200,000/26.5 = $7,547 (table 11-1). This is the required minimum regardless of the beneficiary unless Sally's sole beneficiary is her spouse and he is

more than 10 years younger than she. For the second distribution year, the applicable distribution period is 25.6 (table amount for a 72-year-old participant).

An exception applies if the employee's sole beneficiary is the employee's spouse and the spouse is more than 10 years younger than the employee. In that case, the employee is permitted to use the longer distribution period measured by the joint life and last survivor life expectancy of the employee and spouse (calculated looking at the IRS Joint and Last Survivor Table, a portion of which is reproduced in table 11-2). This exception will apply for any distribution year in which the spouse (who is more than 10 years younger than the participant) is the sole beneficiary as of the January 1 of the distribution year. This means that if the spouse dies or the couple gets divorced after January 1, the joint life table can still be used for that year.

TABLE 11-1
Uniform Lifetime Table

Age of Participant	Distribution Period	Age of Participant	Distribution Period
70	27.4	93	9.6
71	26.5	94	9.1
72	25.6	95	8.6
73	24.7	96	8.1
74	23.8	97	7.6
75	22.9	98	7.1
76	22.0	99	6.7
77	21.2	100	6.3
78	20.3	101	5.9
79	19.5	102	5.5
80	18.7	103	5.2
81	17.9	104	4.9
82	17.1	105	4.5
83	16.9	106	4.2
84	15.5	107	3.9
85	14.8	108	3.7
86	14.1	109	3.4
87	13.4	110	3.1
88	12.7	111	2.9
89	12.0	112	2.6
90	11.4	113	2.4
91	10.8	114	2.1
92	10.2	115 and older	1.9

Example: If Sally's beneficiary in the previous example was her 51-year-old spouse, the minimum distribution would be $200,000/34.2 = $5,848 (table 11-2). In this case, for the second distribution year, the applicable distribution period is 33.2, which is their joint life expectancy calculated at the end of that distribution year.

TABLE 11-2
Joint and Last Survivor Table

Ages	45	46	47	48	49	50	51	52	53	54
68	39.6	38.7	37.9	37.0	36.2	35.3	34.5	33.7	32.9	32.1
69	39.5	38.6	37.8	36.9	36.0	35.2	34.4	33.6	32.8	32.0
70	39.4	38.6	37.7	36.8	35.9	35.1	34.3	33.4	32.6	31.8
71	39.4	38.5	37.6	36.7	35.9	35.0	34.2	33.3	32.5	31.7
72	39.3	38.4	37.5	36.6	35.8	34.9	34.1	33.2	32.4	31.6
73	39.3	38.4	37.5	36.6	35.7	34.8	34.0	33.1	32.3	31.5
74	39.2	38.3	37.4	36.5	35.6	34.8	33.9	33.0	32.2	31.4
75	39.2	38.3	37.4	36.5	35.6	34.7	33.8	33.0	32.1	31.3
76	39.1	38.2	37.3	36.4	35.5	34.6	33.8	32.9	32.0	31.2
77	39.1	38.2	37.3	36.4	35.5	34.6	33.7	32.8	32.0	31.1
78	39.1	38.2	37.2	36.3	35.4	34.5	33.6	32.8	31.9	31.0

Source: Reg. Sec. 1.401(a)(9)-9

Death of the Participant after the RBD

For the participant who dies after the required beginning date, distributions must continue to satisfy the required minimum-distribution rules. In the year of death, the heirs must take the decedent's required distribution (if this distribution was not taken before death) based on the method under which the decedent had been taking distributions.

In subsequent years, the required distributions will depend upon who is the chosen beneficiary. When the beneficiary is an individual who is not the spouse, the applicable distribution period is that individual's life expectancy (using the IRS Single Life Table [table 11-3]) as of the end of the year following death. In subsequent years, the applicable distribution period is the life expectancy from the previous year less one. This means that remaining distributions are now made over a fixed period. This is true even if the beneficiary at the time of death subsequently dies and leaves the benefit to another heir.

TABLE 11-3
Single Life Table

Age	Multiple	Age	Multiple
40	43.6	66	20.2
41	42.7	67	19.4
42	41.7	68	18.6
43	40.7	69	17.8
44	39.8	70	17.0
45	38.8	71	16.3
46	37.9	72	15.5
47	37.0	73	14.8
48	36.0	74	14.1
49	35.1	75	13.4
50	34.2	76	12.7
51	33.3	77	12.1
52	32.3	78	11.4
53	31.4	79	10.8
54	30.5	80	10.2
55	29.6	81	9.7
56	28.7	82	9.1
57	27.9	83	8.6
58	27.0	84	8.1
59	26.1	85	7.6
60	25.2	86	7.1
61	24.4	87	6.7
62	23.5	88	6.3
63	22.7	89	5.9
64	21.8	90	5.5
65	21.0		

Source: Reg. Sec. 1.401(a)(9)-9

Example: John dies at age 82 with an $800,000 IRA account (at the end of the previous year). For the year of death, the required minimum distribution is $800,000/17.1 = $46,783. Assuming that at the end of the year of death, the value of the account is $840,000, and on September 30 of the following year, the sole beneficiary is his daughter Sarah, who is aged 54 at the end of that year, the minimum distribution is $840,000/30.5 = $27,540. The remaining distribution period is now fixed. In the next year, the applicable distribution period is 29.5 (30.5 – 1) and so on in future years. In total, distributions can continue for 30.5 years after the death of the participant. This would be true even if Sarah dies before the end of the period and left the benefit to her heirs.

If there is no designated beneficiary as of September 30 of the year after the employee's death (which would be the case if a nonperson such as a charity or the estate was the chosen beneficiary), the distribution period is the employee's life expectancy calculated in the year of death, reduced by one for each subsequent year.

Example: Sandra dies at age 80 with her estate as the beneficiary. Her account balance at the end of the year of her death is $240,000, and her life expectancy is 9.2 years (10.2 – 1) in the year following death. The required distribution in the year following death is $26,087 ($240,000/9.2). In each following year, the applicable distribution period is reduced by one, until all amounts are distributed after 10 years.

If the participant's spouse is the chosen beneficiary, there are a number of options. In most cases, the spouse will elect to roll the benefit into his or her own IRA (or in some cases, treat the account as his or her own). In this case, subsequent distributions (in the year following death) are calculated using the same methodology as when the participant was alive—with the spouse now treated as the participant.

Example: Rollo dies at age 80 with his spouse Cassandra, aged 75, as the beneficiary. Cassandra rolls the benefit into her own IRA and names their only child, Alexis, as beneficiary. During Cassandra's life, the uniform table is still used to calculate the minimum required distribution. For example, in the year following Rollo's death, the applicable distribution period is 22.0 (see table 11-1 for individual aged 76). Assume that Cassandra dies at age 86 and on the September 30 following the year of her death, her daughter Alexis is the beneficiary. At the end of that year, Alexis is aged 53. The applicable distribution period is 31.4 for that year (see table 11-3). This is now the fixed remaining distribution period, even if Alexis dies prior to the end of that time period. If Alexis were to die before the end of that period, her beneficiaries could continue distributions using the same methodology. Note that in this example, the minimum distributions are spread over a 50-year period.

If the participant's spouse is his or her sole beneficiary as of September 30 in the year following the year of death, and the distribution is not rolled over, the distribution period during the spouse's life is the spouse's single life expectancy, recalculated each year. For years after the year of the spouse's death, the distribution period is the spouse's life expectancy calculated in the year of death, reduced by one for each subsequent year.

YOUR FINANCIAL SERVICES PRACTICE: CLIENT QUERY

Question: Your client, Hope, calls to say that she is approaching age 70 1/2 and has accumulated a significant amount in her Roth IRA. She says she doesn't currently need withdrawals from the plan, but has heard conflicting advice about whether her Roth IRA is subject to the minimum distribution rules. Her husband, Jonathan, is her beneficiary. Assuming that Hope dies before Jonathan and he doesn't need the Roth IRA account for expenses, he will leave the Roth IRA to their three daughters, Amy, Kat, and Andrea.

Solution: Hope is not required to make Roth IRA withdrawals during her lifetime. If she leaves the Roth IRA to her husband Jonathan, he can roll over the Roth IRA into an account in his own name. Since he is then treated as the owner, there will not be any required withdrawals during his lifetime. If Jonathan dies, leaving the Roth IRA to his three daughters, the minimum distribution rules that apply to traditional IRAs in the case of a participant who dies prior to the RMD now apply. This means that the distributions have to be made over 5 years, or if they begin by the end of the calendar year of death, over the life expectancy of the oldest daughter. If the Roth IRA was divided into three accounts by the end of the year following death, each daughter's life expectancy could be used in determining the maximum distribution period.

Annuity Payments

When a defined-benefit pension plan pays out a benefit in the form of an annuity, or if a commercial annuity is purchased to satisfy benefit payments in a defined-contribution plan, the regulations provide a method for determining whether the annuity satisfies the minimum-distribution rules. Under these rules, the determination only has to be made one time—when the annuity payments begin.

If the annuity is meant to satisfy the required minimum distribution rules, payments must begin on or before the participant's required beginning date. Most life annuity and joint and survivor annuities will satisfy the rules as long as the payment interval is uniform, does not exceed one year, and the stream of payments satisfies a nonincreasing requirement. The term *nonincreasing* is defined broadly in the regulations, and variable annuities and annuities that increase due to cost-of-living increases fit within the definition. An annuity with a cash-refund feature also qualifies.

Joint and survivor annuities with a survivor benefit of up to 100 percent are generally allowed. The only exception is for nonspousal beneficiaries who are more than 10 years younger than the participant. In this case, the maximum percentage payable to the beneficiary may be reduced. The maximum beneficiary percentage is based on the adjusted employee/beneficiary age difference. This is determined by first calculating the excess of the age of the participant over the age of the beneficiary in the year the annuity will begin (ages as of the end of year). If the participant is younger than age 70, the age difference determined in the previous sentence is reduced by the number of years that the employee is younger than age 70. Once the adjusted age difference is determined, refer to the IRS table reproduced in table 11-4 to determine the maximum applicable survivor percentage. The example below explains how this works.

TABLE 11-4
IRS Table for Determining the MDIB Maximum Applicable Survivor Annuity Percentage

Adjusted Employee/Beneficiary Age Difference	Applicable Percentage	Adjusted Employee/Beneficiary Age Difference	Applicable Percentage
10 years or less	100%	28	62%
11	96	29	61
12	93	30	60
13	90	31	59
14	87	32	59
15	84	33	58
16	82	34	57
17	79	35	56
18	77	36	56
19	75	37	55
20	73	38	55
21	72	39	54
22	70	40	54
23	68	41	53
24	67	42	53
25	66	43	53
26	64	44 years	52
27	63	and more	

Source: Reg. Sec. 1.401(a)(9)-6

Example:	Zelda, age 65, retires and requests payments in the form of a joint and survivor annuity for her and her daughter Yolonda. The annuity is a 100 percent survivor annuity, payments will be $1,000 a month to Zelda and, upon Zelda's death, $1,000 a month to Yolonda. At the end of the calendar year that the annuity begins, Yolonda is age 36 and Zelda has attained age 66. The adjusted employee/beneficiary age difference is calculated by taking the excess of the employee's age over the beneficiary's age and subtracting the number of years the employee is younger than age 70. In this case, Zelda is 30 years older than Yolanda and is commencing benefits 4 years before attaining age 70, so the adjusted employee/beneficiary age difference is 26 years. Under table 11-4, the applicable percentage for a 26-year adjusted employee/beneficiary age difference is 64 percent. As of the annuity starting date, the plan does not satisfy the MDIB requirement because the monthly payment to Yolonda upon Zelda's death will exceed 66 percent of Zelda's monthly payment.

The life annuity can have a period certain (or the annuity can be a period certain annuity without a lifetime contingency) as long as the period certain does not exceed the joint life expectancy of the participant and beneficiary using the uniform table (or joint and survivor table in the case of a spouse more than 10 years younger than the participant).

Example:	Suppose that Herb, aged 70 (at the end of the first distribution year), chooses a joint and survivor annuity with Sally, aged 80, as the contingent beneficiary. Herb wants to have a period-certain feature and wants to know if there are limitations on the length of the period certain. Because the joint life expectancy under the uniform table for Herb (age 70) is 26.2, this is the maximum length for period-certain payments for an annuity beginning at age 70.

YOUR FINANCIAL SERVICES PRACTICE:
ANNUITIZING AFTER THE REQUIRED BEGINNING DATE

It's quite possible that an IRA participant past the required beginning date would want to purchase an immediate annuity. This transaction is allowed as long as the amount of the distribution satisfies the account plan rules in the year the annuity is purchased, and the annuity purchased satisfies the annuity limitations.

Preretirement Death Benefits

When the participant dies prior to the required beginning date, the general rule is that a participant's entire interest must be distributed by December 31 of the calendar year that contains the fifth anniversary of the date the participant dies. Under this rule, the entire interest could be distributed at the end of the 5-year period.

There are two important exceptions that allow payments over the beneficiary's life expectancy, one that applies to spousal beneficiaries and one that applies to nonspousal beneficiaries. For nonspousal beneficiaries, the minimum-distribution rule is satisfied if distributions are made over the expected lifetime of the beneficiary, as long as the benefit begins by December 31 of the year following the year of death. The calculation of each required distribution is determined using the same methodology as with a nonspousal beneficiary when the participant dies after the required beginning date.

Example: Suppose that Gilligan dies at age 65 and his daughter Ginger is the beneficiary of his IRA. In the year following death, Ginger is aged 40 and her life expectancy is 43.6 years. If the lifetime exception is used and the account balance is $300,000 at the end of the year in which Gilligan dies, the required distribution in the following year is $300,000/43.6 = $6,880. Note that as long as distributions begin by the end of the year following the year Gilligan died, distributions can continue for 44 years. If this deadline is not met, the entire distribution must be made within 5 years!

When the beneficiary is the participant's spouse, the distribution may be made over the life of the spouse, as long as payments begin on or before the later of (1) December 31 of the calendar year immediately after the calendar year in which the participant dies or (2) December 31 of the calendar year immediately after the year in which the participant would have reached age 70 1/2. However, if the spouse dies prior to the commencement of benefit payments, then benefits may be distributed to his or her beneficiary under the same rules that would apply to the participant. Note that the spousal exception is generally not utilized since the spouse will typically elect to roll the benefit into his or her own account.

If the participant does not have a designated beneficiary (chooses a nonperson such as a charity or estate), then distributions must be made over a 5-year period. The lifetime exceptions are not available.

Beneficiary Issues

All the minimum-distribution rules involve identification of the participant's beneficiary. Under the current regulations, the beneficiary used to determine the required distribution is the beneficiary that actually inherits the benefit. Technically, it is the beneficiary identified as of September 30 of the year following death. (See the discussion of post-death planning below.)

Generally, a beneficiary must be an individual (that is, not a charity or the participant's estate) in order to take advantage of the ability to stretch out payments over a beneficiary's lifetime. A nonperson beneficiary (estate, charity, trust) is treated as having no beneficiary, unless the beneficiary is a trust and the following requirements are satisfied:

- The trust is irrevocable at death.
- The beneficiaries under the trust are identifiable.
- The trust document or a statement identifying the distribution provisions is provided to the plan's administrator.

In the case of a trust that conforms to the rules, the beneficiaries of the trust will be treated as the beneficiaries for purposes of the minimum-distribution rules. In most cases, the requirement of notifying the plan administrator does not have to occur until the time the beneficiaries have to be identified.

If there are multiple designated beneficiaries on September 30 of the year following death (and separate accounts for each participant have not been established), the life expectancy of the oldest beneficiary (with the shortest life expectancy) is used for determining the required distributions. If one of those beneficiaries is a nonperson, then the participant is deemed to have no designated beneficiary. If there are multiple designated beneficiaries and separate accounts exist, the minimum distributions of his or her separate share are taken by each beneficiary over the fixed-term life expectancy of each respective beneficiary.

Additional Rules

Multiple Plans

With qualified retirement plans, required minimum distributions must be calculated—and distributed—separately for each plan subject to the rules.

The rules are more liberal with multiple IRAs or 403(b) plans. With IRAs, the minimum distribution must be calculated separately for each IRA, but then the actual distributions can come from any of the IRA accounts. If, however, an individual has accounts in his or her own name as well as inherited IRAs, he or she cannot aggregate the two groups for determining the required minimum distribution. When an individual has multiple 403(b) accounts, the same aggregation rule that applies to IRAs applies to the 403(b) plans.

Rollovers and Transfers

As we have discussed, liberal rules allow participants the right to roll or transfer benefits from one type of tax-sheltered plan to another. This transaction is relatively simple except in the case of the individual rolling over the benefit after attainment of age 70 1/2. In order to ensure that the minimum distributions are made, the rules clarify what to do in this special situation.

Special rules apply to amounts rolled (or transferred) from one tax-sheltered retirement plan to another. From the perspective of the distributing plan, the amount distributed (to be rolled over or transferred) is credited toward determining the minimum distribution from the plan. However, if a portion of the distribution is necessary to satisfy the minimum-distribution requirements, that portion may not be rolled (or transferred) into another plan.

Example: Shirley, aged 71 1/2, receives a single-sum distribution from a qualified retirement plan. She intends to roll the distribution into an IRA. She may not roll the portion of the lump-sum distribution that represents the minimum distribution for the current distribution year into the IRA.

Once the amount is rolled into the second plan, it will count toward determining the participant's benefit for determining the minimum distribution. However, because the minimum distribution is based on the benefit in the previous year, the amount rolled over does not affect the minimum until the following year.

Spousal Rollovers

When the spouse is the beneficiary of the participant's retirement plan benefit, he or she has a unique opportunity to roll the benefit into an IRA in his or her own name. Under the minimum-distribution rules, the rollover is treated as a complete distribution of the participant's benefit, satisfying the minimum-distribution rules from the perspective of the participant's plan. Once the benefit is in the spouse's name, the minimum-distribution rules have to be satisfied with the spouse treated as the participant. The spouse has the opportunity to name a beneficiary and calculate future minimum distributions based on the joint life expectancy of the spouse and the beneficiary.

Grandfather Provisions for Qualified Plans and 403(b) Plans

There are two situations in which the current distribution rules do not apply. In a qualified plan, participants with accrued benefits as of December 31, 1983, were allowed to sign an election form (prior to January 1, 1984) indicating the time and method of distribution of their plan benefit. The benefit election form had to be specific and had to conform to pre-TEFRA rules, which allowed distributions to be deferred much later than age 70 1/2. These grandfather provisions were contained in Sec. 242(b) of TEFRA and are generally referred to as *TEFRA 242(b) elections.*

TEFRA 242(b) election

TEFRA 242(b) elections continue to be valid if benefits are being paid from the original plan in which the election is made, and if the plan distributions follow the Sec. 242(b) distribution election. If it is not followed exactly with regard to the form and timing of the payments, the election is considered "revoked." A substitution or addition of a beneficiary generally does not result in the revocation of the election. If the benefit election is changed or revoked after the individual has reached the required beginning date under the current rules, the participant will be forced to "make up" distributions that would otherwise (absent the Sec. 242(b) election) have been required under the current rules.

Sec. 242(b) elections can delay the timing of required distributions substantially. The retirement planner should be sure to ask if the client has retained an election form in his or her files. As noted above, the election has to be followed exactly in order to avoid having to take a potentially large distribution at some later date.

In a 403(b) plan, a separate grandfathering rule allows the participant to delay the distribution of amounts earned prior to 1987 until the participant attains age 75. There are no special grandfathering exceptions that apply to IRA distributions.

Planning

Under the current rules, the designated beneficiary does not have to be determined until September 30 of the year following the year of the participant's death. This permits some flexibility for determining the post-death minimum required distributions from the retirement plan or IRA. Of course, the decedent's potential beneficiaries are "carved in stone" at the time of his or her death because the decedent can no longer make additional beneficiary choices. However, the use of a qualified disclaimer or early distribution of a beneficiary's share could be effective in changing the designated beneficiary to contingent beneficiaries by the time specified to determine such beneficiary.

Example:	Suppose that Helen dies at age 80. At the time of her death, her son, Bud, from her first marriage, The American College, and her second husband, Saul, are each beneficiaries of one-third of the benefit. Before September 30 of the year following death, Saul rolls his benefit into a spousal IRA, benefits are paid out to The American College, and Bud is the sole beneficiary. This means that subsequent required distributions will be based on Bud's life expectancy. If Helen had also named a contingent beneficiary for Bud's benefit, for example, Bud's child Kelly, Bud could disclaim his benefit in favor of Kelly and the distribution could continue over Kelly's longer life expectancy.

separate account

Another way to limit problems that could arise with multiple beneficiaries is to divide benefits into *separate accounts*. The regulations define acceptable separate accounting to include allocating investment gains and losses, as well as contributions and forfeitures, on a pro rata basis in a reasonable and consistent manner between such separate portion and any other benefits. If these rules are followed, the separate beneficiary of each share determines his or her minimum required distribution based on his or

---

YOUR FINANCIAL SERVICES PRACTICE: BENEFICIARY ELECTIONS

Under the current regulations, taking advantage of maximum deferral is an option that remains open even after the death of the participant, but only if the beneficiary election contains the appropriate list of contingent beneficiaries and qualified disclaimers are made. For a married person with children, the following beneficiary election may be appropriate:

- payable to the spouse
- payable to a credit shelter trust with the spouse as income beneficiary and the children as remainder beneficiaries
- payable directly to the children
- payable to a trust with the grandchildren as beneficiaries

her life expectancy according to his or her age on the birthday that occurs in the year following the year of the decedent's death. The final regulations clearly state that the account can be divided into a separate account for each beneficiary up to the end of the year following the death of the participant.

Because of the ability to disclaim benefits, pay them out, or establish separate accounts after the death of the participant, postmortem planning is possible. However, to effectively use these tools, the participant will have to give careful consideration to the beneficiary election form. For many individuals, this will mean establishing multiple layers of contingent beneficiaries on the designation form in order to provide the most flexibility after the participant's death.

CHOOSING A DISTRIBUTION OPTION

Choosing the best distribution at retirement can be a rather complex decision that involves personal preferences, financial considerations, and an interplay between tax incentives and tax penalties. Planners must keep a myriad of factors in mind in order to render effective advice.

For example, typical considerations include whether

- the periodic distribution will be used to provide income necessary for sustaining the retiree or whether the distribution will supplement already adequate sources of retirement income
- the client has properly coordinated distributions from several different qualified plans and IRAs
- the retiree will have satisfactory diversification of his or her retirement resources after the distribution occurs
- the client has complied with the rules for minimum distributions from a qualified plan

The first step in making a choice is to fully understand the available options. Below is a discussion of the options that are available from qualified plans, SEPs, SIMPLEs and 403(b) plans. Of course, the only way to understand the options for a plan is to read the appropriate documents.

Benefits Available from the Plan

When discussing the options available in tax-advantaged retirement plans, it's important to distinguish qualified plans from those that are funded with IRAs (SEPs and SIMPLEs) and 403(b) plans. Qualified plans are subject to a significant number of limitations while the others are more open ended.

Qualified Plans

Every qualified retirement plan will specify when payments may be made and which benefit options are available. Each plan will also have a default option if the participant fails to make an election. In pension language, the default is referred to as the normal form of benefit. The distribution options are generally quite limited in a qualified plan. This is because any option that is available must be available to all participants. Also, under the anti-cut back rules, options generally cannot be taken away once they are in the plan. To find out when benefits are payable and what the optional forms of benefit are requires a careful review of the plan's summary plan description and, in some cases, a review of the actual plan document.

A qualified plan has a range of options with regard to the timing of payments. Under law, distributions can be deferred until attainment of normal retirement age, but much more typically the plan will also allow payment at attainment of early retirement age, death, or disability. Today, most plans also make distributions available to employees who terminate employment (prior to retirement age) with vested benefits. This is almost always the case in defined-contribution plans, but also is more and more common in defined-benefit plans as well.

involuntary cash-out

When the participant terminates employment with a vested benefit of less than $5,000, the plan can provide that such small benefits will be cashed out in a lump sum—without giving the participant any choice in the timing or form of benefit. Most plans choose this *involuntary cash-out* option to simplify plan administration. A recipient of an involuntary cash-out retains the right to elect a direct rollover to an IRA or to receive the distribution directly. If the involuntary cashout is $1,000 or more and the participant fails to make an affirmative election, the plan administrator is required to roll the involuntary cashout directly to a designated IRA.

When the benefit exceeds $5,000, participants must be given all the benefit options allowed under the plan as well as the right to defer receipt of payment until normal retirement age. (*Planning Note:* Most participants will choose the immediate payout and roll the benefit to an IRA or a new employer's retirement plan. Reasons to stay in the old plan include lower investment costs, favorable investment options such as guaranteed investment contracts or employer stock, or financial penalties for early withdrawal of the benefit.)

In some cases, a plan will also allow withdrawals prior to termination of service. As discussed in chapter 3, this type of provision is not allowed from plans in the pension category, which includes defined-benefit, cash-balance, target-benefit, and money-purchase pension plans. The option is, however, allowed in profit-sharing type plans including profit-sharing, 401(k), stock bonus and ESOP plans. A special rule applies to the salary deferral account in a 401(k) plan—the withdrawals cannot be made unless the participant has a financial hardship (see chapter 3). Since in-service withdrawals result in taxable income, some plans (especially 401(k) plans) also provide for participant loan programs (see chapter 3).

The normal form of benefit for a married individual—in qualified plans that are subject to the qualified joint and survivor annuity rules—must be a joint and survivor benefit of not less than 50 percent or greater than 100 percent and a life annuity for a single participant. In qualified plans, not subject to the rules (generally profit-sharing, 401(k), and stock bonus plans), the normal form of payment is generally a single sum payment. Regardless of the plan's normal-form-of-benefit payment, participants frequently choose one of the alternative forms of distribution allowed under the plan. Options for distributions may include

- annuity payments
- installment payments
- lump-sum distributions

Let's take a closer look at some of the more common options available.

Life Annuity. A life annuity provides monthly payments to the participant for his or her lifetime. Payments from a life annuity completely stop when your client dies and no other benefit is paid to any beneficiary. A life annuity can be an appropriate option for individuals who want the guarantee of lifetime payments but who have no need to provide retirement income to a spouse or other dependent.

joint and survivor annuity

Joint and Survivor Annuity. A *joint and survivor annuity* provides monthly payments to the participant during his or her lifetime and if, at the participant's death, the beneficiary is still living, a specified percentage of the participant's benefit continues to be paid to the beneficiary for the remainder of his or her lifetime. The plan will specify the survivor portion and may allow the participant to choose from a 50 percent to a 100 percent survivor portion. Joint and survivor annuities can be appropriate if there is a need to provide for the continuation of retirement income to a spouse or other beneficiary who outlives the participant.

Life Annuity with Guaranteed Payments. A life annuity with guaranteed payments (sometimes referred to as a life annuity with a period-certain guarantee) provides monthly benefit payments to the participant during his or her lifetime. Payments are made for the longer of the life of the participant or some specified period of time. The plan may offer a 5-year, 10-year, or other specified guarantee period.

Example:	Sandy has elected a life annuity with a 10-year certain in the amount of $1,000 a month. If Sandy dies after 8 years, her designated beneficiary will continue to receive $1,000 a month for 2 years. If instead, Sandy dies 12 years after payments begin, there are no additional payments.

Participants with no real income concern for a beneficiary may still elect guaranteed payments to ensure that, at least, minimum payments are made in case of an untimely death. (*Planning Note:* If a client outlives the guarantee period, he or she has, in effect, gambled and lost because lower monthly benefits will be paid under a life annuity with guaranteed payments than under a straight life annuity.) Also, guaranteed payments can be a good option when the spouse (or some other beneficiary) is ill and has a short life expectancy. For example, if a retiring husband expects to outlive his wife who is in relatively poor health, then a life annuity with a minimum guarantee might be purchased to protect against the unlikely case of the husband predeceasing the wife. The period chosen should reflect, to some extent, the planner's best estimate of the wife's maximum life expectancy and, if applicable, the client's desire to pass on wealth.

Annuity Certain. This annuity provides the beneficiary with a specified amount of monthly guaranteed payments after which time all payments stop (for example, payments for 20 years). An annuity certain continues to be paid whether the participant survives the annuity period or not. If the client dies prior to 20 years, payments will be made to the client's beneficiary. This type of annuity can be appropriate when the participant's income need has a predictable period, such as for the period prior to beginning Social Security payments.

Lump-sum Distribution. This is what it sounds like—the entire benefit is distributed at once in a single sum. A participant interested in rolling the benefit into an IRA will elect the lump-sum distribution option. Some individuals elect this option from qualified plans in order to take advantage of the special tax treatment—10-year averaging for those born before 1936 and deferral of gain for those who receive a portion of their benefit in qualifying employer securities.

installment payments

Installments. The installment option is similar to, but definitely different from, a term-certain annuity. With *installment payments*, the participant will elect a payout length and, based on earnings assumptions, a payout amount will also be determined. Payments will be from the account, not an insurance carrier, and there are no guaranteed payments. If the funds run out before the period is over, payments will stop. If the assumptions are exceeded, the participant typically gets a refund with the remaining account at the end of period.

Value of the Benefit

To understand the value of the benefit provided by the plan, it is important to discuss defined-contribution plans and defined-benefit plans separately. In a defined-contribution plan, the benefit is always based on the value of the account balance. If the participant elects a lump-sum withdrawal, it will represent the entire value of vested account balance. If installment options are elected, the account balance (along with continued investment return) is simply liquidated over the specified time period. If the participant elects an annuity option, the plan will purchase the annuity from an insurance company. Depending upon the service providers involved in investment of plan assets, the plan may be able to get a favorable annuity purchase rate.

actuarial equivalent

In a defined-benefit plan, the value of each benefit is almost always the *actuarial equivalent* of a specified form of payment—most typically a single life annuity. This means that if, for example, the participant chooses a lump-sum benefit, the amount of the lump sum is based on the single sum value of a life annuity using the actuarial assumptions prescribed in the plan. Under current rules, actuarial assumptions must be tied to the PBGC long-term rate, which changes each month. In table 11-5 is an example of the value of a number of benefit options based on a $1,565 monthly benefit. The other annuity options pay less than the life annuity because of the longer guaranteed payout period.

Occasionally, in a defined-benefit plan, all forms of benefit will not be actuarially equivalent. Sometimes a plan will provide an unreduced joint and survivor benefit. For example, if the participant is entitled to a $1,000 life annuity, he or she can also elect a $1,000-a-month 50 percent joint and

TABLE 11-5
Comparison of Optional Benefit Forms
(Defined-benefit plan with a monthly life annuity payment of $1,565, assume both the participant and spouse are aged 65)

Annuity Form	Monthly Benefit
Life	$ 1,565
Life annuity/10-year guarantee	1,494
Life annuity/20-year guarantee	1,360
Joint and survivor (50 percent)	1,418
Joint and survivor (66 2/3 percent)	1,375
Joint and survivor (100 percent)	1,296
Lump-sum payment	$200,000

subsidized benefits

survivor annuity. Forms of payment that are more valuable than the normal form of payment are referred to as *subsidized benefits* It's also not uncommon to see early retirement benefits that are subsidized. For example, the plan may allow an individual age 60 with 30 years of service to receive the full normal retirement benefit payable at age 65 at the earlier age of 60.

IRAs

Typically, form-of-distribution options from IRAs are much more flexible than qualified plans because the individual is the owner and beneficiary. The withdrawals can be made on a discretionary basis or the participant can purchase an annuity. The annuity can be an immediate fixed annuity with one of the payment forms discussed above. It can also be a deferred annuity, or an immediate variable annuity. The attributes of these annuity options are discussed in detail in chapters 8 and 9.

403(b) Annuities

Withdrawal flexibility from 403(b) plans generally falls somewhere between the limited options in a qualified plan and the more open-ended options of the IRA. 403(b) plans have some restrictions on withdrawals prior to termination of employment. Also, if the plan contains employer contributions, the plans are subject to ERISA fiduciary rules and can even be subject to the qualified joint and survivor annuity rules.

Still, the participant may have more distribution options than with a qualified plan, especially if the benefit is funded with an annuity. Here, the participant may have virtually any annuity option commercially available from the insurance carrier, including an immediate variable annuity.

One item that is different for a 403(b) plan than a qualified plan is that the participant can, in many cases, simply maintain the account after termination of employment without selecting a specific cash-out option. This is similar to an IRA. Of course, the participant could also roll the benefit into an IRA account. There are two good reasons to leave the account in the 403(b) vehicle versus an IRA rollover. First, if the participant has accumulated a significant pre-1987 account balance, these amounts are not subject to the normal minimum-distribution rules (payments generally do not have to begin until the participant attains age 75). Second, many carriers will continue to allow participant loans from the 403(b) plan, even after termination of service.

PUTTING IT ALL TOGETHER

Throughout the last two chapters, we have discussed rules that affect pension distributions. Learning this information can be difficult, and integrating it into a cohesive package can be almost impossible. To help with these concerns, we will first review the rules as they apply to qualified plans, IRAs, and 403(b) annuities. After that, we will examine common issues working with different types of clients.

Qualified Plans

Qualified plans must have clear and precise rules regarding the amount, timing, and form of available benefits. The following discusses the tax treatment of these distributions and summarizes the rules that affect qualified plan distributions:

- Distributions are taxed as ordinary income unless the distribution is a lump sum and one of the special tax rules applies (the deferral of gain on employer securities and the grandfathered 10-year averaging and capital-gains rules), or unless the participant has basis. Basis includes after-tax contributions and PS 58 costs.
- The 10 percent premature distribution excise tax applies to the taxable portion of a distribution made prior to age 59 1/2. Exceptions apply if the distribution is made because of death or disability, to pay for certain medical expenses, or if substantially equal periodic payments are withdrawn (after separation from service). Another exception (that does not apply to IRAs) is that of distributions to a terminating participant after attainment of age 55.
- If a participant has a qualified plan balance payable to a beneficiary at his or her death, the value of the benefit is included in the taxable estate. Payments to beneficiaries are treated as income in respect to a decedent—meaning that beneficiaries receiving benefit payments pay income tax but may get a deduction for any estate taxes paid because of the value of the pension.
- In-service distributions are subject to limitations. No in-service withdrawals are allowed from plans categorized as pension plans. Profit-sharing-type plans may allow distributions upon a stated event; 401(k) plans are subject to more limiting hardship withdrawals.
- In lieu of taxable in-service withdrawals, plans may offer participant loan programs. Loans within prescribed limits are not subject to income tax.
- Distributions from most plans are subject to the qualified joint and survivor annuity (QJSA) requirements. A limited exception applies for certain profit-sharing plans.
- Distributions are subject to the minimum-distribution rules. The distribution can be made under the pre-TEFRA (Tax Equity and Fiscal Responsibility Act) distribution rules if the participant made a

written election in 1983. Participants (except for 5 percent owners) who continue working until they are past age 70 can defer the required beginning date until April 1 of the year following the year in which they retire.

- Distributions other than certain annuities, hardship withdrawals from 401(k) plans, and required minimum distributions can be rolled over into another qualified plan, 403(b) plan, 457 plan, or an IRA.

- Qualified plans are required to give participants the option to directly roll over distributions to an IRA or other qualified plan. Distributions that are not directly rolled over are subject to a 20 percent mandatory income tax withholding.

IRAs

The following is a brief review of the distribution rules that apply to IRAs. With one exception (described below), these rules apply to regular IRAs or IRAs associated with SEPs or SIMPLEs.

- Distributions are always taxed as ordinary income unless the participant has made nondeductible IRA contributions (or rolled over after-tax contributions from a qualified plan). None of the special tax rules that apply to qualified plans apply here.

- The 10 percent premature distribution excise tax applies to the taxable portion of a distribution made prior to age 59 1/2. Exceptions apply if the distribution is made because of death or disability, or to pay for certain medical expenses, or if substantially equal periodic payments are withdrawn (after separation from service). With IRAs, there are three additional exceptions: withdrawals to cover medical insurance premiums for certain unemployed individuals, withdrawals to cover post-secondary education expenses, and withdrawals of up to $10,000 for first-time homebuyer expenses.

- With SIMPLE IRAs, the 10 percent penalty tax becomes a 25 percent penalty if withdrawals are made in the first 2 years of participation. So this tax cannot be avoided, SIMPLE IRAs cannot be rolled over or transferred into a regular IRA in the first 2 years of participation.

- If a participant has an IRA account payable to a beneficiary at his or her death, the value of the benefit is included in the taxable estate. Payments to beneficiaries are treated as income in respect to a decedent—meaning that beneficiaries receiving benefit payments pay income tax but may get a deduction for any estate taxes paid because of the value of the pension.

- Participants can make withdrawals from IRAs (as well as SEPs and SIMPLEs) at any time without limitation. No participant loans are available, however.
- Distributions are subject to the minimum-distribution rules under which the required beginning date is always the April 1 following the year of attainment of age 70 1/2.
- The QJSA rules do not apply to IRAs.
- The 20 percent mandatory withholding rules do not apply to IRAs.
- Except for amounts satisfying the required minimum-distribution rules, distributions can be rolled over or transferred to another IRA, a qualified plan, 403(b) annuity, or 457 plan.

403(b) Plans

The following is a brief review of the distribution rules that apply to 403(b) plans:

- Distributions are generally taxed as ordinary income. Although there are no after-tax contributions, it is possible for the participant to have basis due to the PS 58 costs that may be recovered tax free.
- The 10 percent premature distribution excise tax applies in the same way as it does to qualified retirement plans.
- If a participant has a 403(b) account payable to a beneficiary at his or her death, the value of the benefit is included in the taxable estate. Payments to beneficiaries are treated as income in respect to a decedent—meaning that beneficiaries receiving benefit payments pay income tax but may get a deduction for any estate taxes paid because of the value of the pension.
- In-service distributions are subject to limitations. When a plan (funded with annuity contracts) contains a salary-deferral feature, contributions attributable to the deferral election may not be distributed until the employee attains age 59 1/2, separates from service, becomes disabled, becomes a hardship case, or dies. When the plan is funded with mutual fund shares, the special distribution requirements apply to all contribution amounts. The 403(b) plans can have participant loan programs.
- Distributions are subject to the minimum-distribution rules. An exception applies to the portion of the benefit that accrued prior to 1987. That amount can generally be deferred until age 75. In addition, participants (except for 5 percent owners) who continue working past age 70 can defer the required beginning date until the April 1 following the year in which they retire.

- Distributions (other than required minimum distributions and certain annuity payments) can be rolled over into another 403(b) annuity, qualified plan, 457 plan, or an IRA.

- A participant can generally keep the 403(b) vehicle even after termination of employment. This may be a better option than rolling the benefit into an IRA because of the pre-87 exception to the minimum-distribution rules and the ability to continue to take a loan from the 403(b) plan.

- Participants must be given the option to directly rollover distributions to a new trustee or custodian. Distributions that are not directly rolled over are subject to a 20 percent mandatory income tax withholding.

- In some cases, distributions are subject to the qualified joint and survivor annuity (QJSA) requirements.

Working with Clients

Financial service professionals will work with a wide variety of clients, and each of their needs will be unique. The checklist in table 11-6 identifies some client issues. Generally the typical issues that need to be addressed can be divided into two client profiles. The first consists of those clients with limited resources whose primary goal is making their limited resources last throughout their retirement years. The second group is made up of the clients who will not need all the pension assets during their own lifetime. This group will face the dual concern of financing retirement and maximizing the after-tax estate that they leave to their heirs. We will address each of these situations.

Primary Concern: Funding Retirement Needs

For most of us, accruing adequate retirement resources is a daunting task. In many cases, the most significant retirement asset is the company pension. For this reason, it is imperative that the distribution decisions result in maximization of the family's available after-tax dollars. The following materials address the vital issues that apply to clients whose primary concern is affording retirement.

Preretirement Distributions. The major concern for the individual who receives a pension distribution prior to retirement is ensuring that pension accumulations are used to finance retirement and are not spent beforehand. In this regard, participants want to be sure to satisfy rollover rules so that inadvertent taxes do not have to be paid. Meeting the rollover requirements has become much easier now that participants in qualified plans and 403(b)

TABLE 11-6
Checklist of Issues and Decisions at Retirement

1. Do you want an annuity for all or part of your funds?
2. What type of annuity is best for your situation?
3. Can you maximize the monthly payment of your annuity by rolling it into an IRA or another qualified plan—in other words, shop your annuity?
4. Should you delay taxation of a distribution by rolling it into an IRA or another qualified plan?
5. Is a rollover possible from a cash-flow perspective?
6. Is a direct rollover to the new trustee preferable to a rollover?
7. Do you want a lump-sum distribution for part or all of your funds?
8. Are you eligible for either the grandfathered 10-year averaging or capital-gains treatment for pre-'74 income?
9. Should you elect 10-year averaging or the capital-gains treatment?
10. What is the best tax strategy for dealing with the distribution of employer stock?
11. Has the client complied with the rules for minimum distributions from the qualified plan?
12. When do distributions have to begin?
13. Does the beneficiary election form reflect the client's current wishes?
14. In what order should assets be cashed in order to maintain optimum tax shelter and proper asset allocation ratios?
15. Has there been proper coordination of distributions from qualified plans and IRAs?
16. Will the distributions be used to provide necessary income for sustaining your client, or will it supplement already adequate sources of retirement income?
17. Did you meet the need to provide for surviving dependents?
18. Has your client integrated his or her retirement planning with proper estate planning?

---

annuities must be given the option to transfer benefits directly to an IRA or other qualified plan. Note that these direct rollover rules do not apply to IRA-funded plans, including SEPs and SIMPLEs. However, when a participant leaves an IRA-funded plan, there is generally no reason for a rollover.

Still, some clients will be tempted to spend preretirement pension distributions. If you have clients in this position, showing them the power of the compounding return will sometimes convince them otherwise.

Example: Sonny Shortview, aged 40, is changing jobs. He will be receiving a much higher salary in his new job and he is feeling quite well off. Sonny has the opportunity to receive a pension distribution from his old company in the amount of $35,000. Even though he doesn't really need the funds, the amount seems small enough to Sonny that he is considering paying taxes and using the after-tax proceeds for an auto upgrade. Sonny may change his mind when he learns that with a 10 percent rate of return, his $35,000 distribution will grow to $367,687 by the time he reaches age 65.

Another difficult situation arises in the case of involuntary dismissal. An employee who is terminated due to downsizing or other reasons may experience a prolonged period of unemployment. In this case, the individual may need to tap into his or her pension. If the participant is younger than age 59 1/2, he or she must pay the 10 percent premature distribution excise tax unless one of the exceptions applies. The substantially equal periodic payment exception is one way to avoid this tax, but the problem is that distributions must be made for the longer of 5 years or until attainment of age 59 1/2, and this period will probably be much longer than the period of unemployment. This problem can be mitigated somewhat by dividing assets into a number of IRAs. For example, part of the need can be met by using a periodic payment from one IRA and simply paying the excise tax for certain short-term needs from another IRA. If a lump sum is needed, the individual could consider borrowing from another source and repaying the loan with periodic distributions.

Form of Retirement Distribution. For the client living on his or her pension distribution, the two most important decisions are usually when to retire and the form of payment that should be received. In chapter 3, we looked at the effect of retiring at different times—especially retiring early. As we discussed, the effect of early retirement can be quite profound, especially in defined-benefit plans. Even if the plan subsidizes some part of the early retirement penalty, there is always a cost for early retirement. Other timing issues that need to be understood are the consequences of delaying payments to some time after retirement and of retiring after the plan's normal retirement age. Spend time with your clients to make sure they understand these important timing issues—it is rare that a plan participant will fully understand them without your help. Of course, the answers always depend on the specific terms of the plan, so also be sure to review the summary plan description.

Once the client has a full understanding of the timing issues, the next decision is choosing the form of retirement benefits. Almost all individual account-type plans (including qualified plans of the defined-contribution type, SEPs, SIMPLEs, and 403(b) annuities) give the participant the option to receive a lump-sum distribution, which can be rolled into an IRA without tax consequences. This benefit option affords the participant the most flexibility because the participant can take money out as slowly or as quickly as it is needed.

Defined-benefit plans may or may not have a lump-sum option, depending upon the terms of the plan. Also note that a lump sum from a defined-benefit plan is based on the actuarial equivalent of a normal form of payment, usually a life annuity. If the lump sum is calculated with unfavorable assumptions, this option may not be advisable. One way to test the value of the lump sum is to compare the amount payable as a life annuity from the plan to the amount that would result from taking a lump sum, rolling it into an IRA, and then buying a life annuity at commercially available prices.

Many participants will be satisfied with the IRA rollover approach because it provides both investment and withdrawal flexibility. However, this method does not ensure that the participant won't outlive pension distributions. Even with careful distribution planning, investment performance may not meet expectations, or the individual may live too long. To protect against this contingency, retirees should consider having at least a portion of their retirement income payable as some form of life annuity. We reviewed the advantages and disadvantages of various annuity options in the earlier part of this chapter. Participants can generally receive the type of annuity that they want, even if it is not offered by the particular plan involved. They can accomplish this by electing a lump-sum option, rolling the benefit into an IRA, and then purchasing the annuity. Variable annuities should be considered because they can combine the promise of lifetime benefits with the possibility of increasing payments over time to offset the effects of inflation.

Qualified Joint and Survivor Considerations. A married participant receiving a pension distribution in a form other than a qualified joint and survivor annuity generally must have his or her spouse sign a waiver. Unless there is marital discord, receiving an alternate form of benefit generally poses no special concerns. In fact, the disclosure and paperwork involved probably ensure that the participant is carefully considering all the available distribution options. Still, this is a matter that retirees may not understand. Explaining the effect of the joint and survivor form of payment is an excellent way to provide service to the client and solidify the advisory relationship.

Tax Issues

For the individual who receives a distribution from a qualified plan and qualifies for special tax treatment, an issue will be the decision of whether or not to elect special averaging treatment. With smaller distribution amounts, the tax rate using special averaging treatment can look quite attractive; it is possible that the effective rate can be 20 percent or less. Even though this rate is low, remember that it must be compared to the individual's marginal tax rate. The effect of deferring taxes is quite powerful, and taking the benefit as a lump sum has to be examined thoroughly.

If the client receives a lump-sum distribution but does not elect special averaging treatment, then the lump sum should generally be rolled directly into an IRA. As discussed in the previous chapter, it often is appropriate not to roll over the portion of the benefit that represents after-tax contributions. If the distribution includes employer stock, the effect of the net unrealized appreciation rules should be considered before making the rollover election.

Once the rollover occurs, to maximize the benefit of tax deferral, amounts should be distributed only when needed, unless, of course, the minimum-distribution rules require a larger distribution.

Another issue that has become a concern is whether the retiree should elect to convert his or her pension distribution to a Roth IRA. To do this, the distribution first must be rolled or transferred to an IRA and then converted to the Roth IRA. Only single individuals or marrieds filing jointly who have an adjusted gross income of under $100,000 for the year are allowed to convert. As discussed in chapter 4 of the textbook, conversion results in taxable ordinary income in the amount of the conversion. Once in the Roth IRA, growth is tax free as long as the distribution meets certain eligibility requirements. Determining whether to convert is a complex issue that requires a full understanding of the participant's retirement and estate planning concerns. However, there are some general considerations that will affect the participant's decision.

- The Roth IRA conversion becomes more appropriate the longer the period of distributions are stretched out. The individual who is struggling to meet retirement needs will probably require early withdrawals, which means that the Roth IRA will not have time to generate substantial tax-free accumulations.
- The Roth IRA conversion is more appropriate when the income tax rate is the same or higher at the time of distribution than at the time of conversion. For the average person struggling to meet retirement needs, the post-retirement income tax rate is probably lower than at the time of distribution. This factor weighs against conversion.
- Any portion of an IRA can be converted to a Roth IRA. This means that the retiree who has all of his or her retirement income may still want to convert some of it as a hedge against future tax-rate increases.
- For many retirees who are struggling to meet their retirement needs, converting and paying taxes does not seem like an appropriate choice. For this group, it may be more appropriate to put away the maximum allowed into a Roth IRA each year, accumulating amounts in this vehicle prior to their retirement years.

YOUR FINANCIAL SERVICES PRACTICE:
CLIENT QUERY

Question: Your client Wanda is single, aged 73, and has an IRA worth $150,000. Because she does not need to take distributions from the plan to live on, she asks you whether she can avoid taking minimum distributions from the plan. Upon further inquiry, you find out she has three adult children who are all successful financially and six grandchildren. Her goal is to leave the IRA money to her family. You also find out that she has an income of $120,000 a year, but only has AGI of $85,000 because some of her income is from tax-free municipal bonds.

Solution: Wanda sounds like a great candidate for a conversion to a Roth IRA. Once the assets are in a Roth IRA, she can avoid minimum distributions during her lifetime. She will have to pay income taxes at the time of conversion—but the prepaid income taxes also reduce her taxable estate. If she names her six grandchildren as the beneficiaries, at Wanda's death, this account can be divided into six accounts and distributed over the lifetime of each grandchild.

Primary Objective: Maximizing the Estate

When examining the needs of your clients, you will find there is a distinct difference between those who will probably spend most of their assets over retirement and those who can afford to leave an estate to their heirs. Nonetheless, it is impossible to divide the world into two distinct client groups, and the issues will certainly be different for the individual with a $20 million estate than for the person with a $2 million estate. And even for wealthier clients, the first and foremost concern is retirement security, with estate planning as a secondary objective.

However, simply having significant assets in a tax-preferred retirement plan can pose serious problems. As we have learned in the last two chapters, lifetime distributions can be subject to income tax and the 10 percent premature distribution excise tax. If money that is still in the plan is left to heirs, the amount is included in the taxable estate, and distributions are still subject to federal income taxes. If assets are distributed at death, a large portion of the pension asset can be confiscated by taxes. Let's look at an example of the devastating effect that these taxes can have.

Example: Oliver, aged 80, died (without a surviving spouse) with $2 million in his IRA account. Assume Oliver's other assets are large enough that his pension is taxed at the highest marginal estate tax rate of 47 percent (the highest estate tax rate in 2005). Also assume that after Oliver's death, the entire IRA is distributed to his beneficiary, who is in the 35 percent income tax bracket. Looking just at federal taxes, the benefit will be taxed as follows:

Federal estate tax	$ 940,000
47% of $2,000,000	
Income tax on IRA	$ 371,000
35% of ($2,000,000 – $940,000)	
Total reduction	$1,311,000
Net value of IRA for heirs	$ 689,000
Percentage of IRA passing to heirs	34%

Appropriate planning is necessary to minimize this threat. However, it is also important to keep the situation in perspective. Even with the taxes, saving through a tax-sheltered retirement plan will result in larger accumulations than saving on an after-tax basis will.

For example, Daniel, a self-employed individual, is considering whether or not to establish a Keogh plan. He is aged 43 and can afford to contribute $30,000 a year to the plan until he retires at age 65. Daniel wants to compare the effect of saving with a Keogh to saving on an after-tax basis. Because his marginal federal and state income tax rate is 40 percent, his annual after-tax savings would be $18,000. In preparing the illustration, we assumed that plan assets would grow at 10 percent, that inflation would remain at 3 percent, and that the participant would remain in the 40 percent income tax bracket. In both the pretax and after-tax examples, we assumed that none of the accumulated amounts were distributed during Daniel's lifetime (except as required under the minimum-distribution rules). We looked at the value (at death) of the amount that would pass to heirs after all income taxes were paid, and we used the worst-case scenario, meaning that all taxes are paid at the time of death. In this case, we did not subtract out estate taxes. Note, as illustrated in table 11-7, that even with the taxes, Daniel's heirs will end up much better off if Daniel saves using the Keogh plan.

This information is important because it shows that individuals who are faced with income and estate taxes haven't made a mistake in funding their pension plans. However, knowing this is still not that comforting to someone

TABLE 11-7
Comparison of Pretax and Posttax Savings

Client's Age at Death	Net to Heirs Pretax Savings	Net to Heirs Posttax Savings
70	$1,005,830	$ 539,987
75	$1,431,273	$ 722,625
80	$1,975,211	$ 967,036
85	$2,672,980	$1,294,112

faced with a tax rate of 60 percent or more. Fortunately, there are a number of ways to minimize the tax threat. First, under the minimum-distribution rules, it is possible to distribute assets over the remaining life expectancy of the beneficiary after the death of the participant. This method spreads out the payment of income taxes, meaning that the pension asset can continue to generate significant income for the beneficiaries. However, in order to take advantage of the extra deferral period, the pension plan assets cannot be used to pay estate taxes. Readers familiar with estate planning know that the pension asset problem is similar to those that arise with other illiquid assets. In many cases, the solution to the illiquid asset problem is to purchase life insurance—usually using an irrevocable life insurance trust—because the insurance proceeds will not be subject to estate taxes. This approach generates capital for paying estate taxes. In fact, the pension problem is often less difficult to solve than the problem of illiquid assets because distributions from the plan can function as a source of insurance premiums. In many cases, the premiums are simply paid out of distributions that are already required under the minimum-distribution rules.

When the participant is uninsurable or is unwilling to purchase insurance, the problem becomes more difficult to solve. One option is to use pension distributions to fund a family gifting program—taking advantage of the ability to give away $11,000 a year to a beneficiary without estate or gift tax consequences. Another solution for the charitably inclined is to leave the benefit to charity. When a charity receives the benefit, it pays no income taxes and the estate receives an estate tax deduction for the amount of the contribution.

This type of client also needs to consider whether or not to convert some or all of his or her pension assets to a Roth IRA. The major conversion impediment for wealthier clients is that they will earn more than the $100,000 cap. Some advisers are so enthusiastic about the conversion idea that they are looking for ways to reduce the individual's income for a year so that the conversion can occur. The reason that conversion can be so valuable for the wealthier client is that there are no required minimum distributions during the participant's lifetime. If the spouse is the beneficiary, no distributions have to be made over the spouse's lifetime either. After the spouse's death, distributions must be made over the life expectancy of the beneficiaries at that time. This may mean that even if the conversion occurs at age 65, the Roth IRA will grow income tax free for possibly 25 or more years, followed by distributions that can be spread over the next 30 to 40 years (the life expectancy of the beneficiaries). Similar to planning for distributions from traditional IRAs, the Roth IRA conversion works best when estate taxes are not withdrawn from the Roth IRA. Once again, life insurance can be the appropriate means for preparing for this contingency.

Form of Distribution Option. For the client with substantial assets, the IRA rollover option is generally the appropriate choice. This type of client can afford to self-insure against the contingency of living a long life and, therefore, will generally not want to annuitize the benefit. With the IRA, the participant has both investment and distribution flexibility. This strategy is also necessary if the individual wants to convert some or all of the distribution to a Roth IRA.

As discussed in the previous chapter, clients with large pension benefits generally will not elect lump-sum averaging treatment. The effective tax rate is not that attractive for large distributions. Sometimes electing lump-sum averaging is appropriate when an individual is a participant in multiple plans. If, for example, an individual has accumulated benefits of $250,000 in a profit-sharing plan and $1 million in a pension plan, choosing lump-sum tax treatment for the profit-sharing distribution may be appropriate. This strategy should be evaluated carefully because there are a number of traps regarding the aggregation of multiple distributions. Also remember that averaging will be available only to those born before 1936.

12

Housing Issues

Kenn Beam Tacchino

Chapter Outline

Housing issues facing the retiree vary from client to client. In this chapter we will address the major financial and tax concerns involving housing alternatives and relocation that can arise when planning for a retired client. Our focus, of course, will be financial. It is important to remember, however, that retirement is a time of change on many levels. It often means, among other things, adjusting to a new routine and reassessing one's identity. For this reason, some clients cling to their home in retirement as the last bastion of status quo. Planners need to understand that the disposition of the family homestead and the decision of where to reside during the retirement years are, first and foremost, personal choices with a different meaning for every client. The psychological attachment to the home in many cases far outweighs the financial and tax wisdom involved with thinking of the home as an asset. It is in this context that financial service professionals must deal with planning for the disposition of a retired client's home.

WHAT CLIENTS NEED TO KNOW ABOUT THE HOME AS A FINANCIAL ASSET

Despite the caveat raised in the opening paragraph, it is the planner's job to point out the following to his or her client:

- Although one's house remains the same, the character of the neighborhood will be changed during retirement by the deaths and departures of friends. In addition, development in the local area will change the essence of community that once was so familiar.
- The house that was suitable for raising a family may not be suitable for retirement. Instead of being close to schools in the best school district, it might be more important to be close to medical care in a place with lower school taxes.
- The costs of heating, cooling, cleaning, and maintaining a house with empty rooms and a child-sized yard may be prohibitive.
- Even a mortgage-free house can be a financial drain that robs the retiree of income. Here's why: Besides the additional costs involved in maintaining a home, the equity from its sale could be used to provide needed retirement income.

WHAT CLIENTS NEED TO KNOW ABOUT THE TAX OPPORTUNITIES INVOLVED WITH SELLING A HOME

When considering whether or not to move into another living arrangement, clients need to understand the tax implications of selling their home.

YOUR FINANCIAL SERVICES PRACTICE:
ILLUSTRATING THE STREAM OF INCOME AVAILABLE FROM
THE SALE OF THE HOME

Clients need to understand the income that can be provided from any residual amount of money left after subtracting the purchase of the retirement residence from the sale of the preretirement residence. For this reason, it can be a lucrative opportunity to illustrate the projected installment payout, life annuity, or joint and survivor annuity available from freed-up assets. The number crunching will help some clients to make a more informed decision, even if they choose not to cash in on the "home asset." For others, the income stream that can be provided by selling the home asset might mean the difference between just making ends meet and being able to enjoy retirement.

Today the rules are quite liberal, and in most cases the gain will not be subject to federal income tax (note that some states do not follow the federal scheme). This means that if the client would prefer condo living or a smaller home during the retirement years, replacing the old home with a less expensive one will free up assets. The concept of moving to a less expensive, more retirement friendly home and choosing to free up assets is known as *downsizing*. In many cases, downsizing will also yield positive tax consequences. Of course, the tax exemption has rules that must be followed.

downsizing

Code Sec. 121 provides that taxpayers of any age who sell their homes can exclude up to $250,000 of their gain ($500,000 for married taxpayers filing jointly). To qualify for the exclusion, the property must have been owned and used by the taxpayer as a principal residence for an aggregate of at least 2 years out of the 5 years ending on the date of sale. These are known as the ownership and use tests.

For married taxpayers, both spouses have to meet the 2-year use requirement—otherwise the available exclusion is $250,000 rather than $500,000. However, the couple can qualify for the higher $500,000 amount even if just one spouse owns the home. In certain situations, taxpayers may "tack on" periods of ownership and use for purposes of the exclusion. For example, a taxpayer whose spouse has died before the sale date can "tack on" the deceased spouse's period of ownership and use prior to the taxpayer's ownership and use. If a taxpayer receives a home pursuant to a divorce under Sec. 1041, the taxpayer can "tack on" the transferor's period of ownership.

Taxpayers who reside in nursing homes or similar institutions because they are incapable of self-care may treat their stay in such institutions as "use" of their principal residence for up to one year of the 2-year use requirement.

YOUR FINANCIAL SERVICES PRACTICE:
SOLVING ISSUES FOR CLIENTS
WITH TWO OR MORE HOMES

If a client has more than one home, he or she is only entitled to exclude the gain from his or her main home. This is typically defined as the home he or she lives in most of the time. For example, if your client owns a house in the city and a beach house he or she uses during the summer months, the house in the city is the main home.

For some clients the situation may be more complicated, however. For example, they own a house but they can live in another area where they rent a house. In this instance, the rented house is their main home. Also, the time factor may not be so clear cut. In this instance, factors used in determining a client's main home include the place of employment, location of the other family members' main home, the mailing address they use for bills and other correspondence, the address used for tax returns, drivers licenses, car registrations, voter registrations, and the location of the banks, recreational clubs, and religious organizations of which the client is a member.

The exclusion may generally be used only once every 2 years. If a single taxpayer marries someone who has used the exclusion within the past 2 years, that taxpayer is allowed a maximum exclusion of $250,000 (rather than $500,000) until 2 years have passed since the exclusion was used by either spouse. This "once every 2 years" rule is obviously related to the "2 out of 5 years" ownership and use requirement.

If the taxpayer fails to meet the ownership and use rules or the "once every 2 years" rule and the sale of the home is due to a change of employment, change of health, or other "unforeseen" circumstance, a reduced exclusion may still be available. The reduced exclusion is based on the ratio of the amount that the period of ownership and use (or the period between the last sale and the current sale) bears to 2 years. That ratio is then applied to the maximum allowable exclusion ($250,000 or $500,000). For example, if a single taxpayer has $100,000 of gain, owned the home for one year, and sold the home for one of the qualifying reasons, the total gain is excluded from income since $100,000 is less than one-half of $250,000 ($125,000).

amount realized

adjusted basis

Gain on the sale of the house will be determined by taking the amount realized reduced by the taxpayer's adjusted basis. The *amount realized* is the selling price minus selling expenses. *Adjusted basis* begins with the original purchase price of the home but also includes certain settlement or closing costs like attorneys fees, title insurance, recording fees, and transfer taxes. Permanent home improvements also add to basis. Common improvements that add to basis include adding another room, finishing a basement, installing a new heating or central air conditioning unit, adding a new roof, or installing replacement windows. However, repairs that do not add to the value but keep the property in good condition do not add to basis. These include interior or exterior repainting, fixing gutters or floors, repairing leaks or plastering, and replacing broken window panes.

Any depreciation claimed by the taxpayer for periods after May 6, 1997, will reduce the excludible portion of the gain upon sale. This applies in cases where the taxpayer has used the property for rental or business purposes at any time after May 6, 1997, and before the sale of the property.

Finally, note that the exclusion applies automatically unless the taxpayer elects out of it. Generally, information reporting will not be required for sales of homes that result in no taxable gain under the exclusion rules.

PLANNING FOR THE CLIENT WHO MOVES

Up to this point, the discussion has dealt with the tax implications of a retiree selling his or her home and before that the consideration of the home as a financial asset. This discussion has laid the groundwork for many planning opportunities. At the heart of each opportunity is the client's retirement decision either to remain in his or her current residence or to relocate to another. A discussion of these two options will constitute the remainder of this chapter. First, let us consider the client who changes residences.

As we have already seen, a common reason for changing residences at retirement is to downsize—that is, to purchase a retirement residence that costs less than the one being sold in order to transfer a portion of the gain (enhanced by tax breaks) into cash for retirement. At this point, planners should also consider the two other principal reasons that retirees change residences. One reason is to avail themselves of living circumstances uniquely geared to the retired population. These new residences generally reflect changes in lifestyle that are thrust upon the retiree. The residences include life-care communities and other senior living arrangements. (In a later chapter, we will address housing options for those who need current care, such as nursing homes and assisted living arrangements.) The final reason that retirees change residences is to relocate to an area where their dollars can be stretched further because the living costs are lower. In this situation, the planner needs to consider the consequences of his or her client relocating to another state. Let's take a closer look at these issues.

Age-Restricted Housing

Some retirees will be more comfortable living in communities with other retirees. Age-restricted housing options are wide-ranging, including apartment buildings, retirement hotels, condominiums, subdivisions, and mobile home parks. These housing communities can provide safety, companionship, and special services. It is not uncommon to have special recreation and leisure facilities, such as golf courses, craft rooms, swimming pools, game rooms, and libraries. There are also activities to promote community life, such as clubs, volunteer positions, group trips, and entertainment. Many housing communities also contain amenities to make living almost self-contained—for example, food stores, banks, hairdressers, and other services.

Of course, age-restricted housing is not for everyone; some find this type of living sterile and depressing and prefer being in a broader community with a variety of ages. A client will need to weigh this concern with the services offered by the facility.

The legality of age-restricted housing was in question at one time. Today under the Fair Housing Act, however, two exemptions from the nondiscrimination in housing rules may apply. First, a community is allowed to restrict residents to age 62 or older. If this exception is relied on, no residents can be younger than age 62. A second alternative is to limit eligibility to age 55. With this exception, some individuals under age 55 are allowed as long as 80 percent of all residents are 55 or older and at least one resident in each living unit is aged 55 or older.

The client considering age-restricted housing needs to be concerned about which exemption applies. Living in a community with only those aged 62 or

---

**YOUR FINANCIAL SERVICES PRACTICE:
QUESTIONS TO ASK WHEN BUYING
INTO AGE-RESTRICTED HOUSING**

Advise your client to consider the following when looking to move to an age-restricted community:

- Will views and open spaces be preserved? (In other words, what future construction is planned?)
- What kind of additional construction can you do on your home?
- How will you fit in? (How do residents feel about the community? What is the cultural atmosphere like?)
- How does the governance structure work? (What kind of changes do the by-laws permit? What voice do residents have in the community's decision making powers?)
- Is the community family friendly? (Will grandchildren enjoy visiting?)

Also, check accessibility to shopping, recreation, and medical care. Double-check the annual fees and look for hidden costs. Finally, investigate the security of the community and the reputation of the home builder.

---

older provides assurance that the community will have only older residents However, what happens if a retiree's child or grandchild needs housing for a period of time, or if a single person marries someone younger than age 62? If residents buy into the community, then the age-62 restriction could even have a negative effect on property values. In many cases, a community with an age-55 restriction is the better bet.

Life-Care Communities

There are many varieties of life-care communities (also called continuing-care retirement communities) throughout the United States. In fact, because of the number of options that exist, it may be best to explain what life-care communities are by first explaining what they are not. Life-care communities are not simply retirement villages where people over a specified age reside; nor are they simply nursing homes where patients go for custodial and medical care. Life-care communities are a combination of these two extremes and a little bit of everything in between. Moreover, they are often mistakenly thought to be only for the wealthy. The truth is that there are substantial variations in price among life-care communities, and the majority of them are nonprofit organizations.

Like age-restricted housing, life-care communities attract those who are interested in living in a facility designed for older people and who want to enjoy recreational and social activities with their peers. But the candidates for life care are also looking for assistance in daily living that will be available if necessary and the ability to obtain nursing care at market or below market rate.

How They Work

While it is true that facilities, fees, and services vary widely from one life-care community to the next, several common features do exist. Most frequently your clients will pay a one-time up-front fee that can range from modest to expensive depending on the quality of the community and the nature of the contract. In some cases, the fee is nonrefundable; in others, the fee is fully refundable if the individual retiree, couple, or surviving spouse leaves. In still other cases, the fee is refundable based on an agreed-upon schedule. For example, 2 percent of the one-time up-front fee becomes nonrefundable for each month that your client is in residence. If your client leaves after 2 years (24 months), he or she will be entitled to a refund of 52 percent of the fee. In other words, your client will forfeit 48 percent of the fee.

In addition to a one-time up-front fee, residents generally pay a monthly fee that can range from under $1,000 per month up to and over $5,000 per month. The monthly fee depends in part on the dwelling unit chosen and any services rendered. A closer look at the disparity of fees is needed, however.

One reason for the great disparity in both the one-time up-front fee and the monthly fee is that in some cases they interrelate with each other and with any refund policy that applies to one-time up-front fee. In other words, there is a trade-off in these cases between the one-time up-front fee and the monthly fee. In other cases, both types of fees are high because they are used to pay for expensive medical benefits, such as long-term care, that are guaranteed in advance. In yet other cases, both the one-time up-front fee and the monthly fee vary widely because of the variety of services that are provided and the quality of the facility.

Planning Note: It is difficult to do an "apples to apples" comparison between two life-care communities; nonetheless, the planner must be able to assist the client in understanding their similarities and differences.

In return for the payment of fees, your client will get a life-lease contract (sometimes called a residential care agreement) that guarantees some level of living space, services, and lifetime health care. A closer look at these characteristics is in order.

Living Space. The residential accommodation may be a single-family dwelling or an apartment. It can change with the retiree's needs to a skilled-nursing facility or a long-term care facility. Most life-care communities point with pride to the safety of the facility and its accessibility to those who are suffering from one or more diseases associated with aging.

Services. Services may include the following:

- some level of housekeeping, including linen service
- some level of meal preparation (taking one or more meals in a common dining hall)
- facilities for crafts, tennis, golf, and other types of recreation
- transportation to and from area shopping and events
- supervision of exercise and diet
- skilled-nursing care (if needed)
- long-term care, including custodial care (if needed)

extensive contract

modified contract

fee-for-service contract

Lifetime Health Care. One key element to the life-care contract is the guarantee of space in a nursing home if it becomes necessary. The guarantee of long-term care can be approached in several ways. One approach is to pay in advance for unlimited nursing home care at little or no increase in monthly payments (sometimes called an *extensive contract*). Another approach is to cover nursing home care up to a specified amount with a per diem rate paid by your client for usage over and above the specified amount (sometimes called a *modified contract*). A final approach is to cover only emergency and short-term nursing home care in the basic agreement and to provide long-term care on a per diem basis (sometimes called a *fee-for-service contract*).

Additional Concerns

Many retirees enjoy life-care communities because of the opportunity for social interaction with people of like interests and ages. For example, they enjoy having a meal in a common dining room, and they appreciate being checked up on when they do not show up for dinner. Others are less enthusiastic about group living and the regimentation associated with their new "community." For these retirees, it is a comfort to know that they can usually obtain a living unit with its own kitchen and that a coffee shop may be available for alternative dining.

**YOUR FINANCIAL SERVICES PRACTICE:
COORDINATION OF LIFE-CARE COMMUNITY SELECTION WITH
LONG-TERM CARE INSURANCE AND MEDIGAP COVERAGE**

Clients who are involved in a life-care community have definable needs for long-term care insurance and Medigap coverage. Astute planners will best serve these clients by coordinating the medical and long-term care coverage provided by the life-care community with that provided by insurance policies. For example, a life-care community that provides long-term care for a specified period of time and then sets a rate for usage beyond that time can be coordinated with a long-term care insurance contract's waiting period and per diem allowance.

Although no scientific evidence exists to support the contention that retirees who live in life-care communities live longer, many gerontologists share this belief because of the support-group mentality associated with the communities, the high-quality medical care provided, and the quality of life associated with social interaction.

The final concern deals with the tax deductibility of medical costs associated with the life-care contract. The astute planner will learn in advance the amount of the contract construed to be for medical expenses. Many life-care communities omit this fact from the contractual agreement. Inclusion, however, can go a long way in winning (or avoiding) an argument with the IRS regarding the cost of medical expenses.

Hidden Traps

Financial planners need to take special precautions when advising a client on the life-care community he or she should choose. Communities that have gone bankrupt have caused some retirees to lose the one-time up-front fee. Things to look for include whether long-term care costs are being self-insured or whether an outside carrier is involved. Special attention should be paid to how the community sets its fees and whether medical insurance on residents encourages overutilization of services. Also, planners should be wary of communities that undercharged their early residents and must make up the difference from their most recent residents. Planners who practice due diligence at the outset can avoid problems down the road.

In addition, a problem may occur if a married couple has an age disparity and the decision to enter the facility is to meet the needs of the older spouse. If the older spouse dies within a few years, the younger spouse may be left in an unsatisfactory living arrangement. In this case, it's important to understand the refund features of the up-front fee. The couple should consider this issue before choosing a home.

Questions to Ask

Planners may want to ask the following questions when helping a client select a life-care community:

- Who manages the life-care community—owners or an outside profit agency? (Third-party management is less desirable.)
- Is the community owned by a for-profit or nonprofit organization?
- How long has the facility been in operation, and what is the organization's financial condition? Specifically, what is the long-term debt?
- How many units have been rented?
- Does the facility have certifications from the state and leading organizations?

- What is the profile of the resident population?
- Is there a powerful and active residence committee that can influence management decisions?
- What are the health care guarantees provided by the contract?
- What about amortization of the one-time up-front fee? Are the one-time up-front fees of current residents being used to pay current costs?
- How are fee increases determined, and what are they typically?
- What is the refund policy for the one-time up-front fee?
- What are the minimum and maximum age requirements?
- Can the resident either insist upon or refuse nursing care?

Other Alternative Housing Options

In addition to age-restricted housing and life-care communities, retirees have numerous other housing options. Many homeowners who no longer want the responsibility of maintaining a home will choose to rent an apartment. Similarly, those interested in owning may choose to buy a condominium or cooperative. Before jumping in, the homeowner should learn the legal distinctions between the various types of ownership. Both condominiums and cooperatives require cooperative decision making and management of the common areas. There may also be some hidden costs. For example, there could be increases in monthly maintenance fees or special assessments in the near future. Also, cooperatives (and some condominiums) have restrictions on selling the property.

In addition, here are two other housing options that are worth considering:

- *second home*. Retirees with vacation homes may choose to retire into the vacation home and sell the primary home. The exclusion-of-gain provisions generally give the retiree the opportunity to withdraw the gain from the sale without incurring federal income taxes.
- *house swapping*. The retiree could swap living units with a child or even with a stranger, possibly trading a home for a condominium. From an income tax perspective, this transaction is treated as a sale of each property.

YOUR FINANCIAL SERVICES PRACTICE: RESIDENCE CHOICES LITERATURE

The Internet offers easy access to a wealth of information about senior housing. Here are a few ideas. See www.seniorresource.com for housing information for seniors. The American Seniors Housing Association (www.seniorshousing.org) is an organization for those in the senior housing industry. Senior Sites (www.seniorsites.com) lists housing and services offered through nonprofit organizations. New Lifestyles (www.newlifestyles.com) is a resource for senior residential care housing options. Finally, AARP (www.aarp.org) is an excellent resource for a wide range of information for seniors.

RELOCATION OUT OF STATE

domicile

The decision to relocate to another state is often motivated by such factors as climate, location of friends and relatives, and affection for the area itself. For clients considering such a move, some general advice is in order. First, weigh the decision cautiously because it is not easily reversible. Second, consider the prospect of dying in the new state. If one spouse should die, will the other want to cope with another uprooting? Third, consider establishing domicile in a state with lower death taxes. *Domicile* is the intended permanent home of the client. Domicile can be a choice if the client has more than one residence. Such factors as where the client spends time, is registered to vote, has a driver's license, where his or her planner resides, and where his or her will is executed help to determine which residence is the client's permanent home. Fourth, consider state income taxes. Does the state tax base include pension income? Fifth, look carefully at property and transfer taxes. And finally, look to see if the state or local government provides specific tax breaks for the elderly. These tax breaks could include

- an additional exemption or standard deduction
- an income tax credit
- adjusted real estate taxes
- a deferral of real estate taxes until after the retiree's death (at which point the estate will pay the taxes from the sale of the home)
- an exemption of all or part of retirement pay from the state income tax base
- an exemption of all or part of Social Security from the state income tax base
- tax adjustments for renters (homestead credits)
- an exemption of all or part of unreimbursed medical expenses from the state income tax base
- frozen property tax levels for the year the retiree reaches age 65. (In other words, property taxes remain at age 65 rates until the home is sold by the retiree.)

Finally, before any move, the individual should consider looking for a replacement home that is equipped to meet the retiree's needs. Obviously, such changes could later be made to a home, but it would probably be less expensive to purchase a home that already includes such characteristics.

PLANNING FOR CLIENTS WHO WANT TO REMAIN IN THEIR HOMES

A financial planner may look at a client's large, four-bedroom house and see unnecessary heating and maintenance costs. The client, on the other hand, sees the extra rooms as necessary for returning children and visiting relatives. There are other benefits for remaining in a current home. Starting life over in a new location means developing new routines, finding new merchants and service providers, and losing old friends and neighbors who can be relied on for companionship and favors. The value of the retiree's social network is often crucial to his or her sense of well being. If the client has decided that he or she will remain in the house throughout the retirement period, the planner then needs to examine

- whether the house should be modified for senior living
- whether needed services are available
- if house sharing is appropriate
- ways to use the home to create income
- whether or not to retitle the home

Modifying the House for Retirement Living

Retirees who stay in their homes will probably want to make some changes to make the home safer and to minimize ongoing maintenance. The first issue will be making the home safer from falls. This means adding grab bars in the shower and making sure that bathroom and tub floors and other floor surfaces are slip-proof. It also means examining the home for other problem areas (such as narrow walkways) and fixing them. Lighting and even the color scheme (contrasting colors between the floor and walls) can affect the home's safety. The outside of the home should also be examined for cracked or uneven sidewalks and inadequate lighting. Additional handrails or even a ramp may be appropriate both in and outside the house.

Other changes may be helpful to reduce ongoing home maintenance. For example, replacement windows can be easier to clean, and siding can reduce painting costs. Appliances such as dishwashers, garbage disposals and compactors, central vacuuming systems, and water filters (versus bottled water) can reduce daily labor. Even changes to the landscape (like replacing grass with ground cover) can help reduce gardening chores.

Additional welcome changes include having washing machines on the same floor as the home's bedrooms, adding bathrooms on different floors, and even adding bedrooms to the first floor of the home or a stair lift to help climb stars. Appliances should be easy to reach and use, with all operating switches or knobs clearly labeled. Adding an automatic garage door or making parking closer to the entrance can also make life easier. If the retiree has physical restrictions, changes like adding a stair lift or making the home wheelchair accessible may be required. Lighting needs for an aging person can also change, and additional general and specific incandescent task lighting can be an important improvement.

```
┌─────────────────────────────────────────────────────────┐
│            YOUR FINANCIAL SERVICES PRACTICE:              │
│              CHOOSING HOME CARE SERVICES                  │
│                                                           │
│   Hiring in-home service providers is a serious matter    │
│ and individuals, agencies, or organizations should be     │
│ carefully screened. Here's a list of issues your clients  │
│ should evaluate:                                          │
│                                                           │
│   •  Interview the candidate or agency.                   │
│   •  Obtain client references.                            │
│   •  Ask if the care provider or agency is bonded.        │
│   •  Obtain the Department of Motor Vehicles printout     │
│      from the individual's driver's license and ask for   │
│      a felony background check for anyone who will be     │
│      working in the home.                                 │
│   •  Ask for proof of provider worker's compensation      │
│      insurance.                                           │
│   •  Ask for proof of care provider's full professional   │
│      liability insurance.                                 │
│   •  If the care provider is unable to work one day,      │
│      will the care provider (or agency) provide a         │
│      substitute care provider?                            │
└─────────────────────────────────────────────────────────┘
```

Additional Services

Retirees staying in their homes also must be prepared for the possibility of needing additional services. This requires financial readiness, but also research to see what is available in their area. The type of services that may be needed include:

- outdoor home maintenance and gardening
- indoor home maintenance
- cleaning services
- driving
- homecare ranging from meal preparation to help with bathing and dressing
- emergency call/response systems

Sharing a Home

A retiree can share his or her home with others in a number of ways. The term "home-sharing" is generally used to describe an arrangement in which two or more unrelated people share a house or apartment. In a typical arrangement, each of the participants has some private space but also is free to use the common areas of the house, such as the kitchen and living room.

Home-sharing helps people stay independent and reduce their housing costs. Older women show the most interest in home-sharing. They like both the friendships they can make in a home-sharing arrangement and the money they can save on rent. This is important to older women because they are more likely than older men to live alone. They also spend a higher portion of their income on housing, whether they own or rent their home.

YOUR FINANCIAL SERVICES PRACTICE:
CHOOSING TO HOME SHARE

Before deciding on home-sharing, here's a list of issues your clients should evaluate:

- Consider honestly whether you are ready to be assertive with a housemate, openly share your feelings, or negotiate house rules.
- Figure out your needs and preferences concerning where you live, how much space you need, and other important living conditions.
- Determine both the costs and benefits of the home-sharing arrangement.
- Look for a home sharer whose situation complements yours.
- Designate a trial period to determine whether the situation is working out.

In forging a home-sharing arrangement, the client needs to carefully consider what he or she is looking for. Is this arrangement more about friendship and companionship or simply a means of lowering expenses? Either motivation can result in a successful relationship, as long as the parties entering into the arrangement are clear.

Home-sharing with a stranger should be legal in all states, as long as the housing unit is not divided into separate apartments. It will, however, be necessary to review the homeowner's insurance policy in order to determine the implications of sharing the house with an unrelated person.

Sharing a home may also occur with a relative or friend. With close friends and relatives, both parties may be reluctant to enter into a formal arrangement. It is crucial, however, that both parties discuss their expectations as to how the arrangement will work and also agree on how the arrangement will end. This step will help greatly in determining whether the expectations are mutual.

In some cases, the homeowner prefers to divide the home into separate living units. If the home is to be divided into more than one separate living space, there will be zoning implications. Have your clients check zoning laws before renting out space. In some communities, renting out a part of a home to tenants may not be permitted. Again, your client should check his or her homeowners insurance policy to see if additional coverage is necessary.

Creating Income from the Home

Clients who have paid off their mortgages and want to "age in place" may still be able to tap the equity in their homes if they need finances to maintain their current standard of living. For this group there are two primary options, the reverse mortgage and the sale-leaseback. Here, we will introduce these options and familiarize you with the nomenclature.

Also note that if the retiree has a substantial mortgage, it is a good idea to consider refinancing the mortgage. If a careful analysis of expenses shows that the retiree will have difficulty meeting expenses, it may be appropriate to lengthen the terms of the mortgage or otherwise change the terms to lower monthly expenses.

Reverse Mortgages

reverse mortgage

A *reverse mortgage* is a loan against an individual's home that requires no repayment for as long as the individual continues to live in the home. In other words, a reverse mortgage is a strategy that allows a client to live in his or her home and take substantial amounts of money for current needs with no current payments. They are typically available only when all the owners are age 62 or older and when the home is the principal residence. Also, the home must either have no debt or only a small debt that can be paid off with part of the reverse mortgage loan.

The amount of loan payments made to the client depends on the client's age (or clients' joint ages), the amount of equity the home currently has or is expected to have, and the interest rate and fees that are being charged. For example, the U.S. Department of Housing and Urban Development (HUD), in describing the Home Equity Conversion Mortgage (HECM) program, indicated that based on recent interest rates, a 65-year-old could borrow up to 26 percent of the value of the home while an 85-year-old could borrow up to 56 percent. Specific programs will also have maximum loan amounts.

The amount that can be received also depends on the mortgage program selected. In many cases the mortgage program that pays the most is HECM, which is a federally insured program offered by certain HUD-approved lenders. However, in some cases certain special needs loans offered by a state or local government program may be more favorable, and for very expensive homes a private mortgage program may be the best option. The three types of programs are each described in the sections below.

Payment options will vary depending on the specific program, but generally fall into the following categories.

- *Immediate cash advance:* a lump-sum payment at closing.
- *Credit line account:* the option to take cash advances up to the maximum loan value during the life of the loan. Some credit line programs have a fixed maximum while others offer an increasing limit, which increases with a stated interest rate each year.
- *Monthly cash advance:* a definitive monthly payment that can be stated as a specific number of years, as long as the person lives in the home. Some programs will also allow the participant the option to purchase a life or joint and survivor annuity that will make payments over the individual's entire life.

The amount of the debt grows based on the amount paid and accumulated interest. Typically the loan only has to be repaid when the last surviving

---

**YOUR FINANCIAL SERVICES PRACTICE:
TIMING A REVERSE MORTGAGE**

Reverse mortgages best serve your clients from a cash-flow perspective if the following conditions are present:

- a low interest rate environment
- a high home value environment (seller's market)
- an older client and/or spouse

For example, at one point the HECM rate was 3.61 (compared with a 6.5 percent conventional rate). At that rate, a 75-year-old borrowing against a home worth $150,000 could qualify for a $91,590 loan. Contrast this to a year earlier when rates were 5.61 percent and the loan maxed out at $69,190! Furthermore, compare that to an environment when housing prices are depressed and the value would be assessed at significantly less than $150,000.

One last point: Because the value of the loan is based in part on mortality tables, the older the property owner, the larger the loan.

---

borrower dies, sells the home, or permanently moves away. Most loans are nonrecourse, meaning the maximum amount that has to be repaid is the value of the home. If property values have eroded, the borrower has received a windfall and the lender ends up with a loss.

Because these programs are truly loans, if the retiree wanted or needed to sell the home, any equity that exceeded the loan balance is the property of the retiree. If the property is sold at death, the heirs would receive the additional equity. Also, because these are loans, payments received by the retiree as part of the mortgage program are not considered taxable income and interest expense is deductible but only at the time it is paid (when the loan is repaid).

Out-of-pocket costs generally only include an application fee, which covers an appraisal and credit check. Other costs factor into the loan, but these are typically financed. Fees are of the type that are typical in regular mortgage loans, including interest charges, origination fees, and third-party closing costs (title search, insurance, etc.). Cost items can vary from program to program and from lender to lender and need to be evaluated carefully. The Federal Truth-in-Lending Act requires reverse mortgage lenders to disclose the projected annual average cost of the loan.

Home-Equity Conversion Mortgage

Home Equity Conversion Mortgage

The *Home Equity Conversion Mortgage (HECM)* program can enable an older home-owning family to stay in their home while using some of its built-up equity. This is the most popular type of reverse mortgage. The program allows such a household to get an insured reverse mortgage—a mortgage that converts equity into income. FHA insures HECM loans to protect lenders against loss if amounts withdrawn exceed equity when the property is sold. Any lender authorized to make HUD-insured loans, such as banks, mortgage companies, and savings and loan associations, can participate in the HECM program.

To be eligible for HECM, a homeowner must (1) be 62 years of age or older (if married, both spouses must be over age 62), (2) have a very low outstanding mortgage balance or own the home free and clear, and (3) have received HUD-approved reverse mortgage counseling to learn about the program (to ensure that they are not subject to fraudulent practices). An eligible property must be a principal residence, but it can be a single-family residence, a one- to four-unit building with one unit occupied by the borrower, a manufactured home (mobile home), a unit in an FHA-approved condominium, or a unit in a planned unit development. The property must meet FHA standards, but the owner can pay for repairs using the reverse mortgage.

The total income that an owner can receive through HECM is the maximum claim amount, which is calculated with a formula including the age of the owner(s), the interest rate, and the value of the home. Borrowers may choose one of five payment options:

1. *tenure,* which gives the borrower a monthly payment from the lender for as long as the borrower lives and continues to occupy the home as a principal residence
2. *term,* which gives the borrower monthly payments for a fixed period selected by the borrower
3. *line of credit,* which allows the borrower to make withdrawals up to a maximum amount, at times and in amounts of the borrower's choosing
4. *modified tenure,* which combines the tenure option with a line of credit
5. *modified term,* which combines the term option with a line of credit

---

YOUR FINANCIAL SERVICES PRACTICE: FINDING A REVERSE MORTGAGE PROGRAM

To find out more about the HECM program, call (888-466-3487) or visit HUD at www.hud.gov for a list of approved counseling agencies that advise individuals about the program and a list of approved lenders. Additional information is available from two nonprofit organizations: the American Association of Retired Persons' (AARP) Home Equity Conversion Information Center (202-434-6044) and the National Center for Home Equity Conversion (NCHEC) at 7373 147th St., Room 115, Apple Valley MN 55124. To find out about other types of reverse mortgage programs, visit the National Reverse Mortgage Lenders Assn. at www.reversemortgage.org or call 202-939-1765 for an up-to-date list of lenders that clearly tells you which reverse mortgage products are offered by each listed lender.

YOUR FINANCIAL SERVICES PRACTICE:
QUESTIONS TO ASK WHEN CONSIDERING
A REVERSE MORTGAGE

When a reverse mortgage is an option, the following questions should be considered:

- Is staying in the home a realistic and satisfactory long-term option?
- Have you researched all mortgages available in the immediate geographical area?
- Does the monthly payment correspond favorably to the size of the home's equity, the client's life expectancy, and a fair rate of return?
- What distribution options are available under the program?
- If it is a line of credit program, does the line of credit increase over time?
- What are the closing costs involved and how do they compare to other options?
- Does the financial institution require the client to get permission to make renovations?
- Does the financial institution require the client to maintain the property according to contractual specifications?
- Will the financial institution make periodic inspections?

The borrower remains the owner of the home and may sell it and move at any time, keeping the sales proceeds that exceed the mortgage balance. A borrower cannot be forced to sell the home to pay off the mortgage, even if the mortgage balance grows to exceed the value of the property. An HECM loan need not be repaid until the borrower moves, sells, or dies. When the loan must be paid, if it exceeds the value of the property, the borrower (or the heirs) will owe no more than the value of the property. FHA insurance will cover any balance due the lender.

Two mortgage insurance premiums are collected to pay for HECM: an up-front premium (2 percent of the home's value), which can be financed by the lender, and a monthly premium (which equals 0.5 percent per year of the mortgage balance). The lender's loan origination charge can vary, but only up to $1,800 in such charges may be financed by HECM. Borrowers may be charged appraisal and inspection fees set by HUD; these charges can also be financed.

Homeowners who meet the eligibility criteria above can apply through an FHA-approved lending institution, which in turn submits the application to the local HUD field office for approval.

Special-Purpose Loans

A special-purpose loan does not have to be repaid until after the retiree dies, moves, or sells the home. These loans are available for limited purposes such as home repairs or property taxes and are typically made by local government agencies to help low-income retirees remain in their homes. Most of your clients, however, will not be eligible for this type of loan because their incomes will exceed minimum levels.

Proprietary Programs

In addition to the HECM and special purpose programs, there are other reverse mortgage programs. These proprietary programs are developed by private companies that own them and select the lenders who offer them. Typically, these programs will provide larger loan advances than HECM because they are not restricted by FHA and Fannie Mae dollar-lending limitations. In addition, these programs are available on the highest value homes.

Reverse Mortgages Compared with Other Options

For retirees, home equity is an important piece of the financial security puzzle. Some clients may be asset rich but cash poor. Inflation, home maintenance costs, and uninsured medical bills may cause clients to consider cashing in on their home in order to maintain their lifestyle. The question planners face is whether a new mortgage or home-equity loan is more desirable than a reverse mortgage. Table 12-1 compares the options to help make the analysis easier.

Sale-Leaseback

sale-leaseback arrangement

Another means of unlocking the equity tied up in your client's home while allowing the client to remain in the residence is a sale-leaseback arrangement. Under a typical *sale-leaseback arrangement,* your client sells his or her house to an investor and then rents it back from the investor under a lifetime lease. Your client can thus garner extra retirement resources, make use of the home sale exclusion, and still remain in his or her home. In addition, the house is removed from the client's estate. The sale-leaseback agreement can specify future rents or stipulate how changes in the rental rate will be determined (for example, a periodic market value appraisal by a neutral third party).

The most desirable type of a sale-leaseback involves younger family members buying the client's home for investment purposes. The family relationship between the buyer and seller often makes the arrangement run more smoothly. Be cautious, however, because the IRS is sure to audit this type of intrafamily transaction and will expect that all facets of the transaction be conducted in an arm's-length manner. Regardless of who the buyer is, the lease agreement should clearly spell out that it is the new owner's responsibility to pay property taxes, special assessments, insurance, and major maintenance and repairs.

TABLE 12-1
Comparison of Reverse Mortgage with Mortgage/Home-Equity Option

Reasons Favoring the Choice of a Reverse Mortgage	Reasons Favoring the Choice of a Traditional Mortgage over a Home-Equity Loan
1. Mortgages/home-equity loans call for immediate repayment. Reverse mortgages allow the cash up front with deferred repayment.	1. Clients are unaware of the reverse mortgage option.
2. You do not need an income or other assets to qualify for a reverse mortgage. (For most consumer loans you need income or assets.)	2. These loans are much simpler than reverse mortgages.
3. Credit history is not considered, but it will be considered for a traditional mortgage/home-equity loan.	3. The fees for these loans should be much lower than reverse mortgages.
4. The maximum liability is capped at the value of the home (even if payments exceed this value).	4. The mortgage interest/home-equity interest is tax deductible as it is paid up front. The reverse mortgage interest is deductible when paid at the end.
5. The payments made are a loan, so they are not taxed.	5. Interest rates can be locked in and are generally known with a traditional mortgage or home-equity loan. With a reverse mortgage interest rate, charges can change every month or once a year depending on the option chosen.
	6. Restrictions on upkeep of the house may apply to a reverse mortgage. There are no restrictions on a traditional mortgage or home-equity loan.

Example: Jake and Peggy sell their house to their son for $100,000. They receive a down payment of $20,000 and take mortgage payments for 15 years from their son. Jake and Peggy are no longer subject to property taxes and major maintenance costs, their cash flow has improved, and they still have the security of living in "their" home. In the meantime, their son has acquired investment property and receives rental payments. Perhaps more important, however, the home will be kept in the family.

Retitling Property

qualified personal residence trust (QPRT)

While many retirees struggle to make ends meet, wealthier clients also need to be concerned about the estate tax implications of leaving large estates to their heirs. For this group, one useful planning device is the *qualified personal residence trust (QPRT)*. The QPRT allows the homeowner to give away the house, thus removing its value from the estate, while retaining the right to live in it for a specified period without paying rent (rent must be paid if the homeowner wants to stay in the home for a longer period).

The transaction is conducted like this: The homeowner gifts the house to the QPRT (following IRS guidelines). The transaction is treated as a completed gift of the remainder interest in the home. The value of the gift is determined based on IRS tables, and gift tax returns must be filed. The homeowner retains the right to continue living in the home for a specified period. This device is a useful estate planning technique, especially if the home value may appreciate in the future and if the homeowner has an idea of how long he or she wants to use the home.

The QPRT looks even better when contrasted with other options. If the homeowner gives away the property outright, it may remove the property from the estate, but the homeowner loses a sense of security. Staying in the home is then at the consent of the donee. If, to solve this concern, the retiree attempts to retain a life interest in the property in a method other than the QPRT, the value of the home will generally be included in the retiree's estate at his or her death.

CONCLUSION

We end this chapter where we began it, with a caveat about working within your client's emotional framework to help him or her make the best choices. Because home equity is often a major component of a retiree's wealth, planners often aspire to take their clients out of the position of being house rich and cash poor. The client's emotional and other nonfinancial needs must be factored in. Consider everything from caregiving responsibilities to housing needs and work with the client toward the best solution.

13

Insurance Issues for Seniors

Edward E. Graves

Chapter Outline

This chapter will give a brief summary of health insurance and other insurance issues facing seniors. Its intention is to make this book complete as to the subjects relevant to people facing retirement. In-depth coverage of health insurance issues for seniors is found in the HS 351 course, Health and Long-Term Care Financing for Seniors. That course is also required for the CASL designation.

For the majority of the working population, health insurance or managed care coverage is provided through employers. Workers who remain in such covered employment until retirement at age 65 or later make a standard transition from employer-provided coverage to Medicare. The main issue facing these individuals upon retirement is whether or not to purchase Medicare Supplement Insurance (also called Medigap coverage) to go with traditional Medicare coverage or to join a Medicare Advantage plan. Although a significant portion of the population follows this path, there are many other circumstances faced by workers without employer-provided health care or those who lose their health coverage through loss of job, disability, or early retirement.

A growing portion of workers has no health benefits provided through an employer. If these individuals were never covered by a previous employer, their only choice is to obtain health insurance as an individual purchasing coverage from an insurance company because they would not have access to managed care plans. Many self-employed individuals face the same limited options. Individual health insurance can be very expensive and is often beyond the reach of workers in low-paying jobs.

Individuals seeking coverage must make sure that the purported insurance company or managed care provider is in fact a legitimate business operation licensed to provide the coverage in the appropriate state. There have been some significant sham operations where premiums are collected for health coverage on behalf of a fictitious insurance company. When the supposed insured tries to file a claim, he or she finds out that there is no protection and premium payments have been lost. The appropriate state insurance regulator should be able to verify whether or not marketers are representing legitimate insurance companies. Advisors should encourage clients to make these inquiries before paying any premiums for new health coverage.

Individuals seeking coverage may be able to join professional associations or other groups that provide health benefits to members. This can also afford access to group health insurance or managed care coverage, which may prove to be less costly and sometimes even provide more comprehensive protection. Another potential source of coverage for some of these individuals is as a dependent under a working spouse's plan.

HIGH-DEDUCTIBLE HEALTH PLANS AND HEALTH SAVINGS ACCOUNTS

A more recent development is the 2003 Medicare Prescription Drug, Improvement, and Modernization Act that permits health savings accounts (HSAs) in conjunction with high-deductible health plans (HDHPs). These are available to individuals, employees, and the self-employed. The intent is to promote health protection at a lower premium for people who bear more of the up-front costs for health care through a high-deductible plan (at least $1,000 deductible for an individual or at least $2,000 for a family). These deductible amounts will be indexed to inflation and will increase in future years. An additional incentive is provided by enabling participants to make tax-deductible contributions to a tax-advantaged personal HSA (indexed amounts of allowable contributions are over $2,000 annually for individuals and over $5,000 annually for families). Contributions can only be made to these HSAs in a year that the participant is covered by an HDHP and is not a dependent on someone else's federal income tax return. In other words, children are not eligible to set up HSAs unless they are self-supporting. No contributions are permitted to the HSA if the participant is also covered by a non-high-deductible health plan, such as traditional health coverage or Medicare. The funds in an HSA grow tax-free and can accumulate year after year. These funds can be used tax free to pay for qualified medical expenses (expenses covered under the HDHP but not the deductible, COBRA continuation premiums, long-term care premiums, and health plan premiums while the participants is receiving unemployment compensation). HSAs can be maintained even after the individual is no longer eligible to contribute new funds to the account. Distributions from HSAs will only be taxable income if they are used to pay for things that are not qualified medical expenses. Distributions prior to age 65 for non-medical expenses may be subject to a 10 percent tax penalty. The tax penalty does not apply to distributions made after age 65 or after the death or disability of the account owner. At the death of the account owner, the HSA balance can pass income tax-free to a surviving spouse. If anyone other than the surviving spouse receives the balance of the deceased individual's HSA, it will be taxable income to the recipient and the balance will also be included in the estate of the deceased for estate tax purposes.

The HDHP that is necessary before an individual can establish an HSA is permitted to pay for preventive care even before satisfying the high deductible. The law sets an upper limit on the amount of out-of-pocket expenses under these plans that is indexed annually for inflation (over $5,000 for individual coverage or over $10,000 for family coverage in 2005).

Generally, an HDHP cannot provide benefits before the deductible is satisfied, but there is an exception for benefits for preventive care. An HDHP can provide benefits for preventive care services such as immunizations, annual physicals, routine prenatal care, tobacco cessation programs, and weight-loss programs before the insured satisfies the plan's required high deductible.

Consumer-Directed Health Insurance Plans

These combinations of high-deductible health plans and HSAs are known as consumer-directed health insurance plans. The HSA is the successor to the Archer medical savings accounts available through small employers up to the end of 2005. The savings accounts must be administered by a trustee that is either a bank, an insurance company, or other institution eligible to be the trustee or custodian for IRAs. Insurance companies seem to have an advantage if they are also the provider of the high-deductible coverage. They will more easily be able to determine whether or not the criteria for deductible HSA contributions has been satisfied. Non-insurance company trustees will have to rely on the health plan provider to verify that the criteria for deductible HSA contributions has been met.

HSAs were first permitted by law in 2004, but very few were established in that year. The availability of such combination plans is increasing steadily and they are expected to be even more readily available in future years.

These consumer-directed plans appeal strongly to healthy individuals with high incomes who can easily absorb the high deductible. Because they are likely to have few medical expenses, they may not even have to absorb the deductible in some years. They may be able to accumulate significant amounts in the HSA before they ever experience enough qualified medical expenses to justify a withdrawal from the HSA. The HSA balance can continue to accumulate and eventually be used to pay long-term care insurance premiums.

Consumer-directed plans are less attractive to low-income individuals with serious health problems. They are likely to have enough qualified medical expenses every year that they would need to make distributions from the HSA. Low-income individuals will find it difficult to bear the full brunt of the high deductible and thus may be precluded from enjoying any real advantage from such plans.

Qualified medical expenses are likely to increase with age and may eventually become burdensome to those who were very healthy earlier in life. HSAs can be maintained after an individual is covered by Medicare even though no additional deductible contributions can be made to the HSA after Medicare coverage begins.

Health Reimbursement Arrangements

Another form of consumer-directed health plan called a health reimbursement arrangement (HRA) can be established by any size employer. They combine an HDHP with an employer-maintained reimbursement account. The employer makes the contributions to these reimbursement accounts. Employee contributions are not permitted under these arrangements, and the employee is not generally entitled to any reimbursements after termination of employment. Qualified medical expenses (any medical expenses that are eligible for an income tax medical deduction) incurred during employment are eligible for tax-free reimbursement from the employer's reimbursement account.

Employers who establish these plans are not permitted to discriminate in favor of highly compensated employees. If they do discriminate, reimbursements to highly paid employees will be treated as taxable income. Another important limitation on basic HRAs is that they cannot be established by or for self-employed persons.

Critical Illness Insurance

Critical illness insurance policies provide either a lump-sum benefit at the time of diagnosis or, in some cases, a monthly income. The amount of the maximum possible benefit is selected at the time of purchase. The coverage only provides benefits for those illnesses or conditions explicitly identified in the policy. The less generous forms of this coverage only provide benefits in the case of heart attacks, life-threatening cancer, or strokes. The more generous policies expand the benefit eligibility to include Alzheimer's, blindness, deafness, major organ transplants, multiple sclerosis, paralysis, and kidney failure. Clearly this is not comprehensive coverage and it does not attempt to provide any sort of hospital or health-care provider services. The insured is able to use the benefits for any purpose. It could be seen as disability insurance associated with the covered conditions. Such coverage can actually be used to supplement comprehensive health insurance plans to provide cash for additional non-medical expenses incurred.

Hospital Indemnity Insurance

This is another form of very limited protection that provides a specified cash benefit for each day that the insured is hospitalized. The daily benefit amount and the aggregate maximum of total benefits is selected at the time of purchase. This coverage will provide benefits for a wider range of causes than the critical illness insurance. However, it will provide no benefits prior to hospital admissions or after hospital discharge.

Ancillary Health Insurance

These comprehensive health plans provided through employers make available separate coverage for dental and vision. Benefits are usually restricted to preventive care, diagnosis, and basic services.

Continuing Lost Coverage after Job Termination

Individuals who were covered under health plans provided through prior employers with more than 20 workers are eligible to continue that coverage by paying the premiums individually. A federal law commonly referred to as COBRA (Consolidated Omnibus Budget Reconciliation Act of 1986) provides that individuals leaving employment can continue coverage for 18 months. This applies regardless of whether the employment was terminated by the employer or the individual. If the job termination was because of a disability, the coverage can be continued for 36 months.

The premium necessary to continue coverage under COBRA includes both the employee and the employer portion of the premium. This may be significantly higher than the amount the employee was paying while on the job. However, it is likely to be less than the cost of individual coverage providing comparable protection. The savings is likely to be even more pronounced for individuals with poor health who would be charged more under individual coverage based on an evaluation of current health. The ex-employee has the responsibility of paying premiums on a timely basis. The coverage can be terminated if premium payments are not made on time.

A request to continue coverage must be made within 30 days of job termination. It is highly advisable to request continuation immediately after leaving the job and in cases of planned early retirement, the request can be made in anticipation of the early retirement date.

Example:	An employee aged 63 1/2 takes early retirement. By requesting COBRA continuation of coverage, the retiree will have health coverage to age 65, when Medicare eligibility begins. This avoids the need to seek individual coverage prior to the onset of Medicare coverage.

Individuals retiring prior to age 63 1/2 face the problem of obtaining coverage after COBRA protection expires and before Medicare protection begins. Individuals can request a conversion of their expiring COBRA protection to individual coverage under some plans. This option should be compared with other individually purchased coverage available. In nearly every case, the individual coverage will be less comprehensive than that provided under the prior employer's plan even though the premium is likely to be higher.

Employer-Provided Retiree Health Coverage

Some employers with very generous benefit plans provide health plan protection to retirees. Generally this benefit is only available after normal retirement age. However, in very few cases health plan protection may be extended to early retirees. Such arrangements are most common when the employer is offering a package to encourage early retirement of some of the workforce. If the employer contractually agrees to continue such coverage, it cannot later be unilaterally withdrawn. In the case of most retiree health plan coverage, it has been made available by the employer unilaterally and the employer has the right to alter the plan in the future.

Many employers that have previously provided retiree health protection have been recently cutting back on those benefits. In a number of cases, retirees have resorted to litigation in an attempt to retain the past level of benefits, although in most cases, the employer has been successful in reducing or eliminating retiree health benefits. Those cases where the courts have not permitted benefit reductions tend to be those where the company had entered into a contractual agreement with a labor union or other employee group through collective bargaining. Without a contractual agreement to provide benefits, the employer generally has discretion to unilaterally change benefits for both active employees and retirees. Verbal comments by the administration or written statements in an employee handbook promising lifetime health benefits are not regarded as contractual promises by the courts.

For planning purposes, retirees should be aware that any employer-provided health protection in retirement can and may be terminated in the future. For that reason, they should keep themselves informed of the options available (including their costs) because termination could trigger a serious increase in budgetary constraints to cover the cost of lost benefits. The full premium for Medicare supplement policies and the full cost of prescription drugs could be a shock to someone whose previous employer has heretofore provided those benefits but is now discontinuing them.

Example:	An example of a company that terminated retiree health benefits is Bethlehem Steel. As part of bankruptcy proceedings, the company was able to terminate retiree health plan benefits that had previously been agreed to by contract through collective bargaining. The reality is that when a company no longer has the money to pay for the benefits that it had previously agreed to, those benefits will terminate. Then retirees will have to pay for replacement benefits themselves or do without them.

Medicare

In order to best help retired clients plan for their health care needs, financial services professionals must be acutely aware of the ins and outs of the Medicare system. However, contrary to conventional consumer wisdom, there is much more to retiree health care coverage than just Medicare. For many clients, employer-provided health care benefits will help fill the gaps left unfilled by Medicare. For others, Medigap coverage may be useful to make up for the Medicare shortfall. And for those retiring before Medicare coverage kicks in, careful planning—usually using COBRA coverage—is required.

ORIGINAL MEDICARE

Any discussion of planning for a retiree's health care should start with an analysis of the Medicare system. Discussing Medicare is a fairly complex proposition because eligible persons can choose from the original system and a number of other options. First, we will discuss the original program; then we will review the newer options. Finally, we will examine factors involved in choosing the right plan.

The original Medicare program consists of two parts. Part A is the hospital portion of Medicare. It provides benefits for expenses incurred in hospitals, skilled-nursing facilities, hospices (in limited circumstances), and for home health care for a condition previously treated in a hospital or skilled-nursing facility. Part B is the supplementary medical insurance part of Medicare. It provides benefits for physicians' and surgeons' fees, diagnostic tests, certain drugs and medical supplies, rental of certain medical equipment, and home health service when prior hospitalization has not occurred. Let's take a closer look at the entire Medicare system, starting with the question of eligibility.

Eligibility for Medicare

Most of your older clients will be eligible to receive health benefits under the federal government's Medicare program. Part A is available *at no cost* to most persons aged 65 or older. Among those eligible are

- everyone 65 and over who is receiving a monthly Social Security retirement or survivor's benefit
- people aged 65 and over who have deferred receiving Social Security retirement benefits (these people must apply for Medicare—others in "pay status" are automatically enrolled)
- 65-year-old civilian employees of the federal government who did not elect into the Social Security system under the 1983 law
- people who receive or are eligible to receive railroad retirement benefits
- any spouse aged 65 and over of a fully insured worker who is at least aged 62

Any other people (aged 65 or older) who do not meet the requirements to receive Part A at no cost may voluntarily enroll by paying a premium.

Any person enrolled for Part A of Medicare is eligible for Part B. However, a monthly premium of at least $78.20 (2005 figure) must be paid. This annually adjusted premium represents only about 25 percent of the cost of the benefits provided. The remaining cost of the program is financed from the general revenues of the federal government. As a result of the Medicare Prescription Drug, Improvement, and Modernization Act, the Part B premium will continue to equal 25 percent of Part B benefit costs, but only for beneficiaries with modified adjusted gross income under $80,000 for a single person and $160,000 for a couple. Beginning in 2006, higher-income persons will pay a larger premium that increases with income. These increases will be phased in over 5 years, until persons with incomes above $200,000 ($400,000

YOUR FINANCIAL SERVICES PRACTICE:
MISCONCEPTIONS ABOUT MEDICARE ELIGIBILITY

Clients have several misconceptions about eligibility for Medicare that must be corrected. It is important to point out the following:

- Those who retire early and elect to start Social Security at age 62 are *not* eligible for Medicare until they reach age 65.
- Spouses who are younger than 65 and are married to a retiree over age 65 are *not* eligible for Medicare until they turn age 65.
- Despite the Part B premiums, the system offers a relatively good value. In other words, rejecting Part B coverage to avoid paying premiums is not usually the best choice.

---

for a couple) will have a Part B premium equal to 80 percent of the cost of benefits provided. Starting in 2007, these income figures will also be indexed.

If an individual fails to enroll in Part B at age 65, the premium is increased by 10 percent for each full 12 months during which the person could have been enrolled. However, if a person declines to enroll at a time when Medicare is secondary to an employer-provided medical expense plan, the months of coverage under that plan do not apply in determining the amount of the late-enrollment penalty.

Signing Up for Medicare

To enroll in Medicare, clients can contact their local Social Security office (see the phone book for the local address and phone number). Clients can also call 1-800-MEDICARE (1-800-633-4227) or 1-877-486-2048 for hearing-impaired applicants, or go online at www.medicare.gov. Clients should contact Social Security about 3 months before their 65th birthday to sign up for Medicare, even if they are not planning to retire. Those who will be getting Social Security (at age 65 or earlier) will automatically be enrolled for Medicare at age 65 after they apply for Social Security benefits. (Note: Early enrollment does not mean that Medicare benefits start prior to age 65.) In this case, the individual will receive a notice of automatic enrollment. If a client does not want Part B coverage, he or she must reject it in writing within 2 months of receiving the notice.

If a client is not automatically enrolled, he or she has a 7-month window for initially enrolling in Part B of Medicare. It begins 3 months before attaining age 65 and ends 3 months after that month. In order to begin eligibility for benefits at the earliest possible date—the beginning of the month in which age 65 is reached—a person must enroll prior to the first day of that month. Signing up later will result in a one- to 3-month delay in eligibility. Anyone who rejects Part B or who does not enroll when initially eligible may later apply for benefits during a general enrollment period that occurs between

January 1 and March 31 each year. However, because of the possibility of adverse selection, the monthly premium will be increased by 10 percent for each 12-month period during which the person was eligible but failed to enroll. This increase is waived, however, for those who do not enroll because they were covered under an employer plan considered primary to Medicare.

Part A Benefits

Planners need to be aware of the benefits covered by Part A. Covered expenses fall into the following categories:

- hospital benefits
- skilled-nursing-facility benefits
- home health care benefits
- hospice benefits

In addition, planners should be aware of benefits that are excluded under Part A.

Hospital Benefits

benefit period
spell of illness

Part A pays for inpatient hospital services for up to 90 days in each *benefit period* (also referred to as a *spell of illness*). A benefit period begins the first time a Medicare recipient is hospitalized and ends only after the recipient has been out of a hospital or skilled-nursing facility for 60 consecutive days. A hospitalization after that 60-day period then begins a new benefit period. There is no limit on the number of benefit periods a person may have during his or her lifetime, but there is a separate initial deductible for each benefit period.

Example 1:	Angie goes into the hospital for 40 days, goes home for 2 weeks, and returns to the hospital for 85 days. Her 125 days of hospitalization will be considered to be within one benefit period because there was no gap of 60 days between hospital visits.

Example 2:	Ben goes into the hospital for 60 days, goes home for 62 days, and returns to the hospital for 55 days. Both of his stays are fully covered by Part A because they each fall within a different benefit period. In other words, Ben got a clean slate (and a new 90 days of coverage) because he was out for over 60 consecutive days.

lifetime reserve days

In addition to 90 days of hospital coverage each benefit period, Medicare will cover an extra 60 days over an individual's lifetime. These days are referred to as *lifetime reserve days,* and are nonrenewable. In other words, once a lifetime reserve day is used, it cannot be restored for use in future benefit periods.

Example 3:	Angie from example 1 was covered for 90 days under the benefit period rule. In addition, Angie chose to use 35 of her reserve days to cover the full amount of time she spent in the hospital (125 days). Note that Angie has only 25 lifetime reserve days left. However, once she is out of the hospital for 60 days, she will get 90 more days of coverage in the next benefit period in addition to the 25 remaining lifetime reserve days.

Covered services for Part A hospital benefits include the following:

- semiprivate room and all meals (or private room if required for medical reasons)
- regular nursing services
- services of hospital's medical social workers
- use of regular hospital equipment, supplies, and appliances, such as oxygen tents, wheelchairs, crutches, casts, surgical dressings, and splints
- drugs and biologicals ordinarily furnished by the hospital
- intensive care and coronary care
- rehabilitation services, such as physical therapy
- diagnostic or therapeutic items and services ordinarily furnished by the hospital
- operating room costs, including anesthesia services
- blood transfusions (after the first 3 pints of blood)
- lab tests
- X rays

What Is Not Covered. From a planning standpoint, it is just as important to know what is not covered by Part A as to know what is covered. In each benefit period, covered hospital expenses are paid in full for 60 days, subject to an initial deductible of at least $912 (in 2005). This deductible is adjusted annually to reflect the increasing cost of care. Benefits for an additional 30 days of hospitalization are also provided in each benefit period, but the patient must pay a daily coinsurance charge ($228 in 2005). When using lifetime reserve days, patients must also pay a daily coinsurance charge of at least $456 (in 2005). In addition to copayment and deductibles, clients have to pick up the costs of such things as private rooms, private-duty nurses, and a phone or television in the room. Finally, clients should be aware that hospitals are not paid on the basis of actual charges, but are paid a flat fee for each Medicare patient, based on the patient's diagnosis. This has encouraged hospitals to release patients "quicker and sicker."

Planning Note: Hospitals must notify patients of their right to a written discharge plan that advises them about available health resources appropriate for their needs. In addition, patients can appeal premature discharges.

Skilled-Nursing-Facility Benefits

In many cases, a patient may no longer require continuous hospital care but may not be well enough to go home. Consequently, Part A provides limited benefits for care in a skilled-nursing facility. This coverage can be triggered only if a physician certifies that skilled-nursing care or rehabilitative services are needed for a condition that was treated in a hospital within the last 30 days. In addition, the prior hospitalization must have lasted at least 3 days.

When skilled-nursing-facility coverage is used, benefits are paid in full for 20 days in each benefit period and for an additional 80 days with a daily coinsurance charge ($114 in 2005). Covered expenses are the same as those described for hospital benefits.

One very important point should be made about skilled-nursing-facility benefits: Custodial care is not provided under any part of the Medicare program unless skilled-nursing or rehabilitative service also is needed. With that said, however, it is important to note that custodial care can be provided for 100 days in a skilled-nursing facility if your client needs skilled services.

skilled-nursing facility

What Are Skilled Services? A *skilled-nursing facility* may be a separate facility for providing such care or a separate section of a hospital or nursing home. The facility must have at least one full-time registered nurse, and nursing services must be provided at all times. Every patient must be under the supervision of a physician, and a physician must always be available for emergency care.

Home Health Care Benefits

Starting in 1998, Part A and Part B of Medicare began to share the costs of providing home health care. If a patient can be treated at home for a medical condition, Part A will pay up to the full cost for up to 100 home visits by a home health agency, but only if the visits occur after a hospital or skilled nursing facility stay. Home health agencies specialize in providing nursing services and other therapeutic services. Part B covers additional visits or visits that do not occur after a hospital stay. To receive these benefits, a person must be confined at home and treated under a home health plan set up by a physician. The care needed must include skilled-nursing services, physical therapy, or speech therapy.

If one of these services is needed, Part A (or Part B) will also pay for the cost of part-time home health aides, medical social services, occupational therapy, and medical supplies and equipment provided by the home health agency. There is no charge for these benefits other than a required 20 percent copayment for the cost of durable medical equipment, such as iron lungs, oxygen tanks, and hospital beds. Medicare does not cover home services furnished primarily to assist people in activities such as housecleaning, preparing meals, shopping, dressing, or bathing.

Reimbursement levels paid to home health agencies were reduced in recent changes to Medicare. Consequently, some of these agencies have gone out of business, and the supply of these services has declined somewhat. Individuals needing these home services may have to aggressively seek out care from the surviving providers.

Hospice Benefits

hospice benefits

Hospice benefits are available under Part A of Medicare for terminally ill persons who have a life expectancy of 6 months or less. While a hospice is thought of as a facility for treating the terminally ill, Medicare benefits are available primarily for hospice-type benefits provided to patients in their own homes.

respite care

However, short-term (up to 5 days) inpatient care in a hospice is covered. The care is referred to as *respite care,* because it is intended to relieve the family providing home care. It can be provided in a facility, at the organization providing home treatment, or in a hospital or other facility with which that organization cooperates.

In addition to including the types of benefits described for home health care, hospice benefits include drugs, bereavement counseling, and the respite care described above. However, only drugs that are used primarily to relieve pain and to control symptoms are covered. There are modest copayments for some services.

Hospice care benefits are limited to 210 days unless the patient is recer-tified as terminally ill. In order to qualify for hospice benefits, a Medicare recipient must elect such coverage in lieu of other Medicare benefits, except for the services of the attending physician or services and benefits that do not pertain to the terminal condition.

Exclusions from Part A Medicare

In addition to the limitations, copayments, and deductibles described above, planners should be aware that there are some circumstances under which Part A of Medicare will not pay benefits. In addition, there are times when Medicare will act as the secondary payer of benefits. Exclusions under Part A include the following:

- services outside the United States and its territories or possessions. However, there are a few exceptions to this rule for qualified Mexican and Canadian hospitals. Benefits will be paid if an emergency occurs in the United States and the closest hospital is in one of these countries. Note also that a person living closer to a hospital in one of these countries than to a hospital in the United States may use the foreign hospital even if an emergency does not exist.
- elective luxury services, such as private rooms or televisions
- hospitalization for services not necessary for the treatment of an illness or injury, such as custodial care or elective cosmetic surgery
- services performed in a federal facility, such as a veterans' hospital
- services covered under workers' compensation

Under the following circumstances, Medicare is the secondary payer of benefits:

- when primary coverage under an employer-provided medical expense plan is elected by (1) an employee or spouse aged 65 or older or (2) a disabled beneficiary
- when medical care can be paid under any liability policy, including policies providing automobile no-fault benefits
- in the first 18 months for end-stage renal disease when an employer-provided medical expense plan provides coverage. By law, employer plans cannot specifically exclude this coverage during the 18-month period.

Medicare pays only if complete coverage is not available from these sources and then only to the extent that benefits are less than would otherwise be payable under Medicare.

Part B Benefits

In addition to being aware of the benefits and exclusions under Part A of Medicare, planners must be aware of what Part B of Medicare covers and where it falls short for their clients.

Part B: In General

Part B of Medicare provides benefits for the following medical expenses:

- physicians' and surgeons' fees. These fees may result from house calls, office visits, or services provided in a hospital or other institution. Under certain circumstances, benefits are also provided for the services of chiropractors, podiatrists, and optometrists.
- surgical services including anesthesia
- diagnostic tests in a hospital or a physician's office
- physical or occupational therapy in a physician's office, or as an outpatient of a hospital, skilled-nursing facility, or other approved clinic, rehabilitative agency, or public-health agency
- drugs and biologicals that cannot be self-administered
- radiation therapy
- medical supplies, such as surgical dressings, splints, and casts
- rental of medical equipment, such as oxygen tents, hospital beds, and wheelchairs
- prosthetic devices, such as artificial heart valves or lenses needed after a cataract operation
- ambulance service if a patient's condition does not permit the use of other methods of transportation
- Pap smears and yearly mammograms
- flu and pneumococcal vaccine and its administration
- home health services as described for Part A when a person does not have Part A coverage
- emergency room care
- X rays

Part B Exclusions

Although the preceding list may appear comprehensive, there are numerous medical products and services not covered by Part B, some of which represent significant expenses for your senior clients. They include the following:

- custodial care
- most prescription drugs
- drugs and biologicals that can be self-administered (except drugs for osteoporosis)
- routine physical, eye, and hearing examinations, and tests that are part of such exams (except some mammograms and Pap smears)
- routine foot care
- immunizations (except flu or pneumococcal vaccinations or immunizations required because of an injury or immediate risk of infection)

- cosmetic surgery unless it is needed because of an accidental injury or to improve the function of a malformed part of the body
- dental care unless it involves jaw or facial bone surgery or the setting of fractures
- dentures
- eyeglasses
- hearing aids
- orthopedic shoes

In addition, benefits are not provided to persons eligible for workers' compensation or to those treated in government hospitals. Benefits are provided only for services received in the United States, except for physicians' services and ambulance service rendered for a hospitalization that is covered in Mexico or Canada under Part A. Part B is also a secondary payer of benefits under the same circumstances described for Part A.

Amount of Benefits under Part B

With some exceptions, Part B pays 80 percent of the approved charges for covered medical expenses after the satisfaction of a $110 annual deductible. Out-of-hospital psychiatric services are generally limited to 50 percent reimbursement. Annual maximums may also apply to some services, such as psychiatric services and physical therapy.

A few charges are paid in full without any cost sharing. These charges include (1) home health services, (2) pneumococcal vaccine and its administration, (3) Pap smears and mammograms, (4) certain surgical procedures

---

YOUR FINANCIAL SERVICES PRACTICE:
LIMITATIONS ON PHYSICIAN CHARGES

Medicare has an assignment procedure, whereby physicians can agree to accept the Medicare-approved charge amounts as payment in full. (Note that Medicare pays 80 percent; the doctor can still bill the client for the remaining 20 percent.) However, there has been no way to force all physicians to accept assignment.

Now, however, federal law restricts charges of physicians not agreeing to accept assignment to no more than 115 percent of the Medicare-approved charges in 1993 and thereafter. In essence, Congress has limited even noncontracting physicians to a 15 percent surcharge on the Medicare-approved charges for Medicare-covered patients. No surcharge is allowed by physicians who have agreed to accept assignment under Medicare.

These limitations on physician billing are designed to cut down on the out-of-pocket expenses that Medicare patients encounter. In many localities, it has become difficult, if not impossible, to find physicians who accept assignment by Medicare. Furthermore, many seniors report that the law is ineffective in checking doctors' billing practices—in other words, some physicians ask up front for additional compensation!

that are performed on an outpatient basis in lieu of hospitalization, and (5) diagnostic preadmission tests performed on an outpatient basis within 7 days prior to hospitalization.

Since 1992, the approved charge for doctor's services covered by Medicare has been based on a fee schedule issued by the Health Care Financing Administration. A patient will be reimbursed for only 80 percent of the approved charges above the deductible—regardless of the doctor's actual charge. Since late 1990, doctors have been required to submit all bills directly to Medicare regardless of whether they accept assignment of Medicare benefits. Previously doctors could bill patients directly, which required the patients to file the Medicare claims. Since 1991, there have been limits placed on the size of the fees in excess of approved charges that doctors can charge Medicare patients. Nonetheless, balance billing does exist—this is the practice of charging Medicare patients more than the reasonable and customary charge or, in the case of new law, more than 115 percent.

MEDICARE PART C: MEDICARE ADVANTAGE (MEDICARE+CHOICE)

Managed Care Option under Medicare

Medicare participants may now elect to have their Medicare benefits provided by a managed care plan such as a health maintenance organization (HMO), a preferred provider organization (PPO), or an insurance company. These plans are now called Medicare Advantage, but they were previously referred to as Medicare+Choice (a term that will not be used after January 1, 2006). The participant must still pay the part B premium for Medicare and may—in some plans, in some regions of the country—have to pay an additional premium to the managed care plan. Managed care plans in many large cities do not charge a separate or additional premium.

Managed care plans can be in one of four types. First is a plan offered by an HMO. Second is an HMO-provided program with a point-of-service option (POS). A POS option allows the individual to go outside of the HMO for services, but only a portion of the service charges will be reimbursed. The third type is a provider-sponsored organization (PSO). A PSO is a network developed by providers (either doctors only or hospitals and doctors) formed for the purpose of directly contracting with employers. The fourth type is a plan sponsored by a preferred provider organization (PPO). A PPO is an organization that contracts with service providers to provide services at a lower price.

Each managed care plan subcontracts for the Department of Health and Human Services to provide benefits at least equal to and sometimes better than those available under Medicare. Medicare then reimburses the managed care plan for services it provides to participants electing the managed care coverage. The managed care plans usually provide additional benefits, such as prescription drugs, eyeglasses, hearing aids, and routine physical exams;

as well, they usually eliminate deductibles and lower copay amounts to very nominal levels. These additional benefits are often similar to what is provided by Medigap policies. Because of this redundancy, managed care participants tend to drop Medigap policies.

The important factor in managed care plan operations is that services must be provided to participants by qualified providers who are affiliated with or have contracted with the plan. The participant is not able to seek covered services from health care providers outside the plan except in emergencies. By electing the managed care option, the participant gives up the right to covered benefits from any licensed provider of his or her choice. The choices are narrowed to those approved by the specific managed care plan. For these reasons, it may not be advisable for people who travel a lot or live part of the year outside the geographic region of the plan to select managed care.

Persons who elect the managed care option may drop the plan coverage and return to the regular Medicare program by notifying both the local Social Security office and the managed care plan. Medicare coverage will usually be restored within a month of the request.

Returning to regular Medicare benefits can present a problem for persons not healthy enough to purchase a new Medigap policy. This important issue is discussed in more detail later.

Private Fee-for-Service Plans

Retirees can also choose a private insurance plan that accepts Medicare beneficiaries. Generally with these types of plans, the participant may go to any doctor or hospital. The insurance plan, rather than the Medicare program, decides how much to reimburse for the services performed.

A fee-for-service plan may cover extra benefits the original Medicare plan doesn't cover. In this type of plan, the participant pays the Part B premium plus any monthly premium the private fee-for-service plan charges, and an amount per visit or service. Providers are allowed to bill beyond what the plan pays, and the participant will be responsible for paying whatever the plan doesn't cover. These plans will provide benefits for all the Medicare-covered services in the original plan; however, the participant may pay more for some of the services.

Medicare Medical Savings Account (MSA) Plan

This is a permanent option added by the Medicare Modernization Act of 2003. Those eligible under Medicare Part A and Part B can elect into this program. The program consists of two parts: the MSA account, which is a special kind of savings account, and the Medicare MSA policy, which is a high-deductible insurance policy approved by Medicare that covers at least the same services covered by Medicare. The highest deductible amount is

---

YOUR FINANCIAL SERVICES PRACTICE:
THE MEDICARE WEBSITE

The Medicare website can be an invaluable tool for you and your clients (www.medicare.gov). It contains search tools that can help you choose the best Medicare plan option and more. Below are search tools offered as links on the site.

Medicare Personal Plan Finder
Helping you compare health plans in your area

Prescription Drug Assistance Programs
Programs that offer discounted or free medications

Participating Physician Directory
Locate Medicare participating physicians in your area

Helpful Contacts
Find phone numbers and websites

Your Medicare Coverage (coming soon)
Your health care coverage in the original Medicare plan

Medicare Health Plan Compare
Compare health plans in your area

Nursing Home Compare
Compare nursing homes in your area

Dialysis Facility Compare
Compare dialysis facilities in your area

Supplier Directory
Locate Medicare participating suppliers in your area

Publications
View, order, or download Medicare publications

Local Medicare Events
Includes events on Medicare-related topics

Medigap Compare
Locate supplemental insurance policies to cover expenses not paid by Medicare

---

$6,000. (This is the Medicare equivalent of the self-directed high-deductible health plans plus HSAs.)

Medicare pays the premium for the Medicare MSA plan and, at the beginning of the year, makes a deposit to the recipient's Medicare MSA. The amount of the annual deposit depends upon the geographical area and the specific Medicare MSA policy involved. Essentially, the premium savings from the high-deductible coverage (relative to the regular Medicare Advantage plan premium) is contributed to the Medicare MSA. If the recipient uses the money in the MSA to pay for qualified medical expenses, it can be withdrawn tax free. If the withdrawal is for other purposes, it is treated as ordinary income, and in some cases there is a 50 percent penalty tax. If the recipient doesn't use all the money in the Medicare MSA, next year's deposit is added to any remaining balance.

Example: In November of 2004, Jane elects a Medicare MSA plan for 2005 and sets up an account. She chooses a policy with a $5,000 deductible. With this policy, Jane receives an annual deposit (on January 1 of each year) of $1,200 to the MSA account. In 2005, Jane has a routine medical check-up, dental check-ups, and prescriptions filled. She pays $300 from her account for these services. At the end of the year, she has $900 remaining, and at the beginning of the next year, another $1,200 is added to this amount.

Individuals enrolling in a Medicare MSA plan must stay in it for a full year. Enrollment occurs only in November for the following year. The recipient pays the Part B premium. As medical expenses are incurred, the recipient makes withdrawals from the account. Because the amount contributed to the account will generally be less than the deductible, if the account is depleted, the recipient will have to pay the next expenses out of pocket. Once expenses exceed the deductible, then the Medicare MSA plan kicks in.

Medicare MSA plans can have a variety of forms. Some policies allow participants the option to go to any doctor or hospital; some limit participation to a network of providers. A Medicare MSA plan may offer additional benefits that the original Medicare plan doesn't cover. One potential disadvantage from the recipient's viewpoint is that, unlike other Medicare health plans, Medicare MSA plans are not required to have limits on what providers can charge the recipient above the amount paid by the plan. One potential advantage of this program is greater flexibility, because money in the Medicare MSA can be used to pay for things that the original Medicare plan does not cover. This plan is a good choice for the individual who generally has low medical expenses but also has the financial resources to cover the deductible.

Enrolling or Disenrolling in a Medicare Plan

A recipient does not need to do anything to retain his or her original Medicare plan or Medicare managed care plan. If the recipient has one of the Medicare Advantage plans, he or she must disenroll to return to original Medicare. (See table 13-1.)

Medicare Supplement (Medigap) Access

Medigap coverage

The commercial insurance available to supplement Medicare, often called *Medigap coverage*, is not necessary for persons enrolling in a Medicare Advantage plan. However, if anyone who has enrolled in a Medicare Advantage plan later disenrolls, there will be a renewed potential need for Medigap coverage.

Congress expanded the open access to Medigap coverage by mandating that insurance companies provide coverage at standard rates without medical

TABLE 13-1 Enrolling and Disenrolling in Medicare Plans	
How to Enroll/disenroll: Medicare Managed Care or Private Fee-for-Service Plan	How to Enroll/disenroll: Medicare Medical Savings Account (MSA) Plan
Enrollment in a Medicare managed care plan or a private fee-for-service plan can occur at any time. *To enroll:* • Call the plan to request an enrollment form. • Complete and mail the form to the plan. • Receive a letter from the plan identifying when membership begins. • The plan cannot refuse enrollment. *To disenroll:* • An individual may disenroll (leave) a plan at any time for any reason. • Disenroll by calling the plan or the Social Security Administration. • Disenrollment becomes effective as early as the first of the month after a request for disenrollment is received.	Enrollment in a Medicare MSA plan can occur only • during the 3-month period before eligibility for Part A and Part B or • during November of each year *To enroll:* • Set up a special Medicare MSA at a bank/savings institution. • Choose from among available Medicare MSA plans. • Enrollment will be effective January 1. *To disenroll:* File a request for disenrollment for the Medicare MSA plan in November. Disenrollment will be effective December 31.

evaluation to those dropping out of a Medicare Advantage plan. This protection is extremely valuable to persons in poor health who either choose to leave the plan or are forced to leave because the plan is closing down or has become insolvent. There are limitations on this open access.

First of all, the exit from the Medicare managed care plan must take place within one year of having joined the plan. Second, the person must apply for Medigap coverage within 63 days of leaving the Medicare managed care plan. This mandate is not really important for healthy persons. They can easily obtain the coverage at standard rates because of their good health. This open access is essentially the same kind of guaranteed access afforded people during the 6 months following their registration for Part B of Medicare.

Choosing a Medicare Option

The traditional Medicare plan is flexible but does not cover everything. To get more coverage, your client may purchase a supplemental insurance policy, or consider joining a Medicare managed care plan or private fee-for-service plan. Another choice is the Medicare MSA plan. The health plans differ in cost, choice of doctors and hospitals, and benefits. Table 13-2 summarizes the various types of plans.

Cost

All beneficiaries pay the Part B premium. Any additional monthly premiums tend to be lower in Medicare managed care plans than in most supplemental insurance policies (Medigap) and some private fee-for-service plans. Out-of-pocket costs tend to be lower in most managed care plans and the original Medicare plan with some supplemental insurance policies. Total out-of-pocket costs often are higher in the original Medicare plan without a supplemental insurance policy. In *Medicare MSA* plans, there is no monthly premium. Even though the recipient pays for all the costs of services prior to meeting the high deductible for the insurance policy, payment for these services can come from the Medicare MSA. In private fee-for-service plans and Medicare MSA plans, the recipient may be asked to pay extra charges from doctors, hospitals, and other providers who don't accept the plan's fee as payment in full. Table 13-3 is a participant worksheet for comparing the cost features of various plans.

Medicare MSA

Providers

The original Medicare plan, the original Medicare plan with a supplemental insurance policy, private fee-for-service plans, and certain Medicare MSA plans have the widest choice of doctors and hospitals. In most Medicare managed care plans, and in some Medicare MSA plans, the recipient must choose doctors and hospitals from a list provided by the plan. Recipients will want to check if their doctors are on the plan's list and if those doctors are accepting new Medicare patients under that plan. There is no guarantee that a particular doctor will stay with the plan.

The recipient can go to any specialist who accepts Medicare in the original Medicare plan, the original Medicare plan with a supplemental insurance policy, private fee-for-service plans, and some Medicare MSA plans. Most Medicare managed care plans and some Medicare MSA plans require a referral from the primary care doctor to see a specialist. In private fee-for-service plans and Medicare MSA plans, the recipient may be asked to pay extra charges by doctors, hospitals, and other providers who don't accept the plan's fee as payment in full. Table 13-4 is a participant worksheet for comparing provider services.

TABLE 13-2		
Medicare Health Plan Options		
Option	What It Is	Things to Consider
Original Medicare Plan	Traditional pay-per-visit (also called fee-for-service) arrangement available nationwide	Recipient can go to any provider that accepts Medicare. Some services are not covered and the recipient may have to pay some out-of-pocket costs.
Original Medicare Plan with Supplemental Insurance Policy	Original Medicare plan plus one of up to 10 standardized Medicare supplemental insurance policies (also called Medigap insurance) available through private companies	Depending on the standardized policy the recipient buys, he or she will have coverage for at least some deductible and coinsurance costs. There may be coverage for extra benefits not otherwise covered by Medicare. The recipient will have to pay a premium for his or her supplemental policy.
Medicare Advantage Medicare Managed Care Plan	Medicare-approved network of doctors, hospitals, and other health care providers that agree to give care in return for a set monthly payment from Medicare. A managed care plan may be any of the following: a health maintenance organization (HMO), provider-sponsored organization (PSO), preferred provider organization (PPO), or a health maintenance organization with a point-of-service option (POS).	An HMO or a PSO usually asks enrollees to use only the doctors and hospitals in the plan's network. If they do, they may have little or no out-of-pocket cost for covered services. A PPO or a POS usually lets enrollees use doctors and hospitals outside the plan for an extra out-of-pocket cost. Some managed care plans may provide extra benefits. Some plans may charge a premium.
Private Fee-for-Service Plan (PFFS)	Medicare-approved private insurance plan. Medicare pays the plan a premium for Medicare-covered services. A PFFS plan provides all Medicare benefits. Note: This is *not* the same as Medigap.	The PFFS plan (rather than Medicare) decides how much to pay for the covered services received. Providers may bill more than the plan pays (up to a limit) and the recipient must pay the difference. It is likely that recipients will pay a premium for a PFFS plan.
Medicare Medical Savings Account (MSA) Plan	A health insurance policy with a high yearly deductible. Medicare pays the premium for the Medicare MSA plan and deposits money into a separate Medicare MSA an individual establishes. He or she uses the money in the Medicare MSA to pay for medical expenses.	Recipient accumulates money in Medicare MSA to pay for extra medical costs. A corresponding insurance policy has a high deductible. There are no limits on what providers can charge above what is paid by the Medicare MSA plan. Enrollment available only during November. Enrollees must stay in the plan for a full year.

TABLE 13-3
Participant Worksheet for Comparing Plan Costs

For each option does the plan	Plan A	Plan B
Charge a premium in addition to the Medicare Part B premium?		
Charge copayments for doctor visits?		
Pay for prescriptions? How much?		
Charge more if I use a doctor or hospital outside the plan? How much?		
Have maximum amounts it will pay for different services?		
Set limits on what doctors and hospitals charge you?		
Charge a deductible or coinsurance for inpatient hospital services, home health, or skilled-nursing facility services?		

TABLE 13-4
Participant Worksheet for Comparing Provider Services

	Plan A	Plan B
Are my doctors in the plan?		
Is there a selection of the doctors, health professionals, and hospitals that I might need?		
Can I get the doctor I want? Is he or she accepting new patients under that plan?		
Can I see the same doctor on most visits?		
Can I change doctors once I am in the plan?		
What's the plan's policy if it does not have the type of specialist I need?		
Does the plan cover the drugs I use?		
May I use my regular pharmacy?		
Are mail-order pharmacies available?		
What is the annual or quarterly dollar limit on prescription drug coverage?		
Will I have to pay more if I prefer to use brand name instead of generic drugs?		
Is there a maximum out-of-pocket cost for prescription drugs? What is it?		
Does the plan limit the drugs it pays for to those on a list of drugs (called a formulary)?		

Extra Benefits

In Medicare managed care plans or private fee-for-service plans, participants may get extra benefits, like vision or dental care, beyond the benefits covered by the original Medicare plan or the original Medicare plan with a supplemental insurance policy. In lieu of extra benefits, enrollees in Medicare MSA plans receive a deposit in their Medicare MSA from Medicare.

Prescription Drugs

In general, the original Medicare plan does not cover outpatient prescription drugs. Many Medicare managed care plans and a few of the more expensive supplemental insurance policies cover certain prescription drugs up to a specified dollar limit. In general, the original Medicare plan covers only medication while the participant is in a hospital or skilled-nursing facility. Other important things to think about include

- In the original Medicare plan, Medicare pays doctors and other health care providers directly for each service received. For all other Medicare health plans, Medicare pays the health plan a lump-sum amount of money; the plan oversees plan services.
- Plan benefits and costs can change each year. These changes are usually effective the first day of the new year. It is quite possible that a plan will reduce benefits for the following year. For example, some managed care plans have reduced prescription drug benefits as these become more expensive to provide.

MEDICARE PART D: PRESCRIPTION DRUG COVERAGE

Along with numerous other changes to Medicare and the establishment of health saving accounts, the Medicare Prescription Drug, Improvement, and Modernization Act adds a prescription drug program to Medicare— *Medicare Part D*. Until Part D becomes effective in 2006, the act also provides for Medicare-approved drug discount cards. The act also gives employers a financial incentive to provide or continue to provide drug coverage to retirees as an alternative to enrollment in Part D.

Drug Discount Cards

Since spring 2004, most Medicare beneficiaries have been able to purchase a drug discount card. However, the cards are not available to beneficiaries who have prescription drug coverage through Medicaid, TRICARE for Life (for retired military personnel), the Federal Employees Health Benefits Program, or a plan of their current or former employer. In addition, members of Medicare

Advantage plans that already provide discount cards to members cannot purchase another card. Estimates were that a beneficiary's drug costs would be reduced by 10 to 25 percent, but savings for most persons have not been this high. These cards can be sponsored by insurance companies, retail pharmacies, Medicare Advantage plans, and other entities. An individual can purchase only one card and the cost cannot exceed $30. Sponsors are required to pass any discounts they negotiate on the purchase of drugs to cardholders and to publish a price list of the drugs they cover.

Certain low-income seniors will also be eligible for annual subsidies of up to $600 to help them pay the cost of prescription drugs. With the subsidies, this group of older Americans often does enjoy significant savings.

Information on the cost and benefits of available cards, as well as pharmacy locations and drug cost, can be found on the Medicare Web site (www.medicare.gov) or the Web site of the AARP (www.aarp.org).

Prescription Drug Coverage

Medicare Part D

In 2006, *Medicare Part D* will replace Medicare-approved drug discount cards. Part D is a subject of considerable controversy. More liberal members of Congress argue that it does not go far enough in meeting the needs of seniors. More conservative members of Congress contend that its cost will saddle the government with another major entitlement. Part D is also viewed by some as a boon to the pharmaceutical industry. In addition, the rules for this program are very complex. Part D may change before it even becomes effective. Even if no changes are made, many regulations still need to be issued to fully implement the program. Therefore, the following discussion is general, and readers should be aware of developments that take place. One source of this information is the Medicare Web site at www.medicare.gov.

Eligibility and Cost

Part D is a voluntary prescription drug benefit that is available to all Medicare beneficiaries entitled to Part A and enrolled in Part B. This includes persons who participate in any of the various Medicare Advantage plans. The act provides that most eligible persons will have access to at least two privately operated prescription drug plans available in the region in which they live. The plans must meet certain standards and be approved by the Secretary of Health and Human Services. There are provisions in the act for the Secretary to arrange prescription drug coverage on an alternative basis if fewer than two drug plans are approved. Beneficiaries who participate in Medicare Advantage plans would obtain their prescription drug coverage through that plan as long as it was an approved provider.

It is estimated that the premium will average about $35 per month per person. This represents about 26 percent of the actual cost of coverage, with the balance being paid to the drug plan by the federal government. The premium is partially or totally waived for persons with very low incomes.

Covered Drugs

It is expected that each Medicare prescription drug plan will develop a formulary, which is a list of approved drugs that the plan will cover. These formularies do not have to cover every prescription drug. However, they must cover at least two prescription drugs in each therapeutic category and class. Formularies can be changed at any time during the year, but participants may only change drug plans once per year. As a result, some participants may find that there is no longer coverage for a drug that they have been taking.

Benefits

The act provides for a standard prescription drug program but also allows for alternative plans to be approved if certain requirements are met and the plans are at least actuarially equivalent to the standard plans. The standard prescription drug program will have an annual deductible of $250 in 2006. This amount and other dollar figures mentioned below will increase in later years if the expenditures for prescription drugs by Medicare beneficiaries increase.

After the deductible has been satisfied, the plan will pay 75 percent of the next $2,000 of prescription drug costs covered by the plan. Benefits then cease until a beneficiary's total drug costs (including the deductible) reach $5,100. At this point, the beneficiary will have had out-of-pocket costs of $3,600 in addition to the $420 annual premium. The plan will then pay 95 percent of covered drug costs in excess of $5,100.

Medicare beneficiaries with $810 or less in annual prescription drug expenditures will receive no net benefit from Part D. Approximately half of Medicare beneficiaries fall into this category and will need to decide whether they should purchase coverage. The negative side of not signing up when initially

---

**YOUR FINANCIAL SERVICES PRACTICE:
MAKING CLIENTS AWARE OF THEIR RIGHTS**

Medicare beneficiaries have the following rights:

- to receive emergency medical care without prior approval anywhere in the United States if the beneficiary believes that his or her health is at serious risk
- to appeal denied claims
- to have information about all treatment options from the health care provider
- to know how a health plan pays its doctors

eligible is that there will be a financial penalty for enrollment at a later date when a beneficiary might have significantly higher drug costs. This penalty is in the form of a premium that will be higher by at least one percent for every month of later enrollment. The percentage increase may actually be higher if the Secretary of Health and Human Services determines that a larger penalty is actuarially justified.

Medicare Supplement (Medigap) Insurance

After the passage of the initial Medicare legislation in 1965, Medicare supplement policies became as diverse as the companies that sold them. This led to some confusion in the marketplace, especially among the older members of the population—the primary market for these products. It also led to some questionable sales practices and duplications of coverage. As a result, in 1990, the Medicare supplement market became directly subject to federal regulation. However, this legislation does not apply to employer-provided Medicare carve-out or Medicare supplement insurance.

Medicare supplement insurance

Congress directed the NAIC to develop a standardized array of individual policies, all of which would include at least a common core of basic benefits. The technical name of these plans is *Medicare supplement insurance,* but they are often referred to as Medigap policies.

In addition to standardizing Medicare supplement policies, Congress mandated several other features, including a 6-month open enrollment period, limited preexisting-conditions exclusions, prohibition of the sale of duplicate coverage, increased individual loss ratios, and guaranteed renewability. Indeed, when describing the benefits of each of the Medicare supplement policies, insurance companies must use the same format, language, and definitions. They also are required to use a uniform chart and outline of coverage to summarize the benefits in each plan. These requirements are intended to make it easier for beneficiaries to compare policies and to select between them based on service, reliability, and price.

Federal laws have also generated several restrictions on the markets to which Medicare supplement policies may be sold. Under these restrictions, known as antiduplication provisions, it is generally illegal for an insurance company to sell a Medicare supplement policy to

- a current Medicare supplement policyowner, unless that person states in writing that the first policy will be canceled
- a Medicaid recipient
- an enrollee in a Medicare Advantage plan

A violation of these provisions is subject to criminal and/or civil penalties under federal law.

Standardization of Plans

The NAIC adopted 10 standardized plans of benefits called A through J to fill the gaps in original Medicare. Plan A is the basic benefit package. Each of the other nine plans includes the basic plan A package and a varying combination of additional benefits, with plan J providing the most comprehensive coverage of all the plans. (Note that plans A through J are often referred to as policies A through J.). Insurers may offer fewer than the 10 standard plans.

The Basic Benefit Plan. The basic benefits contained in plan A, and that must be included in all plans, consist of the following:

- Hospitalization—Payment of the beneficiary's percentage participation share of Medicare Part A expenses for the 61st through the 90th day of hospitalization and the 60 lifetime reserve days. In addition, full coverage is extended for 365 additional days after Medicare benefits end.
- Medical expenses—Payment of the beneficiary's percentage participation share (generally 20 percent) for Medicare-approved Part B charges for physicians' and medical services.
- Blood—Payment for the first three pints of blood each year.

Additional Medicare Supplement Plan Benefits. The other nine Medicare supplement plans include, in addition to the basic benefits, an array of coverage and benefits that are not included in original Medicare. These additions encompass the following:

- paying the hospital inpatient Part A deductible for each benefit period
- paying the Part A percentage participation share for the 21st through the 100th day of skilled-nursing facility care
- paying the annual Part B deductible
- paying charges for physicians' and medical services that exceed the Medicare-approved amount (either 80 or 100 percent of these charges up to the charge limitation set by Medicare or the state)
- paying 80 percent of the charges after a $250 deductible for emergency care in a foreign hospital (with several limitations) and a $50,000 lifetime maximum
- paying (up to $1,600 per year) for a care provider to give assistance with activities of daily living (at-home recovery) while a beneficiary qualifies for Medicare home health care benefits (with certain limitations)
- paying 50 percent of outpatient prescription drug charges after a $250 deductible to an annual maximum ($1,250 or $3,000 calendar-year

limit). However, this benefit is affected, as explained below, by the new Medicare prescription drug benefit.

Table 13-5 indicates which of these other benefits plans B through J provide.

TABLE 13-5
Benefits Under Medicare Supplement Policies

	A	B	C	D	E	F	G	H	I	J
Basic benefits	X	X	X	X	X	X	X	X	X	X
Skilled-nursing facility (days 21–100)			X	X	X	X	X	X	X	X
Part A deductible		X	X	X	X	X	X	X	X	X
Part B deductible			X			X				X
Part B excess charges						100%	80%		100%	100%
Foreign travel emergency			X	X	X	X	X	X	X	X
At-home recovery				X			X		X	X
Preventive medical care					X					X
Prescription drugs								$1,250	$1,250	$3,000

Medicare Supplement Variations. Except for conformance with the alternative standards in Massachusetts, Minnesota, and Wisconsin, insurance companies cannot offer Medicare supplement policies that differ from these standardized options and cannot change the combination of benefits or the letter names of any of the policies. However, there are two allowable variations: high-deductible policies and Medicare SELECT policies.

High-Deductible Policies. Companies can offer two standard high-deductible Medicare supplement policies. These policies are identical to plans F and J except that they have a high-deductible amount before the plan pays any benefit. Separate annual deductibles for prescription drugs in plan J and foreign travel emergencies in plans F and J also apply. The monthly premium for plans F and J under the high-deductible option is generally less than the monthly premium for plans F and J without a high-deductible option. However, the savings may be offset by the out-of-pocket payments for services required before satisfying the deductible.

Medicare SELECT   *Medicare SELECT. Medicare SELECT* may be any one of the 10 standardized Medicare supplement insurance policies (although plans C, D, and

F are most popular) in which the beneficiary must use the insurance plan's designated hospitals and doctors for nonemergency services to be eligible for full supplemental insurance benefits. Medicare SELECT policies are issued by insurance companies as PPO products and by some HMOs.

In general, Medicare SELECT policies are required to pay full benefits only if a preferred provider is used for nonemergency services. However, Medicare pays its share of approved charges in any case. Medicare SELECT policy premiums are generally 15 to 25 percent less than the monthly premium for the same plan without the required use of a preferred-provider network.

Plan Popularity

Plans A, C, D, and F are the ones most often available in the marketplace. Plan F accounts for nearly half of the Medicare supplement coverage in force. This is probably because it is the most comprehensive coverage without incurring the extremely high premium for prescription drugs. Plans C and D are the next most popular and together account for about one third of all Medicare supplement coverage. Medicare select accounts for less than 10 percent of the Medicare supplement coverage sold.

Changes in 2006

Beginning in 2006, insurance companies may no longer issue new Medicare supplement policies with drug benefits (plans H, I, and J). Persons already insured under these policies have several options. They may continue to renew them with drug benefits included as long as they do not enroll in the new Medicare prescription drug program. If they enroll in the program, they may keep in force their existing Medicare supplement policies but with the drug benefit eliminated and the premium adjusted accordingly. Alternatively, they can purchase another available Medicare supplement policy that has no drug benefit.

The two new Medicare supplement plans (also with no drug benefit), designated as plans K and L, provide the basic Medicare supplement benefits plus the Part A hospital deductible and skilled-nursing facility care for days 21 through 100.

Eligibility

In the absence of any Medicare supplement regulation to the contrary, insurers are free to conduct normal underwriting, including premium rating, preexisting-conditions exclusions, and waiting periods. However, federal regulation creates a broad area of protected enrollment circumstances for beneficiaries who purchase Medicare supplement policies. These protected circumstances are categorized as either normal open enrollment or specified coverage changes. However, even outside of these circumstances, when a beneficiary replaces a Medicare supplement policy, federal requirements may apply.

Open Enrollment. There is an open enrollment period for the purchase of a Medicare supplement policy during the 6-month period beginning when the Part B coverage starts. During this 6-month period, a beneficiary may buy any Medicare supplement policy sold by a company doing Medicare supplement business in the beneficiary's state. The insurance company cannot deny insurance coverage, place conditions on a policy (like delaying the start of coverage), or increase the price of a policy because of past or present health problems. The company can use preexisting-conditions restrictions or exclusion periods for up to 6 months after the effective date of the policy for medical treatments or advice the beneficiary received within 6 months before the date that the policy goes into effect. However, such restrictions are limited, as the company must reduce even this exclusion period for any period of creditable coverage. Thus, if the beneficiary had at least 6 months of creditable coverage, any health problem would be covered immediately. In general, creditable coverage includes medical coverage under a group, individual, or government-sponsored health plan.

Specified Coverage Changes. Three specific situations involving health care coverage changes permit the beneficiary to buy a Medicare supplement policy under protected enrollment circumstances (also known as Medicare supplement protection rights) after the normal Medicare supplement open enrollment period has ended. These circumstances, which are subject to very specific conditions, can be summarized as (1) when existing coverage ends involuntarily, (2) after Medicare supplement coverage is dropped to enter a Medicare Advantage plan for the first time, and (3) when an initially selected Medicare Advantage alternative to the original Medicare program is dropped. In each case, the beneficiary receives the same enrollment protection provided under normal open enrollment with immediate coverage for all preexisting conditions. However, the beneficiary must apply for the new Medicare supplement policy within 63 days after the end of the previous coverage.

After Medicare Supplement Coverage Is Dropped to Enter an Alternative Medicare Plan for the First Time. A protected Medicare supplement enrollment period exists if a beneficiary drops coverage under a Medicare supplement policy to join a Medicare Advantage alternative plan or purchase a Medicare SELECT policy for the first time and then leaves that plan or policy within one year to return to original Medicare.

When an Initially Selected Medicare Advantage Plan to Original Medicare Is Dropped. A protected Medicare supplement enrollment period exists when a beneficiary joins a Medicare Advantage plan after first becoming eligible for Medicare at age 65 and voluntarily leaves that plan within one year to enroll in original Medicare. The beneficiary must be allowed to buy any Medicare supplement policy sold in his or her state.

LONG-TERM CARE INSURANCE

The Need for Long-Term Care

Long-term care insurance addresses the issues of chronic care rather than acute care. It covers short-term recovery after acute care as well as chronic conditions that are likely to continue for the rest of life. Arthritis and Alzheimer's are examples of chronic conditions whose onset is most common in the later years of life. However, chronic conditions can start at much earlier ages as a result of injury or illness.

The primary reason that long-term care (LTC) is a growing market is that the population is aging. The population aged 65 and over is the fastest-growing age group; today it represents about 11 percent of the population, a figure that is expected to increase to between 20 and 25 percent over the next 50 years. The segment of the population aged 85 and over is growing at an even faster rate. While less than 10 percent of the over-65 group is over 85 today, this percentage is expected to double over the next two generations.

Planners should keep in mind that the likelihood of a person needing to enter a nursing home increases dramatically with age. One percent of persons between the ages of 65 and 74 reside in nursing homes, and the percentage increases to 6 percent between the ages of 75 and 84. At ages 85 and over, the figure rises to approximately 25 percent.

A second reason for the rise in popularity of long-term care insurance is cost. Over $103 billion is spent each year on nursing home care. This cost is increasing faster than inflation because of the growing demand for nursing home beds and the shortage of skilled medical personnel. The cost of complete long-term care for a client can be astronomical, with average annual nursing home costs exceeding $70,000.

A third reason for long-term care is the inability of families to provide full care. Traditionally, long-term care has been provided by family members, often at considerable personal sacrifices and great personal stress. However, it is becoming more difficult for families to provide long-term care for the following reasons:

- the geographic dispersion of family members
- increased participation of women in the paid workforce
- fewer children in the family
- higher divorce rates
- the inability of family members to provide care because they, too, are growing old

The Guidelines for Long-Term Care Policies

In order to best understand how long-term care insurance works, it is important to examine the NAIC model legislation regarding long-term care.

Before proceeding with a summary of the major provisions of the NAIC model legislation, however, it is necessary to make three points. First, the model legislation establishes guidelines that are not binding unless and until adopted by the individual states. Insurance companies still have significant latitude in many aspects of product design. Second, many older policies are still in existence that were written prior to the adoption of the model legislation or under one of its earlier versions. Third, not all states have adopted any version, much less the latest version of the model legislation.

The model legislation applies to any insurance policy or rider that provides coverage for not less than 12 consecutive months in a setting other than an acute care unit of a hospital for one or more of the following: necessary or medically necessary diagnostic, preventive, therapeutic, rehabilitative, maintenance, or personal services. The 12-month period has been the source of considerable controversy because, in effect, it allows policies to provide benefits for periods as short as one year. Many critics of long-term care insurance argue that coverage should not be allowed unless benefits are provided for at least 2 or 3 years. Statistics seem to support their views. Approximately 40 percent of all persons who enter nursing homes after age 65 have stays in excess of one year. This figure drops to about 15 percent for stays of 3 years or longer but 8 percent stay longer than 6 years.

The model legislation focuses on two major areas—policy provisions and marketing.

Characteristics of Individual Policies

For many types of insurance, policies are relatively standardized. For long-term care insurance, the opposite is true. Significant variations (and therefore differences in cost) exist from one insurance company to another. A policyowner also has numerous options with respect to policy provisions.

The discussion in this section focuses on issue age, benefits, renewability, and cost. The provisions and practices described represent the norm in that most policies fit within the extremes that are described. However, the norm covers a wide spectrum.

Issue Age

Substantial differences exist among insurance companies with respect to the age at which they will issue policies. At a minimum, a healthy person between the ages of 55 and 75 will be eligible for coverage from most insurance companies. The coverage can be continued for the remainder of life once it has been issued. Most companies also have an upper age of 80 or 85, beyond which new coverage will not be issued. Coverage written at age 85 or older, if available, is often accompanied by restrictive policy provisions and very high premiums.

There is considerably more variation with respect to the youngest age at which coverage will be written. Some companies have no minimum age. Other companies sell policies to persons as young as age 20. Still other companies have minimum ages in the 40-to-50 age range. One reason for not issuing policies to persons under age 40 is the fear of the high number of potential claims resulting from AIDS.

Planning Point

Long-term care insurance coverage is actually very appropriate for younger people as well. The additional cost of assistance (non-acute care) to paraplegic or quadriplegic individuals following an automobile accident are not covered by traditional health plans, which pay for acute care only. Long-term care policies covering these costs to young individuals are available at very reasonable rates.

Benefits

Benefits under long-term care policies can be categorized by type, amounts, duration, ability to restore benefits, and degree of inflation protection.

Types. There are several levels of care that are frequently provided by long-term care policies:

- *skilled-nursing care,* which consists of daily nursing and rehabilitative care that can be performed only by, or under the supervision of, skilled medical personnel and must be based on a doctor's orders
- *intermediate care,* which involves occasional nursing and rehabilitative care that must be based on a doctor's orders and can be performed only by, or under the supervision of, skilled medical personnel
- *custodial care,* which is primarily to handle personal needs, such as walking, bathing, dressing, eating, or taking medicine, and can usually be provided by someone who does not have professional medical skills or training
- *home health care,* which is received at home and includes part-time skilled-nursing care, speech therapy, physical or occupational therapy, part-time services from home health aides, and help from homemakers

adult day care
- *adult day care,* which is received at centers specifically designed for seniors who live at home but whose spouses or families are not available to stay home during the day. The level of care received is similar to that provided for home health care. Most adult day-care centers also provide transportation to and from the center.

```
┌─────────────────────────────────────────────────────────────────────┐
│              YOUR FINANCIAL SERVICES PRACTICE:                         │
│             THE BEST TIME TO SELL LTC INSURANCE                        │
│                                                                        │
│     Many planners feel the best time to sell long-term care insurance  │
│   is when clients are in their late 50s. One reason for this is that    │
│   these clients have often recently undergone the experience of dealing │
│   with the long-term care needs of their parents. More important,       │
│   however, the "numbers" seem to work well for this age group,          │
│   compared to those who are in their mid- to late 60s, because costs are│
│   more reasonable.                                                      │
└─────────────────────────────────────────────────────────────────────┘
```

Most policies cover at least the first three levels of care, and many cover all five. Some policies also provide benefits for respite care, which allows occasional full-time care at home for a person who is receiving home health care. Respite-care benefits enable family members who are providing much of the home care to take a needed break.

It is becoming increasingly common for policies to contain a bed reservation benefit. This benefit continues payments to a long-term care facility for a limited time (such as 20 days) if a patient must temporarily leave to be hospitalized. Without a continuation of payments, the bed may be rented to someone else and unavailable upon the patient's release from the hospital.

Some newer policies provide assisted-living benefits. These benefits are for facilities that provide care for frail insureds who are no longer able to care for themselves but who do not need the level of care that is provided in a nursing home.

Costs. Benefits are usually limited to a specified amount per day that is independent of the actual charge for long-term care. The insured purchases the level of benefit he or she desires up to the maximum level the insurance company will provide. Benefits are often sold in increments of $10 per day up to frequently found limits of $100, $150, $200 or, in a few cases, as much as $450. Most insurance companies will not offer a daily benefit below $30 or $50.

The same level of benefits is usually provided for all levels of institutional care. A high proportion of policies that provide home health care limit the benefit to one-half the benefit amount payable for institutional stays. However, some insurers have introduced home health care limits that are as high as 80 to 100 percent of the benefit for nursing homes.

Some policies are written on an indemnity basis and pay the cost of covered services up to a maximum dollar amount. For example, a policy may pay 80 to 100 percent of charges up to a maximum dollar amount per day.

Duration. Long-term care policies contain both an elimination (waiting) period and a maximum benefit period. Under an elimination period, benefit payments do not begin until a specified time period after long-term care has begun. While a few insurance companies have a set period (such as 60 days), most allow the policyowner to select from three or four optional elimination periods. For example, one insurance company allows the choice of 30, 90, or 180 days. Choices may occasionally be as low as 30 days or as high as 365 days.

(*Planning Note:* The use of an elimination period often keeps policy costs down. Planners should recommend this type of self-insurance and make sure adequate assets are available for the period.)

The policyowner is also usually given a choice regarding the maximum period for which benefits will be paid. For example, one insurer offers durations of 2, 3, or 4 years; another makes 3-, 6-, and 12-year coverage available. At the extremes, options of one year or lifetime may be available. However, a policy with a lifetime benefit will be more expensive than one with a shorter maximum benefit limit. In some cases, the duration applies to all benefits; in other cases, the duration specified is for nursing home benefits, with home health care benefits covered for a shorter time.

A few insurers extend the maximum period (if it is less than a lifetime limit) by a specified number of days (such as 30 days) for each year the insured does not collect any benefit payments. Such an extension is usually subject to an aggregate limit, such as one or 2 years.

A few policies (usually written on an indemnity basis) specify the maximum benefit as a stated dollar amount, such as $250,000 or $500,000.

Restoration. A few policies provide for restoration of full benefits if the insured has been out of a nursing home for a certain time period, often 180 days. However, most policies do not have this provision, and maximum benefits for a subsequent claim will be reduced by the benefits previously paid.

Inflation Protection. Most long-term care policies offer some type of inflation protection that the policyowner can purchase. In some cases, the inflation protection is elected (for a higher premium) at the time of purchase; future increases in benefits are automatic. In other cases, the policyowner is allowed to purchase additional benefits each year without evidence of insurability.

Inflation protection is generally in the form of a specified annual increase, often 5 percent. This percentage may be on a simple interest basis, which means that each annual increase is a percentage of the original benefit. In other cases, the increase is on a compound interest basis, which means that each increase is based on the existing benefit at the time the additional coverage is purchased. Some policies limit aggregate increases to a specified multiple of the original policy, such as two times. Other policies allow increases only to a maximum age, such as 85.

There are two approaches to pricing any additional coverage purchased. Some insurers base premiums on the insured's attained age when the original policy was issued; other insurers use the insured's age at the time each additional increment of coverage is purchased.

Inflation protection is usually less than adequate to offset actual inflation. The maximum annual increase in benefits is usually 5 percent. This is significantly below recent annual increases in the cost of long-term care, which have been in the double digits over the last decade.

Eligibility for Benefits

activities of daily living (ADLs)

Almost all insurance companies now use a criterion for benefit eligibility that is related to several so-called *activities of daily living (ADLs)*. While variations exist, these activities often include eating, bathing, dressing, transferring from bed to chair, using the toilet, and maintaining continence. In order to receive benefits, there must be independent certification that a person is totally dependent on others to perform a certain number of these activities. For example, one insurer lists seven activities and requires total dependence for any three of them; another insurer requires dependence for two out of a list of six.

Newer policies contain a second criterion that, if satisfied, will result in the payment of benefits even if the activities of daily living can be performed. This criterion is based on cognitive impairment, which can be caused by Alzheimer's disease, strokes, or other brain damage. Cognitive impairment is generally measured through tests performed by trained medical personnel. Because eligibility for benefits often depends on subjective evaluations, most insurance companies use some form of case management. Case management may be mandatory, with the case manager determining eligibility, working with the physician and family to decide on an appropriate type of care, and periodically reassessing the case. Case management may also be voluntary, with the case manager making recommendations about the type of care needed and providing information about the sources for care.

Preexisting Conditions

The most common preexisting-conditions provision specifies that benefits will not be paid for a long-term care need within the first 6 months of a policy for a condition for which treatment was recommended or received within 6 months prior to policy purchase. Policies with less restrictive provisions, and perhaps no such provision, are sometimes found but they are usually very strictly underwritten.

Exclusions

Most long-term care policies contain the exclusions permitted under the NAIC model act. One source of controversy is the exclusion for mental and nervous disorders. Other examples are policies that exclude benefits covered by government programs, alcoholism, and drug addiction.

Underwriting

The underwriting of long-term care policies, like the underwriting of medical expense policies, is based on the health of the insured. However, underwriting for the long-term care risk focuses on situations that will cause claims far into the future. Most underwriting is done on the basis of questionnaires rather than on the use of actual physical examinations. Numerous questions are asked about the health of relatives. For example, if a parent or grandparent had Alzheimer's disease, there is an increased likelihood that the applicant will get this disease in the future. In addition, the insurance company is very interested in medical events, such as temporary amnesia or fainting spells that might be an indication of future incapacities.

Underwriting tends to become more restrictive as the age of an applicant increases. Not only is a future claim more likely to occur much sooner, but adverse selection can also be more severe.

Most insurers have a single classification for all acceptable applicants for long-term care insurance, but it is becoming more common to have three or four categories of insurable classifications, each with a different rate structure.

In the past, insurance companies were accused of "underwriting at the time of claims" by denying benefits because of restrictive policy provisions and supposed (or actual) misstatements in the distant past. The regulations of many states regarding preexisting conditions and the mandatory inclusion of an incontestability provision have caused this problem to become less severe over time. The current situation does, however, put many insurance companies in the position of having to underwrite more accurately prior to policy issuance.

(*Planning Note:* An indication of fairly thorough underwriting is the use of an exhaustive set of questions to ascertain potential risk. Companies that do not seek much information at the underwriting stage are more likely to underprice their product and be much more stingy at the time of claims settlement. Poor underwriting practices may necessitate future premium increases or can even threaten the existence of the insurance company.)

Renewability

guaranteed renewable

Long-term care policies currently being sold are *guaranteed renewable*, which means that an individual's coverage cannot be canceled except for nonpayment of premiums. While premiums cannot be raised on the basis of a particular applicant's claim, they can (and often are) raised by class.

Premiums

Premium Payment Period. The vast majority of long-term care policies have premiums that are payable for life and determined by the age of the insured at the time of issue. For example, a policy may have an annual cost of $800 at the time of purchase. Assuming the policy is guaranteed renewable, this premium will not change unless it is raised on a class basis. Long-term care policies of this nature are often advertised as being "level premium." This is misleading because premiums may be (and in a few cases have been) increased by class. As a result, the current NAIC model act prohibits the use of the term "level premium" unless a policy is noncancelable, which means that rates cannot increase.

A few companies have guaranteed renewable policies with scheduled premium increases. These increases may occur as frequently as annually or as infrequently as every 5 years.

While most premiums are paid annually for the insured's lifetime, a few insurers offer other modes of payment. Lifetime coverage can sometimes be purchased with a single premium. Some insurers are now also beginning to offer policies that have premium payment periods of 10 or 20 years, after which time the premium is paid up.

Factors Affecting Premiums. Numerous factors affect the premium that a policyowner will pay for a long-term care policy. Even if the provisions of several policies are virtually identical, premiums will vary among companies. *Planning Note:* Shopping around for price and quality of company can result in rewards.

Age of Policyowner. Age plays a significant role in the cost of long-term care coverage, as shown by the rates in table 13-6. These figures demonstrate that long-term care coverage can be obtained at a reasonable cost if it is purchased at a young age. Not only does the price go up significantly with age, but the underwriting criteria become more difficult to satisfy with increasing age.

TABLE 13-6 Comparison of Long-Term Care Premiums for Similar Policies			
Age	Company A	Company B	Company C
40	$ 680	$ 1,670	$ 1,220
45	850	2,000	1,370
50	1,090	2,450	1,440
55	1,440	3,060	1,830
60	2,010	4,200	2,370
65	2,900	5,750	3,250
70	4,300	7,660	4,650
75	6,290	11,300	6,630
79	9,530	14,710	10,180

Types of Benefits. The benefits provided under a policy have a significant bearing on the cost. Most policies cover care in a nursing home. However, many policies also cover home health care and other benefits provided to persons who are still able to reside in their own homes. This broader coverage increases premiums by 30 to 50 percent.

Duration of Benefits. The longer the maximum benefit period, the higher the premium. The longer the waiting period, the lower the premium. With many insurers, a policy with an unlimited benefit period and no waiting period will have a premium about double that of a policy with a 2-year benefit period and a 90-day waiting period.

Inflation Protection. Policies may be written with or without automatic benefit increases for inflation. All other factors being equal, the addition of a 5 percent compound annual increase in benefits will usually raise premiums by about 50 percent.

Waiver of Premium. Most long-term care policies have a provision that waives premiums if the insured has been receiving benefits under the policy for a specified period of time, often 60 or 90 days. The inclusion of this benefit usually increases premiums by about 5 percent.

Spousal Coverage. Most insurance companies offer a discount of 10 to 15 percent if both spouses purchase long-term care policies from the company.

Deductibility of Premiums

Starting with a federal statute enacted in August 1996, the tax treatment of long-term care (LTC) policies has become more favorable over time. Essentially they are treated like health insurance policies under the federal income tax laws. Employer expenditures on LTC are a deductible business expense, and the employee does not recognize income when the employer pays the premiums. However, the law prohibits individuals from paying LTC premiums through a flexible spending account. This limitation makes it clear that individuals are not allowed to pay the premiums with pretax dollars.

Another limitation in the law prohibits employers from offering LTC policies as a choice under a cafeteria plan for benefits. Employers can provide LTC coverage outside a cafeteria plan. Most existing plans are merely a payroll deduction for premium payments where the employee is paying all of the premium.

Individuals may deduct their LTC premium payments as a medical expense provided that they have enough medical expenses to satisfy the 7.5

percent of adjusted gross income threshold. If the threshold is not satisfied, the deduction will be lost.

The law puts an age-based upper limit on the amount of premium deduction for each covered individual. The amount of premium (if any) in excess of the limit will not be deductible. The age-based upper limits are covered in HS 351, Health and Long-Term Care Financing for Seniors.

Limited Taxation of Benefits

The 1996 statute specifies that qualified long-term care policies will provide benefits that are generally exempt from federal income taxes. There is an unlimited exclusion from income for benefits that reimburse for actual expenses or do not exceed actual expenses. There is a limit on the amount of benefits exempt from income taxes ($240 a day in 2005) when the benefit amount exceeds actual expenses. The latter limitation applies to policies that provide a per diem benefit regardless of actual expenses.

Planning Point

With the numerous variations in long-term care policies, it is very difficult for consumers, life insurance agents, and financial planners to compare policies. In the final analysis, two policies may have the same cost, even though they may differ significantly. In other words, one policy may be clearly superior in certain areas, while the second may have other, more preferable provisions. In such cases, a final selection decision is difficult and highly subjective. To make an informed choice, many factors must be compared as objectively as possible.

To facilitate such comparisons, several states have prepared consumer guides that are usually available upon request.

Example:	A corporate executive and his wife are considering the purchase of long-term care insurance. They have accumulated enough for retirement and probably have enough to pay the cost of long-term care out of their own funds. However, they have a close friend who developed Alzheimer's and has been in a nursing home for more than 9 years. They have determined that it would be more economical to pay the premiums and have other policyowners share the cost if they need custodial care for a long period of time. This would result in less depletion of the retirement funds for either the spouse or the children.

They have determined that they want lifetime benefits for at least $250 per day and inflation protection based on compound interest. They're willing to take the maximum waiting period offered by the insurance company. The policies they are considering provide home care benefits of up to 80 percent of the inpatient benefit amount. They would also provide respite care and bed reservation protection. Because they are purchasing coverage for both husband and wife, there will be a significant spousal premium discount.

LIFE INSURANCE FOR SENIORS

The objective of life insurance is to create cash upon the death of the insured individual. The death benefit is contractually payable to the designated beneficiary or beneficiaries as stipulated in the beneficiary designation. The arrangements may be set up for any one of many possible situations. The common family use is to provide funding for surviving family members, such as minor children and surviving spouses.

In some cases, there may be a long-term need for special children who will never be self-sufficient. Another family use of life insurance that often extends beyond retirement is to create funds for younger family members who will not be inheriting the family business or other valuable family assets, such as a farm or homestead. The objective is often to provide bequests of roughly equivalent value to all children. In some cases, life insurance is used to transfer equivalent amounts to children that offset charitable gifts made by the parents either during their lifetime or at death.

Of course, life insurance can be used to increase the benefits available to charities. The death benefit is payable after the death of the insured, but is likely to be many times more than the aggregate value of premiums paid for the coverage. If a charity owns the policy, contributions to the charity for the purpose of paying policy premiums can be deductible charitable donations. This further lessens the cost of the enhanced benefit. When a charity owns the policy, those proceeds will not be included in the insured's estate. Caution: Transferring policy ownership from the insured will not remove the policy from the estate until 3 years after the transfer due to a provision in the tax law.

Most people approaching retirement have already completed funding the education of their own children. However, some people have started second families late in life or have assumed financial responsibility for grandchildren who are still dependent minors. Having dual responsibility for funding their own retirement and at the same time continuing financial support for dependent minors may justify an ongoing need for life insurance.

On the other hand, if there are adequate funds to provide full funding of both objectives, there may be no need for life insurance to benefit the minor dependents.

Divorce and remarriage occur with increasing frequency among families, resulting in children from different family units. It is not unusual for both persons who are remarrying to have children from a previous marriage. The surviving spouse of a second or third marriage is more likely to direct assets to his or her own progeny rather than sharing with the prior children of the deceased. Life insurance can provide a guarantee that funds will be directed to children from previous marriages if that is desired.

Life insurance can also be used to provide funds to loyal long-term domestic help or other special people, even though they are not related by blood or marriage. These arrangements are contractual and will not be disclosed in public records, such as bequests included in the will. Another advantage is that life insurance death proceeds are paid quickly after proof of death. There is no delay such as may be involved with settling the estate and distributing funds according to the will.

There are definite business uses of life insurance that continue into the later years of life. Business owners often use life insurance to fund a business continuation agreement, which sets forth who will buy the owner's share of the business upon his or her death. These buy/sell agreements usually set forth how the business is to be valued when establishing the price necessary to purchase the interest from the deceased owner's estate. Life insurance to fund such contracts is needed for the remainder of the owner's lifetime unless the business ownership is sold during his or her lifetime. In a typical family business situation, that beneficiary would be a trust or the child or children intended to purchase the business interest from the insured parent's estate. If there is a partnership, the purchaser may be the surviving partners. One of the purposes of business continuation agreements is to facilitate an ongoing business and minimize the likelihood that the business will fail after the owner's death. The surviving partners generally do not wish to share control of the business with the surviving spouse of the deceased partner. Proper buy/sell agreements with associated life insurance funding can ensure that the intentions of the owners will be carried out after one of the owners dies.

The life insurance policies used to fund business buy/sell agreements are usually some form of cash value life insurance. This is because the protection is usually needed up through the later years of life unless the owner sells the business at a relatively young age. After the insured sells his or her business interest, there is no need to continue the life insurance that was put in place to fund the agreement. The coverage may be terminated or, if possible, reconfigured to accomplish another objective. The owner of the life insurance policy may wish to continue the policy at its previous level or reduce the amount of coverage so that the policy can be maintained without the necessity of ongoing premium payments. This may not be possible if the policy is owned by a trust that lacks the authority to redirect or change the policy and/or the beneficiary.

An important end-of-life use of life insurance is to prefund federal estate taxes. Individuals with enough accumulated wealth to trigger estate taxes at death often wish to leave their wealth to surviving family members. They dislike the idea of having that wealth substantially reduced by the payment of federal estate taxes. The way to avoid this problem is to have adequate life insurance in force to pay estate taxes imposed at the time of death. Such coverage is usually some form of cash value life insurance with level premiums that is intended to be kept in force until death. It is usually purchased and owned by a trust so that the value of the life insurance will not increase the amount of the taxable estate. Such uses of life insurance should always be guided by expert tax advice.

YOUR FINANCIAL SERVICES PRACTICE: UNAUTHORIZED ENTITIES

Regulation of insurance products and services varies from state to state. In Florida, for example, regulations prohibit doing business with an unauthorized insurance entity. An unauthorized entity is an insurance company that has not gained approval to place insurance in the jurisdiction where it or a producer wants to sell insurance. These carriers are unlicensed and prohibited from doing business in that state. In most cases where these carriers have operated, they have characterized themselves as one of several types that are exempt from state regulation. It is the financial planner's responsibility to exercise due diligence to make sure the carriers for whom they are selling are approved by the department of insurance in that state.

Proper tax planning is subject to constantly changing tax law and needs intentional flexibility to accommodate future tax law revisions. Persons subject to estate taxes should seek tax advice before obtaining life insurance coverage. Setting it up improperly can significantly increase the tax burden. Correcting improper insurance arrangements may require a redundant purchase of coverage to replace the improperly positioned policy.

Beneficiary Designations

The beneficiary designations on existing life insurance policies should be reviewed periodically to make sure that they still accomplish the desired result. There is always the possibility that the designated beneficiary has predeceased the insured. In such cases, a new beneficiary should be designated.

Another potential problem with beneficiary designations involves those payable to a married child who is undergoing a divorce. If the death proceeds were paid before the divorce is finalized, the death benefit would become part of the property to be divided up in the court proceedings. It would be better to change the beneficiary designation to a trust or to a party who could act as guardian for the funds on behalf of the intended beneficiary. Additional funds channeled into divorce proceedings often motivate attorneys to prolong the fight and thus convert more of the assets to legal fees. After the property settlement is completed and the divorce is finalized, it is again acceptable to name the original child as the beneficiary if that accomplishes the desired outcome. A note of caution: in some jurisdictions, insurance proceeds have been treated as income in the year they were received by a beneficiary parent, which triggered a significant increase in child support obligations.

As the insured ages, there may be more concern about funding education of grandchildren. If the parents and grandparents do not have adequate assets to fully fund such education, they may consider life insurance as a funding vehicle. This may be accomplished by changing beneficiary designations on existing policies so that the policies can be available for the grandchildren's education. Sometimes new policies are purchased by grandparents specifically to provide educational funding if they die before the grandchildren are fully educated.

One of the most problematic beneficiary designations is "wife of the insured" in cases where the insured has divorced and remarried but failed to change the beneficiary designation to the new wife. A number of these cases end up in litigation where both the previous wife and the current wife seek the death benefits. If the intent is to make the new wife the beneficiary, the policy owner should change the beneficiary designation. The insurance company cannot change the beneficiary designation without instructions and authorization from the policy owner. Any dispute over the proper beneficiary will delay the availability of the death proceeds. The insurance company will release the funds to the court, which is to determine who is the rightful recipient after generally lengthy deliberations.

Another form of beneficiary designation that can be problematic is a class designations such as "children of the insured." The objective of such a designation is to include later-born children who were not alive at the time the original designation was made. It does eliminate the need to change the beneficiary designation after each new birth. However, it creates problems at the time of death in determining who is eligible to receive benefits. The insurance company then has the burden of determining every potential member of the class and proving the prior death of any class member who predeceased the insured. This process can take a long time and delays the availability of death benefits to the beneficiary(ies). Consequently, it is advisable to name each beneficiary explicitly and change the beneficiary designation after each birth to include any intended new beneficiary.

It is appropriate to review the amount that will be payable to each beneficiary when there are multiple beneficiaries for a single policy. Adding new beneficiaries will decrease the amount payable to each one. At some point, it may be appropriate to increase the amount of insurance to keep the amount of proceeds in line with the insured's intended objectives.

Most death proceeds are taken as a lump-sum cash settlement. Generally the beneficiary is free to choose either cash in a lump sum or one of a variety of periodic payment arrangements. These include payments for a specified time or payments for the remainder of the beneficiary's lifetime. In some instances, the beneficiary designation will specify periodic payments without the beneficiary having the option to take a lump sum. This is usually the case where the beneficiary is not capable of managing money responsibly. Another approach to controlling funds after the insured dies is to pay the proceeds to a trust where the trustee will have responsibility for deciding when and how much of the funds to dispense. Life insurance companies generally do not get involved in managing funds that will be distributed in a discretionary manner. If a trust is involved, the death benefits are generally payable directly to the trust in a lump sum.

Continuing Existing Coverage

When evaluating coverage, it is important to look at the options already in place. Some people rely on group life insurance coverage through their employer. This coverage generally terminates when employment terminates. Some employer plans allow the individual to convert a small portion of the group coverage to individual coverage that can be continued by the former employee. If the amount that can be retained is not adequate to satisfy the insurance needs after retirement, additional individual coverage may be needed.

Individual life insurance policies also need to be evaluated as to their appropriateness and the future burden of maintaining the current level of coverage. For example, the target premium on a universal life insurance policy may not be sufficient to keep the coverage in force at its current death benefit level after the insured reaches retirement age. Request a policy illustration for the next 20 years of coverage under the existing policy. Such an illustration may demonstrate that the policy will self-destruct unless either premiums are increased or the death benefit amount is decreased.

Individual life insurance policies that have significant cash value accumulated within the contract can be adjusted so that no future premium payments need be made. For whole life policies, this can be accomplished by using nonforfeiture options. The extended term option will keep the same death benefit amount in force as long as the cash value is sufficient to pay the mortality charges. The duration will be less than the remaining lifetime of the insured. The other option is to reduce the amount of coverage so that the policy will be fully paid up and will remain in force as long as the insured lives.

For universal life policies, the owner can always negotiate a reduction in the amount of coverage for purposes of either lowering or eliminating future premium payments. This flexibility makes universal life policies desirable for accommodating future change. Whenever premium payments are terminated under a universal life policy, the policy continues very similarly to an extended term insurance nonforfeiture option under a whole life policy. The mortality charges continue to be deducted from the cash value to keep the coverage in force. The policy will terminate when the cash value is not sufficient to cover mortality charges.

If the death benefit is reduced enough and the cash value is sufficient, it is possible that there would actually be a release of cash value funds as well as elimination of future premium payments. Such arrangements may be more desirable than terminating the coverage outright for its cash value or selling the coverage to a life settlement company.

If the individual coverage is term life insurance, the premiums will increase at each renewal. It is likely that premium increases will eventually be burdensome enough that the owner will decide not to continue coverage. These policies can be converted to a cash value form of coverage with level premiums or they can simply be replaced by the purchase of a new level premium policy. Initially the premium on level premium policies will exceed that previously paid for the term coverage. However, the level premium will eventually be less than would have been paid under the term life insurance contract at some future renewal date.

One thing to keep in mind when considering what to do with existing life insurance policies is to recognize that policies purchased more than 2 years ago provide solid guaranteed coverage. A new policy will be subjected to a 2-year contestable period that can at best delay the benefit settlement and at worst terminate the coverage because of problems with the application. Any death claim that occurs during the first 2 years of coverage will subject the contract and application to extreme scrutiny. Death benefits will not be payable until after a thorough and lengthy evaluation.

Purchasing New Coverage

Existing policies are a known quantity that can be relied on. Proposed new coverage is subject to an underwriting evaluation by the insurance company and the possibility that a crucial step in the contract formation may not be completed. It is not unheard of for people to apply for coverage but suffer a fatal accident before having taken the required physical examination. For these reasons, many agents suggest that old policies be maintained at least until the new coverage has been issued if new coverage is intended to replace an existing policy.

A more conservative suggestion is to maintain the old policy until its replacement has become incontestable. However, a case in Michigan indicated that there can be some risk to this approach. Both the existing policy and the replacement policy were for face amounts in excess of $2 million. The application for the new policy indicated that it was a replacement and the old policy would be discontinued. The insurance company issuing the new policy successfully rescinded coverage after showing the court that the old policy was still being maintained more than a year after the new policy was issued. The combined amount of coverage from both policies exceeded the amount of coverage that the company thought was appropriate.

The availability of new coverage is a function of both age and health of the intended insured. Persons in good health may be able to obtain new coverage well into their 80s. Persons in poor health will find it harder to obtain new coverage and will have to pay higher premiums for that coverage. Insurance companies will refuse to issue coverage to individuals they consider too risky for their underwriting criteria. However, it is important to realize that refusal of coverage from one insurance company does not mean that coverage cannot be obtained from any insurance company. Each insurance company establishes its own underwriting criteria and may be willing to grant coverage to an individual classified as unacceptable by other insurers.

For individuals with severely impaired health, there are specialists who seek out companies that will provide coverage in specific hard-to-insure cases. They are known as substandard market specialists—not because the coverage is substandard but because the life to be insured presents a higher risk to the insurer than the normal underwriting categories. These specialists have a more thorough knowledge of the underwriting classifications of the various insurance companies than most agents. They seek coverage first from the insurance company they believe most likely to issue the coverage. The search for coverage is conducted on a sequential basis if the application is rejected to avoid multiple applications arriving simultaneously on the desks of the Medical Information Bureau (MIB) and reinsurance underwriters. Aggressively applying simultaneously for coverage gives the impression that the purchaser is too eager to obtain protection and increases the likelihood of rejection.

The first step in acquiring coverage is to determine the purpose for which coverage is to be obtained and the amount necessary to satisfy that objective. It is also important to determine how long the coverage will be needed and whether that need will increase, decrease, or stay approximately the same over that time. An example of a need with a relatively short duration may be for the as-yet-unfunded support and education of minor grandchildren. On the other hand, the need to fund a business buy/sell agreement may last a lifetime and represent a steadily increasing need. The pattern of the need will strongly influence the appropriate type of coverage for each situation.

In those cases where the need is likely to terminate within 10 or 15 years, term insurance is probably the appropriate protection. Situations that require protection for more than 15 or 20 years are generally best served with level premium cash value building coverage. Cash value policies that eliminate premium increases are extremely important when considering policies issued at ages 50 and above. However, there can be a problem with universal life policies if a target premium is followed that is not adequate to keep the coverage in force over the full intended period. Clients should be warned of any potential future premium increases if that possibility exists.

Planning Note: Some universal life policies now have a no-lapse guarantee if the target premium is paid on time at all times. There is a wide range of incremental premium increases for this protection. Some actuaries and regulators are criticizing the lowest-priced versions as being inadequately priced and inadequately reserved. Prudence would suggest that the higher-priced versions are more likely to provide adequate guarantees of protection.

When the cash value policies are appropriate, the choice between whole life, universal life, and variable universal life is driven by the same considerations as at younger ages. Whole life has rigid premiums and known future cash values and is backed by investments primarily in bonds and mortgages. Universal life policies provide the flexibility of premiums and partial withdrawals but have much less predictable future cash values. Variable universal life policies combine flexibility of premium with owner-directed financing. This allows higher risk portfolio investments and hopefully higher yields. The risk tolerance of the purchaser is an important factor in determining the suitability of these life insurance contracts. The advisor has the advantage of assessing the client's past behavior with regard to risk-taking and risk tolerance. Obviously the variable universal life policy is best suited to people with a higher risk tolerance threshold. At the other extreme, the very conservative whole life policy is best suited to those with very little risk tolerance.

If life insurance is used to pre-fund potential estate tax liability, survivorship life policies are often used. These are a joint life second-to-die coverage that covers two lives but pays only one death benefit upon the occurrence of the second death.

Any of the cash value forms of coverage are usually suitable for business uses of life insurance. This includes business continuation buy/sell agreements and key person coverages. Lenders sometimes insist that the borrowing business obtain life insurance on one or more key executives as security for the loan.

USING THE "LIVING BENEFITS" FROM A LIFE INSURANCE POLICY

Now let's turn our attention to lifetime withdrawals from life insurance contracts. Some individuals who own cash value life insurance will decide in retirement that either they (1) no longer have a need for the death benefit provided by the life insurance or, more likely, (2) need to tap the policy to meet retirement, long-term care, or other living expenses. Before using the cash value to fund retirement needs, consider the following:

- Life insurance is an efficient and liquid form of inheritance. For this reason, the individual who wants to leave an estate to heirs should probably look to other resources to meet retirement needs before deciding to withdraw or borrow the policy's cash value.
- In some cases, the insured may not have access to the policy cash surrender value (CSV). The policy may have already been assigned to a third party or a trust for income or estate tax purposes.

Those individuals who decide to tap life insurance cash values will want to take full advantage of the tax benefits of life insurance. In this regard, there are two problems with policy structure that may result in adverse tax consequences, although these problems are generally within the control of the insurer and its policy software. The first issue is failure to meet the definition of life insurance because of too much cash value relative to the amount of death benefit.

A policy entered into after 1984 that fails to meet the statutory definition of life insurance provided by IRC Sec. 7702 will result in immediate taxation of the inside CSV buildup. The policy must meet the definition of life insurance under state law, and it must meet one of two alternative federal tests: the cash value accumulation test or the guideline premium cash value corridor test.

To avoid problems at the time the policy is purchased, a statement should be requested from the insurer stating that the policy meets the statutory definition. Note that the issue of qualifying as life insurance could come up again if there is a partial surrender of the policy in the first 15 years (discussed further below).

modified endowment contract (MEC)

The second issue is the *modified endowment contract (MEC)* rule. Any life insurance policy that falls under the definition of a MEC is subject to an "income first" or LIFO (last in, first out) tax treatment with respect to loans and most lifetime distributions from the policy. A 10 percent penalty tax also usually applies to the taxable portion of any loan or withdrawal from a MEC unless the taxpayer has reached age 59 1/2.

A policy will be treated as a MEC if it fails a test called the *7-pay test*. This test is applied at the inception of the policy and again if the policy experiences a "material change." The 7-pay test is designed to impose MEC status on policies that take in too much premium during the first 7 policy years or in the 7 years after a material change. For each policy, a *net level*

net level premium

premium is calculated. If the total premium actually paid into the policy at any time during the 7-year testing period is more than the sum of the net level premiums that would be needed to result in a paid-up policy after 7 years, the policy will be a MEC. Stated simply, the 7-pay test is designed to discourage a premium schedule that would result in a paid-up policy before the end of a 7-year period.

Accessing Value from a Life Insurance Contract

Amounts paid under a life insurance contract while the insured is still living may take one of several forms. The most common of these are policy dividends, withdrawals from the policy's cash value, policy loans, and proceeds from the cash surrender of a policy.

To properly determine the income tax effects of a financial transaction with a policy, the policyowner's tax basis in the policy must first be known.

policyowner's basis

A *policyowner's basis* is initially determined by adding the total premiums paid into the policy and subtracting the policy dividends, if any, that have been paid by the insurer. If nontaxable withdrawals have previously been made from the policy, such amounts would also reduce the policyowner's basis. Policy loans generally have no direct effect on basis unless the policy is a MEC. However, remember that if a policy is surrendered, the principal amount of any loan outstanding against the policy is includible in the surrender value of the policy for tax purposes. Unless specifically mentioned, the discussion below assumes that the policy is *not* a MEC.

Policy Dividends

Policy dividends are treated as a nontaxable return of premium and will reduce basis. If total dividends paid exceed total premiums, dividends will be taxable to that extent. If dividends are used to reduce premiums or are otherwise paid back into the policy (for example, to buy paid-up additions), the basis reduction caused by the payment of the dividend is offset by a corresponding basis increase when the dividend is reinvested in the policy.

Surrender for Cash

If a policy is surrendered for cash, the taxable amount is the total surrender value minus the policyowner's current basis in the policy. Dividends left with the insurer to accumulate at interest are not included in the surrender value for tax purposes because they have already reduced the policyowner's basis in the contract.

Example: Mark Sellers, aged 40, owns a level premium whole life policy. Mark has paid $24,000 in premiums and has received $4,000 in dividends from the policy. The face amount of the policy is $100,000. The total cash value of the policy is $28,000. The policy is also subject to an outstanding loan of $15,000. Mark decides to surrender his policy for cash. The tax effects of Mark's surrender of his policy are as follows:

Surrender Value

Policy loan	$15,000
Net cash value ($28,000 total value less $15,000 policy loan)	13,000
Total surrender value	28,000

Basis

Premium paid	$24,000
Minus dividends	4,000
Total basis	$20,000

Taxable Gain

Surrender value
Minus basis
Taxable gain

Loans

Policy loans are another attractive method for receiving value from the contract. The full CSV minus interest charges until the policy anniversary date is available through the contract's policy loan provisions. The loan is automatically continued even if principal and interest are unpaid as long as CSV is available to cover the interest. The policy interest rate is published annually and is often quite favorable compared to other loan options for the senior client.

For example, the rate of interest payable by the policyowner may be fixed (rates of 5 or 6 percent on older contracts and up to 8 percent on more recent policies) or variable (for example, based on Moody's bond rates), depending on the insurer. The policy loan and interest can be repaid at any time. The death of the insured will reduce the death benefit by the amounts due on policy loans at the time of death.

The policy itself does not terminate unless the outstanding indebtedness equals or exceeds the cash value. The policyowner will then have 31 days to repay amounts sufficient to reinstate coverage. The income tax picture is uniquely favorable here. Unless the policy is a MEC, there is no current income tax even though the loan proceeds are available to the client and gain existed in the policy. Remember that, in many instances, the loan will not have to be repaid while the client is alive. This is why grandfathered single premium contracts are so valuable (and maybe why they were so loathed by Congress). Participants should be careful, however, not to let the policy lapse if they have borrowed more than the basis in the contract. In this case, there will be income tax due even though there is no cash distributed.

Partial Withdrawals

Some whole life contracts permit partial surrenders but require a proportional reduction in death benefits. Some insurers will allow a policyowner to surrender "paid-up additions" (additional blocks of insurance identical to the base policy that are purchased on a no-commissions basis with the policy dividend option) without surrendering the base policy. If a withdrawal is made from a policy that results in a reduction in the policy's death benefit during the first 15 years of the policy, the withdrawal may first be taxed as income to the extent of income earned within the contract. A death benefit reduction resulting from a cash value withdrawal typically occurs in a universal life contract. This "income first" or LIFO (last in, first out) method of taxation is the reverse of the general rule of "basis first" or FIFO (first in, first out) taxation that life insurance typically enjoys. In addition, unfavorable LIFO tax treatment is the rule with respect to withdrawals and loans from policies that are classified as MECs. Because of the potential problems, consider a partial surrender or withdrawal carefully. In most instances, the policy loan provisions provide a better option for the senior client.

Trading for an Annuity Contract

Exchanging a life insurance policy for an annuity contract (fixed or variable) is tax free even if gain exists in the established contract. Thus, an existing life insurance policy can be exchanged for an annuity contract with the same or a different insurer without current taxation. Note that an outstanding loan amount forgiven in the exchange is treated as boot and will be taxed to the extent that the boot exceeds the investment in the contract. Also, a policyowner can take proceeds from a surrender or maturity of a life insurance contract in the form of an annuity and defer income taxes. To receive the maximum favorable annuity tax treatment, the policy benefit payments must be received in periodic installments at regular intervals over more than one year, the policyowner must accept the amounts payable in the form of an annuity, and the annuity option must be elected within 60 days of when the lump sum is payable. The annuity option may be appropriate if the individual desires the lifetime income guarantee of a life annuity or the guarantee of payments over a specified period with a term-certain annuity. Annuities receive favorable creditor protection. From an income tax perspective, there are disadvantages as compared to life insurance. The exclusion of income tax on the basis is spread proportionately over the remaining life expectancy instead of being available to be withdrawn first. Heirs also lose the tax-free status that applies to life insurance. However, note that the income tax treatment for the heirs is disadvantageous relative to life insurance if the annuitant dies prematurely.

Viatical Settlement of a Life Insurance Policy

viatical settlement

There are several other methods for withdrawing living values out of life insurance for long-term care or, perhaps, any emergency cash needs. The life insurance policy may have a long-term care rider or an accelerated death benefit provision. The policy could be transferred to a purchaser in a *viatical settlement* for cash. Under the Health Insurance Portability and Accountability Act of 1996 (HIPAA), the tax treatment of these transactions has been clarified. That Act made the proceeds of an accelerated death benefit or a viatical settlement nontaxable if certain requirements are satisfied.

Under current law, any amount received under a life insurance contract on the life of an insured who is either terminally ill or chronically ill and expected to die within 24 months is treated as if it were paid out at death (and therefore not taxable income). For these purposes, a "terminally ill individual" means an individual who has been certified by a physician as having an illness or physical condition that can reasonably be expected to result in death in 24 months or less after the date of the certification. A "chronically ill individual" has the meaning given to the term by Sec. 7702B(c)(2) (which relates to qualified long-term care contracts), except that this term does not include a terminally ill individual.

viatical settlement provider

If any portion of the death benefit under a life insurance contract on the life of an insured is sold or assigned to a viatical settlement provider, the amount received for the sale or assignment of such portion will be treated as an amount paid under the life insurance contract by reason of the death of the insured (and thus not taxable to the insured). A *viatical settlement provider* in a state that licenses such providers simply means a person who is regularly engaged in the trade or business of purchasing, or taking assignments of, life insurance contracts on the lives of insureds and who has a license in the state in which the insured resides. If the insured does not live in a state that requires licensing, then the provider should satisfy certain requirements of the Viatical Settlements Model Act of the National Association of Insurance Commissioners (NAIC) and meet the requirements of the Model Regulations of the NAIC relating to standards for evaluation of reasonable settlement payments.

Special rules apply for chronically ill insureds with respect to both accelerated death benefits and viatical settlements. In the case of an insured who is chronically ill, the favorable tax status does not apply unless such payments are for costs incurred by the payee for qualified long-term care services (not compensated for by insurance or otherwise) and the contract satisfies the requirements of the tax law that apply to chronically ill individuals. Per diem payments to chronically ill individuals qualify regardless of actual cost, provided they do not exceed a specified daily threshold.

LIFE SETTLEMENTS

Sale of Policy to Investors called Life Settlements

In the past, an insurance company was the only party likely to provide cash for the surrender of the life insurance policy. There was no secondary market for the resale of policies. However, as a result of the viatical sales of policies covering terminally ill persons, a secondary market started emerging. There are now investor groups that will buy life insurance policies seeking a profit at the death of the insured.

The investors pay cash for the policy and pay ongoing premiums to keep the coverage in force until the insured dies. The death benefit is paid to the investors. These investors are seeking a high return (usually more than 20 percent annual equivalent over the remaining lifetime). Consequently, they have some qualification criteria that increase the likelihood of reaching the desired return on their investment, often called a *life settlement*.

life settlement

Generally, these investors require the insured to be at least 65 years of age and that the policy has a significant death benefit amount, such as $1 million or more. The price they are willing to pay may be influenced by the insured's health. A shorter life expectancy will increase the return to the investors and consequently increase the purchase price they are willing to pay. The costs the investors incur in evaluating the insured and paying commissions to the agent as well as the taxes on any gain put a negative pressure on the offering price. The investors are at a disadvantage as opposed to the original policyowner because of the differential tax treatment. The death benefits will be income tax free to the original beneficiary, but the investors will owe income taxes on the difference between the death benefit and the amount invested in the policy.

Once the policy has been sold to investors, the insured has no control over the policy. The investors may choose to resell the policy and the second set of investors may require the insured to undergo a valuation of his or her health before purchasing the policy. There is an incentive for the investors to desire an early death. They have no insurable interest in the insured and the longer the insured lives, the lower their return on the policy will be. The investor group will keep track of the insured so that they can file the death claim as soon as death occurs.

The incentive for a policyowner to sell a life insurance policy is the amount by which the investors' offering price exceeds the cash value available from the insurance company upon termination of the policy. The seller will have no obligation to pay future premiums after the policy is sold. As an example, a policy with a $100,000 cash value that can be sold to investors for $120,000 will provide the policyowner with an additional $20,000 incentive.

If we look at the situation from the perspective of the beneficiary, it would usually be advantageous to retain the policy. The return on the committed funds would be greater because the death benefits are not subject to income tax. While the investors are seeking a return in the neighborhood of 20 percent annually, the return for maintaining the status quo will be even higher. Policyowners may want to consider arrangements that would keep such a high return within the family or offer it to close friends or a charity rather than sell it to an investor group. The potential recipient could pay future premiums and reimburse the policyowner for the difference between the cash value and the offered purchase price. The policyowner could still have access to the cash value.

If the policyowner decides to sell a policy to an investor group, there should be an evaluation of the financial soundness and integrity of that investor group. Many states have enacted statutes and regulations applicable to such policy sales by extending the viatical sales regulations to cover life settlements as well. There is a public policy concern that the purchaser be financially sound and capable of waiting until the insured dies to generate the desired investment return. There is no requirement that the purchaser have an insurable interest in the life of the insured. The policyowner is free to sell the policy to any willing purchaser and should be aware that it can subsequently be resold without limitations.

ADVANCE DIRECTIVES

By law, individuals have the right to make their own medical choices based on their own values, beliefs, and wishes. But what happens if a person has an accident or suffers a stroke and can no longer make decisions? Would the person want to have his or her life prolonged by any means necessary, or would he or she want to have some treatments withheld to allow a natural death? Usually, directives will go into effect only in the event that the person can't make and communicate his or her own health-care decisions. Preparing an advance directive lets the physician and other health-care providers know the kind of medical care the individual wants or doesn't want if he or she becomes incapacitated. It also relieves family and friends of the responsibility of making decisions regarding life-prolonging actions.

advance directive

The term *advance directive* can describe a variety of documents. Living will and health-care power of attorney documents are types of advance directives. Some states also have a document specifically called an advance health-care directive. The term advance directive may be used to refer to any of these specific documents or to all of them in general.

States differ widely on what types of advance directives they officially recognize. Some states require a specific format and content of the advance directive. Moreover, the laws regarding honoring advance directives from

---

YOUR FINANCIAL SERVICES PRACTICE: CHOOSING AN ADULT DAY CARE CENTER

If a client or client's relative needs adult day care services, there are some important questions to ask when visiting a center:

- What are the needs of the family and the member being referred to the center?
- Does the center provide services that match those needs?
- Is the environment conducive to ensuring that the family member remains at his or her maximum level of independence?
- Will the person needing the care and other family members enjoy going there?
- Are the programs geared to the interests of older adults?
- Are the participants treated with dignity?
- Is the center clean?
- Does staff actively interact with clients?
- At the time of the visit to the day care center, are clients sitting alone or sleeping?

one state to another aren't clear. If a person lives in one state but travels to other states frequently, he or she may want to consider having the advance directive meet the laws of other states. A good source of information is the Office of the State Attorney General for each state.

What is uniform across the country is that hospitals and other health-care providers are required under the federal Patient Self-Determination Act to give patients information about their rights to make their own health-care decisions. That includes the right to accept or refuse medical treatment. If an individual has an advance directive, it is appropriate to provide a copy to relevant health-care providers. These directives are more likely to be followed if a friend or family member becomes an active advocate for the patient.

General Considerations

Individuals should keep a number of issues in mind when considering advance directives. First, no one has to have an advance directive if he or she does not want one. Second, if an advance directive is adopted it is crucial to do the following:

- Tell family members and make sure that they know where it is located.
- Tell the person's lawyer.
- Discuss the advance directive with the family doctor before signing it. It's important that both the patient and the doctor are comfortable with the contents. The doctor may have some additional suggestions that the patient hadn't thought to include. Make sure the advance directive is part of the medical records.

- If a person has a durable power of attorney, give a copy of the advance directive to the person holding the power of attorney.
- Be sure to comply with the state's signature and witness requirements. States have various requirements about who can be a witness, how many witnesses are needed, and if the directive must be notarized.
- Keep a small card in the person's purse or wallet notifying emergency medical services (EMS) providers of the person's wishes. (EMS generally refers to ambulance companies and paramedics.) In an emergency situation, however, EMS staff members don't have much time to look for or evaluate different types of documentation. They may only acknowledge cards issued by a state's EMS program, and only when the cards are signed by a personal physician.

An individual may change or cancel an advance directive at any time. Any change or cancellation should be written, signed, and dated. Copies should be given to the doctor and to anyone else who had a copy of the original. Some states allow a person to change an advance directive by oral statement. Even if the advance directive is not officially withdrawn, a patient with a clear mind who is communicating his or her wishes directly to the doctor can carry more weight than a living will or durable power of attorney.

Living Will

living will

A *living will* gives people the opportunity to state whether they want their lives prolonged through medical intervention if they will soon die from a terminal illness or if they are permanently unconscious. In general, a living will indicates whether the individual wants certain treatments withheld or withdrawn if they are only prolonging the dying process or if there is no hope of recovery. Generally, these documents only go into effect if a person is no longer able to make his or her own health-care decisions. The living will is intended for the physician and other caregivers to clarify the patient's wishes.

Health-Care Power of Attorney

health-care power of attorney (HCPOA)

A *health-care power of attorney (HCPOA)* allows an individual to name someone (an agent) to make health-care decisions for the person if he or she is unable to do so. The HCPOA is more flexible than a living will and can cover any health-care decision, even if the person is not terminally ill or permanently unconscious. An HCPOA can apply in cases of temporary unconsciousness or in case of diseases like Alzheimer's that affect decision making. Like a living will, an HCPOA will generally give the person the opportunity to state his or her wishes about certain medical procedures. Also as with the living will, an HCPOA generally goes into effect only when the person is no longer able to make health-care decisions.

Advance Health Care Directive

advance health-care
directive

An *advance health-care directive* combines the features of a living will and a health-care power of attorney with some other options. Some states have a specific advance directive form.

Choosing an agent for the advance directive is a crucial decision because that person generally has the same authority to make decisions about the patient's health care as the patient would normally have. The agent must be someone the person knows well and trusts. He or she should also be someone who cares deeply about the patient's welfare. People often choose their spouse or other close family member to be their agent.

The directive can limit the agent's authority if the person chooses to do so. For example, the document can specify that the agent will not have authority to override the patient's desire not to be put on life-support equipment.

It is also important to make sure that the person selected as agent is willing to take on this role, fully understands the patient's position on care, and is willing to carry out those wishes. It's a good idea to designate an alternate agent in case the agent is not able to act for any reason.

This chapter includes a sample advance health-care directive form from the state of Virginia.

Do-Not-Resuscitate Orders

do-not-resuscitate
order

If a person has a serious or terminal illness, he or she may not want CPR (cardiopulmonary resuscitation) or other forms of resuscitation if they would only prolong death and perhaps increase pain. In such cases, the doctor may write a "DNR" order in the person's medical record. This *do-not-resuscitate order* authorizes other health-care providers to withhold measures to restart the heart or breathing.

Over half of the states now have "prehospital" DNR programs so that a doctor's DNR order can be honored outside of the hospital setting. These programs are usually administered by the state's emergency medical service department or state medical associations. Although the prehospital DNR programs vary from state to state, some common features are as follows:

- standardized documents that responders can recognize quickly. These may be posted prominently in the home; responders know to look for them.
- DNR bracelets or medallions that communicate the individual's DNR status.
- physician involvement. DNR orders generally must be signed by a doctor before responders will honor them.
- comfort treatment not withheld. Responders are still required to alleviate the individual's pain and discomfort even though they are under orders not to resuscitate.

Physicians who are unwilling (for personal, moral, or professional reasons) to issue DNR orders may be required to transfer the care of a patient to another physician who will.

The best place to start for information about prehospital DNR programs is the family physician. He or she should know whether a state has a program and how it works. He or she can also explain what will happen if the person decides to forgo resuscitation and whether it is medically appropriate to do so in a specific case. Other sources include local hospice organizations, state or local EMS offices, and other professionals.

Of course, the DNR order can also be revoked at any time in any way that effectively communicates the person's desire, including

- physically destroying the actual DNR document
- verbally telling emergency responders to disregard the order

More Information

For more information on options for maintaining individual autonomy in health-care decision making, consider taking advantage of the following resources:

- AARP holds education workshops on medical decision making. Call AARP at 1-800-424-3410.
- Contact Choice in Dying, a national organization providing state-specific advance directive forms and instructions, as well as a number of booklets about health-care powers of attorney and living wills. Call 212-366-5540.
- You also can obtain state forms and literature from local hospitals, nursing homes, state or local offices on aging, state bar associations, or medical associations.

VIRGINIA ADVANCE MEDICAL DIRECTIVE

THIS FORM, WITH SLIGHT VARIATIONS, IS THE FORM APPROVED BY THE VIRGINIA GENERAL ASSEMBLY IN THE HEALTH CARE DECISIONS ACT. THE FORM CONTAINS BOTH A "**LIVING WILL**" SECTION AND A "**DURABLE POWER OF ATTORNEY FOR HEALTH CARE**" SECTION. YOU MAY COMPLETE EITHER OF THESE SECTIONS OR BOTH OF THEM. IT IS YOUR RESPONSIBILITY UNDER VIRGINIA LAW TO PROVIDE A COPY OF YOUR ADVANCE DIRECTIVE TO YOUR ATTENDING PHYSICIAN. FOR INSTRUCTIONS ON HOW TO FILL OUT THE FORM AND WHAT TO DO WITH IT, SEE THE OTHER SIDE OF THIS SHEET. VIRGINIA DOES NOT REQUIRE THE USE OF THIS PARTICULAR FORM IN ORDER TO MAKE A VALID ADVANCE DIRECTIVE. *IF YOU HAVE LEGAL QUESTIONS ABOUT THIS FORM, OR WOULD LIKE TO DEVELOP A DIFFERENT FORM TO MEET YOUR NEEDS, YOU SHOULD TALK WITH AN ATTORNEY.*

Advance Medical Directive made this _____ day of _____,
20_____. I, _____, willfully and
voluntarily make known my desire and do hereby declare:

SECTION ONE: LIVING WILL
(CROSS THROUGH IF YOU DO NOT WANT TO FILL OUT THIS PORTION OF
THE ADVANCE MEDICAL DIRECTIVE.)

If at any time my attending physician should determine that I have a terminal
condition where the application of life-prolonging procedures would serve only to
artificially prolong the dying process, I direct that such procedures be withheld or
withdrawn, and that I be permitted to die naturally with only the administration of
medication or the performance of any medical procedure deemed necessary to
provide me with comfort care or to alleviate pain.

OPTION: I SPECIFICALLY DIRECT THAT THE FOLLOWING PROCEDURES
OR TREATMENTS BE PROVIDED TO ME:

_____

_____

In the absence of my ability to give directions regarding the use of such life-
prolonging procedures, it is my intention that this declaration shall be honored by
my family and physician as the final expression of my legal right to refuse medical
or surgical treatment and accept the consequences of such refusal.

SECTION TWO: DURABLE POWER OF ATTORNEY FOR HEALTH CARE
(CROSS THROUGH IF YOU DO NOT WANT TO FILL OUT THIS PORTION OF
THE ADVANCE MEDICAL DIRECTIVE.)

I hereby appoint as my primary agent to make health care decisions on my behalf
as authorized in this document:

_____

(Primary Agent)

_____

(Address)

_____

(Phone Number)

If the above named primary agent is not reasonably available or is unable to act as my agent, I then appoint the following as successor agent to serve in that capacity:

_____

(Successor Agent)

_____

(Address)

_____

(Phone Number)

I hereby grant to my agent, named above, full power and authority to make health-care decisions on my behalf as described below whenever I have been determined to be incapable of making an informed decision about providing, withholding, or withdrawing medical treatment. The phrase "incapable of making an informed decision" means unable to understand the nature, extent, and probable consequences of a proposed medical decision or unable to make a rational evaluation of the risks and benefits of a proposed medical decision as compared with the risks and benefits of alternatives to that decision, or unable to communicate such understanding in any way. My agent's authority hereunder is effective as long as I am incapable of making an informed decision.

The determination that I am incapable of making an informed decision shall be made by my attending physician and a second physician or licensed clinical psychologist after a personal examination of me and shall be certified in writing. Such certification shall be required before treatment is withheld or withdrawn, and before, or as soon as reasonably practicable after, treatment is provided, and every 180 days thereafter while the treatment continues.

In exercising the power to make health-care decisions on my behalf, my agent shall follow my desires and preferences as stated in this document or as otherwise known to my agent. My agent shall be guided by my medical diagnosis and prognosis and any information provided by my physicians as to the intrusiveness, pain, risks, and side effects associated with treatment or nontreatment. My agent shall not authorize a course of treatment which he knows, or upon reasonable inquiry ought to know, is contrary to my religious beliefs or my basic values, whether expressed orally or in writing. If my agent cannot determine what treatment choice I would have made on my own behalf, then my agent shall make a choice for me based upon what he believes to be in my best interests.

Further, my agent shall not be liable for the costs of treatment pursuant to his/her authorization, based solely on that authorization.

OPTION: POWERS OF MY AGENT

(CROSS THROUGH ANY LANGUAGE YOU DON'T WANT AND ADD ANY
LANGUAGE YOU DO WANT.)

The power of my agent shall include the following:

A. To consent to or refuse or withdraw consent to any type of medical care,
    treatment, surgical procedure, diagnostic procedure, medication, and the
    use of mechanical or other procedures that affect any bodily function,
    including, but not limited to, artificial respiration, artificially administered
    nutrition and hydration, and cardiopulmonary resuscitation. This
    authorization specifically includes the power to consent to administration of
    dosages of pain-relieving medication in excess of standard dosages in an
    amount sufficient to relieve pain, even if such medication carries the risk of
    addiction or inadvertently hastens my death;

B. To request, receive, and review any information, verbal or written, regarding
    my physical or mental health, including but not limited to medical and
    hospital records, and to consent to the disclosure of this information.

C. To employ and discharge my health-care providers;

D. To authorize my admission to or discharge (including transfer to another
    facility) from any hospital, hospice, nursing home, adult home or other
    medical care facility; and

E. To take any lawful actions that may be necessary to carry out these
    decisions, including the granting of releases of liability to medical providers.

By signing below, I indicate that I am emotionally and mentally competent to make
this advance directive and that I understand the purpose and effect of this document.
This advance directive shall not terminate in the event of my disability.

_____

(Signature of Declarant)

_____

The declarant signed the foregoing advance directive in my presence. I am not the
spouse or a blood relative of the declarant.

_____

(Witness)

_____

(Witness)

GUIDELINES FOR COMPLETING THE ADVANCE DIRECTIVE FORM

Like all adult Virginians, you have the right to accept or refuse any medical treatment your doctor recommends to you. But what if you are in a coma, through illness or injury, or are otherwise unable to communicate, and a medical decision must be made about your medical care? In such a circumstance, if you have signed an advance directive, the doctor and your family can refer to it and honor your wishes. Thus, through the directive you make decisions about your medical treatment.

This Advance Medical Directive was authorized by the Health Care Decisions Act passed by Virginia's 1992 General Assembly. It has two sections: the 1992 version of the "living will" originally authorized by the General Assembly in 1984 and a durable power of attorney for health care (authorized in 1989.) **You may fill out either the living will section or the durable power of attorney section, or you may fill out both of them.**

If you have already signed a living will or a durable power of attorney for health care and they have been properly prepared and signed, they continue to be valid. You need not re-do them unless there are changes you want to make or unless you prefer this format and wish to make a replacement.

It is wise to discuss this form with your physician before beginning to fill it out. Your physician can explain the medical terms and help you with the optional medical choices. The following guidelines will also help you prepare it properly.

Date the document where shown at the top of the form and enter your name.

The living will section. This section goes into effect only if you are terminally ill. It directs that life-prolonging procedures be withheld or withdrawn and that you be permitted to die naturally with only comfort care and medication to relieve pain. You are given the option of asking for certain procedures and treatments. **If you do NOT want to include the living will section in your declaration, draw a line through it.**

The durable power of attorney for health care. This section applies whether or not you have a terminal condition. It is not limited to life-prolonging procedures but can cover any type of treatment decision. Through this section you give the "power" to make these decisions to an adult person appointed by you as your agent; it is wise to appoint a "successor agent" as backup. **Before filling in the names of your agent/successor agent, talk to the persons you want to appoint.** Explain the directive and what they may be asked to do. It is important to have their understanding and support. **If you do NOT want to include this durable power of attorney section in your declaration, draw a line through the section.** If, however, you want to include the section, you may also give your agent any or all of the specific powers listed A through E. **Draw a line through any of these entries you do NOT want your agent to have.**

Signature. Only one person may sign this form as the "Declarant." If your spouse wants to execute a directive, he/she must prepare a separate form. **Enter the date where indicated and sign your name in the space marked "Signature of Declarant." Two witnesses must be present when you sign your name; they in turn sign their names in the spaces indicated. Neither of these witnesses may be a blood relative or your spouse.** It is not necessary to have the form notarized.

When the form is completed, the law requires that you give a copy of it to your physician, who places it in your medical record. You should also give copies of it to the agent(s) you have named, to members of your family, and, if you wish, to friends who are close to you. Keep a list of the people to whom you have given the form. Keep the original in a place where it can be readily located and tell those you live with where it is. You should review the directive from time to time, especially when there is a change in your health or family status. If you wish to change it, fill out a new form and destroy the earlier one. Distribute copies of the new one, retrieving and destroying the earlier copies.

You may revoke your advance medical directive at any time, but the revocation is effective only when communicated to your physician. The best way to revoke the directive is to destroy or cancel each copy. Or you can revoke it with a signed, dated statement, or by directing someone else to destroy or cancel the directive in your presence, or by stating, preferably directly to your physician, that you want to revoke it. In any case, retrieve and destroy the distributed copies as above.

Virginia law states that, if an advance medical directive is followed and the patient dies, the death is not considered a suicide for purposes of any life insurance that the patient carries.

Even if you have signed this directive, your physician is not obligated to provide care he/she considers ethically or medically inappropriate. However, if the physician's judgment does not agree with your direction or your agent's, the physician must make a reasonable effort to transfer you to another doctor.

Use of this Advance Medical Directive by adults is legal in Virginia. It may not be in another state, depending upon the laws of that state. A lawyer can determine that for you.

This form was prepared as a service to Virginia physicians and their patients by the *Virginia Medical Quarterly*, journal of the Medical Society of Virginia, and the Society's General Counsel. It may be photocopied in any desired quantity.

PROPERTY INSURANCE ISSUES

There are a few issues that warrant periodic review regarding the insurance on homes and automobiles. Although the premiums may not be significant items in budgets of seniors, they provide significant protection of other assets via the liability coverages.

Homeowners Coverages

In addition to the important liability coverages provided by homeowners policies, there are important valuation issues that need to be reviewed. The standard policies provide limited coverage for all types of property generally found in a household. It is important to review the actual values of property contained in a household and compare them with the value limitations in the existing policy. It is quite common for the limitations on silverware, jewelry, furs, cameras, and art objects to be lower than the actual value of the property owned. The solution is to increase the amount of coverage through the appropriate endorsements. A good property insurance agent such as a CPCU can make the appropriate adjustments to make sure the property is adequately protected. Sometimes it's just a matter of increasing the limits and other times it may require the issuance of a separate policy, such as a personal property floater.

The base policy itself also must be reviewed regularly to make sure the coverage is adequate. There are provisions in the coverage that will reduce the benefits if the policy limits do not equal or exceed a specified percentage of the replacement value of the structure. Often this is an 80 percent requirement. If the requirement is not satisfied, all claims will be settled for a portion of the loss rather than the full value of the loss.

Example: The owner of a property has not increased the policy amount for over a decade. The policy requires coverage to equal 80 percent of the replacement value of that structure. Inflation has pushed up the replacement cost to where the amount actually carried is only 40 percent of the replacement value. Consequently, if a loss is suffered, the claim will be settled on the basis of 50 percent of the loss rather than the full value of the loss. If the owner suffered a 100 percent loss of the property, the claim settlement would be limited to the specified policy amount, which is only 40 percent of the amount actually lost. Even though the formula would suggest recovery of 50 percent of the loss, the insurance company will not pay more than the policy limits.

Property owners should consider keeping the amount of coverage in line with the full replacement cost of the structure. Otherwise they run the risk of having less than full coverage in case of a total loss. Property insurance agents have access to valuation information that can help suggest the appropriate amount of coverage. An agent who does not suggest that the amount of coverage be kept in line with property values is not doing the property owner any favors. Failure to increase policy limits may significantly increase the amount of unprotected property risk.

An issue that must be addressed by some retirees is that of extended periods without occupancy while the owner is traveling or residing at another residence. Most homeowner coverage requires that the premises be occupied and sets limits as to how long the protection stays in force if the property is not occupied (such as 30 or 60 days). The coverage will be reduced or terminated if the premises are not occupied more than a specified number of consecutive days. Extending the coverage may require either a housesitter or a specific endorsement to accommodate the actual pattern of occupancy.

Another potential problem is that of part-time or full-time business pursuits conducted out of the home. These activities can negate the coverage under a standard homeowners policy unless it has been endorsed to acknowledge the business pursuits. Salespersons who keep their primary records in the home probably need such a business endorsement, even if customers or clients do not visit the insured premises.

Automobile Issues

Probably one of the most important suggestions is that seniors take a defensive driving course. With the increased congestion and higher rates of travel, many seniors are intimidated by other aggressive drivers on the roads. Driving instructors can help them improve their skills and hopefully reduce their anxiety.

A secondary benefit of taking a defensive driving course is that the instructor can assess the competency of the driver. Response times and alertness may deteriorate with age and some drivers become a threat to both themselves and other drivers. Night driving becomes dangerous for drivers who have cataracts. Most seniors are unwilling to admit that they are no longer competent drivers. It usually takes someone else to suggest that their driving is no longer safe before they will even consider giving up their driving privileges.

Giving up driving means a loss of freedom and independence to most people. Therefore, it is common for drivers to resist any suggestion that they are not safe drivers. Family members often anguish over how to convince an incompetent driver to rely on others for transportation. Sometimes a family physician will suggest that it is no longer safe for the individual to drive. The drivers' license renewal process is being altered in some states to more thoroughly assess driver competency.

Automobile insurance rates are generally reduced for individuals who have taken a defensive driving course. Further discounts are available for ABS braking systems, airbags (especially side air bags), and theft alarm systems. Seniors who qualify for discounts should make sure the agent notifies the insurance company of the eligibility.

Seniors who are semiretired and use their automobile in the pursuit of income may need a commercial auto policy rather than a personal auto policy.

Personal Liability Umbrella Policy

With the extremely high liability judgments being handed down by the courts today, is important to increase the liability protection above and beyond that provided in homeowner and automobile policies. The personal liability umbrella policy extends the liability protection of those two underlying policies. It kicks in whenever a loss exceeds the limits of either the homeowners policy or the automobile policy. The protection is available in increments of $1 million and the premium is quite reasonable.

The intent here is to keep accumulated assets intended for retirement from being squandered to pay court-ordered liability judgments.

14

Estate Planning for Seniors

Constance J. Fontaine

Chapter Outline

ESTATE PLANNING CONSIDERATIONS FOR SENIOR ESTATE OWNERS

Introduction

This chapter on estate planning for competent seniors focuses on financial estate planning concepts that, although not limited only to elder planning, are more specifically directed at that particular group of estate owners. To begin, there are some basic areas that should be addressed for seniors in all instances. This is not to say that all of the succeeding topics are absolutely necessary in all cases, only that they should, at the very least, be considered.

Before delving into actual estate planning thoughts, a discussion of the background for today's seniors is helpful. Presently, people in their 80s and

90s went through the 1930s Depression and were old enough to remember the ramifications of those times. For many, the Depression meant having to live a spartan life as far as food, clothing, shelter, and money were concerned for a impressionable and memorable period of time. For many, this period was fraught with significant worry. Aside from natural vulnerabilities associated with age, those unfortunate times instilled a certain financial mindset in those who are now 80 and older. Many in this age group are anxious about the possible insufficiency of their assets to provide a continuing comfortable existence. These concerns are exacerbated by worries of becoming financial burdens on their children. The Depression seniors are, for the most part, less likely than today's baby boomers to take chances with their money, to play the stock market, and so on. They led what is sometimes today referred to as a *traditional* family lifestyle. The husband-father worked outside of the home and managed the household finances while the wife-mother worked within the home caring for family members. Another complication to add to what is usually some older seniors' financially conservative approach to money is the fact that they typically own properties that were acquired a very long time ago. Often these assets carry a low basis and have appreciated greatly in value over the years. This may make it imprudent from a number of perspectives, including taxes, to use the assets for improved investment diversification. Senior estate planning may benefit with this brief background in mind. Note, however, that the same background does not usually apply to the younger group of seniors, the so-called baby boomers.

Perhaps a more appropriate term for estate planning when it comes to some seniors would be preventive planning. Preventive planning encompasses arrangements made before long-term care is needed and before mental or physical incapacity sets in. Ideally, senior estate planning should be addressed before becoming "older." In the majority of cases, however, individuals do not begin elder planning until past age 60. Younger clients planning for old age are often practical about their plans. Old age is "far off" and they have no difficulty making decisions on senior issues. However, decision-making is less cavalier, more urgent, and sometimes fearful for those beginning the planning process when advanced age is already there or right around the corner. The plans could be as simple as a durable power of attorney, will, and/or trust. Many individuals falsely equate estate planning for seniors with Medicaid planning. Reducing the value of a senior individual's estate for transfer tax and other purposes should not automatically be interpreted to mean spending down for Medicaid eligibility.

Estate planning is an issue for most seniors—not just the wealthy ones. An estate plan does not have to be elaborate or involved. The particulars of each situation drive that determination. Although an estate plan may merely involve executing one or more of the above-mentioned documents, or the review of existing documents, advice concerning gifting, taxation, and other family concerns with an elder law attorney or estate planner, or a financial advisor specifically attuned to senior needs, can be extremely helpful.

Although basic estate planning principles may apply universally to most groups of people, special considerations often need to be taken into account for senior estate owners. Senior estate planning can be unique in several ways. First, unlike planning for young clients, time is more limited, so there is less potential for procrastination. Second, while incompetency should always be an estate planning consideration, seniors' incapacity issues involve more planning urgency. Third, there's a greater concentration of widowed and single clients within the group of senior owners than occurs with estate planning for the typical young and middle-aged clients. While the marital deduction is probably the most significant estate planning device for married couples, for seniors it is frequently unavailable. Fourth, although the focus is on increasing assets for younger owners, for older ones the focus concerns estate reduction methods. Finally, Medicaid issues may require an intricate interweaving of Medicaid and estate planning techniques.

Most of the subjects discussed in this chapter are discussed in greater detail in *Fundamentals of Estate Planning,* the textbook for The College's HS 330 course.

THE NEED FOR ESTATE PLANNING

Many seniors may wonder why they need to be concerned about estate planning. Perhaps they have been moderately successful but have not amassed huge amounts of wealth. It is unlikely that many of them will ever pay high federal estate taxes.

There is far more to estate and financial advising for seniors than just saving taxes. Estate planning considers many more issues that raise questions such as the following:

- How do I want my property distributed?
- What happens if I just do nothing?
- Will there be huge bills to pay?
- Where will the money to pay these bills come from?
- Are there ways to reduce estate settlement costs?
- What will happen if I become ill?
- Who will make decisions about the type of care I receive if I become physically disabled and mentally incompetent?
- Are there sufficient assets to support a surviving spouse?
- Are there ways to ease the financial burdens faced by children?
- Is it possible to help provide for the education of grandchildren?

BASIC ESTATE PLANNING STEPS

Estate planning for seniors is often best approached by following these 10 key steps:

1. inventory of assets and liabilities
2. estimate of asset valuation and estate complexity
3. calculation of current net worth and potential estate taxes
4. goal determination
5. consideration of alternative legal tools to reach goals
6. consideration of alternative forms of property ownership
7. investigation of tax minimization strategies
8. provision for estate liquidity
9. execution of legal documents and planned actions
10. periodic reviews

1.   Inventory of Assets and Liabilities

Seniors need to recognize the assets they own, how they are owned, and what they are worth in order to properly plan their estates. They also need to have an understanding of their debts. This information serves as a starting point to determine what is available for heirs, how such property will currently be distributed, and how estate taxes will be computed. Completing a simple, short fact-finder can expedite this process. (An example of the Fact Finder appears in *Fundamentals of Estate Planning,* The College's textbook for the HS 330 course.)

Assets need to be valued at today's market prices. Current fair market values may differ substantially from the amount paid for assets many years ago. Some seniors may be surprised at their personal net worth and further surprised to learn that their estates face potential estate tax liabilities.

2.   Estimate of Asset Valuation and Estate Complexity

Once all property has been inventoried, the asset values will indicate the estate's complexity and whether or not an estate tax return must be filed. An unusual mix of assets or a mix of assets located in several jurisdictions may require more sophisticated planning.

3.   Calculation of Current Net Worth and Potential Estate Taxes

The next step is to calculate the senior prospect's current net worth, which is done by subtracting liabilities from assets. The resulting figure is a barometer of whether or not the client has accumulated sufficient assets to generate the income needed over his or her remaining life expectancy.

If current estimated net worth is in excess of the current year's estate tax exemption equivalent, there is a potential for federal estate tax liability. Current net worth also provides insight into how much money will eventually be expended for costs associated with death, including funeral costs and estate administration. Once again, consideration must be given as to how these costs will be paid.

4. Goal Determination

Careful deliberation is necessary to formulate exactly what a person wants to do with the wealth that has accumulated over the course of a lifetime in order to determine the direction of a senior's estate plan.

5. Consideration of Alternative Legal Tools to Reach Goals

Tools That Facilitate Lifetime Care and Property Management

- Living trusts
- Powers of attorney

These two tools allow others to step forward and manage a senior's property in cases of physical illness and mental disability.

- Living will
- Health care proxy

These tools, which are components of a last will and testament, can be used to specify wishes about desired health care and provide authority to someone to carry out those wishes.

Tools Used during Life to Transfer Property and Save Estate Settlement Costs

- Lifetime gifts

Property given away is generally not included in a senior's estate. This effectively removes postgift appreciation from estate taxation.

- Irrevocable trust

An irrevocable trust allows seniors to specify their wishes as to the management and eventual disposition of gifted property.

Tools That Focus on the Disposition of Property at Death

- Will

A will is the primary estate planning document for an individual's wishes concerning the disposition of property at death. When a person dies without a will, assets are distributed according to the intestacy laws of his or her state of domicile.

6. Consideration of Alternative Forms of Property Ownership

- Sole ownership
- Tenancy in common
- Joint tenancy with right of survivorship
- Tenancy by the entireties (where permitted)
- Community property

Seniors need to be alert to both the opportunities and pitfalls of different forms of property ownership. Where major changes are planned, competent legal advice should always be sought.

7. Investigation of Tax Minimization Strategies

Although taxes are not usually the primary estate planning concern, most seniors want to investigate ways to reduce income, gift, and estate taxation. The following are three primary techniques to reduce estate and gift taxation:

- marital deduction
- credit exclusion/equivalent bypass trust (CEBT)
- annual gift tax exclusion

Appropriate use of these estate tax savings techniques may allow seniors to redirect additional value to their heirs.

8. Provision for Estate Liquidity

There are costs associated with dying. These include medical expenses associated with a final illness and funeral costs. The administration of an estate typically entails executor allowances and attorney fees. Often, there is a need for the services of an accountant and a professional appraiser. In addition, many seniors die leaving debts. These debts may be small credit card bills or major mortgage loans.

9. Execution of Legal Documents and Planned Actions

More frequently than expected, seniors will take the initiative to meet with their legal advisors, discuss options, have necessary legal documents drafted—and then fail to execute the documents and take the steps necessary to implement plans.

It may be the financial advisor's job to remind seniors of the need to sign legal documents and take necessary action to implement their estate plans.

10. Periodic Reviews

Estate plans should not be considered static. Seniors need to revisit their plans on a periodic basis to make sure that they reflect their current circumstances and needs.

Life-changing events that can trigger the need to revise estate plans include:

- death of a spouse
- remarriage
- serious illness
- marriage of an adult child
- divorce of an adult child
- birth of a grandchild
- a grandchild's college education
- receipt of an inheritance
- sale of the family home
- change in tax laws

PERSONAL ASPECTS OF SENIOR ESTATE PLANNING

In an ideal family setting, all family members are in accord and there are no conflicts, feuds, hard feelings, or relationship remoteness. For many seniors, family harmony means more than assets. Many senior clients approach estate planning from a different perspective than they did when they and their children were younger. Many senior clients could be dealing with three generations or more. There may be second marriages and blended families, sibling rivalries, wealthy and poor adult children, and adult children with numerous to few to no children of their own, to name several possibilities. The variations are endless and yet, besides wanting to be able to provide for themselves financially during the final years so as not to be a burden on their loved ones, senior clients also want to leave a legacy to loved ones and keep family peace in doing so. Because the nature of family relationships often changes, senior clients and their planners need to be creative to keep strife at bay.

Family Estate Discussion

A common suggestion by planners that applies in most, if not all, situations is for senior parents to reveal their intentions to their children (and, perhaps, even grandchildren). The main objective of the family meeting is to reach a level of comfort and to preserve or promote peace. Parents are often reluctant to discuss their estate plans until a health crisis arises. Children are hesitant to introduce conversations about their parents' estate for fear of appearing greedy and intrusive. By openly discussing financial, long-term care, and estate plans prior to death, seniors remove the element of surprise when the will is read after death. Unexpected bequest distributions can ignite family strife. Even when children do not agree with their parent's plans, they have time to adapt to them before they lose the parent. Family holidays, get-togethers, vacations, and even conference calls involving as many family members as possible are good opportunities for the "disclosure" discussion. Open dialogue helps children understand the parent's intentions while he or she is alive, and it gives the parents an opportunity to gauge their children's reactions. Being straightforward with children is usually positive. There is nothing wrong with the parent(s) asking; "Is there any problem with this?" or "Are there any conflicts about what I plan to do?," or stating, "I know this will reduce your inheritances, but I want to make a significant bequest to charity." If disagreements come up, family meetings provide a forum to openly discuss issues without serious discord. It is more beneficial for senior parents to communicate intentions about their wealth throughout the aging process instead of divulging financial information only when there is a crisis. Family financial interaction also serves to make the children feel included and involved in the parent's estate planning process. The upset of a parent's death can magnify even small disagreements. Emotional reactions are more manageable during open discussions while the parent is still living than after the parent's death when everyone is grieving.

Equal versus Unequal Inheritances. Every family situation must be looked at on a case-by-case basis as to whether or not the children should receive equal inheritances. Most seniors want to treat their children equally, but many are also uncomfortable leaving more affluent children the same legacy as less affluent one(s), or the children with few or no children of their own compared to the children who have more mouths to feed, or the child who has cared for and been more attentive to them versus the child(ren) who is more distant geographically and/or less attentive. Depending on the circumstances, it may appear unfair to treat everyone the same from an inheritance standpoint. Equal or unequal, seniors should state their reasons for one way or the other. Children might be more understanding than expected, realizing, especially after hearing from their parent, that one child is not loved more than the others but that for the stated reasons, deserves different or similar treatment. If the senior client's estate consists of assets that are difficult to divide equally among his or her children, purchasing life insurance through a trust can be used to equalize the value each child receives from the estate. A frequent source of potential inequity is the family-owned business in which some children are active and others are not. A solid business succession plan with a buy-sell agreement coupled with life insurance coverage will equalize children's inheritances.

Distributing Personal Family Items

Sibling rivalry often arises over the "small stuff" (Aunt Tessie's porcelain teapot, family picture albums, Grandpa's childhood teddy bear, and so on) than from actual transfers of wealth. Seniors may not even realize how much some family items that have little monetary value mean to their children. To the children, these items are family heirlooms having significant sentimental value. A family discussion often brings out these preferences. If more than one person wants the same object, straws could be drawn or coins flipped, with the losing child or children having other first choices. If this is not workable, the item could be sold or auctioned off and the proceeds divided amongst the contenders.

There are several ways of passing family personal property items to the intended recipients. Many seniors name the beneficiary of specific bequests in the will. Specific bequests, however, are impractical when there are many separate items to be distributed. Also, if the item later is lost, gifted, destroyed, or the testator changes his or her mind about the future recipient, a testator may feel the need to execute a new will or codicil. Consequently, wills can be an impractical way to leave many objects to many persons. In the majority of cases, specific bequests are typically used to leave named stock, cash amounts, collections (coins, figurines, or family tableware, for example), jewelry, and so forth when the number of assets and the number of beneficiaries is not that great. Some states provide that specific bequests are not subject to death taxes. In essence, this means that those tax expenses will be assumed by the residuary beneficiaries, which may or may not be what the testator intended.

External List. Estate owners who have many personal objects that are sought after by multiple family members sometimes will create an external list of the items and the intended beneficiaries of them. Some states allow a signed and dated external directive to be filed with the will, or enforce one if the will makes reference to it; other states do not enforce or recognize an external list of the decedent's wishes. In those states not giving legal recognition to a letter of instruction, however, the executor and family members will usually honor a decedent's letter of wishes, especially if it is handwritten and/or the family was aware that the decedent had documented his or her desires for distribution of personal property items. External documentation may even include pictures of the items. Keeping a record of how you want your assets to be distributed also ensures that more than one beneficiary has not been promised the same items. It provides a reference for knowing what heir gets what asset. The benefit of identifying objects and noting their intended distributions is even more obvious when there are blended families. One thing that is not recommended is for seniors who have remarried to count on the surviving spouse to do "what is right" with respect to passing personal assets to the decedent spouse's heirs. Many unforeseen possibilities can derail the intended plan. Moreover, if the property items have significant value, donors should state whether or not the recipients bear the responsibility for any transfer tax liability.

Outright Lifetime Gift. One of the nontax advantages of gifting during lifetime is that the donor is able to see the donee enjoy the gift and have the assurance that the intended beneficiary received the item, such as a family heirloom. If the donor is confident that he or she will not need the personal property items in the future, giving them away during life allays any fears about the items not being distributed in accordance with the decedent's wishes after death. Lifetime gifting may also reduce potential family friction because transferring the gift clearly demonstrates the donor's intent. The period of time preceding a second marriage is viewed by some advisors as an ideal time to gift sentimental assets and family heirlooms to the donor's children with the first spouse. If clients on the verge of marrying again are concerned about the children from a previous marriage receiving their inheritances and the client can afford to transfer assets during lifetime, planners may recommend giving the children their inheritances then and there.

Upon Death or Incapacity Letter

upon death or incapacity letter

Leaving an *upon death or incapacity letter* of relevant, up-to-date information for family and the estate representative not only felicitates postmortem estate settlement but also further endears the decedent to his or her surviving loved ones. The intent of the letter is to save the survivors time and effort in discovering pertinent information about the decedent. For example, the document should contain the locations of personal papers such as the will, birth certificate, insurance policies, car title, and deeds, as well as banking, brokerage, and credit card account numbers. Since the letter can be tailored to the creator's particular circumstances, it may be simple or very detailed. (See appendix 3.)

Information Gathering

The first place to start with all estate planning is by using a fact finder or some form of asset and personal information form to discover and organize all objective and subjective data pertinent to the client, including a review of the client's family situation, health, personal objectives, testamentary objectives, present assets, existing documents, and current estate plan, if there is one. If the client's spouse has died or the plan under review was designed to correct issues that no longer exist, the primary thrust of the senior owner's estate plan may be a matter of merely simplifying what exists. At the very least, a review of the current plan and client information should ascertain whether or not the senior's estate is likely to trigger the estate tax if he or she died within the next few years. Even if it appears there would be no federal estate tax, state death liability must be considered.

Caution should be taken when significant changes are made in a very elderly person's estate plan or documents. Detailed records containing explanations of the client's reasons for the changes should be maintained so as to avoid later challenges of incapacity and undue influence. Supportive affidavits from the testator's physician and witnesses and, in some cases, videotaping may be warranted.

Elder Advisors

Frequently, elder advisor practitioners recognize an elevated level of concern about a client's potential for disability when they are the parents of special needs children or other family members. This concern is increased by the realization that senior parents are statistically living to even more advanced ages than before. The worry now becomes who will take care of senior parents if their children are unable (for numerous possible reasons) to provide care or make decisions regarding their care. These situations explain why various groups providing senior advice are increasing in numbers. Presently there are several thousand attorneys specializing in elder law, many of whom are members of the National Academy of Elder Law Attorneys (NAELA). NAELA is a professional association of attorneys committed to the improvement of legal services to seniors. At the present time, some states (and more expected to follow) have created state elder law certification programs to meet the growing demand. Elder law attorneys serve seniors in three vital areas: health care and incapacity decision-making, financial management, and estate planning. As with any situation requiring the expertise of an attorney, credentials should be verified, references obtained, and excellent reputation confirmed before the attorney is retained.

MARITAL ISSUES—SENIOR DIVORCE, SEPARATION, AND REMARRIAGE

The institution of marriage has undergone changes, as do all aspects of living. Divorce rates in the United States have increased over the last two decades. As divorce has become more accepted, the stigma that once applied to it is no longer present. An increasing number of divorces also take place among couples in their 60s, 70s, and even 80s (sometimes referred to as "gray divorces"), many of whom have been married for 30 or more years. According to U.S. Census statistics, the divorced senior citizen population increased by close to 35 percent from 1990 to 2000. Divorce and separation percentages have been projected by some to at least double by 2030. Liberalized divorce laws and women's growing presence in the labor force are frequently cited causes.

There are numerous reasons why people divorce or separate in their later years. One reason some divorced couples give is that they have grown personally in different directions and have different aspirations than they once had. With the children grown and gone from the home, the couple determines they no longer have much in common with one another. A large portion of parental energy is devoted to childrearing and careers. When these major undertakings of childrearing and careers are completed, the husband and wife may be left in an interrelationship that has been severely neglected. The lack of interest in one another may have been recognized well before the children were raised but the couple stayed together "for the good of the children." Some couples are bored with one another emotionally, physically, and psychologically. They know all there is to know (or want to know) about the other and continuing as married partners is perceived to be nothing more than mere existence. The parties may just be biding time to get back onto the dating circuit or to live what they believe to be a higher quality of life through regained freedom and peace.

Another reason given for seniors divorcing is derived from individuals having longer life expectancies and remaining in good health during the golden years. Marriage is therefore a longer commitment than it was half a century ago. Some husbands and wives feel that they have tolerated one another long enough and that they deserve some freedom and happiness for their last 20 to 25 years. More than a few older unhappy couples claim their physical health has improved following a divorce.

In addition to longer good health being a factor in senior divorces and separations, women's financial independence is another factor. In previous generations, it was commonplace for the wife to stay home, raise the children, and not work outside of the home. The wife was dependent on her husband's salary and pension benefits for her old age. Presently, with the majority of households having two-career couples, both husband and wife have incomes and pension benefits. There is less interdependence and less need for the other financially.

Effects of Senior Divorce, Separation, and Remarriage

Children

When senior couples divorce, the effects can be devastating on many fronts. It is a common myth that because the couple waited to divorce until the children were grown, the children will not be affected. Even when the father and mother have not gotten along for years and it would seem that the adult children should be prepared for and not upset by their parents ending their union, children are often crushed by the news. Traditions that existed throughout their upbringings are forever disrupted. Family photos will capture only one parent at a time. Family dinners, holidays, and visits will never be the same. In addition, now the children may realize there is a potential future responsibility for one or both parents in the not-too-distant future. Because their parents no longer will be expected to care for one another, perhaps one parent will not be able to make ends meet and will have to move in with a son or daughter's young family. All of these results are likely to produce extended family strain. The strain is exacerbated when one or more of the adult children do not participate to the same degree as their siblings in a parent's personal and financial care. Although contemplating a future burden may lead adult children to encourage their parents to find other partners, the encouragement may stop short of remarriage for a multitude of reasons, including the children's inheritances from their parents. Prenuptial agreements can help to resolve this particular concern. The pre (ante) nuptial is reinforced if it is accompanied by an affidavit signed by a physician attesting to the senior person's mental capacity to make such a decision. If either the husband or wife has age-related problems affecting the mind, divorce may be a moot issue. Marriage and divorce are two areas in which guardians may not act on behalf of their ward. In some cases, however, a guardian *ad litem* may be appointed to protect the interests of an incompetent spouse being sued for divorce. State law and the facts of the particular situation must be carefully reviewed in each case.

Remarriage

Remarriage or cohabitation is not necessarily the goal of divorced seniors. These newly unencumbered individuals may be searching for a part-time, non–live-in companion for the rest of their lives. Freedom and independence mean more to them than having the security of marriage. Perhaps the noncommitted older person avoids remarriage because he or she recognizes the realistic potential of having to take care of a new spouse should health crises arise. Whatever the objectives of the senior divorcee, remarrying in haste out of loneliness, insecurity, fear, or financial concerns is rarely the way to proceed. Although all of those fears are understandable, rushing into another marriage is rarely the answer. This mistake will more likely be made by the spouse who did not request the divorce or is caught off guard by what occurs when there is a divorce. Adjusting to living with someone else after being married to a previous spouse for decades may require more effort than the newly remarried person anticipated. If a senior divorcee is contemplating remarriage, he or she should seek advice from an elder care attorney and/or financial advisor prior to the new marriage and perhaps again after marrying. While all families and the relationships within them are different, in an effort to minimize family conflict and maintain peace, discussing the possibility of remarriage with other family members, especially adult children and even grandchildren, is usually advisable.

Financial Ramifications

In most instances of senior divorce, each former spouse's standard of living may be altered, perhaps drastically. A poorly performing economy can reduce the standard of living even more. Some areas deserving review from a financial perspective for divorcing seniors include the following:

Distribution of Marital Property. No-fault divorce is recognized in the majority of states when both spouses agree they have irreconcilable differences resulting in the breakdown of their marriage. In these situations, the domestic relations court follow a general rule of thumb referred to as equitable distribution. In other words, the marital property is equitably, or nearly equitably, divided between the divorcing couple. The percentage of distribution often depends on the length of the marriage, age, need, and other factors. With senior divorcing spouses, it is not unusual for the wives, especially those who remained at home to raise the children and therefore bypassed outside-the-home careers, to be the less affluent of the two. It may also be likely when seniors divorce for one to pay the other "maintenance"—that is, alimony. The payment amounts can vary according to disparities in individual wealth levels and whether or not the paying spouse (usually the husband) is employed or retired when the couple divorces.

Social Security. A surviving spouse over age 60 (or totally disabled and over age 50) is entitled to Social Security benefits that are predicated on the insured worker spouse's earnings records. This is also the case for a surviving divorced spouse if the marriage lasted for 10 years or longer. If divorce is imminent and the 10-year marriage requirement is not far off, it could be financially beneficial for a "poorer" spouse to stay married until the 10-year threshold is met.

Pensions. Pensions are often a very significant, if not the largest, marital asset. If one of the spouses did not work outside of the home or did not work long enough to accumulate as much in his or her own pension plan as the other spouse, divorce will likely leave a noticeable imprint on this asset. Under the Employee Retirement Income Security Act (ERISA), when one spouse has a qualified pension, the other spouse is entitled to a share of the pension funds. Divorce severs this right unless there is an agreement or court order in the form of a *qualified domestic relations order (QDRO)*. QDRO

qualified domestic relations order (QDRO)

allows the spouse who has not participated in the pension to be named as an alternate payee for pension benefits at the time the benefits are or become payable. Sometimes divorcing parties will substitute other marital assets for rights to the other spouse's pension. It is critical that an actuary value the pension before a property compromise involving the pension is formalized. Divorced spouses must also revisit the beneficiary designated under a pension plan to determine if the designation needs to be changed. If the former spouse is still the named beneficiary after the divorce and the pension holder-employee dies, the benefits will go to the former spouse rather than the new wife or children from the first marriage. The oversight can be costly and contra to the employee's intention.

Wills and Revocable Trusts. Divorce is a life-changing family event which calls for a review of existing wills. Even though in some states divorce automatically results in the revocation or partial revocation of the couple's wills, as soon as the divorce is finalized, the former spouses should create new wills to reflect their changed circumstances.

Life Insurance. Life insurance is another component of many divorcing seniors' lives. It may be necessary to change beneficiary designations and/or policy ownership. If one spouse is dependent on maintenance payments from the ex-spouse, additional insurance on the ex-spouse's life may be advisable to provide continuing financial support when maintenance payments cease at the payor's death. If there is concern on one spouse's part that the ex-spouse-insured will later change the beneficiary designation (from the children of their marriage or the poorer spouse) or cancel the policy, a transfer of ownership or having the beneficiary designation made irrevocable may be the solution.

All of the above areas of concern and review for divorcing senior couples necessitate compliance with the requirements of state and federal law for any changes and new documentation to be effective.

PLANNING FOR INCAPACITY

In many instances, estate planners concentrating on the accumulation, conservation, and distribution aspects of a client's estate overlook discussions about incapacity planning. Estate planning for *in*capacity is just as important as estate planning with capacity. A thorough and comprehensive data collection process incorporates incapacity issues and solutions into a client's overall estate plan. Naturally, incapacity solutions will vary in accordance with the individual's wishes, needs, and asset ownership. Because state statutes often vary with respect to form, requirements, and document execution, planners, as always, need to be knowledgeable of relevant state law.

Before proceeding, the definitions of certain terms commonly used in relationship to incapacity should be addressed. "Incapacity" and "incompetency" may, in most instances, be used interchangeably. Both terms generally pertain to an individual's inability to act in a legal context. Although one's legal inability to act is construed from state statute, the state of lacking capacity is determined typically by relatives, physicians, and other mental health experts. The term "disability," on the other hand, generally pertains to daily physical impairment (for example, an inability to walk, speech difficulties, and so forth). An individual's disablement is usually determined by the individual himself or herself and/or by close family members. A person who is disabled may be completely competent to transact legal matters. Planners should also distinguish between the term "guardian" and "conservator." A guardian is responsible for the personal care matters of a ward, whereas a conservator is responsible for managing the property of a ward.

Asset Management Planning

There are four basic planning methods used for managing an incapacitated person's assets: (1) durable power of attorney, (2) revocable inter vivos (living) trust, (3) guardian of the property/conservator (the choice of title may be according to state law), and (4) special-needs trust (SNT). None of these devices is necessarily mutually exclusive. In other words, an individual may have more than one incapacity-planning techniques employed in his or her incapacity estate plan.

Durable Power of Attorney (DPOA)

Durable Power of Attorney for Property. A durable power of attorney (DPOA) is an excellent estate planning and incapacity-planning document. If the principal (person executing the instrument) wishes, the power for the attorney-in-fact (agent) may become effective upon execution. This type of durable power of attorney is often called a *non-springing durable power of attorney*. A *springing durable power of attorney*, on the other hand, is one that becomes operative only at the time of the principal's incompetency. The terms of the contingency upon which the document becomes effective must be within the terms of the instrument. The contingency typically is based on an independent determination by physicians. Documentation of capacity by independent sources at the time the power is executed is advisable because the principal must be competent at that time. The utility of durable powers of appointment have sometimes been hampered by the refusal of third parties to accept them. Recently, however, some states have enacted laws imposing monetary damages for the failure of third parties to recognize the validity of the durable power. A principal can increase the probability of acceptance by third parties

**non-springing durable
power of attorney
springing durable
power of attorney**

by periodically re-executing the DPOA. In many situations, filing the document with the relevant municipal office or official also encourages credibility.

Durable Power of Attorney for Health Care (DPOAHC). There are two primary techniques by which individuals can plan for their personal care if they become incapacitated: the durable power of attorney for health care (DPOAHC) and the living will. The DPOAHC is referred to in some states as a medical durable power of attorney or medical proxy. Regardless of an individual's other estate-planning initiatives and documents, a necessary safeguard in planning for incapacity is the execution of a DPOAHC. Such a document is extremely flexible and will take effect in any number of health care situations where the incapacitated individual may be unable to give his or her informed consent. Further, the DPOAHC will also take effect in situations other than where the individual is determined to be terminal (as with a living will). The medical contingencies addressed by the DPOAHC can be explicitly listed in the document, although it is much more common that a broad declaration of powers and discretion be given to the named attorney-in-fact to exercise his or her best judgment after evaluating the circumstances at the time. Of course, it is presumed that the document's author has orally discussed his or her medical preferences with the attorney-in-fact beforehand.

A major difference between the DPOAHC and the DPOA is that the former, by its very nature, is always "springing" in its effect, while the latter may also be "non-springing." As long as the patient is able to speak for himself or herself, the medical community will look to the patient for informed consent to any recommended medical procedure. It is only when the individual is unable to provide consent that the authority of the attorney-in-fact/surrogate will be requested, thus providing emotional comfort to individuals who are anxious about delegation of matters as important as one's own physical health.

Some form of the DPOAHC is statutorily recognized in all states. However, state law varies in terms of the protection afforded to health care providers who act on those instructions. Some states, such as California, have statutes permitting health care providers to assume that a DPOAHC is valid in the absence of knowledge to the contrary. Other state statutes are silent regarding the consequences in the event that a physician does not comply with the instructions included in the DPOAHC. In support of a physician's decision to withdraw life-support measures where there is no direction otherwise in a medical directive signed by the patient, the American Medical Association has ruled that such action is appropriate and that the physician should not incur liability. It is conceivable that such thinking may be extended to additional, less threatening procedures that are clearly in the best interest of the patient.

Finally, there is the issue of whether it is preferable to include the legal content of a living will within the DPOAHC. This is permitted in some states and provides for one less document that must be retained by the incapacitated individual. In contrast, the provisions of a DPOAHC should never be commingled with that of a traditional or financial DPOA. They involve very different situations and are drafted for different purposes. In efficient estate planning, the client typically will be offered a choice of separate DPOA and DPOAHC documents, with a charge or fee quoted for the total "package."

Revocable Living Trusts

A living or inter vivos trust also provides financial direction in case of incapacity. As with a durable power of attorney, there may be an independent trustee to provide financial and investment expertise and/or a family member or close associate as trustee. It is through the terms of the revocable living trust that the grantor spells out his or her intentions prior to being unable to do so. Another, less obvious reason for a revocable trust is that, at some point in the aging process, various endeavors that were previously simple to accomplish become increasingly difficult, burdensome, and time consuming. Wise seniors acknowledge that the aging process can take its toll on financial wisdom and management ability. A revocable living trust provides a vehicle for the consolidation of assets, decision-making, and administrative assistance. The senior grantor can be trustee or co-trustee and provide as much or as little input as desired. The property subject to the living trust has the added benefit of being nonprobate property. A revocable trust does not, however, produce any tax savings. Whether the grantor or someone else is the sole or co-trustee, the trust document should always provide for at least one successor trustee.

Seminars on revocable living trusts (living trusts) frequently market them as the ultimate solution for individuals' financial management concerns. Although living trusts are promoted mainly for the flexibility they provide and also as a probate avoidance vehicle, seminar leaders often overlook using this type of trust as an incapacity-planning tool. In other words, the written provisions contained in the trust document will prevail if the grantor becomes unable to act for himself or herself. In the ideal situation, the trust is funded shortly after its creation—that is, the grantor re-titles property in the name of the trustee of the trust. Re-titling is necessary even when the grantor is also the trustee. Sometimes a grantor does not fund immediately after execution and intends to re-title property in the trust's name at a later point in time. When a **standby trust** trust is unfunded, it is referred to as *standby trust*. Caution should be exercised, however, when a revocable living trust is intended for the grantor's incapacity. If the trust remains unfunded until the grantor is unable to act on his or her own behalf, the grantor is no longer capable of carrying out the funding process. A living trust created for incapacity protection must contain a provision concerning an independent determination (usually the agreement of two named physicians) of what the grantor wishes to constitute incompetency.

conservatorship

Having both a will and revocable trust documents helps to forestall, if not prevent, guardianship and *conservatorship* court proceedings in the event of an estate owner's disablement. The guardianship and conservatorship routes are not only time and money consumptive, but are also public in nature. A will, however, is essentially an instrument pertaining to the testator's death, whereas revocable and irrevocable trusts, durable powers of attorney, living wills, health proxies, and so forth pertain to asset and health management and incapacity.

Guardianship or Conservatorship of An Estate

Without other direction, a guardian or conservator must be appointed and continually supervised by a court following a court hearing. This procedure is somewhat streamlined when the ward's planning documents (power of attorney, will, trust) name the individual whom the ward, when competent, wishes to act as his or her agent upon incapacity. In most cases, the guardian or conservator is a member of the ward's family. While it is common for the parents of young children to have a clause in their wills nominating a guardian to act for their children in case of death, nominating a guardian in case of incapacity is often overlooked but is no less necessary than planning for parental deaths.

Special-Needs Trust (SNT)

special-needs trust (SNT)

Special-needs trusts are property management devices used to protect the assets of individuals who expect to be in a long-term disabled condition. Often the subjects of special-needs trusts are children. Ethical considerations abound in discussions of special-needs trusts because they entail arranging beneficiaries' financial interests so as to avail the beneficiaries of government assistance programs such as Medicaid, Supplemental Security Income (SSI), and so forth. In other words, an individual's private assets are put in a special-needs trust in order to keep those assets from being reached by the government for reimbursement. Insulation of the beneficiaries' assets is accomplished by having language in the document prohibiting trust principal from being used in substitution for governmental benefits. A few states view such trusts as against public policy and deny them legal recognition.

- *family SNT*—the most widely used SNT; frequently used as an estate-planning tool for incapacitated persons
- *third-party SNT*—established by nonfamily or interested parties on behalf of an incapacitated person

- *settlement SNT*—funded with personal-injury lawsuit damages received by the incapacitated individual from a court
- *pooled SNT*—funded with assets (including the disabled individual's personal assets) that are pooled with numerous other sources to increase investment results. Each state has a nonprofit organization established to achieve investment benefits.

WILLS

Practically all elder estate planners recommend having a will, even when a living trust is used as a will substitute. Wills are historically considered to be the cornerstone to all estate planning. In cases where the client has a living (inter vivos) trust, having a will in addition to the trust ensures that any property not governed by the trust will pass according to the testator's wishes through the will's residuary provisions. If a will already exists, it should be reviewed with the senior client to be certain his or her objectives have not changed and that it complies with the domiciliary state's statutory requirements. If an existing will remains appropriate but was created more than 10 years ago, many advisors suggest re-executing the will (or other document) by going through the signing, witnessing, and self-proving notarization process at the later and current date of its review. Such actions support the credibility of the document and, with wills, may bolster the terms of the will against potential contests. If the senior client is married, any of the will's marital deduction and credit equivalent bypass trust provisions need to be reviewed to make certain they conform to current estate tax law. Wills are discussed more thoroughly in *The Fundamentals of Estate Planning,* the textbook for The College's HS 330 course.

Living Will

Broadly speaking, a living will and a DPOAHC are both forms of advance medical directives. An advance medical directive is a general term that refers to written instructions about an individual's wishes concerning the continuance or discontinuance of medical care in the event that the individual can no longer speak for himself or herself. Currently, all 50 states allow some form of advance medical directive.

In a living will, a person specifies in writing his or her wishes about medical treatment in situations where they are no longer able to give informed consent. State law may define an individual's choices regarding the continuance of medical treatment (for example, the provision of life support technology); however, the key point to remember in all living will situations is that such provisions are typically only triggered where the individual has been declared to be terminally ill by two or more physicians. This is not the case with a DPOAHC, which may address a great number of additional medical situations where the individual is not terminally ill, but nevertheless is unable to make his or her wishes known through normal means of communication.

In some states (Colorado, for example), a terminally ill individual is also given a choice as to whether to prolong life with artificial nourishment, separate and apart from any life support technology decision. Furthermore, the individual may be given a second election regarding how many days, if any, to use artificial nourishment. There is no easy answer to this question, but there is a general consensus that a prolonged period of time in continuing such nourishment is both unnecessary from a medical perspective and extremely costly. Accordingly, a time period of typically no more than 7 or 10 days from beginning artificial nourishment is frequently used.

Once he or she has completed a living will, an individual should be sure to provide a copy of the document to his or her primary physician. The conclusions specified in writing in the living will should also be discussed orally with the physician. In addition, a second copy of the document should be given to the closest relative of the individual, preferably the person who is also designated the principal's attorney-in-fact in the complementary DPOAHC. In each instance, however, the original of the living will should be retained in a place of safekeeping that is easily accessible to the attorney-in-fact or other family member in the event that the document is needed. Ease of access normally does *not* mean a bank safety deposit box *unless* the designated attorney-in-fact is also a permissible signatory on the box. A planner should be sure to remind his or her clients not to make this common mistake.

Legacy or Ethical Will

Sometimes individuals or couples who have traditional wills and perhaps additional estate planning documents like trusts and powers of attorney, wish to leave something that conveys their personal values, traditions, and/or experiences to following generations. A *legacy or ethical will* may be suggested in such circumstances.

legacy or ethical will

Because the term "ethical will" may, in some respects, be misunderstood, it could be considered a misnomer. For purposes of this chapter, the phrase "legacy will" more realistically imparts the objectives of this type of communication. Instruments exemplifying legacy wills have existed in one form or another for decades. The purpose of these instruments can vary as broadly as one's imagination. Generally, the purpose of legacy wills is for the creator to share

- private knowledge
- passions
- wisdom

- stories
- spiritual feelings
- cherished memories
- mistakes
- good decision-making
- advice
- personal commitments

that gave meaning to his or her life with surviving children, grandchildren, and others. They have been drafted to embrace the creator's life lessons regarding work, marriage, and child raising. It could be said that legacy wills may be used to capture and reflect a person's inner soul for posterity.

Legacy wills are not without some criticism and are not necessarily for everyone. Primary criticisms have included claims that this type of communication may:

- formalize a heavy psychological burden on succeeding generations
- communicate and preserve judgmental attitudes
- place a layer of guilt on surviving, noncompliant family members
- restrain freedom of spirit
- restrict initiative
- attempt to "rule from the grave"

A legacy or ethical will should be kept with a testator's traditional will. Although this type of personal expression is usually written, it can be created in video form. And, as is the case with most declarations, periodic review by the creator is advisable.

GIFTING

Gift-Giving Arrangements

The most important consideration with any gifting program, or any other strategies to save estate tax for that matter, is that senior donors not be deprived of assets they might need for a continued comfortable lifestyle. For wealthy seniors gifting to children, grandchildren, and others is an easy way to reduce an estate.

Many seniors want to provide financial help to grandchildren. Higher education is a key reason why grandparents make gifts to their grandchildren, but it is not the only one. Some grandparents are concerned about the future cost of housing and would like to establish a fund for a grandchild's future home. Others are concerned about more immediate costs, such as the need for specialized or private education at the grammar or high school levels. Still others simply want to provide their grandchildren with a discretionary source of funds.

There are a variety of ways to accomplish gifting objectives. Local property and tax laws and tax rules can affect the feasibility of gift-giving plans. The following arrangements allow seniors to determine how best to structure gifts to grandchildren:

- outright gifts
- Totten trusts
- direct education gifts
- Coverdell Education Savings Accounts
- Sec. 529 qualified tuition programs
- Custodianship—Uniform Transfers (Gifts) to Minors Act (UTMA/UGMA)
- Sec. 2503 (b) trusts
- Sec. 2503 (c) trusts
- Crummey trusts
- Medicaid

Outright Gifts

Holidays and birthdays are often when small amounts of cash are transferred. Although these situations pose few problems, legal, tax, and practical considerations arise when the gifts increase in value. Legally, if the grandchild is a minor, a guardian must be appointed to manage the property depending on the amount or value of the gift. Gift taxes must be considered if the amount transferred to an individual in a year exceeds the gift tax annual exclusion amount.

Example: Marty is a 79-year-old widower who has ten children and grandchildren. In December, Marty makes an annual exclusion gift either outright or in trust with Crummey demand powers to each of his ten family members for a total of $110,000. He makes the same transfers one month later and again in the following January. Within 13 months, Marty has reduced his estate by $330,000. If Marty was married and elected gift splitting, his estate would be reduced by $660,000 without affecting his applicable credit amount.

Distributions from qualified retirement plans and IRAs may be an appropriate source of funds for making annual exclusion gifts. Although deferral of distributions for income tax purposes is commonly accepted tax practice, if senior clients enjoy a comfortable life without the qualified plan or IRA distributions, it may make sense to take current distributions, pay the income tax, and use the distributions to make annual exclusion gifts to children and grandchildren. At the current time, the highest gift and estate tax rate is higher than the highest income tax rate. By giving up deferral of income tax, the senior client has eliminated future estate tax. The difficulty of tax decision-making is further strained by rising applicable credit amounts, possible estate tax repeal, and the potential for future tax changes.

Income tax considerations, such as the kiddie tax rules for children under age 14, can also arise when larger sums are transferred. (The kiddie tax rules are discussed in *Fundamentals of Estate Planning*.) Gifting programs, however, are advisable because property transferred by outright gift is generally not part of the grandparent's estate, which reduces the overall level of estate tax payable. Note that taxes may be due if gifts exceed the lifetime gift-tax exemption amount.

Because few grandparents want youngsters or financially unsophisticated teenagers to handle large sums of money, grandparents often use one or more of the following arrangements for gifting to grandchildren.

Totten Trusts

A Totten trust is basically a bank account into which someone, such as the grandparent, deposits money for the benefit of a minor grandchild; the depositor names himself or herself as trustee. The grandparent retains control over the money in the account while alive. The property automatically passes to the grandchild at the grandparent's death free of probate costs.

Transfers to Totten trusts are not considered taxable gifts as the transfer is not a completed gift because the grandparent retains control. Interest earned on the account is taxed to the grandparent. The assets of the account are included in the grandparent's estate for estate tax purposes.

Direct Education Gifts

One way to make a gift of tuition without paying gift taxes is to take advantage of special qualified transfer provisions in the Internal Revenue Code.

A qualified transfer includes any amount paid to an educational organization as tuition on behalf of an individual. Qualified transfers are not considered gifts for gift tax purposes and also avoid income and estate tax complications. The tuition payments are not treated as income to the grandchild. And, because the money is immediately spent on higher education, there is nothing left to include in an estate that can trigger taxation.

Coverdell Education Savings Accounts

Education IRAs, later renamed *Coverdell Education Savings Accounts (CESAs)*, became available in tax year 1998. A CESA is a trust or custodial account set up specifically for the purpose of paying the qualified education expenses of the designated child beneficiary of the account.

Nondeductible contributions per child under the age of 18 are limited in amount. Earnings and growth are not taxed, and withdrawals used for qualified education expenses are excluded from income. However, if funds in the CESA are not used for educational purposes and/or if the balance of the account is not distributed before the child reaches age 30, the entire amount becomes fully taxable, plus a 10 percent penalty applies.

CESAs represent a limited opportunity for gift giving by grandparents to grandchildren solely to assist with their educational expenses. There are broader gift-giving possibilities with more far-reaching estate tax consequences available in Sec. 529 qualified tuition programs.

Sec. 529 Qualified Tuition Programs

Every state jurisdiction sponsors some type of prepaid, tax-favored savings plan designed to help parents pay for future college expenses.

Under EGTRRA 2001, the funds accumulated in a qualified tuition program grow tax deferred. Also, distributions are tax free as long as the proceeds are used for "qualified" higher education expenses, such as room, board, tuition, books, and supplies. EGTRRA allows accumulated funds to be used at any accredited institution of higher learning in the United States, as well as at many foreign institutions. If funds in the account are not used for higher education, they are subject to income tax and a 10 percent penalty upon distribution.

Some additional tax advantages exist for the donors (parents and grandparents) to the account. For example, the donor maintains full control of the funds in the account even after the child reaches age 18. (Conversely, in an UGMA account—defined below—an "adult" child takes over control at majority age.) Furthermore, donors can contribute up to 5 years' annual gift tax exclusion amounts to a child's account in one single year. This means that currently a grandparent can put as much as $55,000 into a child's Sec. 529 plan in a year without incurring gift tax (married parents and/or grandparents can contribute $110,000 gift tax free), as long as the donor does not make any additional gifts to that beneficiary over that 5-year period. Moreover, the total amount of deposits enjoys tax-free growth in most plans. Furthermore, tax-free withdrawals for qualified expenses can be made from Sec. 529 plans in the same year as withdrawals from CESAs, provided these funds are used for different expenses.

The funding vehicles for these tax-advantaged accounts include mutual funds, which allow for professional management, portfolio diversification, and high return potential over the accumulation period prior to a child's college years. At the present time, Sec. 529 plan holders can change investment options within plans once a year, giving parents even greater flexibility and control over these funds.

Custodianship—Uniform Transfers (Gifts) to Minors Act (UTMA/ UGMA)

These Uniform Acts are frequently utilized for smaller gifts because of their simplicity and because they offer the benefits of management, income and estate tax shifting, and the investment characteristics of a trust with little or none of the document-drafting costs.

Transfers of $11,000 or less to custodial accounts qualify for the annual gift tax exclusion. Income earned on these accounts is subject to the kiddie tax rules.

Custodial accounts do have practical disadvantages when it comes to money management. Beneficiaries are generally entitled to have access to account property once they reach majority, which in most states is age 18.

Sec. 2503(b) and 2503(c) Trusts

To minimize the practical drawbacks involved with most large gifts to minors, such transfers are generally made in trust. There are two basic means to qualify cared-for gifts to minors: Sec. 2503(b) trusts and Sec. 2503(c) trusts. These trusts stipulate how income from them is to be used and gives the trustee no discretion as to its use. The minor receives possession of the trust principal whenever the trust agreement specifies. The 2503(b) trust does not require distribution of principal when the minor reaches age 21, but does require a current (annual) distribution of income. The 2503(c) trust requires distribution of income and principal when the minor reaches age 21.

Crummey Trusts

The final planning arrangement discussed in this section is the Crummey life insurance trust that insures the donor/grantor of the trust (such as a grandparent). It is an irrevocable trust funded with life insurance. Crummey trusts incorporate substantial planning flexibility, including the ability to

- utilize the annual gift tax exclusion
- utilize assets for specific purposes
- manage trust assets beyond the age of majority
- utilize individual tax rates that often prove more favorable to the family unit
- remove assets from a grandparent's estate

Medicaid

Medicaid is a program established for the indigent. It is shared jointly by federal and state governments.

To become eligible for Medicaid, an individual is restricted to retaining assets of low value and minimal income. Therefore, to qualify for Medicaid, each applicant must pass an "asset test" and an "income test." The states determine the threshold amounts of these tests. An applicant's home is exempt from being considered under the asset test if the applicant intends to return at some point in time to the home, even if this is unlikely. Some non-indigent individuals will, with the advice of planners, "spend down" their assets to become Medicaid eligible. If an applicant has made a gift within 36 months (or within 60 months when the gift was made to certain trusts) before seeking Medicaid eligibility, the applicant will be ineligible to receive benefits for a mathematically determined period. The 36- and 60-month periods are referred to as "look-back" periods. The formula used for this calculation divides the value of the gifts during the appropriate "look-back" period by the cost of the average private pay nursing home in the applicant's state of residence.

Example: Ten months before entering a state nursing home facility, Ralph gave his daughter, Kim, a gift of $80,000. At the time Ralph moved into the nursing home, the monthly cost of private pay nursing home care was $5,000. Consequently, Ralph will not be able to avail himself of Medicaid benefits for 16 months. For those 16 months, he must use his own funds to cover his nursing home expenses.

Clearly the concept of spending down one's assets to purposefully take advantage of governmentally provided benefits supported by taxpayers is fraught with ethical issues. Since August 1997, there is a law making it a crime for professional advisors, such as attorneys, financial planners, or accountants, to advise an individual in the intentional transfer of property for the purpose of Medicaid eligibility. This law is somewhat comically referred to as the "Granny's Lawyer Goes to Jail" law. However, Attorney General Janet Reno stated in 1998 that the government has no intention of enforcing the law. This is the status of the law and The Justice Department's position as it stands at the present time.

CONSIDERATIONS FOR LESS AFFLUENT SENIOR CLIENTS

Reverse Mortgages

reverse mortgage

Reverse mortgages are another estate planning option for less wealthy seniors who have a strong desire to remain in the home, are cash strapped, or desire additional money for retirement, gifting, or long-term care. A reverse mortgage is a loan that allows aged 62 or older homeowners to take some or all of their home equity out in cash. The homeowner does not have to pay anything back to the bank until he or she moves out of the home or dies. At that triggering event, whatever amount has been paid out plus interest and any fees for financing the loan must be paid back. Money (the loan amount) received from a reverse mortgage is tax free. There are basically three types of reverse mortgage payments: a lump-sum payment, a line of credit, or an annuity which is a monthly payment for the senior's and/or spouse's life. The amount received is dependent upon the individual's age, prevailing interest rates, and, of course, the appraisal value of the home.

Example:	Rob and Rita, both 75 years old, own a home worth $300,000. Based on their life expectancies, they could perhaps qualify for a lump sum or line of credit of $220,000. If they chose the annuity option based on their life expectancies, their monthly payments would total that amount.

As with regular mortgages, costs are involved, some of which are not readily evident because they are taken from the amount the senior ends up receiving. For instance, in the typical case there is mortgage insurance (it depends on the reverse mortgage arrangement whether or not it is federally insured), closing costs, servicing fees, origination fees, and other potential finance expenses. Interest rates vary. An overly aggressive lender might neglect to spell out these fees in advance in an effort to "seal the deal." At first blush, the reverse mortgage may appear (and may actually be) an appropriate arrangement. However, over the short term financial advantages may be consumed by the costs involved. Seniors or their advisors should do the homework before entering into a reverse mortgage to determine if it is suitable for those circumstances. To estimate potential costs, there is a reverse-mortgage calculator at www.reversemortgage.org, the Web site of the National Reverse Mortgage Lenders Association. It is usually a good idea to discuss this possibility with adult children because their parent(s) may be harboring a false notion that "one of the kids" would like the family home someday. Although reverse mortgages are likely to become less costly with increased popularity in the future, it is doubtful they will ever approximate the lesser costs associated with conventional mortgages.

When contemplating a reverse mortgage, the senior homeowner should understand that for Medicaid eligibility purposes, the home is not a countable asset. When the value of the home is turned into cash, however, the home is transformed into a Medicaid countable asset.

Life Settlements

life settlement

Life settlements are a comparatively recent estate-planning device gaining popularity with less wealthy seniors. Today a senior insured may be able to sell an existing (and often unwanted) life insurance policy to a third-party company engaged in the business of buying policies. The seller then receives an immediate payment representing a portion of the policy's net death benefit. Many types of insurance policies qualify for consideration for a life settlement transaction, including group, universal, variable life, survivorship, and even term. The seller may be a person, a corporation, or a trust. The mechanics of the arrangement are simple. The potential purchasing company gathers the relevant information from the policyowner, determines the policy value for a life settlement, and then makes an offer to the policyowner.

Generally speaking, the life settlement payments representing basis are income tax free, payment amounts over basis and up to cash surrender value are taxed as ordinary income, and amounts in excess of cash surrender value are treated as long-term capital gain. Settlement proceeds may avoid taxation completely if the policyowner is terminally ill. Life settlement agreements are an expansion of viatical settlement agreements that have been previously available. They are an expansion of viatical settlements because a life settlement is possible for a senior citizen, age 70 or more, who is in good

viatical settlement

health, whereas *viatical settlements* are an acceleration of death benefits limited to policyholders who are terminally ill. If a senior is not in good health but is also not terminally ill, a life settlement agreement may be available to someone as early as age 65. The life settlement market has grown from $200 million in 1998 to what is estimated to be a $10 to $15 billion market in 2005.[1]

The sale of a life insurance policy by the policyowner can provide some obvious financial and estate planning benefits and flexibility. Funds that otherwise would not be obtainable by the policyholder during life become available and can be used for a multitude of purposes, such as long-term care, retirement assets, lifetime gifting, charitable contributions, long-term health care insurance, and so forth. Again, remember that any Medicaid eligibility considerations need to be weighed. Once the policy is sold, its value is removed from the owner's gross estate except for what the recipient does not consume. Even if the life settlement amount is not consumed and is therefore included in a decedent's gross estate, the inclusion amount will be less than the full amount of the life insurance proceeds had the settlement never happened. Because the transaction with the funding company is a sale for value, rather than a gratuitous transfer, the 3-year rule of Code Sec. 2035 does not apply.

Pre-need Funeral and Cemetery Trusts

funeral trust

Today funeral and death care is a greater than $20 billion lucrative industry. Funerals, as a business, essentially started in the late 19th century when undertakers were typically carpenters who made coffins on the side of their regular carpentry work. Pre-need *funeral trusts* (also referred to as pre-burial or pre-funeral trusts) are becoming increasingly popular both in the United States and abroad. People, usually seniors, establish funeral trusts so that their funeral service and cemetery plots are paid for without burdening surviving family members.

cemetery trust

endowment care cemetery trust

Funeral trusts are arrangements made with funeral directors and banks by clients who set aside funds to prepay their funerals. Pre-need funeral trust contributions and earnings on investments in a pre-need funeral trust are required to be used to pay the grantor's funeral expenses. *Cemetery trusts*, as the term implies, pertains to pre-needed cemetery arrangements. One type of cemetery trust is an *endowment care cemetery trust*. An endowment care cemetery trust pools individual grantors' contributions to provide for ongoing maintenance of cemetery and gravesite grounds. Usually the cemetery business holds the trust in its own name and is allowed to withdraw earnings from the trust on a regular basis. The principal remains intact. Another type

service and merchandise cemetery trust

of cemetery trust is referred to as a *service and merchandise cemetery trust*. A service and merchandise cemetery trust is similar to a funeral trust in that grantors are able to select and pre-fund items such as burial vaults, gravesite stones, or markers, as well as the funeral service itself. Often these arrangements involve relatively small amounts of money and grantors and/or family members may hold this type of cemetery trust in their own name(s). State law regulates various aspects of the trust, including limitations on amounts placed in the trust.

Some pre-need funeral trusts are revocable and are therefore treated as grantor trusts for tax purposes. Income earned from trust assets is taxable to the owner-purchaser of the arrangement. Income attributed to the grantor from the trust may not result in tax liability because the grantor is below taxable thresholds. If the trust is irrevocable, it still may be treated as a grantor trust because, due to the fact that the funds are set aside to defray a future obligation of the grantor, the funds are treated as a reversionary interest under Sec. 673 of the grantor trust rules. Many pre-funeral trusts are executed for Medicaid purposes. Trust funds are not considered an asset under Medicaid asset test rules.

Under the Taxpayer Relief Act of 1997, Internal Revenue Code Sec. 685 was created to address pre-need funeral trust issues and reporting matters. At this time, the government drafted Form 1041—Qualified Funeral Trust (QFT) to be used when making qualified funeral trust elections. Consequently, the trustee of a pre-need funeral trust may elect to establish a qualified pre-need trust, which is treated as a nongrantor trust for tax purposes. The trustee is responsible for making the election for Sec. 685 treatment. The election is made by filing Form 1041—QFT. State filings are also necessary. The trustee is also responsible for income tax liability on trust earnings. A qualified funeral trust involves a contract that can only be established with someone engaged in the business of providing funeral and burial arrangements. The trust can have no beneficiaries other than the persons for whom the property or services are to be provided at death. Estate planners need to be aware that federal and state tax laws govern the income taxation of funeral and cemetery trusts when trusts are paid out. In addition, many states have changed pre-need trust requirements over the years. With respect to funeral and cemetery trust compliance, it is crucial to meet the requirements in four areas: federal tax law, state tax law, state trust law, and pre-need law. It is the pre-need laws that change the most often and differ from state to state.

senior's sale-leaseback of home with adult child

Senior's Sale-Leaseback of Home with Adult Child

Another potential option for a financially strapped senior is to sell the family home to a child, perhaps as a second home, and then rent it back. A sale to children is much better received conceptually by senior parents than accepting straight out financial assistance from children. The parent is able to remain in the home while continuing to feel that he or she is self supporting and not dependent on an adult child. If the purchasing child pays for the home in installments, the parent has the additional income stream with which to make rental payments. At the time of the sale, the value of the asset is frozen. Any post-sale increase in the value of the home (or any asset sold) belongs to the purchaser and is excluded from the seller's estate. The appreciation avoids gift, estate, and generation-skipping transfer taxes. The parent is also relieved of home ownership responsibilities that often become more onerous with age. If the parent has more than one child, getting an appraisal may be advisable.

From a tax viewpoint, only the unconsumed and present value of remaining installment payment amounts are included in the parent's gross estate at the parent's death. Under the Sec. 121 exclusion of gain from the sale of a principal residence, the parent has gain on only the home's value that is in excess of a $250,000 gain ($500,000 for joint filers). If the arrangement is structured as an arm's length transaction, there are no gift tax ramifications. For the adult child purchaser, on the other hand, the purchase price is the purchaser's basis in the home. Sales within the family result in a higher basis for the younger family member with no corresponding income tax cost to the senior family member. A sale-leaseback may make it possible for children to purchase a home (or other items) they always wanted and hoped to inherit someday. By using a sale-leaseback, the parent has extra cash and the child now has the residence.

Long-Term Health Care Insurance

Long-term health care insurance is a relatively modern addition to the insurance grocery cart of products. Because it is a somewhat new type of insurance, different types of coverage and products are rapidly emerging to fit clients' needs. The role long-term health care insurance plays in estate planning is clear. Having insurance contributions go toward care preserves other estate assets that would otherwise be applied to providing care. Although more than a cursory glance at long-term care insurance is beyond the scope of this chapter, it is definitely an estate planning subject worthy of mention.

Long-term health care insurance is probably not for those having modest assets and incomes because it is comparatively expensive. Of course, the earlier an insured purchases the policy, the lower the premiums, assuming the insured is healthy at the time of application. It should be considered, however, that decreased premiums resulting from an insured's purchase at an early age will be paid over a longer time period. Usually policies are available to persons as young as age 40 and as old as about age 80. Presently, there are policies that cover many levels of care including nursing homes, skilled home care in the senior's place of residence, assisted living institutions, and even for centers providing senior day care. It is possible for long-term care insurance premiums to be income tax deductible if the taxpayer meets certain income tax filing requirements. Without doubt, a purchase of long-term health insurance should only be made after some comparative research.

TRUSTS USEFUL IN SENIOR ESTATE PLANNING

Defective Trusts

intentionally defective trust

Revocable living trusts were mentioned previously in this chapter and also in *Fundamentals of Estate Planning*. An *intentionally defective trust*, on the other hand, is an irrevocable arrangement. A defective trust is drafted so that the grantor or an independent trustee retains certain powers over the trust that cause trust income to be taxable to the grantor. Often this tax result is purposeful but sometimes it is inadvertent, perhaps due to faulty draftsmanship. When a grantor is responsible for the trust's income tax liability, the taxation is called *grantor trust taxation*. The *grantor trust rules* are found in Secs. 671 through 678 of the Internal Revenue Code. Some powers resulting from a grantor trust are: the power to have trust income or principal distributions for the benefit of the grantor or grantor's spouse, the power to reacquire or sell trust property without adequate consideration, the power to borrow against trust property without adequate interest or security, the retention of a reversionary interest greater than 5 percent of the trust's value, the power to use trust funds to purchase life insurance on the life of the grantor or the grantor's spouse, and the power to control beneficial enjoyment of trust income or principal (although an independent trustee having this power will not cause a trust to be defective for income tax purposes).

By creating a defective trust, the senior grantor is able to enhance the benefits of lifetime gifting. Not only is he or she able to remove property from the estate by gifting, but, by also having responsibility to pay income tax on the income generated by the trust due to the defective power, the value of the estate is reduced. The trust beneficiaries receive more and the grantor retains less of the estate. To ensure that the grantor will bear the income tax burden, the trust should not be drafted with Crummey demand powers as these may cancel the benefit of the defective power and result in income taxation to the donees.

Grantor Trust Powers

- Trust income/principal distributions for grantor/spouse
- Reacquire/sell trust property without adequate consideration
- Borrow trust property without adequate interest/security
- Retain reversionary interest greater than 5 percent
- Use trust funds for life insurance on grantor/spouse's life
- Control beneficial enjoyment of income/principal

If any of the above powers require the consent of an adverse party or a party having an adverse interest (someone who has a substantial beneficial—that is, financial—interest in the trust and whose interest will be diminished by consenting to the grantor's exercise of the power), the grantor trust rules do not apply. In other words, the grantor will not have income tax responsibility for the trust income if his or her powers are dependent on the consent of an adverse party. An independent trustee, however, does not constitute an adverse party because an independent trustee does not typically have a beneficial interest in the trust other than routine administrative fees.

Example: Gary Grantor creates an irrevocable trust and expressly provides that under no circumstances is the trust property ever to return to him. The trust provisions direct that the trustee is to distribute income equally to his three sons, but that the grantor, in his sole judgment and without the consent of an adverse party, has the power to vary the percentage interest of any son at any time or wholly exclude any son from sharing in the trust income or principal. This retention of powers by the grantor causes the income to be taxable to Gary under Sec. 674, even though the income is irrevocably payable to others. In addition, the same power causes the corpus to be includible in Gary's estate because of Gary's power to "alter, amend, revoke or terminate" trust property (Code Sec. 2038).

Example: Geraldine Grantor creates an irrevocable trust and funds the trust with securities. The document expressly provides that under no circumstances is the trust property ever to return to her. The trust provisions direct that the trustee is to distribute income equally to her two daughters, but that Geraldine, without the consent of an adverse party, retains the power to reacquire some or all of the securities. If there is no additional trust provision requiring Geraldine to substitute other property or consideration of equal value to the value of the reacquired securities, the income on the trust property will be taxable to Geraldine under Sec. 675 and the value of the trust will be includible in her estate under Sec. 2036 and/or Sec. 2038.

There are a number of ways for a senior client to remove life insurance from his or her estate. If an estate owner/insured has incidents of ownership in significant life insurance, the value of the death benefits will be included and taxed in the insured's estate. If the policy(ies) is gratuitously transferred during lifetime and the transferor dies within 3 years of the transfer, no estate tax savings will result because of Sec. 2035's 3-year rule. The decedent's gross estate will include the policy's face value. The 3-year rule does not apply to sales of life insurance for full consideration, (that is, the policy's interpolated terminal reserve). A problem with sales of life insurance concerns the transfer-for-value rule under Sec. 101. This section requires the purchaser of the life insurance proceeds to pay income tax on the proceeds— not a desirable result. There are some exceptions to the transfer-for-value rule that can lead to a better tax result. The exceptions are transfers of life insurance to a partner of the insured, a partnership in which the insured is a partner, or to a corporation in which the insured is a shareholder or officer. Note, though, that with these types of transfers, the senior seller may have to recognize gain if the policy(ies) had any inherent gain. A sale of the life insurance to a defective (grantor) trust would solve the recognition of gain problem since the trust's income tax liability flows through to the grantor. Therefore, with careful planning and drafting, the insurance policies could be sold to a family limited partnership (FLP), family limited liability company (FLLC), or defective trust to avoid application of the 3-year and transfer-for-value rules and remove the death proceeds from the senior's estate.

irrevocable
grandparent-
grandchild
insurance trust

Irrevocable Grandparent-Grandchild Insurance Trusts

This trust technique is used to reduce a well-off senior's estate. Essentially, the grandparent funds a trust that allows, but does not direct, the trustee to purchase life insurance on the adult child's life. The beneficiary of the trust is one or more grandchildren. When the grandparent's son or daughter dies, the grandchild(ren) receives the death benefits under the policy.

Example: Pop Pop has an estate of $1.5 million and adequate annual income. He transfers $200,000 or assets valued at $200,000 to an irrevocable trust. The trust terms authorize, but do not direct, the trustee to purchase life insurance on the life of his daughter, Dora. The beneficiaries of the trust are Dora's children, Jimmy and Jenny. Assuming Pop Pop has not made prior gifts in excess of his applicable credit amount for federal gift tax ($1 million), Pop Pop does not have any gift tax liability for the transfer to the trust.

Over time, any appreciation generated by the transferred asset escapes estate taxation in Pop Pop's estate. Because Dora has no incidents of ownership in the life insurance policy, the death proceeds are not included in her estate. Additionally, Dora is spared the expense of paying life insurance premiums during her life and has the assurance that Jimmy and Jenny will be well provided for upon her death. Even better, the trust provisions could permit the life insurance proceeds to be available to Dora's estate for liquidity purposes by allowing (but not requiring) the trustee to purchase estate assets or to make loans to the estate. Furthermore, the trust terms could permit, in the independent trustee's sole discretion, to transfer the trust corpus to Dora under as an ascertainable standard without any tax consequences to Dora.

Qualified Terminable Interest Property Trusts (QTIPs)

QTIP trusts are a popular and frequently recommended marital deduction device. With a QTIP, the grantor is able to provide for the surviving spouse for his or her lifetime and make certain the trust principal is transferred to the grantor's children at the surviving spouse's death. This transfer tax savings technique removes concern on the grantor's part that a third party could have access to the trust assets should the surviving spouse remarry. When QTIPs are created for seniors about to embark on another marriage, there are disadvantages that can be somewhat subtle. Since the remaindermen children do not receive the trust corpus until the death of the second (or more) spouse, if the senior groom or bride takes a younger spouse, the children have even longer to wait for their inheritances. The decedent's children may be literally waiting for the stepparent to die, monitoring and resenting his or her every her every expenditure until then. QTIPs involving seniors have the potential to wreak havoc with family harmony. Creating an irrevocable life insurance trust benefiting the children may be the solution. The parent contributes the premium payments to the trust for the trust to purchase life insurance on the parent's life. The face value of the policies are equal to the children's inheritances. The children receive their inheritances at the parent's death and are content knowing that what passes to the stepparent belongs solely to him or her.

Incentive Trusts

More than a few wealthy seniors have concerns that their self-earned wealth will be the ruination of their children and grandchildren's characters.

They are worried that their descendants will suffer from what is humorously referred to as affluenza. The solution to these concerns for some seniors is *incentive trust*—a trust designed to establish and further long-lasting family objectives. Advisors refer to this type of trust by many terms: *legacy trusts, family goals trusts, character trusts,* and *incentive* or *financial incentive trusts.* For the purposes of this chapter, the term "incentive trust" will be used.

Creative estate planning provide incentives for lineal descendants through the use of carefully drafted trusts that are centered on the grantor's values. Such provisions are appropriate for irrevocable life insurance trusts as well as many other estate planning vehicles.

Common Scenario. You are "well off" financially, perhaps downright wealthy, and are respected within your community. Perpetuation of certain personal qualities through generations to follow would be the greatest gift and finest legacy you could leave. Yet you recognize that respect has to be earned—it can't be gifted and it can't be bought. From your perspective, your efforts made you appreciate what you have and what you have achieved. You believe that taking the rough road made you learn to manage life and money. It gave you confidence, values, standards, and self-esteem. You love your children and grandchildren and can afford to lavish them with all sorts of money and privileges that were unavailable to you at their ages.

However, you have noticed signs that the kids take the good life for granted. Your concerns: Will they squander the wealth? Will they "waste" their lives and live off their inheritances? Will your money undermine their personal growth and chances for success? Your wish is that they live up to their individual potentials. You don't want your achievements to be a cause of their inability to lead constructive, respected lives in their own right. The quandary is how to instill a work ethic, promote self-reliance, develop a sense of responsibility, reinforce love, and continue to provide assistance to your lineal descendants. The answer may be found in a type of "character-building" or "personal philosophies" incentive type of trust.

What Should Be Done? A carefully and creatively drafted trust can help develop the grantor's most treasured personal characteristics and family values in his or her lineal descendants. The underpinnings of incentive trusts are quite different from the typical garden-variety trust that is premised on the avoidance of gift and estate taxes and that mandates distributions of income and corpus at predetermined beneficiary ages. The incentive trust will not necessarily pay out income at certain specified intervals, nor will it dole out corpus to lineal descendant beneficiaries upon the attainment of chronological ages. Rather, this trust will make distributions of income and corpus when the beneficiaries have "earned" them in accordance with the personal philosophies of the grantor.

Example: Suppose Greta Grantor considers education to be a primary source for gainful employment and self-worth. Distributions could be related to academic achievements—a college degree, a graduate degree, and so forth. Of course, if the prerequisites for distribution are too narrow—that is, the college degrees must be from certain educational institutions or within certain fields of study—the limitations could discourage the intended beneficiaries from trying to meet the goals Greta would like them to achieve. Therefore, the trust terms should provide latitude. If a beneficiary is not academically inclined, the trust could provide for distributions for the completion of a vocational or trade-oriented program. Perhaps the beneficiary is not a good academic student but is artistically or musically accomplished. In that case, satisfactory progression or completion of art or music school could meet the desired incentives expectation.

Perhaps, on the other hand, Greta Grantor has determined that employment or some form of money-earning endeavor is the foundation for success. After all, she had to work hard to attain success and therefore so should her children. In this case, the trust might provide that every dollar earned in a year is matched with trust money. Limitations could be placed in the trust instructions. For example, earned dollars aren't matched by trust dollars until the beneficiary has earned a certain level of income. Conversely, there could be a limit on the amount of matching to discourage greed. Flexibility can be incorporated into the trust terms by considering inflation and the possible changes in the economy and personal lives.

Trust directions can also anticipate beneficiaries who aspire to government careers or to lives of public service as well as those who wish to give time and effort to philanthropic causes. The possibilities are endless and thought provoking. Clearly the creation of a values-oriented trust can be time consuming and may require a fair amount of ingenuity—guidance of and caring for others usually does.

The incentive trust does not have to (and probably would not be intended to) preclude beneficiaries from receiving any trust benefits unless they have jumped through precise hoops. The trust terms can make provisions for emergency situations, hardships, and extraordinary or changing circumstances. The trust (and the grantor) is likely to be viewed in a positive light when it allows for some flexibility and discretion. Since the wealthy senior probably stumbled several times on the road to success and fortune, the trust terms can provide that beneficiaries will not be denied distributions entirely because of a mistake or two. After all, grantors of incentive trusts wish to instill values such as kindness, understanding, and forgiveness in beneficiaries.

The aim of a personal goals' trust is to encourage beneficiaries to develop qualities and values that will serve them well throughout their lives, years after the grantor is available to provide guidance. However, if a trust that strives for the development of values is too rigid, it may thwart the very purpose for which it was originally created. To avoid the appearance of being too much like a carrot on the end of a stick, the trust directions could grant distributions at specified age intervals when desired accomplishments (for example, a college degree, or full-time employment) have been achieved. Should trust conditions and desired qualities in the beneficiaries not be met, the trust instructions could call for the corpus to pass to charity or to the next generation. Understanding the grantor's intentions, concepts, and reasoning may be enhanced by a family gathering to discuss the trust's directions and provisions.

The selection of a financial advisor and attorney must be done with care because a legacy-style trust may be a more customized document than a conventional trust. Computer software does not contain provisions for this kind of finely tailored instrument. A good balance may be achieved if there is an independent, institutional trustee and also a family or close family friend co-trustee. The corporate trustee has the tax and investment expertise, while the individual trustee provides the personal family insights. A trust that encourages children and grandchildren to reach their potentials and establish sound values is an excellent way of being remembered and way of perpetuating family traditions.

Criticisms. So-called legacy and incentive trusts are not without critics. Some practitioners and psychologists have justifiably noted that accomplishments based on an external motivation are merely a system of rewards and punishments based on money. Claims are made that such trusts are a form of behavior control that, in effect, hinders more than encourages personal achievement.

Estate and Gift Tax Implications. The incentive trust will have some estate and/or gift tax implications because it involves a transfer of property. However, the estate and/or gift tax implications cannot be discussed without addressing the specific circumstances of the transfer or terms of the trust. For example, an inter vivos trust may or may not be a completed gift when it is created, depending on the types of powers retained by the grantor. A completed gift to an inter vivos trust may be included back in the grantor's estate at the time of his or her death under Code Secs. 2036 or 2038 if the grantor, for instance, retains the right to sprinkle benefits or change beneficiaries. A testamentary trust will invariably invoke estate taxation. Due to complexities, a legacy trust should not be created without appropriate legal and tax advice.

MISCELLANEOUS ESTATE PLANNING DEVICES

Most estate-planning techniques pertain to all categories and types of individuals creating estate plans. The following planning methods have been singled out as examples of devices that may be appropriate for senior estate owners. In addition, the estate-planning techniques discussed below are ones that are likely to be implemented by seniors for whom Medicaid considerations are irrelevant.

family limited partnership (FLP)
family limited liability company (FLLC)

Adding to the estate reduction benefits of gifting is the possibility of leveraging the gifts. *Family limited partnershps (FLPs)* and *family limited liability companies (FLLCs)* allow individuals to retain control. Leveraging is achieved by transferring gifts that can be discounted upon transfer. Generally, any property that can be valued may be transferred to these entities created by an estate owner. In return for the contributed property, the FLP or FLLC provides limited partnership or limited liability company interests or "units." The senior client then transfers the units to an irrevocable trust for the benefit of his or her heirs according to the terms of the trust. The limited entity interests have no legal clout, no marketability, and no voting rights. Because the units have restrictions, their value is less than the value of the underlying property the interests represent. This allows the transferor to transfer property (the interests) having a value in excess of its valuation for tax purposes. Depending on the restrictions accompanying the units, typical conservative discounts are in the 15 to 40 percent range. Qualifying the family limited partnership and limited liability company units as present interest gifts for the annual exclusion allows an additional tax bonus for the client.

Example: With a 40 percent discount applied to the FLP or FLLC units transferred to the trust, Marty can make gifts of $550,000 during the same 13-month time period. Caution must be used, however, when using the annual exclusion for gifts of FLPs and FLLCs because the Internal Revenue Service has in the recent past decided to litigate gift tax issues with respect to these transfers. The IRS's approach is that these transfers represent a future interest and therefore the annual gift tax exclusion does not apply. (See PLR 9751002 and *Christine M. Hackl v. Commissioner*, cited 2003-2, USTC.) As with any document, careful drafting by an elder law attorney with expertise in this specialized area is paramount.

Private Annuities

As discussed in *Fundamentals of Estate Planning,* similar to an installment sale, a *private annuity* allows gain to be reported over a period of years. It permits an estate owner to remove property, often low basis property, from his or her estate. The younger family member/buyer receives a basis in the property equal to the value annuity payments the buyer has agreed to make for the rest of the senior family member/seller's life in exchange for the property. The buyer's payments must be unsecured by any collateral other than the transferred property. The payment amounts are determined in accordance with the actuarial factors under Sec. 7520, based on the seller's life expectancy at the time of the transaction. For the private annuity to work according to plan, the value of the life annuity obligation must be the fair market value of the property transferred. The property must be valued carefully, otherwise a taxable gift results—the gift element being the excess of the transferred property's fair market value over the annuity's value.

Unlike a regular installment sale, where the remaining payments are included in the seller's estate if the seller fails to survive the term, with a private annuity, no further payments are due when the seller dies. There is nothing to include in the estate of a seller who dies holding a private annuity agreement. Any annuity payments the seller received and didn't consume before death will be included in the seller's estate.

The estate reduction value of the private annuity is greater if the senior-generation seller dies soon or at least prior to life expectancy after the sale. Clearly, a sizable property interest is transferred at a substantial discount if the seller dies prematurely after receiving only a few payments. As long as the annuity was valued appropriately, the seller's premature death does not result in any additional estate or gift taxes. If, however, at the time of the private annuity the senior seller is not expected to survive for a year, normal valuation rules (that is, the Sec. 7520 actuarial tables) cannot be used.

Aside from transfer tax considerations, the income tax aspects of private annuities must be taken into account. Income taxation for the senior seller has three components (like the installment sale): a return of the seller's basis, tax-free gain (if the transferred property was a capital asset), and ordinary income. The amount of each payment that is excludible from income is the seller's basis divided by the amount of annual annuity payments multiplied by the seller's life expectancy. Capital gain is determined by the excess of the present value of the payment received over adjusted basis divided by the seller's life expectancy. Remaining annuity amounts are ordinary income.

Qualified Personal Residence Trusts

A *qualified personal residence trust (QPRT)* is an alternative estate-planning device involving a residence that is appropriate for some senior clients.

With a QPRT, a gift is made of one or two residences. The residence is transferred to an irrevocable trust placed in trust for the future benefit of the trust beneficiaries, often the transferor's child. The transferor retains the right to live in the home without paying any rent for a stated number of years. The value of the senior transferor's retained interest may be subtracted from the fair market value of the home. The trust beneficiary-remainderman acquires the residence at the end of the term. Because the transferor's interest is subtracted from the value of the residence, he or she only has gift tax on the value of the discounted remainder interest. Frequently the senior's applicable credit/exclusion amount applies and there is no actual gift tax to pay. The retained interest term must be carefully determined because, for the arrangement to be successful, the grantor must survive the term. With QPRTs, tax benefits can be achieved even when the transferor is of advanced age and a relatively short term is used.

Example:	If Harriet is 89 years old, even a 3-year term can produce a satisfactory discount. If the current interest rate under Sec. 7520 was, for instance, 6.5 percent, a QPRT with a 3-year term results in a slightly greater than 50 percent discount. If Harriet outlives the 3-year term and still wants to live in the home, she could pay fair market value rent to the trust. The rent payments allow Harriet to reduce her estate further and do not compromise other annual exclusion gifts to the trust beneficiaries or affect her applicable credit/ exclusion amount. By making the QPRT or successor trust owning the home a grantor trust, there are no income tax consequences resulting from the rent payments.

As long as the QPRT or a successor grantor trust owns the residence, the senior transferor is deemed by IRS standards to be the home owner for income tax purposes. Therefore, real estate taxes, expenses, and so forth are deductions the transferor can take. Because the senior transferor is viewed as the income tax owner, if he or she sells the home to the trust beneficiaries, the seller's IRC Sec. 121 exclusion of gain can be used to shelter $250,000 of gain. The trust beneficiary buyer(s) now owns the home with its full basis step up. When the senior seller later dies or when the trust terminates by its terms, the amount the purchaser(s) paid to the trust to buy the home is recovered by him or her.

CONCLUSION

A common misconception is that estate planning primarily concerns death and estate tax planning. The emphasis of estate planning should be about living, rather than dying. Even though certain aspects of an estate owner's plan may be triggered by death and often entail tax planning, people create estate plans while they are alive for peace of mind and financial confidence during their lifetimes. Estate planning is not dependent on whether or not there is an estate tax or whether or not an individual's estate is subject to tax. What it is about is the coordination of lifetime planning for the security of surviving family members and for transferring various kinds of wealth. Estate planning for seniors may be even more rewarding than planning earlier in life. Having financial and personal structures in place can only enhance clients' golden years. The paramount broad objectives in estate planning for seniors concern preservation of the individual's dignity, independence, and state of control for as long as possible.

Web Sites for Further Information

- www.abanet.org (American Bar Association)
- www.nolo.com
- www.revocible-living-trust.net
- www.uslegalforms.com
- www.findlegalforms.com
- www.yourethicalwill.com
- www.ethicalwill.com
- www.FamilyFight.com
- www.yellowpieplate.umn.edu
- www.naela.org

NOTE

1. Sid Friedman, "Life Settlements: A Big Opportunity and Getting Bigger," *Broker World,* Ocober 2003, 12.

Annuity Table

TABLE VI									
Joint and Last Survivor									
Ages	0	1	2	3	4	5	6	7	8	9
0	90.0	89.5	89.0	88.6	88.2	87.8	87.4	87.1	86.8	86.5
1	89.5	89.0	88.5	88.1	87.6	87.2	86.8	86.5	86.1	85.8
2	89.0	88.5	88.0	87.5	87.1	86.6	86.2	85.8	85.5	85.1
3	88.6	88.1	87.5	87.0	86.5	86.1	85.6	85.2	84.8	84.5
4	88.2	87.6	87.1	86.5	86.0	85.5	85.1	84.6	84.2	83.8
5	87.8	87.2	86.6	86.1	85.5	85.0	84.5	84.1	83.6	83.2
6	87.4	86.8	86.2	85.6	85.1	84.5	84.0	83.5	83.1	82.6
7	87.1	86.5	85.8	85.2	84.6	84.1	83.5	83.0	82.5	82.1
8	86.8	86.1	85.5	84.8	84.2	83.6	83.1	82.5	82.0	81.6
9	86.5	85.8	85.1	84.5	83.8	83.2	82.6	82.1	81.6	81.0
10	86.2	85.5	84.8	84.1	83.5	82.8	82.2	81.6	81.1	80.6
11	85.9	85.2	84.5	83.8	83.1	82.5	81.8	81.2	80.7	80.1
12	85.7	84.9	84.2	83.5	82.8	82.1	81.5	80.8	80.2	79.7
13	85.4	84.7	84.0	83.2	82.5	81.8	81.1	80.5	79.9	79.2
14	85.2	84.5	83.7	83.0	82.2	81.5	80.8	80.1	79.5	78.9
15	85.0	84.3	83.5	82.7	82.0	81.2	80.5	79.8	79.1	78.5
16	84.9	84.1	83.3	82.5	81.7	81.0	80.2	79.5	78.8	78.1
17	84.7	83.9	83.1	82.3	81.5	80.7	80.0	79.2	78.5	77.8
18	84.5	83.7	82.9	82.1	81.3	80.5	79.7	79.0	78.2	77.5
19	84.4	83.6	82.7	81.9	81.1	80.3	79.5	78.7	78.0	77.3
20	84.3	83.4	82.6	81.8	80.9	80.1	79.3	78.5	77.7	77.0
21	84.1	83.3	82.4	81.6	80.8	79.9	79.1	78.3	77.5	76.8
22	84.0	83.2	82.3	81.5	80.6	79.8	78.9	78.1	77.3	76.5
23	83.9	83.1	82.2	81.3	80.5	79.6	78.8	77.9	77.1	76.3
24	83.8	83.0	82.1	81.2	80.3	79.5	78.6	77.8	76.9	76.1
25	83.7	82.9	82.0	81.1	80.2	79.3	78.5	77.6	76.8	75.9
26	83.6	82.8	81.9	81.0	80.1	79.2	78.3	77.5	76.6	75.8
27	83.6	82.7	81.8	80.9	80.0	79.1	78.2	77.4	76.5	75.6
28	83.5	82.6	81.7	80.8	79.9	79.0	78.1	77.2	76.4	75.5
29	83.4	82.6	81.6	80.7	79.8	78.9	78.0	77.1	76.2	75.4
30	83.4	82.5	81.6	80.7	79.7	78.8	77.9	77.0	76.1	75.2
31	83.3	82.4	81.5	80.6	79.7	78.8	77.8	76.9	76.0	75.1
32	83.3	82.4	81.5	80.5	79.6	78.7	77.8	76.8	75.9	75.0
33	83.2	82.3	81.4	80.5	79.5	78.6	77.7	76.8	75.9	74.9
34	83.2	82.3	81.3	80.4	79.5	78.5	77.6	76.7	75.8	74.9
35	83.1	82.2	81.3	80.4	79.4	78.5	77.6	76.6	75.7	74.8
36	83.1	82.2	81.3	80.3	79.4	78.4	77.5	76.6	75.6	74.7
37	83.0	82.2	81.2	80.3	79.3	78.4	77.4	76.5	75.6	74.6
38	83.0	82.1	81.2	80.2	79.3	78.3	77.4	76.4	75.5	74.6
39	83.0	82.1	81.1	80.2	79.2	78.3	77.3	76.4	75.5	74.5

TABLE VI
Joint and Last Survivor (Continued)

Ages	0	1	2	3	4	5	6	7	8	9
40	82.9	82.1	81.1	80.2	79.2	78.3	77.3	76.4	75.4	74.5
41	82.9	82.0	81.1	80.1	79.2	78.2	77.3	76.3	75.4	74.4
42	82.9	82.0	81.1	80.1	79.1	78.2	77.2	76.3	75.3	74.4
43	82.9	82.0	81.0	80.1	79.1	78.2	77.2	76.2	75.3	74.3
44	82.8	81.9	81.0	80.0	79.1	78.1	77.2	76.2	75.2	74.3
45	82.8	81.9	81.0	80.0	79.1	78.1	77.1	76.2	75.2	74.3
46	82.8	81.9	81.0	80.0	79.0	78.1	77.1	76.1	75.2	74.2
47	82.8	81.9	80.9	80.0	79.0	78.0	77.1	76.1	75.2	74.2
48	82.8	81.9	80.9	80.0	79.0	78.0	77.1	76.1	75.1	74.2
49	82.7	81.8	80.9	79.9	79.0	78.0	77.0	76.1	75.1	74.1
50	82.7	81.8	80.9	79.9	79.0	78.0	77.0	76.0	75.1	74.1
51	82.7	81.8	80.9	79.9	78.9	78.0	77.0	76.0	75.1	74.1
52	82.7	81.8	80.9	79.9	78.9	78.0	77.0	76.0	75.0	74.1
53	82.7	81.8	80.8	79.9	78.9	77.9	77.0	76.0	75.0	74.0
54	82.7	81.8	80.8	79.9	78.9	77.9	76.9	76.0	75.0	74.0
55	82.6	81.8	80.8	79.8	78.9	77.9	76.9	76.0	75.0	74.0
56	82.6	81.7	80.8	79.8	78.9	77.9	76.9	75.9	75.0	74.0
57	82.6	81.7	80.8	79.8	78.9	77.9	76.9	75.9	75.0	74.0
58	82.6	81.7	80.8	79.8	78.8	77.9	76.9	75.9	74.9	74.0
59	82.6	81.7	80.8	79.8	78.8	77.9	76.9	75.9	74.9	74.0
60	82.6	81.7	80.8	79.8	78.8	77.8	76.9	75.9	74.9	73.9
61	82.6	81.7	80.8	79.8	78.8	77.8	76.9	75.9	74.9	73.9
62	82.6	81.7	80.7	79.8	78.8	77.8	76.9	75.9	74.9	73.9
63	82.6	81.7	80.7	79.8	78.8	77.8	76.8	75.9	74.9	73.9
64	82.5	81.7	80.7	79.8	78.8	77.8	76.8	75.9	74.9	73.9
65	82.5	81.7	80.7	79.8	78.8	77.8	76.8	75.8	74.9	73.9
66	82.5	81.7	80.7	79.7	78.8	77.8	76.8	75.8	74.9	73.9
67	82.5	81.7	80.7	79.7	78.8	77.8	76.8	75.8	74.9	73.9
68	82.5	81.6	80.7	79.7	78.8	77.8	76.8	75.8	74.8	73.9
69	82.5	81.6	80.7	79.7	78.8	77.8	76.8	75.8	74.8	73.9
70	82.5	81.6	80.7	79.7	78.8	77.8	76.8	75.8	74.8	73.9
71	82.5	81.6	80.7	79.7	78.7	77.8	76.8	75.8	74.8	73.8
72	82.5	81.6	80.7	79.7	78.7	77.8	76.8	75.8	74.8	73.8
73	82.5	81.6	80.7	79.7	78.7	77.8	76.8	75.8	74.8	73.8
74	82.5	81.6	80.7	79.7	78.7	77.8	76.8	75.8	74.8	73.8
75	82.5	81.6	80.7	79.7	78.7	77.8	76.8	75.8	74.8	73.8
76	82.5	81.6	80.7	79.7	78.7	77.8	76.8	75.8	74.8	73.8
77	82.5	81.6	80.7	79.7	78.7	77.7	76.8	75.8	74.8	73.8
78	82.5	81.6	80.7	79.7	78.7	77.7	76.8	75.8	74.8	73.8
79	82.5	81.6	80.7	79.7	78.7	77.7	76.8	75.8	74.8	73.8

TABLE VI
Joint and Last Survivor (Continued)

Ages	0	1	2	3	4	5	6	7	8	9
80	82.5	81.6	80.7	79.7	78.7	77.7	76.8	75.8	74.8	73.8
81	82.4	81.6	80.7	79.7	78.7	77.7	76.8	75.8	74.8	73.8
82	82.4	81.6	80.7	79.7	78.7	77.7	76.8	75.8	74.8	73.8
83	82.4	81.6	80.7	79.7	78.7	77.7	76.8	75.8	74.8	73.8
84	82.4	81.6	80.7	79.7	78.7	77.7	76.8	75.8	74.8	73.8
85	82.4	81.6	80.6	79.7	78.7	77.7	76.8	75.8	74.8	73.8
86	82.4	81.6	80.6	79.7	78.7	77.7	76.7	75.8	74.8	73.8
87	82.4	81.6	80.6	79.7	78.7	77.7	76.7	75.8	74.8	73.8
88	82.4	81.6	80.6	79.7	78.7	77.7	76.7	75.8	74.8	73.8
89	82.4	81.6	80.6	79.7	78.7	77.7	76.7	75.8	74.8	73.8
90	82.4	81.6	80.6	79.7	78.7	77.7	76.7	75.8	74.8	73.8
91	82.4	81.6	80.6	79.7	78.7	77.7	76.7	75.8	74.8	73.8
92	82.4	81.6	80.6	79.7	78.7	77.7	76.7	75.8	74.8	73.8
93	82.4	81.6	80.6	79.7	78.7	77.7	76.7	75.8	74.8	73.8
94	82.4	81.6	80.6	79.7	78.7	77.7	76.7	75.8	74.8	73.8
95	82.4	81.6	80.6	79.7	78.7	77.7	76.7	75.8	74.8	73.8
96	82.4	81.6	80.6	79.7	78.7	77.7	76.7	75.8	74.8	73.8
97	82.4	81.6	80.6	79.7	78.7	77.7	76.7	75.8	74.8	73.8
98	82.4	81.6	80.6	79.7	78.7	77.7	76.7	75.8	74.8	73.8
99	82.4	81.6	80.6	79.7	78.7	77.7	76.7	75.8	74.8	73.8
100	82.4	81.6	80.6	79.7	78.7	77.7	76.7	75.8	74.8	73.8
101	82.4	81.6	80.6	79.7	78.7	77.7	76.7	75.8	74.8	73.8
102	82.4	81.6	80.6	79.7	78.7	77.7	76.7	75.8	74.8	73.8
103	82.4	81.6	80.6	79.7	78.7	77.7	76.7	75.8	74.8	73.8
104	82.4	81.6	80.6	79.7	78.7	77.7	76.7	75.8	74.8	73.8
105	82.4	81.6	80.6	79.7	78.7	77.7	76.7	75.8	74.8	73.8
106	82.4	81.6	80.6	79.7	78.7	77.7	76.7	75.8	74.8	73.8
107	82.4	81.6	80.6	79.7	78.7	77.7	76.7	75.8	74.8	73.8
108	82.4	81.6	80.6	79.7	78.7	77.7	76.7	75.8	74.8	73.8
109	82.4	81.6	80.6	79.7	78.7	77.7	76.7	75.8	74.8	73.8
110	82.4	81.6	80.6	79.7	78.7	77.7	76.7	75.8	74.8	73.8
111	82.4	81.6	80.6	79.7	78.7	77.7	76.7	75.8	74.8	73.8
112	82.4	81.6	80.6	79.7	78.7	77.7	76.7	75.8	74.8	73.8
113	82.4	81.6	80.6	79.7	78.7	77.7	76.7	75.8	74.8	73.8
114	82.4	81.6	80.6	79.7	78.7	77.7	76.7	75.8	74.8	73.8
115+	82.4	81.6	80.6	79.7	78.7	77.7	76.7	75.8	74.8	73.8

TABLE VI
Joint and Last Survivor (Continued)

Ages	10	11	12	13	14	15	16	17	18	19
10	80.0	79.6	79.1	78.7	78.2	77.9	77.5	77.2	76.8	76.5
11	79.6	79.0	78.6	78.1	77.7	77.3	76.9	76.5	76.2	75.8
12	79.1	78.6	78.1	77.6	77.1	76.7	76.3	75.9	75.5	75.2
13	78.7	78.1	77.6	77.1	76.6	76.1	75.7	75.3	74.9	74.5
14	78.2	77.7	77.1	76.6	76.1	75.6	75.1	74.7	74.3	73.9
15	77.9	77.3	76.7	76.1	75.6	75.1	74.6	74.1	73.7	73.3
16	77.5	76.9	76.3	75.7	75.1	74.6	74.1	73.6	73.1	72.7
17	77.2	76.5	75.9	75.3	74.7	74.1	73.6	73.1	72.6	72.1
18	76.8	76.2	75.5	74.9	74.3	73.7	73.1	72.6	72.1	71.6
19	76.5	75.8	75.2	74.5	73.9	73.3	72.7	72.1	71.6	71.1
20	76.3	75.5	74.8	74.2	73.5	72.9	72.3	71.7	71.1	70.6
21	76.0	75.3	74.5	73.8	73.2	72.5	71.9	71.3	70.7	70.1
22	75.8	75.0	74.3	73.5	72.9	72.2	71.5	70.9	70.3	69.7
23	75.5	74.8	74.0	73.3	72.6	71.9	71.2	70.5	69.9	69.3
24	75.3	74.5	73.8	73.0	72.3	71.6	70.9	70.2	69.5	68.9
25	75.1	74.3	73.5	72.8	72.0	71.3	70.6	69.9	69.2	68.5
26	75.0	74.1	73.3	72.5	71.8	71.0	70.3	69.6	68.9	68.2
27	74.8	74.0	73.1	72.3	71.6	70.8	70.0	69.3	68.6	67.9
28	74.6	73.8	73.0	72.2	71.3	70.6	69.8	69.0	68.3	67.6
29	74.5	73.6	72.8	72.0	71.2	70.4	69.6	68.8	68.0	67.3
30	74.4	73.5	72.7	71.8	71.0	70.2	69.4	68.6	67.8	67.1
31	74.3	73.4	72.5	71.7	70.8	70.0	69.2	68.4	67.6	66.8
32	74.1	73.3	72.4	71.5	70.7	69.8	69.0	68.2	67.4	66.6
33	74.0	73.2	72.3	71.4	70.5	69.7	68.8	68.0	67.2	66.4
34	73.9	73.0	72.2	71.3	70.4	69.5	68.7	67.8	67.0	66.2
35	73.9	73.0	72.1	71.2	70.3	69.4	68.5	67.7	66.8	66.0
36	73.8	72.9	72.0	71.1	70.2	69.3	68.4	67.6	66.7	65.9
37	73.7	72.8	71.9	71.0	70.1	69.2	68.3	67.4	66.6	65.7
38	73.6	72.7	71.8	70.9	70.0	69.1	68.2	67.3	66.4	65.6
39	73.6	72.7	71.7	70.8	69.9	69.0	68.1	67.2	66.3	65.4
40	73.5	72.6	71.7	70.7	69.8	68.9	68.0	67.1	66.2	65.3
41	73.5	72.5	71.6	70.7	69.7	68.8	67.9	67.0	66.1	65.2
42	73.4	72.5	71.5	70.6	69.7	68.8	67.8	66.9	66.0	65.1
43	73.4	72.4	71.5	70.6	69.6	68.7	67.8	66.8	65.9	65.0
44	73.3	72.4	71.4	70.5	69.6	68.6	67.7	66.8	65.9	64.9
45	73.3	72.3	71.4	70.5	69.5	68.6	67.6	66.7	65.8	64.9
46	73.3	72.3	71.4	70.4	69.5	68.5	67.6	66.6	65.7	64.8
47	73.2	72.3	71.3	70.4	69.4	68.5	67.5	66.6	65.7	64.7
48	73.2	72.2	71.3	70.3	69.4	68.4	67.5	66.5	65.6	64.7
49	73.2	72.2	71.2	70.3	69.3	68.4	67.4	66.5	65.6	64.6

TABLE VI
Joint and Last Survivor (Continued)

Ages	10	11	12	13	14	15	16	17	18	19
50	73.1	72.2	71.2	70.3	69.3	68.4	67.4	66.5	65.5	64.6
51	73.1	72.2	71.2	70.2	69.3	68.3	67.4	66.4	65.5	64.5
52	73.1	72.1	71.2	70.2	69.2	68.3	67.3	66.4	65.4	64.5
53	73.1	72.1	71.1	70.2	69.2	68.3	67.3	66.3	65.4	64.4
54	73.1	72.1	71.1	70.2	69.2	68.2	67.3	66.3	65.4	64.4
55	73.0	72.1	71.1	70.1	69.2	68.2	67.2	66.3	65.3	64.4
56	73.0	72.1	71.1	70.1	69.1	68.2	67.2	66.3	65.3	64.3
57	73.0	72.0	71.1	70.1	69.1	68.2	67.2	66.2	65.3	64.3
58	73.0	72.0	71.0	70.1	69.1	68.1	67.2	66.2	65.2	64.3
59	73.0	72.0	71.0	70.1	69.1	68.1	67.2	66.2	65.2	64.3
60	73.0	72.0	71.0	70.0	69.1	68.1	67.1	66.2	65.2	64.2
61	73.0	72.0	71.0	70.0	69.1	68.1	67.1	66.2	65.2	64.2
62	72.9	72.0	71.0	70.0	69.0	68.1	67.1	66.1	65.2	64.2
63	72.9	72.0	71.0	70.0	69.0	68.1	67.1	66.1	65.2	64.2
64	72.9	71.9	71.0	70.0	69.0	68.0	67.1	66.1	65.1	64.2
65	72.9	71.9	71.0	70.0	69.0	68.0	67.1	66.1	65.1	64.2
66	72.9	71.9	70.9	70.0	69.0	68.0	67.1	66.1	65.1	64.1
67	72.9	71.9	70.9	70.0	69.0	68.0	67.0	66.1	65.1	64.1
68	72.9	71.9	70.9	70.0	69.0	68.0	67.0	66.1	65.1	64.1
69	72.9	71.9	70.9	69.9	69.0	68.0	67.0	66.1	65.1	64.1
70	72.9	71.9	70.9	69.9	69.0	68.0	67.0	66.0	65.1	64.1
71	72.9	71.9	70.9	69.9	69.0	68.0	67.0	66.0	65.1	64.1
72	72.9	71.9	70.9	69.9	69.0	68.0	67.0	66.0	65.1	64.1
73	72.9	71.9	70.9	69.9	68.9	68.0	67.0	66.0	65.0	64.1
74	72.9	71.9	70.9	69.9	68.9	68.0	67.0	66.0	65.0	64.1
75	72.8	71.9	70.9	69.9	68.9	68.0	67.0	66.0	65.0	64.1
76	72.8	71.9	70.9	69.9	68.9	68.0	67.0	66.0	65.0	64.1
77	72.8	71.9	70.9	69.9	68.9	68.0	67.0	66.0	65.0	64.1
78	72.8	71.9	70.9	69.9	68.9	67.9	67.0	66.0	65.0	64.0
79	72.8	71.9	70.9	69.9	68.9	67.9	67.0	66.0	65.0	64.0
80	72.8	71.9	70.9	69.9	68.9	67.9	67.0	66.0	65.0	64.0
81	72.8	71.8	70.9	69.9	68.9	67.9	67.0	66.0	65.0	64.0
82	72.8	71.8	70.9	69.9	68.9	67.9	67.0	66.0	65.0	64.0
83	72.8	71.8	70.9	69.9	68.9	67.9	67.0	66.0	65.0	64.0
84	72.8	71.8	70.9	69.9	68.9	67.9	67.0	66.0	65.0	64.0
85	72.8	71.8	70.9	69.9	68.9	67.9	66.9	66.0	65.0	64.0
86	72.8	71.8	70.9	69.9	68.9	67.9	66.9	66.0	65.0	64.0
87	72.8	71.8	70.9	69.9	68.9	67.9	66.9	66.0	65.0	64.0
88	72.8	71.8	70.9	69.9	68.9	67.9	66.9	66.0	65.0	64.0
89	72.8	71.8	70.9	69.9	68.9	67.9	66.9	66.0	65.0	64.0

TABLE VI
Joint and Last Survivor (Continued)

Ages	10	11	12	13	14	15	16	17	18	19
90	72.8	71.8	70.9	69.9	68.9	67.9	66.9	66.0	65.0	64.0
91	72.8	71.8	70.9	69.9	68.9	67.9	66.9	66.0	65.0	64.0
92	72.8	71.8	70.9	69.9	68.9	67.9	66.9	66.0	65.0	64.0
93	72.8	71.8	70.9	69.9	68.9	67.9	66.9	66.0	65.0	64.0
94	72.8	71.8	70.8	69.9	68.9	67.9	66.9	66.0	65.0	64.0
95	72.8	71.8	70.8	69.9	68.9	67.9	66.9	66.0	65.0	64.0
96	72.8	71.8	70.8	69.9	68.9	67.9	66.9	66.0	65.0	64.0
97	72.8	71.8	70.8	69.9	68.9	67.9	66.9	66.0	65.0	64.0
98	72.8	71.8	70.8	69.9	68.9	67.9	66.9	66.0	65.0	64.0
99	72.8	71.8	70.8	69.9	68.9	67.9	66.9	66.0	65.0	64.0
100	72.8	71.8	70.8	69.9	68.9	67.9	66.9	66.0	65.0	64.0
101	72.8	71.8	70.8	69.9	68.9	67.9	66.9	66.0	65.0	64.0
102	72.8	71.8	70.8	69.9	68.9	67.9	66.9	66.0	65.0	64.0
103	72.8	71.8	70.8	69.9	68.9	67.9	66.9	66.0	65.0	64.0
104	72.8	71.8	70.8	69.9	68.9	67.9	66.9	66.0	65.0	64.0
105	72.8	71.8	70.8	69.9	68.9	67.9	66.9	66.0	65.0	64.0
106	72.8	71.8	70.8	69.9	68.9	67.9	66.9	66.0	65.0	64.0
107	72.8	71.8	70.8	69.9	68.9	67.9	66.9	66.0	65.0	64.0
108	72.8	71.8	70.8	69.9	68.9	67.9	66.9	66.0	65.0	64.0
109	72.8	71.8	70.8	69.9	68.9	67.9	66.9	66.0	65.0	64.0
110	72.8	71.8	70.8	69.9	68.9	67.9	66.9	66.0	65.0	64.0
111	72.8	71.8	70.8	69.9	68.9	67.9	66.9	66.0	65.0	64.0
112	72.8	71.8	70.8	69.9	68.9	67.9	66.9	66.0	65.0	64.0
113	72.8	71.8	70.8	69.9	68.9	67.9	66.9	66.0	65.0	64.0
114	72.8	71.8	70.8	69.9	68.9	67.9	66.9	66.0	65.0	64.0
115+	72.8	71.8	70.8	69.9	68.9	67.9	66.9	66.0	65.0	64.0

TABLE VI
Joint and Last Survivor (Continued)

Ages	20	21	22	23	24	25	26	27	28	29
20	70.1	69.6	69.1	68.7	68.3	67.9	67.5	67.2	66.9	66.6
21	69.6	69.1	68.6	68.2	67.7	67.3	66.9	66.6	66.2	65.9
22	69.1	68.6	68.1	67.6	67.2	66.7	66.3	65.9	65.6	65.2
23	68.7	68.2	67.6	67.1	66.6	66.2	65.7	65.3	64.9	64.6
24	68.3	67.7	67.2	66.6	66.1	65.6	65.2	64.7	64.3	63.9
25	67.9	67.3	66.7	66.2	65.6	65.1	64.6	64.2	63.7	63.3
26	67.5	66.9	66.3	65.7	65.2	64.6	64.1	63.6	63.2	62.8
27	67.2	66.6	65.9	65.3	64.7	64.2	63.6	63.1	62.7	62.2
28	66.9	66.2	65.6	64.9	64.3	63.7	63.2	62.7	62.1	61.7
29	66.6	65.9	65.2	64.6	63.9	63.3	62.8	62.2	61.7	61.2
30	66.3	65.6	64.9	64.2	63.6	62.9	62.3	61.8	61.2	60.7
31	66.1	65.3	64.6	63.9	63.2	62.6	62.0	61.4	60.8	60.2
32	65.8	65.1	64.3	63.6	62.9	62.2	61.6	61.0	60.4	59.8
33	65.6	64.8	64.1	63.3	62.6	61.9	61.3	60.6	60.0	59.4
34	65.4	64.6	63.8	63.1	62.3	61.6	60.9	60.3	59.6	59.0
35	65.2	64.4	63.6	62.8	62.1	61.4	60.6	59.9	59.3	58.6
36	65.0	64.2	63.4	62.6	61.9	61.1	60.4	59.6	59.0	58.3
37	64.9	64.0	63.2	62.4	61.6	60.9	60.1	59.4	58.7	58.0
38	64.7	63.9	63.0	62.2	61.4	60.6	59.9	59.1	58.4	57.7
39	64.6	63.7	62.9	62.1	61.2	60.4	59.6	58.9	58.1	57.4
40	64.4	63.6	62.7	61.9	61.1	60.2	59.4	58.7	57.9	57.1
41	64.3	63.5	62.6	61.7	60.9	60.1	59.3	58.5	57.7	56.9
42	64.2	63.3	62.5	61.6	60.8	59.9	59.1	58.3	57.5	56.7
43	64.1	63.2	62.4	61.5	60.6	59.8	58.9	58.1	57.3	56.5
44	64.0	63.1	62.2	61.4	60.5	59.6	58.8	57.9	57.1	56.3
45	64.0	63.0	62.2	61.3	60.4	59.5	58.6	57.8	56.9	56.1
46	63.9	63.0	62.1	61.2	60.3	59.4	58.5	57.7	56.8	56.0
47	63.8	62.9	62.0	61.1	60.2	59.3	58.4	57.5	56.7	55.8
48	63.7	62.8	61.9	61.0	60.1	59.2	58.3	57.4	56.5	55.7
49	63.7	62.8	61.8	60.9	60.0	59.1	58.2	57.3	56.4	55.6
50	63.6	62.7	61.8	60.8	59.9	59.0	58.1	57.2	56.3	55.4
51	63.6	62.6	61.7	60.8	59.9	58.9	58.0	57.1	56.2	55.3
52	63.5	62.6	61.7	60.7	59.8	58.9	58.0	57.1	56.1	55.2
53	63.5	62.5	61.6	60.7	59.7	58.8	57.9	57.0	56.1	55.2
54	63.5	62.5	61.6	60.6	59.7	58.8	57.8	56.9	56.0	55.1
55	63.4	62.5	61.5	60.6	59.6	58.7	57.8	56.8	55.9	55.0
56	63.4	62.4	61.5	60.5	59.6	58.7	57.7	56.8	55.9	54.9
57	63.4	62.4	61.5	60.5	59.6	58.6	57.7	56.7	55.8	54.9
58	63.3	62.4	61.4	60.5	59.5	58.6	57.6	56.7	55.8	54.8
59	63.3	62.3	61.4	60.4	59.5	58.5	57.6	56.7	55.7	54.8

TABLE VI
Joint and Last Survivor (Continued)

Ages	20	21	22	23	24	25	26	27	28	29
60	63.3	62.3	61.4	60.4	59.5	58.5	57.6	56.6	55.7	54.7
61	63.3	62.3	61.3	60.4	59.4	58.5	57.5	56.6	55.6	54.7
62	63.2	62.3	61.3	60.4	59.4	58.4	57.5	56.5	55.6	54.7
63	63.2	62.3	61.3	60.3	59.4	58.4	57.5	56.5	55.6	54.6
64	63.2	62.2	61.3	60.3	59.4	58.4	57.4	56.5	55.5	54.6
65	63.2	62.2	61.3	60.3	59.3	58.4	57.4	56.5	55.5	54.6
66	63.2	62.2	61.2	60.3	59.3	58.4	57.4	56.4	55.5	54.5
67	63.2	62.2	61.2	60.3	59.3	58.3	57.4	56.4	55.5	54.5
68	63.1	62.2	61.2	60.2	59.3	58.3	57.4	56.4	55.4	54.5
69	63.1	62.2	61.2	60.2	59.3	58.3	57.3	56.4	55.4	54.5
70	63.1	62.2	61.2	60.2	59.3	58.3	57.3	56.4	55.4	54.4
71	63.1	62.1	61.2	60.2	59.2	58.3	57.3	56.4	55.4	54.4
72	63.1	62.1	61.2	60.2	59.2	58.3	57.3	56.3	55.4	54.4
73	63.1	62.1	61.2	60.2	59.2	58.3	57.3	56.3	55.4	54.4
74	63.1	62.1	61.2	60.2	59.2	58.2	57.3	56.3	55.4	54.4
75	63.1	62.1	61.1	60.2	59.2	58.2	57.3	56.3	55.3	54.4
76	63.1	62.1	61.1	60.2	59.2	58.2	57.3	56.3	55.3	54.4
77	63.1	62.1	61.1	60.2	59.2	58.2	57.3	56.3	55.3	54.4
78	63.1	62.1	61.1	60.2	59.2	58.2	57.3	56.3	55.3	54.4
79	63.1	62.1	61.1	60.2	59.2	58.2	57.2	56.3	55.3	54.3
80	63.1	62.1	61.1	60.1	59.2	58.2	57.2	56.3	55.3	54.3
81	63.1	62.1	61.1	60.1	59.2	58.2	57.2	56.3	55.3	54.3
82	63.1	62.1	61.1	60.1	59.2	58.2	57.2	56.3	55.3	54.3
83	63.1	62.1	61.1	60.1	59.2	58.2	57.2	56.3	55.3	54.3
84	63.0	62.1	61.1	60.1	59.2	58.2	57.2	56.3	55.3	54.3
85	63.0	62.1	61.1	60.1	59.2	58.2	57.2	56.3	55.3	54.3
86	63.0	62.1	61.1	60.1	59.2	58.2	57.2	56.2	55.3	54.3
87	63.0	62.1	61.1	60.1	59.2	58.2	57.2	56.2	55.3	54.3
88	63.0	62.1	61.1	60.1	59.2	58.2	57.2	56.2	55.3	54.3
89	63.0	62.1	61.1	60.1	59.1	58.2	57.2	56.2	55.3	54.3
90	63.0	62.1	61.1	60.1	59.1	58.2	57.2	56.2	55.3	54.3
91	63.0	62.1	61.1	60.1	59.1	58.2	57.2	56.2	55.3	54.3
92	63.0	62.1	61.1	60.1	59.1	58.2	57.2	56.2	55.3	54.3
93	63.0	62.1	61.1	60.1	59.1	58.2	57.2	56.2	55.3	54.3
94	63.0	62.1	61.1	60.1	59.1	58.2	57.2	56.2	55.3	54.3
95	63.0	62.1	61.1	60.1	59.1	58.2	57.2	56.2	55.3	54.3
96	63.0	62.1	61.1	60.1	59.1	58.2	57.2	56.2	55.3	54.3
97	63.0	62.1	61.1	60.1	59.1	58.2	57.2	56.2	55.3	54.3
98	63.0	62.1	61.1	60.1	59.1	58.2	57.2	56.2	55.3	54.3
99	63.0	62.1	61.1	60.1	59.1	58.2	57.2	56.2	55.3	54.3

TABLE VI
Joint and Last Survivor (Continued)

Ages	20	21	22	23	24	25	26	27	28	29
100	63.0	62.1	61.1	60.1	59.1	58.2	57.2	56.2	55.3	54.3
101	63.0	62.1	61.1	60.1	59.1	58.2	57.2	56.2	55.3	54.3
102	63.0	62.1	61.1	60.1	59.1	58.2	57.2	56.2	55.3	54.3
103	63.0	62.1	61.1	60.1	59.1	58.2	57.2	56.2	55.3	54.3
104	63.0	62.1	61.1	60.1	59.1	58.2	57.2	56.2	55.3	54.3
105	63.0	62.1	61.1	60.1	59.1	58.2	57.2	56.2	55.3	54.3
106	63.0	62.1	61.1	60.1	59.1	58.2	57.2	56.2	55.3	54.3
107	63.0	62.1	61.1	60.1	59.1	58.2	57.2	56.2	55.3	54.3
108	63.0	62.1	61.1	60.1	59.1	58.2	57.2	56.2	55.3	54.3
109	63.0	62.1	61.1	60.1	59.1	58.2	57.2	56.2	55.3	54.3
110	63.0	62.1	61.1	60.1	59.1	58.2	57.2	56.2	55.3	54.3
111	63.0	62.1	61.1	60.1	59.1	58.2	57.2	56.2	55.3	54.3
112	63.0	62.1	61.1	60.1	59.1	58.2	57.2	56.2	55.3	54.3
113	63.0	62.1	61.1	60.1	59.1	58.2	57.2	56.2	55.3	54.3
114	63.0	62.1	61.1	60.1	59.1	58.2	57.2	56.2	55.3	54.3
115+	63.0	62.1	61.1	60.1	59.1	58.2	57.2	56.2	55.3	54.3

TABLE VI
Joint and Last Survivor (Continued)

Ages	30	31	32	33	34	35	36	37	38	39
30	60.2	59.7	59.2	58.8	58.4	58.0	57.6	57.3	57.0	56.7
31	59.7	59.2	58.7	58.2	57.8	57.4	57.0	56.6	56.3	56.0
32	59.2	58.7	58.2	57.7	57.2	56.8	56.4	56.0	55.6	55.3
33	58.8	58.2	57.7	57.2	56.7	56.2	55.8	55.4	55.0	54.7
34	58.4	57.8	57.2	56.7	56.2	55.7	55.3	54.8	54.4	54.0
35	58.0	57.4	56.8	56.2	55.7	55.2	54.7	54.3	53.8	53.4
36	57.6	57.0	56.4	55.8	55.3	54.7	54.2	53.7	53.3	52.8
37	57.3	56.6	56.0	55.4	54.8	54.3	53.7	53.2	52.7	52.3
38	57.0	56.3	55.6	55.0	54.4	53.8	53.3	52.7	52.2	51.7
39	56.7	56.0	55.3	54.7	54.0	53.4	52.8	52.3	51.7	51.2
40	56.4	55.7	55.0	54.3	53.7	53.0	52.4	51.8	51.3	50.8
41	56.1	55.4	54.7	54.0	53.3	52.7	52.0	51.4	50.9	50.3
42	55.9	55.2	54.4	53.7	53.0	52.3	51.7	51.1	50.4	49.9
43	55.7	54.9	54.2	53.4	52.7	52.0	51.3	50.7	50.1	49.5
44	55.5	54.7	53.9	53.2	52.4	51.7	51.0	50.4	49.7	49.1
45	55.3	54.5	53.7	52.9	52.2	51.5	50.7	50.0	49.4	48.7
46	55.1	54.3	53.5	52.7	52.0	51.2	50.5	49.8	49.1	48.4
47	55.0	54.1	53.3	52.5	51.7	51.0	50.2	49.5	48.8	48.1
48	54.8	54.0	53.2	52.3	51.5	50.8	50.0	49.2	48.5	47.8
49	54.7	53.8	53.0	52.2	51.4	50.6	49.8	49.0	48.2	47.5
50	54.6	53.7	52.9	52.0	51.2	50.4	49.6	48.8	48.0	47.3
51	54.5	53.6	52.7	51.9	51.0	50.2	49.4	48.6	47.8	47.0
52	54.4	53.5	52.6	51.7	50.9	50.0	49.2	48.4	47.6	46.8
53	54.3	53.4	52.5	51.6	50.8	49.9	49.1	48.2	47.4	46.6
54	54.2	53.3	52.4	51.5	50.6	49.8	48.9	48.1	47.2	46.4
55	54.1	53.2	52.3	51.4	50.5	49.7	48.8	47.9	47.1	46.3
56	54.0	53.1	52.2	51.3	50.4	49.5	48.7	47.8	47.0	46.1
57	54.0	53.0	52.1	51.2	50.3	49.4	48.6	47.7	46.8	46.0
58	53.9	53.0	52.1	51.2	50.3	49.4	48.5	47.6	46.7	45.8
59	53.8	52.9	52.0	51.1	50.2	49.3	48.4	47.5	46.6	45.7
60	53.8	52.9	51.9	51.0	50.1	49.2	48.3	47.4	46.5	45.6
61	53.8	52.8	51.9	51.0	50.0	49.1	48.2	47.3	46.4	45.5
62	53.7	52.8	51.8	50.9	50.0	49.1	48.1	47.2	46.3	45.4
63	53.7	52.7	51.8	50.9	49.9	49.0	48.1	47.2	46.3	45.3
64	53.6	52.7	51.8	50.8	49.9	48.9	48.0	47.1	46.2	45.3
65	53.6	52.7	51.7	50.8	49.8	48.9	48.0	47.0	46.1	45.2
66	53.6	52.6	51.7	50.7	49.8	48.9	47.9	47.0	46.1	45.1
67	53.6	52.6	51.7	50.7	49.8	48.8	47.9	46.9	46.0	45.1
68	53.5	52.6	51.6	50.7	49.7	48.8	47.8	46.9	46.0	45.0
69	53.5	52.6	51.6	50.6	49.7	48.7	47.8	46.9	45.9	45.0

TABLE VI
Joint and Last Survivor (Continued)

Ages	30	31	32	33	34	35	36	37	38	39
70	53.5	52.5	51.6	50.6	49.7	48.7	47.8	46.8	45.9	44.9
71	53.5	52.5	51.6	50.6	49.6	48.7	47.7	46.8	45.9	44.9
72	53.5	52.5	51.5	50.6	49.6	48.7	47.7	46.8	45.8	44.9
73	53.4	52.5	51.5	50.6	49.6	48.6	47.7	46.7	45.8	44.8
74	53.4	52.5	51.5	50.5	49.6	48.6	47.7	46.7	45.8	44.8
75	53.4	52.5	51.5	50.5	49.6	48.6	47.7	46.7	45.7	44.8
76	53.4	52.4	51.5	50.5	49.6	48.6	47.6	46.7	45.7	44.8
77	53.4	52.4	51.5	50.5	49.5	48.6	47.6	46.7	45.7	44.8
78	53.4	52.4	51.5	50.5	49.5	48.6	47.6	46.6	45.7	44.7
79	53.4	52.4	51.5	50.5	49.5	48.6	47.6	46.6	45.7	44.7
80	53.4	52.4	51.4	50.5	49.5	48.5	47.6	46.6	45.7	44.7
81	53.4	52.4	51.4	50.5	49.5	48.5	47.6	46.6	45.7	44.7
82	53.4	52.4	51.4	50.5	49.5	48.5	47.6	46.6	45.6	44.7
83	53.4	52.4	51.4	50.5	49.5	48.5	47.6	46.6	45.6	44.7
84	53.4	52.4	51.4	50.5	49.5	48.5	47.6	46.6	45.6	44.7
85	53.3	52.4	51.4	50.4	49.5	48.5	47.5	46.6	45.6	44.7
86	53.3	52.4	51.4	50.4	49.5	48.5	47.5	46.6	45.6	44.6
87	53.3	52.4	51.4	50.4	49.5	48.5	47.5	46.6	45.6	44.6
88	53.3	52.4	51.4	50.4	49.5	48.5	47.5	46.6	45.6	44.6
89	53.3	52.4	51.4	50.4	49.5	48.5	47.5	46.6	45.6	44.6
90	53.3	52.4	51.4	50.4	49.5	48.5	47.5	46.6	45.6	44.6
91	53.3	52.4	51.4	50.4	49.5	48.5	47.5	46.6	45.6	44.6
92	53.3	52.4	51.4	50.4	49.5	48.5	47.5	46.6	45.6	44.6
93	53.3	52.4	51.4	50.4	49.5	48.5	47.5	46.6	45.6	44.6
94	53.3	52.4	51.4	50.4	49.5	48.5	47.5	46.6	45.6	44.6
95	53.3	52.4	51.4	50.4	49.5	48.5	47.5	46.5	45.6	44.6
96	53.3	52.4	51.4	50.4	49.5	48.5	47.5	46.5	45.6	44.6
97	53.3	52.4	51.4	50.4	49.5	48.5	47.5	46.5	45.6	44.6
98	53.3	52.4	51.4	50.4	49.5	48.5	47.5	46.5	45.6	44.6
99	53.3	52.4	51.4	50.4	49.5	48.5	47.5	46.5	45.6	44.6
100	53.3	52.4	51.4	50.4	49.5	48.5	47.5	46.5	45.6	44.6
101	53.3	52.4	51.4	50.4	49.5	48.5	47.5	46.5	45.6	44.6
102	53.3	52.4	51.4	50.4	49.5	48.5	47.5	46.5	45.6	44.6
103	53.3	52.4	51.4	50.4	49.5	48.5	47.5	46.5	45.6	44.6
104	53.3	52.4	51.4	50.4	49.5	48.5	47.5	46.5	45.6	44.6
105	53.3	52.4	51.4	50.4	49.4	48.5	47.5	46.5	45.6	44.6
106	53.3	52.4	51.4	50.4	49.4	48.5	47.5	46.5	45.6	44.6
107	53.3	52.4	51.4	50.4	49.4	48.5	47.5	46.5	45.6	44.6
108	53.3	52.4	51.4	50.4	49.4	48.5	47.5	46.5	45.6	44.6
109	53.3	52.4	51.4	50.4	49.4	48.5	47.5	46.5	45.6	44.6

TABLE VI
Joint and Last Survivor (Continued)

Ages	30	31	32	33	34	35	36	37	38	39
110	53.3	52.4	51.4	50.4	49.4	48.5	47.5	46.5	45.6	44.6
111	53.3	52.4	51.4	50.4	49.4	48.5	47.5	46.5	45.6	44.6
112	53.3	52.4	51.4	50.4	49.4	48.5	47.5	46.5	45.6	44.6
113	53.3	52.4	51.4	50.4	49.4	48.5	47.5	46.5	45.6	44.6
114	53.3	52.4	51.4	50.4	49.4	48.5	47.5	46.5	45.6	44.6
115+	53.3	52.4	51.4	50.4	49.4	48.5	47.5	46.5	45.6	44.6

TABLE VI
Joint and Last Survivor (Continued)

Ages	40	41	42	43	44	45	46	47	48	49
40	50.2	49.8	49.3	48.9	48.5	48.1	47.7	47.4	47.1	46.8
41	49.8	49.3	48.8	48.3	47.9	47.5	47.1	46.7	46.4	46.1
42	49.3	48.8	48.3	47.8	47.3	46.9	46.5	46.1	45.8	45.4
43	48.9	48.3	47.8	47.3	46.8	46.3	45.9	45.5	45.1	44.8
44	48.5	47.9	47.3	46.8	46.3	45.8	45.4	44.9	44.5	44.2
45	48.1	47.5	46.9	46.3	45.8	45.3	44.8	44.4	44.0	43.6
46	47.7	47.1	46.5	45.9	45.4	44.8	44.3	43.9	43.4	43.0
47	47.4	46.7	46.1	45.5	44.9	44.4	43.9	43.4	42.9	42.4
48	47.1	46.4	45.8	45.1	44.5	44.0	43.4	42.9	42.4	41.9
49	46.8	46.1	45.4	44.8	44.2	43.6	43.0	42.4	41.9	41.4
50	46.5	45.8	45.1	44.4	43.8	43.2	42.6	42.0	41.5	40.9
51	46.3	45.5	44.8	44.1	43.5	42.8	42.2	41.6	41.0	40.5
52	46.0	45.3	44.6	43.8	43.2	42.5	41.8	41.2	40.6	40.1
53	45.8	45.1	44.3	43.6	42.9	42.2	41.5	40.9	40.3	39.7
54	45.6	44.8	44.1	43.3	42.6	41.9	41.2	40.5	39.9	39.3
55	45.5	44.7	43.9	43.1	42.4	41.6	40.9	40.2	39.6	38.9
56	45.3	44.5	43.7	42.9	42.1	41.4	40.7	40.0	39.3	38.6
57	45.1	44.3	43.5	42.7	41.9	41.2	40.4	39.7	39.0	38.3
58	45.0	44.2	43.3	42.5	41.7	40.9	40.2	39.4	38.7	38.0
59	44.9	44.0	43.2	42.4	41.5	40.7	40.0	39.2	38.5	37.8
60	44.7	43.9	43.0	42.2	41.4	40.6	39.8	39.0	38.2	37.5
61	44.6	43.8	42.9	42.1	41.2	40.4	39.6	38.8	38.0	37.3
62	44.5	43.7	42.8	41.9	41.1	40.3	39.4	38.6	37.8	37.1
63	44.5	43.6	42.7	41.8	41.0	40.1	39.3	38.5	37.7	36.9
64	44.4	43.5	42.6	41.7	40.8	40.0	39.2	38.3	37.5	36.7
65	44.3	43.4	42.5	41.6	40.7	39.9	39.0	38.2	37.4	36.6
66	44.2	43.3	42.4	41.5	40.6	39.8	38.9	38.1	37.2	36.4
67	44.2	43.3	42.3	41.4	40.6	39.7	38.8	38.0	37.1	36.3
68	44.1	43.2	42.3	41.4	40.5	39.6	38.7	37.9	37.0	36.2
69	44.1	43.1	42.2	41.3	40.4	39.5	38.6	37.8	36.9	36.0
70	44.0	43.1	42.2	41.3	40.3	39.4	38.6	37.7	36.8	35.9
71	44.0	43.0	42.1	41.2	40.3	39.4	38.5	37.6	36.7	35.9
72	43.9	43.0	42.1	41.1	40.2	39.3	38.4	37.5	36.6	35.8
73	43.9	43.0	42.0	41.1	40.2	39.3	38.4	37.5	36.6	35.7
74	43.9	42.9	42.0	41.1	40.1	39.2	38.3	37.4	36.5	35.6
75	43.8	42.9	42.0	41.0	40.1	39.2	38.3	37.4	36.5	35.6
76	43.8	42.9	41.9	41.0	40.1	39.1	38.2	37.3	36.4	35.5
77	43.8	42.9	41.9	41.0	40.0	39.1	38.2	37.3	36.4	35.5
78	43.8	42.8	41.9	40.9	40.0	39.1	38.2	37.2	36.3	35.4
79	43.8	42.8	41.9	40.9	40.0	39.1	38.1	37.2	36.3	35.4

TABLE VI
Joint and Last Survivor (Continued)

Ages	40	41	42	43	44	45	46	47	48	49
80	43.7	42.8	41.8	40.9	40.0	39.0	38.1	37.2	36.3	35.4
81	43.7	42.8	41.8	40.9	39.9	39.0	38.1	37.2	36.2	35.3
82	43.7	42.8	41.8	40.9	39.9	39.0	38.1	37.1	36.2	35.3
83	43.7	42.8	41.8	40.9	39.9	39.0	38.0	37.1	36.2	35.3
84	43.7	42.7	41.8	40.8	39.9	39.0	38.0	37.1	36.2	35.3
85	43.7	42.7	41.8	40.8	39.9	38.9	38.0	37.1	36.2	35.2
86	43.7	42.7	41.8	40.8	39.9	38.9	38.0	37.1	36.1	35.2
87	43.7	42.7	41.8	40.8	39.9	38.9	38.0	37.0	36.1	35.2
88	43.7	42.7	41.8	40.8	39.9	38.9	38.0	37.0	36.1	35.2
89	43.7	42.7	41.7	40.8	39.8	38.9	38.0	37.0	36.1	35.2
90	43.7	42.7	41.7	40.8	39.8	38.9	38.0	37.0	36.1	35.2
91	43.7	42.7	41.7	40.8	39.8	38.9	37.9	37.0	36.1	35.2
92	43.7	42.7	41.7	40.8	39.8	38.9	37.9	37.0	36.1	35.1
93	43.7	42.7	41.7	40.8	39.8	38.9	37.9	37.0	36.1	35.1
94	43.7	42.7	41.7	40.8	39.8	38.9	37.9	37.0	36.1	35.1
95	43.6	42.7	41.7	40.8	39.8	38.9	37.9	37.0	36.1	35.1
96	43.6	42.7	41.7	40.8	39.8	38.9	37.9	37.0	36.1	35.1
97	43.6	42.7	41.7	40.8	39.8	38.9	37.9	37.0	36.1	35.1
98	43.6	42.7	41.7	40.8	39.8	38.9	37.9	37.0	36.0	35.1
99	43.6	42.7	41.7	40.8	39.8	38.9	37.9	37.0	36.0	35.1
100	43.6	42.7	41.7	40.8	39.8	38.9	37.9	37.0	36.0	35.1
101	43.6	42.7	41.7	40.8	39.8	38.9	37.9	37.0	36.0	35.1
102	43.6	42.7	41.7	40.8	39.8	38.9	37.9	37.0	36.0	35.1
103	43.6	42.7	41.7	40.8	39.8	38.9	37.9	37.0	36.0	35.1
104	43.6	42.7	41.7	40.8	39.8	38.8	37.9	37.0	36.0	35.1
105	43.6	42.7	41.7	40.8	39.8	38.8	37.9	37.0	36.0	35.1
106	43.6	42.7	41.7	40.8	39.8	38.8	37.9	37.0	36.0	35.1
107	43.6	42.7	41.7	40.8	39.8	38.8	37.9	37.0	36.0	35.1
108	43.6	42.7	41.7	40.8	39.8	38.8	37.9	37.0	36.0	35.1
109	43.6	42.7	41.7	40.7	39.8	38.8	37.9	37.0	36.0	35.1
110	43.6	42.7	41.7	40.7	39.8	38.8	37.9	37.0	36.0	35.1
111	43.6	42.7	41.7	40.7	39.8	38.8	37.9	37.0	36.0	35.1
112	43.6	42.7	41.7	40.7	39.8	38.8	37.9	37.0	36.0	35.1
113	43.6	42.7	41.7	40.7	39.8	38.8	37.9	37.0	36.0	35.1
114	43.6	42.7	41.7	40.7	39.8	38.8	37.9	37.0	36.0	35.1
115+	43.6	42.7	41.7	40.7	39.8	38.8	37.9	37.0	36.0	35.1

TABLE VI
Joint and Last Survivor (Continued)

Ages	50	51	52	53	54	55	56	57	58	59
50	40.4	40.0	39.5	39.1	38.7	38.3	38.0	37.6	37.3	37.1
51	40.0	39.5	39.0	38.5	38.1	37.7	37.4	37.0	36.7	36.4
52	39.5	39.0	38.5	38.0	37.6	37.2	36.8	36.4	36.0	35.7
53	39.1	38.5	38.0	37.5	37.1	36.6	36.2	35.8	35.4	35.1
54	38.7	38.1	37.6	37.1	36.6	36.1	35.7	35.2	34.8	34.5
55	38.3	37.7	37.2	36.6	36.1	35.6	35.1	34.7	34.3	33.9
56	38.0	37.4	36.8	36.2	35.7	35.1	34.7	34.2	33.7	33.3
57	37.6	37.0	36.4	35.8	35.2	34.7	34.2	33.7	33.2	32.8
58	37.3	36.7	36.0	35.4	34.8	34.3	33.7	33.2	32.8	32.3
59	37.1	36.4	35.7	35.1	34.5	33.9	33.3	32.8	32.3	31.8
60	36.8	36.1	35.4	34.8	34.1	33.5	32.9	32.4	31.9	31.3
61	36.6	35.8	35.1	34.5	33.8	33.2	32.6	32.0	31.4	30.9
62	36.3	35.6	34.9	34.2	33.5	32.9	32.2	31.6	31.1	30.5
63	36.1	35.4	34.6	33.9	33.2	32.6	31.9	31.3	30.7	30.1
64	35.9	35.2	34.4	33.7	33.0	32.3	31.6	31.0	30.4	29.8
65	35.8	35.0	34.2	33.5	32.7	32.0	31.4	30.7	30.0	29.4
66	35.6	34.8	34.0	33.3	32.5	31.8	31.1	30.4	29.8	29.1
67	35.5	34.7	33.9	33.1	32.3	31.6	30.9	30.2	29.5	28.8
68	35.3	34.5	33.7	32.9	32.1	31.4	30.7	29.9	29.2	28.6
69	35.2	34.4	33.6	32.8	32.0	31.2	30.5	29.7	29.0	28.3
70	35.1	34.3	33.4	32.6	31.8	31.1	30.3	29.5	28.8	28.1
71	35.0	34.2	33.3	32.5	31.7	30.9	30.1	29.4	28.6	27.9
72	34.9	34.1	33.2	32.4	31.6	30.8	30.0	29.2	28.4	27.7
73	34.8	34.0	33.1	32.3	31.5	30.6	29.8	29.1	28.3	27.5
74	34.8	33.9	33.0	32.2	31.4	30.5	29.7	28.9	28.1	27.4
75	34.7	33.8	33.0	32.1	31.3	30.4	29.6	28.8	28.0	27.2
76	34.6	33.8	32.9	32.0	31.2	30.3	29.5	28.7	27.9	27.1
77	34.6	33.7	32.8	32.0	31.1	30.3	29.4	28.6	27.8	27.0
78	34.5	33.6	32.8	31.9	31.0	30.2	29.3	28.5	27.7	26.9
79	34.5	33.6	32.7	31.8	31.0	30.1	29.3	28.4	27.6	26.8
80	34.5	33.6	32.7	31.8	30.9	30.1	29.2	28.4	27.5	26.7
81	34.4	33.5	32.6	31.8	30.9	30.0	29.2	28.3	27.5	26.6
82	34.4	33.5	32.6	31.7	30.8	30.0	29.1	28.3	27.4	26.6
83	34.4	33.5	32.6	31.7	30.8	29.9	29.1	28.2	27.4	26.5
84	34.3	33.4	32.5	31.7	30.8	29.9	29.0	28.2	27.3	26.5
85	34.3	33.4	32.5	31.6	30.7	29.9	29.0	28.1	27.3	26.4
86	34.3	33.4	32.5	31.6	30.7	29.8	29.0	28.1	27.2	26.4
87	34.3	33.4	32.5	31.6	30.7	29.8	28.9	28.1	27.2	26.4
88	34.3	33.4	32.5	31.6	30.7	29.8	28.9	28.0	27.2	26.3
89	34.3	33.3	32.4	31.5	30.7	29.8	28.9	28.0	27.2	26.3

TABLE VI
Joint and Last Survivor (Continued)

Ages	50	51	52	53	54	55	56	57	58	59
90	34.2	33.3	32.4	31.5	30.6	29.8	28.9	28.0	27.1	26.3
91	34.2	33.3	32.4	31.5	30.6	29.7	28.9	28.0	27.1	26.3
92	34.2	33.3	32.4	31.5	30.6	29.7	28.8	28.0	27.1	26.2
93	34.2	33.3	32.4	31.5	30.6	29.7	28.8	28.0	27.1	26.2
94	34.2	33.3	32.4	31.5	30.6	29.7	28.8	27.9	27.1	26.2
95	34.2	33.3	32.4	31.5	30.6	29.7	28.8	27.9	27.1	26.2
96	34.2	33.3	32.4	31.5	30.6	29.7	28.8	27.9	27.0	26.2
97	34.2	33.3	32.4	31.5	30.6	29.7	28.8	27.9	27.0	26.2
98	34.2	33.3	32.4	31.5	30.6	29.7	28.8	27.9	27.0	26.2
99	34.2	33.3	32.4	31.5	30.6	29.7	28.8	27.9	27.0	26.2
100	34.2	33.3	32.4	31.5	30.6	29.7	28.8	27.9	27.0	26.1
101	34.2	33.3	32.4	31.5	30.6	29.7	28.8	27.9	27.0	26.1
102	34.2	33.3	32.4	31.4	30.5	29.7	28.8	27.9	27.0	26.1
103	34.2	33.3	32.4	31.4	30.5	29.7	28.8	27.9	27.0	26.1
104	34.2	33.3	32.4	31.4	30.5	29.6	28.8	27.9	27.0	26.1
105	34.2	33.3	32.3	31.4	30.5	29.6	28.8	27.9	27.0	26.1
106	34.2	33.3	32.3	31.4	30.5	29.6	28.8	27.9	27.0	26.1
107	34.2	33.3	32.3	31.4	30.5	29.6	28.8	27.9	27.0	26.1
108	34.2	33.3	32.3	31.4	30.5	29.6	28.8	27.9	27.0	26.1
109	34.2	33.3	32.3	31.4	30.5	29.6	28.7	27.9	27.0	26.1
110	34.2	33.3	32.3	31.4	30.5	29.6	28.7	27.9	27.0	26.1
111	34.2	33.3	32.3	31.4	30.5	29.6	28.7	27.9	27.0	26.1
112	34.2	33.3	32.3	31.4	30.5	29.6	28.7	27.9	27.0	26.1
113	34.2	33.3	32.3	31.4	30.5	29.6	28.7	27.9	27.0	26.1
114	34.2	33.3	32.3	31.4	30.5	29.6	28.7	27.9	27.0	26.1
115+	34.2	33.3	32.3	31.4	30.5	29.6	28.7	27.9	27.0	26.1

TABLE VI
Joint and Last Survivor (Continued)

Ages	60	61	62	63	64	65	66	67	68	69
60	30.9	30.4	30.0	29.6	29.2	28.8	28.5	28.2	27.9	27.6
61	30.4	29.9	29.5	29.0	28.6	28.3	27.9	27.6	27.3	27.0
62	30.0	29.5	29.0	28.5	28.1	27.7	27.3	27.0	26.7	26.4
63	29.6	29.0	28.5	28.1	27.6	27.2	26.8	26.4	26.1	25.7
64	29.2	28.6	28.1	27.6	27.1	26.7	26.3	25.9	25.5	25.2
65	28.8	28.3	27.7	27.2	26.7	26.2	25.8	25.4	25.0	24.6
66	28.5	27.9	27.3	26.8	26.3	25.8	25.3	24.9	24.5	24.1
67	28.2	27.6	27.0	26.4	25.9	25.4	24.9	24.4	24.0	23.6
68	27.9	27.3	26.7	26.1	25.5	25.0	24.5	24.0	23.5	23.1
69	27.6	27.0	26.4	25.7	25.2	24.6	24.1	23.6	23.1	22.6
70	27.4	26.7	26.1	25.4	24.8	24.3	23.7	23.2	22.7	22.2
71	27.2	26.5	25.8	25.2	24.5	23.9	23.4	22.8	22.3	21.8
72	27.0	26.3	25.6	24.9	24.3	23.7	23.1	22.5	22.0	21.4
73	26.8	26.1	25.4	24.7	24.0	23.4	22.8	22.2	21.6	21.1
74	26.6	25.9	25.2	24.5	23.8	23.1	22.5	21.9	21.3	20.8
75	26.5	25.7	25.0	24.3	23.6	22.9	22.3	21.6	21.0	20.5
76	26.3	25.6	24.8	24.1	23.4	22.7	22.0	21.4	20.8	20.2
77	26.2	25.4	24.7	23.9	23.2	22.5	21.8	21.2	20.6	19.9
78	26.1	25.3	24.6	23.8	23.1	22.4	21.7	21.0	20.3	19.7
79	26.0	25.2	24.4	23.7	22.9	22.2	21.5	20.8	20.1	19.5
80	25.9	25.1	24.3	23.6	22.8	22.1	21.3	20.6	20.0	19.3
81	25.8	25.0	24.2	23.4	22.7	21.9	21.2	20.5	19.8	19.1
82	25.8	24.9	24.1	23.4	22.6	21.8	21.1	20.4	19.7	19.0
83	25.7	24.9	24.1	23.3	22.5	21.7	21.0	20.2	19.5	18.8
84	25.6	24.8	24.0	23.2	22.4	21.6	20.9	20.1	19.4	18.7
85	25.6	24.8	23.9	23.1	22.3	21.6	20.8	20.1	19.3	18.6
86	25.5	24.7	23.9	23.1	22.3	21.5	20.7	20.0	19.2	18.5
87	25.5	24.7	23.8	23.0	22.2	21.4	20.7	19.9	19.2	18.4
88	25.5	24.6	23.8	23.0	22.2	21.4	20.6	19.8	19.1	18.3
89	25.4	24.6	23.8	22.9	22.1	21.3	20.5	19.8	19.0	18.3
90	25.4	24.6	23.7	22.9	22.1	21.3	20.5	19.7	19.0	18.2
91	25.4	24.5	23.7	22.9	22.1	21.3	20.5	19.7	18.9	18.2
92	25.4	24.5	23.7	22.9	22.0	21.2	20.4	19.6	18.9	18.1
93	25.4	24.5	23.7	22.8	22.0	21.2	20.4	19.6	18.8	18.1
94	25.3	24.5	23.6	22.8	22.0	21.2	20.4	19.6	18.8	18.0
95	25.3	24.5	23.6	22.8	22.0	21.1	20.3	19.6	18.8	18.0
96	25.3	24.5	23.6	22.8	21.9	21.1	20.3	19.5	18.8	18.0
97	25.3	24.5	23.6	22.8	21.9	21.1	20.3	19.5	18.7	18.0
98	25.3	24.4	23.6	22.8	21.9	21.1	20.3	19.5	18.7	17.9
99	25.3	24.4	23.6	22.7	21.9	21.1	20.3	19.5	18.7	17.9

TABLE VI
Joint and Last Survivor (Continued)

Ages	60	61	62	63	64	65	66	67	68	69
100	25.3	24.4	23.6	22.7	21.9	21.1	20.3	19.5	18.7	17.9
101	25.3	24.4	23.6	22.7	21.9	21.1	20.2	19.4	18.7	17.9
102	25.3	24.4	23.6	22.7	21.9	21.1	20.2	19.4	18.6	17.9
103	25.3	24.4	23.6	22.7	21.9	21.0	20.2	19.4	18.6	17.9
104	25.3	24.4	23.5	22.7	21.9	21.0	20.2	19.4	18.6	17.8
105	25.3	24.4	23.5	22.7	21.9	21.0	20.2	19.4	18.6	17.8
106	25.3	24.4	23.5	22.7	21.9	21.0	20.2	19.4	18.6	17.8
107	25.2	24.4	23.5	22.7	21.8	21.0	20.2	19.4	18.6	17.8
108	25.2	24.4	23.5	22.7	21.8	21.0	20.2	19.4	18.6	17.8
109	25.2	24.4	23.5	22.7	21.8	21.0	20.2	19.4	18.6	17.8
110	25.2	24.4	23.5	22.7	21.8	21.0	20.2	19.4	18.6	17.8
111	25.2	24.4	23.5	22.7	21.8	21.0	20.2	19.4	18.6	17.8
112	25.2	24.4	23.5	22.7	21.8	21.0	20.2	19.4	18.6	17.8
113	25.2	24.4	23.5	22.7	21.8	21.0	20.2	19.4	18.6	17.8
114	25.2	24.4	23.5	22.7	21.8	21.0	20.2	19.4	18.6	17.8
115+	25.2	24.4	23.5	22.7	21.8	21.0	20.2	19.4	18.6	17.8

A1.18   *Financial Decisions for Retirement*

TABLE VI
Joint and Last Survivor (Continued)

Ages	70	71	72	73	74	75	76	77	78	79
70	21.8	21.3	20.9	20.6	20.2	19.9	19.6	19.4	19.1	18.9
71	21.3	20.9	20.5	20.1	19.7	19.4	19.1	18.8	18.5	18.3
72	20.9	20.5	20.0	19.6	19.3	18.9	18.6	18.3	18.0	17.7
73	20.6	20.1	19.6	19.2	18.8	18.4	18.1	17.8	17.5	17.2
74	20.2	19.7	19.3	18.8	18.4	18.0	17.6	17.3	17.0	16.7
75	19.9	19.4	18.9	18.4	18.0	17.6	17.2	16.8	16.5	16.2
76	19.6	19.1	18.6	18.1	17.6	17.2	16.8	16.4	16.0	15.7
77	19.4	18.8	18.3	17.8	17.3	16.8	16.4	16.0	15.6	15.3
78	19.1	18.5	18.0	17.5	17.0	16.5	16.0	15.6	15.2	14.9
79	18.9	18.3	17.7	17.2	16.7	16.2	15.7	15.3	14.9	14.5
80	18.7	18.1	17.5	16.9	16.4	15.9	15.4	15.0	14.5	14.1
81	18.5	17.9	17.3	16.7	16.2	15.6	15.1	14.7	14.2	13.8
82	18.3	17.7	17.1	16.5	15.9	15.4	14.9	14.4	13.9	13.5
83	18.2	17.5	16.9	16.3	15.7	15.2	14.7	14.2	13.7	13.2
84	18.0	17.4	16.7	16.1	15.5	15.0	14.4	13.9	13.4	13.0
85	17.9	17.3	16.6	16.0	15.4	14.8	14.3	13.7	13.2	12.8
86	17.8	17.1	16.5	15.8	15.2	14.6	14.1	13.5	13.0	12.5
87	17.7	17.0	16.4	15.7	15.1	14.5	13.9	13.4	12.9	12.4
88	17.6	16.9	16.3	15.6	15.0	14.4	13.8	13.2	12.7	12.2
89	17.6	16.9	16.2	15.5	14.9	14.3	13.7	13.1	12.6	12.0
90	17.5	16.8	16.1	15.4	14.8	14.2	13.6	13.0	12.4	11.9
91	17.4	16.7	16.0	15.4	14.7	14.1	13.5	12.9	12.3	11.8
92	17.4	16.7	16.0	15.3	14.6	14.0	13.4	12.8	12.2	11.7
93	17.3	16.6	15.9	15.2	14.6	13.9	13.3	12.7	12.1	11.6
94	17.3	16.6	15.9	15.2	14.5	13.9	13.2	12.6	12.0	11.5
95	17.3	16.5	15.8	15.1	14.5	13.8	13.2	12.6	12.0	11.4
96	17.2	16.5	15.8	15.1	14.4	13.8	13.1	12.5	11.9	11.3
97	17.2	16.5	15.8	15.1	14.4	13.7	13.1	12.5	11.9	11.3
98	17.2	16.4	15.7	15.0	14.3	13.7	13.0	12.4	11.8	11.2
99	17.2	16.4	15.7	15.0	14.3	13.6	13.0	12.4	11.8	11.2
100	17.1	16.4	15.7	15.0	14.3	13.6	12.9	12.3	11.7	11.1
101	17.1	16.4	15.6	14.9	14.2	13.6	12.9	12.3	11.7	11.1
102	17.1	16.4	15.6	14.9	14.2	13.5	12.9	12.2	11.6	11.0
103	17.1	16.3	15.6	14.9	14.2	13.5	12.9	12.2	11.6	11.0
104	17.1	16.3	15.6	14.9	14.2	13.5	12.8	12.2	11.6	11.0
105	17.1	16.3	15.6	14.9	14.2	13.5	12.8	12.2	11.5	10.9
106	17.1	16.3	15.6	14.8	14.1	13.5	12.8	12.2	11.5	10.9
107	17.0	16.3	15.6	14.8	14.1	13.4	12.8	12.1	11.5	10.9
108	17.0	16.3	15.5	14.8	14.1	13.4	12.8	12.1	11.5	10.9
109	17.0	16.3	15.5	14.8	14.1	13.4	12.8	12.1	11.5	10.9
110	17.0	16.3	15.5	14.8	14.1	13.4	12.7	12.1	11.5	10.9
111	17.0	16.3	15.5	14.8	14.1	13.4	12.7	12.1	11.5	10.8
112	17.0	16.3	15.5	14.8	14.1	13.4	12.7	12.1	11.5	10.8
113	17.0	16.3	15.5	14.8	14.1	13.4	12.7	12.1	11.4	10.8
114	17.0	16.3	15.5	14.8	14.1	13.4	12.7	12.1	11.4	10.8
115+	17.0	16.3	15.5	14.8	14.1	13.4	12.7	12.1	11.4	10.8

TABLE VI
Joint and Last Survivor (Continued)

Ages	80	81	82	83	84	85	86	87	88	89
80	13.8	13.4	13.1	12.8	12.6	12.3	12.1	11.9	11.7	11.5
81	13.4	13.1	12.7	12.4	12.2	11.9	11.7	11.4	11.3	11.1
82	13.1	12.7	12.4	12.1	11.8	11.5	11.3	11.0	10.8	10.6
83	12.8	12.4	12.1	11.7	11.4	11.1	10.9	10.6	10.4	10.2
84	12.6	12.2	11.8	11.4	11.1	10.8	10.5	10.3	10.1	9.9
85	12.3	11.9	11.5	11.1	10.8	10.5	10.2	9.9	9.7	9.5
86	12.1	11.7	11.3	10.9	10.5	10.2	9.9	9.6	9.4	9.2
87	11.9	11.4	11.0	10.6	10.3	9.9	9.6	9.4	9.1	8.9
88	11.7	11.3	10.8	10.4	10.1	9.7	9.4	9.1	8.8	8.6
89	11.5	11.1	10.6	10.2	9.9	9.5	9.2	8.9	8.6	8.3
90	11.4	10.9	10.5	10.1	9.7	9.3	9.0	8.6	8.3	8.1
91	11.3	10.8	10.3	9.9	9.5	9.1	8.8	8.4	8.1	7.9
92	11.2	10.7	10.2	9.8	9.3	9.0	8.6	8.3	8.0	7.7
93	11.1	10.6	10.1	9.6	9.2	8.8	8.5	8.1	7.8	7.5
94	11.0	10.5	10.0	9.5	9.1	8.7	8.3	8.0	7.6	7.3
95	10.9	10.4	9.9	9.4	9.0	8.6	8.2	7.8	7.5	7.2
96	10.8	10.3	9.8	9.3	8.9	8.5	8.1	7.7	7.4	7.1
97	10.7	10.2	9.7	9.2	8.8	8.4	8.0	7.6	7.3	6.9
98	10.7	10.1	9.6	9.2	8.7	8.3	7.9	7.5	7.1	6.8
99	10.6	10.1	9.6	9.1	8.6	8.2	7.8	7.4	7.0	6.7
100	10.6	10.0	9.5	9.0	8.5	8.1	7.7	7.3	6.9	6.6
101	10.5	10.0	9.4	9.0	8.5	8.0	7.6	7.2	6.9	6.5
102	10.5	9.9	9.4	8.9	8.4	8.0	7.5	7.1	6.8	6.4
103	10.4	9.9	9.4	8.8	8.4	7.9	7.5	7.1	6.7	6.3
104	10.4	9.8	9.3	8.8	8.3	7.9	7.4	7.0	6.6	6.3
105	10.4	9.8	9.3	8.8	8.3	7.8	7.4	7.0	6.6	6.2
106	10.3	9.8	9.2	8.7	8.2	7.8	7.3	6.9	6.5	6.2
107	10.3	9.8	9.2	8.7	8.2	7.7	7.3	6.9	6.5	6.1
108	10.3	9.7	9.2	8.7	8.2	7.7	7.3	6.8	6.4	6.1
109	10.3	9.7	9.2	8.7	8.2	7.7	7.2	6.8	6.4	6.0
110	10.3	9.7	9.2	8.6	8.1	7.7	7.2	6.8	6.4	6.0
111	10.3	9.7	9.1	8.6	8.1	7.6	7.2	6.8	6.3	6.0
112	10.2	9.7	9.1	8.6	8.1	7.6	7.2	6.7	6.3	5.9
113	10.2	9.7	9.1	8.6	8.1	7.6	7.2	6.7	6.3	5.9
114	10.2	9.7	9.1	8.6	8.1	7.6	7.1	6.7	6.3	5.9
115+	10.2	9.7	9.1	8.6	8.1	7.6	7.1	6.7	6.3	5.9

TABLE VI
Joint and Last Survivor (Continued)

Ages	90	91	92	93	94	95	96	97	98	99
90	7.8	7.6	7.4	7.2	7.1	6.9	6.8	6.6	6.5	6.4
91	7.6	7.4	7.2	7.0	6.8	6.7	6.5	6.4	6.3	6.1
92	7.4	7.2	7.0	6.8	6.6	6.4	6.3	6.1	6.0	5.9
93	7.2	7.0	6.8	6.6	6.4	6.2	6.1	5.9	5.8	5.6
94	7.1	6.8	6.6	6.4	6.2	6.0	5.9	5.7	5.6	5.4
95	6.9	6.7	6.4	6.2	6.0	5.8	5.7	5.5	5.4	5.2
96	6.8	6.5	6.3	6.1	5.9	5.7	5.5	5.3	5.2	5.0
97	6.6	6.4	6.1	5.9	5.7	5.5	5.3	5.2	5.0	4.9
98	6.5	6.3	6.0	5.8	5.6	5.4	5.2	5.0	4.8	4.7
99	6.4	6.1	5.9	5.6	5.4	5.2	5.0	4.9	4.7	4.5
100	6.3	6.0	5.8	5.5	5.3	5.1	4.9	4.7	4.5	4.4
101	6.2	5.9	5.6	5.4	5.2	5.0	4.8	4.6	4.4	4.2
102	6.1	5.8	5.5	5.3	5.1	4.8	4.6	4.4	4.3	4.1
103	6.0	5.7	5.4	5.2	5.0	4.7	4.5	4.3	4.1	4.0
104	5.9	5.6	5.4	5.1	4.9	4.6	4.4	4.2	4.0	3.8
105	5.9	5.6	5.3	5.0	4.8	4.5	4.3	4.1	3.9	3.7
106	5.8	5.5	5.2	4.9	4.7	4.5	4.2	4.0	3.8	3.6
107	5.8	5.4	5.1	4.9	4.6	4.4	4.2	3.9	3.7	3.5
108	5.7	5.4	5.1	4.8	4.6	4.3	4.1	3.9	3.7	3.5
109	5.7	5.3	5.0	4.8	4.5	4.3	4.0	3.8	3.6	3.4
110	5.6	5.3	5.0	4.7	4.5	4.2	4.0	3.8	3.5	3.3
111	5.6	5.3	5.0	4.7	4.4	4.2	3.9	3.7	3.5	3.3
112	5.6	5.3	4.9	4.7	4.4	4.1	3.9	3.7	3.5	3.2
113	5.6	5.2	4.9	4.6	4.4	4.1	3.9	3.6	3.4	3.2
114	5.6	5.2	4.9	4.6	4.3	4.1	3.9	3.6	3.4	3.2
115+	5.5	5.2	4.9	4.6	4.3	4.1	3.8	3.6	3.4	3.1

TABLE VI
Joint and Last Survivor (Continued)

Ages	100	101	102	103	104	105	106	107	108	109
100	4.2	4.1	3.9	3.8	3.7	3.5	3.4	3.3	3.3	3.2
101	4.1	3.9	3.7	3.6	3.5	3.4	3.2	3.1	3.1	3.0
102	3.9	3.7	3.6	3.4	3.3	3.2	3.1	3.0	2.9	2.8
103	3.8	3.6	3.4	3.3	3.2	3.0	2.9	2.8	2.7	2.6
104	3.7	3.5	3.3	3.2	3.0	2.9	2.7	2.6	2.5	2.4
105	3.5	3.4	3.2	3.0	2.9	2.7	2.6	2.5	2.4	2.3
106	3.4	3.2	3.1	2.9	2.7	2.6	2.4	2.3	2.2	2.1
107	3.3	3.1	3.0	2.8	2.6	2.5	2.3	2.2	2.1	2.0
108	3.3	3.1	2.9	2.7	2.5	2.4	2.2	2.1	1.9	1.8
109	3.2	3.0	2.8	2.6	2.4	2.3	2.1	2.0	1.8	1.7
110	3.1	2.9	2.7	2.5	2.3	2.2	2.0	1.9	1.7	1.6
111	3.1	2.9	2.7	2.5	2.3	2.1	1.9	1.8	1.6	1.5
112	3.0	2.8	2.6	2.4	2.2	2.0	1.9	1.7	1.5	1.4
113	3.0	2.8	2.6	2.4	2.2	2.0	1.8	1.6	1.5	1.3
114	3.0	2.7	2.5	2.3	2.1	1.9	1.8	1.6	1.4	1.3
115+	2.9	2.7	2.5	2.3	2.1	1.9	1.7	1.5	1.4	1.2

TABLE VI
Joint and Last Survivor (Continued)

Ages	110	111	112	113	114	115+
110	1.5	1.4	1.3	1.2	1.1	1.1
111	1.4	1.2	1.1	1.1	1.0	1.0
112	1.3	1.1	1.0	1.0	1.0	1.0
113	1.2	1.1	1.0	1.0	1.0	1.0
114	1.1	1.0	1.0	1.0	1.0	1.0
115+	1.1	1.0	1.0	1.0	1.0	1.0

Form 4972 and Instructions

Form **4972**

Department of the Treasury
Internal Revenue Service (99)

Tax on Lump-Sum Distributions
(From Qualified Plans of Participants Born Before January 2, 1936)
▶ Attach to Form 1040 or Form 1041.

OMB No. 1545-0193

2004

Attachment
Sequence No. **28**

Name of recipient of distribution

Identifying number

Part I Complete this part to see if you can use Form 4972

			Yes	No
1	Was this a distribution of a plan participant's entire balance (excluding deductible voluntary employee contributions and certain forfeited amounts) from all of an employer's qualified plans of one kind (pension, profit-sharing, or stock bonus)? If "No," **do not** use this form	**1**		
2	Did you roll over any part of the distribution? If "Yes," **do not** use this form	**2**		
3	Was this distribution paid to you as a beneficiary of a plan participant who was born before January 2, 1936?	**3**		
4	Were you **(a)** a plan participant who received this distribution, **(b)** born before January 2, 1936, **and (c)** a participant in the plan for at least 5 years before the year of the distribution?. . . . . If you answered "No" to both questions 3 **and** 4, **do not** use this form.	**4**		
5a	Did you use Form 4972 after 1986 for a previous distribution from your own plan? If "Yes," **do not** use this form for a 2004 distribution from your own plan	**5a**		
b	If you are receiving this distribution as a beneficiary of a plan participant who died, did you use Form 4972 for a previous distribution received for that participant after 1986? If "Yes," **do not** use the form for this distribution	**5b**		

Part II Complete this part to choose the 20% capital gain election (see instructions)

6	Capital gain part from Form 1099-R, box 3	**6**	
7	Multiply line 6 by 20% (.20) . . . . ▶	**7**	

If you also choose to use Part III, go to line 8. Otherwise, include the amount from line 7 in the total on Form 1040, line 43, or Form 1041, Schedule G, line 1b, whichever applies.

Part III Complete this part to choose the 10-year tax option (see instructions)

8	Ordinary income from Form 1099-R, box 2a minus box 3. If you did not complete Part II, enter the taxable amount from Form 1099-R, box 2a.		**8**	
9	Death benefit exclusion for a beneficiary of a plan participant who died before August 21, 1996		**9**	
10	Total taxable amount. Subtract line 9 from line 8		**10**	
11	Current actuarial value of annuity from Form 1099-R, box 8. If none, enter -0-		**11**	
12	Adjusted total taxable amount. Add lines 10 and 11. If this amount is $70,000 or more, **skip** lines 13 through 16, enter this amount on line 17, and go to line 18		**12**	
13	Multiply line 12 by 50% (.50), but **do not** enter more than $10,000 .	**13**		
14	Subtract $20,000 from line 12. If line 12 is $20,000 or less, enter -0-	**14**		
15	Multiply line 14 by 20% (.20)	**15**		
16	Minimum distribution allowance. Subtract line 15 from line 13		**16**	
17	Subtract line 16 from line 12		**17**	
18	Federal estate tax attributable to lump-sum distribution		**18**	
19	Subtract line 18 from line 17. If line 11 is zero, **skip** lines 20 through 22 and go to line 23 . .		**19**	
20	Divide line 11 by line 12 and enter the result as a decimal (rounded to at least three places).	**20**	.	
21	Multiply line 16 by the decimal on line 20	**21**		
22	Subtract line 21 from line 11	**22**		
23	Multiply line 19 by 10% (.10)		**23**	
24	Tax on amount on line 23. Use the Tax Rate Schedule in the instructions		**24**	
25	Multiply line 24 by ten (10). If line 11 is zero, **skip** lines 26 through 28, enter this amount on line 29, and go to line 30		**25**	
26	Multiply line 22 by 10% (.10)	**26**		
27	Tax on amount on line 26. Use the Tax Rate Schedule in the instructions	**27**		
28	Multiply line 27 by ten (10)		**28**	
29	Subtract line 28 from line 25. Multiple recipients, see instructions . . . . ▶		**29**	
30	**Tax on lump-sum distribution.** Add lines 7 and 29. Also include this amount in the total on Form 1040, line 43, or Form 1041, Schedule G, line 1b, whichever applies . . . . . ▶		**30**	

For Paperwork Reduction Act Notice, see instructions.   Cat. No. 13187U   Form **4972** (2004)

A2.3

General Instructions

Section references are to the Internal Revenue Code.

Purpose of Form

Use Form 4972 to figure the tax on a qualified lump-sum distribution (defined below) you received in 2004 using the 20% capital gain election, the 10-year tax option, or both. These are special formulas used to figure a separate tax on the distribution that may result in a smaller tax than if you reported the taxable amount of the distribution as ordinary income.

You pay the tax only once, for the year you receive the distribution, not over the next 10 years. The separate tax is added to the regular tax figured on your other income.

Related Publications

Pub. 575, Pension and Annuity Income.

Pub. 721, Tax Guide to U.S. Civil Service Retirement Benefits.

Pub. 939, General Rule for Pensions and Annuities.

What Is a Qualified Lump-Sum Distribution?

It is the distribution or payment in 1 tax year of a plan participant's entire balance from all of an employer's qualified plans of one kind (for example, pension, profit-sharing, or stock bonus plans) in which the participant had funds. The participant's entire balance does not include deductible voluntary employee contributions or certain forfeited amounts. The participant must have been born before January 2, 1936.

Distributions upon death of the plan participant. If you received a qualifying distribution as a beneficiary after the participant's death, the participant must have been born before January 2, 1936, for you to use this form for that distribution.

Distributions to alternate payees. If you are the spouse or former spouse of a plan participant who was born before January 2, 1936, and you received a qualified lump-sum distribution as an alternate payee under a qualified domestic relations order, you can use Form 4972 to make the 20% capital gain election and use the 10-year tax option to figure your tax on the distribution.

See *How To Report the Distribution* on this page.

Distributions That Do Not Qualify for the 20% Capital Gain Election or the 10-Year Tax Option

The following distributions are not qualified lump-sum distributions and do not qualify for the 20% capital gain election or the 10-year tax option.

● A distribution that is partially rolled over to another qualified plan or an IRA.

● Any distribution if an earlier election to use either the 5- or 10-year tax option had been made after 1986 for the same plan participant.

● U.S. Retirement Plan Bonds distributed with the lump sum.

● A distribution made during the first 5 tax years that the participant was in the plan, unless it was paid because the participant died.

● The current actuarial value of any annuity contract included in the lump sum (Form 1099-R, box 8, should show this amount, which you use only to figure tax on the ordinary income part of the distribution).

● A distribution to a 5% owner that is subject to penalties under section 72(m)(5)(A).

● A distribution from an IRA.

● A distribution from a tax-sheltered annuity (section 403(b) plan).

● A distribution of the redemption proceeds of bonds rolled over tax free to a qualified pension plan, etc., from a qualified bond purchase plan.

● A distribution from a qualified plan if the participant or his or her surviving spouse previously received an eligible rollover distribution from the same plan (or another plan of the employer that must be combined with that plan for the lump-sum distribution rules) and the previous distribution was rolled over tax free to another qualified plan or an IRA.

● A distribution from a qualified plan that received a rollover after 2001 from an IRA (other than a conduit IRA), a governmental section 457 plan, or a section 403(b) tax-sheltered annuity on behalf of the plan participant.

● A distribution from a qualified plan that received a rollover after 2001 from another qualified plan on behalf of that plan participant's surviving spouse.

● A corrective distribution of excess deferrals, excess contributions, excess aggregate contributions, or excess annual additions.

● A lump-sum credit or payment from the Federal Civil Service Retirement System (or the Federal Employees' Retirement System).

How To Report the Distribution

If you can use Form 4972, attach it to Form 1040 (individuals) or Form 1041 (estates or trusts). The payer should have given you a Form 1099-R or other statement that shows the amounts needed to complete Form 4972. The following choices are available.

20% capital gain election. If there is an amount in Form 1099-R, box 3, you can use Form 4972, Part II, to apply a 20% tax rate to the capital gain portion. See *Capital Gain Election* on page 3.

10-year tax option. You can use Part III to figure your tax on the lump-sum

distribution using the 10-year tax option whether or not you make the 20% capital gain election.

Where to report. Report amounts from your Form 1099-R either directly on your tax return (Form 1040 or 1041) or on Form 4972.

● If you do not use Form 4972, report the entire amount from Form 1099-R, box 1 (Gross distribution), on Form 1040, line 16a, and the taxable amount on line 16b (or on Form 1041, line 8). If your pension or annuity is fully taxable, enter the amount from Form 1099-R, box 2a (Taxable amount), on Form 1040, line 16b; do not make an entry on line 16a.

● If you do not use Part III of Form 4972, but use Part II, report only the ordinary income portion of the distribution on Form 1040, lines 16a and 16b (or on Form 1041, line 8). The ordinary income portion is the amount from Form 1099-R, box 2a, minus the amount from box 3 of that form.

● If you use Part III of Form 4972, do not include any part of the distribution on Form 1040, lines 16a and 16b (or on Form 1041, line 8).

The entries in other boxes on Form 1099-R may also apply in completing Form 4972.

● Box 6 (Net unrealized appreciation in employer's securities). See *Net unrealized appreciation (NUA)* on page 3.

● Box 8 (Other). Current actuarial value of an annuity.

If applicable, get the amount of federal estate tax paid attributable to the taxable part of the lump-sum distribution from the administrator of the deceased's estate.

How Often You May Use Form 4972

After 1986, you may use Form 4972 only once for each plan participant. If you receive more than one lump-sum distribution for the same participant in 1 tax year, you must treat all those distributions the same way. Combine them on a single Form 4972.

If you make an election as a beneficiary of a deceased participant, it does not affect any election you can make for qualified lump-sum distributions from your own plan. You can also make an election as the beneficiary of more than one qualifying person.

Example. Your mother and father died and each was born before January 2, 1936. Each had a qualified plan of which you are the beneficiary. You also received a qualified lump-sum distribution from your own plan and you were born before January 2, 1936. You may make an election for each of the distributions; one for yourself, one as your mother's beneficiary, and one as your father's. It does not matter if the distributions all occur in the same year or in different years. File a separate Form 4972 for each participant's distribution.

An earlier election on Form 4972 or Form 5544 for a distribution before 1987 does not prevent you from making an election for a distribution after 1986 for the same participant, provided the participant was under age 59½ at the time of the pre-1987 distribution.

When You May File Form 4972

You can file Form 4972 with either an original or amended return. Generally, you have 3 years from the later of the due date of your tax return or the date you filed your return to choose to use any part of Form 4972.

Capital Gain Election

If the distribution includes a capital gain, you can (a) make the 20% capital gain election in Part II of Form 4972 or (b) treat the capital gain as ordinary income.

Only the taxable amount of distributions resulting from pre-1974 participation qualifies for capital gain treatment. The capital gain amount should be shown in Form 1099-R, box 3. If there is an amount in Form 1099-R, box 6 (net unrealized appreciation (NUA)), part of it will also qualify for capital gain treatment. Use the NUA Worksheet on this page to figure the capital gain part of NUA if you make the election to include NUA in your taxable income.

You may report the ordinary income portion of the distribution on Form 1040, line 16b (or Form 1041, line 8) or you may figure the tax using the 10-year tax option. The ordinary income portion is the amount from Form 1099-R, box 2a, minus the amount from box 3 of that form.

Net unrealized appreciation (NUA). Normally, NUA in employer securities received as part of a lump-sum distribution is not taxable until the securities are sold. However, you can elect to include NUA in taxable income in the year received.

The total amount to report as NUA should be shown in Form 1099-R, box 6. Part of the amount in box 6 will qualify for capital gain treatment if there is an amount in Form 1099-R, box 3. To figure the total amount subject to capital gain treatment including the NUA, complete the NUA Worksheet on this page.

Specific Instructions

Name of recipient of distribution and identifying number. At the top of Form 4972, fill in the name and identifying number of the recipient of the distribution.

If you received more than one qualified distribution in 2004 for the same plan participant, add them and figure the tax on the total amount. If you received qualified distributions in 2004 for more than one participant, file a separate Form 4972 for the distributions of each participant.

If you and your spouse are filing a joint return and each has received a lump-sum distribution, complete and file a separate

Form 4972 for each spouse's election, combine the tax, and include the combined tax in the total on Form 1040, line 43.

If you are filing for a trust that shared the distribution only with other trusts, figure the tax on the total lump sum first. The trusts then share the tax in the same proportion that they shared the distribution.

Multiple recipients of a lump-sum distribution. If you shared in a lump-sum distribution from a qualified retirement plan when not all recipients were trusts (a percentage will be shown in Form 1099-R, boxes 8 and/or 9a), figure your tax on Form 4972 as follows. (Box numbers used below are from Form 1099-R.)

Step 1. Complete Form 4972, Parts I and II. If you make the 20% capital gain election in Part II and also elect to include NUA in taxable income, complete the NUA Worksheet below to determine the amount of NUA that qualifies for capital gain treatment. Then, skip Step 2 and go to Step 3.

Step 2. Use this step only if you do not elect to include NUA in your taxable income or if you do not have NUA.

- If you are not making the capital gain election, divide the amount in box 2a by your percentage of distribution in box 9a. Enter this amount on Form 4972, line 8.

- If you are making the capital gain election, subtract the amount in box 3 from the amount in box 2a. Divide the result by your percentage of distribution in box 9a. Enter the result on Form 4972, line 8.

- Divide the amount in box 8 by the percentage in box 8. Enter the result on Form 4972, line 11. Then, skip Step 3 and go to Step 4.

Step 3. Use this step only if you elect to include NUA in your taxable income.

- If you are not making the capital gain election, add the amount in box 2a to the amount in box 6. Divide the result by your percentage of distribution in box 9a. Enter the result on Form 4972, line 8.

- If you are making the capital gain election, subtract the amount in box 3 from the amount in box 2a. Add to the result the amount from line F of your NUA Worksheet. Then, divide the total by your percentage of distribution in box 9a. Enter the result on Form 4972, line 8.

- Divide the amount in box 8 by the percentage in box 8. Enter the result on Form 4972, line 11.

Step 4. Complete Form 4972 through line 28.

Step 5. Complete the following worksheet to figure the entry for Form 4972, line 29:

A. Subtract line 28 from line 25 . _____

B. Enter your percentage of the distribution from box 9a . _____

C. Multiply line A by line B. Enter here and on Form 4972, line 29. Also, write "MRD" on the dotted line next to line 29 . _____

NUA Worksheet (keep for your records)

A. Enter the amount from Form 1099-R, box 3 . . . . **A.** _____

B. Enter the amount from Form 1099-R, box 2a . . . . **B.** _____

C. Divide line A by line B and enter the result as a decimal (rounded to at least three places) . . . . **C.** __._____

D. Enter the amount from Form 1099-R, box 6 . . . . **D.** _____

E. Capital gain portion of NUA. Multiply line C by line D . . . . . **E.** _____

F. Ordinary income portion of NUA. Subtract line E from line D . . . **F.** _____

G. Total capital gain portion of distribution. Add lines A and E. Enter here and on Form 4972, line 6. On the dotted line next to line 6, write "NUA" and the amount from line E above. . . . . **G.** _____

Death Benefit Worksheet (keep for your records)

A. Enter the amount from Form 1099-R, box 3, or, if you are including NUA in taxable income, the amount from line G of the NUA Worksheet **A.** _____

B. Enter the amount from Form 1099-R, box 2a, plus, if you are including NUA in taxable income, the amount from Form 1099-R, box 6 . . **B.** _____

C. Divide line A by line B and enter the result as a decimal (rounded to at least three places) . . . . **C.** __._____

D. Enter your share of the death benefit exclusion* . . . . . . **D.** _____

E. Multiply line D by line C . . . . **E.** _____

F. Subtract line E from line A. Enter here and on Form 4972, line 6 . . **F.** _____

*Applies only for participants who died before August 21, 1996. If there are multiple recipients of the distribution, the allowable death benefit exclusion must be allocated among the recipients in the same proportion that they share the distribution.

A2.5

Part II

See *Capital Gain Election* on page 3 before completing Part II.

Line 6. Leave this line blank if your distribution does not include a captial gain amount or you are not making the 20% capital gain election, and go to Part III.

Generally, enter on line 6 the amount from Form 1099-R, box 3. However, if you elect to include NUA in your taxable income, use the NUA Worksheet on page 3 to figure the amount to enter. If you are taking a death benefit exclusion (for a participant who died before August 21, 1996), use the Death Benefit Worksheet on page 3 to figure the amount to enter on line 6. The remaining allowable death benefit exclusion should be entered on line 9 if you choose the 10-year tax option.

If any federal estate tax was paid on the lump-sum distribution, you must decrease the capital gain amount by the amount of estate tax applicable to it. To figure this amount, you must complete line C of the Death Benefit Worksheet on page 3, even if you do not take the death benefit exclusion. Multiply the total federal estate tax paid on the lump-sum distribution by the decimal on line C of the Death Benefit Worksheet. The result is the portion of the federal estate tax applicable to the capital gain amount. Then, use that result to reduce the amount in Form 1099-R, box 3, if you do not take the death benefit exclusion, or reduce line F of the Death Benefit Worksheet if you do. Enter the remaining capital gain on line 6. If you elected to include NUA in taxable income, subtract the portion of federal estate tax applicable to the capital gain amount from the amount on line G of the NUA Worksheet. Enter the result on line 6. Enter the remainder of the federal estate tax on line 18.

 If you take the death benefit exclusion and federal estate tax was paid on the capital gain amount, the capital gain amount must be reduced by both the procedures discussed above to figure the correct entry for line 6.

Part III

Line 8. If Form 1099-R, box 2a, is blank, you must first figure the taxable amount. For details on how to do this, see Pub. 575.

If you made the 20% capital gain election, enter only the ordinary income portion of the distribution on this line. The ordinary income portion is the amount from Form 1099-R, box 2a, minus the amount from box 3 of that form. Add the amount from line F of the NUA Worksheet if you included NUA capital gain in the 20% capital gain election.

If you did not make the 20% capital gain election and did not elect to include NUA in taxable income, enter the amount from Form 1099-R, box 2a. If you did not make the 20% capital gain election but did elect to include NUA in your taxable income, add the amount from Form 1099-R, box 2a, to the amount from Form 1099-R, box 6. Enter the total on line 8. On the dotted line next to line 8, write "NUA" and the amount of NUA included.

 Community property laws do not apply in figuring tax on the amount you report on line 8.

Line 9. If you received the distribution because of the plan participant's death and the participant died before August 21, 1996, you may be able to exclude up to $5,000 of the lump sum from your gross income. If there are multiple recipients of the distribution not all of whom are trusts, enter on line 9 the full remaining allowable death benefit exclusion (after the amount taken against the capital gain portion of the distribution by all recipients—see the instructions for line 6) without allocation among the recipients. (The exclusion is in effect allocated among the recipients through the computation under *Multiple recipients of a lump-sum distribution* on page 3.) This exclusion applies to the beneficiaries or estates of common-law employees, self-employed individuals, and shareholder-employees who owned more than 2% of the stock of an S corporation. Pub. 939 gives more information about the death benefit exclusion.

Enter the allowable death benefit exclusion on line 9. But see the instructions for line 6 if you made a capital gain election.

Line 18. A beneficiary who receives a lump-sum distribution because of a plan participant's death must reduce the taxable part of the distribution by any federal estate tax paid on the lump-sum distribution. Do this by entering on line 18 the federal estate tax attributable to the lump-sum distribution. Also see the instructions for line 6.

Lines 24 and 27. Use the following Tax Rate Schedule to complete lines 24 and 27.

Tax Rate Schedule

If the amount on line 23 or 26 is:		Enter on line 24 or 27:	Of the amount over—
Over	But not over—		
$ 0	$1,190	- - - - - 11%	$ 0
1,190	2,270	$130.90 + 12%	1,190
2,270	4,530	260.50 + 14%	2,270
4,530	6,690	576.90 + 15%	4,530
6,690	9,170	900.90 + 16%	6,690
9,170	11,440	1,297.70 + 18%	9,170
11,440	13,710	1,706.30 + 20%	11,440
13,710	17,160	2,160.30 + 23%	13,710
17,160	22,880	2,953.80 + 26%	17,160
22,880	28,600	4,441.00 + 30%	22,880
28,600	34,320	6,157.00 + 34%	28,600
34,320	42,300	8,101.80 + 38%	34,320
42,300	57,190	11,134.20 + 42%	42,300
57,190	85,790	17,388.00 + 48%	57,190
85,790	- - - - -	31,116.00 + 50%	85,790

Paperwork Reduction Act Notice. We ask for the information on this form to carry out the Internal Revenue laws of the United States. You are required to give us the information. We need it to ensure that you are complying with these laws and to allow us to figure and collect the right amount of tax.

You are not required to provide the information requested on a form that is subject to the Paperwork Reduction Act unless the form displays a valid OMB control number. Books or records relating to a form or its instructions must be retained as long as their contents may become material in the administration of any Internal Revenue law. Generally, tax returns and return information are confidential, as required by section 6103.

The time needed to complete this form will vary depending on individual circumstances. The estimated average time is:

Recordkeeping . . . . 52 min

Learning about the law or the form . . . . 19 min

Preparing the form . . . 1 hr., 11 min

Copying, assembling, and sending the form to the IRS . . 20 min

If you have comments concerning the accuracy of these time estimates or suggestions for making this form simpler, we would be happy to hear from you. See the instructions for the tax return with which this form is filed.

Upon Death or Incapacity Letter

To My Family and Executors:

This is my Upon Death or Incapacity Letter containing information you will need after I am gone. This is not a legal document. It is intended to provide you with the information you will need in order to save you time and effort finding the information without guidance.

Name _____

To Do First

1. Call_____to help.
    (relative/friend)   (phone)

2. Notify my employer at_____
                              (phone)

3. Make funeral arrangements with _____

4. Ask for at least 10 copies of the death certificate from the funeral director.

5. Call my lawyer _____
                        (name)   (phone)

6. Notify local Social Security office.

7. Obtain and process my insurance policies.

8. Contact my bank(s) _____

Beneficiaries' Expectancies

From my employer _____
                    (person/department to contact)   (phone)

_____
(life insurance)   (profit sharing)

_____
(accident insurance)   (pension plan)

_____
(other benefits)
From insurance companies _____
                            (total amount)
From Social Security _____
                        (lump sum plus monthly benefits)
From the Veterans' Administration _____
                                    (inform VA)
From other sources _____

Social Security

Name _____ Card Number _____

Location of card _____
File a claim immediately to avoid possibility of losing any benefit checks. Call local Social Security office for appointment _____ .
                              (phone)
Expect a lump sum of about $_____, plus continuing benefits for children under 18, or until 22 for full-time students.

Personal Computer

Location _____
Password _____
E-mail address(es) _____
_____
List of important documents stored on computer _____
(with file name/title of each document)

Location of Personal Papers

Last will and testament _____
Birth certificate _____
Marriage certificate _____
Military records _____
Naturalization papers _____
Other _____

Safe Deposit Box

Bank _____
Address _____
Under the name of _____ Phone _____
Location of key _____
Contents _____

Post Office Box

Address _____
Owner(s) _____ Number _____
Location of key/combination _____

Checking Accounts

Bank _____

Address _____

Name(s) on account _____

Account number _____

Type of account _____

Online account user name _____

Online account password _____

Location canceled checks/statements _____

(Note: Repeat for each account)

Savings Accounts/Certificates

Bank _____

Address _____

Name(s) on account _____

Account number _____

Type of account _____

Location passbook/certificate receipt _____

Online account user name _____

Online account password _____

Special instructions _____

(Note: Repeat for each account)

Doctors' Names/Addresses

Doctor(s) _____
          (name, address, phone)

_____

_____

_____

_____

Dentist(s) _____

_____

Credit Cards

(Note: All credit cards in my name should be canceled)

Company_____
               (name)   (phone)
Address _____
Name on card _____
Location of card _____
Credit card company's phone number _____
Online account user name_____
Online account password _____
Company_____
               (name)   (phone)
Address _____
Name on card _____
Location of card _____
Credit card company's phone number _____
Online account user name_____
Online account password _____
(Note: Repeat for each card)

Non-Mortgage Loans Outstanding

Bank _____
Address _____
Name on loan _____
Account number _____Collateral, if any _____
Location of papers_____
Life insurance on loan: Yes_____   No_____
(Note: Repeat for each loan)

Debts Owed to Me

Debtor _____
Description _____
Terms _____
Balance _____
Location of documents _____
(Note: Repeat for each debt)

Car

Year, make, model _____

Body type_____Cylinders_____Color_____

Identification number _____
                          (title, registration)

Location of car keys _____

Income Tax Returns

Location of previous returns—federal, state, local_____

_____

Tax preparer _____
                    (name, address, phone)

Determine whether quarterly taxes are due

Investments

Stocks

Company_____

Name on certificate(s)_____

Number of shares _____

Certificate number(s) _____

Purchase price and date_____

Location of certificates _____

(Note: Repeat for each investment)

Bonds/Notes/Bills

Issuer_____

Issued to _____
              (owner)

Face amount $_____Bond number_____

Purchase price and date _____

Maturity date_____

Location of certificates _____

Mutual Funds

Company_____
Name on Account _____
Number of shares or units_____
Location of statement(s), certificate(s) _____

Online Accounts

Brokerage _____
User name _____
Password_____
(Note: Repeat for each account)

Funeral and Burial

(Note: There may be a separate Funeral and Burial Letter for important preferences)

Cemetery Plot

Location _____
Purchase date_____Deed number_____
Location of deed _____
Other information _____
                    (perpetual care, etc.)

Facts for Funeral Director
(Note: Bring this with you; also bring cemetery deed, if possible)

My full name_____
Residence_____Phone _____
Marital status_____Spouse_____
Date of birth_____Birthplace _____
Father's name/birthplace_____
Mother's maiden name _____
Length of residence in state_____In U.S._____
Military service   Yes_____   No_____When_____
(Note: Bring veterans' discharge papers if possible)
Social Security number_____Occupation_____
Burial insurance (bring policy if proceeds will be used for funeral expenses)_____

_____
(company name and policy numbers)

Life Insurance

Location of all policies _____

Policy _____ Whose life is insured _____
     (amount)

Insurance company _____

Company address _____

Type of policy_____ Policy number_____

Beneficiaries _____

Issue date _____ Maturity date_____

Payout method _____

Other options on payout _____

Other options on payout _____

Other special facts_____
(Note: Repeat information for each policy)

For $_____in veterans' insurance call local Veterans' Administration office at phone
_____

Other Insurance

Accident

Company_____ Agent_____

Address _____

Policy number_____ Coverage_____

Beneficiaries _____

Location of policy_____

Car, Home, Household

Coverage_____

Company_____ Policy Number _____

Address _____

Location of policy_____

Term (when to renew) _____ Agent_____
(Note: Repeat for each policy)

Medical

Company_____Coverage _____
Address _____
Policy number _____Agent_____
Location of policy_____
Through employer or other group_____
(Note: Repeat for all medical insurance policies)

House, Condo, or Co-op

In whose name _____
Address _____
Lot_____Block_____on map called _____
Location of statement of closing, policy of title insurance, deed, land survey, etc._____

_____
Location of house keys _____

Mortgage

Bank held by_____
Amount owed $ _____Method of payment _____
Location of payment book/payment statements _____
Life insurance on mortgage   Yes_____Policy # _____No _____
Notify bank of my death-unpaid amount will be paid by insurance.

House Taxes

Amount $ _____

Purchase Price of House

Amount $ _____

Itemized House Improvements

Improvement_____Cost_____Date _____

Improvement_____Cost_____Date _____

Improvement_____Cost_____Date _____

Location of bills _____

If Renting   Yes_____   No_____

Location of lease_____Expires _____
                                                                                        (date)

Household Contents

Name of owners _____

Form of ownership _____

Location of documents _____

Location of inventory _____

Important Warranties/Receipts

Item_____

Location of warranty/receipt_____

Additional Information/Wishes

_____

_____

_____

Dated _____Signed _____

Glossary

account plan method of calculation • under the minimum distribution rules, the account plan rules govern the minimum distribution calculation for all account-type plans except when a commercial annuity is purchased

accumulation value • the annuity value before any surrender charges

active life expectancy • the number of years a person can expect to live without a disability

active participant • an individual who is deemed to participate in an employer's retirement plan—but nonqualified plans are not counted. Active participant status affects the individual's ability to receive a deduction for contributions to an IRA.

activities of daily living (ADLs) • the criteria used to establish benefit eligibility under a long-term care contract—in other words, the telling signs of the need for nursing home care. They include eating, bathing, dressing, transferring from bed to chair, using the toilet, and maintaining continence.

actuarial equivalent • the value of different benefit options is altered to accommodate the uniqueness of the benefit form. This means that if, for example, the participant chooses a lump-sum benefit, the amount of the lump sum is based on the single sum value of a life annuity using the actuarial assumptions prescribed by the plan.

adjusted basis • typically starts with a home's purchase price, but includes certain settlement or closing costs, such as attorney's fees, title insurance, recording fees, and transfer taxes

adult day care • day care provided at centers specifically designed for seniors who live at home but whose families are not available to stay at home for the day. All offer social activities; some also provide health and rehabilitation services.

advance directive • a document that combines the features of a living will and a health-care power of attorney. Some states have a specific advance directive form.

affiliated service group rules • rules requiring aggregation of multiple companies for discrimination testing of qualified plans when related businesses work together to provide goods or services to the public

Age Discrimination and Employment Act (ADEA) • makes it illegal to discriminate against workers over 40 based on age

age-restricted housing • The Fair Housing Act allows communities to have age restrictions for residents as long as the restrictions conform with either an age 62 restriction or an age 55 restriction

AIME • *See* average indexed monthly earnings.

AIR • *See* assumed investment return.

ALE • *See* applicable life expectancies.

allocation formula • a profit-sharing plan formula that allows the employer to make discretionary contributions, which must contain a definitely determinable allocation formula. This formula determines how the contribution is allocated among the plan's participants.

amount of benefit • for minimum distribution calculations, the benefit amount of an IRA is the value of the benefit as of the last day of the year prior to the year for which the minimum distribution is being calculated

amount realized • typically the selling price minus selling expenses

AMR • *See* arithmetic mean return.

annual contract charge • an annual fee charged against the account value of fixed-interest annuities and variable annuities

annual reset indexed annuity • compares the positive change in the index from the beginning of the policy year to the end of the policy year. It provides incremental protection on the growth by locking in the previous year's anniversary value.

annuitant • the person whose life is the measuring life for an annuity

annuitization • the process by which a deferred annuity is transformed into a guaranteed payout stream (for example, a life income with 10 years period certain). However, the amount of the income payments is not guaranteed with variable income annuities.

annuity • the annual payment of an allowance or income for a lifetime or a specified number of years

annuity certain or term certain • an annuity payout over a specified period of time—for example, 20 years

annuity/LTCI combination • a relatively new product that combines asset protection with asset preservation by creating two products within one contract—one to create an annuity account and one to address long-term care insurance needs

annuity method of calculation • under the minimum distribution rules, an annuity benefit payable from a defined-benefit plan or a commercial annuity purchased in any account-type plan must satisfy the annuity method of calculating the required minimum distribution

annuity unit • a measure for valuing a variable annuity during its liquidation stage. The dollar value of each unit fluctuates with the investment performance of the separate account underlying the annuity.

applicable distribution period • when calculating required minimum distributions, planners will use the appropriate period from the Uniform Lifetime Table

applicable life expectancies • the minimum distribution calculation under the minimum distribution rules is based on the life expectancies of the participant and a chosen beneficiary. The ages used are generally based on the ages of those individuals as of the last day of the year for which the minimum distribution is calculated.

arithmetic mean return (AMR) • the average return found by dividing the sum of the separate per-period returns by the number of periods over which they were earned

asset allocation • process of setting the portfolio proportions for major asset categories

asset fee • the amount assessed by an insurance company on indexed annuities. The fee is applied against the growth in the index and reduces the amount of interest the insurer credits to the annuity.

assumed investment return (AIR) • the return that the investment portfolio must earn on a variable annuity in order for benefit payments to remain level

average indexed monthly earnings (AIME) • an individual's wage history (capped at the taxable wage base and indexed for inflation) is averaged and the resulting average indexed monthly earnings are used to generate a person's primary insurance amount under Social Security

baby boomer • an individual born between 1946 and 1964

back-end load • a sales charge at the time of a withdrawal from a variable deferred annuity as a percentage of the amount withdrawn. *Also known as* a surrender charge or contingent deferred sales charge.

basis • a complex term that refers to the amount of capital invested by the taxpayer plus any adjustments made under tax law. In theory, a taxpayer should pay taxes on gain only when property is sold at an amount in excess of basis. When it comes to the sale of a home, basis includes the purchase price (including adjustments from prior rollovers) and the cost of capital improvements made to the house. The cost of repairs and home maintenance is not included in basis.

beneficiary • the person who normally inherits the annuity proceeds at the death of the annuitant

benefit carve-out plan • a way for an employer to provide retiree health care benefits. This plan is designed around the same benefit program that applies to active employees.

benefit period • under the Medicare system, a benefit period begins the first time a Medicare recipient is hospitalized and ends only after the recipient has been out of the hospital or skilled-nursing facility for 60 consecutive days. There is no limit on the number of benefit periods a person may have during his or her lifetime, but Medicare coverage is limited to 90 days in each benefit period.

benefit statement • a statement provided to plan participants notifying them of the dollar value of their benefits

beta • a measure of the systematic risk of an asset or portfolio. Beta can be represented as either the mathematical ratio of the asset's covariance with the market divided by the variance of the market or as the slope of a regression line that relates the return of the asset to the return on the market.

bond default premium • the additional return received for the additional risk of investing in corporate bonds rather than government bonds of equal maturity

bond maturity premium • the additional return received for the interest-rate risk incurred by investing in long-term government bonds rather than Treasury bills

bonus interest rate • extra amount of interest granted to new purchasers of fixed-interest deferred annuities that is paid in addition to the normal stated interest rate

"bottom-up" analysis • investment approach concentrating on the individual company's characteristics, with less emphasis on economic/market and industry/sector factors

break-even holding period • the amount of time that would have to lapse before one would be indifferent between saving in a nonqualified account and saving in an IRA account

break-even life expectancies • the point at which it is economically desirable to take full Social Security benefits at normal retirement age rather than reduced benefits at early retirement age

capital asset pricing model (CAPM) • an extension of portfolio theory that contends that in an efficient market, investors should be compensated for incurring systematic risk, measured as beta, but not for incurring unsystematic risk because unsystematic risk can be eliminated through diversification

capital-gain provision • a special grandfather rule that applies to lump-sum distributions from qualified plans in the case of an individual born before 1936. The rule provides for a special 20 percent tax rate for the portion of the lump-sum distribution attributable to pre-1974 plan participation.

capital market line (CML) • the line formed by combinations of the risk-free asset and the market portfolio

capital preservation model • a capital needs analysis method that assumes that, at life expectancy, the client has exactly the same account balance as he or she did at retirement

cap rate • the upper limit on the amount of interest the annuity can earn

cash balance pension plan • a defined-benefit retirement plan characterized by an annual contribution made by the employer for each enrolled employee. Once deposited, funds accrue interest.

cash or deferred arrangement (CODA) • a qualified plan, usually part of a profit-sharing or stock bonus plan, that gives an employee the option to contribute some of his or her salary to the plan. A 401(k) plan is one example.

cash-out provision • a retirement plan provision that allows for the payment of a single-sum distribution upon termination of employment that occurs prior to attainment of normal retirement age, death, or disability

cemetery trust • used to fund preneeded cemetery arrangements. *See also* endowment care cemetery trust, service and merchandise cemetery trust

COBRA • the Consolidated Omnibus Budget Reconciliation Act of 1985, which established health insurance continuation for employees changing jobs or retiring

CODA • *See* cash or deferred arrangement.

Code Sec. 401(a)(4) • mandates that qualified plans cannot discriminate in favor of highly compensated employees

COLA • *See* cost of living adjustment.

conduit IRA • an IRA that is created solely with a rollover distribution from a qualified plan. If no other amounts are contributed, amounts can be rolled back from the conduit IRA to a qualified plan at a later date.

conservatorship • a court-appointed and supervised party that is used when neither a will nor a revocable trust document is present

constant relative risk aversion • the assumption that a person has the same risk tolerance despite the amount of wealth that he or she currently has

continuity theory • stresses the persistence of personal identity through the expansion of other roles. People who experience this will have an easier time adjusting to retirement.

contrarian investing • investment approach in which the investor identifies a widely accepted view and then invests as if that view were incorrect

controlled group rules • rules requiring aggregation of multiple employers for discrimination testing of qualified plans when there is a sufficient amount of common ownership

coordination plan • a way for an employer to provide retiree health care benefits. This plan factors in the amount the insurer would make after applying the deductible and coinsurance payments and then may reduce that amount so that the plan payments plus Medicare payments are equal to total expenses.

cost of living adjustment (COLA) • generally speaking, an increase in a payment stream typically based on the consumer price index (CPI). Under Social Security, it refers to an increase in the CPI for the one-year period ending in the third quarter of the prior year. This is the amount by which Social Security benefits are typically increased to keep pace with inflation.

covariance • a measure of the degree to which random variables move in a systematic way relative to each other, either directly or inversely. In portfolio theory, reduction of risk is achieved more rapidly by combining assets that have small or even negative covariances with each other.

Coverdell Education Savings Account (CESA) • a trust set up specifically for the purpose of paying the qualified education expenses of the designated child beneficiary of the account

crisis theory • views the occupational role as the major source of personal validation. People who experience this will have a difficult time adjusting to retirement.

current assets future value factor • a factor that is determined by looking at the assumed rate of return on investments prior to retirement and the number of years until retirement

decline in purchasing power (DIPP) • assets that are not indexed for inflation will have a diminishing ability to buy goods and services over time. The DIPP fund is the amount saved to prevent this decline from happening.

deferred annuity • an annuity contract that starts payment in the future beyond the first contract year

defined-benefit pension plan • a category of qualified retirement plan that specifies a stated benefit to which eligible participants are entitled. The employer is responsible for making contributions in amounts sufficient to pay promised benefits.

defined-benefit present value factor • determined by looking at the assumed rate of return on investments after retirement and the expected duration of retirement

defined-contribution plan • a retirement plan in which employer contributions are allocated to participants' accounts. The participant's benefit is based on the account balance, which consists of the employer's contributions and investment experience.

DIPP • *See* decline in purchasing power.

direct rollover • a distribution from a qualified plan that is transferred, at the request of the participant, directly to an IRA or other qualified plan

disability insured • at a minimum, disability-insured status requires that a worker (1) be fully insured and (2) have a minimum amount of work under Social Security within a recent time period.

distribution year • under the minimum distribution rules, a minimum distribution must generally be made for the calendar year in which a participant attains age 70 1/2 and for each subsequent year. Each year for which a distribution must be made is referred to as a distribution year.

diversifiable risk • *See* unsystematic risk.

diversification • spreading one's portfolio funds among many different assets in many different categories to reduce risk

dollar-cost averaging • process of adding a specified amount to the portfolio on a regular basis, regardless of whether the portfolio value is tending up or down; results in a lower average price per share since more shares are purchased when prices are low and fewer shares are purchased when prices are high

domicile • the intended permanent home of a client. Important for state estate tax purposes, it is determined by such factors as where the person spends the majority of his or her time, where he or she is registered to vote, the state his or her driver's license is from, and where his or her will is executed.

do-not-resuscitate order • a document signed by a patient authorizing health-care providers to withhold measures to restart the heart or breathing

downsize • to sell a home and move to a less expensive abode to free up assets for retirement

early-distribution penalty tax • *See* Sec. 72(t) penalty tax.

early retirement reduction • regarding Social Security retirement benefits, a reduction of 5/9 of one percent per month prior to the employee's normal retirement age

Earnings and Benefit Estimate Statement • an annual statement sent by the Social Security Administration to workers over 25 (who are not currently receiving benefits) concerning their Social Security benefit

earnings test • a restriction in Social Security pay status applied to people who earn over a threshold amount. These people will "lose" some of their Social Security benefit.

echo boomer • an individual born between 1977 and 1994

efficient frontier • a set of portfolios, each of which offers the highest expected return for a given risk and the smallest risk for a given expected return

efficient market hypothesis • the theory that new information is quickly incorporated into security prices

eldercare locator • allows clients, caregivers, and planners to call a toll-free number and speak with people who can facilitate help with eldercare issues

elderly dependency ratio • the number of persons 65 or older per 100 persons of working age

eligible rollover distribution • the term used to describe a distribution from a qualified plan that qualifies for rollover treatment

employee stock ownership plan (ESOP) • a qualified plan that is categorized as a defined-contribution plan. The plan must invest primarily in securities of the sponsoring employer.

endowment care cemetery trust • pools individual grantors' contributions to provide for ongoing maintenance of cemetery and gravesite grounds

equity risk premium • the additional return received for the additional risk of investing in common stocks (as represented by the Standard & Poor's 500 index) instead of investing in Treasury bills

ERISA Sec. 404 (c) • grants fiduciary relief in the case of a participant exercising independent investment discretion over his or her own account

ESOP • *See* employee stock ownership plan.

exclusion plan • a way for an employer to provide retiree health care benefits. This approach pays benefits based only on the portion that Medicare does not cover.

exclusion ratio • the ratio or percentage applied to an immediate annuity payment to determine how much of the payment is excluded from income taxation

executive bonus life insurance plan (Sec. 162 plan) • employer pays a bonus to the executive for the purpose of purchasing cash value life insurance

expected return • a factor in the calculation of the exclusion ratio for immediate annuities. The expected return is the total amount of payments the policyowner can expect to receive from the immediate annuity. The total investment is divided by the expected return to produce the exclusion ratio.

expense method • to measure a person's financial need by using a retirement budget

extensive contract • a life lease contract that pays in advance for unlimited nursing home care at little or no increase in monthly payments

family limited liability company (FLLC) • *See* family limited partnership.

family limited partnership (FLP) • adding to the estate reduction benefits of gifting is the possibility of leveraging the gifts FLPs allows individuals to retain control and achieve leveraging by transferring gifts that can be discounted upon transfer. In return for the contributed property, the limited partnership provides interests or units.

family maximum • the maximum benefits that are paid out under the Social Security system when different types of benefits are paid to two or more members of a family

FASB 106 • an accounting rule that requires employers to put future liabilities for retiree health care benefits on their current books

fee-for-service contract • a life lease contract that covers only emergency and short-term nursing home care in the basic agreement. It typically, however, provides guaranteed space for long-term care on a per diem basis.

FICA tax • Federal Insurance Contributions Act (Social Security tax). A 1.45 percent rate is applied for all income for Medicare and 6.2 percent rate is applied for the taxable wage base for old age, survivors, and disability benefits.

first-death reduction joint and survivor annuity • an annuity in which payments are reduced at the first death, regardless of whether the participant or the beneficiary dies first

first distribution year • the first year for which a distribution must be made under the minimum distribution rules. Generally a minimum distribution must be made for the year in which the participant attains age 70 1/2, even if the required beginning date is the following April 1.

fiscal welfare • an indirect payment made to an individual through the tax system

fixed-amount annuity • annuity in which the purchaser pays a premium and selects the periodic payment amount the insurance company is to pay

fixed-interest annuity • the simplest type of deferred annuity, which offers a guaranteed interest rate for a certain period of time

fixed-period annuity • annuity in which the purchaser pays a premium and selects the period of time the insurance company is to make periodic payments

flexible-premium annuity • an annuity that allows additional contributions (beyond the initial contribution) at the time by the policyowner

FLLC • *See* family limited liability company.

FLP • *See* family limited partnership.

Form SSA-7004 • a request for earnings and benefit estimate statement from the Social Security administration

401(k) plan • a profit-sharing-type plan that allows employees to make salary-deferral-type contributions on a pretax basis

403(b) plan • a tax-sheltered annuity program with similar tax advantages to those of qualified plans but that can be sponsored only by a tax-exempt organization or public school. The plan is similar to a 401(k) plan in that participants may make pretax contributions through salary deferral elections and the employer may make contributions on a discretionary basis.

free-corridor amount • a maximum amount of money that a contract owner can withdraw from the contract each year before the end of the surrender charge period without incurring a surrender charge

free-window period • the period at the end of an annuity contract term during which there are several options open to the owner of the annuity

front-end load • a percentage taken from money coming into the contract as a charge for entering into the contract

full cash refund feature • a feature of an annuity in which a specified refund payment is made if the stream of annuity payments is less than a specified dollar amount

full retirement age • the age at which full Social Security benefits are paid

fully insured • term used under Social Security to refer to a type of eligibility status. To be fully insured, an individual generally needs to complete 40 quarters of coverage.

fundamental analysis • process of identifying investments that will have high risk-adjusted returns by evaluating their underlying economic factors

fund expense • an asset-based fee for management operations of the various subaccounts

funeral trust • separate funds set aside to pay for final expenses

general account • the investment option in a variable annuity that guarantees the owner's principal and a stated level of interest earnings. It can also be referred to as the guaranteed account.

geometric mean return (GMR) • the effective annual rate of return over multiple time periods, computed as $GMR = [(1 + PRR_1)(1 + PRR_2)\ldots(1 + PRR_n)]^{1/N} - 1$

geriatric care manager • a social service professional with expertise in devising, monitoring, and coordinating care plans for seniors

golden handshake • an incentive offer by an employer made to an employee to encourage early retirement

growth rate • *See* step-up rate.

guaranteed minimum accumulation benefit • a benefit available in variable deferred annuities that guarantees that the value of the annuity can be stepped up to a certain amount on a specified date, whether or not the contract owner annuitizes

guaranteed minimum income benefit • a benefit offered in variable deferred annuities that increases the owner's investment by some compounded percentage—typically between 3 and 6 percent. At the end of a specified period, the increased amount may be used to turn the contract into an immediate annuity.

guaranteed minimum interest rate • the lowest interest rate established in a deferred annuity that the insurance company promises it will always pay. Traditionally, 3 percent has been the guaranteed minimum interest rate, but recently, states are lowering this amount due to the prolonged time frame of low interest rates during which insurance companies have been operating.

guaranteed minimum return of premium benefit • a benefit offered in variable deferred annuities that guarantees that the owner may take back the premium after a specified number of years if the investment is more than the account value

guaranteed renewable • in a long-term care contract, a provision that allows an insurance company to revise premiums on a class basis

health-care power of attorney • a document in which an individual names someone (an agent) to make health-care decisions if the individual is unable to do so

high-water mark indexed annuity • an indexed annuity that uses a crediting method in which the growth in the index is credited by comparing the index point at the end of each policy year to the last highest anniversary point within each contract term. If the current point is higher, then interest is credited from the last highest point to the current point.

Home Equity Conversion Mortgage • a reverse annuity mortgage program sponsored by the federal government

hospice • a facility for treating the terminally ill. Medicare does, however, provide hospice care benefits for a person at home

hospice benefits • benefits paid under Part A of Medicare for terminally ill persons who have a life expectancy of 6 months or less. Benefits can be provided at a hospice or for patients in their own homes.

human capital • refers to a person's ability to generate income

immediate annuity • an annuity contract with an immediate payout or one with payments that begin within one year of the contract date

incentive stock options (ISOs) • options to purchase shares of company stock at a stated price over a limited period of time. Different from nonqualified stock options in that the rules governing ISOs are quite strict and the tax treatment is more favorable to the executive.

incentive trust • a trust designed to establish and further long-lasting family objectives. *Also known as* legacy trust, family goals trust, character trust, and financial incentive trust.

income requirement assumption • represents the planner's estimation of the level of income needed by retirees to sustain the standard of living they enjoyed just prior to retirement through their retired life

independence • in portfolio theory, refers to the absence of any relationship between the historical (or projected) periodic returns of two assets. Such assets would have no covariance with each other.

Index of Leading Economic Indicators • set of 11 economic statutes that the government uses to forecast economic activity

indexed annuity • ties the earnings in the annuity to an outside index. An indexed annuity has more growth potential than a fixed annuity.

individual retirement account (IRA) • a retirement plan established by an individual that receives special tax treatment

inflation bias • tendency to overstate the degree to which one has a favorable personality trait

in-service distributions • distributions from a qualified plan to a participant payable for any reason prior to termination from service

installment payout • participants in a plan elect a payout length and, based on earnings assumptions, a payout amount will also be determined

instrumental activities of daily living (IADLs) • abilities that include performing light housework, preparing meals, grocery shopping, using the telephone, using transportation, keeping track of money or bills, and managing medicines

intentionally defective trust • an irrevocable arrangement under which a defective trust is drafted so that the grantor or an independent trustee retains certain powers over the trust that cause the trust to be taxable to the grantor

interest rate guarantee period • the amount of time the interest rate is guaranteed in a deferred annuity. It is often tied to the length of the annuity's surrender charge period.

involuntary cashout • when a participant terminates employment with a vested benefit of less than $5,000, the plan can provide that such small benefits will be cashed out in a lump sum

IRC Sec. 121 • the provisions for the exclusion of gain on the sale of a personal residence

irrevocable grandparent-grandchild insurance trust • a way to reduce the estate in which the grandparent funds a trust that allows, but does not direct, the trustee to purchase life insurance on the adult child's life, with the beneficiary of the trust being one or more grandchildren

IRS Form 1099R • the tax form that reports a payment from a qualified plan, IRA, SEP, or 403(b) plan to both the IRS and the participant

ISO • *See* incentive stock options.

joint and survivor annuity • provides monthly payments to the participant during his or her lifetime, and after his/her death provides a benefit to the survivor (if still alive)

joint and survivor annuity with pop-up feature • in contrast to the conventional joint and survivor annuity, if the beneficiary dies before the participant, the monthly benefit pops up to what it would have been had the participant chosen a single-life annuity rather than the joint and survivor annuity

joint and survivor life annuity • a type of immediate annuity payout in which the policyowner and another person chosen by the policyowner are the measuring lives over which the annuity payments are made. The annuity payments will continue in full or in a reduced amount as specified in the contract upon the death of the first annuitant and will cease upon the death of the second annuitant.

joint and survivor life annuity with installment or cash refund • a type of immediate annuity payout in which the policyowner and another person chosen by the policyowner are the measuring lives over which the annuity payments are made. Under the installment refund option, the insurance company will refund the remaining balance of the deposit by continuing payments to the named beneficiary after the second annuitant's death until the full deposit is returned. Under the cash refund option, the insurer will refund the discounted present value of the remaining payments in a lump sum.

joint and survivor life annuity with period certain • a type of immediate annuity payout in which the policyowner and another person chosen by the policyowner are the measuring lives over which the annuity payments are made. The annuity payments will continue until the death of the last annuitant, with a minimum payment period—generally 5, 10, 15, 20, 25, or 30 years.

Keogh plan • a qualified retirement plan sponsored by a partnership or self-employed individual

LCI • *See* life-cycle investing.

legacy or ethical will • a document that conveys personal values, traditions, and/or experiences to following generations

lentigo • discoloration that occurs on the face, backs of hands, and forearms of people over 50

life annuity • *See* life-only annuity.

life annuity with cash refund • a type of immediate annuity in which the insurance company will pay the policyowner payments for the entire life of the annuitant. In the event the policyowner dies before receiving back in payments the amount of premium paid, the insurance company will pay the difference between the dollar amount of the original premium and the total payments paid prior to death in a lump-sum payment to the beneficiary.

life annuity with guaranteed payments • an annuity that pays benefits over the longer of the participant's lifetime or a specified time period

life annuity with installment refund • a type of immediate annuity in which the insurance company will pay the policyowner payments for the entire life of the annuitant. In the event the policyowner dies before receiving back in payments the dollar amount of the premium originally paid, the insurance company will continue payments to the named beneficiary until the dollar amount of the original premium has been paid.

life annuity with period certain • a type of immediate annuity in which the insurance company will pay the policyowner payments for the entire life of the annuitant. In the event the annuitant dies before the end of a specified period (5, 10, 15, 20, 25, or 30 years) beginning with the issuance of the policy, the insurance company will continue payments to the named beneficiary for the rest of that period.

life-care community • sometimes called continuing-care retirement communities. These are villages that provide housing and services (including long-term care) to retired parties in exchange for up-front and monthly fees.

life-cycle investing (LCI) • process of tailoring the investment portfolio to fit the individual's phase in the life cycle

life-lease contract • sometimes called a residential-care agreement, this is the contract issued by a life-care community. These contracts generally guarantee living space, services, and the availability of lifetime health care.

life-only annuity • a stream of payments over the life of the participant

life settlement • selling an existing (and often unwanted) life insurance policy to a licensed third party

life span • the maximum potential age of human beings (somewhere around 120 years)

lifetime reserve days • Medicare coverage is provided for up to 90 days in each benefit period. Medicare recipients, however, are given 60 extra lifetime reserve days to tack on to the end of this period. These days are nonrenewable (use them and/or lose them).

living will • a document that specifies the types of medical intervention a person will want if the person will soon die from a terminal illness or if he or she is permanently unconscious

long-term care benefit rider • provides the owner of an annuity contract with access to cash values if the annuitant has to enter a long-term care facility

long-term care insurance • insurance that provides per diem allowances for nursing home costs

long-term care ombudsmen • local offices that investigate nursing home complaints, advocate for residents, and mediate disputes. Ombudsmen often have extensive knowledge about the quality of life and care inside each nursing home in their area.

lump-sum distribution • a distribution from a qualified plan that is eligible for special income tax treatment

market portfolio • the theoretical portfolio of all assets, to which individual assets and portfolios can be compared in modern portfolio theory. Typically, the Standard & Poor's 500 or another broad-based stock market index is used as a surrogate for the market portfolio.

market risk • *See* systematic risk.

market timing • attempt to anticipate significant market movements and to make major changes in asset allocation accordingly

market value adjustment (MVA) • an increase or decrease in the annuity's value, depending on the overall level of interest rates in the United States economy relative to the interest rate in the specific annuity. If the policy's interest rate is 8 percent and the market is earning only 4 percent, the policy's values would be adjusted upward under this feature if the owner surrenders early.

matching maturities • selecting an asset that matures at the same time that the funds will be needed

maturity date • the insurance company's designated maximum age at which distributions must begin

MDIB • *See* minimum distribution incidental benefits.

mean reversion process • a particularly high (low) rate of return in one time period is more likely to be followed by a low (high) rate of return in the next period

means testing • to reduce or eliminate Social Security benefits for individuals with a certain amount of income or assets

Medicare medical savings account (MSA) • an alternative to the original Medicare program that includes both a high-deductible insurance plan and a medical savings account

Medicare Part A • the hospital portion of the federal health insurance program for seniors

Medicare Part B • the doctor and service provider portion of the federal health insurance program for seniors

Medicare Part D • voluntary prescription drug benefit available to all Medicare beneficiaries who are entitled to Part A and enrolled in Part B

Medicare SELECT • a Medigap insurance policy that requires the recipient to use doctors or hospitals within its network in order to receive full benefits

Medicare Supplement Insurance • *See* Medigap coverage.

Medigap coverage • insurance that provides services not covered by Medicare

mental accounts • the set of information and experience that may cause an individual to select a financial alternative based on its relative, rather than absolute, monetary benefit

minimum distribution incidental benefits • the intent of the minimum distribution incidental benefit rule is to ensure that the participant who attains age 70 1/2 and begins retirement distributions does not defer payment of a large portion of the benefit until after his or her death. The rule applies only when the beneficiary is not the spouse and is more than 10 years younger than the participant.

minimum distribution rules • rules that require payments from qualified plans, IRAs, SEPs, and 403(b) plans to begin within a specified period of time. The rules generally require that retirement benefits begin at age 70 1/2. The rules also specify how quickly distributions must be made after the death of the participant.

min-max range • the range of returns for a specific asset type for a holding period of a specific length within a specific time frame

minimum participation rule • rule stating that an employer's plan will not be qualified unless it covers (1) 50 employees or (2) 40 percent of the employer's eligible employees, whichever is less

modern portfolio theory (MPT) • a set of quantitative approaches to explaining the risk-return relationship, portfolio diversification, and asset selection

modified cash-refund annuity • a life annuity with the possibility of a refund to a chosen beneficiary if annuity payments have been less than a specified amount

modified contract • a life-lease contract that provides a specified amount of nursing home care with a per diem rate paid for usage above the specified amount

modified endowment contract (MEC) • special tax treatment applies when a life insurance policy is characterized as a MEC. A policy will be treated as a MEC if it fails the so-called 7-pay test.

money-purchase pension plan • a defined-contribution type qualified plan in which the employer contribution is specified and benefits are based on the participant's accumulated account balance

mortality and expense (M&E) charges • asset-based charges against investment subaccounts in a variable deferred annuity

MPT • *See* modern portfolio theory.

MVA • *See* market value adjustment.

net level premium • used in calculating whether a life insurance contract is characterized as a modified endowment contract (MEC)

net unrealized appreciation • the portion of a distribution that may not be subject to current income tax treatment when employer securities are part of a lump-sum distribution made to a participant

noncancelable provision • in a long-term care contract, a provision for establishing premiums in advance that cannot be changed

nonqualified annuity • an annuity in which the money placed in it has already been taxed

nonqualified retirement plan • an employer-sponsored deferred-compensation plan that does not receive the same special tax treatment as a qualified plan but that is subject to fewer restrictions. Generally these plans are established only for a small group of executives.

nonqualified stock options • options granted by the company to the executive to purchase shares of company stock at a stated price over a given limited period of time

nonspringing durable power of attorney • becomes effective upon execution

normal distribution • distribution corresponding to the shape of the normal (bell) curve

OASDHI • acronym for the old age, survivors, disability, and health insurance portions of Social Security

Older Americans Act • a law that assists senior citizens in living independently

partial surrender • an amount of money taken from a deferred annuity contract before the annuity reaches its maturity date

participation rate • the proportionate amount of the percentage change that is used to determine the actual interest rate that will be credited to an equity-indexed annuity for the contract term

passive investing • attempt to duplicate the risk-reward characteristics of a well-known stock indicator series by creating a stock portfolio that is nearly identical to that implied by the indicator series

Patient Self-Determination Act • a federal statute giving patients the right to make their own health-care decisions, including the right to refuse medical treatment

pay-as-you-go • current payroll taxes are used to pay current benefits

pension plan • a qualified retirement plan that must state the level of contributions or benefits provided, and are not allowed to make distributions except upon death, disability, termination of employment, or attainment of the plan's retirement age

percentage change • the change in the index from the beginning of the contract term to the end of the contract term, expressed as a percentage

phantom stock • the employer promises to pay the executive the value of some stated number of shares of stock at some later specified date. The stock is not actually set aside, only entered as a promise, and payment may be in cash or possibly in shares of stock.

phased retirement • a reduction in hours and commitments rather than a complete removal from the workforce

PIA • *See* primary insurance amount.

point-to-point indexed annuity • an indexed annuity that uses an indexing method that credits interest earnings by measuring from one particular index point to a second particular index point

policyowner's basis • a way to properly determine the income tax effects of a financial transaction with a life insurance contract. Determined (initially) by adding the total premiums paid into the policy and subtracting the policy dividends.

portfolio success rate • a function of portfolio composition and withdrawals rates; can be defined as 100 percent minus the portfolio failure rate

preference reversal • change in a client's ranking of alternatives, depending on how the alternatives are presented

premium bonus • a dollar amount of money sometimes available in deferred annuities that is applied on top of the amount of premiums paid by the policyowner. The addition of a premium bonus will often increase the surrender charges in the policy and/or the length of the surrender charge period.

pre–59 1/2 IRS penalty tax • a 10 percent tax assessed against annuity owners who take withdrawals or surrenders from their policies prior to age 59 1/2 and do not fall within one of the exceptions to the rule. The tax is assessed against the amount of the withdrawal that is subject to ordinary income tax.

preretirement inflation factor • determined by looking at the assumed annual inflation rate prior to retirement and the number of years until retirement

price indexing • the first-year benefits for retirees would be calculated using inflation rates, instead of the increase in wages over a workless lifetime

primary insurance amount (PIA) • a benefit amount that is used to determine most Social Security benefits. The primary insurance amount is determined by applying a formula to the individual's AIME.

private annuity • similar to an installment sale, it allows gain to be reported over a period of years

principal residence • a place where a person lives, as distinguished from a vacation residence. It is the exclusive permanent home.

profit-sharing-type plans • qualified retirement plans, including profit-sharing plans, ESOPs, stock bonus plans, and 401(k) plans, that allow for discretionary employer contributions, but the contributions must be allocated in a specified way. Distributions may be made at termination of employment but in-service distributions are permitted if certain conditions are met.

prospectus • a document that provides the complete details of the product, including investment features, options, fees, other costs, death benefits, and payout options

provisional income • a taxpayer's adjusted gross income plus tax-exempt interest income plus 1/2 of Social Security income

purchasing power preservation model • attempts to have the purchasing power of the portfolio at life expectancy equal the purchasing power of the portfolio at the time of retirement

put option • when an ESOP or stock bonus plan is sponsored by a company whose stock is not publicly traded, the company must offer to buy back any stock distributed to participants. This buy-back offer is called a put option.

qualified annuity • an annuity that accepts pretax dollars from an employer-sponsored retirement program or IRA

qualified domestic relations order (QDRO) • a court order as part of a divorce proceeding that requires the plan administrator to pay benefits to an alternate payee, who can be the participant's former spouse, child, or other dependent

qualified joint and survivor annuity (QJSA) • the required form of payment for any benefits paid from a qualified plan to a married plan participant

qualified personal residence trust (QPRT) • allows the homeowner to give away the house, thus removing its value from the estate, while retaining the right to live in it for a specified period without paying rent

qualified preretirement survivor annuity (QPSA) • the required preretirement death benefit payable to the spouse of a married plan participant

qualified retirement plan • an employer-sponsored retirement plan eligible for special tax treatment. Common types of qualified plans include profit-sharing plans, defined-benefit plans, and money-purchase pension plans. Special tax treatment includes employer deduction at the time contributions are made to the plan's trust, no income tax on the trust, and deferral of taxation to the employee until the time of distribution to the employee.

quarter of coverage • the measuring stick used for Social Security eligibility

question framing • manner in which a question is posed, which often influences the client's response

random walk hypothesis • the theory that security prices move in a manner that cannot be predicted by prior price changes

real riskless rate • the rate of return on Treasury bills, adjusted for inflation, as measured by the consumer price index

replacement ratio • level of income stated as a percentage of final salary

replacement ratio approach • the measure of a person's financial need as a percentage of final salary

required beginning date • the latest date that a minimum distribution must begin. Generally it is the April 1 of the year following the calendar year in which the participant attains age 70 1/2.

residential care facilities • adult homes that provide safety, shelter, and companionship

residual risk • *See* unsystematic risk.

respite care • enables caregivers to be temporarily relieved from their caregiving responsibilities

restricted stock plan • stock payments from the company to the executive that are nontransferable and forfeitable until some future specified date. Forfeiture usually occurs if the executive ceases employment prior to retirement age or some other specified age.

retirement income needs • the total amount of savings that allows a client to sustain the standard of living enjoyed just prior to retirement throughout the retirement period

retirement income shortfall (RIS) • the result of subtracting the projected annual need from existing sources stated in terms of annual income provided at retirement

retirement needs present value factor • determined by looking at the assumed annual inflation rate after retirement, the expected duration of retirement, and the assumed rate of return on investments after retirement. Subtract the assumed investment rate after retirement from the assumed inflation rate after retirement, then look at the duration of retirement.

retirement village • age-restricted housing development that often provides recreational opportunities and maintenance services for common ground

return/return tradeoff • to increase the expected return on a portfolio by adopting a more aggressive posture

reverse mortgage • a way to stay in the same home while capitalizing on the home's equity. The homeowner enters into an agreement with a lender to receive payments in exchange for a secured interest in the home's equity.

RIS • *See* retirement income shortfall.

rising floor death benefit • a death benefit in a variable deferred annuity in which the benefit is equal to the larger of the account value or the premiums paid plus interest

risk-free withdrawal rate • withdrawal rate based only on net investment income

risk premium • the additional return received for the risk incurred by investing in a given asset category rather than a safer alternative

risk tolerance • a willingness to incur risk, especially in monetary matters

risky shift • the tendency for a group decision to be riskier than the decisions of the individuals in the group

rollover • a payment made to a participant from one type of tax-advantaged retirement plan that is subsequently deposited within 60 days into another tax-advantaged retirement plan

Roth IRA • type of individual retirement account in which contributions are made on an after-tax basis, but earnings are not taxed and qualifying distributions are tax free

Roth IRA conversion • a rollover from a traditional IRA to a Roth IRA. This transaction triggers income tax, but not the 10 percent premature distribution excise tax.

salary reduction plan • a nonqualified retirement plan that allows participants to defer current salary with the objective of deferring taxation until a later date

sale leaseback arrangement • an arrangement under which a person sells his or her home to an investor and rents it back. The seller/renter gets the advantage of removing the home from the estate and freeing up equity from the home.

SARs • *See* stock appreciation rights.

savings incentive match plan for employees (SIMPLE) • a simplified retirement plan that allows employees to save on a pretax basis, with limited employer contributions

savings rate factor • determined by looking at the number of years until retirement, the average annual rate of return expected, and the savings step-up rate

SECA tax • Self Employment Contributions Act (Social Security tax on self employeds). Doubles the rates applied to FICA taxes.

Sec. 1035 exchange • allows the annuity purchaser to move funds from one insurance company to another without making it a taxable event

Sec. 72(t) penalty tax • a 10 percent penalty for premature distributions from a tax-advantaged or qualified plan

Sec. 162 plan • *See* executive bonus life insurance plan.

Sec. 529 Qualified Tuition Programs • prepaid, tax-favored savings plans designed to help parents pay for future college expenses

security market line • the linear relationship between systematic risk (beta) and expected return according to the capital asset pricing model (CAPM)

Senior Protection in Annuity Transactions Model Regulation • a model regulation adopted by the National Association of Insurance Commissioners in 2003 to set standards and procedures for recommendations of annuity products to consumers aged 65 and older

senior's sales-leaseback of home with adult child • a senior sells the family home to an adult child and then rents it back

SEP • *See* simplified employee pension plan.

separate account • a strategy used to limit problems that could arise with multiple beneficiaries under the minimum distribution rules. If certain rules are followed, the separate beneficiary of each share determines his or her minimum required distribution based on his or her life expectancy on the birthday that occurs in the year following the year of the decedent's death.

separation theorem • the idea that the decision of what portfolio of risky assets to invest in can be separated from the selection of an appropriate risk-return tradeoff. In this scenario, all investors would select the market portfolio.

SERP • *See* supplemental executive retirement plan.

service and merchandise cemetery trust • similar to a funeral trust in that grantors are able to select and prefund specified items (for example, burial vaults and gravesite stones). Typically these arrangements involve relatively small amounts of money and the trust may be held in the client's own name.

SIMPLE • *See* savings incentive match plan for employees.

simplified employee pension plan (SEP) • employer-sponsored retirement plan in which contributions are made to the IRA of each participant. The SEP is an alternative to a profit-sharing plan.

single-premium annuity • an annuity structured to allow only one contribution in the contract

skilled-nursing facility • a facility for patients who no longer require continuous hospital care but are not well enough to go home. The facility must have at least one full-time registered nurse, and nursing services must be provided at all times. Patients must generally be under the supervision of a physician.

small stock premium • the additional return received for the additional risk of investing in small capitalization stocks rather than investing in Standard & Poor's 500 stocks

social assistance • social benefits with eligibility criteria designed in part to encourage the able-bodied poor to work

social desirability bias • the tendency to overstate the degree to which one has a favorable personality trait

Social Security • the old age, survivors, disability, and health insurance (OASHDI) program sponsored by the federal government

special-needs trust • a property management device used to protect the assets of individuals who expect to be in a long-term disabled condition

special-purpose loan • a loan that does not have to be repaid until after the retiree dies, moves, or sells his or her home

special situation analysis • identification of investments with high potential returns and lower-than-commensurate risk due to market inefficiencies; usually associated with financially troubled companies

SPD • *See* summary plan description.

spell of illness • *See* benefit period.

spousal benefit • Social Security retirement benefit paid to a nonworking spouse. The benefit is based on the working spouse's primary insurance amount (PIA).

spousal consent • the consent required for a participant to elect out of a qualified joint and survivor annuity or a qualified preretirement survivor annuity

spousal IRA • a separate individual retirement plan for a married individual who does not receive employment income (and therefore cannot maintain his or her own IRA).

springing durable power of attorney • becomes operative only at the principal's incapacity

standard deviation • a measure of the degree of dispersion of a distribution

standby trust • a trust that is not funded immediately after execution

step-up rate • the rate by which savings are increased each year. The rate usually parallels expected salary increases.

stepped-up death benefit • a death benefit in a variable deferred annuity in which the benefit is updated on specific policy anniversary dates by the policy value as of that date, if higher. Step-up dates can occur every year or at specified intervals, depending on the policy's design (also referred to as a ratcheted death benefit).

stock appreciation rights (SARs) • a benefit program that gives participants the right to receive cash or stock in the amount of the stock's appreciation over a limited period of time.

stock bonus plan • a profit-sharing plan that delivers benefits to employees in the form of stock instead of cash

straight life annuity • *See* life-only annuity.

subaccounts • similar to mutual funds, accounts that are part of the separate account of a variable annuity contract. The subaccounts offer investment funds into which the policyowner allocates his or her premiums.

subsidized benefits • forms of payment of an annuity that are more valuable than the normal form of payment. For example, if the participant is entitled to a $1,000 life annuity, he or she can also elect a $1,000-a-month 50 percent joint and survivor annuity.

substandard (impaired risk) annuity • a special type of immediate annuity in which the insurance company requires annuitants to undergo medical underwriting to show that their life expectancy is less than normal. The substandard annuity pays higher income because the insurer will not be making the annuity payments for as long as normally expected.

substantially equal periodic payments exception • under this exception to the 10 percent penalty tax for premature plan withdrawals, payments can begin at any age to meet ongoing financial needs as long as certain requirements are met

suitability • a concept of appropriateness that has been required in the sale of variable annuities but that has not been required in the sale of fixed or indexed annuities until 2003. Suitability was addressed in 2003 in the sale of both fixed and variable annuities through the NAIC's adoption of the Senior Protection in Annuity Transactions Model Regulation.

summary plan description (SPD) • a brief, easy-to-read document summarizing the terms of a retirement plan that must be given to participants of any plan covered by ERISA

supplemental executive retirement plan (SERP) • a nonqualified retirement plan paid for by the company and intended to supplement other retirement income

supplemental security income (SSI) • a benefit program administered by the Social Security administration that pays monthly income to clients who are 65 or older, blind, or disabled. In order to qualify, the client's income and assets must be minimal.

"sure thing" principle • the tendency for people to put too much emphasis on selecting a choice with a certain outcome and too little emphasis on choices that have outcomes of moderate or high probability

surrender • a full surrender provision in a deferred annuity contract allows the policyowner total withdrawal of funds prior to maturity of the contract. *Compare* partial surrender.

surrender charge • charge imposed by an insurance company to encourage purchasers to make long-term commitments. The charge penalizes premature withdrawals.

surrender charge period • the length of time from the issuance of a deferred annuity during which the insurance company will impose a fee for amounts withdrawn or surrendered. Surrender charge periods usually last for 7–10 years.

surrender value • the actual amount the owner would receive upon a complete and total surrender of the policy

systematic risk • the part of risk that is related to the market as a whole and cannot be diversified away. As investors add assets to their portfolios, they diversify away the unsystematic risk. If investors continue to diversify, the portfolio will eventually resemble the market portfolio and will retain the risk that is inherent in the market portfolio, which is systematic risk. Systematic risk can also be represented as the relative tendency for an asset's return to track the market's return, or beta.

target-benefit pension plan • a qualified retirement plan categorized as a defined-contribution pension plan that is a hybrid between a defined-benefit and a money-purchase pension plan. The plan has a stated benefit formula that is used to determine annual contributions. However, the actual benefit is based on accumulated contributions and actual investment experience—not the stated benefit in the plan.

target replacement ratio • postretirement annual income divided by the preretirement annual income, where each income provides the same standard of living

tax deferral • allows for the accumulated money in a deferred annuity contract to be free of taxation until it is withdrawn

taxable wage base • the maximum dollar amount of wages is subject to Social Security taxes

technical analysis • identifying underpriced investments by looking at the market itself, especially at supply and demand for the investment

TEFRA 242(b) election • grandfathered favorable tax treatment for qualified plan and 403(b) distributions

temporary annuity • an annuity that expires at the earlier of death or a specified period of time

ten-year averaging • special tax treatment for eligible lump-sum distributions from qualified plans that is available only to individuals born before 1936

terminal illness rider • generally makes annuity values available to the policyowner if the annuitant becomes terminally ill

thrill seeker • personality type that is prone to take risk in all categories of life situations

"top-down" analysis • fundamental analysis approach in which analyst evaluates sequentially (1) economic and market factors, (2) industry/sector factors, and (3) company characteristics

top-heavy plan • a plan in which 60 percent or more of benefits go to key employees

total expense ratio • used to compare the expenses for variable deferred annuities to those for regular mutual funds

TRR • *See* target replacement ratio.

trustee-to-trustee transfer • assets from one IRA are routed directly from one trustee (or custodian) to another

trust fund • assets held in a trust, which is a legal arrangement wherein an individual gives fiduciary control of property to a person or institution for the benefit of beneficiaries

unrealized appreciation • a term used to describe a special tax rule that applies to lump-sum distributions from qualified retirement plans. The rule allows the benefit recipient to defer paying taxes on the appreciation on the value of distributed employer securities.

unsystematic risk • the part of an asset's total risk that is independent of movements in the general market. In practice, unsystematic risk represents investment-specific characteristics. For a stock investment, such factors include the company's relative reliance on government contracts, potential foreign currency losses, potential competition, management depth, financial leverage, and a myriad of other factors. Unsystematic risk, also called diversifiable risk and residual risk, can be reduced by diversifying among many assets.

upon death or incapacity letter • a document that provides pertinent information on the location and status of a decedent's financial information. The letter should contain the location of personal papers such as the will, birth certificate, and insurance policies, as well as banking, brokerage, and credit card numbers.

variable annuity • a deferred annuity that allows the annuity purchaser to participate in the investment of the annuity funds by determining how much of the contribution will be invested in a series of accounts

variable immediate annuity • annuity in which the periodic payments received from the contract vary with the investment experience of the underlying investment vehicle

variable life annuity • type of life annuity in which the periodic payments depend on the performance of an underlying asset, such as a stock portfolio

vesting schedule • a schedule that determines whether an employee who terminates employment will be eligible to receive qualified plan benefits

viatical settlement • the transfer of an insurance policy in anticipation of death to a third party for cash

viatical settlement provider • a person who is regularly engaged in the trade or business of purchasing, or taking assignments of, life insurance contracts on the lives of insureds and who has a license in the state in which the insured resides

wealth relative • a term used when calculating compound returns, which is simply the end-of-period value divided by the beginning-of-period value

withdrawal • *See* partial surrender.

Index